A COMPLEX FATE

A Complex Fate

William L. Shirer
and the American Century

KEN CUTHBERTSON

McGill-Queen's University Press
Montreal & Kingston · London · Ithaca

© McGill-Queen's University Press 2015
ISBN 978-0-7735-4544-1 (cloth)
ISBN 978-0-7735-9723-5 (ePDF)
ISBN 978-0-7735-9724-2 (ePUB)

Legal deposit second quarter 2015
Bibliothèque nationale du Québec

Printed in Canada on acid-free paper that is 100% ancient forest
free (100% post-consumer recycled), processed chlorine free.

McGill-Queen's University Press acknowledges the support of
the Canada Council for the Arts for our publishing program.
We also acknowledge the financial support of the Government
of Canada through the Canada Book Fund for our publishing
activities.

This book has been published with the help of a grant from
Furthermore: a program of the J.M. Kaplan Fund.

Library and Archives Canada Cataloguing in Publication

Cuthbertson, Ken, author
    A complex fate : William L. Shirer and the American
century / Ken Cuthbertson.

Includes bibliographical references and index.
Issued in print and electronic formats.
ISBN 978-0-7735-4544-1 (bound). – ISBN 978-0-7735-9723-5 (ePDF). –
ISBN 978-0-7735-9724-2 (ePUB)

    1. Shirer, William L. (William Lawrence), 1904–1993.
2. Novelists, American – 20th century – Biography. 3. Journalists –
United States – Biography. 4. War correspondents – United States –
Biography. I. Title.

PS3537.H913Z85 2015   070.92   C2014-908472-2
                                          C2014-908473-0

This book was typeset by True to Type in 10.5/13 Sabon

In memory of William L. Shirer (1904–1993)
and Eileen (Shirer) Dean (1938–2011)

Contents

Foreword

MORLEY SAFER

History with its flickering lamp stumbles along the trail of the past, trying to reconstruct its scenes, to revive its echoes, and kindle with pale gleams the passion of former days.

Winston Churchill[1]

It would not be overstating it to say the period 1937 through 1945 encased *the* story of the twentieth century. For reporters, the run-up to the Second World War and the war itself was an irresistible story. It had everything. It was a movable feast, a feeding frenzy of sabotage and espionage, mad men and statesmen, duplicity and cowardice and heroics, and millions upon millions of lives lost in unimaginable slaughter.

And, despite wartime censorship, this was the first time the public could share the immediacy of events as they happened thousands of miles away, all due to the coming of age of the newfangled medium of radio. Among the first to realize the journalistic potential of radio was Edward R. Murrow, a young aspiring executive of the Columbia Broadcasting System (CBS).

William S. Paley, a programming genius and owner and chairman of CBS, was so impressed with Murrow that he appointed him director of Public Affairs and sent him to London. His mission: to find European voices – statesmen, poets, people of influence, even children's choirs from Eastern Europe, all recruited for "talks" intended to give Paley's network a touch of class, a sense of global reach and worthiness that would be attractive to American listeners and advertisers.

Murrow fulfilled his mission, but he also had other things on his mind. By 1937, he was alarmed by what was happening in Europe. Murrow kept up with events reading wire service dispatches from Berlin written by a feisty American reporter named William L. Shirer. The product of the rough-and-tumble bare-knuckled journalism of the *Chicago Tribune*, Shirer pulled no punches and was a master of his craft.

There was little doubt about Hitler's intention to create a "New World Order." He had rearmed Germany while the Western alliance – Britain and France – dithered. Appeasement was in the air. In Germany, all opposition had been brutally silenced. It was obvious to Ed Murrow that there was a vitally important story to be told, and he decided that Bill Shirer was the man to help him tell it.

Murrow invited Shirer to dinner at Berlin's legendary Adlon Hotel to discuss the possibility of a job as a correspondent for CBS's fledgling radio news operation. Shirer was dubious, considered radio an effete medium with actors reading copy rather than hard-nosed reporters reporting. He would have no part in it. But over dinner and drinks Murrow convinced Shirer that he intended to launch serious broadcasts that would keep America informed.

Murrow combined a certain scholarly gravitas with a country boy's earthy sense of humor. Shirer had been laid off from his job that very day, and with his wife expecting their first child, he found Murrow's offer impossible to resist. The two men became colleagues and fast friends.

Shirer was the very first CBS News correspondent Murrow hired and the first of the news team that came to be known as "the Murrow Boys" – eleven men (and one woman, at least briefly). Most of the "boys" oozed charm; most of them, unlike Shirer, were impeccably dressed in bespoke suits and shirts; but all of them were immersed in world affairs and passionate about their journalism, all of them ultimately making their reputations covering almost every aspect of the biggest story ever covered. So big, that although the Second World War ended seventy years ago, books about it continue to be published by the dozen annually. And virtually any book with "Hitler" in the title seems to reach the bestseller list.

In addition to Shirer, among the Murrow Boys were the immensely talented Eric Sevareid, Charles Collingwood, Winston Burdett, and Richard C. Hottelet, each of whom I later worked with at CBS, along with Alexander Kendrick, another Murrow hire who joined CBS in 1947. I owe a debt of gratitude to these six men – and indirectly, of course, to Ed Murrow and Bill Shirer.

When I was invited to join CBS in late 1963, the remaining Murrow Boys and Alexander Kendrick accepted me as one of their own – in particular

Charles Collingwood, who became a mentor guiding me through the labyrinth of corporate journalism. Beginning in 1965, we covered Vietnam together, and in 1968 we covered the "Prague Spring" and the subsequent Soviet invasion. His generosity to the new kid on the block was immeasurable. Charles was known to his colleagues as "the duke." It was an apt nickname. He had that formal yet nonchalant bearing that only the royals can conjure up; in that regard, he was the polar opposite to Bill Shirer, who was a scrapper. Each man was enormously talented but displayed his talents in totally different ways. It almost goes without saying they also had egos to match.

London-based Ed Murrow and Bill Shirer in Nazi Berlin pretty much owned the war story for CBS in the run-up to September 1939 when the Germans invaded Poland. Murrow's reports from London rooftops as the Battle of Britain and the Blitz raged on were cool, terse, descriptive essays about the effects of the bombing and the stoic resistance of Londoners. Shirer roamed the battlefields with the German shock troops as they rolled through Western Europe. He witnessed the Battle of Britain from the German side, and he was there in June 1940 when the French capitulated. There is a remarkable photograph (on the cover of this book) that shows Shirer batting out his copy in the forest north of Paris at Compiègne. Behind him, German and French officers are milling about, while inside a nearby railway car the generals are formally signing the documents of the French surrender.

By December 1940, worn down by the workaday stresses of life in Hitler's Germany and virtually gagged by Nazi censorship, Shirer packed up and went home. Back in the United States, CBS gave him a lucrative contract to broadcast a weekly fifteen-minute program of news and analysis. He was in clover for the next seven years. But in 1947, in his tenth year with CBS, his life was turned upside down.

It was the beginning of the plague years in America, the birth of McCarthyism and the Red Scare. When the advertising agency for the corporate sponsor of Shirer's newscast complained to CBS President Bill Paley that Shirer was leaning too far to the left, his days with the network were numbered. Shirer was already in Paley's bad books. He ordered Murrow to fire him.

Murrow mounted only a half-hearted defense of his old friend before caving in and letting Shirer go. Furious that he had lost his job at CBS, Shirer went public with what he regarded as an abuse of freedom of speech. There were demonstrations. CBS was picketed, accused of caving in to right-wing extremists. Ed Murrow was devastated.

Despite his towering accomplishments and status as one of the iconic figures of American broadcasting, Murrow would come to feel a gut-wrenching sense of remorse about the end of his friendship with Shirer. It haunted him to the end of his life, as did his later surrender in signing the 1951 loyalty oath that all CBS employees were forced to agree to if they wanted to keep their jobs.

An embittered Bill Shirer eventually bounced back after thirteen long, lean years in which he struggled to earn a living. But his 1960 book *The Rise and Fall of the Third Reich* was a towering international success that remains in print to this day. Ed Murrow, frail with the cancer that in 1965 would claim his life, made one last attempt to reconcile with Shirer, but sadly the trust and kinship between the two men had been broken, and it remained so.

This is a book that in its own way has an almost Shakespearian quality: larger-than-life characters, broken friendships, pride and regret, all set against a background of war and depredation. And, in Murrow's case, a combination of Henry V and his St Crispin's Day speech and of Hamlet's dreadful indecision. And for Shirer, revenge of sorts in his own rise and fall and rise again – and, almost as a chorus, a group of loyal noblemen, both scholars and heroes, all doing their duty.

This book is also an *in memoriam* to an era of brilliant reporting, which to this day remains elegant, accurate, and admirable. Sad to say, we live in an era in which shoddy gossip tries to pass as journalism, in which shouting has become the norm, in which the media we had come to depend on have been reduced to mere shadows by the economics and culture of our time. I was pilloried a few years ago for saying publicly that I would trust citizen journalism as much as I would trust citizen surgery.

No matter. I also say with considerable pride that, at CBS, we cling to the same lofty standards that Ed Murrow, Bill Shirer, and the rest of the Murrow Boys set for us. May it ever be so.

William L. Shirer as a toddler, circa 1906. All photos are courtesy of the Literary Trust of William L. Shirer, unless otherwise indicated.

A teenage Bill Shirer during one of his summers as a Chautauqua crewman.

Bill Shirer in 1921, his freshman year at Coe College.

Tess Stiberitz as she looked in 1930, when Shirer met her.

William L. Shirer (*second from right*), dining with the Emir of Buchara, during the coronation ceremonies of Nadir Khan as king of Afghanistan, Kabul, October 1930.

Shirer (sixth from right, centre), the Swiss photographer Walter Bosshard (second from right, holding camera in his left hand), and an assortment of other guests who attended the coronation (*Archiv für Zeitgeschichte* ETHZ: NL Walter Bosshard/145).

The "stomach turning" sight of the corpses of some of Nadir Shah's enemies, hanged in Kabul's central bazaar, October 1930.

Chicago Tribune ad touting Shirer's "exclusive" reports on the coronation of Nadir Khan, 1930.

An unhappy William Shirer posing for a photo outside the Doge's Palace in Venice, before sailing to India in February 1931.

Shirer riding in a rickshaw in India, 1931.

Chicago Tribune ad touting Shirer's "exclusive" coverage of Mahatma Gandhi and the Indian independence movement, 1931.

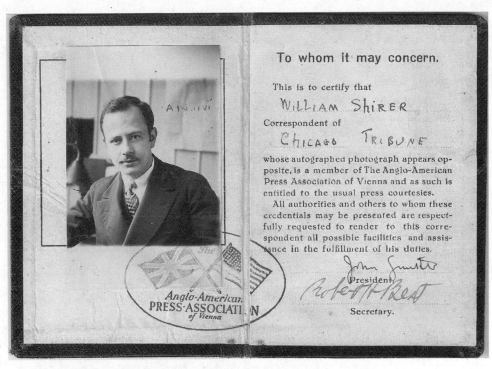

To whom it may concern.

This is to certify that

WiLLiAM ShiRER

Correspondent of

Chicago TRiBUNE

whose autographed photograph appears opposite, is a member of The Anglo-American Press Association of Vienna and as such is entitled to the usual press courtesies.

All authorities and others to whom these credentials may be presented are respectfully requested to render to this correspondent all possible facilities and assistance in the fulfillment of his duties.

President.

Secretary.

Shirer's *Chicago Tribune* press card, Vienna, circa 1932.

Tess Shirer captured this image of her husband striking a pensive pose, circa 1932.

Tess and Bill Shirer on a Vienna street, circa 1932.

Tess Shirer posing among the springtime blossoms, Berlin, 1936.

Shirer smoking and reading, early 1930s.

John Gunther in 1937, the year after publication of his book *Inside Europe* became a runaway best-seller (from *Inside: The Biography of John Gunther* by Ken Cuthbertson).

Shirer broadcasting from Bahnhof Friedrichstrasse, Berlin, 28 September 1938.

Shirer broadcasting live from St Peter's Square, Rome, 3 February 1939.

Shirer (*left*) and Murrow, having drinks and ice skating (with unidentified child) during a 19 January 1940 get-together in Amsterdam, arranged by Mary Marvin Breckinridge (*right*).

CBS colleagues (left to right) Thomas Grandin, Murrow, and Shirer relaxing at a Paris café, circa 1939 (Edward R. Murrow papers, Digital Collections and Archives, Tufts University, MS025.002.045.002616.00002).

A COMPLEX FATE

Introduction

Sometimes people call me an idealist. Well, that is the way I know I'm an American. America is the only idealistic nation in the world.

US President Woodrow Wilson[1]

For a free, self-governing people, something more than a vague familiarity with history is essential if we are to hold onto and sustain our freedoms.

Historian David McCullough, 2003[2]

The Chicago-born, Iowa-raised and -educated William L. Shirer was a member of the great exodus of idealistic young Americans who migrated to Europe in the 1920s. Like them, he rejected prohibition and what he saw as the soul-sucking materialism, prudery, and insularity of America in the Jazz Age. As a member of Gertrude Stein's so-called "Lost Generation" Shirer went looking for something greater in life, something more soulful, more fulfilling.

Eric Sevareid, the celebrated broadcaster who was Shirer's friend and co-worker at Columbia Broadcasting System (CBS), mused about "that extraordinary band of American journalists, some with Midwest hayseed still in their hair … scholars and linguists, who rampaged through Europe in their twenties and thirties somehow ended up on a first-name basis with kings and bartenders … More than diplomats or politicians, it was [these journalists] who told America what was happening and what was going to happen to the civilization of the west."[3] Theirs was a WASP, middle-class worldview; it was also one with unmistakably messianic undertones, for its hallmarks – so distinctly and undeniably American – were an abiding faith in liberal democracy, free enterprise, and the dignity and worth of the individual – the core values of the "American way." At the time, the United States and all that it stood for were almost universally admired, albeit begrudgingly so at times. It was no mere hyperbole when in February 1941 *Time-Life* magazine publisher Henry R. Luce boldly proclaimed the twentieth century to be "the American Century."[4]

Shirer was a child of the American empire at the zenith of its power, wealth, and global influence. Progressive in his politics, he believed in the fundamental honesty and decency of the American people and in the inherent strengths and goodness of the democratic ideals the Founding Fathers had enshrined in the remarkable document that is the United States Constitution. That William Shirer's unflinching insistence on remaining true to those same principles brought him perilously close to ruin was the crowning irony in a life that brimmed with ironies. "As an observer abroad Shirer had recorded some of the worst years of our time," historian Barbara Tuchman notes, "but it was in his own country that he was to experience personally, as a victim, the effects of fear and evil."[5]

In many ways, Shirer was an enigma, a puzzling bundle of contradictions whose flaws were as pronounced as his virtues. In that regard, he was not unlike the land of his birth. That was a reality that he understood and accepted. In his 1990 memoir, *A Native's Return,* Shirer observed, "It was a complex fate, maybe, as Henry James said, to be an American and one, I realize, not especially admired by some in other countries and cultures, who perceived us as 'the ugly Americans.' Still ... I am glad it was mine."[6]

The narrative arc of Shirer's life is as sprawling, voluminous, and dramatic as a Henry James novel. It was also as complex and wondrous as his times. Not only was he one of the foremost American print journalists of the twentieth century, he was one of the pioneers of news broadcasting and the author of sixteen books – two of which rightly are regarded as modern classics. As a *Boston Globe* writer once noted, *Berlin Diary* and *The Rise and Fall of the Third Reich* "will ensure [Shirer's] reputation as long as humankind reads."[7]

That said, it is impossible to forget that for all of his many accomplishments and his admirable qualities, like all of us, Shirer had failings. He was by times vain, impulsive, and headstrong to a fault. Thrice married, too often he hurt himself and those he loved. Yet, Shirer was at heart a good man, principled, intelligent, caring, and compassionate. He was also a larger-than-life figure whose adventures – and misadventures – stand as a vivid reminder of the ups and downs of fortune that can make or break any person.

Shirer's life, recounted here for the first time in its unvarnished entirety, is worth considering for a number of reasons. For one, in this age of social media and the citizen journalist, his career offers lessons on the nature and role of journalism and journalists in a democratic society. For another, part and parcel with that, the critical reception that professional historians accorded Shirer's writings raises intriguing questions about the legitimacy and value of "popular history" as a literary form and of the journalist as "historian." And finally, the circumstances of Shirer's departure from CBS highlight the dangers inherent in corporate involvement in the dissemination of "news," and the dark realities of his 1950 blacklisting underscore concerns that continue to resonate in our own uncertain post-9/11 world: the fraught intersections of democracy, patriotism, and paranoia. Indeed, William L. Shirer's life story stands as a cautionary tale about what can happen when a good person – or a good nation – stumbles, loses direction, and fails to grasp or heed the lessons of history.

When I began work on this biography in 2006, I never dreamed I was setting out on a research trail that would see me journey from Shirer's birthplace in Chicago, to his childhood home in Cedar Rapids, Iowa, and then on to London, Paris, New York, and Lenox, Massachusetts, where he lived in his twilight years and is buried. In addition, I used the telephone, internet, and the mail service to access resources in other far-flung spots where Shirer worked and lived.

I was fortunate enough to meet and talk with Shirer himself one day back in November 1986 when I visited him at his home in Lenox. He was eighty-two at the time, but still in possession of all his faculties and pleased to talk with a visitor. I interviewed him about his friendship with journalist John Gunther (about whom I was writing). At the time, I had no way of knowing my conversation with Shirer would, two decades later, provide me with both the creative spark and a starting point for a book on his own life.

William Shirer was a prolific writer – he worked at his craft almost every day of his adult life – and so his articles, books, and broadcast scripts were the logical jumping-off point for my research. In addition to the wealth of information that I gleaned from those sources, I interviewed many people who knew or knew *of* Shirer. It was through their eyes that I've been able to widen my lens and craft a more complete, well-rounded portrait of the man and his times.

I also gained valuable insights and understanding of Shirer from the wealth of archival materials to which I had access. These included the collection of Shirer's personal papers, correspondence, draft manuscripts, photographs, and secondary material that is housed in the archives of the Stewart Memorial Library at Coe College, Cedar Rapids; boxes of unsorted, uncatalogued personal papers, letters, clippings and photographs that remain in the possession of the Literary Trust of William L. Shirer; declassified Federal Bureau of Investigation files on Shirer that I obtained under the United States Freedom of Information Act; and other snippets of worthwhile information that I uncovered in archives and libraries as far afield as Chicago, New York, Boston, Dallas, London, and Geneva.

No biographer can ever give a reader more than a glimpse into the life of the subject he or she writes about. However, as Virginia Woolf once noted, "By telling us the true facts, by sifting the little from the big, and shaping the whole so that we perceive the outline, the biographer does more to stimulate the imagination than any poet or novelist save the very greatest."[8]

1

Midwestern Beginnings

His parents' plan had been to give him a patriotic name. William Lawrence Shirer's father was a rising star in the ranks of the Republican Party in Chicago. His mother was related to the Lawrences of Massachusetts, one of the most prominent blue-blood families in the early history of New England. Had he been born a few hours earlier – on 22 February, the birthday of George Washington – baby William would have been called George. Instead, from his first breath, Seward and Elizabeth Shirer's elder son did things his own way, stubbornly declining to make his appearance until the wee hours of the morning of 23 February 1904. That dogged determination, a distinguishing characteristic of Shirer's personality, would be at once his greatest shortcoming and greatest strength. It would lead to no end of turmoil in his personal life, yet it would also serve him well in his chosen vocation. He would emerge as one of the foremost American journalists of the twentieth century and as one of the pioneers of news broadcasting.

In both regards, it is fitting that William Shirer was born in the Woodlawn neighborhood of Chicago, that most quintessentially American of cities. The exact location was an upstairs bedroom of his family's South Greenwood Avenue home, a five-minute walk south of the University of Chicago campus. At the time, the leafy streetscapes here were prosperous and awash in hope. The same neighborhood today is much less upscale and decidedly less fashionable. Like the core areas of so many other big American cities, Woodlawn suffered through a slow, painful period of urban decay in the latter decades of the twentieth century. However, in 1904, with the effervescent President Teddy Roosevelt in the White House, America itself was different, and all things seemed possible. Especially in Chicago.

Barely a century removed from its beginnings as the remote military outpost, America's so-called "Second City" was a bustling metropolis of 1.8 million people. This was the great American melting pot personified. Three out of every four residents of the city were foreign-born or were first-generation Americans. Immigrants from the four corners of the globe lived alongside tens of thousands of black Americans from the Old South, former slaves and their sons and daughters, who had migrated north seeking jobs and freedom from the corrosive racial intolerance of the day.

As the hub of the nation's vast economic heartland, Chicago was a place where life's possibilities seemed as limitless as the Midwestern skies, and a man with pluck, luck, and drive could grab a handful of the future and of the American dream for himself. There was no mistaking that this was very much a *man's* world. Poet Carl Sandburg dubbed Chicago the "City of Big Shoulders,"[1] and the nickname was apt. Chicago's sprawling stockyards, factories, rail yards, and wharves were among America's busiest. Here was a gritty, blue-collar town. Yet, paradoxically, Chicago was also a place in which the arts – music, painting, and literature, especially – flourished, and where architecture rose to dizzying new heights, literally as well as figuratively.

Seward S. Shirer, the father of the baby William, was in his element here. An attorney by vocation, he was handsome, well-spoken, and personable. Seward was also bright, ambitious, determined, and upwardly mobile. The proud father recorded the details of the arrival of his first son in his diary: "Five minutes to three – Baby Boy born. Weighed 7¾ lbs. William Lawrence Shirer. Born 6500 Greenwood Avenue."[2]

William, the child's given name, was that of his paternal grandfather. Lawrence, his middle name, was drawn from his mother's side of the family. "Billy," as his parents affectionately called him, was the middle child of three siblings. His older sister, Josephine, named after her maternal grandmother, had been born on 8 September 1900. A younger brother, John, arrived two years after him, on 29 April 1906.

William L. Shirer always remembered his Chicago childhood as being happy and secure; the Shirers were solidly middle class, a loving, stable, and closely knit family. Seward Shirer, the patriarch, seemed destined for success, perhaps even greatness, if a cruel and tragic turn of fate had not cut short his life.

In order to understand and appreciate who William Shirer was, we must look at his family history, which was the archetypal American immigrant experience of the day. His genealogical roots were in the Palatinate area of the Rhineland, in the southwest corner of modern Germany. The family historian, Donald Boyd, has speculated that the "Scheurers" – as the Shirers originally were known – traced their origins to an area near the German border with Switzerland, where the Scheurer surname is common.[3] William Shirer's namesake uncle, William G., informed him in a 1931 letter, "While the family was pretty much of the farmer type, they were sufficiently elevated above the common herd so that the men ... were in the habit of holding minor offices under the Grand Duke [who ruled the area], such as Keepers of the Black Forest. Your great grandfather and his father before him did this sort of thing." William G. also speculated that a man named Scheurer who served as president of Switzerland during World War One may have been "a not far-distant relative of ours."[4]

In one of the largest influxes of European settlers of the pre-Revolutionary era, as many as 30,000 Palatine Germans came to North America. Among them were Seward Shirer's grandparents, who bypassed the big cities of the Eastern Seaboard to travel up the Hudson River to Herkimer County, ninety miles northwest of Albany. Here Johann Frederick Scheurer, his wife Marie Eva (née Brennizer), and their four children settled and began farming about 1844.[5] Seward Shirer's father, William Walter Scheurer, was born in 1846. Being the fourth son in the family, his prospects were limited, and so he left home at fifteen, mere weeks before the April 1861 opening salvos of the Civil War. William W. headed west in search of youthful adventures and farmland to call his own. Sometime in the course of his travels, his Scheurer surname became Anglicized. "My grandfather attached no importance to the [spelling] change," William L. Shirer wrote many years later. "It was done mainly because the town officials and tradesmen mistakenly kept writing it the way they thought it sounded, and it was simpler to go along with them."[6]

In the mid-nineteenth century, Anglo-Saxon influences dominated North American society, and the imperative for immigrants to amend the spelling of "foreign-sounding" surnames was strong. However, that does not seem to have been a factor in William W.'s acquiescence, for he continued to speak German at home.

William W.'s travels took him to Will County, south of Chicago. There, in 1868, he took as his wife twenty-year-old Caroline Triem, a native of Canton, Ohio, who had been a student at Northwestern College in Plainfield, Illinois. Like her husband, she was a first-generation American, her maternal family members also being Palatine Germans who had settled in Ohio.[7]

Following their marriage, Carrie and William W. joined Carrie's parents, Ludwig and Elizabeth Triem, and her grandparents, Henry and Margaret Huppert, in a westward migration that took them south of Lake Michigan, across the flatlands of western Illinois, and into the rolling farm country of the Iowa frontier. At the time, a frenzied land rush was underway there.

Iowa had become the twenty-ninth state in the Union in 1846, the year William W. was born. The population grew quickly as land-hungry white settlers staked out homesteads and displaced the indigenous Indian tribes, save for the Sioux, whose warriors were too proud and too stubborn to surrender without a fight; the other tribes sold their land – and arguably their dignity and way of life – to the United States government. In his 1978 memoir, *Twentieth Century Journey*, William L. Shirer recalls experiencing the legacy of these developments a generation later: "We were brought up to believe that 'the only good Indian was a dead Indian' … and nothing was said to us in those days of the cruel and savage slaughter and the robbery of the Indians by the white Americans, one of the darkest sides of our history."[8]

By 1860, the population of Iowa was 700,000 and growing. The prospect of owning a chunk of the world's best farmland was a powerful draw for William W. and Carrie Shirer and their kin. Having crossed the Mississippi River, they traveled about ninety miles farther north and west before stopping in Benton County. There they staked a claim near the community of La Porte City, which is fifteen miles southeast of Cedar Falls.

After building a sod hut and putting a first crop into the ground, William W. and Carrie started a family. The eldest of their four children, daughter Lillian V(ictoria), was born 3 January 1870; son Seward S(mith) followed on 17 September 1871; daughter Mabel M(ay) on 4 March 1876, and a second son, William G(arfield), on 11 September 1880. Walter and Carrie's patriotism and political inclinations were underscored when they named their eldest son after former New York governor William Seward, the outspoken abolitionist who had served as Secretary of State in the Republican administrations of presidents Abraham Lincoln and Andrew Johnson. Similarly, they gave their younger son the middle name Garfield, in honor of the ill-fated President James A. Garfield, the former GOP Congressman from Ohio – America's last "log cabin" president – who was fated to die by an assassin's hand in 1881.

However, Washington, presidential politics, and indeed the rest of the world were distant realities for the Shirers and other Iowa homesteaders. Their windswept farms were isolated, miles from the nearest neighbors. Travel was by horse and wagon or on foot. For that reason, and because money was tight, prairie settlers learned to be self-sufficient. What little social life there was for the farm families in the vicinity of La Porte City revolved around the local Evangelical Church, which most of the German families in the area faithfully attended.

The Shirer siblings grew up with a keen appreciation of the value of resourcefulness and of an honest day's toil. The girls helped their mother with housework, while the boys and their father worked the land and tended the livestock. There was never a shortage of chores to be done, and days during the growing season were endlessly busy and tiring. The Shirers grew corn, vast acres of it, to be used as feed for the livestock that became the family's main source of income.

As the Shirers' farm prospered and the children grew, William W. Shirer immersed himself in the area's political life, serving in various capacities: school trustee, justice of the peace, and township clerk. He also passed along to his children, especially to his son, Seward, a keen sense of civic duty. Despite the family's deep ties to their rural community, the Shirers regarded farming as a means to another end: the chance for a better life for themselves and their children. When it became evident that daughters Lillian and Mabel May were keen to take voice and piano lessons, and that sons Seward and William were more interested in books than agriculture, the Shirers made a decision in spring 1889 that must have seemed bold, even foolhardy, to friends and neighbors.

William W. Shirer was forty-three, Carrie forty-one, when shortly after Seward's graduation from the LaPorte High School, the Shirers sold their farm and moved fifty miles southeast to the town of Mount Vernon, Iowa. Here the children would have opportunities to continue their educations at Cornell College. The school, started by the Methodist Church in 1852, was typical of the dozen or so institutions of higher learning that were scattered around Iowa at that time. All had been founded as religious seminaries in the middle decades of the nineteenth century. While the quality of the educational experiences offered depended on each school's resources – especially where the sciences were concerned – most students received a solid grounding in the liberal arts and humanities. In autumn 1889, with tuition just twelve dollars per term, a college education for their children was within reach of most farm families in the area, including the Shirers.

Seward, eighteen and burning with intelligence and ambition, enrolled at Cornell, while his sister Lillian began five years of study at the College's music conservatory. Younger sister Mabel attended prep school during the 1893–94 school year and then study at Cornell for a year, while their brother William ("Willie," to his family and friends) attended the College for four years, graduating in 1903.[9]

After spending his freshman year in a sciences program, Seward Shirer switched his major to Classics. Oratory was one of the subjects in which he excelled, winning a cash prize in a regional competition and serving as the class salutatorian on graduation day in 1893.

Public speaking skills and a solid liberal arts education were not all that Seward Shirer took away from Cornell. In his senior year, he had also won the heart of Elizabeth Tanner, a twenty-one-year-old music student who hailed from nearby Cedar Rapids. "Bessie," as her family and classmates called her, was of Welsh-English stock.

Bessie Tanner and Seward Shirer were a stark example of the principle that opposites attract; the two could not have been more different in demeanor or physical appearance. A photo of Bessie taken during this period depicts an almost mournful-looking young woman of slight build. Though her features were plain, there was a beguiling delicacy to her, a wispiness even. The roundness of her face and the prominence of her nose were offset by a finely featured mouth and jawline. There was a gentleness to her that was reflected in her large eyes.

Bessie, being a talented pianist, preferred music to words. Reserved to the point of being shy, she clearly regarded the prospect of having her photograph taken with the same trepidation that she felt when first she caught the eye of Seward Shirer, one of the most engaging and popular young men at Cornell.

Six feet tall, willow-rod lean, and fit from his farm labors, Seward cut an impressive figure. He was a top student, an eloquent orator, and a talented athlete; he starred on the Cornell College varsity baseball team. As such, teachers and classmates had tabbed him as "most likely to succeed." His graduation photo depicts a dark-haired young man with a strong handsome face and a finely chiseled nose and jawline. The distinctive Shirer eyes, probing and alert beneath dark, full eyebrows, gave him an air of seriousness and intelligence. Seward was cerebral, but he was no bookworm. He was outgoing, bubbled with self-confidence and emanated an infectious enthusiasm for life. His personality and his oratorical skills prompted suggestions that he become an attorney, an idea that he liked. However, because he had no money for law school tuition, he was obliged to follow the legal career path of so many impecunious young men of the day: Seward set out to pass the state bar examination by "reading law" for a year or two in the office of an established attorney.

After graduating from Cornell, Seward found a job as the principal at a preparatory school in Blairstown, Iowa. He studied law in his spare time, and after passing the state examinations he was admitted to the Iowa bar in spring 1894. In the year he spent practicing law in Estherville, a small town northwest of Cedar Rapids, Seward managed to scrape together the money for tuition at the Lake Forest University law school in Chicago. Working part-time as a teacher in the city's public school system paid the bills while he was a law student. And teaching continued to be his fallback vocation in the first lean years after he graduated from Lake Forest in June 1896 and gained admittance to the Illinois bar. Hoping to save enough money so that he and Bessie Tanner could marry, Seward toiled for the next two years to establish himself in Chicago by expanding his social and business networks and joining the Republican Party.

Meanwhile, back in Iowa, Bessie attended the Cornell music conservatory for a year after her fiancé's graduation. She then returned to her parents' home in Cedar Rapids, where she waited for Seward. With most of her girlfriends and schoolmates already married, these were anxious times for Bessie.

The couple finally wed on the evening of 20 January 1899 in a ceremony that was held in the parlor of the Tanner home in Cedar Rapids, which had been "simply but effectively decorated with palms and festoons of evergreens."[10] The groom was twenty-seven, his bride two years younger. The newlyweds settled in Chicago, where they initially rented an apartment in a building at 333 East 62nd Avenue. Seward evidently was doing well in his career, for the following year the couple moved to a more upscale building at 6500 Greenwood Avenue, and here they started their family. However, once there were three children to raise, Seward and Bessie Shirer decided it was time for a bigger house of their own. This residence, with newfangled electric lights and the luxury of central heating, was at 6612 Lexington Avenue, a few blocks north and east of where they had been living. Their new abode overlooked then-fashionable Jackson Park and it was a short walk from the University of Chicago campus.[11]

As was customary at the time, the bulk of the responsibility for child rearing in the Shirer household fell to Bessie Shirer. She was, by all accounts, a loving and devoted mother with an at-times playful disposition. Shirer's daughter, Eileen ("Inga") Shirer Dean, recalled her grandmother telling her how one day when Seward was at the office she had discovered a trunk full of old clothing in the attic. In a moment of whimsy, she got dressed up and waited at the door. When Seward arrived home, he was neither amused nor did he share in the fun. Whether he was having a bad day or simply did not see the humor in the situation is unclear.[12]

This is not to say that Seward Shirer was not a good husband or a devoted family man. He was both. Each summer, the Shirers took a family vacation, usually at Portage Lake in northern Michigan. During these idyllic interludes, Seward taught the children to swim, fish, row, sail, and pick berries. He took so much delight in these activities that Bessie teased him about "acting like a schoolboy." But Seward's devotion to his family was not confined to vacation periods. When the dinner dishes had been cleared away each evening, he loved to sit in the parlor reading the newspaper to all three children, who gathered on the floor around his chair. That all three Shirer siblings grew up with an awareness of politics, government, and world affairs in no small measure was due to their father's actions. "Certain happenings ... [about] which [he] read to us before we were old enough to follow the newspapers ourselves, were as exciting to us as the coming of the motorcar, the airplane, and the wireless," William Shirer recalled.[13]

The Shirer siblings also absorbed many of their father's political opinions. Seward was a staunch Republican and a "progressive" in the manner of Teddy Roosevelt, who became president in September 1901 when President McKinley was assassinated, and he remained in the White House until 1909. Seward Shirer proudly served as a sergeant-at-arms at the 1904 GOP convention in Chicago, where delegates nominated Roosevelt as the party's presidential candidate for that year's election. Afterward, in the months leading up to the November vote, Seward worked part-time for the Republican National Committee at a salary of $20 a week. Two years later, he involved himself in the re-election campaign of district Congressman James R. Mann, who achieved national prominence as the author of the Mann Act, a law aimed at prohibiting "white slavery."

William Shirer later speculated that Mann was grooming Seward Shirer to be his eventual successor. That seems likely, for Seward was highly regarded by Chicago's Republican power brokers. As a result, in 1906 his partisanship earned him a job as an Assistant United States Attorney, with an annual salary of about $2,500. This was a comfortable wage in an era when most industrial workers toiled six days per week and were lucky to take home $500 per year. Within a few years, Seward's annual salary had risen to almost $5,000.

Despite this, money was never a driving force in his life. Seward Shirer was an idealist, a committed Christian with an abiding sense of morality. He also had a fervent belief in the fairness and virtue of the American political system, which he insisted could exert a positive influence on people's lives and bring about a more just and equitable society. Seward, who subscribed to the notion that "The Republican Party of Lincoln is the party of the future," had an unshakable faith in the "American way." These were core values that he passed on to his children, a reality that would prove pivotal in the life and career of his older son.

Bessie Shirer shared her husband's outlook and his commitment to community involvement. She was an outspoken supporter of the women's suffrage movement and of efforts to relieve the suffering of the less fortunate. Bessie and Seward supported various charities, and each December they packed hampers full of food and clothing for Christmas Eve delivery to poor families living in the south-side slums that were home to workers from the city's stockyards. Such visits to "the other side of the tracks" had a profound impact on the Shirer children. They grew up with a keen, deep-seated sense of social justice.

Seward Shirer loved to debate income inequities and other issues of the day. Sometimes he invited other attorneys and male friends home for drinks, cigars, and lively conversation. Among the visitors to the Shirers' parlor was Seward's colleague Clarence Darrow, who at the time was one of America's most famous attorneys. He and Seward Shirer were courtroom adversaries, yet the two men shared a mutual respect, had similar views on many issues, and were avid baseball fans. Being too young to join in or truly comprehend the talk he overheard, young Bill Shirer was only vaguely aware of Darrow's celebrity: "I have often regretted that I was not old enough to absorb some of their talk ... It was only years afterward, when I had read some of Darrow's great courtroom speeches and read his books, that I was able to grasp the greatness, the goodness, the courage, of this rough-looking, humane, civilized man."[14]

The Shirer children's interest in public affairs took on a whole new degree of engagement when their father began involving himself in municipal politics. Seward felt that Chicago's political system was corrupt and in dire need of reform. "Brothels, gambling joints, and saloons abounded, as did whores in the busy streets," William Shirer recalled, "and the notorious First Ward, in the heart of the city, was the fiefdom of two legendary characters my father ... used to talk about as Hinky Dink [Michael Kenna] and Bathhouse John [Coughlin]." These two corrupt city councilors "not only ran the First Ward, which included the business and amusement district, for half a century – from 1890 to about 1940 – but often had control of the whole city."[15]

Determined to involve himself in the crusade to help clean up City Hall, Seward set out to win the Republican nomination for alderman in Chicago's seventh ward. Throwing himself into that task, he campaigned tirelessly throughout autumn and the early weeks of the New Year. His older son, William, would often tag along on these outings, and the experiences were ones he never forgot: "Away from the shelter of home, it gave me one of my first glimpses of the world of grownups ... I felt six-foot tall."[16]

Sadly, Seward Shirer never realized his dream of winning elected office. He fell ill the last week of January. Doctors surmised that he was suffering from exhaustion, or else had come down with a stomach ailment, possibly the flu. Either diagnosis seemed reasonable. After all, he had been putting in extraordinarily long hours for several months. In addition to his after-hours efforts on the municipal campaign trail, in his job at the District Attorney's office, Seward was working on a complicated legal case against a big oil company; the high-profile trial was front-page news in Chicago's newspapers.

When the prescribed medicines had no effect on Seward's condition, his pain and discomfort worsened. In desperation, Bessie Shirer called in a specialist who realized Seward was suffering from acute appendicitis, a condition that today can usually be treated with antibiotics, if it is diagnosed in time. In 1913, the condition was far more problematic. Seward Shirer's appendix burst in the ambulance on the way to the hospital. After the emergency surgery, he lay critically ill for ten long, agonizing days. For a time, it seemed as if he might pull through. In fact, the *Chicago Evening Post* newspaper carried a report on 12 February 1913 that suggested as much. "Seward S. Shirer, Assistant United States District Attorney, is pronounced out of danger by physicians in attendance at the Washington Park Hospital, Mr Shirer was operated on for appendicitis about two weeks ago. His condition had been critical and for a time his life was despaired of."

However, Seward was suffering the effects of peritonitis – the same deadly condition that in 1926 claimed the life of legendary magician Harry Houdini. Although a specialist performed a second surgery on Seward, it was already too late; the poison had spread throughout his body. Early on the morning of 18 February, Seward Shirer died. He was only forty-one and in the prime of life.[17]

The Shirer children could scarcely believe their father was gone. Nine-year-old William was numb to the words of Seward's friends and colleagues who delivered the eulogies at a memorial service held at Woodlawn Park Masonic Lodge and to the intonations of the Presbyterian minister who presided over the funeral service in the parlor of the Shirers' family home. Afterward, Seward's body was shipped back to Cedar Rapids for burial.

While his father was a devoutly religious man who had accepted his fate as "God's will," young William Shirer was not nearly as submissive: "It seemed to me such a senseless thing – then and forever after … The more I thought about it as I grew older, the more it confirmed for me the meaninglessness of life, its pointlessness … The world itself died with my father in 1913, or shortly thereafter, for the next year there came the Great War, which left the world my father had known in shambles."[18]

2

Cedar Rapids

Seward Shirer's sudden death brought about pivotal changes for his family. He left the proceeds of a $10,000 life insurance policy and clear title to the family's home, valued at $6,500. However, Bessie Shirer's long-term financial situation was tenuous, and so in spring 1913 she rented out the house in Chicago, packed up her children, and moved home to Cedar Rapids. William Shirer recalled many years later, "I felt a complete stranger as we, my mother, brother, sister, and I alighted from the train at Union Station [in Cedar Rapids] into the welcoming arms of my gray-haired grandparents, who helped gather our baggage and drove us away in a horsedrawn cab. My mother looked as depressed as I felt. She had not yet recovered from the trauma of her husband's sudden death and the collapse of all her dreams."[1]

The necessity of a return to Cedar Rapids was a bitter pill for Bessie to swallow. In 1913, the prospects for a thirty-eight-year-old widowed homemaker with three young children were anything but bright. However, in Cedar Rapids she could depend on family.

Bessie's parents, Frank and Josephine Tanner, had worked hard to build a comfortable life for themselves after arriving in Cedar Rapids in 1868. Iowa was still pulsating at the time with the land rush that also had lured Seward Shirer's parents westward. Frank Tanner's forebears, like so many other immigrants from southwest England and Wales in the late eighteenth century, came to America seeking freedom and a better life. In many ways, the Tanners' history in North America reflects that of the Thirteen Colonies and of America in its formative years. William L. Shirer detailed his maternal family's trials and tribulations in his memoir *Twentieth Century Journey*.[2]

Suffice it here to report that Frank Tanner was born near Cooperstown, New York, in 1844[3] and fought for the Union in the Civil War. He served four years as a member of the 106th New York Infantry Company, seeing action in some of the war's bloodiest battles, including Gettysburg. Wounded three times, he returned to Cooperstown at war's end and there married the sweetheart he had left behind. Josephine Lawrence, New Hampshire-born and two years older than her husband, claimed to be related – at least distantly – to the Lawrences of Massachusetts, one of the most prominent families in the early history of New England. Frank Tanner sometimes referred to the Lawrences as "damned Anglicans and Methodist bishops," whether in fun or scorn is unclear. What is clear is that Grandmother Tanner shared a common trait of the Lawrences, who, as William Shirer notes, had "rather bulbous noses with flaring nostrils."[4]

Shirer also surmised that, apart from taking Josephine Lawrence's hand in marriage, the biggest adventure of Grandfather Tanner's life was his four years in the Union army. Seized with an insatiable restlessness, in 1868 Frank Tanner had packed up his wife and their one-year-old son, Charles – affectionately known as "Dode" – and they had joined the long caravans of homesteaders headed to the Western frontier. The Tanners settled briefly in the town of Anamosa, Iowa. It was there, on 7 July 1871, that their second child, daughter Elizabeth "Bessie" – was born.

Not long afterward, the Tanners moved thirty-five miles southwest to Cedar Rapids. The coming of the transcontinental railway, which brought industry and prosperity to the town proved key to Frank's livelihood. He found work the Lyon and Tomlinson glove company as a commercial traveler, ranging far-and-wide across the American Midwest. With a "gift of the gab," he prospered in his labors, so much so that in just a few years, he and Josephine saved enough money to buy their own house. The dwelling, at 811 Second Avenue,[5] was in one of Cedar Rapids' most desirable neighborhoods. Among their neighbors were the Van Vechtens, who were a well-to-do banking family. The younger of the Van Vechtens' two sons, Carl, was nine years older than Bessie Tanner and was gay. Not surprisingly, even as a boy he felt out of place in his hometown.

Dissimilar though they were, Carl Van Vechten and Bessie Tanner shared a common dream: to escape their small-town beginnings. Bessie married Seward Shirer; Carl Van Vechten went away to study at the University of Chicago. He then pursued a journalism career in New York, winning fame and celebrity in the 1920s as a music critic, novelist, and

portrait photographer. Although he was a zealous convert to big-city living, Van Vechten never entirely escaped his roots. His 1924 roman à clef,
The Tattooed Countess, was a book that bubbled with unflattering depic-
tions of Cedar Rapids in the 1890s. When Van Vechten returned home
for a visit in October 1924, William Shirer, who was a student journalist
at the time, sought him out for an interview. Van Vechten advised Shirer
to "get the hell out of [town] as quickly as possible" if he wanted to succeed in life.[6]

The Tanner house in Cedar Rapids, a spacious two-story Victorian-style
frame dwelling, boasted a large front porch, a spacious parlor, five bed-
rooms, and a second-floor bathroom, which was a luxury at the time.
Although it was smaller than and relatively modest when compared to
many of the other dwellings along Second Avenue, the Tanner home was
well built and comfortable. Nonetheless, Shirer's life here was far from
easy; he worked hard in his youth. However, viewed through the lens of
today's sensibilities, any description of life in Cedar Rapids circa 1913
evokes sepia-toned mental images of the middle-America that artist Norman Rockwell depicted in his iconic *Saturday Evening Post* magazine covers. William Shirer spent his formative years, from age nine to twenty-one,
in this world. Idyllic though this now sounds, the reality is that he was
unsettled, for he had a love-hate relationship with his grandparents; the
Shirer brothers loved their grandfather, disliked their grandmother, a wisp
of a woman who ruled her home with an iron hand. Her personality
stood in marked contrast to that of her husband.

Frank Tanner was easy-going and genial. A big man with a bushy wal-
rus moustache and a gentle manner, he was like a second father to his
grandsons, especially young William. The two were kindred spirits, for
each had been nine when they lost their fathers.

By the time daughter Bessie returned home with her three children in
tow, Frank Tanner was age seventy and retired. Nothing much troubled
him. He had settled into a familiar routine that included afternoon sessions in his study, where he sat smoking his pipe and reading books about
the Civil War. Before dinner each evening, he would don his derby hat and
stroll down to the neighborhood saloon. There he would sit drinking and
talking with his chums, many of whom were fellow Civil War veterans.
These late-afternoon outings were an ongoing source of friction between
Shirer's grandparents. Josephine Tanner, a militant teetotaler, railed
against the evils of the "demon rum" and chided her husband for his
drinking. Grandfather Tanner took little notice of his wife's henpecking;

but other family members could not tolerate her stridency, especially young William. This proved problematic both for grandmother and grandson.

At age seventy-two, it could not have been easy for Josephine Tanner to have two bright, active, and independent minded boys living under her roof. For his part, Shirer decried his grandmother as being ill-tempered and mean. Josephine disciplined her grandsons by cuffing them about the ears. This went on until the day that young William fought back. According to an account of the incident, which Shirer wrote many years later, he and his grandmother got into an argument. As their tempers rose, Grandmother Tanner lashed out. A blow she struck knocked her grandson to the floor. Springing to his feet, he retaliated. A slap to the cheek and a shove sent the old lady sprawling. Not surprisingly, the commotion brought the rest of the family running, Shirer watched in horror as his mother and sister revived Grandmother Tanner with smelling salts and helped her to her bedroom. Shirer was awash in guilt and shame, but his grandmother "never hit me again, and her scolding dropped way off. And though my mother gave me a good bawling out, I felt that secretly she sympathized."[7]

The veracity of Shirer's account is questionable. In fact, his daughter, Inga Shirer Dean, doubts that the incident ever happened – at least not as Shirer described it. If it did occur, Dean said her father probably exaggerated, either for dramatic effect or because after sixty years of replaying the scene in his mind it had become real to him: "My father was not a violent man. He never hit his own kids, never even came close to doing so. I doubt he ever actually struck his grandmother. But the fact he said he *did* was a measure of how upset she made him."[8]

Given Shirer's antipathy toward Grandmother Tanner, it is not surprising that he was profoundly dismayed when his grandfather died after suffering a cerebral hemorrhage on the evening of 18 June 1914. Shirer was devastated. He had now lost the two male role models in his life within a span of less than a year. These experiences steeled him to the cruel caprices and uncertainties of life – both of which he would see more than his share of in coming years.

Like her husband, Josephine Tanner died unexpectedly, falling victim to a heart attack on the morning of 14 April 1917. Bessie Shirer inherited the Tanner family home, but her financial situation remained tight; fortunately for her, she and her three children by now had settled into life in Cedar Rapids. During the long, hot Iowa summers, the Shirer siblings played in the neighborhood, earned pocket money doing odd jobs, and sometimes traveled by train to visit their Uncle Dode and his wife, who lived "out west" in Miles City, Montana. Bessie's brother, big, fat, jovial, and childless, was a foreman on the Milwaukee Railroad.

When school began in autumn, young William and his brother John attended Jackson Elementary School, a few blocks from home. Sister Josephine, older and in the ninth grade, was a student at Washington High School, an imposing three-story edifice on Greene Square in the heart of the Cedar Rapids business district. In her youth, Bessie Shirer had gone to the same schools as her children now did.

During his own years at Jackson, William Shirer gave little indication that he would one day become famous or that he would accomplish anything of any importance. He was an indifferent student. Reading, writing, history, and geography were his favorite subjects, arithmetic his bane. Despite his undistinguished academic record, Shirer's early schooling had a pivotal impact on his life. This was largely due to the efforts of two outstanding teachers: Principals Frances Prescott of Jackson School and Abigail Abbott from Washington High. "These two remarkable women ... in those public schools in this rural town, had, by their friendship, by their encouragement, by their faith in me, done more for me than they probably ever realized."9

Both Prescott and Abbott saw that Shirer, who was headstrong, impulsive, and undisciplined as the prairie winds, burned with a fierce intelligence. Following the deaths of his father and grandfather and the disruption of the move from Chicago to Cedar Rapids, the boy was struggling to find himself. Books were his anchor in life; like his father before him, he was a voracious and dedicated reader.

It was around this same time that Shirer also started to develop a passion for writing, which became his emotional and creative outlet. He delighted in reading aloud his composition exercises to teachers and classmates. As his ability to express himself grew, so too did his ambitions. Thus Shirer was bitterly disappointed when in his sophomore year at Washington High he was not invited to join either of the school's two males-only Greek-letter "literary" fraternities. Frat boys dated the prettiest girls and filled most of the spots on the school debating team and the editorial staff of the student newspaper. Both of these latter extracurricular activities were ones at which Shirer might well have excelled if given the chance. Principal Abbott consoled him by suggesting that he start his own fraternity. Shirer, never a joiner, declined. Nonetheless, the principal's idea set her young charge thinking about positive ways to deal with rejection. It also spurred him to press ahead with his writing. As a result, by the time that he was sixteen and in his junior year at Washington High, he had already moved beyond writing for a high school newspaper. He was the "high school correspondent" for the *Daily Republican*, one of Cedar Rapids' two newspapers.

Shirer's restlessness spilled over into other areas of his life; he was impatient to leave school, find a real job, and grow up. In summer, he mowed lawns and weeded gardens, sold vegetables he grew in a backyard garden and eggs laid by some chickens he kept. In winter, he shoveled snow and tended furnaces for neighbors. Shirer strove to live up to his role as the man of the house.

His job prospects brightened considerably in April 1917, when America entered the war in Europe. The nation was ill-prepared for total mobilization; as industry was gearing up to meet those needs, nine million young men aged twenty-one and older were being drafted into the military. When many of them went overseas to fight, the country faced a labor shortage. Shirer, still just thirteen, was full of bravado and tall for his age. Too young to join the army, he had to be content to don an army uniform, take part in drills, and learn to shoot as a member of the Reserve Officers' Training Corps (ROTC) at Washington High.

The Armistice that ended the war on 11 November 1918 came all too soon for Shirer, who resented having missed the opportunity to prove his manhood in battle. To make up for it, he lied about his age in summer 1919 in order to attend the ROTC camp at Funston, Kansas. At least initially, the experience was heady stuff to a fifteen-year-old boy who was eager for adventure, and the $100 monthly salary seemed like a small fortune to him.

Shirer dutifully recorded many of the mundane details of his experiences in a pocket-sized notebook. Two things are abundantly clear from his pencil jottings. For one, peacetime army life was more tedious than eventful; Shirer's journal entries became fewer and further between as the summer wore on and the novelty of the fourteen-hour workdays, endless marching and drilling, and cautionary films about the dangers of sexually transmitted diseases waned. The other thing Shirer's journal entries underscore is the fact he was not cut out to be a soldier. In a test of his rifle-range marksmanship, when shooting from twenty-five yards in a prone position, he scored only nineteen hits out of a hundred shots; it was, he conceded in his diary, a "rotten" performance.[10] Adding injury to insult, a few days later, Shirer keeled over on the parade square in the searing heat of a July afternoon.[11]

Despite such misadventures, Shirer was loath to return home for his junior year at Washington High. For a time, after his ROTC training ended, Shirer stayed on as a civilian army field clerk earning $100 per month. He left the job and returned to Cedar Rapids only because his mother was adamant that he do so. However, he sewed a red discharge stripe on the sleeve of his tunic, and for several weeks at the start of the fall term – until Principal Abbott dissuaded him – Shirer wore his army uniform to school, as many returning veterans did. That summer he had also taken up pipe smoking, a habit that made him appear older and more pensive than many of his friends and classmates.

Shirer's career aspirations changed abruptly and often during his high school years. By continuing to lie about his age and with pipe stem clenched firmly between his teeth, he succeeded in landing adult jobs that filled his free time. One summer, he worked on a freight terminal loading dock. Another summer, he put in ten-hour days at the National Oats factory, where many of his co-workers were women who had found employment in the wide-open job market that existed during the First World War. Working alongside adults of both sexes was a crash course in the ways of the world for Shirer, still barely old enough to shave. The women at the factory swore, smoked, and drank like soldiers. Their newfound sense of freedom extended to their sexuality. After work Shirer's female co-workers sometimes "would invite you over to nearby Daniels Park 'for a drink and a roll' – an invitation I appreciated but was too exhausted and especially too afraid, in my Boy Scout purity, to accept."[12]

Fueled by such earthy experiences, Shirer grew up quickly. By 1920, he was eager to see the world, and his adolescent wanderlust was in full bloom. Thus, he landed a $20-per-week summer job with the Redpath-Vawter Lyceum Bureau, which staged traveling Chautauqua assemblies. That Bessie Shirer supported and abetted her son in his ambitions is clear. Because he was still a minor, Bessie was obliged to sign a release allowing "young Bill" to go on the road for three months. The contract she signed for his second summer stated that he was eighteen years of age on 23 February 1921.[13] In fact, he was only seventeen.

The Chautauqua phenomenon is now as quaint and long-gone as the Edison phonograph or the horse and buggy. However, in the latter decades of the nineteenth century and the early years of the twentieth, these traveling tent shows were all the rage across the United States and areas of southern Canada. Chautauqua was akin to vaudeville with a sprinkling of educational content; lectures and music were staples of the shows, which were touted as enlightening, wholesome family entertainment.[14] That reality was reflected in the "rules governing crew men," which were conspicuously printed at the end of that two-page employment contract Bessie Shirer signed on her son's behalf. All male Chautauqua workers were required to sleep in the crew's tent. In addition, they were restricted from leaving the job site without the boss's permission and were forbidden to swear or engage in "girling." ("This is not a social event but a summer's work," a cautionary note warned.)

Shirer reveled in the footloose lifestyle and the camaraderie of his Chautauqua workmates, most of whom were college students or former servicemen who were older and worldlier than a high school kid from Cedar Rapids. Shirer spent three summers traveling with Chautauqua companies. In 1920, his first year on the road, he worked in the mailroom sending out promotional brochures; the next two he toiled as a roustabout, erecting and collapsing the tent and moving the tons of show equipment: "I loved the traveling, the variety of the land as we jolted along in a [railway] day coach through the rolling cornfields of Iowa, the lake-studded countryside of Minnesota, the flat wheatlands of the Dakotas, [and] the hills of Missouri with its faint flavor of the South."[15]

Apart from being liberated from maternal controls and family responsibilities, the summers Shirer spent on the Chautauqua circuit were significant for another reason. His experiences opened his eyes and led him to subscribe to the scathing depiction of small-town life writer Sinclair Lewis presented in his 1920 satirical novel *Main Street*. That book, which rocketed the Minnesota-born author to national literary fame, lampooned the conformity, piety, and hypocrisies of life in a fictional Midwestern community called Gopher Prairie. Shirer's reading of *Main Street* fueled in him the same restless stirrings that his own parents had once felt. For the first time, he began to dream of a future working as a journalist in Chicago, or farther afield – in New York, London, or perhaps even Paris. These ambitions gave Shirer ample food for thought during the long days he spent on the road with Chautauqua. He had become "aware of girls,"[16] and in summer 1921 he met a pretty young co-worker named Peggy O'Neal who had graduated from college that spring. Dark-haired, blue-eyed, and alive with Irish vitality, she set Shirer's heart aflutter. Despite their employer's rules, a serious relationship blossomed during the three months he and Peggy worked side by side.

As the end of the summer drew near, she began musing aloud about their future together. That included marriage, a family, and settling down in a small college town where they could run a book or art shop. However, William Shirer was not ready to marry or settle down. Not yet. Maybe not ever, he decided. He was intent on going to college. However, he faced a huge problem in fulfilling that ambition.

3

More Questions than Answers

With money being tight at home, William Shirer's post-secondary educational options were limited. Thus, in autumn 1921 he enrolled at Coe College in Cedar Rapids, where tuition fees were sixty dollars per year. The campus was only a ten-minute walk from the Tanner family home. Shirer's sister Josephine was a senior at the school, and Shirer's brother John enrolled two years later. "Most of the students [at Coe] were like me. They came from solid families of modest means, many fresh off the farm and from the small towns. Most had to earn at least part of their way."[1]

Coe College had about 900 students at the time. In later years, Shirer lamented what he perceived to be the school's many shortcomings: geographical isolation, the inadequate library and lab facilities, and teachers who were poorly paid, and – at least in his opinion – poorly trained. Founded in 1851 as a Presbyterian seminary, Coe had severed its formal ties to the Presbyterian Church in 1881, but religion remained at the core of campus life; Coe president Harry Morehouse Gage was fervent in his belief that a solid grounding in theology was one of the essentials of a quality education. The two years of Bible study that were compulsory for all students grated on Shirer: "Both pupils and teachers and, of course, the administration and the trustees were proud of the Christian atmosphere of the campus ... as if that made up for the intellectual and cultural deficiencies."[2]

Coe was by no means unique in embracing traditional values. In the 1920s, religion occupied an even more prominent role in America than it does today. In a postwar world rife with turmoil and cynicism, the Christian faith offered stability and a measure of certainty at a time when the nation was ill prepared for the return to "normalcy" and the demobilization of two million veterans. It was in some measure due to the changed attitudes and loosened morality of those returning veterans that on 29 January 1919 Congress ratified the Eighteenth Amendment of the Constitution, the Volstead Act. The much-ballyhooed "noble experiment," which began one year to the day later, made illegal the "manufacture, sale, or transportation of intoxicating liquors within, the importation thereof into, or the exportation thereof from the United States."[3]

Adding impetus to the changes sweeping America were the new attitudes of women. Many of those who had had their first real taste of equality during the war years were loath to return to their submissive roles as housewives and mothers only. Three decades of agitation for gender equality culminated in the August 1920 ratification of the Nineteenth Amendment, which finally gave women the vote. This initiative was part of a broader process of intellectual ferment that prompted Americans young and old alike to reexamine many of their traditional values. As a result, the postwar years were characterized by a conservative backlash against many of the developments and trends that were reshaping American society.

Mobilization had brought about an unprecedented growth in the power of the federal government. This left conservatives and Jeffersonian democrats alike – young William Shirer being among the latter group – feeling uneasy. Meanwhile, the war had given rise to widespread suspicion toward immigrants, particularly those of German heritage. Fears of sabotage attacks had spurred Congress to pass legislation that was restrictive as well as repressive. The Espionage Act of 1917 and the Sedition Act of 1918 imposed fines and jail terms on anyone who was deemed to be "disloyal." These laws, which the Supreme Court ruled constitutional, resulted in more than 6,000 arrests and 1,500 convictions for "antiwar activities."

Further enflaming the social unrest sweeping postwar America, inflation was running rampant. Workers, strikebreakers, and troops clashed in the streets of America's cities. At the same time, racial tensions were simmering as large numbers of southern blacks who had migrated to northern cities seeking work in the burgeoning industrial sector clashed with demobilized veterans who were no less hungry for jobs.

Many Americans, tired of Europe's seemingly endless conflicts and suspicious of "foreigners" and their strange ideas, resented the wartime sacrifices the nation had made both at home and "over there." That disquiet was reflected in the results of the 1920 presidential election, when voters rejected President Woodrow Wilson's "abstract patriotism" and internationalist outlook. After eight years of Democratic rule, the electorate returned the Republicans to power. The new man in the White House was an ineffectual, small-town conservative who campaigned on a promise of a smooth return to normalcy. Ohio senator Warren Gamaliel Harding handily defeated Democratic challenger James Cox, winning more than 60 percent of the popular vote. Those who felt that the country should retreat into a kind of self-imposed isolationism now held power in Washington. This move "back to the future" was easier said than done, of course, and in a scenario that is eerily reminiscent of events in the wake of both the Second World War and the 9/11 terrorist attacks, a mass paranoia gripped America. This suspicion of foreigners – an unfathomable irony if ever there was one, in a nation settled, populated, and built by immigrants – resulted in a phenomenon that became known as "the Red Scare."

Life in Cedar Rapids, while somewhat insular, was not unaffected by national events. However, Iowans – as always – remained hard working, down-to-earth, deeply spiritual, and conservative. Those bedrock values shaped campus life at Coe College and dictated William Shirer's experiences during his four years there, even if he did not accept or subscribe to them as most of his classmates and teachers did: "In the beginning I was a practicing Presbyterian, green and ignorant, a country bumpkin, except that my mind may have matured a little from a good deal of extracurricular reading of novels and history in books."[4] Shirer's Coe experiences were only the beginning of his education, teaching him an essential lesson he would never forget: in life, there are many more questions than answers.

Despite the fact that making, selling, and transporting alcoholic beverages was illegal, the law did little to stem America's thirst for drink, and so the unintended effect of Prohibition was to spawn the growth of a vast underground criminal economy. Illegal alcohol was as available in Cedar Rapids as anywhere else, and drinking was a problem at Coe College, especially among the members of the campus fraternities. Despite this and despite the unrest and intellectual ferment bubbling around him, Shirer was happy at Coe, even if he declined to embrace the "rah rah" spirit of campus life. In later years, he professed his scorn for classmates who returned to their alma mater for reunions. In his mind, they were people "who never grew up." (Although he vowed never to be one of them, he eventually acceded, returning "home" to Coe for his 50th class reunion in 1975.)

Academically, Shirer was an inconsistent student; the transcript for his first three years at Coe includes marks ranging from As to Es, although he had no actual course failures. However, by his senior year, he was a solid B-average student. He excelled in English and History and earned top grades in Argumentation and Debate, which was not surprising, and in

Bible Studies, which *was*. His indifferent results in "military training" and gym class served as another reminder that he was unsuited for any career that involved robust physical activity. If Shirer distinguished himself at all during his Coe years, it was in his extracurricular activities. In addition to his fraternity involvements, he had passing engagements with the choir, the debating society, and the track-and-field team – the last because he was expected to compete rather than because he was athletically inclined.

The activity in which Shirer really made his mark was student journalism. He wrote for the campus newspaper, the *Coe College Cosmos*, taking on ever-more responsible roles. Shirer was sports editor in his sophomore year, managing editor in his junior year, and editor-in-chief in his senior year, 1924–25 – a reflection of his writing talents and his relationships with Coe College President Harry Morehouse Gage and Ethel Outland, his journalism professor.

Outland, one of the legendary figures in the college's history, was a 1909 Coe graduate, who taught English and journalism to generations of students in the thirty-eight years from 1911 to 1949; for more than a quarter century she served as the mentor to and den mother of the student journalists of the *Cosmos*. Outland recognized William Shirer's talents and encouraged him in his dreams of a journalism career and in his involvements with the *Cosmos*. It is evident that he felt comfortable in his relationship with her, for in their dialogues he often was critical of the Coe administration. "Frankly, I am disgusted and discouraged," Shirer wrote in a July 1924 letter to Miss Outland. "Sometimes I think that Coe in its anxiety to meet its liabilities in a financial way has lost sight of the fact that it is also supposed to be an educational institution."[5]

By necessity, William Shirer held part-time jobs during the four years he was a student at Coe. Sometimes he earned extra money a stagehand at Greene's Opera house in downtown Cedar Rapids; other times he toiled at manual labor, as he did in August 1922 when he worked on the Nebraska wheat harvest. And later that autumn, with the help of Ethel Outland, he landed a job in the newsroom of the Cedar Rapids *Daily Republican*, which provided his basic training in the world of workaday journalism. For three hours each morning, Shirer edited the newspaper's sports pages before heading to classes. The $25 he took home each week enabled him to contribute to his family's household budget, buy clothes and other personal necessities, and still have a few dollars to court girls on weekends.

In summer, when Shirer's hours at the newspaper became full-time, his job responsibilities increased correspondingly. Typically, he worked as many as sixty-five hours per week editing the sports pages, covering the games of the local semi-pro baseball team, and writing feature articles. For his efforts, he banked thirty-five dollars weekly during his first summer on the job, fifty dollars the second.

By all accounts, Shirer distinguished himself during his time at the *Daily Republican.* He was already displaying a keen nose for news, an eye for telling detail, and an ability to write quickly and well. His skills were on full display on 5 August 1923, when he covered the mid-morning arrival in Cedar Rapids of the train carrying the body of President Warren Harding, who had died suddenly while visiting San Francisco. Another Shirer article written a few weeks later caused even more of a stir. He scored a journalistic coup when he got an exclusive interview with boxer Jack Dempsey, the heavyweight champion of the world. Dempsey had won his title by knocking out opponents; Shirer earned his "scoop" by rousing Dempsey from a state of unconsciousness. When the stationmaster at the Cedar Rapids railway station tipped off Shirer that Dempsey's private Pullman car was part of a train that had stopped in town for a few hours, Shirer saw an opportunity. "In the best fashion of the cub reporter,"[6] Shirer talked his way into the Champ's stateroom and woke the boxer from a sound sleep. When Dempsey finished glaring at Shirer and accepted that the train was still in Iowa, he agreed to answer a few questions. Dempsey said nothing of any real importance, but Shirer's account of the interview appeared on page 1 of the next day's issue of the *Daily Republican*. That Shirer was becoming a local celebrity because of his journalism was made clear by the fact that even the editor of the rival *Gazette* stopped him on the street to congratulate him on his work.

Emboldened by his successes, Shirer sought out other visiting celebrities. They included several locals who had "made good," such as the aforementioned writer Carl Van Vechten, painter Grant Wood, and evangelist Billy Sunday. Shirer also got to know many of Cedar Rapids' leading citizens. Because he was making a name for himself as a journalist, in autumn 1924 Ethel Outland approved Shirer's bid to become managing editor of the *Cosmos*. His performance in the job did not disappoint her. Shirer proceeded to further distinguish himself by tackling a wide variety of topical issues in the columns for the editorial page of the campus newspaper. Some were typical student journalism, sophomoric and silly; others were well reasoned, informed, and displayed a depth of understanding that belied his youth. All were lively, provocative, and attracted readership both on campus and in the broader community. Shirer's rants earned him a reputation as a "crusading editor," as he is described in a

1951 edition of the alumni magazine that commemorated Coe College's centennial.

Shirer served as editor-in-chief of the *Cosmos* in his senior year. Inspired by the examples of two of his heroes – journalist H.L. Mencken and satirist Mark Twain – Shirer continued to ruffle feathers: he decried Coe's annual class executive elections as a farce; he chided the College's administration for various policies (including one that mandated compulsory attendance at the daily chapel services); and he called for updating the "outdated curriculum" of the English department. His criticisms did not stop at the boundaries of the Coe campus. Shirer sniped at larger targets when he chided Cedar Rapids politicians and civic leaders and voiced pointed opinions on topics of the day. On one occasion, in a retrospective article on the influential figures who had died in 1924, Shirer favorably compared Russian Bolshevik leader Vladimir Lenin to United States President Woodrow Wilson and Italian classical composer Giacomo Puccini. Such youthful pronouncements were too much for some irate college trustees and members of the local Chamber of Commerce – "the Bolshevik hunters around these parts," as Shirer dismissed them[7] – who complained to Coe President Harry Morehouse Gage about Shirer's "radicalism."

Unlike his predecessors, Coe President Harry Gage was no ordinary clergyman. He was also a distinguished academic, having earned a doctorate degree in divinity at Union College in New York before pursuing graduate studies at Columbia University. Gage, who was forty-two when he became president of Coe in 1920, was determined to transform the college into a first-class academic institution. Gage, like Ethel Outland, held Shirer in high regard. The president encouraged his young charge to read widely, think critically, and express his opinions forcefully, while also being tolerant of the actions and opinions of others. Life was about standing up for your beliefs, while also being willing to compromise, Gage patiently explained. For Shirer, brimming with youthful fire and enthusiasm, that was "a lesson that was hard for me to learn."[8]

Shirer and Gage spent many hours talking and debating issues of the day, and in the process Gage emerged as a father figure and mentor to Shirer. In the circumstances, it is not at all surprising that Coe's president declined to muzzle or discipline his young charge for his at-times intemperate outbursts. Gage correctly sensed that Shirer was struggling to find direction in life, particularly where matters of personal faith were concerned. In fact, two months before beginning his senior year at the college, Shirer confided in his diary. "I find myself without conviction toward everything making for life. In the matter of morals and religion and politics and education ... I find myself expressing grave doubts. I am at sea."[9]

Outwardly, at least, Shirer was an opinionated – twenty-one-year-old who exuded a self-confidence that prompted him to hold forth on a wide range of topics.[10] For example, in an essay – for which he earned a grade of A minus – he dismissed the need for and the value of Coe students actually studying, something "that the school authorities" did not want or expect and which only earned "measly, meaningless numbers known as grades."[11]

In a final display of bravado, he scrawled a handwritten signature in pencil across page 2 of the 10 June 1925, bound office copy of the *Cosmos*, which featured his final editorial ("We Fade from the Picture"). In that same farewell offering, Shirer paid tribute to Ethel Outland, to whom he acknowledged "We owe her a great deal more than she will ever know. To her we have gone with our little troubles on more than one occasion."

During his year as editor-in-chief, Shirer occasionally mused in print about his youthful doubts and confusions. In his final editorial he admitted his uncertainties and even poked fun at his own skepticism: "We doubt not that our critics have been right. We admit to being too often controversial and sometimes even sour ... But youth sometimes is that way and we will blame it on our tender age. A few years of experience will affect a change of viewpoint, our friends tell us. We believe them."[12]

In no aspect of his life was this truer than where theology was concerned. Shirer already harbored doubts that Christianity, or any faith, could be *the* one true religion. Shirer wrestled with questions of faith and tolerance all his life. It was with such unresolved, and unresolvable, questions still swirling in his mind that he graduated from Coe College in June 1925 – with no long-term goals, no firm career path in mind, other than the vague notion that he hoped to earn a living as a journalist. First, however, he yearned to spend a summer traveling to some of the cities he had dreamed of visiting: New York, London, and Paris. Especially Paris.

Following the commencement ceremony, where he received his Bachelor of Arts degree, Shirer waved goodbye to family, friends, and the tearful young woman he had been dating.[13] He had scraped together $200, which was just enough for a summer in Europe. That sum included $100 awarded by his paternal uncle and namesake, William G. Shirer, and a $100 loan that Harry Morehouse Gage had spotted him. Shirer caught a ride into Chicago with his uncle, who had driven in his flivver to Cedar Rapids to see his favorite nephew graduate from college. After a few days in the Windy City, Shirer set off by train for New York, where he spent a week seeking a job as a newspaper reporter, took in a Broadway show, and looked up a few acquaintances. On 4 July, he traveled by train to Montreal, where he met up with a friend from Coe College named George H. Latta.[14] The two hoped to sign on as deckhands on a cargo ship bound for England or Europe.

Although they were impatient to be off, they cooled their heels for nine days in a grungy boarding house near the docks, surviving on meals of bread and cheese, and passing time on park benches or hanging around the campus of McGill University. Finally, early on the morning of 14 July 14 they departed for England aboard a cattle boat, the S.S. *Manchester*. Their grand adventure had begun.

4

Paris

The years between the two great wars of the last century were the golden age of ocean liners. For North America's well-heeled and the burgeoning middle class, overseas travel had never been more affordable, convenient, or comfortable. However, William Shirer and George Latta had no choice but to work their way across the Atlantic. In an ersatz diary that he kept on scraps of paper, Latta recorded the details of their voyage aboard the *Manchester Importer*. The work they did shoveling manure out of the cattle stalls and feeding the animals was hard, dirty, and hot, but Latta and Shirer were well fed – soup, boiled potatoes, and beef three times per day – even if cleanliness was not part of the cook's routine; one day, Latta found a piece of dishrag in his soup.

The weather being fair and the seas calm, neither Shirer nor Latta suffered from any extended period of seasickness. The twelve-day voyage was mostly uneventful, although the two travelers did spot a school of porpoises, numerous icebergs, and even the carcass of a dead whale. Shirer and Latta filled the hours between work sessions playing cards, writing letters, reading, and joining the other members of the crew in raucous debates about life, women, and politics. Latta, a talented artist, did pencil sketches of people and shipboard scenes. Regrettably, his sketchbooks have been lost, but he also took photos using an old Brownie camera that he carried on the trip. One of his grainy snapshots shows a coverall-clad Shirer leaning against the ship's railing, smoking a cigarette and looking every bit a hard-working crewman.

Both Shirer and Latta were tired of shoveling cow manure by the time the *Manchester Importer* reached port on 28 July. Quickly disembarking, the pair made their way to London by rail. Then, after seeing the sights in the British capital, visiting Oxford University and Shakespeare's hometown of Stratford-on-Avon, they traveled to France, where they stopped off to tour some World War One battlefields and cemeteries.

The French capital was *the* destination of choice for Shirer and Latta, as it was for all footloose American tourists, British people fleeing the dreariness of postwar London, impoverished Russian nobility displaced by the 1917 Bolshevik revolution, and an eclectic assortment of intellectuals and other dreamers and schemers of all nationalities. Paris in the 1920s was the venue for a flowering of the arts: performance, visual, and literary. The city was alive with gaiety, romance, history, and the legendary French *joie de vivre*. There was no prohibition in France – or anywhere else in Europe – and indeed the French regarded America's ban on alcohol consumption with a mixture of amusement and scorn.

Paris was wonderfully affordable for those with greenbacks to spend, the exchange rate being pegged at about four francs to the dollar. Small wonder American tourists – and Canadians – flocked to the city; tens of thousands of them took up residence for extended periods. Hotels, shops, bars, and cafés catered to Americans, as did three English-language daily newspapers. English was the "second language" on the terraces of many of the cafés and bistros in the famous Latin Quarter. Nowhere was this more the case than at popular American hangouts such as the Café Du Dome, the Deux Magots, the Rotonde, the Sélect, and the Closerie des Lilas, where the young Ernest Hemingway often sat as he wrote in the mornings.

Malcolm Cowley, the celebrated literary critic and chronicler, has noted that while Hemingway's star has dimmed with the passing of years, changing tastes, and "posthumous assaults on his reputation,"[1] in the early 1920s he was on his way to becoming one of the – if not *the* – world's most famous and popular authors. His influence on an entire generation of writers is undeniable; and Hemingway was the role model for Shirer and many other wannabe novelists of the day. "Most American writers on the Left Bank ... merely talked of writing," Shirer observed, "but Hemingway worked hard and took his writing with deadly seriousness."[2]

Hemingway, like the other American writers and artists who flocked to Paris at the time were members of the "lost generation," as poet and self-styled literary guru Gertrude Stein dubbed them. Like Shirer, they had rejected what they saw as the monotony, provincialism, and hypocrisy of postwar American society: "Civilization in America, they proclaimed, had gone all wrong ... Life had become tawdry, vulgar, uncreative, a mad grab for the dollar. Artists and writers – and creative individuals – could not grow on such barren soil. They must flee abroad, to Paris, if possible. Only there could they fulfill themselves."[3]

Patrons of the Left Bank cafés sometimes encountered Hemingway and fellow American expatriate writers, including F. Scott Fitzgerald, E.E. Cummings, Ezra Pound, John Dos Passos, Edith Wharton, Willa Cather, Hart Crane, and the aforementioned Gertrude Stein. By the mid-1920s, Paris had become the cultural mecca and ersatz home of a who's who of American literature. As Hemingway put it in a 1950 letter to a friend, "If you are lucky enough to have lived in Paris as a young man, then wherever you go for the rest of your life, it stays with you, for Paris is a moveable feast."[4] That wonderfully evocative descriptor, "a movable feast," has become synonymous with Paris in the 1920s.

William Shirer could certainly relate to those words. Ever after, he would cherish the memories of being twenty-one, utterly free, and having had the opportunity to savor the pleasures of a cornucopia of Parisian sights, sounds, tastes, and emotions: those "were the happiest and most wondrous, if not the most important and eventful, years of my life."[5]

There was no shortage of inexpensive accommodation in the Left Bank neighborhoods of Paris. Shirer and George Latta spent the summer of 1925 living in a pension on Boulevard Port Royal, a few blocks from the Sorbonne. With little money to spare, they stayed up late, slept in most mornings, and idled away afternoons in the Luxembourg Gardens, the sprawling sixty-acre park in the heart of Paris. The two young Americans contented themselves by lolling about on the grass and benches in the park. Latta sketched; Shirer smoked his pipe, basked in the sunshine, and read inexpensive editions of the French classics that he purchased at book-stalls along the Seine. He also honed his language skills by chatting up friendly shopgirls and secretaries who ate lunch in the park.

In the evenings, Shirer and Latta joined the crowds on the terraces of the Left Bank cafés and bistros. Here they watched the world go by, smoked, flirted, read, talked with new friends, and drank wine when they had the money, or when someone else bought. Years later, Malcolm Cowley recalled the young William Shirer of this period as having "his hair ... neatly parted a little left of center to correspond with his opinions."[6] It was a wonderfully carefree time, albeit a formative one for Shirer. However, as the summer slipped away and his money dwindled, Shirer's scheduled 20 August departure for home loomed like a grim shadow.

Shirer and Latta had booked return passage on the same cattle boat on which they had come over. Compounding Shirer's reluctance to go home was the fact he did not want to return to Cedar Rapids; his only real option was to hope for newspaper work in Chicago or New York. Even more daunting than any job hunt was the unappealing reality of life back home: "The bigotry and the banality, the inanities of a society dominated by quacks, by fundamentalism, Puritanism, and the puerility of President Coolidge were not what a youngster looked forward to returning to and trying to live with, to live the only life given to you."[7]

Desperate to remain in Paris, he made a last round of the city's English-language newspapers, magazines, and news agency offices. The editor of one newspaper Shirer had visited had showed him a file bulging with the résumés of hundreds of job seekers; other editors had invited him to leave his résumé, while cautioning that his chance of getting hired were slim to none.

On their last night in town, the sun was coming up as he and Latta stumbled back to their pension exhausted and hung-over. Their plan was to grab a few hours of sleep before catching the noon boat-train for London. However, as Shirer stumbled into their room he spotted an envelope that had been slipped under the door. Too tipsy to pick it up, Shirer collapsed onto his bed. It was only after he stirred a few hours later that he remembered the envelope, which bore the logo of the *Chicago Tribune*. Shirer had visited the newsroom of the *Tribune*'s Paris edition, a crowded, bustling workplace on the third floor of the *Petit Journal* building at 5 Rue Lamartine. Here Shirer had spoken with city editor David Darrah. Being not much older than the young job seeker before him, Darrah was cordial, but he had offered little hope of a job. So Shirer was surprised and delighted that Darrah had sent him a note to let him know that if he was still looking for work, he should drop by the newsroom some evening soon at about nine o'clock.

Despite the vagueness of Darrah's invitation and the fact he was all but broke, Shirer ignored George Latta's warning. Having opted to stay on in Paris, Shirer waved goodbye to his friend as Latta boarded a train at the Gare du Nord. Alone now, Shirer returned to the pension intent on resting for a few hours. However, finding he was too keyed-up to sleep, he got dressed and walked the streets until dinner hour. He then he used a few of his remaining francs to buy a meager dinner and half liter of wine, the latter to fortify his courage.

It was exactly 9 p.m. when Shirer appeared in the *Tribune* newsroom, where David Darrah was already hard at work. After greeting the nervous young job applicant, the city editor asked how much experience Shirer had working as a copyeditor. "Two years," Shirer replied. True, he had done a bit of copyediting during his summer stints in the sports department of the Cedar Rapids *Daily Republican* and during his days at the *Coe College*

Cosmos, but that was it. Shirer also stretched the truth when Darrah asked about his ability to function in French. Part of the *Tribune* job involved translating articles from Havas, the French news agency.

Darrah explained that he was in dire need of a copyeditor, preferably someone with ties to or knowledge of Chicago. Setting aside the doubts he surely must have had, Darrah looked Shirer in the eye and cautioned him that he could only expect to make about sixty dollars per month at the *Tribune*. It was a starvation wage, but Shirer was determined to make do regardless. He was grateful to have found a job: "On such a slender thread does the course of one's whole adult life hang … From the age of twenty-one mine would follow a path quite different from the one it had been on."[8] In good measure that was due to his work with the *Chicago Tribune* and his at-times stormy relationship with the newspaper's irascible hands-on publisher Colonel Robert McCormick.

The Paris edition of the *Chicago Tribune* employed twenty people in 1925, nine of them in the newsroom, which was perpetually short-staffed. The reason was simple: of the three English-language newspapers in Paris at the time, the *Tribune* paid its employees the least and so staff turnover was high. "You knew … that whatever else happened [at the *Tribune*], *somebody* would be certain *not* to show up for work because he was drunk, and that this extra burden would fall on the other members of the staff. You [also] knew … that *somebody* would be certain *to* show up because he was drunk,"[9] notes writer Harold Stearns.

This was the same Harold Stearns whose 1922 book *Civilization in the United States* had inspired Shirer and many other young Americans to seek intellectual salvation abroad. Having heeded his own advice, Stearns was among the first of the would-be expatriates to sail for Europe. Like Shirer, Stearns found work at the *Tribune*. He was hired to write a daily horseracing column. And like Shirer, Stearns came to understand how physically and mentally draining workaday journalism could be, especially for those who toiled in the employ of the *Chicago Tribune*, the self-anointed "World's Greatest Newspaper."

While any such claim was debatable, there is no denying that in 1925 the *Tribune* was one of America's most influential dailies or that the Tribune Company was one of America's great media empires. Its ascendancy was orchestrated by Colonel Robert Rutherford McCormick, the newspaper's irascible, autocratic, and xenophobic publisher. McCormick was as strong-willed as he was eccentric; a dark streak ran in the family. One of his grandfathers had died in an insane asylum, and McCormick's brother Joseph took his own life. Alluding to this, William Shirer wrote, "'All of the McCormicks,' [the Colonel] would say, 'are crazy – except me,' though some of us who worked for him wondered about the validity of the exception."[10]

McCormick ruled his *Tribune* empire with an autocrat's iron hand until his death in 1955. Being an unabashed Chicago booster, he was acutely aware of the rivalry between New York and America's "Second City." Although he was adamantly isolationist, during World War One he had launched a four-page Army Edition tabloid that was published in Paris. When the newspaper hit the streets on 4 July 1917 McCormick trumpeted it as being a patriotic gesture intended to boost the morale of soldiers in the American Expeditionary Force; he conveniently ignored or forgot that the army itself produced its own newspaper, *The Stars and Stripes*.

Two months after its appearance, the Army Edition became a full-size newspaper. As the circulation grew, a cable service from Chicago was launched, and the original staff of three more than doubled in size. Not surprisingly, given this success, McCormick opted to continue publishing his Paris edition after the war ended, avowing in an editorial that the paper was "dedicated ... to a new role, as the remaining link of communications, in both directions, between the old world and the new."[11] Cynics suspected that McCormick planned to use the newspaper as a platform in Europe from which to trumpet his opposition to the League of Nations, an institution to which he was adamantly opposed; the Colonel was suspicious of anything "foreign." Other observers noted the possibility, not unreasonable given McCormick's sizeable ego, that he simply wanted to maintain an overseas presence to prove to the world that the *Tribune* could compete with the other six American newspapers that had foreign news services, especially the arch-rival *Chicago Daily News*, and the four that were New York based – *The New York Times*, the *New York Herald Tribune*, the *World*, and the *Evening Post*. (The Boston-based *Christian Science Monitor* was the other.)

The *Chicago Tribune* and the other American newspapers with foreign news services did not have the field to themselves. Competition was intense. As yet, there were no broadcast correspondents; however, there were three rival American news agencies: the Associated Press (AP), the United Press (UP), and one operated by the Hearst newspaper chain. Each of these agencies maintained bureaus and networks of paid contacts in various overseas capitals. These men and women reported breaking news to their agency and its subscribers, which included thousands of newspapers across North and South America, the *Tribune* being among them.

This left correspondents in the employ of the *Chicago Tribune* Foreign News Service (FNS) free to focus on writing articles that provided context and background color to the day's top stories.

The system for gathering foreign news at the time is worth noting since the journalism to which it gave rise would have a huge impact back in the USA. These journalists – there were only about 300 of them in total – exerted profound influence on public opinion and, arguably, on the United States' foreign policy, for their articles informed, colored, and shaped the worldview of successive generations. Shirer was destined to become one of the leading lights of this select group of opinion leaders.

Overseas news operations have always been expensive, labor intensive, and time consuming. That was especially so in the 1920s, when cable was used to convey breaking news across the seas. It cost as much as a dollar a word for a telegram, and so most features articles were sent via the postal service. With cables being prohibitively expensive, a kind of shorthand language known as "cablese" evolved. This gave birth to some odd new words. A man with a Vandyke beard was described as being "vandyked," while a shooting victim was said to have been "revolverized."

However, those were the idiosyncratic exceptions rather than the rule. For the most part, cablese was limited to everyday words; codes were seldom used because of the time needed to decipher them and because of the possibility of mistakes happening. The use of cablese died out with the coming of new communication technologies, yet its impact was significant since it shaped the writing style of a generation of journalists and of former journalists, Ernest Hemingway being the most notable example. His sinewy prose style, journalistic in tone with simple declarative sentences and a paucity of adjectives and adverbs, became hugely influential and popular with readers. Legend has it that after being chided for having taken an unscheduled leave, Hemingway quit his job as a *Toronto Star* correspondent by cabling *Star* publisher Harry Hindmarsh, "ADVISE YOU UPSTICK JOB ARSEWARDS."[12] The veracity of that anecdote is uncertain. What is not is that Hemingway's bare-bones style contributed to the decline of the flowery Victorian-era prose that characterized so much American writing in the early decades of the twentieth century. By summer 1925 he had published two books, and the American expatriate literary community in Paris was abuzz with gossip about Hemingway, who already was projecting a carefully cultivated image as a larger-than-life character.

Shirer encountered Hemingway in person for the first time when the two met one day on the patio of the Closerie des Lilas café. Hemingway was sitting with Ezra Pound when Shirer and two of his *Tribune* work-mates happened along. The trio got into a conversation with Pound about the merits of the various Paris literary magazines. Pound, who at the time was regarded as one of America's greatest poets, was helping writer Ford Madox Ford with the editing of a journal called the *Transatlantic Review*. Hemingway was a star contributor, whom Pound obligingly was hailing as America's best young prose writer.

As the discussion between Pound and Shirer's companions deepened, Hemingway and Shirer struck up a conversation. Shirer had heard of Hemingway and was in awe of him. And so he was surprised that Hemingway did not look or talk like a writer: "He was big and athletic, with a ruddy complexion and bright, lively eyes."[13] When Hemingway learned Shirer was a fellow Chicagoan who had worked as a sports reporter, he quickly turned the conversation to boxing, cycling, and tennis, which were some of his favorite sports. "He said not a word about writing, which I was hoping he would, for like most of the young Americans in Paris, I was already trying to write poems and short stories and finding it more difficult than I had anticipated."[14]

Shirer's first encounter with Hemingway was memorable, albeit mundane. His introduction to another of Paris's most famous American expatriate writers was much more noteworthy. F. Scott Fitzgerald, only twenty-nine years old but already speeding along the road to literary immortality, alcoholism, and self-destruction, was drunk the night he clambered up the stairs and staggered into the *Tribune* newsroom. Plopping himself down at the copy desk, Fitzgerald announced that he had come to help his friend James Thurber get "the god-damned paper" out. Thurber, perpetually short of money and at age thirty-five still struggling to find his literary feet, had joined the *Tribune* staff a few months earlier.

Thurber had taken young Bill Shirer under his wing, and so it was to him that Shirer now turned for guidance. Puzzled over the identity of the clean-cut, smartly dressed young visitor, he whispered a query in Thurber's ear. Thurber responded by announcing in a voice loud enough for all to hear that their uninvited "guest" this night was *Mister* Scott Fitzgerald. "Never heard of him, eh?" the drunken writer shouted, casting a challenging glance Shirer's way. But Shirer *had* heard of Fitzgerald and proclaimed it in a no-less-loud voice. Shirer had read Fitzgerald's 1920 debut novel *This Side of Paradise*. He had also read Fitzgerald's latest book, *The Great Gatsby*, which had been published just a few months earlier to mixed reviews.

Gatsby's creator insisted on staying put on this night, even when the copyeditor in whose chair Fitzgerald was sitting returned from a break.

Unfazed, Fitzgerald proceeded to sing loudly and set about tearing up any sheets of copy paper that were within his reach, including articles written for the next edition of the newspaper. Despite the distraction, the *Tribune* staff managed to put out a paper. A group that included Shirer, Eugene Jolas, Elliot Paul, and Thurber then set out to escort their guest to his home. En route they stopped at various cafés for drinks. When Fitzgerald finally passed out, his rescuers loaded him into a taxi. He came to just as they were arriving at his apartment building, and there ensued a raucous confrontation between Fitzgerald and his pajama-clad wife Zelda. Angry now, Fitzgerald turned on Thurber, whom he was intent on bashing on the head with a chunk of iron grating he had seized upon. Fortunately for Thurber, who was blind in one eye, Jolas tackled Fitzgerald. Shirer and Paul then disarmed him before carrying him upstairs to his flat.

Shirer was understandably nonplussed by his introduction to the man some critics today regard as one of the best American writers – if not *the* best – of his generation: "I was not yet grown up enough to realize, I guess, that it mattered not a damn how much of a nuisance a writer could make of himself, especially when drunk … The only thing that counted was how he wrote, and Fitzgerald wrote as well as anyone and often, as in Gatsby, better."[15]

By autumn 1925, William Shirer had settled into his new life in Paris. With a regular paycheck – even if it was only fifteen dollars a week – he could afford more permanent lodgings. So he rented a housekeeping room in the Hotel de Lisbonne, a historic inn located near the corner of rue Monsieur-le-Prince and rue de Vaugirad, in the heart of the Left Bank: "By the time I arrived, [it] was full of Americans, mostly from the Paris *Tribune* … Nearly half our staff had settled down there and this made the place very convivial though it detracted from one's privacy. Each knew pretty much what the others were up to, especially romantically, but at our early age that did not seem to matter greatly."[16]

Ned Calmer, another *Tribune* reporter who later became a CBS radio news commentator and war correspondent, immortalized life at the hotel in his 1961 novel *All the Summer Days*. If Calmer's novel is memorable for anything, it is the author's description of Paris in the 1920s and life in the Hotel de Lisbonne. The eighteenth-century building was an oddity in that it had central heating, a rarity for Paris. Otherwise, as Ned Calmer noted, the Lisbonne was showing its age. A plaque (which is still there) mounted on the wall near the front door, commemorates the building as the one-time residence of two of the most celebrated French literary figures of the nineteenth century: Charles Baudelaire (1821-1867), the father of the symbolist movement in French poetry, and Paul Verlaine (1884-1893), who is regarded as being Baudelaire's artistic and intellectual heir.

For about ten American dollars per month, Shirer rented a spacious, high-ceilinged room that was sparsely furnished, but bright and functional. The only thing the Lisbonne lacked was proper bathrooms. Those who wished to take a bath or shower were obliged to go across the street to use the facilities at one of Paris's many public bathhouses. Next to the stairwell on each floor of the Hotel de Lisbonne was a closet-sized communal "Turkish toilet." These facilities consisted of a cement mound on the floor with a four-inch hole in the middle. "On each side was a raised footrest, similar to one on a bootblack's stand ... The trick was to achieve a proper balance without keeling over."[17]

Apart from its colorful past, a kind of frat-house atmosphere, and the central heating, which proved invaluable during the bitterly cold winter of 1925–26, what made the Hotel de Lisbonne a desirable address was its convenient location. The building was a short walk from the Luxembourg Gardens and the cafés, restaurants, and bookshops of the Latin Quarter. Among the latter was Sylvia Beach's now-legendary Shakespeare and Company at 12 Rue de l'Odéon, where Hemingway, Ezra Pound, and James Joyce were among the regular customers. Shirer was too cash-strapped to buy, or even to rent, many books. However, when he could afford it, he read inexpensive editions of the French classics – Hugo, Molière, Zola, et al. He also spent time taking courses at Collège de France and chatting-up the young female students and office workers he met in cafés and on the benches in the Luxembourg Gardens. Shirer found French women irresistible. The attraction was mutual. "They certainly were not waiting for marriage in order to enjoy making love ... I learned a great deal from them that first year in Paris, and in the process greatly improved my French."[18]

Shirer's journalism apprenticeship was also continuing apace in his work with the *Tribune*. He learned the lessons of the writer's craft and forge lifelong friendship with some of his co-workers and with other journalists he met. Among the latter were fellow Chicagoans John Gunther, a correspondent for the rival *Chicago Daily News*, and Vincent ("Jimmy") Sheean, who had been fired by the same paper for insubordination and now sometimes wrote for another English-language daily called the *Paris Times*. "We were, the three of us, Chicago kids, and we all had a lot of luck," Shirer recalled many years later.[19]

5

The World's Dizziest Newspaper

William Shirer's first year in Paris passed in a blur. Despite his chronic shortage of cash and his frustrations as a writer of fiction or poetry, he was content to hone his journalistic skills at the *Tribune*. At the time, the twenty-member staff was all-male. Newcomers were thrown into the deep end to either swim or sink. The pay was poor, and staff turnover was high; however, those who stuck it out came to share a deep and abiding sense of comradeship. During its storied seventeen-year existence (1917–34), the newspaper was home to a remarkable roster of characters and literary talents. In addition to Shirer, Root, and Thurber, the impressive list of now well-known writers who were on staff or sometimes contributed articles includes Henry Miller, Gertrude Stein, Ford Madox Ford, Kay Boyle, Elliot Paul, and Vincent Sheean. Despite this, the newspaper's historical reputation has been exaggerated; as Waverley Root observes, "[It] seems to have benefited by comparison with the relatively colorless [Paris] *Herald*."[1]

While the *Tribune*'s offices were located on the Right Bank, its sensibilities were firmly rooted in the bohemian culture of the Left Bank. Daily circulation was about 8,000, most of which were read by American expatriates and tourists, and so the editorial staff churned out a selection of domestic news content, articles about the Parisian social scene, interviews with local and visiting celebrities, sports stories, and even a daily one-page supplement for the Riviera during "the season." The latter was printed in Nice and inserted into the copies of the newspaper when they arrived aboard the morning train from Paris.

As a new hire, William Shirer's nightly duties in the Paris newsroom – from eight p.m. to two a.m. – involved editing articles culled from various news services, writing headlines, and rewriting news stories cribbed from French newspapers. The work was often tedious, but the people were endlessly interesting and often funny. The *Tribune*'s music critic, Irving Schwerke, described the publication as "the world's dizziest newspaper." He was right about that. Produced on a shoestring budget, the *Tribune* was as much a work of imagination as of journalism.

Most of the editorial content was wire copy sent from the London office of the Chicago *Tribune* FNS. Out of this raw material, a few paragraphs of cablese, each night the staff of the Paris edition spun enough domestic "news" to fill much of the front page and several columns inside the eight-page newspaper. Even letters to the editor were created; so much for journalistic integrity or any pretensions of it.

James Thurber was a master at expanding the nightly news cable from New York. Other *Tribune* writers, Shirer among them, also became adept at generating "creative" editorial material. Just a few days after he started working at the newspaper, one of the editors prevailed upon him to craft a news story out of a ten-word account of the crash of a dirigible in Ohio. He did such a wondrous job that a few weeks later, the same editor had him invent the details of a maritime accident that led to the loss of an American navy submarine and its thirty-four crewmen. Shirer's efforts won him the job as the *Tribune*'s unofficial "disaster specialist."

In summer 1926, William Shirer returned to a job as a beat reporter. The move away from the night shift in the newsroom might have been viewed as a demotion had Shirer not volunteered for it. The departures from Paris of his good friends James Thurber and the Iowa-born painter Grant Wood – both of whom had returned home to the States – prompted him to change the direction of his own life. He decided his work with the Paris edition might be his stepping-stone to a more prestigious job with the FNS. Foreign correspondents were paid in American dollars rather than French francs, and they routinely traveled throughout Europe and even into Asia, something Shirer was keen to do. However, before he could even hope to catch on with the FNS, he faced some significant problems. For one, competition for jobs with the service was intense. For another, at age twenty-two, Shirer was regarded as being too young to be a foreign correspondent. And finally, he'd had no dealings or relationship with Henry ("Hank") Wales, the service's Paris bureau chief. This cigar-smoking curmudgeon from New Jersey – a self-described "really mean guy" – enjoyed a well-deserved reputation as the archetypal foreign correspondent, even if he boasted that for most of his career he never owned a trenchcoat, the iconic symbol of his vocation. Wales was known less for his sartorial style than for his credentials as a shrewd, no-nonsense newsman.

Shirer settled on a couple of strategies in hopes of impressing Wales. One was to master the technical skill of writing in cablese. The other was even more pragmatic: he set out to distinguish himself both by the quantity and quality of his writing. Predictably, the former proved easier than the latter. Important news stories, headline-grabbers about politics, crime, and juicy scandals, generally were the preserve of FNS correspondents. Shirer and the other two staff reporters of the Paris edition wrote about more mundane matters, usually life in the American community in Paris and the activities of visitors to the city. In his youthful hauteur, Shirer increasingly found himself embarrassed, appalled even, by what he felt was the loutish behavior of his fellow countrymen. Adopting the same cheeky tone he had affected during his student days as editor of the *Coe College Cosmos*, Shirer was not shy about injecting caustic opinions about this and other matters into his journalism. His at-times acerbic tone was indicative of his mindset; he had grown tired of his work. However, working days afforded Shirer more time to socialize, and he soon became involved in a love affair with a dark-haired Frenchwoman he identifies in his writings only as Yvonne. She earned a living writing freelance articles, and in later years, she reportedly worked as Ernest Hemingway's secretary whenever he was in town, typing his manuscripts and helping him with his correspondence. "[Yvonne] was Parisian to the bone," Shirer recalled, "chic, sophisticated, witty, bursting with energy and animation, and yet underneath rather contemplative, full of wonder about life, exhaustively curious about it, but always skeptical, and determined to make the best of it that she could."[2]

At age twenty-seven, Yvonne was five years Shirer's elder. She was also infinitely worldlier. For one thing, she was married. That revelation came as a shock to Shirer, since it called into question the integrity of his own youthful rejection of the socially conservative values of his Midwestern upbringing. He was also frustrated, for he correctly sensed that the future of his relationship with Yvonne was tenuous at best. Despite this, she sometimes traveled with him on his foreign assignments, which by now were becoming more frequent. Ironically, this development came about not because of the quality of Shirer's work in Paris, but rather because of his experience as the sports editor back in Cedar Rapids.

The FNS assigned, "as needed," a reporter from the Paris bureau to cover high-profile sporting events. When the journalist who usually handled these stories quit, Hank Wales tabbed Shirer as the emergency replacement. Reporting on boxing matches and golf and tennis tournaments heightened Shirer's profile. It also opened unexpected doors for him and led to the opportunity that he needed to win a full-time job with the *Tribune*'s foreign news service.

Europe was abuzz in spring 1927 in anticipation of impending attempts by daredevil aviators to fly between New York and Paris. A $25,000 prize offered by a Franco-American philanthropist named Raymond Orteig, international fame, and bragging rights would all go to anyone who would be the first to make that perilous 3,800-mile flight. The name Charles Lindbergh was mentioned only in passing in all of the hoopla. Despite the fact the twenty-five-year-old airmail pilot was the son of a flamboyant multi-term congressman, Lindbergh was a virtual unknown when he announced his intention to attempt a solo crossing of the Atlantic in a single-engine plane, a feat most observers felt would prove to be suicidal. Reporters referred to Lindbergh as the "Flying Fool." Regardless, he took off from New York a few minutes before eight o'clock on the morning of 20 May 1927. By four p.m. the next day, Lindbergh's tiny silver-colored Ryan monoplane, *The Spirit of St. Louis*, had reached Ireland, and excitement began to build in the French capital as word spread of Lindberg's imminent arrival.

In the Paris newsroom of the *Tribune*, managing editor Bernhard Ragner failed to grasp the significance of the drama that was unfolding only a few miles away. Hank Wales, having a far more discerning nose for news, realized that the Lindbergh story might be one of the biggest of his career, and he wanted to be ready if it was. Wales and his assistant, Jay Allen, spent Friday night in the FNS office reading newspaper clippings, telephoning sources for quotes, and making plans to get a news story to New York ahead of the competition. Shirer volunteered to help out, after having expressed interest in covering Lindbergh's arrival for the Paris edition. Bernhard Ragner had already assigned city editor Jules Franz to write the story, but Ragner agreed to let Shirer go along with Wales and Allen – if he first wrote his assigned article for the day.

In his memoir *Twentieth Century Journey*, Shirer has left us a vivid first-hand account of his own adventures and the pandemonium at Le Bourget airfield, northwest of Paris. Lindbergh's plane touched down on the floodlit runway a few minutes after ten o'clock on the night of Saturday, 21 May 1927, a little more than thirty-three hours after leaving New York City. The world – and Lindbergh's life – would never be the same.

It is difficult nowadays, if not impossible, to grasp the impact of Lindbergh's accomplishment on our grandparents' generation. Social historian Frederick Lewis Allen writes that Charles Lindbergh exemplified all that was best about America and the American way of life. Fearless, modest as the Minnesota farm boy that he was, and bubbling with optimism, Lindbergh was very much the man of the moment. "A disillusioned nation fed on cheap heroics and scandal and crime was revolting against the low estimate of human nature which it had allowed itself to entertain … Something that people needed, if they were to live at peace with themselves and with the world, was missing from their lives. And all at once Lindbergh provided it. Romance, chivalry, self-dedication – here they were, embodied in a modern Galahad for a generation which had foresworn Gallahads."[3]

Intent on scooping the competition on the Lindberg story, Shirer and Wales rushed off to cable their reports to Chicago, leaving Jay Allen at Le Bourget airfield to pursue a possible interview with America's newest hero. Finding the roadway snarled in a massive traffic jam, Shirer and Wales jogged most of the four miles back to Paris. Wales immediately made for the offices of a cable company. Having already written most of his story and made the arrangements to send it, he set to work writing the rest of it. Meanwhile, Shirer returned to the *Tribune* newsroom to tap out his own account of Lindbergh's dramatic landing. Jules Franz being caught up in the traffic jam, managing editor Ragner informed Shirer the story was his to write for page 1 of the next morning's edition of Paris edition. "But don't make it too long," he cautioned.[4]

Two hours later, with his own article complete, Shirer returned to the cable office to help Hank Wales pull together FNS coverage of the night's events. By now, Jay Allen had attended a two a.m. Lindbergh press conference at the American embassy. The pajama-clad aviator, now dog-tired and running purely on adrenalin, had sat on the edge of his bed answering the questions put to him by a dozen journalists. When Shirer reached Jay Allen by telephone, he scribbled down some Lindbergh quotes and passed them on to Wales. Ever enterprising, the crusty newsman plugged Lindbergh's words into his news story and tacked the word "Exclusive" after the place-line of his report, which was headlined "'Am I Here?,' He Asks as City Goes Wild with Frenzy of Joy."[5] The implication, of course, was that the *Chicago Tribune*'s intrepid correspondent had sat down with the pilot for a one-on-one interview.

Having finished their work for the day, Shirer and Wales adjourned to an all-night café for some coffee and croissants. Despite his fatigue, Wales was buoyant, for he had already received a cable from Colonel McCormick in Chicago congratulating him on his coverage of the Lindbergh landing and on having beaten the competition on the story; Wales's "scoop" appeared above the fold on page 1 of a special edition of the newspaper. Picked up by scores of newspapers across the American heartland that subscribed to the *Tribune*'s wire service, the story played a pivotal role in shaping the initial impression that millions of Americans had of Charles A. Lindbergh.

As Wales sipped a coffee and reviewed his young helper's front-page article in that morning's Paris edition, he nodded. "Not bad," he muttered. When he had finished reading, Wales looked his helper in the eye. Prior to this, while he had read Shirer's sports stories, he had not regarded him as candidate for a FNS job. Shirer's work on the Lindbergh story changed all that. "Willy, I think maybe you've got what it takes," Wales said. "The secret of this business is to turn it out fast under pressure. Maybe ... maybe I can find room for you."[6]

Wales was true to his word. Next day, William Shirer left his job at the Paris edition for a staff position with the *Chicago Tribune*'s FNS. At the tender age of twenty-three, he had realized his dream of becoming a foreign correspondent.

6

Gabardine Trenchcoats and Late-Night Trains

William Shirer's career as a foreign correspondent began much as his stint with the Paris *Tribune* had ended: reporting more of the "good news" story of Charles Lindbergh's post-flight adventures. The scale and enthusiasm of the receptions Lindbergh enjoyed in Paris, Brussels, and London was but a precursor to the surging crowds that awaited his triumphant home-coming; a crowd of four million people greeted him upon his return to New York City. Sadly, the impact of his unbridled celebrity proved ruinous, both for Lindbergh-the-man and Lindberg-the-legend. His life had changed forever. And so, too, had William Shirer's.

His promotion to the *Tribune*'s FNS brought a substantial raise and a change in his duties. As the junior man in the office, he now worked a late shift, from three p.m. to three a.m. At six o'clock each evening, Hank Wales headed off to his favorite café, leaving Shirer alone in the FNS office. By now, thanks to his ongoing relationship and pillow talk with Yvonne, he had become proficient in French. This was a handy skill when it came to following up on interesting news stories he spotted in the various French newspapers.

Whenever there was important breaking news, Shirer's standing orders were to track down his boss and apprise him of the latest developments. Wales seldom returned to the office in the evening, even when he was sober enough. Instead he issued instructions and left it to Shirer or Jay Allen, the bureau's number 2 man, to write an article under Wales's byline and then wire it home to Chicago, six time zones away. Whenever a story ghostwritten by Shirer made page 1 or Wales received a congratulatory telegram (or a bonus payment), as occasionally happened, Wales would clap Shirer on the back and announce with a good-natured chuckle, "Good work, Willy! Chicago likes your stuff."

If this bothered Shirer or Jay Allen, they kept silent about it. The two were generally content with their jobs and with their salaries, which were enough to live on. Shirer was earning fifty dollars American per week, rather than the fifteen he had taken home as a member of the staff of the Paris edition, who were paid in French francs, which were subject to the ups and downs of currency fluctuation.

Seattle-born and four years Shirer's senior, Jay Allen had earned a Master of Arts degree in French literature at Harvard before he married and in 1925 made his way to Paris and a job with the *Tribune*'s FNS. Like Shirer, Jay Allen aspired to become a novelist. The two men spent countless hours discussing and debating politics, the arts, and the writings of French authors and of many of the Americans who were living and writing in Paris. Shirer later recalled that while he and Allen were "probably little more than Jeffersonian liberals in our outlook on life,"[1] this eventually – and inevitably – would put them at odds with Colonel McCormick, the xenophobic, autocratic proprietor of the *Chicago Tribune* and its FNS. However, in 1927, as far as their employer was concerned, both men were still just faceless names on the list of editorial employees that was posted on a wall of the *Tribune* newsroom. That doubtless explains some of the bizarre assignments with which Shirer was tasked.

On one occasion, he was sent to the Cantigny area, north of Paris, on a futile search for a pair of binoculars McCormick supposedly had lost in summer 1918. The Colonel claimed to have left them and other personal belongings in a barn as American Expeditionary Force was pursuing retreating German forces. On several occasions, Shirer was assigned to entertain McCormick's septuagenarian mother on her visits to Paris.[2] Their conversations often proved interesting, especially when the McCormick matriarch reminisced about her early life. One afternoon, she asked Shirer to send a cable to the White House on her behalf. Dutifully taking out his pencil, Shirer recorded in his notebook her dictation about the current political situation in Europe; the intended recipient, Mrs McCormick announced, was President Abraham Lincoln, whom she claimed to have known in her childhood. Although he was perplexed by such a bizarre request, Shirer continued jotting down her message. Upon his return to office, he asked Hank Wales what to do about the cable. Taking the cigar from his mouth, Wales stared at Shirer for a long moment. "Forget it. Mr Lincoln, I believe, is dead," he growled.[3]

Following Charles Lindbergh's departure from Europe, Shirer became a Paris-based FNS roving correspondent, traveling the Continent and making frequent stops in London. Beginning in 1927, he spent three consecutive summers at the *Tribune* office on Fleet Street, filling in for vacationing FNS staff. Shirer found the city drab and lifeless – never more so than on Sundays, when restaurants, pubs, and theaters were closed. Shirer was also lonely without Yvonne, who remained in Paris with her husband.

If pressed, Shirer would have admitted that at the time London was an interesting place for any young journalist to work; the city had eighteen daily newspapers and more than forty weeklies. What is more, Shirer was not impressed by the editorial quality of many of these publications. Apart from *The Times of London*, the staid voice of "the British Establishment," there was little pretense of objectivity in British journalism, even when compared to the editorial content of such owner-driven American newspapers as the *Chicago Tribune*. Recognizing this, Shirer applauded the fact by the mid-1920s in the United Kingdom radio was emerging as a potential competitor to the print media. Back home in the States, broadcasting was strictly the preserve of the private sector. Not so in England, where the state-run network, the British Broadcasting Corporation (BBC), enjoyed a statutory monopoly.

Shirer applauded the facts the BBC's programming was commercial free and was neither "dumbed down" nor subject to advertiser interference – a concern that ultimately played a key role in Shirer's own broadcasting career and, indeed, in his life. At the same time, Shirer admitted that he sometimes found listening to the BBC tedious. With no competition for listeners, the public broadcaster had little incentive to improve its programming, innovate, or even to ensure the integrity of its newscasts; government-appointed "controllers" kept a wary eye on the content of news reports while selectively approving the "facts."

Shirer was similarly scornful of the class divisions in English society and of the hierarchies within the hierarchies. Class was still a vital concern in a land in which less than 1 percent of the population owned two-thirds of the wealth. Being at heart a Jeffersonian liberal, Shirer marveled that England's ruling class had managed to maintain its power, and yet, paradoxically, democracy had taken root and developed here. Shirer's own observations and his reading of British history led him to conclude that this had come about because the English oligarchy had usurped the powers of the Crown while convincing "the lower classes" to support them.

This situation in the United Kingdom stood in marked contrast to that of many other nations at the time, especially Russia. There, the 1917 Bolshevik revolution had swept away the tottering Romanov dynasty. The Tory governments in England eyed with distrust, hostility even, the communist Union of Soviet Socialist Republics and what a cynical Shirer aptly describes as "the Bolshevik bogey[man], which I would later see exploited to fool the populace in other countries ... above all, my own."[4]

Washington and London were as one in their antipathy toward the Bolsheviks. Yet despite their many areas of common interest, relations between the two wartime allies often were frosty. Shirer concluded the differences had its roots in the simmering resentments held by the British ruling class, who felt England's former colony was an opportunistic upstart that had become too powerful, too wealthy, and too influential in the decade after the Great War. At the same time, there was a widespread feeling in America that the westward postwar shift in the balance of power had an air of historical inevitability to it.

Any such a notion was unpalatable for the British, the French, and other Europeans to countenance, much less accept. Despite the isolationist tendencies of the Coolidge administration in Washington, there was little doubt that America had eclipsed Europe's old colonial powers in power and influence. However, all was not quite as it seemed, for the foundations of America's postwar economic prosperity were flimsy at best. Much of the new wealth that was being created was the product of unbridled speculation; playing the stock market and buying "on margin" in hopes of getting rich quick had become the new national pastime. America's prosperity was a bubble, wondrous to behold, but hollow to its core. By 1929, despite a decade of supposed prosperity, only 2 percent of American families had incomes of more than $10,000 per year, while 60 percent of families lived below the poverty line, surviving on less than $2,000 per year. With wages low and prices relatively high, the gap between rich and poor had become an unbridgeable chasm. It was only a matter of time until the bubble of prosperity burst; when it did, the results were disastrous and painful.

If there was a dominant theme in American foreign policy in the 1920s, it was isolationism. However, more Americans than ever before were traveling abroad and the nation's reputation as a bastion of liberty and equality was soaring to unprecedented heights; the United States was almost universally regarded as a land of opportunity and a beacon of hope in a troubled world. Being American was a source of pride. So it was, much to the dismay of Shirer and many like-minded observers, that neither the politicians in Washington nor a majority of Americans were ready to acknowledge – much less embrace – the nation's newly won political, military, economic, and moral ascendancy. In November 1919, the Republican-dominated Senate had rejected Democratic President Wilson's plans for American involvement in the League of Nations, which was Wilson's brainchild.

At the same time, even as successive Republican administrations in Washington in the 1920s were pursuing an isolationist foreign policy and implementing protectionist tariffs, the nation's cultural and sporting ties were flourishing globally. Americans had suddenly become sports crazy, in good measure because the country's athletes were dominating many international competitions, the Olympics in particular. As a result, media coverage and public interest grew.

Tribune editors in Chicago, knowing Shirer's background as a sportswriter, began assigning him to cover high-profile sporting events – including the two Olympic Games that were held in Europe in 1928. At the same time, Shirer was also dispatched to report on meetings of the League on Nations. The latter experience was enlightening but also disheartening: "Though my Wilsonian illusions were quickly dampened, it was educational to watch the world statesmen floundering about in a sea of hypocrisy."[5]

By now, Shirer was reveling in his status as a foreign correspondent and had made many friends and contacts among the ranks of the journalistic community. Officially, other correspondents were his competitors, but everyone knew everyone (all too well at times), and because they ate, socialized, and traveled together, many of them became close friends. In times of need, they often helped each other out. For example, when *New York Times* reporter Wythe Williams, one of Shirer's pals, left his post to tend to urgent personal business, Shirer covered for him. Several articles he did appeared on page 1 of *The Times* under Williams's byline; it was the only time Shirer ever wrote for that newspaper. This sort of ghostwriting was not uncommon, as Shirer's experiences working in the Paris bureau of the FNS had made clear.

Shirer and several of his associates were celebrating his twenty-fourth birthday on 23 February 1928, when the arrival of a cable from Hank Wales interrupted their evening of drinking and gambling at a Geneva casino. Shirer was summoned back to Paris *post haste* on orders from Colonel McCormick himself. The *Tribune*'s capricious owner had disapproved of Shirer's League of Nations articles, angrily dismissing them as being too sympathetic and "left-leaning."

Shirer returned to Paris feeling embarrassed and utterly deflated. To his surprise, he was not fired. Colonel McCormick either had changed his mind about sacking him, or else he simply had forgotten about the incident. Shirer never learned which it was; however, it presaged events that ultimately led to the end of his career with the newspaper.

While Shirer was no longer reporting on the League of Nations, he was back to covering sporting events. Thus he spent two busy weeks in Amsterdam reporting on the 1928 summer Olympics, and more specifically on the exploits of the United States team, which was under the direction of General Douglas A. MacArthur, still a relatively unknown figure at the time.

When Shirer's girlfriend Yvonne arrived from Paris, he spent every spare moment with her. This time was precious to Shirer, who was still in love and was naive and vain enough to believe Yvonne would jettison her husband to be with him. That was never going to happen, of course. Shirer, who now was traveling constantly, learned the hard way that failed marriages, shattered love affairs, and lonely nights on the road were some of the occupational hazards of life as a foreign correspondent. Never was that truer than in the interwar years. As Shirer's friend and colleague John Gunther notes, these journalists "were strictly on [their] own" when they traveled.[6] The hours were long, the work demanding, and the competition – fueled by testosterone, egos, and the dictates of the newspaper business – was intense, regardless of friendships. Shirer and every other foreign correspondent engaged in the perpetual game of trying to outdo each other in the search for a "scoop." As Waverly Root once quipped, "All's fair in love, war, and newspaper competition."[7]

Success as a foreign correspondent required the ability to get the facts, and then to write a story quickly, accurately, and colorfully. One had to be resourceful, tough-minded, self-confident, and independent of mind; those who were not did not last long in the business. This was before the instant communications technologies we now take for granted; in 1928, long-distance telephone service was still uncertain in many European countries, particularly in areas of the Balkans and in Mediterranean lands. Even the act of traveling was a challenge. Overnight trains were the sole reliable, reasonably priced means of getting around in Europe. Mechanical breakdowns, border delays, and other irritants were common. It was a grueling sixty-eight-hour ride from Paris to Constantinople (which officially became known as İstanbul in 1930) even aboard the fabled Simplon-Orient Express, which often averaged little more than twenty-five miles per hour on its 1,600-mile journey; other less glamorous trains, the so-called "milk runs" that linked the cities of Europe, made no better time.

Journalists on the road paid their expenses in cash or else they carried letters of credit, which were honored at hotels and restaurants where they were personally known. Europeans tended to move about more than did North Americans in those days, yet ordinary people on both sides of the Atlantic generally stayed close to home and paid cash for most purchases. There was no such thing as a credit card.

In the popular imagination, fed by books, articles, and countless Hollywood films, mention of the term "foreign correspondent" summoned to mind an entire job description. It also evoked images of exotic locales, trenchcoat-clad men in wide-brimmed fedoras, late-night trains, beautiful women, spies, mystery, and intrigue. True, Shirer and his colleagues traveled endlessly, met newsmakers, and often had front-row seats as history was being made. However, for the most part their lives were solitary, routine, and onerous; writing a news story is seldom the stuff of high adventure. Being a foreign correspondent was less a job than a way of life. That fostered the strong sense of camaraderie, *esprit de corps* even, that existed among the members of the fraternity. When they got together, they tended to party as hard as they worked.

There was a price to be paid for the competitive nature of the foreign correspondent's lifestyle, the constant deadline pressure, and the peripatetic lifestyle. To fill the long, lonely hours spent in hotel rooms in far-flung cities or sitting on the overnight trains, many journalists drank or smoked, often both and to excess. And they wrote letters, sometimes by the ream. They wrote to wives, family, and other loved ones, to colleagues, and to editors in the home office; it was not unusual for William Shirer to dash off as many as six personal letters in a day.

Sex was just another diversion for many journalists; philandering and infidelity were very much a part of the transient lifestyle. When Shirer began traveling, he doubtless did so with the same cynical advice in mind that his colleague George Seldes reported the conductors on the Orient Express had offered him: Beware of the "famous, but fictitious, slinky beautiful blondes with whom we might get in trouble. The caveat was that in your compartment it's rape. In theirs, it's commerce."[8]

Despite the relatively permissive European attitudes toward sex in the 1920s and 1930s, the management of many hotels tended to frown upon unmarried couples sharing rooms. This was especially true in conservative-minded countries and in smaller cities and towns everywhere. Since desk clerks, on orders from the police, asked foreigners to show their passports when checking in, some creativity was called for when unmarried heterosexual couples were traveling together. Renting separate rooms was a common, albeit expensive, ruse.

Small wonder that failed marriages and divorces were the rule rather than the exception for those journalists who lived life on the road. It took a special kind of person indeed – and a rock-solid relationship – to cope with, let alone survive, the workaday stresses, travails, and loneliness of living out of a suitcase for weeks at a time.

By autumn 1928, after only sixteen months as a roving correspondent, William Shirer had already grown weary of the perpetual travel. He was also beginning to question the newsworthiness of some of the stories he was tasked to write; he resented being obliged to waste time on what he regarded as trivialities. When he was not reporting on high-profile athletic events, Shirer traveled to cities from one end of Europe to the other reporting on scandals and celebrity news. Typically, in the first week of October he found himself in Rome for the wedding of American heavyweight boxer Gene Tunney and his bride Mary J. "Polly" Lauder, who had fled to Italy in hopes of avoiding the media spotlight back home. The Tunney-Lauder wedding held little allure for Shirer, who was far more interested in talking with the groom's best man: novelist and playwright Thornton Wilder, whose 1928 novel *The Bridge at San Luis Rey* had won the Pulitzer Prize for fiction. "In truth, I was getting tired of having to report on the goings on of American notables in Europe," Shirer lamented. "In Paris and London and on the Riviera or at Deauville or Biarritz we had to spend too much time keeping track of their marriages and divorces and other games."[9]

Shirer remained in Rome for two months after the Tunney wedding, subbing for vacationing bureau chief David Darrah (the man who had hired him to work at the *Tribune*'s Paris edition). Shirer relished his time in Rome, for he continued to be fascinated by questions of spirituality and religion. These were concerns he wrestled with his whole life: "I was baptized in the Presbyterian Church and went to Sunday school and church regularly as a child … In College, the first doubts began to rise. And they grew rapidly as I went abroad as a correspondent and came into contact with other cultures, other religions. I found it increasingly difficult to believe in the very foundations of the Christianity that I had been born into."[10]

Shirer's cynicism only grew when he was accorded a crash course in the realities of Vatican power politics and intrigue. Assigned the task of writing a series of feature articles about the arcane world of papal finances, he turned to the only readily available source of information on the topic: a paid informer. The man, an erudite monsignor who was friendly with many of the American journalists in Rome, professed to have knowledge of the Vatican's innermost workings. The more the informant was paid, of course, the juicier the information he provided; some of it *may* even have been true. The monsignor insisted that he used the fees he collected for his services to support his elderly mother and other relatives. Shirer suspected otherwise; rumor had it the wily cleric spent the money on his mistresses and his other guilty pleasures.

The Vatican and spiritual concerns certainly were not Shirer's only intellectual fascinations during his stay in Rome. Keen to understand the burgeoning mass appeal of Benito Mussolini, Shirer was one of the first American journalists to assess the leader of Italy's National Fascist Party. Mussolini, an erstwhile socialist, had stormed to power in 1922 and then proceeded to use a deft combination of political guile and brute force to restore order to a nation that had been tottering on the brink of political and economic chaos. He subdued Italy's left and boasted that he had once again "made the trains run on time." Thus, many people who should have known better hailed Mussolini as a great leader. For example, American inventor Thomas Edison declared Mussolini to be "the greatest genius of the modern age."

Shirer was intrigued by the cult of personality that had grown up around the Italian dictator. What was the essence of his hold on the Italian people? Would an American understand it? It was with those questions in mind that Shirer went to the Piazza Venezia one cool October evening to hear Mussolini address a large crowd that had gathered in to celebrate the sixth anniversary of the Italian fascists' rise to power. During the youthful summers he had spent working as a member of Chautauqua tent crews, Shirer had listened countless times to soaring oratory of the silver-tongued William Jennings Bryan and evangelist William A. "Billy" Sunday. On this night in Rome, Shirer came away disappointed by the performance of Mussolini, whom he adjudged to be more style than substance: "The pitch of his voice was too high and the pace of his words too feverish. He screamed at his listeners ... You could see at once though, that he was a born actor ... [and] an artful manipulator of the masses."[11]

When Shirer left Rome in mid-December, he took some time off and rendezvoused with Yvonne for a romantic pre-Christmas tryst in the French Alpine resort of Grenoble. In Shirer's eyes, his lover had never looked more beautiful, and their time together was magical. However, the spell was broken when Shirer renewed his demands that Yvonne divorce her husband and marry him. She refused, chiding Shirer for "being bourgeois and foolish." That was the beginning of the end for their love affair. Back in Paris for Christmas, Yvonne spent the holiday season with her family, leaving Shirer to brood alone.

Hank Wales, thinking he was doing "young Willy" a favor, early in the New Year dispatched him to Nice, the resort town on the French Riviera. Shirer's assignment was to report on the funeral of the Grand Duke Nicholas, the exiled cousin of the Tsar Nicholas II, whom the Bolsheviks in 1917 had murdered along with his family. The Grand Duke's death dashed the last hopes of the exiled Russian nobility for a revival of the Romanov dynasty. While Shirer grasped the historical significance of the moment and was moved by the tragic story of the Russian imperials, he had little sympathy for their political cause. Nor did he accept that the United States was one of the few nations that had not yet recognized the Soviet Union; Shirer regarded this as an unwise, even hypocritical, strategy as Washington had extended diplomatic recognition to other despotic regimes, most of which were on the political right. In light of the accusations that was hurled Shirer's way in the late 1940s, it is worth noting that Shirer *never* was an admirer of the Soviet Union – unlike the many American journalists, intellectuals, and artists who voiced support for Stalin's "great Socialist experiment." However, Shirer did support the idea of recognizing the Bolshevik regime for pragmatic rather than ideological reasons – Communist Russia could be a counterbalance to a rising fascist tide in Europe, he reasoned. Recognition of any government, he argued, did not imply approval of a regime.

Following the Grand Duke's funeral, Shirer remained in Nice to cover "the social season." This job, the plum that his friend James Thurber had coveted, held little appeal for Shirer. Imbued, as he was, with a no-nonsense Presbyterian work ethic and a disdain for "the smart set," it was all he could do to suppress his revulsion with the conspicuous consumption, frivolity, and pomposity: "Watching the idle rich convinced you that there was something wrong with the distribution of wealth in this world, and that maybe the socialists, who wanted to redistribute it and give a little more to those who toiled, were right … Obviously in this field I was a lousy journalist, refusing to acknowledge that what bored me titillated our readers in Chicagoland."[12]

The prospect of spending several weeks in Nice left Shirer glum. At age twenty-five, he was still hungry for the big scoop that he hoped would make his name and his journalism career. Complaining to Wales got him nowhere. Frustrated and morose, Shirer retreated to his hotel room most evenings, passing the long hours writing letters and reading the novels of Proust, Balzac, and Stendahl. When he ventured out, it was to gamble in the casinos at nearby Monte Carlo or to seek out the companionship of the French-speaking journalists who gathered at a neighborhood café.

Happily for Shirer, his Rivieran exile was cut short when Hank Wales ordered him to Vienna to fill in at the FNS bureau in the Austrian capital for a few weeks. The assignment developed into something much more significant, for it marked the end of Shirer's time in Paris. As one literary critic correctly notes, "Although Shirer did not publish any poetry or fiction during the years he lived [there], as he had originally hoped to do, his Paris experience was pivotal in his life. It changed him from a relatively inexperienced, although well-read, youth to a journalist with wide interests and a concern for careful research. These traits, combined with a clear and vigorous writing style gave him unprecedented success as a journalist-historian."[13]

Vienna: A Capital without a Nation

Even before the onset of the Great Depression, Vienna was a city in decline, having fallen on hard times in the years following World War One. On the day in February 1929 that William Shirer arrived there for the first time, the city had been blanketed by snow and was enduring a record-setting cold snap. Despite the inclement weather, Shirer fell in love with the historic capital of the Hapsburg Empire: "After the French, the Austrians and especially the Viennese were the most attractive people I had seen, the women particularly."[1]

As was his habit whenever he arrived in city for the first time, Shirer went on a walking tour, confirming what he had heard: music and baroque were the essence of Viennese life. Immersing himself in the city's culture, Shirer quickly came to appreciate Vienna's musical heritage. Chamber music became one of his passions. Another was the food served in the dining room of Sacher's, Vienna's most famous hotel and the perennial favorite of Austria's ruling elite. At John Gunther's suggestion, Shirer introduced himself to the elderly proprietress; Frau Sacher knew everyone who counted in Vienna. Taking Shirer under her wing, she introduced him to military men, politicians, bureaucrats, and sundry aristocrats. That is how Shirer met "a fading countess" who invited him to escort her to the annual military ball at the Hofburg palace. Curiosity having got the better of him, Shirer shelved his cynicism about Austrian nobility to accept the invitation. Despite "the odor of mothballs" that hung over the gala event – figuratively, if not literally – the evening was memorable; it was Shirer's first exposure to what the Viennese refer to as *gemütlichkeit* – a sense of frivolity and carefree indulgence. This was all strange, yet seductive, to a twenty-five-year-old American from a dour Protestant Midwestern background:

"For a few hours that evening in the great chandeliered halls, those remnants of a bygone day forgot the bleak present and faded back to the past with all its frivolous trappings, dancing the night through to the waltzes of Johann Strauss."[2]

Not long afterward, while attending a diplomatic tea party, he met yet another countess, a dark-haired Hungarian whom he identified in his writings only as "Zora." Although she was at least a decade his elder, there was instant chemistry between them. After leaving the gathering, the pair spent a passionate night together before going to the *Tribune* office early next morning so Shirer could do his job. His command of German was still tenuous, and so Zora helped him translate the news from Vienna's morning newspapers.

Like Yvonne in Paris, Zora was married. However, she and her aristocratic husband had drifted apart after a decade as a couple. He was now living on his country estate, while she had taken an apartment in town and announced her intention to end the marriage, even if obtaining a divorce was difficult in Austria, a staunchly Roman Catholic country. None of this much troubled Shirer, who was smitten. When Zora invited him to move in with her, he did so and was still encamped there in April, when Hank Wales ordered him to go to England. His assignment: to cover some sporting events there and then spend the summer in London filling in for *Tribune* bureau chief John Steele when he went on vacation.

After a tearful parting from Zora, Shirer left Vienna the last week of April. Any sadness he felt during the sixty-hour train ride back to Paris vanished the moment he arrived at La Gare du Nord, for there on the station platform waiting for him was Yvonne. In his eyes, she had never looked more beautiful, and so they resumed their romance after a five-month hiatus. However, it did not take long for old differences between them to resurface. Emotions were still raw a few days later when Shirer packed his bags and left for London. Having spent the two previous summers there, he knew the routine and felt more at home on this stay. His spirits were further buoyed when Zora arrived unexpectedly from Vienna: "We were openly 'living in sin,' after all – it was not so prevalent nor so widely accepted then as now – and she was happy among my more bohemian and working class friends."[3]

His London social circle was a varied one, both politically and intellectually. He had developed a friendship with two members of Parliament from the British Labour Party: a feisty Welshman named Aneurin

"Nye" Bevan and a spirited young Scottish woman named Jennie Lee. The pair were linked politically and romantically; they married in 1932. Shirer routinely dined with the couple and their friends at a restaurant in the Soho area of London. The talk among this eclectic group of politicians, union leaders, academics, journalists, and theater people was spirited and lively. One of the regulars in summer 1929 was the African-American singer Paul Robeson, who was in town to star in a production of *Show Boat.*

These roundtable gatherings continued for many years, and Shirer joined in whenever he was in London. On one especially memorable occasion in June 1943, Bevan asked him to invite John Steinbeck to dine with the group. The novelist, a darling of the liberal-left at the time, was in London in connection with his work as a *New York Herald Tribune* war correspondent. New to the job and eager to build a network of contacts, Steinbeck came to dinner. He was taken aback by the passion of the after-dinner debate that raged around him. As Shirer recalled, "There was so much shouting that John, a peaceful, amiable and rather apolitical man, feared we would come to blows."[4]

Although Shirer's summer in London was relatively carefree, it ended on a downbeat. Still in turmoil over the emotional uncertainties of his relationship with Yvonne, he refused to make a commitment to Zora. Heartbroken, she drifted away, and after securing a divorce she wed a Hungarian diplomat.[5] Sadder but wiser after the split, Shirer was still despondent when he returned to Paris that autumn. Taking a month's leave, he traveled home to the United States. A visit with family and friends would give him the much-needed opportunity to clear his mind and take stock of his life. Or so he hoped.

The cool, rainy weather that greeted Shirer in New York matched his dark mood, as did the doom-and-gloom economic news about the Wall Street crash of two weeks earlier. Contrary to President Herbert Hoover's assurances that the economy was fundamentally sound, the reality was alarmingly different. America's prosperity in the 1920s had been an illusion of epic proportions, and on that now-infamous "Black Tuesday" – 29 October 1929 – when the American economy crumbled, the financial shockwaves echoed worldwide.

Shirer had seen poverty and hardship in Europe, yet he was still unprepared for the despair he encountered on the streets of New York. It had been an article of faith for him, indeed for all Americans, that theirs was a nation of boundless opportunity and plenty; this is what set the land of his birth apart from the rest of the world, what supposedly made it superior. In the wake of Wall Street crash, the initial disbelief and shock soon gave way to widespread feelings of confusion, fear, and anger. "Men and women, shabbily dressed, but with good, strong American faces that had a bewildered look, were standing on the curb selling apples ... I scarcely recognized the proud country and the proud people I had left only four years before. The good citizens, recently so cocky, seemed stunned. They couldn't grasp what had hit them, nor could I."[6]

As the full impact of the Great Depression swept tsunami-like across the continent, America's agricultural heartland was hit hard. Like investors everywhere, Iowans lost heavily in the market collapse; Shirer's mother was among them. Bessie Shirer was all but wiped out financially. Shirer's brother had graduated from Coe College in 1927 and had found work in New York as an economic statistician. Armed with his newfound knowledge of the market, John Shirer had invested his mother's life savings in "rock-solid" blue-chip stocks. They were not rock-solid, of course; more than half of the Shirer matriarch's retirement nest-egg disappeared in the Wall Street crash. At age fifty-eight, she again was struggling to make ends meet. The sense of despair her elder son felt over this turn of events and the sad plight of millions of other ordinary Americans morphed into a bewildered, simmering anger. Shirer wondered how and why the wealthiest and most bountiful nation on the planet had been reduced to such a sorry state.

The reason, he concluded, was the "appalling inequities" that were inherent in America's economic system; "Prosperity to be real and lasting [has] to be shared."[7] Critics pointed out that a small number of people had accumulated enormous wealth in the 1920s, while 60 percent of Americans lived below the poverty line – existing on an annual income of $2,000 or less.

William Shirer was a man with a profound sense of social justice; this trait had its roots in the deep soil of his Presbyterianism and his Midwestern upbringing. Seward and Bessie Shirer had raised their three children to be honest, hard-working, and independent, However, they also taught them the justness of the Christian virtue of "doing unto others" and of sharing with the less fortunate. From the day he had left home in 1925, Shirer sent money to his mother each and every payday. Even in the wake of the Wall Street crash, having resolved to continue doing so regardless, he was true to his word. Bessie Shirer was thankful. She was also proud of her elder son. When he came home for a visit in that troubled autumn, she marveled at his mastery of French, and, although Prohibition was still in effect, she sipped from the bottle of Benedictine liqueur that he had smuggled home from Paris for her. Everywhere Shirer went in Cedar Rapids – while visiting old friends, strolling familiar streets, or dropping by the Coe College campus to pay his respects to his former professors and to speak to a journalism class – he was hailed as a hero, a hometown boy who had made good. Reporters from the local labor newspaper, the *Coe College Cosmos,* and the Cedar Rapids *Gazette* sought him out for interviews. In his mind, all of this made him realize how much he had changed since leaving home: "Everything in Cedar Rapids seemed smaller than I remembered."[8]

Shirer also spent an afternoon visiting artist Grant Wood. After his 1926 return home from Paris, Wood had set about painting what he knew best: the ordinary scenes and faces of Iowa life. The day Shirer visited his friend's studio, the artist had several works-in-progress sitting on his easels; one of them was the painting *American Gothic,* which was destined to become his signature work and one of the iconic images in modern American art. Although all of this was still ahead, Shirer understood that, while returning home had been the right decision for Wood, his own future lay elsewhere. Already he was restless to return to Europe; however, first he had an appointment in Chicago.

Prior to leaving Paris, Shirer had heard from Hank Wales that it would be prudent for him to drop by the *Chicago Tribune* offices when he was home; Colonel McCormick had let it be known he wanted to meet "young Shirer." Thus, when he appeared at the *Tribune* newsroom, Shirer was ushered into a lunch with the Colonel, managing editor Ed Beck, and the newspaper's senior editors. Shirer was on edge, fearful his bosses had decided he was too inexperienced to be a foreign correspondent. His anxieties only grew when lunch ended and McCormick invited him to come to his office for "a private chat." The two men took the elevator to the thirty-sixth floor of the *Tribune* Tower. Once there, in his wood-paneled office, McCormick settled in behind his desk and told his young employee to take a seat. Shirer did so, and then being nervous as a mouse, he lit a cigarette. "Put that damned thing out!" McCormick barked. "No one smokes here!"

Shirer was certain he was about to be fired. His dread grew as he watched the Colonel leaf through a file of newspaper clippings and inter-office correspondence. When finally the *Tribune* owner looked up, he did not fire Shirer; instead, he complimented him on his work (apparently having forgotten his earlier criticisms of Shirer's writings). The Colonel then beckoned for Shirer to follow him over to a wall map of Europe. Stabbing a finger at the dot on the map that represented Vienna, McCormick announced, "I want you to go there. I want you to take over *that* bureau." Then, in the next breath, he added two caveats: Shirer should avoid being "taken in" by the Austrian aristocrats, whom the Colonel was sure he would encounter. The other caution proved to be more significant and ominous, although it seemed innocuous enough at the time: "Don't fall for all those Socialists and Communists there."

Following a brief exchange of pleasantries and a perfunctory hand-shake, McCormick returned to his desk. As Shirer turned to go, his smile melted away for he realized he had no idea where the door was. After scanning the wall of the large wood-paneled room in vain, the *Tribune*'s new Vienna correspondent sheepishly had to ask his boss how to get out of the office. "It's right behind you, Shirer!" said McCormick. Then, reaching under his desk, he pressed a button. A camouflaged door open-ed, and as Shirer exited and the panel slid shut behind him, he heard McCormick chuckling. "A queer duck," Shirer thought. "But he gave me Vienna!"[9]

Shirer's mid-December return to work was delayed for a month when he suffered an attack of appendicitis on the return voyage to Europe. Haunt-ed by memories of his own father's death from the same affliction, Shirer feared for his life. However, the ship's doctor correctly diagnosed Shirer's ailment, and so an ambulance was waiting on the dock when the ship arrived at the French port at Cherbourg. Shirer was rushed to the Ameri-can Hospital in Paris, where his emergency surgery went well, and he then spent the Holiday Season convalescing, which gave him yet another oppor-tunity to plead with Yvonne to leave her husband and be with him. When she remained adamant in her refusal, Shirer resolved to end the relation-ship. It was with a heavy heart, but a fresh sense of resolve and emotional freedom, that in mid-January he traveled to Vienna to begin his new job.

Being based in Vienna meant that in addition to Austria, his "beat" was a sprawling territory that included the five other countries of Central Europe: Bulgaria, Yugoslavia, Hungary, Romania, and Czechoslovakia. Like Austria, all of these nations in whole or in part – except for Bulgaria – had been part of the Hapsburg Empire, and all had fallen on hard times. It was now Shirer's job to travel throughout the region, visiting with the network of paid informants who were his eyes and ears in the various countries.

As had been the case when he had worked in Paris, the cost of living in Vienna was relatively inexpensive. Shirer could afford to live comfortably on his fifty-dollar-per-week salary, and so he quickly settled into a comfortable routine, renting a room at the aptly named Grand Hotel, taking meals at Sacher's and other fine restaurants, and dating local ladies.

John Gunther of the rival *Chicago Daily News*, who arrived in town with his wife Frances in June 1930, wrote an article for *Harper's* magazine in which he described the routine and lifestyle of a Vienna-based foreign correspondent.[10] Every day was a working day that began early and ended late.

Housing being in short supply, most Viennese lived in tiny apartments. Because they had little disposable income, they gathered in the coffeehouses to socialize, a cup of java being an affordable treat. "The coffee house is ... the inner soul of Vienna, the essential embodiment of the spirit of the town," Gunther observes. "It is ... much more than just a place to drink coffee ... you have also literature, conversation, and peace of soul and mind."[11]

There was a coffeehouse on every street corner in Vienna, or so it seemed, and each one catered to a different clientele. Foreign journalists favored the Café Louvre, on the corner of Wipplinerstrasse and Renngasse. The L-shaped interior was bright, had high ceilings, and about forty booths where patrons sat. Oversized Gothic windows offered a panoramic view of passersby and street traffic. The Café Louvre had one great attraction other coffeehouses did not: it was just a few doors away from the studios of Radio Austria and from the telegraph office. This was why Shirer, Gunther, and their colleagues gathered here each day to exchange information and socialize. Journalists also used the café's telephone to dictate articles to Paris or London, or else they wrote at a quiet corner table and then sent a waiter to the telegraph office to send the article by cable.

Apart from Shirer and Gunther, other Café Louvre regulars included Whit Burnett and his partner Martha Foley, the *New York Sun* syndicate's Vienna correspondents; Marcel Fodor of the *Manchester Guardian*; and Robert Best, the United Press's man in Vienna and the head of the local foreign press association. Best dominated the daily gatherings; it was in his booth, his *stammtisch*, where the journalists congregated. A big, genial, bon vivant from South Carolina, Best had lived in Vienna since 1923, spoke excellent German, and had an extensive network of news contacts. The Café Louvre was Best's dining room, social center, and ersatz office. "In all the time he was in Vienna ... he virtually lived there.

It would never have occurred to anyone to telephone or meet him any-place else – at any time of the day or night," Shirer later recalled. "The café was not only his office but his real home."[12] Best was everyone's pal, but he also had a dark side: to the dismay of many of his friends, he was stri-dently pro-Nazi.

Many of the Café Louvre regulars officially were "rivals." However, those who congregated at Robert Best's *stammtisch* were colleagues and friends. Thus, when Whit Burnett and Martha Foley lost their jobs, the Café Lou-vre regulars chipped in enough money to tide them over until they could regain their financial footing.

Marcel "Mike" Fodor was one of the journalists who came to the aid of Burnett and Foley and of many others who were in need. "The Balka-ns have been the training ground for more foreign correspondents than any other area in the world," a writer for *Time* magazine noted in 1944. "And of those trained there in the last quarter century, most have learned from Fodor."[13] Hungarian-born and English-educated, Fodor was fluent in five languages, well connected, reliable, and principled. He had set up shop in Vienna in 1921 and remained there long enough that he became a fixture and mentored young journalists, John Gun-ther and William Shirer among them. Shirer welcomed the help for he was well aware that he faced a steep learning curve as the *Tribune*'s new Vienna bureau chief.

Some of the pressure Shirer felt to do well was of his own making. Despite Colonel McCormick's enthusiasm for the city, by 1930 the news-paper's editors in the Chicago newsroom – like their counterparts at other American newspapers – regarded the Austrian capital as a backwater. The prevailing wisdom was that the real action, the breaking news, was hap-pening in London, Paris, Rome, and Berlin. Nonetheless, American and British newspapers and news services reflexively maintained their bureaus or contacts in the city because the competition did and because the steady stream of well-known foreign visitors suggested that Vienna still merited some attention. American and British statesmen, diplomats, politicians, and writers came to see for themselves the great socialist experiment that was underway in the city, the same experiment that the Colonel had cau-tioned Shirer against "falling for."

One of the writers who turned up in Vienna and whom Shirer rel-ished the opportunity to meet was Sinclair Lewis. He and his wife, Dorothy Thompson, spent the winter of 1932–33 in the city. They came because their marriage was failing, and they hoped spending time together here might help to save it. Thompson, who spoke fluent German, felt very much at home in Vienna, her husband much less so. Lewis – "Red" to his friends – was an at times taciturn, sullen character with a pockmarked complexion and dark view of the world. His acerbic wit surfaced whenever he drank, which was often; he was an alcoholic. Being ill at ease socially, Lewis was moody and imbibed heavily much of the time that he was in Vienna. It did not help that he "betrayed a dislike for political argument, abstract discussion, journalistic excitement and table pounding," particularly if the talk turned to Hitler and the Nazis.[14] Nor did it help that Dorothy Thompson, bisexual and flirtatious, had developed an infatuation with a German woman writer. Thompson being otherwise occupied, Lewis retreated to a villa on the Semmering, the popular Alpine ski resort near Vienna. There, he proceeded to lose himself inside a bottle; his breakfast usually included a tumbler of brandy.

Shirer still aspired to become a novelist, and so one day he approached Lewis for advice. At age forty-five, he was happy to have a young drinking companion, especially one who was ready to talk about Lewis's favorite topic: Harry Sinclair Lewis. The writer expounded on current events, other writers, and the creative process. Shirer, starry-eyed, held Lewis in high regard – so much so that he hailed him as being America's greatest novelist and as someone who had made more lasting literary impact than Fitzgerald, Hemingway, Dos Passos, and Faulkner *combined*: "No other writer ... captured and recorded as he did the nature of American life, its foibles, its frustrations, its aspirations, its generosity, its hocus-pocus, its speech and its wonderful absurdities."[15]

Lewis was the first American to win the Nobel Prize in Literature (1930), and on the strength of novels such as *Main Street* (1920), *Babbitt* (1922), *Arrowsmith* (1925), and *Elmer Gantry* (1927) there can be no argument that he was one of the major writers of the twentieth century. However, Lewis's books are little read today, and few literary historians concur with Shirer's inflated assessment of Lewis's place in the pantheon of American greats; Shirer was a far better journalist than literary critic.

Author interviews aside, there was always plenty of news to report from Vienna, and so Shirer threw himself into his work. In a busy week, he often cabled as many as five articles to Chicago. However, because sending long telegrams was cost prohibitive and the news agencies supplied details of breaking news, the FNS editors preferred that their far-flung correspondents write articles that provided analysis and background color to the latest news. *Tribune* management was so concerned about controlling expenses that Colonel McCormick himself kept an eye on all spending.

Stories detailing scandals, crime, sex, and news oddities were the favored fare from FNS foreign correspondents. And all copy was written with an eye to Midwestern sensibilities. With that in mind, Shirer reported on an eclectic variety of topics. A common element in all of these articles was their lack of time sensitivity. Advisedly so, for these "mailers" took at least a week to reach Chicago.

The nine-hour time difference between the American Midwest and Austria meant that Shirer's workday was ending just as Chicago was waking up each morning. This remoteness also accorded him a considerable degree of latitude in terms of what he wrote about and how he spent his days, although like all FNS correspondents Shirer was obliged to fill out and submit endless forms detailing his monthly expenses down to the penny.

The Colonel had dispatched Shirer to Vienna with instructions to "build up the bureau." While managing editor Ed Beck knew the marching orders, it is unclear how well he conveyed this information to the newspaper's editors or senior FNS staff overseas. That much is clear from the correspondence that passed back and forth between Shirer and Paris bureau chief Hank Wales, the FNS's top man in Europe. "I expect [John] Steele will want you in London again this summer for sports," Wales advised in a March letter. "You would of course return to your bureau [in Vienna] in the autumn."[16]

In his reply, Shirer questioned Wales about what events he was expected to cover and the timing of his return to Vienna. He was intent on making the most of the opportunity Colonel McCormick had given him, but he had another motivation for wanting to remain in Vienna in summer 1930: Shirer had fallen in love. Vienna-born Theresa "Tess" Stiberitz was nineteen and a fledgling photographer, drama critic, and would-be journalist. Shirer had met her through their mutual association with George Gedye, a British journalist who was the Vienna correspondent for *The New York Times* and various British newspapers. Gedye (rhymes with "ready") was married, but he had a roving eye. When he set to work on the first of the four books about Austria and Austrian politics, Gedye hired Tess Stiberitz as his research assistant. She was of average height – five-foot, four inches tall, according to her passport – blond-haired, with blue-gray eyes,[17] and bubbling with ambition. Tess had an artistic flair and a gift for languages. In addition to a proficiency in her native German, she spoke English and

Danish, which she had learned as a child, and in later years she picked up Spanish, French, and Greek.

While Tess Stiberitz never hid her past, she never trumpeted it. As a result, much of the Stiberitz family history has been forgotten. Tess's two daughters acquired only a vague knowledge of their mother's youthful years. "From an early age, she wanted to escape her roots and never seemed to be nostalgic for her Vienna life and family," her older daughter Inga Shirer Dean recalled.[18]

Tess Stiberitz was eager to leave the past behind, though not because she came from a background of poverty or hardship. Indeed, the Stiberitzes were burghers, people of solid middle-class stock. Tess attended private schools ("Everyone who could go went to private school because the [public] schools weren't very good"[19]) and studied dance, until she hurt her back in a fall.

Tess's father, Johann, was a low-level functionary in the Austrian civil service whose job involved enforcement of the laws and regulations that governed baking, hence his job title: *brotführer*. Linda Shirer Rae, the younger daughter of Tess and William Shirer, recalls, "My father ... sometimes would tease my mother about her 'petit bourgeois' roots. In keeping with his leftish views, I suspect he'd have loved it if my grandfather had been a baker. That would have been much more in keeping with his respect for blue-collar work and with his impatience with the lower-middle-class attitudes and bureaucracy in general."[20]

The specifics have been forgotten, but Johann reportedly served in the Austrian army during the First World War. Taken prisoner by the Russians, he did not return home until about a year after the fighting had ended. In his absence, Grandmother Stiberitz – who also was named Theresa – took her two children, Tess and her younger brother Freddie, who had been born in 1914, and returned home to live with her parents. Despite the tenor of the times, the Stiberitzes were still relatively well-to-do; family legend has it that they had once done well as carriage makers. Regardless, these were leaner times for the extended family, and Tess especially did not see eye-to-eye with her grandmother. "My maternal great grandparents lived in one of those large apartment houses ... [with] a central courtyard and four or five balconied stories surrounding it," Linda Shirer Rae notes. "My mother said that she and her cousins would play in the courtyard, and this was the only time in her life when he had the experience of a communal life."[21] Inga Shirer Dean had similar recollections of conversations with her mother: "She told me [that her grandparents' home] was filled with relatives, and whenever she crossed the courtyard on her way out, her mother would know in seconds."[22]

Austria, like Germany, suffered badly in the closing months of the First World War, and food shortages became so severe that many Austrian children were sent to live with relatives or sympathetic foster families in other countries. Both Tess and her brother Freddie joined this exodus. They were separated when sent to live in Denmark; neither of them ever forgot the resulting trauma. For her part, Tess was well cared for and, as her daughter Linda Shirer Rae explains, "[She] fell in love with her Danish family and they with her. They invited her back for many years."[23]

Tess came to feel so much at home in Denmark, that at one point in her teenage years she was engaged to a young Danish man. Freddie fared less well. Being four years younger than his sister, he had forgotten much of his native German by the time he and Tess returned to Vienna, which he did when Johann Stiberitz was released from the prisoner-of-war camp in Russia and was able to resume his job. Johann then moved his wife and two children into their own apartment. The family were still sufficiently affluent that both Tess and Freddie attended private school, and when she was sixteen Tess lived for a year in Paris, where she learned French.

Out of these youthful experiences Tess began to dream of making a career for herself that would allow her to travel. A career in journalism offered that promise. Working for and socializing with George Gedye and with his associates must have seemed endlessly exciting to Tess Stiberitz. Although Gedye was fourteen years William Shirer's senior and already the author of two books, Shirer was determined to woo Tess away from him and from other potential suitors. Shirer was in love and rebelled against the prospect of spending yet another summer in London. Hence his objections when Hank Wales proposed that assignment.

Rather than countermand McCormick's orders, Wales found another reporter to go to London, and Shirer remained in Vienna. That was just as well because the *Tribune* editor-publisher was now taking a keen interest in the news coverage his young charge was providing. Having spent some time in Austria when his father served in the American diplomatic core, McCormick fancied himself an expert on the city and on Balkans affairs. As a result, he took to dashing off notes to Shirer on all manner of topics. In mid-May, for example, he sent a message suggesting his Vienna bureau chief keep an eye on "the efforts of oppressed minorities to maintain themselves." In his tactfully worded reply, Shirer thanked the Colonel for the "reminder" and agreed to do as he had suggested. Then in a postscript, he pointed out, "Your letters to me still are addressed to the Paris office, and those to [the former Vienna bureau], who is in London, continue to be sent here."[24]

To say that the inconsistencies of McCormick's management style were puzzling is an understatement. He was intent on micro-managing FNS operations and "beating" the competition, yet he seems to have had little real awareness – much less an understanding – of the details of the service's editorial operations or even of who was staffing which bureau when. Ultimately, this became painfully apparent to Shirer; it played a role in terminating his career as a *Tribune* foreign correspondent.

8

"SHIRER FLY INDIA"

The summer of 1930 was a magical interlude in the life of William Shirer. It also proved to be the proverbial calm before the storm. The weather in Vienna was hot; after a flurry of activity in June and early July, life settled into a lazy routine. With no major news stories developing, Shirer had time to court Tess Stiberitz. The couple idled away lazy afternoons sunbathing and picnicking, often in the company of John Gunther and his wife Frances and with Mike and Martha Fodor. In the evenings, they socialized at the Café Louvre or went out on the town. The life-changing development that ended this idyllic interval for Shirer was as sudden as it was unexpected.

When he traveled to Paris in mid-August on business, Tess tagged along for a romantic five-day getaway. Afterward, Tess returned to Vienna, while Shirer stayed on for a few days of work in the *Tribune*'s Paris bureau. While he was there, an urgent telegram arrived from Chicago. Colonel McCormick instructed Hank Wales to send Jay Allen to India to report on the dramatic developments that were occurring there. Indian nationalists were rising up against their British colonial masters, and a classic David-and-Goliath struggle was developing, one instigated by the most unlikely of revolutionaries: Mahatma Gandhi, the pacifist leader of the Indian National Congress political party.

Never before had a subjugated people attempted to throw off the yoke of imperial dominance without resorting to violence. Yet Gandhi, a dusky-hued enigma in a loincloth, seemed determined to do so armed only with the sheer power of his will. Colonel McCormick, was keenly interested in Gandhi who was quickly emerging on the international scene as "a personality." *The New York Times*' India correspondent Upton Close noted, "If picturesqueness be an indication of personality, Gandhi can well supply this."[1] McCormick, an avowed Anglophile, was also intrigued by the challenge that Gandhi presented to the British Empire.

However, there was one major flaw in McCormick's plan for *Tribune* coverage of the story of Gandhi's nascent rebellion. The Foreign News Service reporter who would normally have been assigned to the story was gravely ill. Jay Allen, his replacement, was down with a debilitating liver ailment and was in no shape to make the long journey to India, let alone to deal with the heat and difficult living conditions there. *Tribune* management was inclined to dismiss any illness that was less than life-threatening as being an occupational hazards that was part-and-parcel with being a foreign correspondent. However, Wales was sympathetic to Allen's suffering. So after considering his options – which included flying to India himself, or assigning George Seldes or Shirer to the story – he opted to send Shirer. As the junior man in the news operation, Shirer was the logical candidate. He was also single and presumably could travel at a moment's notice. Wales also figured the upheaval in India might be the "big story" that Shirer had been seeking in order to make a name for himself.

"Ordinarily ... I'd like to go," Shirer confided in a letter to Tess. "But now that I have you, sweetheart, I can't bear to be away from you for so long."[2] He was also reticent for another reason, one he dared not mention. Shirer suspected that George Gedye was still intent on employing and possibly romancing Tess. And in Shirer's absence, Hank Wales planned to have Jay Allen stand in for him in Vienna. This was gasoline on the fires of Shirer's jealousy. Allen also had eyes for Tess, and the attraction may have been mutual. It is unclear if Tess knew Allen was married, although it is unlikely that Shirer would not have informed Tess of that. "I felt so jealous about you last night. Jay came back [to Paris] to find three or four letters from you and also [a] card," Shirer lamented in a letter to Tess. Then, in a clumsy effort to win her sympathy, he continued, "I did not know you wrote him so often, and it hurt me tho it is none of my business, and I am small even to mention the matter."[3]

McCormick's response to Wales's decision that Shirer should be the one to go to India was not long coming. The terse cable that Shirer received from Chicago was a model of penny-pinching clarity and conciseness. It read: "SHIRER FLY INDIA."

"[The Colonel's] message, though I could not know it at that instant, would transform my life. It would quickly lead to a widening and deepening of my understanding of the world and its turmoil, giving me my first actual experience of a revolution, dispelling much of the 'mystery' of

Asia and the Asians, and bringing me into a lasting friendship with the greatest revolutionary, after Lenin, of our age, and the greatest man, a frail little Hindu, half-clad in a loincloth, a saint and at the same time a shrewd politician and a charismatic leader of the masses, Mahatma Gandhi."[4]

Although he continued to be based in Vienna, William Shirer spent much of the next two years reporting the momentous developments that were reshaping India. He became fascinated by Gandhi and his tireless efforts to win independence from the British Empire. This diminutive leader, who preached his own unique gospel of nonviolent civil disobedience, possessed the patience and puissance of an ant struggling to push a boulder uphill. What made his efforts even more remarkable was Gandhi's method and physical appearance, both of which were in stark contrast to the characteristics of the fascist dictators – Hitler in Germany, Mussolini in Italy, and Franco in Spain – who were busy shattering Europe's old order and sending the world hurtling toward the bloodiest war in history.

Gandhi's guiding philosophy, a mélange of what British historian Jan Morris has described as "foibles, dogmas, and contradictions – political ambition, social theory, religious precept, racial pride, [and] personal intuition,"[5] was known as *Satyagraha*. Translated literally from Hindi, the word means "force of truth." The essence of Gandhi's message was that one could conquer an enemy, no matter how unyielding or ruthless, through nonviolent personal sacrifice and suffering. That simple notion, as powerful as truth itself, ultimately confounded the rulers of the mighty British Empire. It also gave rise to a series of unprecedented political developments.

Many British people who were living and working in India at the time were at least in some measure sympathetic to the nationalist cause in principle, if not action; even the viceroy, Lord Irwin, was among them. However, most colonial officials, military leaders, and politicians in London regarded Gandhi with a mixture of skepticism, scorn, and bemusement. Like his many political enemies in India, the country's British masters underestimated the mahatma. Indeed, convincing London to grant India its freedom was not Gandhi's only challenge. He was also struggling to unite fractious elements of the Indian National Congress, to break down the pervasive, age-old caste system that has been described as the "inner citadel of Hinduism" in India, and to contain the flames of Hindu-Muslim strife. These were the same fires of hatred and intolerance that ultimately consumed Gandhi himself and that smolder to this day – witness the uncertainties that greeted the May 2014 election victory of the Narendra Modi-led Bharatiya Janata Party (BJP), which has been accused of championing hardline Hindu fundamentalism.

The mahatma was painfully aware that the British stoked the fires of sectarian hatreds in India, playing Hindu against Muslim in the same "divide and rule" strategy that originally had enabled the British to conquer the vast subcontinent. In the 1930s India accounted for one fifth of the world's population, yet an astoundingly small cadre of a few thousand colonial officials and soldiers collaborated with Indian allies to govern the colony on Great Britain's behalf. However, for all their imperial knowhow the British were tentative and unsure when it came how best to deal with Gandhi. Should they do so with displays of brute force? By negotiating with him? Or simply by ignoring him, this seemingly frail little man who was such an unknown? In part, at least, the uncertainties were due to the fathomless cultural and religious differences between Britain and India.

The same misunderstandings, suspicions, and hatreds that pervaded India's patchwork society also influenced the British and clouded any critical assessments of India and of the mahatma. Even Winston Churchill, as savvy a politician as there was at that time, failed to grasp the realities of the colony's political situation or the essence of Gandhi's mass appeal.

With the Labour Party in power in London, Conservative leader Stanley Baldwin, Churchill, and their political colleagues sat on the Opposition benches in Parliament. Yet Churchill spoke for many of his countrymen when he voiced his indignation at the prospect of Gandhi sitting down with Lord Irwin, the viceroy of India, to discuss Indian self-rule. The mere thought of Gandhi or any Indian nationalist leader intruding in colonial governance was galling to imperialists of the old school. "It is alarming and also nauseating to see Mr Gandhi, a seditious Middle Temple lawyer, now posing as a fakir of a type well known in the East, striding half-naked up the steps of the Viceregal palace, while he is still organizing and conducting a campaign of civil disobedience, to parlay on equal terms with the representative of the King-Emperor," Churchill thundered.[6]

While Gandhi's followers revered him, Churchill and other skeptics, who included Gandhi's political and sectarian foes – Muslim and Hindu alike – vilified him as a hypocrite and as an implacable impediment to peace. What they found incomprehensible, maddeningly so, was how his positions on issues shifted depending on the dictates of the fluid political situation.

Shirer and other American journalists found Gandhi no less enigmatic. However, their views of the man and his message tended to be far more favorable than those of their British counterparts. While the United States had no emotional or political stake in the fate of India, Gandhi's struggle against the might of the British Empire resonated, for it echoed the challenges that George Washington and his compatriots had faced in 1776. As a result, Indian independence became a cause célèbre for American liberals in the early 1930s. However, despite the inherent justness of Indian grievances and the compelling spectacle of Gandhi's efforts to end British domination of the country, most Americans paid scant, if any, attention to what was happening in India. There was little history of contact between the United States and Britain's largest colony. For another, America still had not emerged from the self-imposed isolationism of the 1920s. When that crazy, carefree decade came screeching to a halt with the onset of the Great Depression in October 1929, Americans had far more immediate and pressing concerns than the political turmoil in distant lands. Shirer was atypical in his interest in such goings-on.

He had job-related reasons for concerning himself with overseas events, of course. But he also had inherited his parents' concern for issues of social justice and the rights of the "common man," and so he took a keen interest in developments in India. Shirer's fascination with Gandhi's teachings was rooted in his own search for spirituality and a deeper understanding of life. As a lad, he had blithely subscribed to his parents' religious beliefs. That was until his father's untimely death at age forty-one planted in Shirer's mind the seeds of doubt about the existence of an omnipotent, all-powerful God and the merits of organized religion: "I was baptized in the Presbyterian Church and went to Sunday school and church regularly as a child ... In college, the first doubts began to rise. And they grew rapidly as I went abroad as a correspondent and came into contact with other cultures, other religions."[7]

Shirer recognized Mahatma Gandhi's charisma; however, as a skeptic and a rationalist, he also recognized the inherent contradictions in the Indian leader's message and methodology. There was no shortage of either. Despite this, Shirer sensed Gandhi was someone who merited attention. He saw that beneath the humble exterior was a shrewd political strategist, and so the more Shirer learned about the man, the more eager he was to meet him: "For years, ever since I had read of his first imprisonment in India in 1922 and had been overwhelmed by the eloquence of [Gandhi's] words in his own defense at [his] famous trial, and then more recently read his autobiography and followed as best I could in the Western press his efforts to free India ... I had had a feeling that perhaps he was the greatest living man on our planet."[8] However, Shirer's initial meeting with Gandhi ended up being delayed for almost a year.

Having received Colonel McCormick's cable ordering him to fly to India, Shirer began making hasty travel plans. After getting booster shots for everything from cholera to typhus and plague to smallpox, he booked a ticket on Imperial Airways' tri-weekly service to India. In 1930, this was the world's longest commercial airline route.

Imperial Airways had only been flying for six years, the first passenger service between London and Paris having been inaugurated in 1924; flights from London to the farthest corners of the British Empire began three years later. The service to Karachi (in what is now Pakistan) took to the air in 1929. For a variety of reasons – the relatively short distances, the military imperative, and public acceptance being among them – air travel for passengers caught on sooner in Europe than it did in the America.

The aircraft that Imperial Airways flew on its long-distance routes was a bulky three-engine flying boat called a Short S8 Calcutta. The plane, which could take off from or land on a runway or on water, flew at speeds up to one hundred and eighteen miles per hour.[9] Passengers took the train from London to Paris and from there to the Mediterranean coast, where the aircraft were based. The cost was prohibitive for the time: almost $600, plus a forty-dollar surcharge for the visas that were required to pass through the various countries along the way.

The flight on which William Shirer flew – his ears stuffed with cotton balls to muffle the roar of the airplane's engines – departed early on the morning of 9 August 1930, a Saturday. It did so carrying a ton of mail and seven passengers, although there was room for fifteen passengers. As was the case with American air carriers at that time, the human cargo was really an afterthought; Imperial Airways' primary business was hauling the Royal Mail. Because the flying boat could only carry enough fuel for five hours aloft, it landed frequently on a meandering 6,000-mile route that took it from France to Vienna, Belgrade, Athens, and then across the Mediterranean to Alexandria, Egypt. From there, it continued its southeast odyssey, flying over the deserts of Syria, Iraq, and Persia (modern-day Iran), to a touchdown in Karachi, then the main port for the northwest of India. En route, the plane was buffeted by storms, held up by customs delays, and experienced heart-stopping motor trouble over Greece. The pilots made up for two days of lost time by crossing the desert at night. With no navigational beacons for guidance and with kerosene flares as the only runway lights when the plane landed or took off in the dark, it is an understatement to describe Shirer's aerial passage to India as "an adventure."

Veteran United Press correspondent Webb Miller, who had flown with Imperial Airways on the same route three months earlier, recalled the journey as being one of the most harrowing and trying experiences of his life. The entire flight had to be made at low altitudes, where the winds, the weather, the deafening drone of the engines, and the extreme heat made conditions trying. Even two thousand feet in the air, daytime temperatures routinely soared well above a hundred degrees Fahrenheit, and the Imperial Airways aircraft were unpressurized – that innovation still being years in the future.[10] In daylight hours, the glare of the sun heated the interior of the plane like an oven; passengers and flight crew alike felt as if they were being slowly baked. What is more, flying over the deserts of Arabia, Persia, and Iraq at low altitudes is not for the faint of heart or stomach; "Great patches of outcropping rock became heated in the furnace-like sun much faster than the surrounding sand and set up great chimneys of ascending air like a stupendous chimney," as Web Miller notes. "Air flowed down the edges of the rising currents to fill the vacuum. When our plane struck these vertically rising and descending currents of air, they carried our nine-ton machine hundreds of feet upwards or downwards like thistledown. At times, we fell five-hundred feet within a few seconds."[11]

Shirer was understandably relieved finally to land in Karachi late on the afternoon of 15 August, a Friday. Despite being dog-tired and sapped by the oppressive heat, he promptly cabled an article home to Chicago in which he recounted the details of his journey from London to the Indian subcontinent in *just 6.5 days*. He made no mention of the physical discomforts or terrors he had experienced, preferring instead to marvel in the wonders of aviation technology: "Vasco di Gama, the first European to visit these parts, took eleven months in sailing from Lisbon, and the best speedy mail boats do it now in three weeks."[12] *Tribune* editors, no less awed by the wonders of modern air travel, published his dispatch in a prominent spot above the fold on page 1 of the Sunday edition.

Unfortunately for Shirer, the rest of his initial visit to India was markedly less auspicious and successful. Gandhi was incommunicado. The British had locked him up in Yeravda prison in early May, and there he remained for nine months, all through the long, hot summer and autumn. Shirer was left to poke around in India and send a series of "mailers" home to Chicago; the lack of breaking news left him frustrated. Adding misery to woe was his inability to shake the malaria and chronic dysentery that he had contracted. He was also impatient to get back home to Vienna, where he desperately hoped to find Tess waiting for him.

Shirer was in Bombay the first week of October preparing for the ocean voyage home when a chance encounter with a young man from Afghanistan prompted him to change his travel plans. Shirer was at a diplomatic party when he met sixteen-year-old Mohammed Zahir Khan, the crown prince of Afghanistan.[13] Zahir Kahn, a member of the Pashtun tribe, spoke French but only a few words of English. As a result, none of the other Western journalists at the gathering, most of whom were British, could talk with him. When Shirer and the prince began chatting in French about their mutual experiences in Paris, the young man revealed that two days hence he was leaving for Kabul, the Afghan capital, where his father was about to be crowned as the new king of Afghanistan. Shirer, ever hungry for an exclusive, smelled opportunity.

Afghanistan was a land that few Americans at the time had heard of, much less visited. In fact, when a United States diplomat arrived in Kabul in the mid-1920s, the king du jour, a tribal warlord named Amanullah Khan,[14] informed the diplomat that he was the third American *ever* to visit the city. It is striking how little this remote land has changed over the years. Owing to endless tribal conflicts and its landlocked location astride the ancient trade and invasion routes connecting Central Asia in the north to India in the south, Afghanistan has a tortured, often bloody, past. The Russians and the British, who ruled the country in the nineteenth century, have a long history of involvement there.

The crown prince's father, Mohammad Nādir Shah – also known as Nādir Khan – had seized power in 1929 and then moved to formalize his rule. It was to his coronation that his son was traveling when Shirer met him in Bombay. When Shirer suggested he would like to attend the festivities, the prince agreed to help him do so, although he almost certainly had pegged his new "friend" as being an American spy. Many of the foreign journalists in India at the time were suspected of being agents of their governments, as some indeed were. Regardless, the prince and his advisors assumed Shirer was a man of importance who could help influence Washington to look favorably on the new Afghan regime. As the new king himself told Shirer, "[America] is the one great country in the world which has no political interests in Afghanistan. If we can establish commercial relations with you, why not diplomatic relations? Perhaps you can mention this in Washington. I have no one there to do it."[15] In the 1930s, the few Afghans who had traveled to the West had no more knowledge of the United States than Americans had of Afghanistan.

There was yet another reason the Afghan prince was willing to befriend Shirer: he was eager to thumb his nose at the British, who had relinquished control over Afghanistan's affairs in 1919.[16] India's colonial overlords maintained tight control over traffic through the Khyber Pass, the famous north-south land route between Afghanistan and the Indian sub-continent. The British had allowed no foreign journalists to visit Afghanistan for more than two years. The way around this travel ban that Shirer and the prince hit upon was to include him in the Afghans' "official party." Thus, Shirer accompanied the prince and his party on 8 October when they boarded the Frontier Express train in Bombay bound for Peshawar. That city, the bustling capital of the northwest frontier, was the southern terminus of the camel caravans – the *kafilahs*, some of them several miles long – that since time immemorial had carried trade goods through the Khyber Pass. From Peshawar the prince's entourage set off for Kabul in a decidedly more modern caravan, one consisting of four automobiles and a baggage truck. As expected, the British soldiers manning the checkpoint at the southern end of the Khyber Pass tried to turn Shirer away; the British were well aware of and disapproved of his reporting on Gandhi and of recent events in India. However, when the prince insisted his American "guest" be allowed entry, the British officer in charge had no choice but to comply.

All along the pass's thirty miles of serpentine, rock-strewn roadway, the prince's party came under sporadic rifle fire from hostile tribesmen who sniped at them from atop the mountain ridges. On the Afghan side of the border, the prince's caravan rendezvoused with a ragtag but fierce-looking contingent of Afghan troops who escorted them the rest of the way on the three-day journey to Kabul. There, awaiting the prince and his party, was a throng of jubilant Pashtun tribesmen and the prince's uncle, the new prime minister. Shirer recalled how when the motorcade proceeded to the royal palace for a reception, he lost any appetite he might have had for the proffered tea and sweets. Nādir Khan was still settling scores with his enemies, and the evidence of this was on display for all to see: "My stomach had turned a little at the sight in the great central bazaar ... [of] a dozen bodies dangling stiffly from ropes that stretched down from the roof of the dome, the heads turned slightly ... a gruesome grin on the waxen faces, the hands still tied."[17]

Exactly how tenuous was the new king's hold on power became clear on the day Shirer attended a luncheon in his Bavarian-style palace at Paghman, the Afghan summer capital, which is located in the mountains, a few miles north of Kabul. The meal was interrupted by the appearance on a nearby mountain ridge of a horde of enemy tribesmen, who swept down the slope toward the palace on horseback firing their rifles. With bullets flying in all directions, the Royal Guard held off the attackers long enough for Nādir Shah and his guests to escape. This was the first time that William Shirer had ever come under fire, and he later admitted that he was terrified.

Apart from this incident Shirer was in little real danger during his official stay in Afghanistan; suicide bombings, improvised roadside explosives, or the barbaric kidnappings and murders of foreign visitors by Islamic fundamentalists were all still years in the future. After enduring the heat of India, Shirer felt revived by the cool mountain air, even if conditions in Kabul still were less than comfortable. Shirer stayed at the town's only hotel, which he claimed was the shabbiest he ever encountered in all his years of travel as a foreign correspondent. However, the grand spectacle of the coronation ceremony and the subsequent celebrations more than made up for his physical discomforts. Shirer was the only Western journalist in town, although a Swiss photographer-adventurer named Walter Bosshard and an Austrian writer named Harold Lech were also present. The three of them, along with other foreign guests – representatives of the British, French, Russian, and Turkish governments, as well as assorted Western businessmen who had come to Kabul in hopes of courting commercial dealings with the new Afghan government – donned whatever formal attire they could muster for the celebrations. Shirer borrowed a dinner jacket from a member of the French legation. He then joined the new king, his family, government officials, and the foreign guests as they watched an epic parade of more than twenty thousand motley soldiers, some mounted, some walking barefoot. A few of the marchers sported uniforms, most wore traditional Afghan robes, baggy trousers, and turbans. There were scores of camels and even an elephant corps. The scene, like something out of a Rudyard Kipling story, was grand theater. Afterward, Shirer wrote a three-thousand-word dispatch describing the parade and detailing Afghanistan's political turmoil during the kingdom's most recent political isolation. The story was any young newspaperman's dream since it was an "exclusive." But Shirer faced a major problem: conveying his story to far-off Chicago.

There was no response when the Kabul radio-telegraph operator attempted to contact Peshawar. Shirer suspected British sabotage, and he was probably correct. So he debated, albeit only briefly, the idea of radioing his "scoop" directly from Kabul to Chicago at the cost of a dollar per word. Given his employer's concerns about expenses, Shirer feared that he would be fired if he did this. Another option was to accept the help of a secretary in the Soviet legation who had offered to cable the article to Chicago via Moscow; however, Shirer knew if he did so, the Soviet Union's Tass news agency would his steal his story, and he would get no credit for it. Instead, he waited patiently for the radio operator in Peshawar to respond, and each day he shortened his article by several hundred words. Finally on the fourth day, word came back that the dispatch, now half its original length, had been received and had been forwarded on to London for transmission to Chicago. The *Tribune* published it on 20 October 1930, as a page 1 exclusive under the headline "Warrior Takes Afghan Throne Amid Glitter." When the same article was reprinted in London by the *Daily Telegraph*, members of the Afghan legation in the British capital initially complained that the report was false. Like the rest of the world, they learned of the latest political developments in Kabul by reading Shirer's dispatch.

Shirer never again visited Afghanistan, but he was well aware that in 1933 Nāder Shah fell victim to an assassin and was succeeded on the throne by his son. Zahir Khan proved his political savvy by ruling his country for forty years, until July 1973, when finally he, too, was deposed in a Marxist coup that abolished the monarchy. This period marked a high point in Cold War intrigues in Central Asia, and the Soviet Union was intent on exerting control over the region. When the Red Army invaded in 1979, just as the British had done a century before, Afghanistan descended into the chaos and bloodshed from which it is still struggling to free itself.

William Shirer's stay in Kabul ended the first week of November when he and the Swiss photographer-adventurer Walter Bosshard set off on the return journey to India. A dozen years Shirer's senior and an old Asia hand, Bosshard displayed an Indiana Jones-like flair for adventure. He spoke Pashtu, possessed nerves of steel, and was not in the least intimidated by the fierceness of the local tribes. On one occasion, Bosshard and Shirer were driving at night when they came upon a group of local tribesmen. The men were blocking the entrance to a bridge that spanned a small mountain gorge. As Shirer and Bosshard's car came to halt, the tribesmen pointed their rifles and demanded the two men get out. Bosshard, who carried a pistol, promptly did so. After greeting the men in Pashtu, he negotiated the fee to cross the bridge and then returned to the car. The Afghans took the money but continued to block the roadway. Bosshard, angry now, jumped out and approached the men again. This time, he cursed them roundly. Then, to Shirer's horror, Bosshard slapped their leader in the face. Amazingly, this had the desired effect: the men stood aside and allowed the car to pass. As Bosshard later explained, brute force was a language the locals understood and respected.

Bosshard displayed a similar presence of mind the next day in Jalalabad, a town in southern Afghanistan. He was taking pictures in the market-place when a couple of mullahs appeared and, in a gesture that seems all too familiar today, they suddenly began denouncing the *kafirs*, the non-believers. In a heartbeat, the atmosphere changed. The same people who moments earlier had been smiling and mugging for the camera grew angry and menacing. When someone threw a stone at Bosshard and Shir-er, others quickly joined in. "I had never been stoned before ... It was something one read about in the Bible."[18]

Shirer's instinct was to turn and make a run for it. Bosshard dissuaded him; doing so, he warned, would only embolden their attackers. Instead, Bosshard drew his pistol. Holding the weapon in the air at arm's length above his head, he and Shirer backed away from the crowd while doing their best to ward off the shower of stones flying at them. In this way, they made their way back to the parked car with the howling mob in pursuit until Bosshard fired a couple of shots into the air. In the ensuing confusion, he and Shirer jumped into the car and sped off amid a hail of stones that bounced off the roof and trunk of the vehicle.

The rest of the drive back to Delhi was less eventful, although it again was an adventure to traverse the Kyhber Pass, where marauding bandits lay in wait to rob or kill unescorted travelers. Fortunately for Shirer and Bosshard, they encountered a British army patrol that accompanied them to Peshawar, the southern terminus of the road to Kabul.

Once he was safely back in India, Shirer rested in Delhi in an effort to shake off the after-effects of malaria and dysentery, both of which had dogged him for months. He also wrote a series of mail articles about his Afghan adventures, to which *Tribune* editors gave prominent treatment and which prompted Colonel McCormick to publish a full-page adver-tisement proclaiming how "Only one correspondent, a *Tribune* man, saw Nadir Khan become king [of Afghanistan]!" The advertisement featured an inset map and a large pen-and-ink illustration of a parade of motorcars edging its way through a crowd on both sides of a narrow street that looked like a scene out of *The Arabian Nights*. The text of the advertise-ment points out how once again the *Tribune* had provided its readers with a "scoop" and concluded by noting how "Only by spreading its own writ-ers over the world can the *Tribune* make certain of information uncolored by propaganda or external prejudice. Far-flung, experienced, its staff ensures reliable news from foreign countries."[19] Such puffery, which was standard fare for the self-proclaimed "World's Greatest Newspaper," inevitably took on a bitter irony for Shirer. His cynical view, shared by most other *Tribune* FNS correspondents, was that "reliable news" was really a euphemism for any news that fit with McCormick's own narrow view of the world. As events soon proved, that notion was all too accurate.

After almost three months in India, Shirer was physically exhausted and worn down by illness and mental fatigue. The fact that each day he was writing multiple letters to Tess is indicative both of how much he missed her and of how unsure he was that she still cared for him; with romantic rival George Gedye on hand, and Jay Allen sometimes standing in for him in the *Tribune*'s Vienna office, that no longer seemed a certainty.

Shirer was desperate to return home. Knowing his employer's fascination with history and exotic places, Shirer proposed what he hoped was an intriguing plan. With Gandhi still in prison and India quiet for now, Shirer suggested that he could return to Vienna via a portion of the overland route that Marco Polo had followed in the thirteenth century, the fabled Silk Road; he would travel through the port of Basra in southern Iraq, by rail to Babylon, Baghdad, and Constantinople. Just as Shirer hoped, that idea appealed to McCormick, who was eager for more of the kind of colorful exclusives Shirer had sent from Kabul. Thus, with the Colonel's blessing, Shirer left Bombay the last week of November aboard a British ship carrying British officers newly returned from home leave and now bound for Karachi and their postings along the six-hundred-mile northern frontier. From Karachi, Shirer continued on to Basra, the site of much fighting during and after the two Gulf Wars in 1990–91 and 2003–11. The British had driven a Turkish army out of the city in November 1914, and had then modernized the port and established a strong military presence to protect their oil interests in the region. "Under the new treaty with the 'independent' state of Iraq, Great Britain retains its naval air base, guarding the air route to India and commanding the Persian Gulf,"[20] Shirer noted. In 1930, the Middle East and oil concerns were of scant interest to Americans.

When Shirer traveled the 400 miles northwest to Baghdad via rail, he was far more interested in reporting on the archaeological dig he chanced upon at a place called Ur-Junction, the birthplace of the Biblical patriarch Abraham. A professor named C. Leonard Wooley was directing a joint dig at Ur jointly sponsored by the British Museum and the University of Pennsylvania. Wooley believed he had uncovered evidence of the great flood that prompted the building of Noah's Ark. One of Wooley's assistants, a young British scholar named Max Mallowan – newly married to mystery writer Agatha Christie – was somewhat less certain of what they had discovered. Regardless, the archaeologists were suspicious of Shirer and his motives in showing up in such an out-of-the-way place. Wooley feared Shirer would scoop him on news of what was being unearthed at Ur, the professor having committed to write "an exclusive" for *The Times* of London. When Shirer agreed not to publish anything about the dig until after Wooley's report appeared, he was welcomed with open arms. Wooley even granted the American visitor access to his notes. Thus, upon his arrival in Baghdad a few days later, Shirer sent off a length "mailer" to Chicago recounting the story of the Ur dig. He assumed the story would be front-page news in Chicago, but to his dismay *Tribune* editors buried the article at the back of the Sunday travel section.

The remainder of Shirer's trip home was memorable, but journalistically inauspicious. In Baghdad, he used his French-language skills to interview King Feisal, the ally of T.E. Lawrence – Lawrence of Arabia – during his desert campaign against the Turks in the First World War. At age forty-five Feisal "had a finely chiseled, aristocratic face, still handsome [and] bearded ... but there was a sadness and a weariness" to him.[21] Lawrence and Churchill had promised Feisal that he would become the leader of the Arabian Peninsula after the war; however, the king had been outmaneuvered politically by Ibn Saud, the head of the Wahhabis, a fundamentalist Muslim sect. Saud founded the country that in 1932 became the modern state of Saudi Arabia. Feisal, a weary figure, was resigned to his fate. Shirer empathized; like Feisal, he felt buffeted by events beyond his control. However, unlike Feisal, Shirer was impatient to learn what the future held for him and was eager to be back in Vienna in time to spend Christmas with Tess. He continued his journey homeward via train across the Kurdish areas of northern Iraq to Constantinople, where he boarded the Orient Express. Any doubts Shirer had about his future with Tess Stiberitz vanished the moment the train pulled into the station at Budapest in the wee hours of a snowy morning a few days before Christmas. There waiting there for him on the platform was Tess. She had traveled from Vienna to meet him and had rented a hotel suite, arranged a festive meal, presents, and even a Christmas tree. "We fell into each other's arms," Shirer later wrote. "By the time we proceeded on to Vienna a couple of days later, we had decided to marry."[22]

9

Mahatma Gandhi

William Shirer and Tess Stiberitz married on 31 January 1931 at Vienna city hall in a ceremony presided over by the city's socialist deputy mayor: "Emil Vadnai [*sic*], a Hungarian friend who worked for *The New York Times* [as George Gedye's assistant],[1] and his lovely dark-haired Viennese wife were our only witnesses."[2] However, Shirer's memories of that Saturday afternoon were faulty. The marriage certificate reveals that Vadnay and Thomas R. Flack, the American vice-consul in Vienna, served as the official witnesses.[3] None of the Stiberitz family attended; as Inga Shirer Dean explains, "My mother told me that her parents weren't thrilled with the match, but they were laid back about their children, and so they didn't get too upset when Tess decided to go ahead with [getting married]."[4]

Despite the circumstances, the day was not without gaiety or humor. The wedding ceremony was conducted in German; with Shirer's language skills being limited, Tess nudged him whenever he was required to say "Ja." When the necessary "I do"s had been uttered and the official documents signed, the newlyweds, accompanied by Vadnay and his wife, adjourned to Schoener's, Vienna's finest restaurant, for a champagne lunch.

The Shirers had rented a modestly priced, furnished flat, "a lovely, quite modern joint," as Shirer described it in a letter to his mother. "Our only difficulty is that we can never take a place for very long."[5] His words proved to be prophetic, for the ink on the apartment lease was barely dry when a cable arrived from Chicago. Colonel McCormick wanted to know if Shirer was well enough to return to India and resume his coverage of the Indian nationalist movement, the British finally having released Gandhi from prison. When Shirer begged off, Hank Wales in Paris begrudgingly tabbed another reporter to take on the assignment.

Shirer regretted missing out on the chance to return to India, but he was still afflicted with chronic abdominal cramps and diarrhea. Fortunately for him, fears that he had contracted tuberculosis proved groundless. Those health concerns aside, Shirer was keen to spend time with his bride, and he was intent on resuming his efforts to build the Vienna bureau. He hoped to get help from Tess, whose language skills and flair for photography were proving helpful to him. "[Tess] is very young, not 21 yet," Shirer gushed in a letter to his brother John. "She devours books with a hunger which I envy ... [and] has a strange hankering for lectures sometimes. She studies queer things, as at present where she is taking a course in anatomy at the university. She likes sports. She swims, and skates, and hikes up mountains, provoking me to great exertion to keep up with her. When we come to America you will be able to talk with her for her English is quite perfect."[6]

Shirer could scarcely believe his good fortune in having won Tess's hand and felt he was leading a charmed life. True, he carped about his job and about the working conditions – the mediocre pay, the miserly expense allotments, the constant travel, and the lack of job security – but every American foreign correspondent in Europe in 1931 was in the same situation. Nonetheless, all things considered, the *Tribune* was a relatively good employer, being ahead of the times in terms of employee benefits.

Whenever he considered his career situation, Shirer had to concede that he was better off than many other people. Letters he received from back home painted an increasingly sorry picture as the Great Depression deepened and North America's economic woes mounted. Shirer's mother in Cedar Rapids was struggling to make ends meet (even though Shirer, ever the dutiful son, continued to send her a monthly check), while his sister Josephine, who was out of work, had returned to university for graduate studies. This was a course of action Shirer regarded with disdain. At age twenty-six, he had little patience for academia or for "dull textbooks." He confided in a letter to his mother, "Tess sometimes argues that I apply myself too much to the modern scene without bothering to understand the past. Admittedly, I do, as do most of my generation. But I hold that that, at least, is the less objectionable of the two. Better understand the world around us than the past, which already has been fairly well figured out by historians ... [O]nly dull pedants or the stupid revel in their knowledge of the past."[7]

Shirer's employer was of a like mind. Colonel McCormick often was fixated on his own narrow – and fanciful – version of the history. Yet at other times he was obsessed with whatever news story was breaking; in the blind rush to best the competition, nothing else mattered. Thus, in the last week of January 1931 McCormick's attention turned to the events that were unfolding in India, specifically the spectacle of Gandhi's defiance of the British Empire. When the idea of dispatching someone other than Shirer to India proved unworkable, McCormick reverted to his original plan. On 1 February, one day after Shirer's wedding, the Colonel sent him a three-word cable. The message could not have been clearer, more succinct, or more painful: "SHIRER, RETURN INDIA."

His initial reaction to this order was one of disbelief. Then he became angry. It was not until he discussed the situation with Tess and consulted with his doctor that his rage lessened. Shirer was filled in turn with despair, a profound feeling of sadness and betrayal, and finally a bitter acceptance of his situation. Given the economic realities of the day and the scarcity of jobs, quitting the *Tribune* was not a realistic option. Shirer had no choice but to accept his latest Indian assignment. Such was the life of a young American foreign correspondent working for the self-proclaimed "World's Greatest Newspaper" in the mean winter of 1931. Many years later, sadder and infinitely wiser, Shirer recalled the corrosive impact of his job dictates on his marriage: "All our fond hopes of living together [had been] suddenly crushed. From the very beginning of our marriage ... the pattern of our life together for the next 14 years was fixed."[8]

Bright and early on the morning of 2 February 1931, Tess and Bill Shirer traveled by train to the Semmering. There the newlyweds spent the afternoon on the ski slopes before pressing on that evening to Venice for a one-day stopover, their ersatz honeymoon. Next day, in the Adriatic port of Trieste, Shirer boarded the SS *Ganges* for the long journey to Bombay. His parting from Tess was tearful. Afterward, he lingered in the ship's bar imbibing coffee and brandy as he read and reread Tess's farewell letter. Even in the midst of the bon voyage party, Shirer had never felt sadder, lonelier, or more miserable: "[W]hen I could stand it no longer [I] got up and went out on the deck where the excited Italians still were loading the cargo. I was glum," he reported in a letter to Tess.[9]

Shirer was at sea, physically and emotionally, for the next ten days. He passed the hours writing baleful, plaintive letters to Tess and to family and friends. "This sudden and unexpected separation [from Tess] has been one of the worst blows on my life, but one from which I am confident I will not crack," he confided to his brother John. "Nor will the girl I married ... You would think that marriage coming so seldom in one's life, that I would have been spared the heartbreak of a separation so soon after our union. The Shirers have never won prizes for good luck thrust upon them, but how could I expect fate to be quite so cruel? Well, it has been, bitterly so. The woman, as usual, has saved me from utter despondency; from throwing up my job even and seeking to lead my own life with her for a year on my meagre savings."[10]

Despite his efforts to remain upbeat, Shirer's letters to his wife reveal a grim, almost painful, uncertainty about their ability to remain true to one another. His angst grew with each passing day. Their separation, he knew, would be trying, especially with George Gedye persisting in his efforts to press his relationship with Tess; Shirer was convinced Gedye's intentions went beyond business. At the same time, Shirer had grown suspicious of John Gunther, who also had developed a rapport with Tess and was sharing with her the intimate details of his own troubled marriage; both he and his wife Frances were undergoing psychotherapy.

Shirer's trepidation about the situation in Vienna only grew when he overheard an alcohol-fueled discussion among some of his fellow passengers on the SS *Ganges*; they had concluded cynically that infidelity was a given in any marriage. Prompted by his own insecurities, Shirer sent Tess as many as three letters per day, repeatedly vowing to remain true to her: "Incidentally, I never seem to have had quite so much faith in you as I have now."[11]

When he was not penning plaintive missives or agonizing over the long-term prospects for his marriage, Shirer whiled away the days at sea by reading about political developments in India during the six weeks he had been away. Shirer knew that the British authorities had detained Gandhi indefinitely in May 1930 for having dared to defy the century-old law that obliged Indians to buy their salt only from government suppliers.

Gandhi, sly as a fox, understood the importance of symbolic gestures in a land where so many people were illiterate and poor. Challenging the salt tax was a unifying act that resonated throughout the land; Hindus and Muslims alike were filled with resentment of the British imperial rulers and their Indian collaborators. Gandhi had been sentenced to nine months in prison as punishment for his campaign against the salt tax. When finally he was freed, it was only because Lord Irwin, the all-powerful viceroy of India, was a religious man who was intrigued by Gandhi, whom he likened to Jesus. Irwin also felt that negotiations offered the only real hope of quelling India's seething religious violence and mass unrest. Gandhi, too, understood the urgency of the situation and the difficulties in restoring calm.

Shirer was intent on reporting the outcome of Irwin's talks with Gandhi. Thus, even though he was bone-weary when he arrived in Bombay on yet another stiflingly hot, humid day, he immediately boarded the *Frontier*

Mail train for the 750-mile journey north to the capital, Delhi. There he hoped finally to meet and interview Gandhi. His timing proved serendipitous; a few days earlier, while Shirer was still at sea, the Indian leader had attended the first of a series of eight meetings with Lord Irwin at the viceroy's palace, and he was keen to talk about it. The spectacle of this little barefoot brown man conferring with Irwin was grand political theater. With the world suddenly paying attention to what was happening in India, Gandhi was eager to court foreign support for his cause – especially from America. Thus, when Shirer's request for an interview arrived, Gandhi immediately agreed to talk with "the esteemed correspondent of the *Chicago Tribune*." The mahatma was nothing if not media savvy.

Their initial meeting took place late on the afternoon of 22 February 1931 at the home of one of Gandhi's prominent Muslim supporters. Shirer arrived to find the mahatma on the veranda, squatting before a spinning wheel. In this, the hour before his daily prayer meeting, he was turning out his self-imposed 200-yard daily quota of cotton thread. This symbolic gesture was intended as a protest against the importation into India of British textiles. Gandhi "greeted me warmly, with a smile that lit up his face and made his lively eyes twinkle ... The welcome was so disarming, his manner so friendly and radiant, that my nervousness evaporated before I could say a word."[12]

Foregoing the chair that was offered to him, Shirer sat on the floor cross-legged as he recorded Gandhi's words and assessed the man. Although Shirer had seen photos of the mahatma, he was struck by the disparity between Gandhi's humble appearance and his political influence. The diminutive rebel who was confronting and confounding India's imperial rulers, and who inspired the fanatical loyalty of millions of followers in his efforts to change the course of history through the sheer power of his will, was disarmingly unpretentious. Reading Shirer's account of his firsthand impressions of Gandhi, today it is difficult *not* to envision a mental image of British actor Sir Ben Kingsley's portrayal of Gandhi in the eponymous 1982 Academy Award-winning movie. (Vince Walker, the American journalist character played by actor Martin Sheen in that big-screen epic, reportedly is a composite, the chief inspiration for which was William Shirer.)

Gandhi was physically slight, his wiry physique having been whittled lean by years of ascetic lifestyle and vegetarianism. To Shirer's Western eyes, the mahatma looked emaciated. Yet at age sixty-one, he was surprisingly fit; he walked a brisk four or five miles every morning. "Fasting, [the] Indian sun, and the strain of years in prison, of long hard, nervous work, had obviously taken their toll, turned the nose down, widened it at the nostrils, sunk in his mouth just a little so that the lower lip protruded, and the teeth were missing – I could see only two ... His hair was closely cropped, giving an effect of baldness. His large ears spread out, rabbit-like. His gray eyes lit up and sharpened when they peered at you through his steel-rimmed spectacles and then they softened when he lapsed, as he frequently did, into a mood of almost puckish humor. I was almost taken aback by the gaiety in them."[13]

Dressed in a simple loincloth of homespun cotton, or *khadi*, with a white shawl draped over his shoulders to ward off the evening chill, Gandhi looked like central casting's idea of the stereotypical Hindu holy man. Nonetheless, whenever he spoke English in his conversations with British officials and with Shirer and other Western journalists, Gandhi's soft, lispy voice betrayed his upper-class roots and British legal education.

The mahatma was as complex and contradictory as any political leader who ever lived. His fallibilities, foibles, and inconsistencies only added to the intrigue he held for Indians and for Shirer and many other Westerners. In this, their initial meeting, Shirer was intent on probing Gandhi's philosophy. When Shirer asked him to explain how it was that he had managed to shake the mighty British Empire to its very foundations, Gandhi smiled coyly. "By love and truth," he replied. "In the long run, no force can prevail against them."[14]

Refusing to be satisfied with such "highfalutin' generalities," as he called them, Shirer pressed Gandhi for specifics. Wily as a chess master, Gandhi replied that he could *not* be more specific, insisting he and the Viceroy had agreed not to make any public statements that might prejudice their ongoing negotiations. At the same time, Gandhi allowed that he understood how difficult it was for Westerners to understand or accept that a revolution could be empowered by the sheer force of the human spirit. "Believe me," he assured Shirer, "*Satyagraha* is a very practical weapon."[15]

Although Shirer's hour-long conversation with Gandhi was repeatedly interrupted by aides and other interlopers, the two men covered a wide range of topics, including the mahatma's hopes for a postcolonial India. The interview ended when it came time for Gandhi's evening prayers with the crowd of 500 followers who had gathered outside.

Like the handful of other Western foreign correspondents in Delhi, William Shirer waited impatiently for the outcome of the negotiations between Gandhi and Irwin. Those sessions were lengthy, involved, and at times emotional. With Gandhi and other Indian Congress leaders remaining tight-lipped about the progress of the talks, Shirer set to work building relationships with figures in the National Congress's inner circle, its Working Committee. In particular, he befriended Mahadev Desai, Sarojini Naidu, and Jawaharlal Nehru, all of whom were Hindus and key advisors to Gandhi.

Jawaharlal Nehru was one of Gandhi's most trusted confidants. Like Gandhi, Nehru had gone to school in England, first at Harrow and then at Cambridge, where he read Law. Unlike Gandhi, who was twenty years his senior, Nehru was thoroughly westernized, and at age forty-one was a handsome man with "a sensitive look and manner, a jauntiness even."[16] He dressed well and was cultured and articulate. Women found him attractive. Despite the differences between them, Gandhi had anointed Nehru as his likely successor. Shirer reported in a letter to Tess that Nehru was "India's coming great man."[17] Indeed, he became the first prime minister of an independent India (1947 to 1964).

Among those in Gandhi's inner circle, Nehru was one of the few people willing to provide information to foreign journalists, even if most of his comments were "off the record." Nehru confided in Shirer that he was angered by the slow pace of the talks between Gandhi and Irwin, which were becoming bogged down over the logistics of the transfer of powers from Great Britain to India, over details of the financial arrangements of any transfer of power, and over future relations between India's Muslims and Hindus: "[Nehru] struck me in our talks as a somewhat sad and disillusioned young man, in continual battle with himself to suppress not only his doubts about himself but his disagreements with Gandhi to whom he was utterly loyal."[18]

It was increasingly apparent to Shirer that many of Gandhi's advisors shared Nehru's misgivings about the pace of talks and were impatient for a breakthrough in the negotiations. Serious internal rifts were starting to appear in the ranks of the Indian National Congress leadership. A bloc led by Nehru, pressed Gandhi, arguing that he was too conciliatory and was making too many concessions to the British. While the mahatma, through force of character, was able to convince his supporters to have faith in him a while longer, he stiffened his bargaining position.

A parallel process was taking place on the British side, where the viceroy was under pressure not to give away too much too soon. It seemed inevitable that the talks would reach an impasse, and so Shirer's cable dispatch to Chicago for the evening of 28 February reflected this: "There is to be no peace in India."[19] In fact, he had spoken too soon. The echoes of this latest setback sent Gandhi and Irwin scurrying back to the negotiating table with a renewed sense of urgency. The mood surrounding their talks fluctuated daily. On 3 March, it appeared some form of tentative agreement had been reached, but then it fell apart. After a heated meeting of the National Congress Working Committee that extended late into the night, Gandhi emerged to assure waiting foreign journalists that nothing had been settled. "So, my dear Mr Shirer, you can go home and get some sleep," the mahatma advised. Patting the *Chicago Tribune*'s India correspondent on the shoulder, Gandhi explained, "I do not plan to see the Viceroy until tomorrow." The sequence of events proved important.

Shirer, weary, increasingly depressed at being away from Tess, afflicted with various physical ailments, and exhausted by the heat and the dust, trudged back to his room at the Hotel Cecil. There he sat down to tap out the daily 500-word dispatch that he planned to send to Chicago, a dozen time zones away, he was interrupted by a knock on the door and the arrival of an urgent, jolting cable from his employer. Reading it, Shirer felt sick. The Associate Press correspondent in India had already announced to the world that Gandhi and Irwin had signed an agreement and that "peace had settled over India." It did not matter that the news was premature. What mattered was that it *looked* as if the competition had "scooped" the *Tribune*, and Colonel McCormick was not happy about it. "I did my best to swallow my wounded pride," Shirer later wrote. "Gandhi's agreeing to call off his massive civil-disobedience movement was what counted. What I needed to do was to try to assess its historical significance."[20]

Indeed, people on both sides of the struggle were going through the same thought process. Despite this, few observers grasped the essence of the 5 March agreement between Gandhi and the viceroy, which halted the violence that was tearing India apart and led to the release of thousands of imprisoned nationalists. "More than one of [Gandhi's] younger followers, just out of jail, called it a 'complete surrender,'" Shirer reported, "and a spokesman for the Indian government did not conceal his satisfaction with the terms under which it was able to terminate the revolution which threatened British domination in India."[21]

Meanwhile in far-off London, staunch imperialists railed against the concessions that Irwin had granted. Hardliners recognized that by negotiating with Gandhi, the British had conceded de facto recognition of the cause of Indian nationalism. Gandhi, too, sensed this. He was now more convinced than ever that time and history were on his side; the question was no longer *whether* the British would withdraw from India, but rather *how* and *when*.

Gandhi reiterated his beliefs at a meeting with Shirer and a half-dozen other foreign journalists. The "half-naked little holy man" patiently answered reporters' questions as he sat eating a meal of dates and orange slices, which he washed down with goat's milk sipped from a prison jug. Gandhi repeated that he was a "man of peace" and that his agreement with the viceroy for now had restored calm to India. Whether or not India remained peaceful really was up to the British, Gandhi insisted. Then, canny as a chess grandmaster, he made a direct appeal for support to Shirer and his millions of American readers. The mahatma had never been to the United States, although he spoke of visiting one day; like untold millions of the world's poor and oppressed people, he regarded the nation of Jefferson and Lincoln as a land of hope and promise. Clichéd and trite though that sounds in our own cynical times, that was very true in 1931. "I should like to appeal to the people of the great American republic," Gandhi told Shirer. "I know this struggle based as it is upon truth and non-violence ... has fired the imagination of Americans and excited their curiosity."[22]

Shirer knew he was being used as a pawn in the chess game between India and Great Britain. What he did not see – and he was not alone in this regard – was the real significance of the Gandhi-Irwin agreement, or the nuances of the mahatma's vision for India. "I admit I was slow to comprehend what seemed so evident to [Gandhi] ... Even the Indian leaders around him, Nehru above all, were terribly disillusioned. They went along with Gandhi and publicly praised him for what he had 'won' because ... there was nothing else to do. In private, and sometimes to me, they spoke of Gandhi's 'surrender.'"[23] Shirer eventually came to realize that "For the first time the British acknowledged that Gandhi represented the aspirations and indeed the demands of most of the Indians for self-government. And ... from then on, he, and the Indian National Congress he dominated would have to be dealt with seriously."[24]

It is understandable that Shirer's analytical skills in the early months of 1931 were not as acute as they might otherwise have been. For one thing, with a front-row seat to the history, he was awed – overwhelmed even – by the epic sweep of the events playing out before him. For another, although he recognized that Gandhi was "too clever in turning every idea to his own way of thinking to impress you as a purely God-man,"[25] he could not help but admire the mahatma. Shirer had fallen under the man's spell.

Ever since his own father's untimely death eighteen years earlier, William Shirer had been skeptical about his Christian faith and about organized religion in general. However, being a spiritual person, he continued to search for higher truth and meaning in life. Despite his anger at the circumstances of his being in India, he was endlessly curious about the eclectic brand of Eastern religion and philosophy that Gandhi preached. In one of his letters to Tess, Shirer reported that he had read *Lives of a Bengal Lancer*, a popular 1930 novel by Francis Yeats-Brown, a major in the British army. If that book is remembered today, it is only because it served as the basis for a 1935 Academy Award-winning film starring the American actor Gary Cooper; however, the theme of the original book was something quite different from what was presented on screen. Shirer described the story as being about a British military officer who "soars to the heights of Hindu philosophy." Shirer "throbbed with joy"[26] as he read the tale, for he felt that it afforded him fresh insights into Gandhi.

He felt a similar exhilaration each time he was in Gandhi's presence. The mahatma's message was intriguing as the man himself, for he was a bundle of quirks, confounding contradictions, and paradoxes. Sensing Shirer's interest, Gandhi cultivated a friendship with "his young American friend," inviting him to go on early morning walks, during which the two men engaged in rambling conversations that were more life lessons than media interviews. Gandhi assumed the role of the teacher and spiritual counselor to Shirer, the inquiring student who dutifully followed the prescribed lesson plan. It included readings from the holy books of the world's great religions – the Bible, the Koran, and the Bhagavata-Purana, among others. On one memorable occasion, Gandhi enlisted Shirer and his portable typewriter to record a personal statement that he wanted to make to the world. Shirer was flattered: "Gandhi already had done so many personal kindnesses, had been so generous of his time with me, that I was glad to do this little chore … Every moment in his luminous presence, despite my moments of skepticism, was precious to me."[27]

There can be no doubt that Shirer's admiration for Gandhi influenced his reporting of events in India. So, too, did the traumatic developments shaking Shirer's personal life. The eighteen-hour days he was working – typically from eight a.m. each day until two a.m. the next morning – the exotic diet, the lack of hygiene, and the incessant heat wore him down physically, to the point of near exhaustion. Inevitably, his health continued to suffer. It did not help that he felt downcast at the prospect of an indefinite separation from his bride. He remained painfully aware that back in Vienna, British journalist George Gedye was continuing his efforts to woo Tess. In his letters home, a jealous Shirer implored her not to work for Gedye, although he was aware she was troubled by her own health problems and was desperately short of cash, so much so that she was considering abandoning their apartment. The landlord was threatening to sue if she did.

Far from home and feeling impotent, distraught, and angry, Shirer appealed to his employer for relief. Instead, he received a testy letter from the business manager of the FNS's Paris office, a Mr Elsfelder, who wrote to remind Shirer that the newspaper only allowed its foreign correspondents fifty dollars per month for rent and that staff were subject to transfer on short notice and were under orders not to sign leases or take on long-term financial commitments: "Since you were called away from Vienna, the normal thing for you to have done ... would have been to immediately [sublet] the apartment."[28]

Small wonder Shirer was increasingly distracted and glum. "I can get up little enthusiasm for my work," he confided in a letter to Tess written barely a week after his arrival in India. "I had some the first few days [here], but it is gone now."[29] His mood darkened if a day passed with no mail from home. Shirer wrote to Tess whenever he had a spare moment. His letters, passionate and filled with longing, were also tinged with an uncertainty, a desperation even, that reflected his inner turmoil. At one point, he told Tess how in anticipation of their next reunion he had been reading a self-help book called *Married Love*, which was a 1930s version of a sex manual. The volume, written by an English woman named Marie Strope, had created a sensation, but Shirer was disappointed with what he read: "She writes about prudish English lasses and their more prudish men."[30]

Shirer lived for Tess's letters. Whenever one arrived, he read and reread it endlessly, searching for any hint that his marriage *might* be in trouble. A casual turn of phrase by his wife, no matter how innocent or offhand, gave him cause for hours of introspection and worry. In a typical letter written the first week of March 1931, he demanded, "You say: 'There are cases when one falls in love and just can't help it.' And have you? And how? And with whom?"[31]

For better and worse, Shirer was distracted from his own woes in mid-March, when Gandhi set off on another tour aimed at mobilizing fresh support for the nationalist cause and spreading awareness of his opposition to India's caste system. At Gandhi's invitation, Shirer tagged along: "You will never get to know the real India until you get out of Delhi, Bombay, and the other cities and see how the overwhelming mass of Indians, half-starved and in rags, pass their lives."[32]

The tour reminded Shirer how perilously close India was to spinning out of control. That was evident from the behavior of the chaotic, surging crowds that greeted Gandhi wherever he went. Occasionally, these gatherings turned violent, as National Congress supporters battled both Hindu and Muslim extremists. Such bloody turmoil was emotionally draining for

Gandhi, his associates, and the foreign journalists who witnessed the chaos. Shirer returned from this latest sojourn bone-weary and deathly ill with the now-chronic ailments that had laid him low on his first visit to India the previous year. He was suffering from malaria, an undiagnosed inflammation of the intestines, a tropical skin condition, and an aching tooth. Increasingly, he was forced to take to his bed, and at times was too weak and despondent to tap the keys of his typewriter. When Shirer's plans for some prolonged downtime were thwarted by Colonel McCormick's refusal to grant him a leave, Shirer cabled Tess to ask her to join him in India. He proposed that they enjoy a proper honeymoon in Simla, the viceroy's summer capital in the cool Himalayan heights north of Delhi. To his delight, Tess agreed with that plan. Thus, Shirer was in improved spirits in mid-April when he reported on the arrival in India of a new viceroy, Irwin's five-year term having expired: "All the lords, ladies, knights, dames, maharajahs, nawabs, and other potentates and notables who [had grown] fat off this weird land of starving millions, gathered in Bombay tonight to bid the parting viceroy, Lord Irwin, and to welcome the new viceroy, Lord Willingdon."[33]

Fresh from a stint as governor general of Canada, Willingdon was eager to tackle the challenges of ruling India; however, he was ill-suited for the task. As Shirer reported, the new viceroy was "a little pompous and somewhat shallow."[34] Another observer described him as having "a thin, gray, deeply depressing face and a narrow, trembling frame ... The inadequacy of his presence was emphasized by the uniforms, top hats, medals, and carriages by which he was clothed, decorated, or moved."[35]

Willingdon brought with him to Bombay a letter from British Prime Minister Ramsay MacDonald to Gandhi, inviting him to London for a round table conference on Indian self-rule. As Gandhi and the Indian Congress leadership debated their response to the invitation, Willingdon settled in as viceroy, and Shirer took some much-needed time off in hopes the rest would help him regain his health.

Following Tess's mid-May arrival in Bombay, the Shirers spent a joyous week in the city. Sarojini Naidu, Gandhi's well-to-do Indian Congress colleague and friend, "the flashing, witty poetess," as Shirer described her,[36] entertained Tess, introduced her around town, and took her shopping. With her gift for languages, Tess picked up enough Hindustani to begin conversing with locals and to gather information for freelance articles.

The Shirers' stay in the summer capital, an ersatz, make-believe English village – one compete with tea rooms and a street mall – 8,000 feet above sea level in the Himalayan foothills, started out promisingly enough. However, when Tess fell ill with dysentery, her condition soon deteriorated. As a result, she collapsed aboard the train as the Shirers were returning to Delhi the first week of August. Rushed to hospital by ambulance, in the 100-degree-plus Fahrenheit heat and humidity Tess was stricken with a high fever and was dehydrated. She clung to life for a week as her British doctors struggled to treat her. When her fever finally broke after two weeks, her health improved enough that the Shirers were able to return home to Vienna, Chicago finally having granted Shirer's request for a sick leave.

The Shirers retreated to an alpine resort in southern Austria, where the cooler climate, familiar food, and improved sanitary conditions helped both of them to recuperate. By the second week of September, Tess was well enough to return to Vienna, while her husband resumed work. He was waiting at the port of Marseilles on 11 September when Gandhi arrived there aboard the British liner RMS *Rajpuiana*. Having accepted MacDonald's invitation to take part in a round table conference, the mahatma was en route to London.

In India, only a handful of foreign journalists had followed Gandhi's activities, hence William Shirer's easy and at times cordial relationship with him. However, the moment Gandhi set foot in Europe, a throng of British, American, and European reporters and photographers dogged his every step. Startled by the media crush and all of the public attention, Gandhi retreated to his second-class cabin, where he sat spinning while meeting one-on-one with selected journalists. When Shirer sat down with him, Gandhi was cordial and accorded him special treatment, inviting Shirer to travel to London as a member of the Indian delegation. Furthermore, when Shirer quizzed Gandhi about his strategy for the London conference, the mahatma was candid: "Since you have been good enough to report my words truthfully from India, even though they have often confused you, my dear Shirer, I will tell you."[37]

Gandhi proceeded to outline his three key demands: complete independence for India, equal status with Great Britain in any future dealings, and various safeguards to be put in place during the transitional phase as India moved to nationhood. Gandhi, in a buoyant mood, confided that when the London conference was over and his ends had been achieved he hoped to visit America for a lecture tour during which he would talk about poetry. Gandhi was being playful and was having fun with Shirer and his readers. However, the last laugh was not Gandhi's. His lecture tour never happened, for there was never any chance of him achieving success at the London conference. The British government had seen to that.

Regardless, the mahatma's arrival in England created a sensation. Photos of him striding through London streets clad only in his trademark loincloth and sandals appeared on the front pages of the country's newspapers. Curiosity aside, most residents of the British capital were not sympathetic to Gandhi or his message. As Shirer reported, "To sophisticated London, Gandhi has been more the freak, the butt of jokes in the newspapers, the cause of laughter at the news reel movies – in short, a funny little man who wears a loin cloth and spins and pretends to put demands to the great British empire."[38]

Ramsay MacDonald was no less disdainful of Gandhi and the idea of an independent India. The Labour prime minister's strategy was tried and true: divide and conquer. After two weeks of talks, MacDonald "chided the Indian leaders, including the 'holy man' about their quarrels,"[39] as Shirer reported. MacDonald announced that, given the deep schisms within Indian society, it was inconceivable that the British would ever withdraw or grant the colony self-rule. The London conference, he said, was consultative only; no negotiations of any substance would take place there.

Gandhi was humiliated; he knew MacDonald had outmaneuvered him. Nonetheless, the mahatma lingered in London for a month before returning home in the first week of December. He remained intent on resuming his struggle, but he knew the British were in no mood for further negotiations. Willingdon's response to renewed sectarian violence was direct and unequivocal: he began a new crackdown. Gandhi, Nehru, other leaders of the Indian National Congress, and more than 60,000 Indian nationalists were jailed.

With Shirer no longer in India to report on these developments, Gandhi sent him a cable from Poona Prison, in which he announced his intention to fast "unto death" if necessary. That message was further evidence that Gandhi, like Shirer's employer, had been favorably impressed by his coverage of the Indian independence movement. In fact, Colonel McCormick had gone out his way to laud Shirer's work, publishing full-page ads in the *Tribune* to tout the timeliness, objectivity, and quality of his reports. At the same time, McCormick praised his Vienna correspondent frugally sending his reports to Chicago by mail. Shirer was pleased, but he was also well aware of his employer's fickle nature. Despite this, he had no idea of how soon this capriciousness would bring his career with the *Chicago Tribune* to a crashing, ignominious end.

10

Termination

Misfortune, like death, more often than not arrives unannounced. And so it was for William Shirer. Once the London round table conference adjourned, Shirer returned to Vienna intent on resuming his efforts to build the bureau and advance his career. However, a life-altering injury dealt his plans and hopes a crushing setback.

Tess, an avid skier, had introduced her husband to the sport, and whenever they had time to spare, the Shirers traveled by train to the Semmering ski resort. They were there the last weekend of March 1932, skiing with *New York Times* correspondent John MacCormac and his wife Molly. On the slopes, Shirer fell awkwardly while trying to avoid a collision with another skier. The sharp end of one of his ski poles jabbed him squarely in the right eye.

Shirer spent the next ten days in a Vienna hospital with bandages covering both eyes. Doctors initially feared he would lose his sight entirely, and it was touch-and-go until finally, the vision in his left eye began to clear. However, the ski pole had damaged Shirer's optic nerves, and a blood clot that formed in his injured right eye proved problematic; various treatments and surgical procedures were unsuccessful. Ophthalmologists with whom he consulted were concerned about the possibility that the "sympathetic optic nerve" in his left eye might fail, perhaps leaving him totally blind. For that reason, in May 1944 he had his damaged right eye removed in an operation performed at the Presbyterian Medical Centre in New York City. In 1932, all of this was still far in the future. For two weeks after the accident, Shirer was bedridden. Tess filled in for him at the office, with help from the office assistant, a man named Emil Maass.

Shirer was back on the job in time to cover the municipal elections in Vienna the third week of April. With the incumbent socialist government expected to win re-election, Shirer wrote an article explaining why – for one thing, he stated, the city council had improved living conditions for many residents: "Before [the First World War] the workers of Vienna lived like cattle. Their slums were probably the worst in Europe."[1]

In far-off Chicago, Colonel McCormick fumed when he read those words. With America's economic crisis deepening and dissatisfaction with the Hoover administration growing, McCormick was obsessed with fears of civil unrest in the streets of America's cities and with notion that "the Reds" were taking over in Washington. The Colonel viewed the situation in dire, apocalyptic terms, thundering in his editorials that the end of Western civilization was nigh. Oblivious to political reality, he demonized FDR as a dangerous radical and a demagogue.

Despite the much ballyhooed "objectivity" of the *Tribune*'s foreign news coverage, McCormick, petulant, myopic, paranoid, and as authoritarian as any of the dictators who were on the march in Europe, allowed no pro-New Deal reporting in his newspaper. Nor did he tolerate any comment that so much as hinted at sympathy for socialist or leftist political ideology. Thus, a week after writing his report on Vienna's municipal elections, Shirer received in the mail a reprimand in the form of a clipping of the offending article. Across the sentence in which Shirer stated that Vienna's slums "probably" had been "the worst in Europe" prior to the socialist city council taking steps to improve the situation, McCormick demanded, "Mr Shirer: How do you know this?"

A longer letter from the Colonel arrived a few days later. "I cannot imagine how you could know what conditions in Vienna were like before the War." Assuming the tone of an angry parent scolding an errant child, the Colonel continued, "Reading your article I gathered the impression that you were either reading the New York papers pretty assiduously or associating with New York newspapermen. They are not good teachers. New York [journalists] are pretty well confirmed in the habit of parlor socialism. It is nothing but a form of mental laziness somehow translated into dreamy egotism. Writers of the parlor socialist type do not bother to seek the facts, and their small entourage does not want facts: it wants ecstasy. The principal achievement of the *Chicago Tribune* in the last fifteen years has been to insist on facts on economic and semi-historic narrative. A blanket approval of Bolshevism in the abstract furnishes many a man an excuse for not supporting his family. You should be careful not to get in the frame of mind where a similar approval of all the effects of Vienna socialism justifies you in your own mind in not doing a real day's work."[2]

Shirer, never shy about speaking up if he felt slighted or that he had been criticized unjustly, was also stubborn – and principled – to a fault: "I should have been mature enough *not* to answer the Colonel's aberrations."[3] Instead, he responded to the scolding from McCormick with a letter in which he coyly pointed out that there were no "New York newspapermen" in Vienna to lead him astray; the correspondents for both the *New York Herald Tribune* and *The New York Times* were British.

None of this was what McCormick wanted to hear, of course, and so from this point onward, Shirer was a marked man. Nonetheless, there were times when it seemed the *Tribune* publisher had forgotten the incident. Or it may have been the case that his attentions were diverted elsewhere; after all, the *Chicago Tribune* empire had more than 4,000 employees. It was Shirer's misfortune that two other incidents in autumn 1932 further stoked the flames of McCormick's wrath.

In the first, in mid-September Shirer wired to Chicago a gossipy four-paragraph news story reporting that Chinese-American actress Anna May Wong, a popular Hollywood star of the day, had been involved in a motor vehicle accident in a village near Vienna. Then, as now, stories of crime, celebrity scandals, and sex were media staples. The article Shirer wrote stated that the car in which Wong and an American songwriter friend named Rudolph Friml were driving had hit a child: "Miss Wong, who was driving at the time of the accident, was booked on a charge of driving without a license, a serious offense in Austria. If the child dies she will be charged with manslaughter."[4]

The shoddy grammar aside, Shirer's brief article received prominent play in the *Tribune* along with a three-column photo of Anna May Wong in a bathing suit and a head-and-shoulders photo of Friml that was as large as the news story itself.[5] The source of Shirer's information was the Vienna newspapers. In picking up the story and relaying it to Chicago, he was doing what he did as a matter of daily routine. Unfortunately, on this occasion, Shirer's sources named the wrong Wong. The woman involved in the accident was actually a Chinese-American named Mary Wong. Upon learning of the erroneous news report, Anna May Wong's lawyer served notice that their client intended to sue the *Chicago Tribune* for libel.

When word of this reached McCormick's ears, he demanded that Shirer provide an explanation of what had happened and how. Managing Editor Edward Beck advised the Colonel in a memo that the mistake was the product of a simple case of mistaken identity: "I have written to Shirer telling him what an indefensible position he got the paper into, and have turned the letter from [Wong's lawyers] over to [our lawyers]."[6]

The second incident that got Shirer into hot water had no legal or financial repercussions, but it was a black mark against the *Tribune*'s credibility. A prominent Chicago businessman named Samuel Insull had fled to

Europe after a grand jury indicted him on criminal charges that involved the alleged theft of a large sum of money. Insull, holed up in Italy, received $2,500 that was wired to him by family. Putting the money to use, he sought refuge in Greece, a country that at the time had no extradition treaty with the United States. All of this was front-page news in the *Tribune* and other Chicago newspapers, and so *Tribune* editors sent their European correspondents in search of Insull.

Shirer traveled to Athens and from there reported some erroneous information about the wanted man, which was repeated in subsequent *Tribune* articles. It is not clear if Shirer fell victim to a deliberate scheme to discredit him and the *Tribune* – the newspaper business was cutthroat – or if he misinterpreted the information provided by an unscrupulous Greek contact who was also working for the rival Hearst news syndicate. Regardless, Colonel McCormick was unforgiving. Where Shirer was concerned, the *Tribune*'s senior management decided, it was a case of three strikes and their Vienna correspondent was out. On 17 October, Shirer received a terse telegram from Edward Beck. It read: "SHIRER THIS NOTIFICATION YOUR SERVICES WITH *TRIBUNE* TERMINATES TODAY OCTOBER SIXTEENTH STOP YOU WILL BE PAID ONE MONTHS SALARY COVERING TO NOVEMBER SIXTEENTH." With that William Shirer's career as a *Chicago Tribune* foreign correspondent came to an abrupt and decidedly inglorious end.

Autumn 1932 was an inopportune time to be out of work, especially in Vienna. The Austrian nation, teetering on bankruptcy and lurching from one economic crisis to the next, was plagued with an unemployment rate of 30 percent; people were starving in the streets. In addition, political tensions and violence were on the rise while socialists and fascists – the latter doing Hitler's bidding – fought bloody street battles.

Despite the quickening pace of events in Europe, in addition to the *Chicago Tribune*, only three American newspapers still had correspondents on the continent: the archrival *Chicago Daily News*, *The New York Times*, and the *New York Herald Tribune*; none was hiring. Neither were any of the three American news agencies with bureaus in Europe: the Associated Press, the United Press, and the Hearst service.

Shirer's firing came as a shock, especially since it happened on the very day the *Tribune* was planning to publish another full-page advertisement touting his latest scoop, which was the cable Gandhi had sent Shirer from Poona Prison. Despite this, the ad was pulled just as the newspaper was about to go to press.

In a desperate bid to save his job, Shirer appealed to *Tribune* managing editor Ed Beck, who had always been cordial toward him. Shirer explained the reason for the Insull misinformation and pleaded for an explanation of his firing. He also dashed off letters to various colleagues relating his unhappy news and doing his best to put on a brave face. "Well, I got mine last night, as you probably heard," Shirer told John Steele, the *Tribune*'s London correspondent. "I don't understand it, but I'm not going to do any whining ... at 28, I cannot convince myself that I am finished yet."[7]

A sympathetic response from Steele was cold comfort for Shirer, as were the letters he received from other friends and colleagues. Despite the kind words, the reality was that Shirer had become a statistic. Like millions of other able-bodied men and women, he was now jobless. Tess Shirer continued to find piecemeal work, but the couple's bills quickly piled up. Adding insult to injury for Shirer, the promised month's severance pay from the *Tribune* failed to materialize. This only added to his bitterness and anger toward his former employer.[8]

It was five weeks before Ed Beck's reply to Shirer's letter arrived. In it, the managing editor tried to justify Shirer's firing by explaining that the newspaper had been obliged to pay $1,000 to settle Anna Mae Wong's threatened libel action. Beck went on to claim that *Tribune* editors had been concerned about the alleged shoddiness of Shirer's work prior to his dismissal. The managing editor's rationale for the firing was self-serving at best. Other newspapers in Europe and the United States – including *The New York Times* – had also carried the Wong news report; however, all had been quick to apologize for the error. The *Tribune* had not. Beck also failed to mention, let alone to explain, why if management was unhappy with Shirer's work, he received no warning of it. Nor did Beck explain why the newspaper had continued publishing advertisements touting the high quality of Shirer's news coverage. The reality was that Shirer had been fired on a spur of the moment decision by the imperious Colonel McCormick. While Shirer suspected as much and scoffed at Beck's limp explanation, the bottom line was that he remained unemployed.

With no other options, Shirer resolved to spend his days writing. He set to work on a nonfiction book and a stage play, both of which were based on his Indian experiences. In a letter to his brother, Shirer admitted that there was at least one positive aspect his firing: "It came in time for me yet to make something of my life." In addition to the writing projects he had in mind, there were "a lot of spiritual and intellectual cravings which my job has not allowed me to satisfy. There are books one has wanted all his life to read."[9]

Bespectacled, prematurely balding, and with his ever-present pipe clenched between his teeth, in 1932 Shirer looked – and sometimes acted – more like an academic than foreign correspondent. For all his intellec-

tual acuity and journalistic talent, the despair of being unemployed quickly eroded Shirer's self-confidence and his health. Falling ill with strep
throat, he landed in hospital where he underwent a tonsillectomy. Adding
to his woes, the Shirers' landlady was threatening to sue them for back
rent; they'd had the misfortune of renewing their lease the day before
Shirer was fired.

These were dark days for Tess and Bill Shirer, and their unhappiness
only deepened when their friends the Gunthers backed out of a planned
Christmas-time ski trip, opting instead to attend a lavish alcohol-fueled
party being thrown by Dorothy Thompson, which rolled on for ten days.
A bender was the last thing Shirer needed just then. As the shock of being
fired faded, it gave way to a lingering bitterness that was tinged with
despair. In hopes of a fresh start, the Shirers decided to use their savings –
about $1,000 – to pay for a year in Spain, where the climate was warm and
the cost of living low. Shirer hoped to write the novel that would help him
establish himself as a successful author. He was also musing about becoming a teacher, even if the prospect of returning to academia to earn a graduate degree held little real appeal for him.

The Shirers were still in the midst of planning their departure from
Vienna when a bizarre, almost surreal, letter arrived from Chicago. Writing
on 30 December 1932, more than two months *after* he had ordered Shirer's dismissal, Colonel McCormick commented, "You did some excellent
work in India, but since then you have almost vanished from the picture as
a European correspondent. Is it that your health is so bad, or do you think
that your field is non-productive? We might transfer you elsewhere if that
is so." McCormick continued in a similar vein, pointing out to Shirer that
there was much happening in Central Europe that might be of interest to
Tribune readers "although heaven knows, you haven't made it so."[10]

Shirer was thunderstruck. And confused. Did this letter mean that
McCormick had reconsidered and was now offering to rehire him? Had
Shirer's firing all been some sort of bizarre misunderstanding? Or was the
Colonel so out of touch with reality that he had completely forgotten
Shirer was no longer a *Tribune* employee? "Is the world mad? Or am I
going crazy?" Shirer asked in a letter to John Steele. "What does this letter
from the Colonel ... mean? You know him better than I do. What do you
think?"[11] Steele, too, was at a loss to explain.

Ready to swallow his pride if it meant getting his job back, Shirer dispatched a cable to let the Colonel know that he was mailing a response to
the 30 December letter. In his reply, Shirer explained how surprised he
had been to receive the Colonel's query when he had been fired ten weeks

earlier. Shirer went on to admit that he would welcome his old job back because there *was* a lot of news to cover in Central Europe.

Convinced the events of recent weeks had all been forgotten and that he was about to be rehired, Shirer treated his wife to a celebratory dinner at one of Vienna's finest restaurants. However, their celebration was short-lived, for they arrived home afterward to find a cablegram in their mailbox. The message it delivered was short and to the point: "SHIRER DISREGARD LETTER 13TH. MCCORMICK." A follow-up letter, dated 11 January, arrived the next week. In it, McCormick's secretary advised Shirer to ignore the Colonel's letter of 30 December; it had been a mistake. When he wrote it, the secretary explained, the Colonel did not realize that Shirer was no longer working for the *Tribune*.

This latest McCormick outrage prompted Shirer to dash off a flurry of queries to friends and former colleagues in the hope that someone could provide him with a lead on a new job. Predictably, no one could offer anything more than encouragement to "hang in there." That is what the Shirers did, remaining in Vienna until 19 February, the day they left for Spain jamming the nineteen suitcases that held everything they owned into a cramped third-class compartment. En route to the Italian port of Ancona, from where they had booked passage on a Barcelona-bound ship, the Shirers stopped on the Semmering for a last day of skiing and an expected farewell get-together with the Gunthers and with Dorothy Thompson and Sinclair Lewis. However, the Shirer's farewell to Austria, the Semmering, and their friends was anticlimactic. John Gunther had raced off to Berlin to report on the recent election victory of Hitler and the Nazis; Lewis again was lost in drink, and Thompson was in the midst of another one of her wild parties. The Shirers dropped by to say hello, but being in no mood for false merriment they left quickly. Shirer lamented in his diary that Thompson had grown too full of herself: "I do not like her very much … I feel the feeling is mutual."[12]

The Shirers reached Spain on 3 March 1933 after a desultory ten-day voyage from Ancona. Bad luck continued to dog them; upon their arrival in Barcelona they learned that banks back home were closed for the day. With the American financial system on the brink of collapse, outgoing Republican President Herbert Hoover had persuaded the governors of all forty-eight states to declare a banking holiday. In Washington early the next day, Franklin D. Roosevelt took the oath as president of the United States. Resolute and confident, he did his utmost to reassure the American people that there were better times ahead. "This great nation will endure as it has endured, will revive and prosper," FDR declared in his inaugural address. "The only thing we have to fear is fear itself."[13]

Half a world away, as Shirer notes in his diary, he and Tess were feeling "damned low, and very depressed,"[14] as they anxiously waited to see what impact, if any, the new president's brave words would have. In Europe, that proved to be little, at least initially. The Spanish banks refused to convert greenbacks into Spanish pesetas until the new exchange rate was set. Luckily for Shirer a check arrived from a Paris bank where he kept an account, the balance having been converted to pesetas a few days earlier. That money, about $250 American, was enough to tide the couple over until the arrival of the balance of their $1,000 in savings.

Shirer had asked friends, some of them in the United States diplomatic corps, for advice on suggested venues for their planned year in Spain. The consensus was that the area known as Costa Brava was a good bet, and that proved to be correct. About a hundred miles northeast of Barcelona the Shirers came to the Catalonian fishing village of Lloret de Mar. Perched on a sandy crescent-shaped beach with the Mediterranean to the east and the snow-capped Pyrenees as the backdrop in the west, the town was sleepy, picture-postcard idyllic, and inexpensive.

The house the Shirers rented was half of a three-story seaside villa owned by a Barcelona medical professor. With its ten furnished rooms, complete with a living room with fireplace, two bathrooms, and central heating – a rarity in Spain. The dwelling was palatial. The rent being just fifteen dollars American per month, Shirer paid for a full year in advance. He and Tess then settled into the kind of carefree life they long had dreamed of.

The Spanish sunshine proved to be a tonic, warning their bodies and restoring their optimism that life could and would get better. Tess and Bill Shirer swam in the sea, explored the village and surrounding area, idled away days at the beach, and read whatever books they fancied. They also put to use their nascent Spanish-language skills, socializing with the locals. Among them was their neighbor, the classical guitarist Andrés Segovia. The diminutive musician took to dropping by the Shirers' house each evening to socialize and drink wine. "[Segovia] proved to be as fine a person as he was a musician, courtly and generous, like most Spaniards, modest and simple in his manners and extremely considerate," Shirer recalled years later.[15]

Bespectacled and erudite, Segovia loved to talk about books and writing. He was also keen to listen to the collection of gramophone records Shirer had acquired on his travels to India, Afghanistan, and Turkey; Segovia found Asian music exotic and fascinating. Often, his evening visits with the Shirers also included a rare treat: an impromptu performance in which Segovia played the music he spent his days composing.

Segovia and other neighbors were not the only visitors the Shirers entertained in Lloret de Mar. A steady stream of relatives and friends appeared at their door. Tess's brother Freddie, now a student at the University of Vienna, arrived on his bicycle and stayed all summer. The Gunthers came for weekends whenever they were in the area. So did Madrid-based *Chicago Tribune* correspondent Jay Allen and his wife. On at least one occasion, the Allens brought with them the painter Luis Quintanilla, a friend of Ernest Hemingway's and a fiery proponent of the political revolution that was underway in his native Spain.

Whenever the Shirers sat down with their guests the talk inevitably turned to the arts, culture, and, of course, politics; it was impossible to ignore events either in Spain or the United States. Back home, Roosevelt was intent on implementing the New Deal, his wide-ranging and controversial program of economic and political reform. The political situation in Spain, no less unsettled, was growing ever more polarized as the country drifted toward civil war.

No matter how much they tried, by autumn 1933 the Shirers could not escape or ignore the realization that their Spanish interlude soon would end; they had only enough money for a one-year stay. Knowing this, Shirer adopted a disciplined work schedule in his efforts to become self-supporting. Each morning he sat down at his typewriter at eight o'clock and wrote until early afternoon. He was working on an autobiographical novel, some short stories, and articles about recent political events in Europe. The latter he submitted to magazines in the New York and London. To his dismay, despite the fact he had retained to represent him the well-known New York literary agent Carl Brandt – to whom John Gunther had introduced him – Shirer had no luck selling *any* of his articles. Even more problematic was the fact that self-doubt, the blight that affects all writers at some point, had begun to sap his self-confidence. Inevitably, Shirer concluded the novel he had been struggling with was no good: "Only later did I see that it was dreadfully immature and sentimental."[16]

As the Shirers' remaining time in Spain dwindled, William Shirer grew increasingly gloomy, both about his own prospects and of those of the Spanish republic, with which he had come to sympathize. The political situation across the rest of Europe was no less depressing. In Germany, Adolf Hitler and the Nazis were consolidating their hold on power. In Italy, Benito Mussolini was growing more bellicose by the day, and to the east, Soviet dictator Joseph Stalin was busy purging political opposition and murdering or imprisoning his enemies.

Ignoring their dire financial situation, the Shirers traveled to London for the 1933 holiday season, staying as guests in the Hyde Park-area home of Pat and Russell Strauss, a well-to-do Labour MP. The Strausses were well connected politically and socially, and so the Shirers met many prominent left-leaning British politicians, writers, journalists, editors, and artists of the day, most notably the sculptor Henry Moore and the eminent socialist thinker, author, and educator Harold Laski.

Despite the gaiety of the cocktail chatter, Shirer found himself dismayed by the insularity of his British friends and many of the people he met at the Strauss's home. Few of them seemed aware of – much less cared about – the situation in Spain or the dangers posed by the rise of Hitler, Mussolini, and Stalin.

The Shirers were down to their last $100 by the time they returned to Lloret de Mar the second week of January. The winter weather on Spain's Mediterranean coast is often cool, gray, and wet, and so with their bank account and spirits at rock bottom, the couple tried to economize. They gave up eating meat and stopped heating the house. Fortunately, their rent was paid to the end of April. With no other options or prospects, they were determined to stick it out until then. Inevitably, with each passing day their mood darkened and their relationship began to show renewed signs of the stress. While Shirer did his utmost to maintain a positive outlook, lurking in the recesses of his mind were rage and cynicism, hints of which came out from time to time. For example, a reply to a letter from Ethel Outland, who had taught Shirer English and journalism at Coe College, reveals how cynical and embittered he had become: "Really, isn't it unbelievable what our bankers ... got away with? ...And they were the boys whom I was taught to look up to as God's own. They were the ones who endowed our colleges, made the commencement speeches, chased out 'radical' college editors, and in general wove the patterns of our lives. And what a bunch of crooks they were."[17]

Despite his despair, Shirer was still contemplating the idea of a return home, if for no other reason than the lack of a viable option. The problem was that he and Tess no longer had enough money to pay for their passage. What is more, Shirer knew once they crossed the Atlantic, with ten million Americans still out of work his chances of finding a job were slim.

However, just when the situation seemed bleakest, Shirer received a cable from Eric Hawkins, the editor of the Paris-based English-language newspaper the *Herald*, offering him a job. Although the position, as a copyeditor, was a step down from his work with the *Tribune* FNS, Shirer accepted immediately. He celebrated by buying coal for the furnace and by splurging on some wine and food. A few days later, Shirer left Tess to close up the house and pack up their belongings while he traveled ahead to find an apartment and begin his new job.

Shirer's return to his beloved Paris was anything but joyous, for he was downcast and in an introspective mood. For that reason, he began keeping a daily journal of a sort, "a record" as he described it. His entry for 1 February 1934 reveals his angst and self-doubts. Shirer recounted how while he was dining in one of his favorite Paris restaurants, a small family-owned café near the Pantheon, the owner's teenage son came by his table to say hello. Shirer was taken aback to realize that eight years had passed since he had last seen the boy: "I sat in the same seat in the same restaurant thinking: 'I'm doing almost the same work for almost the same awful pay today as then – eight years ago … Has there been no change in my life, no progress, no direction or have I fulfilled a cycle, being now approximately where I started?"[18]

Shirer had to admit to himself that, try as he might, he could not force himself to contemplate the future. His problems were too immediate, too pressing. Tess had sent him a worrisome letter, the tone of which to him "seemed frigid." At the same time, she had forwarded a telegram from their friends the Vadnays, who were still living in Vienna. The message congratulated the Shirers on their third anniversary, which had passed unmarked on 31 January.

"Despite the ups and downs, they've been good years … I love Tess deeper now than ever before, much deeper than then, three years ago."[19] He could not have known, although he must have suspected, how the events of coming months would continue to test the limits of that love.

Shirer was relieved finally to have found a job, especially one in Paris, even if it was a blow to his self-esteem to be forced to return at age thirty to the same work at the same entry-level pay he had earned in 1926: "It hurt my pride and laid me low with a deadening sense of failure."[20] Compounding his frustration and dismay was the realization that Paris, the city he had known and loved, had changed. Many of his friends had left, and those who were still there were now, like him, older, sadder, and wiser. Some were still working for the Paris edition of the *Tribune*, which was on its last legs. Despite the fact that daily circulation had grown to 25,000 (outselling the rival *Herald* by 5,000 copies), the newspaper was still a money loser. Thus, at the end of November 1934, Colonel McCormick sold the

Tribune's assets to the owners of the *Herald*, and the two newspapers merged to become the Paris *Herald Tribune*.[21]

Just as journalism in Paris had a new face, so, too, did France, the country that Shirer had always regarded as Europe's most civilized and enlightened. If there was a dominant theme in French society during the mid-1930s it was the ever-increasing politicization and polarization of daily life. As this happened, those who sought simplistic solutions to complex problems looked for scapegoats. In France, as was the case in Germany, Italy, Russia, and several other nations, Jews became a target of their hatred. Despite the fact that Jews were less than 1 percent of the population, anti-Semitism was on the rise in France.[22]

The tensions in French society were symptomatic of a much deeper malaise that was affecting the country and its government. Indeed, when Shirer returned to Paris in early 1934, France was struggling to find new direction and national purpose. Many people were convinced the time for drastic change had come, but there was no political consensus on what form that change should take. The French political scene of the 1930s was endlessly complex. On 28 January 1933, the day Hitler came to power in Germany, France was without a government. The latest governing coalition had unraveled a few days earlier; in the eighteen months between June 1932 and January 1934, France went through six governments.

It was into this maelstrom of political unrest that Shirer now found himself immersed as he reentered the world of workaday journalism. The latter was a wakeup call that reminded him of how much he missed the challenges and the adrenaline rush – not to mention the higher pay and prestige – of life as a foreign correspondent.

Being less industrialized than some other nations, France initially escaped the worst effects of the Great Depression. By late 1931, two years after the crash, the situation had taken a turn for the worse. The economy was stagnant; the national government was running a deficit, and unemployment was soaring. When state-imposed production quotas and wage-and-price controls proved to be as unsuccessful as they were unpopular, the opposition at both ends of the political spectrum organized protests that quickly turned violent. Shirer was on the streets of Paris watching as rampaging mobs of communists and their allies attacked government buildings. The ensuing deaths of sixteen people – among them a woman who been standing mere paces from Shirer when she was hit in the head by a police bullet – prompted the resignation of Premier Édouard Daladier. Shirer later wrote, "Imagine Stalin or Mussolini or Hitler hesitating to employ troops against a mob trying to over throw their regimes!"[23]

11

From Paris to Berlin

He was thankful to have a job again, but William Shirer had grown restless within mere weeks of his return to Paris. Increasingly, his attention was focused on events in Germany, where Adolf Hitler was emerging as a man to be watched and feared in the wake of the bloody purge – the now-infamous "Night of the Long Knives" – in which the Nazi dictator orchestrated the murders of hundreds of erstwhile allies and political enemies. Then a few months later, following the death on 2 August of the country's aged President Paul Von Hindenburg, Hitler declared himself to be chancellor and president of Germany.

As he followed these developments from Paris, Shirer longed to be in Berlin, where he felt the real action was. Having confided his frustrations to Tess, he set to work contacting friends and colleagues in the German capital's foreign press corps in hopes of finding a job there. To his surprise, his efforts paid off; Shirer was at his desk in the *Herald* newsroom one afternoon in early August when he got a phone call from Arno Dosch-Fleurot, the chief of the Hearst-owned Universal News Service (UNS) bureau in Berlin. Dosch-Fleurot was calling with a job offer, which Shirer accepted on the spot. After promptly giving the required notice at the *Herald*, he then headed across the street to celebrate at the nearest bar. For the first time in almost two years, Shirer felt that his career was again moving forward, prompting him to ebulliently quip, "I'm going from bad to Hearst."[1]

Nazi propaganda ministry officials, having learned of Shirer's hiring, dispatched two agents from the *Geheime Staatspolizei* – the Gestapo – to greet him and Tess upon their arrival at Berlin's Friedrichstrasse Bahnhoff on 25 August. The agents examined Shirer's passport and questioned him about what he would be doing in Berlin, even though in all likelihood they already knew all that.

Puzzled by the secret police's unexpected interest in him, Shirer sought out his old friend Hubert R. Knickerbocker to ask his advice. The veteran newsman, who had been reporting from Berlin for American newspapers since 1923, could only speculate that it was a case of guilt by association: Shirer was known to be an associate of Dorothy Thompson, whom the Nazis had declared persona non grata; by coincidence, they had expelled her from the country merely two hours before the Shirers arrived in Berlin. Knickerbocker surmised that the attention Shirer received was intended to intimidate him and put him on notice that he, too, was being watched. "All through my [time] in Berlin I was conscious of walking a real, ill-defined line. If you strayed too far off it, you risked expulsion. One soon got the feeling of how far one could go ... I made up my own mind ... that as long as I could tell the essential story of Hitler's Germany, fully, truthfully, and accurately, I would stay, if I were allowed to. Once that became impossible I would go."[2]

Telling what Shirer termed the "essential story of Hitler's Germany" proved to be a challenge. The world was a very different place for America and for American citizens in 1934. The age-old tyranny of distance still ruled in all matters of travel, trade, and communications. Hence, American-German relations in this period were characterized by a mutual lack of awareness. On the German side, this was largely due to the myopia of Hitler and the key men around him. As George Messerschmidt, the American Consul to Germany in the early 1930s, observed, Nazi leaders "know practically nothing of the outside world."[3]

At the same time, the dominant theme in American foreign relations in the 1930s was isolationism. Despite the Roosevelt administration's antipathy for Nazism, most Americans who were not of German heritage had scant interest in events in that country, as Shirer was dismayed to learn. Preoccupied with bread-and-butter concerns, disillusioned in the wake of America's involvement in the Great War, and reassured by a noisy pro-fascist lobby, most Americans believed the Nazis posed no direct threat to the United States or its interests. Furthermore, many American conservatives – like their French counterparts – actually *admired* the way Hitler and Italian dictator Benito Mussolini were tackling their nations' economic ills, curbing the power of the trade unions, and clamping a lid on social unrest. (American songwriter Cole Porter even wrote a popular tune in which one of the lines went: "You're the tops. You're Mussolini.")

The Nazis sought to capitalize on such sentiments, and so prior to Pearl Harbor and America's entry into the war, German diplomats, propagandists, and agents worked to ensure that Washington would maintain its official neutrality or even tilt in favor of Germany in its quarrels with England and France. As Shirer's colleague Howard K. Smith pointed out, "It was, after all, through the eyes of a relatively small corps of reporters in Berlin that America saw Germany."[4] Being well aware of this, Nazi officials went out of their way to cultivate good relations with receptive journalists, offering quid pro quo "favors."

Surprisingly, there was no censorship of the cables that American print journalists sent home. Instead, German representatives who were stationed in the United States scanned local newspapers for content they considered "objectionable," and when they found it they notified Berlin. It was with the outbreak of war in September 1939 that the situation took a more sinister turn. Censorship was introduced in Germany, and the long arm of the Gestapo reached out to exact revenge upon those foreign journalists who were particularly nettlesome. Several of Shirer's colleagues and friends – H.R. Knickerbocker and Edgar Mowrer among them – were expelled, while others were intimidated, received anonymous threats, or were even attacked and beaten by "unknown assailants."

When William Shirer officially began his new job in Berlin on 26 August 1934, one of his first assignments was to report on that fall's Reichsparteitag, the annual convention of the Nazi party. Initiated in Munich in 1923, from 1933 to 1938 these events were held each September. Nazi leaders chose the venue – the historic Bavarian city of Nuremberg – for its central location, vast zeppelin field, and the strength of the local Nazi party organization. Albert Speer, Hitler's personal architect and the creator of some of his gaudiest and most grandiose imperial dreams, planned these rallies as awe-inspiring celebrations of the power of the Third Reich. As such, they were theater on an epic scale.

The Nuremberg rallies grew ever larger for each of the five years after Hitler's 1933 rise to power. By 1938, more than half a million uniformed party faithful and members of the German military were taking part. The 1934 Nuremberg rally was William Shirer's introduction to this collective madness, and a dramatic introduction it was. All of Germany was on edge; merely two months had passed since Hitler's mass purge of his enemies, and rumors were rampant that rebellious members of the SA were intent on avenging the murder of their leader, Ernst Röhm. Like everyone, Shirer was keen to see what would happen in Nuremberg; however, he was no less interested in observing Hitler up close.

Shirer detailed his initial impressions of the Nazi dictator in the news stories he wrote at the time and in his subsequent writings. Nowhere did he do so more graphically or dramatically than in his 1984 book *The Nightmare Years*. His eyewitness account of the Nuremberg rally is a chilling read that evokes a vivid sense of the time, place, and mood. It also serves as a vivid reminder of Shirer's superb reportorial skills.

His initial assessment of Hitler, which was anything but favorable, would not change. Shirer described the Nazi leader as a "vulgar, uneducated, fanatically bigoted Austrian, who had risen from the gutters of Vienna."[5] Yet Shirer also sensed that here was a man not to be taken lightly or to be dismissed as being someone of passing importance, as many foreign observers were all too ready to do. Shirer came to this conclusion as he stood among the adoring crowds that gathered to watch Hitler's motorcade navigate an eight-kilometer route leading to his hotel in the historic heart of Nuremberg: "Like a Roman emperor he rode into the medieval town at sundown, past solid phalanxes of wildly cheering Germans who packed the narrow streets ... Thousands of swastika flags blotted out the Gothic beauties of the city's architecture, the facades of the old houses, the gabled roofs. The streets, hardly wider than alleys, were a sea of brown and black uniforms."[6]

The führer, clad in a weathered gabardine overcoat, stood in the back of an open car. Repeatedly, he raised his right arm in the Nazi salute. In Shirer's estimation, the gesture was more perfunctory than passionate. "His face, which was rather flabby, had no particular expression – I expected it to be much stronger – and I wondered what there was in his almost modest bearing, in his rather common look, that unleashed such hysterical acclaim in the mob ... their faces contorted in a way I had never seen before."[7]

Shirer had another, more prolonged, opportunity to observe Hitler the next day, when the Nazi leader addressed 30,000 party faithful who packed a cavernous arena. The event had all of the color, pageantry, and fervor of a mass religious service or a revival meeting. Hitler's speech was a frenzied denunciation of the Bolsheviks and Jews, whom he professed to be battling in his efforts to "save Germany" and all of Europe. Hitler's audience repeatedly rose as one to roar their approval of his words.

Shirer witnessed similar scenes of mass adulation all week. Each event in Nuremberg was staged and choreographed to stir German pride and a sense of awe at the sheer number of participants. Among the most memorable of these displays was one that took place on the fourth night of the rallies. A sea of 200,000 uniformed Nazis gathered in Albert Speer's torchlit cathedral of light. The awe-inspiring spectacle was recorded for posterity by film crews directed by Leni Riefenstahl, Hitler's personal filmmaker. Her documentary, *Triumph des Willens* (*Triumph of the Will*), is a chilling glorification of the Nazi Party that film historians now regard as a classic of cinematic propaganda. The black-and-white film depicts Hitler in his element, speaking before a sea of fanatical admirers. As his words echo from the loudspeakers, periodically he pauses for dramatic effect. Each time he does so, as if on cue the crowd erupts into thunderous applause and resounding shouts of "Sieg Heil!" or "Heil Hitler!"

Later that same night, Shirer looked on as 15,000 of the most rabid Nazis, recruited from the crowd at the zeppelin field, paraded through the medieval streets of Nuremberg in a torch-lit procession; the Nazis loved the spectacle, which they adopted when they hosted the 1936 Olympic Games in Berlin. Hitler took the salute from a viewing stand in front of the train station. "It was the first such parade I had ever seen," Shirer later recalled. "It stirred the feelings of the marchers and spectators alike ... I was a little stirred myself as I watched the endless ribbon of bobbing torches pass by and dissolve into the night, the successive bands blaring out the old German martial tunes and the tramping men singing the old Nazi marching songs."[8]

Shirer attended all of Hitler's public appearances during the week of the Nuremberg rallies, often seated mere feet away from the Nazi dictator; Ernst "Putzi" Hanfstaengl, the Nazis' foreign press chief – a Harvard grad who was half-American and an acquaintance of Teddy Roosevelt, FDR, Charlie Chaplin, and many other well-known people – provided American and British journalists with prime seats.[9] From such vantage points, Shirer had the opportunity to see for himself that Hitler was not "the brutish, raving lunatic" his detractors insisted he was. "You have to go through one of these [party rallies] to understand Hitler's hold on the people, to feel the dynamism in the movement he's unleashed and the sheer, disciplined strength the Germans possess."[10]

However, the truly puzzling thing for Shirer – and what continues to fascinate political theorists, historians, and psychologists – was the essence of Hitler's mass appeal. What was the nature of his hold on the German people? Was this adulation the product of some diabolical plan? Was it the result of a unique confluence of historical events and personalities peculiar to Germany alone? Or was it an incongruity – a hideously deformed European phenomenon that was the offspring of the marriage of twentieth-century technology with nineteenth-century romanticism? Nazism was the first totalitarian movement with access and the desire to utilize radio and film as tools of mass communication.

Both Hitler and FDR grasped the potential of radio to spread a message and mold public opinion. Roosevelt used his gift for good, Hitler to weave an evil cult-like spell the likes of which the world had never seen before. While he was not a born orator, Hitler spent many years honing his platform skills to the point where style triumphed over substance. To Shirer's ears and those of most other non-Germans, much of what the führer said was utter nonsense, yet it appealed to Germans in a visceral way that was both puzzling and frightening.

Another enduring element of Hitler's mystique was the disparity between his undistinguished appearance and the cult-like devotion he inspired. The Nazi leader did not fit the stereotypical image of the leader as a man with commanding physical presence, exemplary character, or great intellect. Shirer commented on this in his writings, noting that Hitler was in many ways nondescript. To begin with, he was of average size: about five feet, nine inches tall and 150 pounds. "His legs were short and his knees turned in slightly so that he seemed to be a bit knock-kneed … He had well-formed hands, with long, graceful fingers that reminded one of those of a concert pianist, and he used them effectively, I thought, in his gestures during a speech or when talking informally with a small group."[11]

Hitler was not handsome; there was no debating that. His nose was bulbous with thick, flared nostrils, and Shirer mused that perhaps he had grown his trademark Charlie Chaplin "little tramp" mustache to soften the harshness of his facial features, the dominant features of which were his eyes. They were hypnotic and made up for many of his other shortcomings. Martha Dodd, the daughter of then-United States ambassador to Germany William E. Dodd, once advised Shirer to pay special attention to Hitler's "unforgettable eyes." When Shirer followed that advice at Nuremberg, he found himself agreeing with Dodd's assessment. "What hit you at once was their power." Hitler's eyes "stared at you. They stared through you. They seemed to immobilize the person on whom they were directed, frightening some and fascinating others, especially women, but dominating them in any case."[12]

Hitler's bluster and guile carried him safely through at the 1934 Nuremberg rallies, In fact, the entire week was a triumph for him, for it left no doubt in anyone's mind that he was firmly in control of the Nazi Party and of the German nation. Having seen this for himself, Shirer returned to Berlin feeling numbed by all of the goose-stepping and mass gatherings of Nazis that he had witnessed, but also with fresh awareness of the dangers posed by Hitler and the mass movement he had forged. While this all is self-evident today, it was not so at the time.

Germany was relatively calm in summer and early autumn 1934. During this lull in the gathering storm, the Shirers settled into their new lives in Berlin and set about trying to make sense of the madness that was all around them. Shirer strove to improve his German-language skills, develop news sources, and build a social network. Among the friendships he and Tess forged was one with the aforementioned Martha Dodd, who despite her own pro-Nazi leanings became their friend. Dodd remembered the Shirers in a 1939 memoir, writing that while Tess and Bill Shirer were "too young and too poor to give elaborate parties"[13] she enjoyed their company and made it a point to invite them to social gatherings at the American embassy. This widened the Shirers' social circle and provided William Shirer with entrée to the diplomatic community, which proved invaluable as he went about his work.

Dodd's description of the Shirers provides a revealing literary snapshot of the couple at the time. Tess "was a beautiful, shy, and glowing Viennese girl with great intellectual integrity, firmness, and discrimination."[14] Dodd's opinion of Shirer was no less favorable: "Bill was by far … the best and clearest thinkers to the economic implications of Fascism, among the group on Berlin. He was a cultured person as well, having followed and participated in new writing and publishing ventures (as, for instance, Whit Burnett and Martha Foley's *Story* [magazine]) in Vienna, and read voluminously in almost every field."[15]

Dodd's observation that the Shirers were not inclined to socialize "with the crowd" echoes the assessments of others who knew the couple during this period. The photographic evidence underscores this point. In a snapshot of the Shirers taken in Berlin – one in which they are posed with a group of friends that includes Martha Dodd, *New York Herald Tribune* correspondents Joe Phillips and Joe Barnes, and Barnes's wife Esther – Tess is standing with arms folded across her chest, clearly uncomfortable with being photographed. Her husband is at her right shoulder, a reassuring hand resting on her back. Bespectacled and with a pencil-thin moustache, a scarf wrapped around his neck, and a beret perched jauntily atop his head, Shirer looks more like the archetypal Parisian artist than an American foreign correspondent. "[The Shirers] were happy in themselves, read and worked together, arrived at conclusions about life and social progress that did not fit well into the picture they found themselves involved in … They didn't like artificial or stupid people – they definitely felt no kinship with German Nazis, and were shy in making friends among their own group. However, they had a small circle … with whom they were content and productive."[16]

Tess and Bill Shirer would need the friendship and support of friends and colleagues in the difficult, dangerous times that lay ahead. This was the period Shirer himself described as his "nightmare years."[17] A telling entry in his diary confides, "I miss the old Berlin of the Republic, the care-free, emancipated, civilized air, the snub-nosed young women with short-bobbed hair and the young men with either cropped hair or long hair – it made no difference – who sat up all night with you and discussed anything with intelligence and passion. The constant Heil Hitler's [*sic*], clicking of heels, and brown-shirted storm troopers or black-coated S.S. guards marching up and down the street grate me."[18] Things would get much worse for him and for Germany. How much worse, he could never have dreamed.

12

The Nightmare Years

William Shirer's life in Berlin revolved around his journalism colleagues and select members of the diplomatic community with whom he had established relationships. Most nights, they gathered at a faux-Italian eatery known as the Ristorante Italiano. Much of the spot's appeal was its location, which was handy to both the telegraph office and the propaganda ministry. "The [Ristorante Italiano] has become an institution for the British and American correspondents here, helping us to retain some sanity and affording an opportunity to get together informally and talk shop – without which no foreign correspondent could long live," Shirer wrote in his diary.[1]

The regulars congregated at a *Stammtisch* – reserved table – informally presided over by Norman Ebbutt until August 1937, when the Nazis expelled the correspondent of *The Times of London* from Germany. "Everybody else in the restaurant is watching [the foreign reporters] and trying to overhear what they are saying," the Anglo-American writer Christopher Isherwood observed. "If you have a piece of news to bring them – the details of an arrest, or the address of a victim whose relatives might be interviewed – then one of the journalists leaves the table and walks up and down with you outside, in the street."[2]

Shirer's Ristorante Italiano circle included H.R. Knickerbocker of the *New York Evening Post* (until the Nazis expelled him from Germany) and Sigrid Schultz, the veteran *Chicago Tribune* correspondent – the only female journalist, although not the only female, at the table. Martha Dodd, being literary-minded and an aspiring writer, had gotten into the habit of dropping by regularly. She was, as Shirer describes her, "pretty, vivacious, [and] a mighty arguer."[3]

It was Dodd who introduced Shirer to many visiting literary figures, including novelist Thomas Wolfe, who visited Berlin in September 1935 and had a romantic fling with Dodd. The day that Shirer, Dodd, and Wolfe sat down over lunch, Shirer engaged Wolfe – as he had Ernest Hemingway, F. Scott Fitzgerald, Thornton Wilder, and Sinclair Lewis – in a wine-fueled discussion about writing and why so many of America's best writers "dried up" in middle age, at a time of life when logic suggested they should have been doing their best work. Shirer was favorably impressed by Wolfe, who was physically big, bubbling with energy, and "a very genuine person."[4] Unfortunately, Shirer did not record the specifics of their conversation. Wolfe's comments would make for fascinating reading, given his experiences and the fact his own life and literary career ended prematurely. Wolfe fell victim to pneumonia in 1940 at age forty, just as he was entering what should have been his most productive years as a writer.[5]

Martha Dodd was not the only figure from the diplomatic community to frequent the Ristorante Italiano; some of the junior staff from various embassies showed up from time to time, as did Nazi press officials and sometimes even Gestapo Chief Rudolf Diels, with whom Martha Dodd also was romantically involved. At the time, the relationship between journalists, diplomats, and government officials was decidedly more casual and less inhibited than it is today. Several of the young diplomats who came to the Ristorante Italiano did so because they were aspiring writers who liked to associate with journalists. Among the latter, was a then-unknown secretary at the American embassy named George Kennan. Milwaukee-born and Princeton-educated, he was thirty-two in 1936, the same age as William Shirer. Like Shirer, he was still struggling to decide if he had taken the right path in life. "[Kennan] struck me as having too good a mind to be in the diplomatic service … and indeed, for a time he confided to me his doubts about remaining in it. He was attracted by the prospects of a literary career."[6]

Kennan remained in the service of the State Department for twenty-six years and in 1952-53 served as the American ambassador to Soviet Union. Fluent in Russian, he won a well-deserved reputation as one of the most knowledgeable and influential American experts on Soviet affairs. Kennan was also the chief architect of the policy of containment, the controversial Cold War-era doctrine that informed American foreign policy in its efforts to halt the spread of Communism through diplomacy. At the same time he was serving his nation as a diplomat, Kennan was also pursuing his literary ambitions, eventually winning a National Book Award and a Pulitzer Prize.[7]

This is worth noting for it was Kennan who opened Shirer's eyes to the realization that the translations of Russian literary classics he had read in his youth were "quite inadequate." This awareness spawned a desire in Shirer's mind to discover what he had missed. This enduring curiosity would have an unexpected and significant impact on him in his twilight years.

Given the fluid nature of life in journalism and life in the diplomatic corps, it is not surprising that an ever-changing cast of characters dined at Norman Ebbutt's Ristorante Italiano table. Among the Americans who came and went were Ralph and Joe Barnes, two fellow journalists with whom Shirer became good friends. Although they shared a surname and both worked for the *New York Herald Tribune*, the two were not related. However, both men were destined to play significant roles in Shirer's life.

Shirer had met Ralph Barnes in Paris; now, because their employers were not in direct competition, they routinely cooperated on stories, sometimes with help from Tess. As well, the two men and their wives socialized. Barnes and his wife Esther had two young daughters, while the Shirers were thinking of starting a family of their own.

When Ralph Barnes moved on in mid-1939, Joe Barnes replaced him as the *Herald Tribune*'s Berlin correspondent. Harvard educated, cerebral, and left-leaning politically, he and Shirer discovered they were kindred spirits. Like George Kennan, Joe Barnes was fluent in Russian, and he and Shirer spent many hours discussing Russian literature. As we shall see, after leaving journalism to work as a senior editor with Simon and Schuster publishing in New York, a quarter century later Joe Barnes played a vital role in the editing of several of Shirer's books, including the one that would rescue his career and forever change his life.[8]

After working for more than a decade in Europe, William Shirer felt comfortable serving as a mentor to cub journalists. As such, he befriended several of the eager young men who came to work in Berlin with the UP news service, an employer that paid starvation wages and therefore was constantly looking for new staff. Among these recruits was Louisiana-born Howard K. Smith, a twenty-three-year-old graduate of Tulane University. After joining UP in London, he had worked there and then in Copenhagen before being assigned to Berlin in 1940. Smith, like Shirer, was intelligent, outspoken, highly principled, and staunchly anti-Nazi. Despite their ten-year age difference, the two men became colleagues and lifelong friends.[9]

Another junior UP bureau staffer in Berlin was a "rather innocent, naïve, gentle, charming young man," as Shirer recalled him. Richard Helms was a native of St Davids, Pennsylvania, who had attended high school in Switzerland (where he became fluent in French and German) before graduating from Williams College in Williamstown, Massachusetts. Like Kennan, Helms aspired to be a writer. Unlike Kennan, he abandoned his dreams to travel a different career arc, one that included stops in newspaper advertising and wartime service in the Office of Strategic Services, before he embarked on a career in the Central Intelligence Agency (CIA). The latter culminated in him serving as director of the Agency from 1966 to 1973.[10]

Shirer's roster of professional contacts during this period was as eclectic as his social circle. Despite the obvious dangers, he built a wide and varied network of informants. Among them were Germans who risked their lives to oppose Hitler, as well as some paid tipsters, loose-lipped bureaucrats, and even a few Nazi Party officials. One reason Shirer was able to meet and cultivate contacts within the ruling party's hierarchy and bureaucracy was because Alfred Rosenberg, the Estonian-born "official philosopher" of the Nazi Party (who, ironically, was Moscow-educated) hosted regular "beer nights." Some foreign correspondents and foreign diplomats attended these gatherings, where Nazi leaders came to talk about their recent activities. Afterward, alcohol having loosened their tongues, they and their underlings circulated among the crowd, drinking and talking informally. It was at these sessions, held every four to six weeks, that Shirer became familiar with most of Hitler's top deputies and henchmen, including Hermann Göring, the number 2 man in the Nazi hierarchy; Rudolf Hess, the Fuhrer's "deputy"; Joachim von Ribbentrop, soon to become Germany's foreign minister; SS chief Heinrich Himmler; American-born Baldur von Schirach, the leader of the Hitler Youth movement; and various generals in the German army's high command. The only top Nazi leaders who absented themselves from the Rosenberg-organized gatherings were Hitler and propaganda minister Joseph Goebbels. Hitler never socialized outside his select inner circle, while Goebbels loathed Rosenberg and preferred to hold court on his own terms.

Shirer got to know Göring better than most of the other top Nazis. Being vain, ambitious, and surprisingly energetic despite his immense girth, the deputy-führer was addicted to the limelight. As excessive as Hitler was frugal, Göring had a fondness for showy uniforms, palatial houses, trophy girlfriends, rich food, and drugs. His excessive appetites made him the butt of derisive humor, although never to his face. And with good reason. A classic psychopath, Göring was utterly ruthless, impulsive, and bloodthirsty. Yet he was one of the Nazi leaders whom Shirer found to be approachable; if it suited his purposes he was eager to talk to foreign journalists.

The evening they met for the first time, Göring suggested Shirer drop by his office next day "for a chat." Shirer's bosses in New York had approached Göring about writing a regular column for the UNS, and he was eager to talk money. Göring implored Shirer, "Come on, your Mr Hearst is a billionaire, *nicht wehr* [isn't he]? What's a thousand or two more dollars per article to him?"[11]

What is intriguing about these negotiations is that they reveal the lengths to which the American media were willing to go in courting top Nazi leaders to write articles or to speak on radio. The practice was common. For example, in 1932, Ed Murrow's predecessor as CBS's man in Europe, César Saerchinger, convinced Adolf Hitler to do "a talk" for CBS. However, when Saerchinger notified his bosses in New York of the Nazi leader's demand for a $1,500 speaker's fee, William Paley sent a cable informing him "Unwanted Hitler at any price."[12] Similarly, a 1933 bid by NBC's Max Jordan to get Hitler to make an appearance on that network failed, albeit for a very different reason: once he had had taken power in Germany, Hitler lost all interest in appearing on American radio.[13]

Shirer recognized that while his "slight business relationship" with Göring put him in touch with the Nazi leadership, the link was tenuous and of little actual benefit. Göring, ever the opportunist, was intent only on milking money out of the UNS, and he regarded Shirer as his conduit. At one point, as a friendly gesture, the Nazi leader offered to sell Shirer some Expressionist paintings at a "good price." Shirer politely and prudently declined, suspecting – correctly, as it turned out – that the artworks had been stolen from their Jewish owners.

Throughout this period, Shirer kept notes of his interactions with Göring and other Nazi leaders, as well as a daily journal in which he recorded the minutia of his own life. Initially, he drew upon this material for his UNS articles. Later, he recycled this information and reported it in more detail in first-hand accounts of his experiences living under the Third Reich. In addition to two books chronicling his Berlin years – *Berlin Diary* (1942) and *End of Berlin Diary* (1947) – Shirer also wrote his 1960 signature work *The Rise and Fall of the Third Reich*, still arguably one of the best books ever written on the Nazis, and the 1984 bestseller *The Nightmare Years: 1930–1940*. Shirer, the consummate journalist, approached his work with a keen eye for human detail and an informed appreciation for the grand sweep of history. Thus, he eventually was able to write the most informative "inside" account of the madness of the Third Reich that any foreign observer has ever produced. Those writings are essential reading for anyone who seeks to understand how Hitler rose to power and mobilized an entire nation to do his evil.

One of the truly puzzling aspects of life in Nazi Germany for William Shirer was the way in which ordinary people were able to compartmentalize their lives and carry on even as the country began its descent into totalitarianism. In the early years of Hitler's rule, most Germans were not directly affected by Nazi excesses. This was true even in Berlin, a vibrant capital city of 4.2 million residents. With the chaos of the Weimar years now behind them, Hitler was making good on his promise to banish the humiliations of Germany's defeat in the First World War, and the nation hummed with fresh purpose. Six million workers had been unemployed when Hitler came to power; by 1937, that number had been pared to just one million. Most ordinary Germans were happy to lie low and avoid moral culpability by turning a blind eye to the escalating political violence and to the Third Reich's persecution of the "enemies of the state" – Jews, gays, leftists, Jehovah's Witnesses, and union leaders, in particular.

Political scientist Hannah Arendt explains in her classic 1951 study *Origins of Totalitarianism*[14] that a distinguishing trait of authoritarian regimes is the use of terror to control and divide an uninformed or uneducated population. The wisdom of Arendt's observations remains both clear and relevant. Witness the reliance on terror by "back to the future" zealots – Islamic fundamentalists – and by cruel despots in North Korea, Burma, Zimbabwe, Syria, and elsewhere to eliminate their enemies and to control people by sowing fear and mistrust. Nazi Germany set the bar for brutish, barbaric, and cult-like state-sanctioned intimidation.

Shirer struggled to come to reconcile his own Germanic heritage and the grim realities of the Nazis excesses: "What surprised me at first was that most Germans, so far as I could see, did not seem to mind that their personal freedom had been taken away, that so much of their splendid culture was being destroyed and replaced with mindless barbarism, or that their life and work were being regimented to a degree never before experienced even by a people accustomed for generations to a degree of regimentation."[15] To Shirer, the evil banality of Nazi rule was claustrophobic and depressing: "Perhaps it was partly because I had seen a little of Berlin when it had been a carefree place during the heyday of the Weimar Republic."[16]

Politics aside, there were many mundane challenges to life in Nazi Germany. Finding a place to live was one of them, at least it was for Shirer and any other foreign journalists who shunned the "favors" doled out by Propaganda Ministry officials. Rental accommodation was scarce, largely because of Hitler's grandiose dreams of reshaping the capital of the Third Reich as a modern-day Rome. Much of Germany's available resources and manpower were devoted to the construction of grand public buildings and infrastructure. So many public buildings were being refurbished or razed to make way for planned developments that a popular refrain heard on Berlin streets went, "Renovate, rejuvenate, and incidentally change the date."[17]

Upon their arrival in the Nazi capital, the Shirers rented a furnished studio apartment from a Jewish couple who had fallen on hard times. With the lady of the house unemployed, and her sculptor husband no longer allowed to sell his works to Aryans, the couple fled to England. Shirer arranged to make rent payments in British pounds sterling via a bank in London, although he knew doing so was *verboten* under the terms of the Nazis' currency exchange laws. This was not the only instance of the Shirers doing what they could to help Jewish friends and associates.

Like many of his colleagues in the foreign press corps, William Shirer was appalled by the Nazis' persecution of Jews and other so-called "enemies of the state." Shirer used his contacts in the embassies of the United States and other friendly nations to help some at-risk Germans – Jews and Gentiles alike – secure exit visas. Among the former was a Jewish woman named Helene ("Hella") Katz. Polish born, she had moved to Vienna with her parents in 1915 and built a career as a photographer, opening a studio in the fashionable neighborhood around the city's hotels and tourist attractions and winning plaudits with her portraits of musicians, ballet dancers, and others who were involved in the city's vibrant performing arts scene. Tess Shirer, who was interested in photography and the arts, became one of Katz's pupils, as did John Gunther's wife Frances.

By autumn 1938, with mass deportations of Austrian Jews underway, the government there confiscating Jewish businesses and personal property, and Nazi-instigated anti-Semitic violence on the rise, in desperation Katz wrote to the Shirers pleading for help in obtaining a visa to go to the United States. William Shirer responded by enlisting the help of John Gunther, who was now living in New York, having left journalism for a successful career as an author.

With help from the Shirers and John Gunther, Katz succeeded in escaping Austria, finally arriving in England in April 1939. From there, she was one of the fortunate Jewish refugees who made her way to safety and a new life in America. For that, in some good measure, she had the Shirers to thank.[18]

Sometimes Tess and William Shirer also provided safe haven in their home to imperiled Jewish friends and even to strangers. "These efforts, we had to face it, were but a drop in the bucket," Shirer later lamented. "For most Jews there was no help."[19] That realization and the realities of the situation in Germany left the Shirers emotionally drained and at times depressed. Did they want to do more for those people they knew were in danger? The answer to that question is undoubtedly yes. *Should* they have done more? In hindsight, yes. But *could* they have done more? The answer to that question is no, not even if they had been fully aware of the extent of the Nazi's persecution of Jews and other undesirables. Shirer's situation was complicated by personal circumstances.

Because he routinely traveled in his job and spoke to many people, Shirer knew the Gestapo kept a close eye on him. Even if he was not under constant surveillance, the secret police wanted him to *think* that he was; as Hannah Arendt noted, fear is an integral element of any totalitarian state's control over its citizens and visitors alike. Thus, agents of the secret police routinely called upon Shirer and other foreign journalists in their homes and offices. Nazi double agents and informers lurked everywhere, and, as Shirer knew from firsthand experience, propaganda minister Joseph Goebbels denounced those members of the foreign press corps who dared incur his wrath, threatening them with expulsion. Or worse.

No less worrisome in Shirer's mind was the Nazi practice of rounding up Germans who were seen associating with foreign journalists. Those who were arrested as "spies" faced severe punishments. Jewish detainees were dispatched to the "work camps" that were being set up around the country. Aryans were jailed; some were executed. This latter reality hit home with Shirer with gut-wrenching clarity one morning, when he read a newspaper report about how the Nazis had beheaded two young German women he knew. They had dared to criticize the regime. "[Breakfast that day] was a meal I never finished," Shirer later wrote. "I was numbed at the thought of their heads – dark hair and lovely, refined faces – being chopped off."[20]

Such brutality terrorized and demoralized all who were opposed to Nazi rule. The dangers were immediate and visceral, and so the possibility that he might have played a role, however inadvertent, in another person's imprisonment or murder haunted Shirer. "I soon learned how important it was to be careful to protect my sources, the men and women who at great risk furnished me with news the government tried to suppress … When sometimes one of my sources did get nabbed … I would walk the streets of the capital, dazed and despairing, searching my conscience and my memory to try to discover if anything I had done, any slip I might have made, could possibly have implicated him."[21]

Heightening Shirer's uncertainties was the awareness that no one was immune from Nazi persecution or harassment. He and Tess saw that for themselves in June 1935 when they moved from their studio apartment into a comfortable, airy house on the southern outskirts of Berlin. Their new place, a short drive from Tempelhof airfield, belonged to a retired military man whom Shirer met through their mutual friend H.R. Knickerbocker. Captain Hermann Köhl was second only to Hermann Göring as a hero of Germany's World War I air corps. Köhl, a deeply moral man who maintained friendships with foreigners and made no secret of his anti-Nazi views, paid a steep price for doing so: he lost his job and received death threats. Fearing for their lives, Köhl and his wife fled Berlin.

In September 1935, being sorely in need of a vacation, William Shirer sailed home to the United States. It was a measure of how precarious his financial situation was that he could scarcely afford a return ticket to New York. There was no money for Tess to accompany him, even if they both traveled third class.

Despite his circumstances, Shirer's time in America was worthwhile, vocationally and personally. In addition to meeting with his UNS bosses, he visited his brother John, who, like their older sister Josephine, was living in New York. When Bessie Shirer, still active and healthy at age sixty-four, arrived by train from Cedar Rapids, mother and all three children enjoyed a brief but joyous family reunion. For the first time in more than a decade, they were all together.

Shirer's homecoming served as a vivid reminder of how tense and controlled was his life in Nazi Germany. While the Great Depression was now into its sixth year and America remained mired in an economic morass, Shirer was struck by how free he felt in New York: "From the moment I stepped off the boat ... I felt the enormous vitality of the teeming city ... There was electricity in the clear, early autumn air. The place and the people seemed wonderfully alive."[22] Despite this, there *was* one aspect of life here that Shirer found disconcerting, alarming even.

He was stunned to discover how little awareness or interest most Americans had in what was transpiring in Nazi Germany. Many supposedly "informed people" Shirer spoke with – politicians, journalists, broadcasters, academics, and artists – seemed indifferent to Europe's changing political landscape and the growing dangers posed by fascism. This gave Shirer reason to wonder: was he overreacting, or were most Americans downplaying the seriousness of the situation? Either way, Shirer felt a growing sense of disquiet; he realized he felt more "at home" in Europe than in the land of his birth. Not that it much mattered; once he was back in Germany he had little time to dwell on such concerns.

When Arno Dosch-Fleurot, the UNS bureau chief in Berlin, was transferred to Rome, Shirer suddenly found himself in charge of the Berlin bureau. The added responsibility and workload brought heightened job pressures, especially since there were rumors the UNS was in trouble financially, all of this at a time when the Nazis were growing more belligerent in their treatment of critics, especially foreign journalists. The dangers of the situation had been underscored in January 1936, when the American correspondents in Berlin met with then-Ambassador Dodd and the visiting Under-Secretary of State William Phillips. The diplomats had cautioned Shirer and his colleagues that they were "on their own" when it came to dealing with Nazi officials; Washington, Phillips warned, could do nothing to prevent the Gestapo from harassing or expelling them.

When Germany won the right to host both the 1936 winter and summer Olympics games, in November 1935 Shirer had written a series of articles outlining Nazi plans to use the games for propaganda purposes. The winter Olympics, scheduled for February in the Bavarian alpine resort of Garmisch-Partenkirchen, were to be a dress rehearsal for the much larger summer games, to be held in Berlin in August. The Nazis dialed down their "Jew baiting," as Shirer termed it, during the time the world's eyes were focused on Germany. This was part of a deliberate strategy, for as diplomatic historian Geoffrey S. Smith notes, "The Nazi hierarchy decided upon a policy of restraining American interest in foreign politics by relying on tourist and cultural propaganda."[23]

The participation of American athletes in the 1936 winter and summer Olympic Games was an undeniable public relations coup for Hitler that served to further embolden him at home and on the world stage. If today we now recall anything about only the Berlin Olympics, it is black American sprinter Jessie Owens's four gold medals. What is forgotten, as Shirer later pointed out, was how on the morning of the 400-meter relay race, American Olympic officials dropped two Jewish runners from the track-and-field team – Sam Stoller and Marty Glickman – replacing them with Owens and another black athlete named Foy Draper. True, Owens was lightning-quick afoot, but Stoller had faster qualifying times than did Draper; the only reason to drop the Jewish runner from the American team was to placate the games' German hosts. Regardless, the strategy worked from a competitive standpoint. The American team won the gold medal in record time, even if the way it did so "left a bad taste in many an American mouth," as Shirer put it.[24]

All of these developments were still nine months in the future when he wrote his articles outlining Hitler's plans to use the Olympic Games for political ends. Nazi officials were incensed, and so a propaganda Ministry official telephoned Shirer to berate him for his Olympic Games articles. Shirer generally kept his cool when dealing with bureaucrats and Nazi functionaries, but he had a temper that flared if he felt he had been wronged or was being bullied. When the Nazi official accused him of being a liar, Shirer responded angrily. After a torrent of shouting and foul language, the phone call ended abruptly. Predictably, the repercussions came quickly.

Next morning, Shirer found himself being denounced in articles that appeared in various Berlin newspapers and in broadcasts heard on German radio. Incensed by this and figuring that he was about to be expelled from Germany and therefore had nothing to lose, Shirer sought out the Propaganda Ministry functionary who was responsible. The ensuing confrontation quickly grew heated, with Shirer thumping his hand on the official's desk and demanding an apology and a correction.

The outcome of all this sound and fury was surprising: cooler heads prevailed, and a hasty compromise was reached. The Nazi official agreed to stop denouncing Shirer and to allow him to remain in the country. The quid pro quo was that Shirer would discontinue his protest, something he was content to do; he had made his point. When Shirer later queried his contacts within the Propaganda Ministry he learned the only reason he had not been kicked out of the country was because Joseph Goebbels had decided that Herr Shirer had been taught "a lesson." What is more, Goebbels surely must have known that Shirer's articles, while problematic for the Nazis, had not swayed American public opinion, at least not enough to convince United States Olympic committee officials to boycott the upcoming games.

The pro-German lobby in America was busy trumping negative press reports about the Nazi regime in Germany. Shirer received yet another reminder of that reality when aviator Charles Lindbergh and his wife, Anne, traveled to Berlin for the Olympic summer games. Being unabashed admirers of the Third Reich and skeptical of media reports about Nazi excesses, the couple attended public events, one of which was a lavish reception thrown by Goebbels.

The Lindberghs were not the only prominent American visitors to Berlin who questioned news coverage of the Nazi regime. Far from it. For example, Norman Chandler, the conservative-minded owner of the *Los Angeles Times*, and a group of his peers and associates joined the chorus when they came to town. At a lunch with Shirer and Ralph Barnes of the *Herald Tribune*, Chandler demanded to know why the orderly and outwardly prosperous conditions in Germany, which he and his companions had seen "with their own eyes," were at odds with articles written by American journalists. "They had talked to Göring," Shirer noted, "and he had told them that we American correspondents in Berlin peddled nothing but lies about National Socialist Germany."[25]

Small wonder Nazi leaders decided that anything Shirer and his colleagues were writing was of little importance, for now at least. Goebbels's decision to allow the UNS's bureau chief to remain in Berlin ultimately proved pivotal, both to Shirer and to the world's understanding of the evils of the Nazi regime. Had he been expelled in 1936, Shirer would not have had a front-row seat from which to report from a uniquely American perspective Germany's descent into madness, Europe's drift to war, and the opening salvos of the bloodiest conflict in human history.

13

A Change of Direction

Life under the Third Reich was trying and uncertain for foreigners, but the Shirers did their best to adapt. Tess found work as a freelance translator and photographer and sometimes aided her husband in his job. Having "inherited" a pro-Nazi German office assistant whom he neither liked nor trusted, Shirer welcomed his wife's help; the competitive pressures of his job were a grind, his pay was barely adequate, and his fourteen-hour days were exhausting. Nonetheless, he believed the work he was doing was important. On a more elemental level, with the Depression into its seventh year in 1936, journalism jobs for American expatriates in Europe remained scarce. The realization in May that Tess was pregnant only underscored Shirer's need for a regular paycheck.

As bureau chief, he could set his own hours, and so he made time to be with Tess. Together they escaped the city whenever possible. With that in mind, Shirer paid 400 marks for an eighteen-foot sloop he bought from man in a pub. By mooring the vessel at a marina on the Havel River, south of the city, the Shirers could enjoy warm-weather leisure days on the water. Neither of them knew much about boats, but they learned quickly. Ever after, they remembered these idyllic sunlit days as being among the happiest of their life together: "Tess was twenty-six that summer, and I was thirty-two, a wonderful age for married love and much too early for time and circumstances to take their toll."[1]

Occasionally, they took longer trips, traveling Europe by train. That was the case the third week of June 1936 when they vacationed in the historic Croatian city of Dubrovnik in the company of H.R. Knickerbocker and his wife Agnes. What started out as a romantic getaway came perilously close to taking a tragic turn when for the second time in less than two months Tess had a brush with death. Both incidents, though unrelated, involved aircraft crashes.

In mid-April a press agent from the German company that operated the *Hindenburg* zeppelin had telephoned the UNS office in Berlin with a tempting offer: a "freebie" – a free promotional flight to the United States. Although he dearly wanted to accept, Shirer declined the free trip, citing work commitments and the fact he had already written about the zeppelin's operations. Undeterred, the press agent extended his offer to Tess, who had done the research for the articles her husband had written about zeppelin passenger service the previous year. It was fortunate that Shirer was busy and neglected to forward the invitation because on 6 May 1936, the *Hindenburg* crashed in flames as it was docking at Lakehurst, New Jersey; thirty-six people lost their lives. Had she been on that board, Tess might well have been among the casualties.[2]

She had another close encounter with death in Dubrovnik. Early one morning, Tess took her Leica camera to the central market to take photographs. In the skies above the town on this day, a young Yugoslavian air force pilot lost control of his plane while doing risky low-level acrobatics in a bid to impress a girlfriend. The daredevil pilot, his co-pilot, and eight people on the ground died when the bomber crashed into the crowded marketplace. Having witnessed the accident from afar, Shirer rushed to the scene. Seeing emergency workers carting away the dead and wounded, he feared the worst. To his immense relief, he found Tess shaken, but otherwise unharmed. Ever resourceful, she was busy taking news photos of the carnage.

Shirer, who was by nature introspective and prone to periods of melancholy self-reflection – and even depression – could feel himself being slowly worn down by the cumulative effects of such misadventures, his job stresses, and the oppressiveness and uncertainties of life in Nazi Germany. His precarious financial situation only added to his angst, especially in light of persistent rumors that his employer was in financial trouble. To ease his fears when he asked about this and to reward his good work, in March 1937 his employer had bumped his weekly salary from $75 to $89, plus $36 for expenses. He was now earning $125 per week. "I know you realize the tribute which is being paid you by this increase," Shirer's boss in New York insisted.[3]

Shirer was appreciative. He knew he was taking home a decent wage relative to what the average German worker earned, yet the fact remained that Shirer was perpetually in debt. The realization that he and Tess were about to become parents only added to his anxieties. Although he could scarcely afford to do so, ever the dutiful son, each month Shirer continued sending $25 to his mother in Cedar Rapids.

In a bid to earn extra income, he began writing freelance articles for American publications. He also stepped up his efforts to find a job that paid better and had more stability. However, for now, with no firm offer forthcoming he had no choice but to make the best of his situation.

Like every other American journalist in Europe, Shirer fantasized about writing the book that would make him rich and famous. John Gunther was among the select few who hit upon the elusive magic formula, and it changed his life. Gunther and Shirer, "two Chicago boys" had made a mutual pledge to be successful novelists and to quit the newspaper business by the time each of them they were thirty-two. Gunther was thirty-five when finally he was in a position to leave his job with the *Chicago Daily News*. It was to his surprise and everlasting dismay that he did so not as a novelist but rather as the author of a work of nonfiction. Shirer, three years younger, clung to his dream of writing "the Great American Novel," and so he spent almost a year of his spare time working on a tale based on his experiences in India. When in spring 1937 the novel was done, Gunther obligingly introduced Shirer to his own literary agent in New York, Berenice Baumgarten of Brandt and Brandt. However, much to Shirer's chagrin, she had no luck finding a publisher for his book. This was a bitter pill for him to swallow, for he begrudgingly had to accept Tess's critical assessment of the manuscript as being too preachy and not very good. Shirer reluctantly concluded that he was not yet mature enough to write quality fiction. To his credit, he did not dwell on his literary frustrations.

Working conditions for foreign journalists in Berlin grew ever more restrictive as the Nazis tightened their hold on power. Like a schoolyard bully, Hitler's bluster grew louder as one by one, he renounced the punitive obligations the Allies had imposed upon Germany in 1919. With each success, his popularity among the German people soared. Emboldened by this, he adopted an increasingly bellicose foreign policy. Shirer, like many foreign observers, was puzzled and dismayed by the reluctance or inability of the Allies to check Hitler's aggression, especially when it was clear that diplomacy was ineffective when dealing with him.

That point had been underscored in March 1936 when Hitler announced Germany would no longer be bound by the terms of the Locarno Treaty of 1925, one of which had established the Rhineland as a neutral zone. Even as Hitler was standing before cheering delegates in the Reichstag to announce his latest gambit, the German army was already reoccupying the Rhineland. "At the [Ristorante Italiano] tonight one of the French correspondents cheered us up by stating positively that the

French army would march tomorrow," Shirer wrote in his diary on 7 March. "Why it doesn't march, I don't understand. Certainly, it is more than a match for the Reichswehr. And if it does, that's the end of Hitler."[4]

After too much beer, two plates of spaghetti, and a lengthy debate, it was three a.m. when Shirer went home to bed feeling certain that this time Hitler had miscalculated and would pay the price. Not so. He was aghast next day when the French failed to respond: "Hitler has got away with it! France is *not* marching ... Instead it is appealing to the League [of Nations]! ... Oh, the stupidity (or is it paralysis?) of the French! I learned today, on absolute authority that the German troops [who] marched into the demilitarized zone of the Rhineland yesterday had strict orders to beat a hasty retreat if the French army opposed them in any way. They were not prepared or equipped to fight a regular army."[5]

An emboldened Hitler was making plans to annex Austria and setting his agents to work stirring up trouble in Poland, Czechoslovakia, and neighboring Baltic states. Farther afield, reveling in his self-appointed role as defender of Christian Europe against the godless Communist menace, Hitler was determined to thwart Soviet efforts to influence events in Spain. The German military backed pro-fascist Nationalist rebels in their civil war against the Republican loyalists, sending money, "volunteer" troops, and waves of military aircraft to join the fight. The Spanish conflict was a training exercise for the tactics of the Blitzkreig – "lightning war" – that enabled the German army to sweep across Western Europe in the opening months of the Second World War.

These were heady days for Hitler. As biographer John Toland notes, "If Hitler had died in 1937, on the fourth anniversary of his coming to power ... he would undoubtedly have gone down as one of the greatest figures in German history. Throughout Europe he had millions of admirers."[6] Indeed, Hitler's influence extended to America, where members of the German-American Bund wore swastika-festooned uniforms, and aviator Charles Lindbergh and other influential public figures praised Germany's economic and military successes. Fascism was on the march around the globe.

Despite the dizzying swirl of international events, the pace of life in Berlin slackened during the hot, languid days of summer, when Hitler and other Nazi leaders adjourned to their vacation homes. Tess and Bill Shirer seized the opportunity to take a holiday of their own, traveling to England and France in early July 1937. While the main purpose of the trip was to visit friends, Shirer also hoped to meet with senior representatives from *The New York Times* and the *Chicago Daily News*, both of whom had expressed interest in hiring him.

In England, the Shirers stayed with the Knickerbockers, who were now living near London. It was to the Knickerbocker house that Shirer's long-time friend Jay Allen and Carroll Binder, the foreign editor of the *Chicago Daily News*, dropped by one evening for drinks. Shirer was confident that Binder would offer him a job. However, that did not happen. What *did* happen, and it proved to be far more significant, was that Jay Allen gave Shirer the business card of the European representative of the New York-based Columbia Broadcasting System (CBS) radio network. The man, Edward R. Murrow, had asked Allen to have Shirer call him when he was in London; Murrow, an academic-turned-newsman with no journalism experience, was looking for an experienced American foreign correspondent to help him in his work. Journalist Raymond Gram Swing, a mutual friend, had recommended Shirer as the ideal candidate.

Shirer had never heard of Murrow and was not inclined to return his call. Like most print journalists of the day, Shirer had little regard for radio broadcasters or their newfangled medium. Many newspapers and news agencies forbade their staff from being interviewed or speaking on air; the UNS was not among them. Shirer had already made one news broadcast for CBS, but it had not gone at all well and he had vowed not to do another.

The day the *Hindenburg* crashed in New Jersey the network's representative in Berlin had asked Shirer to do a fifteen-minute report on German reaction to the disaster. His reluctance proved to be well founded. He hated the experience and bristled when his script had to be vetted by Air Ministry officials. Even more problematic was Shirer's stage fright when speaking on live radio. "I swallowed. I tried to clear my throat," he later recalled. "I began, my quivering voice skipping up and down the scale, my lips parched, [and] my throat dry."[7]

The two main American radio networks of the day – CBS and the rival National Broadcasting Corporation (NBC) networks, Red and Blue – had no news-gathering capabilities, and so they routinely invited print journalists to comment whenever there was major news out of Europe. Nonetheless, live transatlantic broadcasts were still a novelty owing to the technological limitations of the medium, time differences between Europe and North America, and other logistical concerns.

Commercial shortwave radio signals from the United Kingdom and the Continent were usually beamed to London. From there a transmitter relayed them west across the Atlantic to receiving stations in the New York City area. The process was technologically awkward, weather dependent, and subject to political interference and censorship.

All of this was swirling in the background when Jay Allen handed

Edward R. Murrow's business card to Shirer, who suspected the CBS man wanted to pump him for information about recent events in Germany. So Shirer never gave the idea of calling Murrow a second thought. He and Tess joined the Knickerbockers on a trip out to Salcombe, Devonshire, where they spent a weekend at the country home of sportswriter-turned-author Paul Gallico and his wife Pauline. Gallico, like John Gunther, had left the newspaper business to seek his fame and fortune writing books and freelance articles. His articles and short stories regularly appeared in leading American magazines, and he wrote a book a year for the next forty years, including his three best-known works: *The Snow Goose* (1941), *Lou Gehrig: Pride of the Yankees* (1942), and *The Poseidon Adventure* (1969), all of which became Hollywood films.

Gallico was living every journalists' dream, and Shirer envied and desperately wanted to emulate him. However, for now at least he remained tied to his job and the security of a steady paycheck. For that reason, the Shirers next traveled from England to Paris. There Shirer met with UNS managing editor Seymour Berkson, who was visiting from New York. Once more, Berkson reassured his Berlin bureau chief that the rumors about Universal folding were baseless. Buoyed by that news, the Shirers and the Knickerbockers spent ten carefree days sunbathing and swimming on the French Riviera. When the time came for their husbands to return to work, Tess and Agnes Knickerbocker lingered in the sunshine. Unfortunately for Tess, her plans for a relaxed September return to Berlin were about to be altered by an unexpected development half a world away: the fallout from a financial crisis in the business affairs of one of America's wealthiest and most powerful men.

On the afternoon of Saturday, 14 August 1937, William Shirer was working in the UNS office when a telegram arrived from the home office in New York. That was nothing unusual, but the curt message it delivered was: effective immediately the UNS was ceasing operations. As part of this "readjustment" all UNS staff were now working for the International News Service, a sister operation that provided European news for evening papers in the Hearst newspaper chain. Shirer understandably felt betrayed and angry; his boss's assurances about the future of the UNS had been as hollow as press baron William Randolph Hearst's troubled finances. "I keep my job, but [INS correspondent Pierre Huss] is [now] in charge. That is no reflection on me," Shirer explained in a letter to Tess. "The order simply made all the INS men in charge of all the combined bureaus. I must swallow my pride until I find something better."[8]

That was easier said than done. Adding insult to injury, the INS bureau chief, who was pro-Nazi, warned Shirer to "watch [his] step" where the German government was concerned.[9] Shirer was intelligent, savvy, and a top-notch journalist, but he could also be headstrong to a fault. Predictably, it did not take long for him to get on Huss's bad side – two days, in fact.

The Nazis finally had ordered Norman Ebbutt to leave the country. *The Times* of London's Berlin correspondent was being expelled in retaliation for the British having ordered some German correspondents out of London. As was customary when an American or British member of the journalistic community was banished, his or her colleagues went to the train station to see him or her off. In Ebbutt's case, Joseph Goebbels himself had made it known that any such farewell gathering would be considered to be an "unfriendly" act. Knowing this, Huss cautioned Shirer not to go to train station. However, because he was stubborn and regarded it as a matter of principle to show solidarity with his fellow journalists, Shirer ignored Huss's order and was among the well-wishers who went to the station to bid farewell to Ebbutt when he departed on the evening of 16 August.

A week later, Shirer was working in the INS office when a telegram arrived from New York. It read, "SHIRER DEEPLY REGRET BUT NECESSITY CONSOLIDATING FORCES REQUIRES THAT WE DISPENSE WITH YOUR SERVICES AFTER THIS WEEK STOP MANAGEMENT HAS APPROVED PAYMENT OF ONE MONTHS SALARY AS DISMISSAL STOP DEPOSITING THIS MONEY YOUR ACCOUNT PARIS."[10] Shirer was stunned. This was the third time in four years that he had lost his job, and it hurt. Especially now. After finishing the dispatch that he was writing – a gesture that speaks volumes about his professionalism – Shirer went for a walk to clear his head and consider his job prospects, which were not good. With his bank account depleted after his recent holiday, bills to pay, and a baby on the way, Shirer could ill afford to be unemployed.

He was still dazed and feeling utterly deflated when he returned to the INS office. It was then, with his spirits at rock bottom that he made a serendipitous discovery: he chanced to notice on his desk a telegram from Salzberg, Austria. It had arrived earlier in the evening, when he had been too busy to open it. Doing so now, he discovered the sender was Edward R. Murrow, the pesky CBS radio representative who had asked him to meet with him a few weeks earlier in London. Murrow was coming to town on Friday, three days hence, and he invited Shirer to dine with him at the Adlon, Berlin's poshest hotel. History remembers the Adlon as "the crossroads where journalists, diplomats, spies, and government officials all congregated."[11] Murrow had chosen the Adlon as the ideal venue in which meet with Shirer, whom he was out to impress. "I'd heard of [Murrow], but I'd never met him. My first reaction was that he was one of these VIPs coming into Berlin and he wants to pick the brains of us correspondents who were there so he could make a talk. Well, I figured we'd have a drink anyway, and a meal, and that's it."[12]

That spur of the moment decision to have dinner with Ed Murrow proved to be a pivotal moment in Shirer's life. It led to developments that brought his days as a newspaperman to an end and launched him on a career as a broadcast journalist. Network radio was about to emerge as news medium that would revolutionize and forever change journalism. And Shirer was about to become a pioneer.

14

An Unlikely Duo

William Shirer was in a dark mood and was prepared to dislike Edward R. Murrow, the man who had invited him to dinner at Berlin's Adlon Hotel on the evening of 27 August 1937. Still smarting after his dismissal from the INS, Shirer was also frustrated that Frederick Birchall of *The New York Times* was continuing to stall on a promised job offer.

Murrow had nothing to do with any of this, of course. The fact was that, where radio was concerned, like most print reporters at the time, Shirer had a chip on his shoulder. Never mind that he had no real understanding of the new medium, having left the United States in 1925. That was a year before the birth of the National Broadcasting Corporation (NBC), with its two networks, the Red network and the Blue network (the colors used as a means of mapping the areas in which each service's programming would be heard).

As cultural historian Frederick Lewis Allen observes, "Radio ... was destined ultimately to alter the daily habits of Americans as profoundly as anything that the [1920s] produced."[1] However, living in Paris as he was then, Shirer was oblivious to these developments. Nothing had changed in that regard by 1937. "I had never given much thought to radio ... In Berlin I tuned in occasionally for spot news and the weather. And once in a while I had snatched an hour to listen to a symphony concert or an opera. I had no idea of what radio was like at home."[2] What he did understand was that it was an "upstart medium," one that threatened to become a competitor of newspapers, even if most print reporters regarded broadcasters as would-be or pseudo-journalists.

Murrow, the European director of talks for CBS, was painfully aware of the scorn with which print journalists regarded broadcasters. He had not forgotten the disdain with which American foreign correspondents had treated him upon his arrival in London in May 1937. They had rejected out of hand his application to join their association. "I wasn't even allowed to attend the meetings, much less become a member."[3] That rebuff only served to steel Murrow's resolve to show his detractors what he was made of. His dapper appearance belied his blue-collar roots. Murrow was a scrapper who, in true Horatio Alger-like fashion, had risen above his hardscrabble beginnings through pluck, luck, and hard work.

The man the world would come to know as Edward R. Murrow – and who would play a pivotal role in the life and career of William Shirer – was born at Polecat Creek, a now-faded dot on the map of Guilford County, North Carolina. The youngest of the four sons of Roscoe and Ethel (née Lamb) Murrow, he carried the given name of his father and of his eldest sibling, Roscoe Jr, who had died only a few days after being born. It was not until 1904, seven years later, that Ethel Murrow gave birth again. That child, a boy named Lacey, was four years old, and his brother Dewey was two when Egbert Roscoe Murrow was born on 25 April 1908. "He was a little character from the start," writes biographer Anne Sperber, "the runt of the litter, in the family mold – bright, self-assertive, an individual."[4] There was ample reason for that. The Murrows had a well-deserved reputation for being independent minded.[5]

Egbert Murrow's maternal grandfather, a slave owner, had fought for the Confederacy during the Civil War. Other members of the extended Murrow family were Quaker abolitionists who dared to vote Democrat in a staunchly Republican state. The icing on the proverbial cake was that the family opposed the growing and selling of tobacco, one of Guilford County's principal crops. It was the height of irony that at age eighteen Egbert Murrow took up smoking, becoming a three-pack-a-day man. Given that he was afflicted with asthma, his weakness for tobacco would ultimately prove to be the death of him.

In 1913, the Murrows moved to the Pacific Northwest, settling near Blanchard, Washington, a farming and logging community thirty miles north of Seattle. For a time, the family lived in a tent they pitched on land owned by one of Ethel's cousins. Roscoe Murrow worked as an agricultural laborer before he found a job on a logging railway, first as a brakeman and then as a locomotive engineer.

It was Ethel Murrow, as determined as she was diminutive, who held the family together during its many lean times. A devout Methodist, she also had an unshakable sense of right and wrong. As such, she was determined to instill this same moral certainty in her boys and followed the advice offered in Proverbs 23:13–14 ("Withhold not correction from the child ...

Thou shalt beat him with the rod, and shalt deliver his soul from hell.") To ensure that her boys learned the Scriptures, each night Ethel Murrow listened as each one read aloud a chapter of the Bible. Murrow's biographers have speculated that it was this experience that instilled in him a love of the English language and the spoken word. Perhaps, but at the same time, his brothers also exerted a profound, albeit less lofty, influence on his development. As various biographers have pointed out, Murrow's brothers taught him to use his fists and gave him reason to use them.

All three Murrow boys earned top grades in high school and helped supplement the family's meager income by working part-time for local farmers or at the town sawmill. In the summer months, they toiled in lumber camps in hopes of saving money for college. The work was hard and dangerous. It was also eye opening. The ranks of their co-workers included itinerant laborers, many of whom were supporters of the radical labor union known as the International Workers of the World (iww) – the Wobblies. During the First World War, strikes were regarded as being treasonous, and in the anti-Red hysteria of the postwar years, conservative politicians, business leaders, and police condemned the iww and its leaders as Bolsheviks. Labor violence in the Pacific Northwest was widespread and bloody.

The Wobblies were in retreat by the time Egbert Murrow was old enough to go to work in the lumber industry. However, the working environment remained emotionally charged. Given his own family background and the dangerous conditions in which he labored, it is not surprising that Murrow was pro-union or that he grew up quickly. By age fourteen, he was already square-shouldered, six-feet, two inches tall, with dark-haired good looks that women found appealing.

It was during these same formative years that Murrow adopted the name "Ed." He had decided that it sounded more "manly" than Egbert. He also preferred it to "Egg," the pet name his parents called him, or to "Eber Blowhard," the nickname hung on him by schoolmates, who teased him about his at-times effusive personality. Despite the fact that he was restless, feisty, and sometimes was moody to the point of being depressed, Ed Murrow was an academic high achiever who also excelled at everything from glee club and the school orchestra, to athletic teams and debating; in his senior year, he won election as student president.

When he graduated from high school in spring 1925, Murrow wanted to go on to university; however, like Bill Shirer, he could not afford the tuition. So foregoing school temporarily, Murrow took a full-time job as an axe man on a forestry crew. In autumn 1926, at a time when Shirer had already been working in Paris for a year, Murrow enrolled at Washington State College in the town of Pullman. He paid his own way by working part-time as a janitor in a sorority house (sleeping on a cot in the basement) and unloading freight at the town's railway station. In retrospect, given his situation and his blue-collar background, it is understandable that partway through his freshman year Murrow abandoned business administration studies, opting instead to major in speech.

Although he continued to spend summers working on a lumber crew, Murrow had learned to speak eloquently, for he had a quick mind and a wonderfully resonant voice (which he put to use working as a sportscaster for a local radio station). As his self-confidence grew, he took to dressing with style, immersed himself in extracurricular activities, and became the archetypal big man on campus. He was his school's representative on the Pacific Student Presidents Association and attended the 1930 convention of the National Student Federation of America (NSFA). A speech he made there in support of a resolution calling upon American students to take more interest in national and world affairs so impressed the NSFA executive that they drafted him to seek the presidency. The position was unpaid, but Murrow saw it as an opportunity, and so he agreed to stand as a candidate in the election, which he won handily.

When Murrow graduated in spring 1930, he accepted an offer to run the NSFA's national office in New York City. The position provided a paltry twenty-five-dollar-per-week living allowance. That was of scant concern to Murrow who felt having a job of any kind beat standing in a bread line. Among his duties were the task of finding speakers and acting as on-air host for a series of NSFA-sponsored lectures on the CBS radio program *University of the Air*. The weekly offering, which focused on topical issues of the day, was regarded as part of the network's public service commitment, something CBS boss William Paley took seriously.

As the NSFA's director of talks Murrow arranged for visiting scholars and academics – Albert Einstein among them – to appear on the show. Murrow also worked with the CBS contact in London, a man named Fred Willis, to convince important international newsmakers to address CBS listeners via transatlantic shortwave hookup.

Murrow remained with the NSFA until late 1931, when he took a paying job with the Institute of International Education (IIE), which worked closely with the NSFA and other students' groups in North America and Europe to promote overseas academic exchange programs. Murrow joined the IIE as the assistant to director Stephen Pierce Duggan. The retired College of the City of New York professor was an outspoken advocate of the peace movement, did some broadcasting for CBS, and sat as a member of the Council on Foreign Relations and on the editorial board of its journal, *Foreign Affairs*.

During the three years Murrow worked with Duggan, the older man became his intellectual mentor and treated him like a son. Murrow ate meals with the Duggan family, and Stephen Duggan introduced him to friends and colleagues, who included a who's who of East Coast academics, journalists, government bureaucrats, judges, and business figures. It was through Murrow's work with IIE that he met his future wife, Janet Huntington Brewster, whom he married on 27 October 1934. And Murrow's friendship with Fred Willis blossomed when Willis moved to New York to work as an assistant to CBS President William Paley. When Paley decided to hire someone to look after the non-sponsored public service-type programming that made up half of the CBS schedule at the time, Willis recommended his friend Ed Murrow.

According to biographer Robert Edwards, in 1934 Murrow was casting around for a better job, and so he had applied to be president of Rockford College in Illinois. He was the preferred candidate – that is until school officials looked into the details of his curriculum vitae and discovered Murrow had lied about his age: he was twenty-six, not thirty-one, as he claimed to be. Even more significantly, he had also fudged his academic credentials.[6]

Edwards reports that Murrow repeated the deception in September 1935, when he applied to CBS. Again, he added five years to his age. He also claimed to have majored in political science and international relations at Washington State and to have earned a Master of Arts degree at Stanford.[7] This time, no one bothered to delve into the veracity of his résumé, and Murrow got the job when veteran newspaperman Raymond Gram Swing, the preferred candidate, turned it down after learning that he would *not* be allowed to go on the air himself. Unlike Swing, Murrow did not care if he was allowed to broadcast; the career opportunity and pay raise were too attractive to turn down.[8]

Falsifying academic credentials, employment history, and other relevant details is an old game, one that was widespread in an era before such information could be verified with a telephone call or a few clicks of a computer mouse. In this instance, Murrow got away with his ruse – another of the great ironies in the life of this complex, contradictory, and supremely talented man whose reputation as a broadcaster was built on his personal integrity. Regardless, it was fortunate for all concerned that Murrow caught on with CBS. His hiring proved to be a watershed moment in his life. His organizational skills and on-air presence proved crucial to the growth and popularity of the CBS network, and, if not for Murrow, the arc of William L. Shirer's life would have been profoundly different.

America was still wallowing in economic despair in 1935, yet CBS prospered. Times were tough, and radio – the "dream factory of the airwaves" – offered a product for which there was an insatiable demand: free entertainment. With 30 million radio receivers in use in America, CBS was building a mass audience on the star power of such popular performers as Burns and Allen, Al Jolson, and Kate Smith. William Paley could boast of having ninety-seven affiliated stations in his operation, more than either of rival NBC's Red or Blue networks.[9]

For a variety of reasons, many of which had to do with the ability of newspaper owners to influence government regulators in Washington, neither CBS nor NBC had a news department per se. Initially, William Paley had little interest in news programming. However, that all changed when NBC began attracting listeners with its newscasts. Paley responded in 1930 by hiring a coolly efficient but humorless former *New York Times* night editor named Ed Klauber. A firm believer in the potential of news as a ratings builder, Klauber earned the title of network vice-president when he convinced Paley of the value of news as a corporate asset and of the need for "balanced coverage." What Klauber was really touting was "objectivity," an elusive journalistic ideal that is every bit as slippery as "the truth." Ethereal though these concepts may be, straying from the pursuit of them carried risks for CBS and for all broadcasters. Ever the shrewd businessman, Paley was intent on maximizing profits, not using CBS to spread the opinions of news commentators; controversy could alienate some listeners and prompt the meddlesome politicians in Washington to further regulate the broadcasting industry. Thus Paley's actions were guided as much by a wary pragmatism as by any belief in the virtues of free speech.

Determined to compete with NBC in developing his news programming, Paley recruited a gruff, brash, hard-drinking former UP wire service reporter named Paul White to act as CBS's first news editor. White was well qualified for the job, being a graduate of the Columbia journalism school, a champion debater in his student years, and an experienced print journalist. However, being competitive by nature and training, he tended to regard co-workers – including Ed Klauber – as potential rivals in the fight to climb the CBS corporate hierarchy. Despite this, Klauber and White were obliged to work together as a team.

By the time Ed Murrow joined the network in autumn 1935 the network's daily broadcast schedule included only three newscasts: five-minute broadcasts at noon and 4:30 p.m., and a fifteen-minute summary each night at eleven o'clock. cbs's jack-of-all-trades chief announcer and newscaster at the time was Robert Trout, whose dulcet-toned baritone voice was his calling card. Trout, like other radio newscasters at that time, did little more than read the day's headlines. For any additional information or insights, listeners were advised to check out their local newspaper, or to listen to cbs's star news commentators, both of whom rivaled nbc's Lowell Thomas for audience and influence. One was fast-talking *Brooklyn Eagle* newspaper columnist-turned-broadcaster Hans von Kaltenborn. The other was Philadelphia-based Boake Carter, an irascible Irishman whose anti-Roosevelt, pro-Nazi ranting eventually became so over-the-top that William Paley could tolerate no more and canceled his program.

Seeking to capitalize on the public's appetite for news, Paley and Klauber decided the best way to compete with the print media was to use radio's immediacy to maximum advantage. cbs began airing debates between high-profile newsmakers – the sort of people print journalists quoted in their writings. The fact Ed Murrow had been recruiting speakers in his work with the iie figured in his hiring at cbs. He already had the necessary job skills, expertise, and contacts.

Paul White regarded Murrow warily, but the new director of "talks" made a positive and lasting impression on William Paley. Murrow had an excellent radio voice and would have been a superb newscaster, but he had few chances to go on air, even if he would have welcomed a chance to do so.

During his first year with cbs, Murrow arranged more than 300 talks from twenty-seven countries. Even if he did not realize it at the time, the experience and network of overseas contacts he was building proved pivotal to advancing his career at cbs, the profitability of the network, and ultimately the fortunes of William Shirer.

The cbs-nbc rivalry was ratcheted up several notches in December 1936 during England's abdication crisis, which ended with King Edward VIII renouncing his throne in order to marry the American divorcee Wallace Warfield Simpson. nbc's coverage of this real-life royal soap opera was a huge ratings winner, and, because audience numbers drove advertising revenues, William Paley was determined to fight back. With fascism on the march in Europe, Japan and China at war in the Far East, and the world's political situation becoming more perilous by the day, the cbs president recognized the growing likelihood of another major war. The Roosevelt administration officially maintained a foreign policy of neutrality, and the American public had no appetite for becoming involved in any of the Old World's troubles. But Paley realized this did not mean CBS listeners had no interest in overseas news; America was, after all, a nation of immigrants. Thus, in February 1937 Paley offered Murrow a new job: director of European operations for CBS. He replaced César Saerchinger, who had quit to return home to the States. After six years in Europe and at age forty-eight, he felt that he stood a better chance of advancing his broadcasting career back in New York. It was a decision he lived to regret.

William Shirer knew little about CBS and nothing of Ed Murrow when he accepted the CBS representative's dinner invitation. Murrow was well aware of Shirer's reputation as one of the top American journalists in Europe. He also knew – or soon would – that at age thirty-three Shirer was out of work again and struggling to put food on the table for himself and his pregnant wife. As Murrow biographer Joseph Persico noted, Murrow's first impression of Shirer was that here was "a stocky, balding, rumpled figure who wore a beat-up fedora and who spoke with the flat, uninflected speech of the prairie."[10] At the same time, Murrow took note of Shirer's lively gaze and quick mind. And there was *something* about him that Murrow liked.

For his part, all of Shirer's prejudices and preconceptions seemed to be confirmed when he met Murrow; in his crisp Savile Row suit he looked more like a Hollywood film star than a working journalist. "As I walked up to him I was a little taken aback by his handsome face ... Just what you would expect from radio, I thought."[11]

His words speak volumes about his own prejudices and ignorance of radio as a medium. However, much to his surprise – and credit – Shirer quickly sensed that he had been hasty in his initial assessment of Murrow. When the two men sat down for drinks, Shirer found himself warming up to the young CBS man; he realized they had mutual friends and held similar views on life and politics. "Obviously, we liked the same sort of people: the more liberal and intelligent of the American foreign correspondents, the Labour Party people in England, the New Deal crowd at home."[12] These words, smug though they may seem now, are revealing of Shirer's beliefs and of his personality, albeit in a different way, from his prejudices about radio broadcasters. They were not evidence of mere hubris, although in 1937 there's no question that Shirer had a chip on his shoulder. But context is everything. He wrote those words more than four decades later, in 1984. By then, he was an octogenarian, sadder, wiser, and not at all inclined to soften or qualify his opinions.

Shirer was never a typical journalist. For better and worse in an era when anti-intellectualism was so widespread as to be almost de rigueur among print journalists, Shirer was an intellectual, even if he was loath to admit it. During his periods of unemployment, he occasionally had set aside his ambivalence and considered returning to university for graduate studies, as his economist brother John had done. Ultimately, Shirer had rejected that possibility and with it any idea of a teaching career. There was too much newspaper ink in his veins to allow him to return to academia: "If I had more than a BA, I might try it. But I refuse to go through the nonsense of acquiring more degrees."[13]

All indications are that Shirer would have been a first-rate social scientist had he chosen that career path. With his probing intellect, his at-times Zen-like self-discipline, and his ability to analyze and make sense of people, ideas, and complex situations, he had the skills needed to excel in the lecture hall and as a writer of scholarly papers and books. Yet those same qualities, when combined with his restless nature, verbal dexterity, and a profound sense of the fundamental absurdities of life were the same ones that made him such a gifted journalist.

As Shirer and Murrow continued their conversation in the dining room of the Adlon Hotel that fateful night in August 1937, Murrow revealed that he was not there to gather information for a broadcast as Shirer had assumed, but rather to offer Shirer a job. Having concluded that the pace of events in the United Kingdom and Europe was quickening as the clouds of war gathered, Murrow was intent on broadening the scope and tone of CBS's news coverage. He was under no illusion that this would be easy. After all, radio was regarded as entertainment; that is what attracted listeners and advertising dollars. Hence, William Paley had dispatched him to London with instructions to arrange "entertaining" programming – that included sporting events, musical concerts, and those talks by well-known public figures.

Murrow nodded and went along with that, but the truth was that he had little patience for such frivolities; he confided as much to his wife Janet and to some of his friends, one of them being the English political economist Harold Laski, whom he had encountered on the voyage to England aboard the SS *Manhattan*. Murrow had met Laski during his time with the IIE, and so the two men spent time at sea playing ping pong, drinking, and talking. Murrow told Laski he was not fond of England or its snooty class system. He was planning, he said, to make CBS broadcasts from there more "down to earth." Despite the technical challenges, Murrow hoped to take a microphone out onto the streets and into the pubs and parks – to do what the British technicians who handled the technical details called "outside broadcasts" – in order to give American listeners the opportunity to hear what the "average man" in England was thinking and doing.[14] Laski, a dedicated socialist, applauded this populist imperative.

Democratizing radio was not Murrow's only goal. He had also concluded that in order to succeed in his new job he would need help, especially when it came to knowing what was happening in Europe and whom to call upon to arrange for the use of broadcasting facilities. The latter was a challenge. In most European countries the government controlled the shortwave broadcasting transmitters; in order to gain access to them, it was necessary to deal with bureaucrats and also to have contacts among the politicians and the journalists who could give talks. The rival NBC network had a head start in all regards, already having its own man in London. That man was Fred Bate, a "handsome, graying American expatriate"[15] who had lived in England for more than two decades. So well connected was Bate that he personally knew the king and socialized with him. Being personable and easy going, Bate was taken aback by Ed Murrow's feistiness. The day a mutual acquaintance introduced the two men in the lobby of a London hotel, Murrow looked Bate in the eye and suggested that they step outside "then and there" to settle any differences they *might* have. Bate, unsure if the younger man was serious or merely joking, tactfully (and prudently) declined. As it happened, he and Murrow eventually became good friends. Officially, they were competitors, but they developed a healthy mutual respect and admiration.[16]

Bate's associate, "the Continental European representative" of NBC, was decidedly less genteel. German-born, American-educated Max Jordan was based in Basel, Switzerland. Like William Shirer, he had worked as an INS wire service reporter, having covered the European political scene in the 1920s and early 1930s before joining NBC in 1934. "Ubiquitous Max," as he was known, was an inveterate newshound who traveled constantly and was crafty, coolly efficient, and ultra-competitive. Jordan knew all the right people when it came to "getting the story" and giving NBC an edge on the competition. The latter was crucial. Exclusivity had become a crucial; it did not matter how newsworthy or interesting a broadcast was if it was not "exclusive."

In addition to his head start in the field, Max Jordan had another important advantage over his CBS competition: his employer permitted him to go on the air himself whenever there was breaking news. "Between

1935 and 1937, Jordan's voice was frequently heard [on NBC] reporting the news of Europe, as well as offering feature sidelights."[17]

Knowing this, Ed Murrow set out to adopt NBC's organizational blueprint and to find CBS's answer to Max Jordan. Soon after his arrival in England, he began asking friends and contacts for suggestions on the names of American journalists in Europe whom he might recruit to help him build a CBS presence there. The one name that came up repeatedly was that of William L. Shirer. Having worked in Europe for a dozen years, he had many friends and contacts in the journalism world, and word had spread that he was in the market for a new job. Shirer had not bothered to respond to Murrow's initial request for a meeting when he had been in London in July. However, it was fortunate for Shirer that CBS's new man in London was persistent. A month after being snubbed, Murrow was traveling on the continent and knew he would be stopping in Berlin. Hence the telegram he sent Shirer inviting him to have dinner. Murrow's timing was impeccable.[18] And it could not have been more serendipitous for either man.

When finally they sat down to talk, Murrow was favorably impressed. He "found that Shirer was everything he'd been told ... sharp, knowledgeable, and well-connected."[19] Thus reassured, Murrow wasted little time in making his pitch; Shirer recalls that Murrow "said he was looking for an experienced foreign correspondent to open a CBS office on the Continent. He could not cover all of Europe from London."[20]

Shirer could barely contain his excitement when Murrow promised that, if he signed on with CBS, the network would pay him the same salary he had been making at INS. "Tess and I could continue to live all right on [that] $125 a week. Even with the addition to the family. [Frederick] Birchall had balked a little at [The New York] Times paying even that ... It felt good, after the uncertainty of the last few days, just to be offered a steady job."[21]

Satisfied that they had a deal, the two men settled down to enjoy a meal at CBS's expense. It was only when they were savoring a smoke and after-dinner glasses of brandy that Murrow cleared his throat and announced there was one small detail about Shirer coming to work at CBS that he had neglected to mention. It was a formality, really: Shirer would have to audition, do a sample broadcast, so CBS president William Paley and other network brass back in New York could assess his voice. This was nothing to worry about, Murrow assured him; Shirer could discuss the Nazi's upcoming annual rally at Nuremberg or any other news story he felt comfortable talking about.

Shirer still had vivid memories of the CBS broadcast he had done when he reported German reaction to the Hindenburg disaster. That experience had been a real-life nightmare; he had been petrified with fear and vowed never to do any more radio work. He regarded the idea of auditioning for a job as being silly, demeaning even: "Who ever heard of an adult with no pretensions to being a singer or any other kind of artist being dependent for a good, interesting job on his voice? And mine is terrible. I'm positive of it."[22]

Despite Murrow's insistence that how Shirer sounded on-air would not be a problem – even if his voice was "as squeaky as Gandhi," as Shirer joked it might be[23] – Murrow left nothing to chance. The two men spent a morning going over Shirer's audition script, and they talked at length about how Shirer would go about his job. "[Murrow] seemed so optimistic about the prospects that we talked for hours ... with him proposing as my first job a joint trip with him, starting [in Berlin], and going thru Austria to Italy, lining up broadcasts," Shirer told Tess in a letter. "Now I hate like hell to count on anything before it's clinched, but this guy enthuses me with what we could do over here, if only [my voice] passes."[24]

Despite his misgivings about working in radio, Shirer was in dire straits financially and had no choice but to go through with the audition if he wanted the job with CBS. That trial broadcast took place on 5 September, nine days after his dinner with Murrow. To say that things did not go well in the broadcast studio would be an understatement. To begin with, the person who was making the technical arrangements, a woman name Claire Trask (who also had arranged his Hindenburg talk on CBS), forgot the script for her introductory words in the café where she and Shirer met beforehand. Trask left him alone in the broadcast studio while she retrieved her missing papers, returning with only a minute to spare before the scheduled airtime.

Adding to Shirer's anxieties was the fact that in 1937 most radio broadcasts were done blind. The person speaking had no headphones to hear instructions or even to know if and when others were talking. All he or she knew was that once the red light atop the broadcast technician's control panel lit up, it was time to start speaking. Then, as the allotted broadcast time was running out, the technician would wave and begin to count down remaining seconds on his fingers. What happened during a broadcast was all up in the air, literally as well as figuratively. In the era before satellite telecommunications, transmitting a shortwave radio signal across the Atlantic was very much an inexact science, one dependent on a still-primitive technology, split-second timing, and the uncertainties of weather and atmospheric conditions.

Radio was an adventure at the best of times, doubly so for any inexperienced or nervous would-be broadcaster. Shirer endured the added angst of not being able to perform in the relative comfort of the state broadcasting studios – remember, NBC had a right of first refusal on those facilities. Instead, he was obliged to speak from a makeshift studio in the Ministry of Post and Telegraph. "When we got there to do this, I was nervous. And the microphone was standing about seven feet high … We couldn't find a stool or anything to stand on, and we didn't know what we were going to do. I saw some old piano boxes in the corner, and we rolled one of those out and climbed up on top of that."[25]

Perched atop that lofty wooden crate, his legs dangling, to ensure that his mouth was level with the microphone, Shirer struggled with his words. He was also trying "to remember the points Murrow had made in the previous weekend of coaching: to speak slowly, to pause frequently, to stress certain words and phrases, and to keep the talk on a relaxed, conversational tone – above all, *not* to sound as if I were reading a script."[26]

That was easier said than done, and so the audition was an ordeal, just as he had feared. Shirer managed to endure, but afterward, he went home feeling glum. He was convinced he had blown his chances of a job with CBS. Fortunately for him, he had no time to feel sorry for himself. Shirer had agreed to a last-minute request from his friends Webb Miller and Fred Oechsner of the United Press to help with their coverage of the Nazis' annual Nuremberg rally.

Murrow had asked Shirer not to accept another job offer for at least two days, until he had heard back from him. At the same time, Frederick Birchall continued to stall on the promised job with *The New York Times*. Shirer grew ever more frustrated and angry. Finally, he'd had enough. "To hell with CBS, and to hell with *The Times*," he decided. "As soon as I finished in Nuremberg, I would catch the first boat for New York and start job hunting there."[27]

It was five days before Murrow got back to Shirer. His assertion that the audition would be a "mere formality" had been wishful thinking. CBS news editor Paul White had balked at hiring Shirer, whose voice, White insisted, was reedy and too soft-spoken; his Midwestern intonation was as flat and uninteresting as a prairie grain field. In reality, there was more to it than that. White regarded Murrow as a potential rival in the CBS hierarchy and had been happy to see him posted to Europe. Now White was intent on showing the younger man who was boss. Murrow was no less determined to do things his way and to grow his job. In order to do that, he was intent on hiring the right people, ones he felt comfortable working with and had confidence in, regardless of how they sounded on air. Murrow biographer Ann Sperber reports that Janet Murrow recalled many years later that her husband was "appalled" at White's attitude.[28]

The disagreement between Murrow and White became a macho contest of wills. For a week, telephone calls and telegrams flew back and forth across the Atlantic, until finally White gave in. He sent word to Murrow that yes, he could hire Shirer if that was *really* what he wanted to do. Having made his point, White was now ready to let Murrow see the error of his ways. Or it perhaps it may have been that Fred Klauber or even William Paley himself intervened on Murrow's behalf. What we do know is that he got his way on this and on other future hiring decisions. On the evening of 10 September, when Murrow finally telephoned Shirer in Nuremberg to tell him the good news, he said nothing about his squabble with Paul White. Murrow said only, "The bastards in New York finally came through … They think you're terrific."[29] To cement the deal, Murrow sent Shirer a letter in which he confirmed the offer of a $125-per-week job starting 1 October.[30]

While it is unlikely that Shirer believed Murrow's kind words about his potential as a broadcaster, he was relieved to have another job, any job. Buoyed by the good news, he dashed off a telegram to Tess, who was in Paris, after her extended vacation in southern France. She was suffering through a difficult pregnancy. Shelving any concerns he may have had, Shirer rushed off to the zeppelin field where Hitler was speaking to another mass gathering of his brown-shirted Nazi faithful. "This was the show where they make a cathedral of blue lights from one hundred and fifty-four search-lights that stretch eight miles into the heavens – indescribable – but I didn't get drunk over it," Shirer said in a letter to his "beautiful Tessie."[31]

In the journalists' seating area Shirer sat beside Frederick Birchall. When Shirer announced he was going to work with CBS, *The New York Times*' man "put on a queer face," and tried to dissuade him.[32] Birchall insisted his bosses in New York were about to offer Shirer a job as the newspaper's Moscow correspondent. He warned Shirer that if he joined CBS he would be wasting his talents. However, Shirer was undeterred. Murrow's enthusiasm was infectious, and Shirer had made up his mind: after losing a newspaper job three times in less than five years, he was ready for a change, and he was determined to succeed in this new line of work.

"[Shirer and Murrow] made an unlikely couple," writes Ann Sperber. "Shirer, shorter and stocky, a news veteran, hair already wearing thin, the classic picture of the rumpled reporter, peering at the world through thick, metal-rimmed glasses; Murrow, tall and thin, with his Savile Row look, knifelike crease in his trousers, not a hair out of place."[33] In photos taken at the time, clad in his overcoat, a wide-brimmed fedora atop his head, the ever-present cigarette in hand, Murrow looks as if he had been sent by central casting at a Hollywood Studio to play the role of the intrepid foreign correspondent.

While Shirer and Murrow were an unlikely duo, they were a terrific team; each brought complementary skills to their working relationship. "Murrow had fired me with a feeling that we might go places in this new-fangled radio-broadcasting business ... We would have to feel our way. We might find a new dimension for reporting the news. Instantaneous transmission of news from the reporter to the listener ... There was no time lag, no editing, no rewriting, as in a newspaper. A listener got [it] straight from a reporter, and instantly, what was taking place."[34]

Shirer was the first of the group of talented reporters whom Ed Murrow recruited as he built the cbs radio news operation in Europe. "The Murrow boys," as they came to be known, were about to change forever not just broadcasting, but the very essence of modern journalism. Joseph Persico, another of the Murrow biographers, said it succinctly and well when he wrote that "they created the standards for radio and later television journalism which were to give cbs news its durable supremacy" for many years to come.[35]

15

Return to Vienna

William Shirer acted quickly upon his return to Berlin from Nuremberg, dashing off a letter to Ed Murrow verifying his formal acceptance of the CBS job offer: "As I told you on the telephone, I am delighted." Shirer also promised to send a photograph of himself to New York. "So far, I can only find one taken in a sweat-shirt. I imagine Columbia would prefer one in a business suit, and I shall do my best."[1]

Shirer and Murrow had already made some preliminary decisions about the specifics of Shirer's employment. For one thing, he would be based in Vienna. That was something Tess Shirer applauded; she had never warmed to Germany or to the German people, especially the Nazis. For his part, her husband was eager to relocate, although he felt there was still much to do in Berlin. "Somehow, I feel that, despite our work … there is little understanding of the Third Reich … It is a complex picture and it may be that we have given only a few strong, uncoordinated strokes of the brush, leaving the canvas as confusing and meaningless as an early Picasso."[2]

The Shirers had done their utmost to insulate themselves from the ugliness of Nazi rule, finding refuge in their life together. When they socialized, it was with Shirer's journalism colleagues and their families or with select members of the foreign diplomatic corps. Despite this, Shirer felt the strains of life in Nazi Germany were wearing him down emotionally and mentally. And what better place than Vienna to recover and safely monitor the madness that was enveloping Europe? The Austrian capital had always been one of his favorite cities. True, the cost of living there was relatively high, but there were compelling reasons to make Vienna the base of CBS's European operations. For one, it was centrally located, and, because Austria was still officially neutral, radio broadcasts originating there were not subject to Nazi censorship. From a personal standpoint, with a baby due in February and her husband on the road so much of the time, Tess Shirer welcomed the support of her family in Vienna.

Shirer left his wife to set up their new apartment while he traveled to London to meet with Ed Murrow. The two men spent the time planning CBS's coverage of European affairs, and they met again in Nice, France, in November to draft a list of CBS broadcasts for 1938. Things began promisingly in this regard, but Shirer's initial euphoria about his new job was short-lived. Having reconciled himself to the notion that he was now working in radio, he was dismayed to learn that neither he nor Murrow would speak on air. Instead, Murrow informed him, their job was to arrange public service broadcasts and to recruit politicians, intellectuals, and print journalists to do talks whenever there was breaking news. Like Murrow, Shirer was to be a behind-the-scenes organizer, facilitator, and producer, *not* an on-air reporter. As a veteran foreign correspondent, one who was among the top-tier of American journalists in Europe at the time, Shirer found this unfathomable and even demeaning. Often he knew more about what was happening than did the reporters he recruited to speak on air. He made no secret of his dismay at this and could not help but wonder if he *would* regret leaving print journalism for radio, as Frederick Birchall had predicted.

CBS management had its own rationale for the restricting Shirer and Murrow's activities. Political and financial concerns that affected the radio industry in the United States came into play. Officially, the Roosevelt administration remained neutral in its foreign policy, even though the president and many of his advisors already had concluded it was only a matter of time until America would be drawn into Europe's quarrels. However, for now Washington was determined to do nothing to hasten that development, and so the government opposed having representatives of America's radio networks "editorializing" – or even appearing to take sides – when they reported the news from overseas. State-owned national broadcasting networks being the rule in Europe and the United Kingdom, politicians and government bureaucrats there tended to assume the same situation existed in America. Representatives of the *National* Broadcasting Corporation did nothing to dispel this notion; the "national" descriptor opened doors for NBC's representatives and won them preferential treatment in a day when America's reputation was still sky high and countries courted Washington's favor.

Broadcasting in America was ruled by the dictates of the marketplace, although not exclusively. The federal government maintained a measure of control through its regulatory agency, the Federal Communications Commission (FCC), which had been established in February 1934. Ironically, America's newspaper barons – the supposed champions of free enterprise and an unfettered press – lobbied for more government control of broadcasting, having decided that radio was their mortal enemy. Why would readers buy a newspaper or magazine when they could get their news free via the airwaves?

Prior to 1930, the prevailing wisdom in the corporate offices of America's fledgling radio networks was that the medium was essentially an entertainment vehicle. That was certainly the case with the onset of the Great Depression, when radio's popularity soared. The combined annual gross revenue of NBC and CBS in 1930 totaled only $19 million. By 1935, those of NBC alone had jumped to $31.4 million, those of CBS to $17.6 million.[3]

What little news coverage there was in the early days of network radio in America consisted mostly of "special events" broadcasting and "bulletins" on breaking news. Shortwave broadcasts of overseas events were still a novelty; the first regularly scheduled program, in February 1929, was part of a symphony concert from London. At the time, there were only a few shortwave transmitters in Europe powerful enough to beam a signal across the North Atlantic. Within a decade, there were more than 100 such transmitters, and so overseas broadcasts became a regular feature of the on-air schedules of the American networks.[4]

In April 1930 CBS had appointed the aforementioned César Saerchinger, a former newspaperman, as its London rep. Diminutive, bespectacled, and erudite, Saerchinger set about arranging CBS broadcasts, usually by speakers or special events such as symphony concerts and choir recitals. When Saerchinger's territory grew to include all of Europe, in 1931 rival NBC dispatched one of its executives to Europe to find its own representative. By 1932, NBC grabbed the lead in the competition for overseas cultural and political programming, with Fred Bate as its man in London and Max Jordan on the continent.

Meanwhile back in the United States, the first regularly scheduled network newscasts were weekday summaries read by Lowell Thomas on NBC's Blue network (as yet, the Red network carried no news programs), which debuted in autumn 1930. Taking note of Thomas's growing popularity and of the public's appetite for information, CBS boss William Paley responded by increasing the frequency of Hans von Kaltenborn's news commentaries to thrice weekly and by adding newscasts read by Boake Carter and Edwin C. Hill.

In April 1933, newspaper owners responded to the sudden popularity of radio newscasts; the Associated Press stopped making its wire service available to radio stations. CBS's response was to announce plans to set up its own news-gathering service. A peace accord signed by newspaper owners and radio industry representatives that stalled this venture was but a temporary truce. The ink was barely dry when William Paley, intent on overtaking NBC in the networks' ratings war, began looking for ways around the deal. One was to make ever more use of news bulletins and educational or public service programming. Enter Ed Murrow, whom Paley hired in 1935 to increase the frequency and improve the quality of CBS's offerings.

In retrospect, network radio's move into news reporting seems to have been inevitable, both for business reasons and because of the free speech provisions of the American constitution. However, at the time that was not entirely clear. As a result, then – even more than is the case nowadays – advertisers were reluctant to sponsor any program that might stir controversy or alienate consumers.

If reporting the news created the perception that a network was "committing" itself editorially, executives at CBS and NBC were content to avoid potential trouble. They went to great lengths to differentiate between news commentaries and news reports from the network's correspondents in the field. Regardless, the distinction was less one of substance than of perception and semantics. Ed Murrow understood this, as did Bill Shirer. However, Murrow was more adept at hiding his frustrations than was his broadcast partner. "The idiocy of it staggered me," Shirer fumed. "I felt let down by Murrow and the CBS brass led by William S. Paley. And I had thought – and Murrow had told me – I had been hired because of my knowledge and experience as a veteran foreign correspondent."[5]

Given his own journalistic credentials and temperament and Murrow's uneasy working relationship with Paul White, it is understandable that Shirer did not have much respect for the CBS news director or that he was unhappy within the parameters of his new job but felt he had no choice other than to grin and bear it. For now. Nonetheless, there was one consolation: he had decided that Ed Murrow would be "a grand guy to work with. He was sensitive, serious, intelligent, with a warmth behind his reserve and a droll sense of humor."[6] Stanley Cloud and Lynne Olson, the authors of the book *The Murrow Boys*, quote Shirer's elder daughter Inga Shirer Dean as saying, "Ed was the only close friend [my] father ever had."[7] However, Dean lamented that, in their rush to categorize the nature of the relationship between her father and Ed Murrow, the authors misinterpreted her words. In so doing, they painted a misleading picture of the real William Shirer.

As noted earlier, his erstwhile *Chicago Tribune* colleague George Seldes – a man known for his at-times self-destructive insistence on speaking his version of the unvarnished truth – once observed that Shirer "was *never* one of the boys."[8] Seldes's words square with Shirer's own self-image and with his friends' perceptions of him. For instance, Martha Dodd, who spent a lot of time with the Shirers during their Berlin years, recalled that the couple were selective in their friendships but certainly not reclusive.[9] William Shirer loved good conversation, literature, and the arts, especially chamber music. He was very much a people person, when he wanted to be. Thus, the notion that Murrow was Shirer's "only close friend" is dubious, especially when you consider the longevity of Shirer's career, his zest for life, and the nature of his relationships with old friends and colleagues such as Jay Allen, Joe Barnes, Marcel Fodor and, in particular, "the Chicago kids" – John Gunther and Vincent ("Jimmy") Sheean. Like Shirer, the latter duo were Windy City-born and were Shirer's friends to the end of their lives.[10]

While the uniqueness of the Shirer-Murrow friendship is debatable, its intensity and significance are not. Although both men had sizeable egos, there is no doubt or denying that they quickly became best friends. In part, this was due to their similar temperaments and liberal outlooks on life. In part, it was because of the work they were doing together. The two faced the same challenges and frustrations, shared a sense of common purpose, and savored the same successes. During the four years they worked as a team in Europe, they met in person as often as possible. They talked on the telephone almost every day. And they socialized frequently – often in company with their wives, Tess and Janet. Inga Shirer Dean aptly likened the relationship of her father and Murrow to that of "foxhole buddies."

Being the first of the Murrow boys, Shirer occupied a special place in Ed Murrow's life and in his psyche. Murrow biographer A.M. Sperber says it well, "For both men, their relationship [was] unique. For Murrow it was the only true peer relationship among his CBS colleagues in his broadcast career, marked if anything, by a measure of deference. Shirer was the more sophisticated, the great newspaperman, with the legitimizing experience of print that he, Murrow, had never had. Murrow was the greater broadcaster. They had been complementary and also, at a subtle level, rivals. With Bill Shirer he could never act as boss."[11] That is what made inevitable and so very traumatic the rift that eventually destroyed their friendship.

While William Shirer was Vienna-based, his beat was most of Europe – including Germany – where he arranged coverage of events and recruited speakers. His job was immeasurably complicated by the sweetheart agreements Max Jordan had negotiated with the German state broadcasting service. NBC enjoyed first call on Berlin studio time and broadcast feeds.

In the circumstances, Shirer initially made little headway in challenging NBC's preferred status in Germany. He enjoyed more success in that other fascist dictatorship, Italy. There, money bought airtime at the Vatican radio service's studios. The *monsignori* in charge of the facility let Shirer know all that he wanted in return for cooperation was an initial lump sum payment of a few hundred dollars followed by "a modest annual contribution to [the Vatican's] well-being."[12] Shirer was willing to ante up, especially when he learned from contacts in Rome that Pope Pius XI, at age eighty and in failing health, was moribund. Shirer was eager to ensure that CBS had reliable sources within the Vatican and that the network's contact in Rome, INS reporter Frank Gervasi, would be able to broadcast timely reports on the Pope's death. William Paley initially objected to paying what amounted to bribe money for information or studio access in Rome, especially when it was demanded by members of the clergy. He changed his mind only when Shirer explained that, like it or not, that is how things were done in Italy (and many other European countries), especially with competition heating up among CBS, NBC, and the upstart Mutual Broadcasting System, which had gone on the air in 1934.

Ed Murrow was buoyed by the progress he and Shirer were making to build CBS's European profile. However, he continued to be irked by NBC's cozy relationship with German state radio. When Murrow demanded that he and Shirer be allowed to meet with Nazi propaganda minister Goebbels to discuss the situation, NBC's Max Jordan quietly used his influence in Berlin to thwart any such palaver.

Murrow and his bosses in New York still had a lot to learn about how things were done in Europe, but they could not have had a better teacher than William Shirer. Whatever he may have lacked in terms of visual perspective (he had lost the sight of his right eye in that March 1932 skiing accident), he more than made up for with the acuity of his observations, his intelligence, and his expertise. With more than twelve years' experience as a foreign correspondent, Shirer's news instincts were accurate and razor sharp. He spoke fluent French and German and passable Spanish and Italian. Furthermore, he had inside contacts, knew the political landscape, and had personal relationships with many key players in Germany, France, Spain, Austria, and Italy.

Shirer, never one to suffer fools gladly, grumbled whenever he was assigned to arrange CBS coverage of events that he regarded as being trivial or unworthy of his time. Still, he and Murrow retained their sense of humor. On one occasion, Murrow cabled him: "Please contact vaudeville agencies ascertain whether any parrot available willing talk microphonely." When Shirer asked if the creature had to be English-speaking, Murrow replied, "German parrot okay."[13]

It was not always so easy to grin and bear it. That was the case in October 1937 when Shirer's assignment was to follow the Duke and Duchess of Windsor on their tour of Germany and to convince the Duke to do a talk for CBS. In Germany, the Duke met with Hitler, and much to the delight of propaganda ministry officials the couple toured the country, ostensibly to study labor conditions. Shirer was being diplomatic when he suggested to his CBS bosses that the Duke's visit to Germany had been "ill advised." In conversations with Ed Murrow and other colleagues, Shirer was considerably more forthright, scornful even. Having met the Duke and observed him at close range, Shirer concluded the royal was a weak character and "a very stupid man."[14] At the same time, Shirer puzzled over Edward's fascination with Mrs Simpson, for whom he had renounced the throne the previous December. Shirer had decided the Baltimore-born divorcee was neither beautiful nor glamorous. Nor was she very bright. Like her husband – who opined that Hitler was not "such a bad chap"[15] – Mrs Simpson knew nothing of politics and seemed to be either incapable of or uninterested in learning.

In the end, the Duke and Duchess abandoned their mission after being embarrassed by a storm of public criticism back home in the United Kingdom and in the United States, where the protests of Jews, organized labor, and anti-fascist groups made it clear they were not welcome. Shirer was pleased by this turn of events, which relieved him of the task of trailing after the royals. He was impatient to cover stories with more gravitas, in particular the growing turmoil in Austria. It was apparent to Shirer that living conditions there had deteriorated in the four years he and Tess had been away. With political unrest and violence rampant, the mood was increasingly grim. Anti-Semitism was growing, unemployment soaring, and the gap between rich and poor widening. In fact, the situation was so dire that people literally were starving to death on Vienna's streets. Austria was a nation teetering on the brink of ruin. However, with greenbacks to spend, the Shirers were relatively well off, and so they were able to rent a spacious third-floor apartment in the upscale Plösslgasse neighborhood, next door to the Rothschild family's palatial home. Both husband and wife were happy to be back in Vienna, despite the growing turmoil.

It was readily apparent to Shirer and many other observers that Hitler would not be content until Austria was part of the Third Reich. The only real questions were how and when that would happen. After a second Nazi putsch failed in January 1938 – as had one in 1934 – Hitler ran out of patience. Because his generals initially were reluctant to invade Austria, Hitler took matters into his own hands, summoning Austrian chancellor Kurt von Schuschnigg to a February meeting. Amid the scenic splendors at Hitler's alpine mountain retreat at Berchtesgaden, the Nazi leader flew into a rage, haranguing his visitor and insisting that he agree to a series of demands that effectively would bring about an Anschluss – the political union of Austria and Germany.

The high-stakes political wrangling continued until 11 March when Hitler issued an ultimatum: von Schuschnigg must call off a planned plebiscite and resign, or else the German army would invade Austria. Von Schuschnigg had no choice but to comply with Hitler's demands, after which 100,000 German troops who rolled into Austria on 12 March made the Anschluss a reality. The nations of Europe reacted with predictable shock and outrage, but none – most notably Great Britain and France – was ready to take action that would force Hitler to back down. In Washington, Secretary of State Cordell Hull told reporters that the Roosevelt administration was "concerned" about the Austrian situation, but the United States was not planning to get involved in any way.[16]

Thus, Hitler's bold gamble paid off, and he achieved his greatest foreign policy triumph to that time. Shirer, like most other foreign journalists in Vienna, viewed these developments with profound dismay. His every instinct as a newsman had been to report the story he saw emerging; however, when he had asked for airtime on CBS to relate the exclusive "inside" story of what went on behind closed doors at the meeting between Hitler and von Schuschnigg, his request was denied. Instead, he was told to proceed with business as usual – namely the task of organizing a broadcast from Bulgaria of a children's choir concert and a talk by the king of that country. Shirer, livid at missing out on reporting the Anschluss story, had no time to press his concerns. He had other work to tend to, and Tess was due to give birth any moment. "But I went [to Sofia], spending my [thirty-third] birthday, 23 February, on the Orient Express as it puffed its way down through the snow-covered Balkans." Shirer added with a hint of bitterness, "No foreign correspondent let his personal life interfere with his assignments, however asinine. Despite having acquired a wife, and the both of us being young, I had had little personal life the last few years."[17]

Upon his return to Vienna on the afternoon of 26 February, Shirer found his colleague Ed Taylor waiting for him at the train station. Taylor had good news and bad news to share. The former was that Tess had given birth to a baby girl that morning. The latter was that it had been a difficult delivery. The hospital was Roman Catholic, and the nurses caring for Tess, many of whom were nuns, maintained that childbirth should be a natural experience, sans medical intervention or pain relief (undoubtedly because none of them had ever given birth!). Tess was in labor for an incredible forty-eight hours, and her agony ended only when a Jewish obstetrician performed an emergency cesarean operation that saved the lives of mother and child, a daughter the Shirers named Eileen Inga.[18] But Tess still was not doing well. She was exhausted from her ordeal and had developed phlebitis, clotting in the outer veins of the legs, a condition which can be fatal if not properly treated. It was Tess's misfortune to experience her medical difficulties just as Austria was descending into the political abyss. With Nazis rioting in the streets of Vienna and anti-Semitism now at a fever pitch, those Jews who had sufficient means fled for their lives. Among them were doctors and other staff from the hospital where Tess was a patient. As a result, the level and quality of her medical care was less than adequate.

Shirer remained at his wife's bedside day and night, until her condition stabilized. However, eleven days after giving birth, even with Tess still in critical condition, Shirer was obliged to travel to Slovenia to arrange yet another CBS *Columbia School of the Air* broadcast by yet another children's choir. In far-off New York, Paul White continued to ignore the political developments rocking Austria. For that reason, on the evening of 9 March, when Austrian Chancellor von Schuschnigg announced his decision to hold the plebiscite on unification with Germany, Shirer was on the overnight train for Ljubljana, the Slovenian capital. There he remained blissfully unaware of the political crisis that was brewing in Austria. For the next two days, Shirer went about his business. By the time he returned to Vienna, the city was in chaos. Everyone was talking about the upcoming vote, and mobs of Nazi thugs were rampaging through city streets.

After a quick stop at home and a hospital visit to see Tess, who still had a worrisome fever thirteen days after having given birth, Shirer had hurried over to the café in which foreign journalists were now gathering to talk shop and socialize. They had abandoned the Café Louvre, where the pro-Nazi Bob Best still held court nightly. By now, he had become intolerably loud and bellicose in his support of Hitler.

Colleagues brought Shirer up to date on what had happened in his absence, but they had misread the situation when they anticipated that von Schuschnigg's planned plebiscite would be peaceful and that most Austrians would vote to remain separate from Germany; if so, they assumed that for now, at least, Hitler's plans to seize the country would be shelved. Shirer was far less certain of that, especially when he saw that Vienna's police were doing nothing to curb the excesses of the brown-shirted Nazis who had taken over the streets of the old city; some police had even donned Swastika armbands. Shirer's worst fears had been realized when he heard the plebiscite was off, and von Schuschnigg was resigning. Arthur Seyss-Inquart, a Nazi sympathizer and Hitler proxy, had succeeded him as chancellor. This meant that Hitler had won: the Anschluss was a reality. "Austria is finished," Shirer wrote in his diary. "Beautiful, tragic, civilized Austria! Gone."[19]

Austrian Nazis were gleeful. At the Café Louvre, Bob Best gloated; while listening to him sing Hitler's praises, Shirer was angered by the sight of his former office assistant, Emil Maass, who marched in shouting, "Heil, Hitler!" Maass had pretended to be a staunch anti-Nazi – enabling him to spy on Shirer and other foreign journalists. He now revealed his true sympathies, declaring it was "about time" that Austria and Germany were united. Then, smirking, he proudly showed his former employer the Swastika button he had pinned to his lapel. Seeing this, Shirer struggled to control his emotions. He knew this was no time to speak out, regardless of how much these developments were affecting him personally.[20] His work was one thing; his concerns for the welfare of his wife and infant daughter were quite another. Both were in danger.

Rampaging Nazi gangs entered the hospital where Tess was being treated; floor by floor, ward by ward, they roamed in their search of Jews, whom they beat before dragging them off to be shipped to the concentration camps the Nazis were now setting up. So terrorized was one Jewish woman who was on the same maternity ward as Tess that she threw herself and her baby out a window. Those few Jewish doctors – Tess's among them – or staff who had not already fled for their lives now did so, with the result that the quality of patient care deteriorated still further.

Amid all of this turmoil and tragedy, Shirer sat at home in the wee hours of the morning of Saturday, 12 March 1938. He had never felt more powerless, alone, or frustrated. "Impossible to sleep, so will write. Must write something ... The Nazis will not let me broadcast. Here I sit on one of the biggest stories of my life. I am the only broadcaster in town."[21]

The Anschluss and the imminent arrival of a triumphant Hitler in Vienna were by far the most exciting events that had developed since Shirer joined CBS. This was his golden opportunity finally to go on air with a live news report. With NBC's Max Jordan out of town, the story would be a CBS exclusive. However, before that could happen, Shirer faced a whole new problem.

William Shirer's frantic efforts to get through to Paul White in New York proved fruitless; the Nazis controlled the telephone lines into and out of Vienna. Likewise, Shirer had no luck in reaching Ed Murrow, who was busy arranging a musical broadcast in Warsaw. Acting on his own, Shirer set out for the studios of the Austrian state broadcasting system, RAVAG, in hopes of sending a shortwave transmission to New York by way of Geneva, London, or even Berlin. He hoped CBS staff in New York would air his report.

It was shortly after 11 p.m. on 11 March – five p.m. in New York – when Shirer arrived at the RAVAG studios. The situation he encountered was chaotic. Shirer managed to talk his way past the armed guards at the building's main entrance. Once inside, he was dismayed find that the Nazis – "harmless, excited boys of 17 or 18 mostly, though fooling dangerously, I noted with their rifles and revolvers" – had seized control of the facilities in anticipation of a midnight broadcast by Hitler.[22] Erich von Kunsti, the director of the RAVAG, was under arrest, and all shortwave transmissions out of Vienna were now being streamed through Berlin. Although Shirer was fearful, he remained undeterred. However, when he sought out von Kunsti, with whom he had had a good working relationship, the Austrian said he could do nothing to help. Shirer next approached the "scar-faced chap" in a Nazi uniform who was issuing orders.[23] The man stopped long enough to listen to Shirer's request and then promised to telephone Berlin for permission and technical facilities for a CBS broadcast. He then told Shirer to come back later; with that, he was escorted out of the building. When Shirer later tried to re-enter the broadcast center, he was repeatedly turned away by the guards at the door: "About two in the morning it became evident that I was a nuisance. I was a foreigner, unknown to the Nazis. Maybe I was a spy ... About three a.m. someone came out and told me it was no use waiting any longer. I was *invited* to leave. I have never been a man to argue with bayonets. I left."[24]

Leaving frustrated Shirer beyond measure. He was an eyewitness to one of the biggest news stories of his career, and yet he had no way to report it. Unable to sleep, Shirer consoled himself with a bottle of beer. He was drinking a second one when the telephone rang. It was Ed Murrow calling from Warsaw. The two men spoke in a kind of code they hoped would confuse the Gestapo agents whom Shirer was certain were tapping his phone:

"The enemy has crossed the goal line," Shirer told Murrow.

"Are you sure?" replied Murrow.

"I'm paid to be sure," said Shirer.[25]

Murrow had already conferred with New York, and Paul White finally had agreed to get Shirer's report on the air as soon as possible. With that in mind, Murrow suggested Shirer fly to London; from there he could render an uncensored account of the day's dramatic developments. Murrow would travel to Vienna, where he would cover for Shirer and wait for the Nazis to lift their broadcasting ban.

While all of this was happening, Tess Shirer remained in hospital, where she continued to battle phlebitis. Shirer had the welfare of his wife and infant daughter in mind as he and Murrow made their plans. However, for better and worse, his journalistic instincts had kicked in. Like a thoroughbred racehorse that is bred to run, Shirer could not help himself. After throwing a few belongings into a suitcase, he tried to call the hospital to leave a message for Tess. When he was unable to reach her, he dashed off a note that he left for a woman they employed as a part-time maid; Shirer asked her to deliver the message to Tess first thing next morning. By the time that happened, Shirer was at the Vienna airport. There he encountered a repeat of the situation of last night's scene at the broadcasting center; the facility, now awash in Nazi flags and banners, was under German control. Gestapo agents with help from SS officers were restricting civilian flights. "Then they cleared the London plane ... But I could not get on. I offered fantastic sums to several passengers for their places. Most of them were Jews and I could not blame them for turning me down."[26]

Priority was being given to German military aircraft, with one notable exception: Berlin-bound planes from Lufthansa, the German state airline, were still flying. Shirer, ever resourceful, was able to book the last seat on the morning plane. Once he was in Berlin, he caught a connecting flight to Amsterdam, and from there another one that took him to London. Having written his script en route, at 11:30 p.m. on that Saturday night –

after sixteen hours in transit – Shirer sat down in a BBC broadcasting studio to do a fifteen-minute report for CBS in which he offered what he thought was the first eyewitness account of the developments that had rocked Austria. However, his joy was short-lived. Shirer was crestfallen to learn that that NBC's Max Jordan, "Ubiquitous Max," had beaten him on the story. Having "slipped back into Vienna" while Shirer was still in the air bound for London, Jordan had convinced Austria's new Nazi masters to allow him to deliver a news report, albeit a censored one, to listeners in America. Barely ten minutes into his own broadcast, Jordan learned from an Austrian broadcasting technician that RAVAG was about to carry an address by Hitler, who had entered Austria and was speaking to a crowd of 300,000 delirious supporters in the city of Linz. Thus, America heard Hitler's speech live, with Max Jordan doing simultaneous translation.[27]

The novelty of NBC's coverage – an unplanned, serendipitous broadcast – was such that newspapers across the country, including *The New York Times*, carried accounts of it. The extent of Shirer's disappointment at being scooped can be gauged by the fact that in subsequent writings he never mentioned Jordan's triumph, not even in the privacy of his own diary or correspondence to friends. He preferred instead to focus on the remarkable events of the following day. On that day, he and Ed Murrow presented a half-hour broadcast that became one of those once-in-a-lifetime eureka moments. In the process, they redefined their roles with CBS radio, put William Paley's network on the road to two decades of preeminence in American news broadcasting, and forever change broadcast journalism. In retrospect, what they did seems like a no-brainer, the only logical thing to do in the circumstances. At the time, it was a bold and unprecedented experiment.

16

"We now take you to London..."

CBS President William Paley did not like to lose. At anything. And so he was angry that rival NBC had scooped his network on news of the Anschluss. Knowing this, Fred Klauber and Paul White scrambled to find a more timely way to present the news from Europe. "One of [their] first decisions was to allow Murrow and Shirer to broadcast their reports themselves," notes Paley biographer Lewis J. Paper. "There simply was no time to package their information for others to read, and besides, the firsthand accounts would have more drama if related by those who had actually witnessed the events. The next step was to schedule the reports to be aired over the CBS radio network, and on that point Paley himself took charge."[1]

Although he was abed with a case of the flu when the Nazis seized control of Austria on 12 March, Paley insisted on being kept informed about what was happening there. Shirer's request to use the RAVAG studios to broadcast a report having been denied, Paley personally telephoned Erich von Kunsti, the director general of the Austrian state broadcasting service; the two men had met once and had gotten along well. When Paley's call somehow made it through to von Kunsti's office, the CBS president appealed for studio time. "I told him how distressing it was that his organization was not allowing us the use of the facilities we needed to broadcast from there," Paley later recalled. Von Kunsti tearfully explained that he was under arrest and was no longer in charge: "I cannot do anything ... I would if I could."[2] The telephone line then went dead.

Paley was stunned. The emotional conversation and the abruptness with which it had ended personalized the Austrian crisis for the CBS president and underscored for him the impact of the momentous events that were reshaping Europe. It occurred to Paley "that every capital in Europe must be seething in reaction to Hitler's takeover of Austria. Whether or not we could hear from captured Vienna, it would be interesting if we could switch from one capital to the other and give reports from all. But was it technically feasible?"[3]

When William Paley rang Fred Klauber early on the morning of Sunday, 13 March, to discuss the situation, Paley was determined "to regain the face [CBS] had lost as a result of Max Jordan's on-scene reports from Vienna for NBC."[4] Responding to his boss's questions, Klauber said he thought it "probably" would be possible to do the broadcast Paley had in mind. This was a news program that would pull together the disparate elements of the Austrian story – live, eyewitness accounts from Shirer, Murrow, and knowledgeable print journalists, a statement by a prominent British political figure, as well as any other commentary that would help listeners make sense of what clearly was a fluid and volatile situation.

Both CBS and NBC had featured European news roundups in past, but each of these broadcasts had taken weeks to organize. Paley wanted the CBS broadcast on the air that night. Today, such a program can be organized in minutes. In March 1938, broadcasting technology was still rudimentary, and the venture Paley envisioned was unprecedented. When Klauber was reluctant to assure Paley that his staff could pull off something this complex with so little lead time, Paley fumed. "I said, Goddamnit, there's no reason in the world I can think of why it can't be done. It *has* to be done."[5]

It fell to Klauber and news director Paul White to make the roundup broadcast happen. What William Paley wanted, William Paley got; he was not someone to take "no" for an answer. So White had no choice but to shelve his doubts about the network's ability to pull together such a program and any personal reservations he had about raising the profile of Ed Murrow, whom he continued to regard as a potential career rival.

It was about seven a.m. in New York time when White telephoned Shirer in London, where it was already noon. After explaining that Paley wanted a half-hour European news roundup on the air that evening, White asked Shirer a blunt question: could he and Murrow make it happen on such short notice? White was relieved and surprised when Shirer said yes. This was the opportunity for which he had been waiting. "The truth was I didn't have the faintest idea of how to do it ... I put in a call to Murrow in Vienna, and as I waited for him to call back I pondered what to do."[6]

On the plus side, because Shirer knew most of the American and British journalists in Berlin, Paris, and Rome, he was confident he could convince one of them in each city to take part in the CBS broadcast, if they could get permission from their home offices in time. On the negative side, Shirer realized he and Murrow had less than twelve hours to recruit reporters, arrange telephone lines to link the five cities involved, write a script, and secure transmission times with the state broadcasters in Germany, France, Italy, and the United Kingdom. The logistics of all of this would have been a challenge at any time. The difficulties were now compounded by the disruptions caused by the German army's move into Austria and by the fact it was a Sunday. The offices of the state broadcasting agencies in most European countries were closed, and no studio technicians were available. In London, many politicians and Foreign Office decision-makers had retreated to their country homes for the weekend. "It seemed to be an English custom that could not be altered, no matter how great a crisis suddenly broke on the continent of Europe," Shirer noted.[7]

He and Murrow forged ahead regardless. Shirer made optimum use of the telephone lines, his language and journalistic skills, and his personal contacts to set the wheels in motion for that evening's broadcast. He lined up live reports from his friends Edgar Mowrer, the Paris correspondent of the *Chicago Daily News*; Frank Gervasi of the INS agency in Rome; and Pierre Huss of INS in Berlin. Meanwhile in Vienna, Ed Murrow was working the phones to sort out the myriad technical details of the planned broadcast. It took considerable negotiating, but he managed to persuade the German officials who were now in control of Austria's telephone and broadcasting systems to grant him use of a phone line to Berlin. There, CBS rep Claire Trask had arranged for Murrow's report to be transmitted to New York by shortwave radio.

Not surprisingly, there were a few problems that neither Shirer nor Murrow could solve in time for the broadcast. For one, Frank Gervasi was frustrated in his efforts to arrange studio time in Rome. Instead, he resorted to dictating his report over the telephone to Kay Campbell, Murrow's secretary at the CBS office in London; Shirer would read Gervasi's words on air. Similarly, when it proved impossible to find a suitable broadcasting facility in Paris, Mowrer telephoned his report to the BBC's London studios. From there, it was relayed by shortwave to New York.

With all possible arrangements in place, telephone lines booked, split-second time and audio cues set, and people standing by in five cities (and six time zones), Shirer took a deep breath as he settled in front of a BBC microphone in London. Through his headphones he heard the calm, reassuring voice of CBS announcer Bob Trout in New York, "The Voice of CBS News," introducing the program. It was two a.m. Monday morning in Vienna, where Ed Murrow sat with his ear glued to the telephone as he awaited his cue to speak. It was one a.m. Monday in London, eight p.m. Sunday evening in New York when Trout intoned, "Columbia begins its radio tour of Europe's capitals with a transoceanic pickup from London. We now take you to London..." William Shirer never forgot how, at that instant, "All the fatigue of the last 48 hours disappeared [and] I felt a tinge of excitement."[8] He also had the presence of mind and sufficient sense of perspective to realize that they were making broadcasting history.[9]

Shirer opened the overseas portion of the program by reporting that it was unlikely the British would do anything to stop the German takeover of Austria, other than to register a diplomatic protest. He went on to speculate – correctly, as it turned out – that Czechoslovakia, with its ethnic German minority, would be the next target of Hitler's aggression.

Labour MP Ellen Wilkinson, a friend of Ed Murrow's, echoed Shirer's opinions, explaining that the official British reaction to developments in Austria was one of "interested curiosity," nothing more. Wilkinson predicted that Great Britain would take no action to check Hitler's aggression. In Paris, Edgar Mowrer spoke about the "brutal, naked force" the Nazis were using to subdue Austria, and he warned the "collapse of the 1918 [Versailles] peace" posed a danger to all the countries of Europe, and by implication to the interests of the United States.

In Vienna, Ed Murrow spoke of the impact of the Nazi takeover of Austria: "It's now nearly two-thirty a.m. [here] and Herr Hitler has not yet arrived ... There isn't a great deal of hilarity, but at the same time there doesn't seem to be much feeling of tension. Young storm troopers are riding about the streets, riding in trucks and vehicles of all sorts, singing and tossing oranges out to the crowd. Nearly every principal building has its armed guard, including the one from which I am speaking."[10] In this remarkable broadcast, the first of the more than 5,000 he would make for CBS over the course of the next three decades, Murrow spoke with a Nazi censor monitoring his every word; in the Austrian capital, "They lift their arms here a little higher than in Berlin, and the 'Heil Hitler' is said a little more loudly."[11]

Shirer read Frank Gervasi's report from Rome. One of the unknowns, Gervasi noted, was how Mussolini would react to Hitler's incursion into a country the Italian dictator regarded as being within his own sphere of influence. The answer to that question was the same as it was for the other nations of Europe: Italy would (and could) do nothing. "The Duce ... had joined the Führer's camp," Shirer noted.[12]

Alone among the CBS commentators on this night, the pro-Nazi Pierre Huss in Berlin framed his assessment of the Anschluss in positive terms, reporting that most Germans believed Hitler's assertion that a majority of Austrians were eager to become part of the Third Reich because of their historic ties to Germany. The half-hour CBS broadcast ended with Democratic Senator Lewis Schwellenbach, of Washington, a New Deal supporter and member of the Senate Foreign Relations Committee, reiterating the Roosevelt administration's determination to stay out of the fray: "If the rest of the world wants to involve itself in [a] brawl, that is its business."[13]

Huss's comments aside, Shirer and Murrow were delighted with how the CBS broadcast had come together. In New York, Paley, Klauber, and White were ecstatic, especially when they learned that audience reaction to the broadcast was swift and enthusiastic. Predictably, CBS corporate executives were eager to take credit for the program's success. In his 1947 book *News on the Air*, Paul White related his own role in the broadcast and in so doing implied that he had been in control and had shepherded Shirer and Murrow along.[14] Years later, Paley himself claimed that *he* had been the one responsible for this historic broadcast. That was true; the idea had been his and his alone. "For the time it was an extraordinary feat of logistics and planning. Each correspondent reported live, some thousands of miles away from each other and each of their reports had to be scheduled precisely to the second ... In 1938 this technique was immediately recognized as an unusual event in the news. By bringing together in one program an anchorman at studio headquarters and correspondents on location, we were doing something that would become the important format of modern news broadcasting."[15]

Indeed, this was no mere hyperbole. The basic format for that original CBS roundup broadcast, in which a news anchor introduced reports from correspondents in the field, has become the standard model that ever since has been the worldwide standard in news broadcasts, on both radio and television. At CBS radio, the European roundup evolved to become *World News Roundup*, a flagship news program that was destined to become the "longest running continuous broadcast on network radio," as Robert Trout describes it.[16]

William Shirer, though ever ready to give credit where it was due, always felt that he and Murrow were more responsible for the success of the broadcast and the change of direction it represented than was anyone in New York. "[Murrow and I] took advantage of [the Anschluss]," he told broadcasting historian David Hosley in a 1980 interview. "As I recall, we didn't even ask them; we just went on the air and they were glad to have us. And that changed the whole thing. It was just one of those accidents that happened. If it hadn't been a big event like that, the networks were too stupid to change their policy, I think."[17]

Shirer's memory was a tad too selective. Although his role, in particular, was pivotal, there can be no denying that first CBS European roundup was very much a team effort. It could not have succeeded otherwise. Lynn Olson and Stanley Cloud are correct when they observe, "The idea for a roundup had originated in New York, but Shirer and Murrow had made it happen and made it work."[18]

Regardless of who was responsible, the reality was that in that watershed half-hour of programming CBS had reasserted its credibility as a news source and succeeded in grabbing the limelight back from NBC. In his diary, Shirer stated, "This crisis has done one thing for us. I think radio talks by Ed and me are now established. Birth of the 'radio foreign correspondent,' so to speak."[19]

Within days of the Austrian broadcast the CBS promotions department had produced a glossy advertising brochure entitled "Vienna, March: A Footnote to History," which touted the network's prowess in covering events in Europe and its reliability as a news source. The underlying message was that from now on not only would CBS provide listeners with news reports and commentary, it would do so with a timeliness that newspapers and magazines could never hope to match. As Murrow biographer Alexander Kendrick notes, "In [that] half hour radio came into its own as a full-fledged news medium, the most immediate and forceful yet devised, reaching across 3,000 miles of ocean and hundreds of miles of Europe in several directions, to bring a sense of history into the American home."[20]

One essential point that neither Paley nor any of the commentators then or since has mentioned is that the news roundup CBS aired on the evening of 13 March was uniquely and distinctively American. The irony is that at the time isolationist sentiments ruled the day in Washington, and the Roosevelt administration continued to espouse a policy of neutrality in its foreign policy. Yet none of the national broadcasting systems in Europe could have aired the kind of broadcast CBS had, even if the idea had occurred to their people; it took an innovator with William Paley's vision, determination, and financial resources. It took the creativity, talents, and grit of professionals such as William Shirer, Ed Murrow, and the other members of the CBS team to make it a success. In 1938, despite the hardships wrought by eight long years of the Great Depression, the remarkable thing is that so many Americans still bubbled with a giddy, unbridled sense of optimism that anything was possible.

No sooner had CBS's inaugural European news roundup broadcast ended than Paul White was on the phone instructing Shirer to organize another one for the next evening. Exhausted, but still on an adrenalin high, he readily agreed.

Ed Murrow was back on the air with a solo report from Vienna on Monday afternoon, and then just a few hours later, he and Shirer took part in another CBS roundup broadcast. Because this one, a reprise of Sunday's program, was well advertised, millions listened to the more than 125 CBS-affiliated stations in the United States and Canada.

Buoyed by their successes, Shirer remained in London all week to organize and arrange CBS broadcasts. At one point, Winston Churchill, who in 1938 was very much a political pariah, even in his own Conservative Party, rose in the House of Commons to chide Labour Prime Minister Neville Chamberlain for his policy of appeasement, which Churchill decried as being shortsighted and dangerous. Shirer felt this hawkish message, which ran counter to the prevailing mood in London, was important enough to be reported to an American audience. When William Paley agreed, he authorized Shirer to offer Churchill fifty dollars for a public service talk. Knowing something of Churchill's financial situation, Shirer was skeptical he would bite. In fact, now – as was the case for much of his life – Churchill lived one step ahead of his creditors. His journalist son, Randolph, had confided to Shirer that his father's main source of income at the time was a syndicated newspaper weekly newspaper column, which netted him about $1,500 per week. For most people, that would have been a lot of money. For a man with Churchill's spending habits and lifestyle, it was scarcely enough to make ends meet. The man who described himself as a "private member of Parliament, but of some prominence" was in need of money.[21] Shirer tried to explain this to Paley, but the CBS president was adamant: he would pay Churchill no more than fifty dollars to speak.

When Shirer rang Churchill to invite him to speak on CBS, he was ready to accept. That is, until he heard the proposed fee. Churchill snorted derisively: "Tell your boss I'll be happy to do it for $500 – £100, that is."[22]

While Churchill never delivered that public service talk on CBS, the network did continue to report on Europe's deepening political crisis. Among the highlights of the news programming that third week of March 1938 were Ed Murrow's reports on Adolf Hitler's triumphant arrival in Vienna and the subsequent storm of Nazi hatred and violence against Austria's Jews. Murrow, who made as many as three solo broadcasts each day that week, was sickened and angered by the brutality he witnessed. In the circumstances, his stay in Vienna was neither easy nor pleasant. Not only was he working around the clock, he also felt obliged to visit and comfort Tess Shirer, who remained in hospital in critical condition. Each evening when he called London to confer with Shirer, Murrow provided his colleague and friend with a medical update on his wife.

Shirer flew back to Vienna on 19 March. When the two CBS men returned from the airport to the Shirers' apartment in the upscale Plössl-gasse neighborhood, they were dismayed to find armed SS guards block-ing the building's entrance. Shirer, exhausted after his journey and angry at what was happening in Austria, demanded to see the soldiers' com-manding officer. He and Murrow were directed next door to the Roths-childs' palace, which SS troops were busy looting.[23] The bemused officer who was overseeing the thievery listened to the Americans' complaints. He then had one of his men escort Shirer and Murrow upstairs to the Shirers' apartment. "You'll have to stay put there – at least for a while – until this little operation is finished," the SS man warned.[24]

They did as they were told. Drinks in hand, Shirer and Murrow stood at a window watching as SS troops loaded booty onto waiting trucks. When finally the Germans had gone, Shirer and Murrow ventured out. Shirer, eager to see for himself the impact of the Nazi takeover of Vienna, was stunned by the changes that had taken place in just a week. Swastika banners and flags now festooned every public building, while the mood on the streets was ugly and ominous. Jews, even those who merely *looked* Jewish, were being stop-ped and questioned, and in some cases beaten and arrested by the groups of uniformed Nazis thugs, who were everywhere. The changes in the Austrian capital, Shirer observed, were "almost unbelievable."[25]

Many buildings and homes in the city's Jewish neighborhood had been vandalized. Windows were smashed, walls scarred by pro-Nazi graffiti, and stores looted. Vienna's Jewish population, more than 180,000 people prior to the Anschluss, already had been reduced by half. Those Jews who had realized early on what was happening wisely had fled the country. Others, who were swept up in the maelstrom but had enough money, bought their way out. The trade in selling safe passage out of Austria became so lucrative and so well organized that the SS set up the "Office for Jewish Emigration."

Those Jews who were less affluent went into hiding or were rounded up by Nazis. Some were killed immediately. Many more were shipped off to concentration camps. Shirer was appalled to see that Austria's Nazis were even more fanatical about this than were their new German masters. The Viennese, who had always been so easy-going, hospitable, and friendly, overnight had become cold, ruthless, and uncaring. The change was as profound as it was saddening; *gemütlichkeit*, that legendary Viennese sense of frivolity, indulgence, and joy of life that Shirer and so many other Americans had loved was no more.

Regardless, when Ed Murrow departed for London on the morning of 20 March, Shirer did his best to resume his CBS duties and his life in Vienna. The Nazis had relaxed their control over Austrian broadcasting, but they had instituted censorship; Hitler was incensed by the world outcry over the Anschluss, which he blamed on the "lies" being spread by the foreign media. With censorship now in place the Nazis were confident that they could control and direct the message that was getting out. Shirer was no less intent on outwitting the censors in hopes of providing complete and accurate news reports on the run-up to rigged plebiscites Hitler had ordered held in Austria and Germany in a bid to legitimize his actions.

In the midst of all this turmoil, Shirer had personal issues to deal with. He was still concerned about the health of Tess and the baby, both of whom were released from hospital two days before that 10 April vote. Although he had to carry them both from the street up the three flights of stairs to their apartment, Shirer was relieved to have his family home. In his diary on 8 April, Shirer predicted, "The worst is over."[26] However, that proved to be wishful thinking, for Tess was still in much pain, and her fever persisted. In a desperate bid to discover the cause, Shirer took her back to the hospital for more tests and X-rays. The latter yielded a shocking discovery. The obstetrician who had done the emergency cesarean operation that had saved the lives of both mother and child had left a medical instrument inside Tess's abdomen. The doctor treating her, who was not a surgeon, advised that the obstetrician who had performed the C-section should do corrective surgery. However, there was a big problem: because he was Jewish, the doctor was now in hiding.

Shirer used his contacts to help locate the man and to persuade him to do the vital corrective surgery, which was performed secretly late one night at a clinic located in a Roman Catholic convent on the outskirts of Vienna. Afterward, Tess's medical condition improved steadily, albeit slowly. As it did, the Shirers began making plans to leave for Switzerland, William Shirer and Ed Murrow had decided Geneva would be the new base for cbs's operations in Europe. That historic Swiss city, censorship-free and home to the League of Nations, was centrally located for rail and air travel throughout the continent.

With Austria now being part of the Third Reich, Shirer and Murrow surmised that Czechoslovakia, with its sizeable German-speaking minority, would be the next target of Hitler's aggression. "[It] will certainly be next on Hitler's list. Militarily it is doomed now that Germany has flanked it on the south as well as the north," Shirer wrote in his diary on 14 April, four days after the rigged plebiscite that had "legitimized" the Anschluss, with 99.75 percent of Austrian voters and 99.08 percent of Germans approving of the German takeover.

The American public's appetite for European news had peaked during the Austrian crisis. Audiences for the coverage that both CBS and NBC were now providing soared as tensions escalated and the number and frequency of overseas news reports grew. "It was almost amusing how often CBS now put us on the air to report," Shirer quipped.[27] Even so, it would be wrong to think that some miraculous epiphany had caused network executives in New York suddenly to see the potential of radio as a news vehicle. The reality was that events in Europe were still no more than a passing concern in the executive offices of CBS and NBC. Thus, as tensions between Germany and Czechoslovakia escalated during spring and summer 1938, entertainment remained the name of the game for America's radio networks. The only regularly scheduled CBS news programming was a nightly commentary by Boake Carter; listeners in the New York area could also tune into a couple of five-minute newscasts, one at 7:30 p.m., the other at 11 p.m. Lead announcer Bob Trout, who had distinguished himself during the Austrian crisis, was now hosting a weekly quiz show.

All of this was a source of frustration for Shirer and Murrow, especially with William Paley praising their work and CBS's ratings soaring. "They were two young people covering a continent in turmoil," writes Murrow biographer A.M. Sperber, "their only backup their stamina, imagination, and professionalism, in recognition of which the prestigious Headliners Club [in New York] had presented them with the Silver Plaque for their reporting of the *Anschluss*."[28] Regardless, the two CBS men still were obliged to arrange concerts by children's choirs, talks by sundry speakers, and coverage of various "special" events. When Shirer traveled to Rome the first week of May to report on an important meeting between Hitler and Mussolini, Paul White instructed him to locate some "singing birds" for a novelty broadcast. Shirer reported that he could find no melodious Italian birds – if he had even bothered to look.

The frivolity of such assignments was not the only aggravation CBS's man on the continent endured. Another rub, one that had a fundamental effect on how he and Murrow went about their business, was William Paley's insistence that all broadcasts be done live for "authenticity" sake and because sound recording technology was still complex and expensive. Paley also feared that introducing recorded sound to radio would cause labor strife with the musicians' unions, which insisted that all musical performances be live; in retrospect, why voice reports would have been an issue is as unclear as it is puzzling. State-run European radio broadcasters routinely made use of pre-recorded reports and music; CBS did not. "As Europe lurched down the road to war, Ed and I tried in vain to get Paley to allow us to record," Shirer later recalled.[29] The CBS president's intransigence on this issue posed no end of logistical difficulties for the network's news staff. Given the relatively primitive state of broadcast technology at the time, the unpredictability of shortwave broadcasting – due to weather, atmospheric conditions, and magnetic disturbances – and the split-second timing issues involved in airing live news reports, Shirer and Murrow had to be creative. On more than one occasion, they were obliged to ad lib when they were cued to go on air too early or late.

This proved to be especially problematic as the pace of events in Europe quickened once again. With Hitler ratcheting up his rhetoric against Czechoslovakia, war seemed increasingly likely. Then, as now, were there is conflict the media inevitably follow, and so a large contingent of foreign journalists descended upon Prague. Reporters from many of America's leading newspapers and news agencies were among them, as was Shirer, who arranged for a talk on CBS by Eduard Beneš, the president of the Czech Republic, and Alice Masaryk, the daughter of Thomas Masaryk, one of the country's co-founders. Beneš had agreed to include in his speech some comments about Czech-German relations, but "technical difficulties" of undetermined origin disrupted that portion of the broadcast, which was being beamed across the Atlantic to New York via Germany since the Czech state did not yet have its own state-operated shortwave radio transmitter. This incident underscored a couple of emerging realities for Shirer. One was that with the growing public profile he and Murrow enjoyed in America, the Gestapo was now paying closer attention to their activities. That became apparent the first week of May 1938, when Shirer traveled to Rome to report on that aforementioned meeting between Hitler and Italian dictator Benito Mussolini. The SS guards who searched Shirer's train at the Austrian-Italian border and invaded his sleeping compartment quizzed him at length and then relieved him of all his foreign currency. The Nazis had slapped tight controls on how much money travelers could carry with them when they were leaving Austria – the limit was just twelve dollars American; while it may have been that Shirer simply got swept up in a routine check, subsequent events suggest he was now receiving special attention from the secret police. That was certainly the case on 10 June, the day that he and Tess finally left Vienna.

Relations between Germany and Czechoslovakia had reached a breaking point, with Hitler having manufactured a crisis over what he termed the "need for a square deal" for three-million German-speaking, pro-Nazi residents in the Sudetenland. That industrialized, mineral-rich area in the northwest corner of Czechoslovakia, formerly part of Germany, had come under Czech control after World War One. When thousands of German troops massed along the border the last week of May, the world held its collective breath. Surprisingly, this time Hitler backed down in the face of an allied coalition that had rallied to the defense of Czechoslovakia.

Amidst this climate of heightened tensions, Gestapo agents spent two days at the Shirers' apartment rummaging through the books, papers, and personal effects the family were packing for their move to Switzerland, which could not come a moment too soon for Tess Shirer's liking. Sickened by the German takeover of her homeland, she was barely able to hide her contempt for the Nazis. In a gesture of defiance, she refused to trade her Austrian passport for a German one, as she was now obliged to do. To obtain the necessary exit visa for her and the baby, Shirer was obliged to appeal to officials in the American legation, who helped obtain the documents from the German ministry. Even so, when the Shirers, with baby and an Austrian nanny in tow, appeared at the Vienna airport to board the noon-hour flight to Zürich, they came under intense scrutiny. The Gestapo agent who processed their paperwork demanded to know why Tess, an Austrian national, was not carrying a German passport. Her exit visa, which was due to expire that very day, was acceptable only because it had been stamped by the head of the Gestapo in Vienna. Even so, the chief of airport security was still suspicious and insisted Tess be searched prior to boarding her flight. When Shirer protested angrily, Gestapo agents hauled him aside. After searching him and peppering him with questions, they left him locked in an interview room while they turned their attentions to his wife. What followed was one of the most harrowing, infuriating, and terrifying ordeals of Shirer's life.

He could only grit his teeth and cuss as the female Gestapo agents stripped Tess naked, forcing her to submit to a full body search. Indifferent to the risk of infection, the zealous officers even made her remove some of the bandages on her abdomen. The Gestapo suspected her husband was engaged in money smuggling, and they hoped to catch him in the act. The Shirers were fortunate to escape without having false evidence planted in their bags. They were also fortunate that the captain of the Swiss airplane understood what was happening and delayed his takeoff for a half-hour, until the Shirers and the nanny were safely on board. "Flew blind in storm clouds along the Alps all the way from Vienna to Zürich, the plane pitching and tossing and most of the passengers sick and scared," Shirer wrote in his diary. "Then there was Zürich down there, Switzerland, sanity, and civilization again."[30]

17

Radio News Comes of Age

As the simmering war of words between Germany and Czechoslovakia over the Sudetenland escalated, it became increasingly obvious that war was inevitable. "Militarily [Czechoslovakia] is doomed now that Germany has it flanked on the south as well as the north," Shirer noted in his diary.[1]

Ed Murrow agreed, and so in early August he suggested that Shirer hasten to Prague to report on the British-mediated talks taking place there between the leaders of the political party representing the Sudetendeutsch and Czech officials. Shirer did as Murrow wanted; however, he was dismayed that he and Murrow were obliged to continue pleading with CBS news chief Paul White for airtime. As yet, White had little interest in what was happening in the Sudetenland.

By the last week of August, with the Prague peace talks on the verge of collapse, Shirer departed for Berlin, where on 25 August he witnessed the biggest German military parade he had ever seen. Afterward, despondent and fearful, he returned to Geneva to spend the first week of September with Tess and Eileen, who were planning to leave for New York at month's end. Tess hoped to establish residence in the States, so as to enable her to qualify herself and her daughter for American passports, their old ones being invalid now that Austria was part of the Third Reich. At the same time, there was another, even more pressing, reason for the sojourn: "I thought it well to get Tess and [Inga] out of [Europe] until we knew whether there would be peace or war."[2]

In hindsight, the significance of the political developments that rattled Europe in spring and summer 1938 is apparent. That was not so at the time, even when Hitler seized the moment and upped the ante yet again by announcing that he would talk about the Sudeten situation in his keynote address at the closing session of the Nazi Party's annual Nuremberg rally. A half-century later, Shirer recalled, "I can still feel in my bones ... the almost unbearable tension that gripped Europe through the whole month of September."[3]

There was enormous anticipation of Hitler's address, and so Shirer and a group of colleagues gathered in Prague on the evening of 12 September to listen to the radio broadcast. Delivered to a surging crowd of a half million Nazi Party zealots who filled the massive "palace of lights" stadium in Nuremberg, Hitler's words were beamed live across Europe and North America. In the United States, many people were angered when both NBC and CBS pre-empted their usual afternoon programming – soap operas, military music, and Betty Crocker's household tips – to air the speech in which the Nazi dictator worked himself into a frenzy, demanding that the 3.4 million Sudetendeutsch be allowed to determine their own future by voting in a plebiscite. "I have never heard the Adolf [sic] quite so full of hate, his audience quite so on the borders of bedlam," Shirer wrote in his diary. "What poison in his voice when at the beginning of his long recital of alleged wrongs to the Sudeteners he paused: 'Ich spreche von der Czechoslovakei!' His words, his tone, dripping with venom."[4]

CBS responded to the growing air of crisis by broadcasting the first of the many European news roundups on "the Sudeten crisis." Murrow reported from London and Shirer from Prague, with stringers – American newspaper journalists recruited for the occasion – chiming in from Paris and Berlin.

For two days after Hitler's speech, the world held its collective breath. Shirer, along with other foreign journalists and the British envoy to the Czech peace talks, Lord Runciman, remained in Prague. There they hunkered down and waited for the German air raids that the world felt certain would be forthcoming. Thousands of Jews, at least those who could afford to do so, fled Prague, which was awash in rumors. Shirer was frustrated that he could confirm none of them; Czech was one of the few European languages he neither read nor understood.

When British Prime Minister Neville Chamberlain met Hitler on 15 September at the Nazi leader's retreat in the mountains above the Bavarian town of Berchtesgaden, Shirer was intent on being there to report what transpired. However, with train travel now restricted continent-wide, he instead paced the lobby of the Ambassador Hotel in Prague, which had become the ersatz headquarters of the foreign media. Shirer passed the hours by smoking, drinking in the hotel bar, and talking with his colleagues. From time to time, a spokesman for the Czech government or the Sudetendeutsch dropped by to hand out media releases or to field questions. Each visit sent the assembled journalists scrambling to the telephones to report the latest news, the details of which were difficult, if not impossible, to confirm. About all Shirer could say with any degree of certainty, despite having toured the Sudetenland by car, was that the border region was in chaos. His efforts to broadcast the latest developments were thwarted by atmospheric conditions. NBC had no such difficulties. Abel Schechter, the network's director of News and Special Events, revealed in a 1941 memoir that NBC's technical staff had figured out a way around the problem: they relayed their shortwave signals south to Capetown, South Africa, across the Atlantic to Buenos Aires, and from there north to New York. "Inasmuch as we ordered up that circuit, it was our very own, and for several days we had the rival broadcasting systems mystified as to how we could get programs through from Europe when they couldn't."[5]

Shirer was obliged to cable his reports to New York until atmospheric conditions improved enough for transatlantic radio contact to be reestablished. By then, it was becoming painfully apparent that Shirer and Murrow's prediction was accurate: the Czechs were on their own in resisting Nazi aggression. In hindsight, the folly of the British and French unwillingness to stand up to Hitler is evident. What is too often forgotten today is that, for all the Nazi dictator's malevolence, there was considerable sympathy for his demands, even in England. After all, the British royals had their roots in Germany, and there was a widespread sentiment among the ruling elite in the United Kingdom that the Treaty of Versailles had unfairly punished the German people. Influential voices argued that under Hitler a resurgent Germany would provide a vital European bulwark against the growing menace posed by Soviet dictator Joseph Stalin.

Shirer and Murrow, being immersed in the situation, followed events in Europe far more closely than did their bosses in New York. Thus, when Shirer arrived in Prague to cover the reaction to Hitler's speech on 12 September, he again had to plead for airtime to report the latest news. Paul White begrudgingly agreed to air a five-minute daily report, but not before extracting from Shirer a promise that he would, as Shirer recalled, "cable beforehand when I think the news does not warrant my taking the time."[6]

The men in New York who ran America's radio networks still regarded their core business as serving up entertainment to Depression-weary listeners. All of that would all change overnight as the Sudeten crisis flared suddenly and spectacularly. "For once, soap operas couldn't compete with the drama and excitement of what was happening abroad," note Cloud and Olson.[7]

Paul White responded to the quickening pace of events by setting up a CBS crisis-coverage team. Popular news commentator Hans Kaltenborn was installed as the chief analyst and anchorman for the roundups and news bulletins that were pouring in from Europe. Robert Trout, and two other staff announcers read some newscasts, but Kaltenborn did the bulk of the work. So busy was he that at the height of the crisis he all but lived in the studio at 485 Madison Avenue, taking his meals there and napping on a cot next to his microphone. "From Studio 9 Kaltenborn would throw out the cue, 'Calling Edward Murrow, come in Ed Murrow', and a voice that was becoming increasingly familiar to the public would cut through the short-wave static: 'Hello, America, this is London calling', the standard opening from overseas," Sperber recalls.[8] Similarly, Kaltenborn cued Shirer's reports from wherever he was in Europe on that particular day. "Come in, William Shirer," the CBS anchorman would call out. Then Shirer's voice would be heard, sometimes distantly as it emerged from the crackling static: "Hello, America, this is Berlin calling..."

The voices of Shirer and Murrow, CBS's two star foreign correspondents, were fast becoming as familiar as those of family members to the millions of listeners across North America who were transfixed by the radio news reports from Europe. Shirer and Murrow were now speaking on the air several times each day.

As it became apparent that Britain and France, without consulting with their Czech ally, had agreed to accept Hitler's demands, Shirer and Murrow struggled to control their anger and dismay. "Mr Chamberlain is meeting Hitler at Godesberg [a scenic town located on the Rhine River, just south of Cologne] on Wednesday [21 September]," Murrow told Shirer, "and we want you to cover that. If there's a war, then you can go back to Prague."[9]

Murrow set to work reporting on the fast-breaking developments in London, where a rising chorus of politicians both from within Chamberlain's own Conservative caucus and the opposition Labour Party were voicing doubts about the policy of appeasement. Meanwhile, Shirer hastened to Godesberg. He was certain history was about to be made there, and he was correct.

Czech leaders, isolated and having no real options other than to fight or comply with Hitler's demands, reluctantly announced they would accept the Anglo-French proposal to cede to Germany those areas of the Sudetenland where the Sudetendeutsch were in a majority. However, even that was not enough to satisfy Hitler, who was in no mood to be conciliatory.

Czech concessions only served to further embolden him. Thus, when Chamberlain arrived in Godesberg on 22 September for talks, Hitler had a surprise waiting for him and for the world.

That same morning, Shirer chanced to have a memorable encounter with the Nazi dictator. Shirer had seen Hitler many times over the course of the past four years, but always on occasions that had been carefully choreographed. This time was different, and in this unguarded moment Shirer grasped for the first time that Herr Hitler's swagger and bluster were elements of a masterful performance by a man who was under enormous pressure; he had not yet developed the supreme self-confidence – and hubris – that ultimately led to his downfall and ruin. The Nazi leader had risked everything in this make-or-break gamble, and evidently knew it. Shirer and an Austrian colleague were having breakfast in the riverside terrace of a Godesberg hotel when Hitler unexpectedly strode past the journalists' table. As they watched wide-eyed, Shirer's companion whispered, "Look at his walk!"

"On inspection it was a very curious walk indeed," Shirer wrote in his diary. "Dainty little steps ... every few steps [Hitler] cocked his right shoulder nervously, his left leg snapping up as he did so. I watched him closely as he came back past us. The same nervous tic. He had ugly black patches under his eyes. I think the man is on the edge of a nervous breakdown."[10]

Suddenly, all of the rumors that were flying around made sense. Like everyone, Shirer had heard that Hitler was prone to flying into a rage at the mere mention of Czech President Eduard Beneš's name or of the word Sudetenland. It was said that when this happened Hitler would begin shaking uncontrollably and would fall to the floor, hence the derisive nickname *Teppichfresser* – the carpet-eater.

Regardless of his mental state, Hitler caught Chamberlain by surprise when he informed the British prime minister that their previous agreement was off. Instead, he announced that the German army would occupy the entire Sudetenland eight days hence, on 1 October. All Czech government officials and troops must leave the region by then, or else Germany would declare war. This was no negotiating ploy; it was a demand.

Stunned and angry, Chamberlain stormed out of the meeting. He remained closeted in his hotel, conferring with advisors until late that evening when he again met with Hitler. This session lasted three hours, but nothing came of it. Hitler held firm in his demands. As a result, the mood on both sides was apprehensive. Media observers speculated that Hitler finally had overplayed his hand and now there was no way out for either side. Shirer was about to go on the air to report this when Nazi Propaganda Minister Goebbels and Eugen Hadamovsky, the head of the German radio service, burst into the porter's room that had been turned into a makeshift broadcast studio for foreign journalists. The Nazi officials, in a surly mood, forbade Shirer from reporting anything that had not been mentioned in the official communiqué, which simply stated that Chamberlain had agreed to convey to Prague a German memorandum in which Hitler's demands were set out.

Next morning, 24 September, Shirer and many of his colleagues returned to Berlin. The warm, sunny weather there matched the mood of Nazi officials and of the German public, who blithely accepted media assurances that Hitler and Chamberlain were working to find a peaceful solution to their differences. The situation was markedly different in London and Paris; in both capitals there was burgeoning opposition to the appeasement policy. However, as history tells us, in the end, the Czechs alone refused to give in to Hitler's demands.

Eduard Beneš, knowing he had lost control of the situation, stepped down as president of the Czech Republic. His replacement, General Jan Syrový, promptly ordered the mobilization of the country's army and the drafting of an additional half-million men. When Syrový announced that Czechoslovakia would resist any German aggression, most observers felt the die had been cast and war would begin at any moment. The evidence is that Hitler agreed; on the evening of 26 September, he worked himself into a red-faced frenzy before an audience of 15,000 party faithful in a Berlin sports arena. The Nazi dictator shrieked. He ranted. Spittle flew as he pounded the lectern with his fist. He left no way out for himself or the world when he declared that on 1 October the Sudetenland would be in German hands "by peace or war." Shirer, who was doing a live broadcast of the event, was astonished: "For the first time in all the years I've observed him, [Hitler] seemed tonight to have completely lost control of himself."[11]

If Hitler was to be believed, not only was he intent on seizing the Sudetenland, he was determined to wipe Czechoslovakia off the map. However, just when it seemed there was no avoiding a war, perhaps sensing how tentative his position was – we now know the German army and a majority of Germans still had no enthusiasm for a fight – Hitler surprised everyone by inviting Chamberlain, Daladier, and Mussolini to meet with him in Munich. The four men would sit down together in a last-ditch bid to find a peaceful way out of the Sudeten impasse; no representative from the Czech government was invited. Historians have endlessly analyzed the events of the Munich conference, where the British and French betrayed the Czechs, who now realized the futility of further resistance.

The four-power agreement signed at Munich did nothing to ensure a lasting peace. In giving in to Hitler's demands, the Allies only delayed the inevitable for another year. Sensing this, William Shirer had only scorn for the British and French leaders. He left the conference feeling even more disillusioned, downcast, and angry. He was convinced the German military still was not yet ready to fight another war, and yet the Allies had meekly given Hitler everything he demanded. Shirer could only shake his head in disbelief and applaud from afar when Winston Churchill, "the lone, unheeded prophet," rose in the British House of Commons to denounce the Munich Agreement as "a total, unmitigated defeat" for Britain and France.[12]

Shirer had another, far more personal, reason to feel sullen. He had suffered a huge embarrassment in Munich when yet again he was outmaneuvered by NBC's Max Jordan, who had obtained a copy of the final text of the agreement an hour before any of his competitors. Shirer attributed Jordan's success to "his company's special position in Germany," which had enabled him to gain "exclusive use of Hitler's radio station in the *Führerhaus*, where the conference was taking place" and to having posed as a German official.[13] The truth was that Jordan's success was due to his own ingenuity rather than to any deception or sweetheart arrangement that NBC enjoyed with the German broadcasting service.[14]

Jordan was on the air reporting his exclusive while Shirer and his colleagues cooled their heels at the broadcast center as they waited for delivery of their official copies of the conference communiqué. In Shirer's own mind, getting scooped was an unforgettable lapse on his part, a shortcoming for which his former employer, Colonel McCormick of the *Chicago Tribune*, would have sacked him on the spot. Adding insult to injury, Shirer later learned that he had missed the details of yet another development in Munich. Before departing for home British Prime Minister Neville Chamberlain had visited Hitler one last time to get his signature on an agreement pledging that Germany and Britain would negotiate their way around any future disagreements and would never go to war against one another. While the document proved to be not worth the paper it was printed on, Chamberlain made much of it at the time; upon his arrival in London, he stood on the balcony at 10 Downing Street and waved the paper above head, declaring he had secured "peace with honor ... peace in our time."

If Ed Murrow is to be believed, CBS officials were unconcerned that Max Jordan had beaten Shirer on coverage of the news out of Munich. "There is neither criticism nor blame in connection with our being whipped at

Munich," he advised Shirer. "Don't take it too seriously because I don't and things change pretty fast."[15] Shirer accepted Murrow's reassurance. In his diary and in private conversations, he downplayed the disappointments and embarrassments he had suffered, particularly the details of how Max Jordan had "scooped him" on the wording of the final agreement. Shirer was gracious in conceding this and even offered a grudging praise to Jordan in a September 1940 article for *Atlantic Monthly*.[16] However, in later years Shirer refused to accept – or was it to believe? – that Jordan's triumph was the fruit of his pluck and a bit of luck.

Ultimately, as Ed Murrow noted, Jordan's ingenuity and the precise wording of the formal document signed at Munich did not count for much. Far more significant was the accord's immediate impact. In London, Murrow ended his broadcast on the night of 30 September observing that "At this critical juncture the Czech government is placing the interest of civilization and world peace before the distress of its own peoples and is resolved to make sacrifices which never in history were expected from an undefeated state."[17]

That story is what Shirer set off to report next. After a hasty departure from Munich aboard the overnight train to Regensburg, he traveled by bus to the town of Passau, on the Austrian-Czech border. There he embedded himself with the German troops who were "picnic marching" into the Sudetenland. Because he was riding in a German military vehicle, Shirer had no way of doing a broadcast; he instead cabled his reports to New York. It was not until he was back in Berlin that Shirer again was able to take to the airwaves to report what he had seen and heard. By then, it was clear that the threat of war in Europe had abated, for now.

As the world breathed a collective sigh of relief, the level of tension dropped. In America, public interest in the Sudeten crisis evaporated as quickly as it had developed. When Shirer called from Berlin on the evening of 2 October to report that German military censors were willing to let him resume broadcasting, Paul White told him there was no need to do so: "Forget it. Take a rest." Ordinarily, Shirer would have been angered to receive such an order, not now. He was tired and depressed. He'd had enough: "Can stand some sleep ... and a change from these Germans, so truculent and impossible now."[18]

Broadcast historian Elizabeth McLeod notes, "Coverage of the Czech crisis is considered the defining moment of broadcast news in the 1930s."[19] She also points out that, with the passing of time and in the shadow of Ed Murrow's reputation as a broadcasting legend, the details of how the two major networks covered the story are largely forgotten. Both CBS and NBC had provided round-the-clock coverage. The anchor for the NBC broadcasts was veteran announcer Lowell Thomas with Fred Bate, Max Jordan, and various newspaper journalists reporting from overseas. According to McLeod, in the nineteen days between 10 September and 29 September, NBC's team made 147 shortwave broadcasts, while Murrow, Shirer, and their CBS colleagues made 151.[20]

NBC enjoyed the edge in the technical quality of its offerings, and there is no question that its on-air talent was inventive, energetic, and dedicated. However, leaving aside Max Jordan's scoop at Munich, listeners across North America preferred CBS's coverage. As Cloud and Olson note, "There was no question that overall CBS had outshone NBC, not to mention the other, smaller network, Mutual."[21] There were several reasons.

CBS's competitive edge came in the quality of the reporting done by its two brightest stars: Murrow and Shirer. Murrow took to the airwaves thirty-five times during the crisis, reporting the latest developments from London or Paris and interviewing newsmakers who provided commentary and vital context. At the same time, Shirer did dozens of broadcasts and logged thousands of miles as he shuttled back and forth between Prague and Berlin or visited Munich, the Sudetenland, and the other places where the news was being made. Together, he and Murrow took part in fourteen European roundup broadcasts.

"As the *Anschluss* crisis established the European and later the 'world news roundup,' with separate reports from several cities abroad, so the Munich crisis established the news round table, in which correspondents in four or more cities, linked together by shortwave circuits and land lines could carry on a spontaneous continuing conversation, instead of reading from separate scripts," Alexander Kendrick notes. "Thus questions could be raised from the United States which had not occurred to those in Europe, and could be answered."[22]

The entire CBS news team – the on-air personalities, technicians, and network executives – gained in experience and confidence with each broadcast. In the past, when the unexpected happened or atmospheric conditions prevented a European shortwave broadcast from reaching New York, an announcer in the network studios had been left to fill the dead air by adlibbing, or else technicians had resorted to the time-honored practice of interjecting a "musical interlude." No more. When a signal was unavailable, CBS engineers now were ready to change direction on the fly. If Shirer's broadcast from Berlin was not available, Murrow was standing by in London to fill in, or vice versa. If Shirer, Murrow, or one of the network's stringers were not on the line, Kaltenborn stepped into the breach without listeners ever being aware this was not the plan. The process of broadcasting the overseas news was quickly becoming seamless, or at least as seamless as it could ever be in the era of shortwave reports and live radio.

The senior CBS management team, Paul White and Fred Klauber in particular, played vital roles in making all this happen. They provided the necessary resources – the cost was high for cables, transatlantic telephone calls, shortwave broadcasts, and all of the ancillary needs – and helped to foster a working environment in which excellence in all aspects of news coverage was not only encouraged, but demanded.[23] This approach fostered the kind of creative thinking that continued to push the envelope. Even Ed Murrow's peers at the venerable BBC admired the work he and Shirer were doing. CBS was building its reputation as a world leader in broadcast journalism, raising the bar for radio news coverage and ensuring American pre-eminence. The CBS network was unsurpassed in terms of the rigor with which stories were covered and in the creativity that went into its news broadcasts. "The CBS reporters ... gave their words a dramatic resonance lacking in the thin, clipped voices of Jordan and Bate. Critics in the United State noticed this and lauded the CBS effort while giving passing mention to the NBC reporters," writes Elizabeth McLeod.[24]

The perception that CBS's news coverage was without peer was furthered by the efforts of the network's publicity department, which went into overdrive to promote its on-air personalities as being larger-than-life characters. To a considerable extent, this was true. Hans Kaltenborn, authoritative, multilingual, knowledgeable, and tireless, was the ideal news anchor. In the field, Murrow and Shirer were a superb reporting team; their talents and temperaments complemented one another perfectly at this stage in each of their careers. The two men grew together, each in his own way, and in the process they helped to change the way Americans got and consumed news. In the December 1938 issue of *Scribner's Magazine*, Robert Landry turned the spotlight on the changing nature of the media and in particular Murrow's role in that process.[25] CBS's "man in London" Murrow fast was emerging as the preeminent news broadcaster of his generation.

Listening to the scratchy recordings of Murrow's voice from this period, what is now most striking is the theatricality of his delivery. To modern ears, his voice sounds stilted and artificial. However, that style appealed to audiences of the day, and there is no mistaking that Murrow was a natural broadcaster. His diction was impeccable. His sense of pacing was incomparable, his delivery smooth as silk, and his gift for simplifying and humanizing complex events was unsurpassed. Murrow had no formal training as a journalist, but with Shirer's help and guidance, he was honing his reporting skills and becoming a first-rate newsman.

Shirer was not in Murrow's league when it came to on-air performance or presence; of that, there is no question. Yet there were few, if any, foreign correspondents working in Europe in 1938 – American or other – who could match Shirer's depth of knowledge, contacts, linguistic talent, or journalistic skills. Nonetheless, given his reedy Midwestern twang and the initial tentativeness in his delivery, CBS never would have hired him had not been for Ed Murrow's perseverance in making it happen. It was also Murrow who helped Shirer refine his on-air technique to the point where he was more than competent in his role as a broadcaster.

Just as the internet has today all but displaced both print and conventional broadcasting as North America's preferred source of information and entertainment, radio eclipsed print in the late 1930s. In the last three weeks of September 1938, with tensions in Europe escalating, millions of listeners in the United States and Canada turned to radio as their main source of news. As A.M. Sperber notes, "At the workaday level, [a new] force was emerging: the radio correspondent, uniting in one person the functions of news gatherer, writer, and broadcaster, neither a commentator nor a news reader, but a staff reporter – a figure new to communications."[26]

For CBS, Ed Murrow and Bill Shirer were those figures, and both had become celebrities. William Paley understood that. "Columbia's coverage of the European crisis is superior to competitors, and probably the best job ever done in radio broadcasting," he told Murrow in an effusive congratulatory cable.[27]

18

The Gathering Clouds of War

In the wake of the Munich crisis, William Shirer again began to question the trajectories of his career and personal life. He and Ed Murrow had become two of America's most popular and influential radio personalities, but Shirer was painfully aware that his newfound celebrity had come at a steep price: "My job in radio was now keeping me on the road most of the time ... I loved the work, though I did wish I could be with my family more, especially now that we had a young child. When did family life start? I was 35. But one had to face it: a roving correspondent over these last years of crisis in Europe had little personal life."[1]

Shirer's mood reflected his profound sense of loss and foreboding. For the first time in his career, he was too downcast to work. Ed Murrow empathized. Like Shirer, he was prone to bouts of depression, and his mood was now dark. Murrow and Shirer decided to meet for a weekend in Paris. Ostensibly they were there to talk business, in particular the need for CBS to hire more full-time staff in Europe. But their real intent was to commiserate and to "drown our sorrows in champagne."[2]

Neither man had any enthusiasm for discussing work-related issues when they arrived in the French capital on 8 October. The two longed to recapture some of the joie de vivre they had experienced on previous visits to Paris, which had always been one of Shirer's favorites cities. However, he now found Paris a "frightful place, completely surrendered to defeatism with no inkling of what has happened to France."[3]

CBS's star correspondents stayed up late two nights running. They talked endlessly, downing bottle after bottle of champagne as they wandered the Paris streets, trekking from one old haunt to the next. Try though they did, they could not shake the sense that the world as they had known it was forever changed. Their conversation kept returning to the European political situation and to the slim prospects for a lasting peace. Shirer wrote in his diary, "We agree on these things: that war is more probable now than ever, that it is likely to come after the next harvest, [and] that Poland is next on Hitler's list."[4]

With the weekend done, Murrow returned to London to pack for a trip to New York and a scheduled meeting with the Paley, White, and Klauber. The CBS management team were planning to discuss the network's coverage of another European war that now seemed inevitable. Shirer returned to an empty flat in Geneva, since Tess, Eileen, and the Swiss nanny were still away. Alone, he passed the time by learning to play golf, and he began to write a stage play, a cathartic work with the working title *The Foreign Correspondent*.

It took a couple of weeks of downtime for Shirer to recharge his batteries and get back to work in a serious way. Whenever possible, he was now traveling by air on long trips, and so after flying visits to Warsaw, Brussels, and Belgrade, he flew to Rome, where eighty-one-year-old Pope Pius XI was moribund after suffering a heart attack. Paul White, sensing yet another opportunity to show off CBS's newfound prowess in reporting the breaking news from Europe, was eager to ensure the network would have timely coverage of the drama that was unfolding at the Vatican. However, the Pope did not die, not yet anyway, and so with other business to tend to, Shirer hastened to Paris to greet his family upon their return from the States. The reunion was not entirely a happy one, for Tess's trip had been an exercise in frustration.

She, Eileen, and the nanny had enjoyed a three-month stay with John Shirer and his German-born wife, Erna, at their home in Virginia. Tess's frustrations had come about because she had spent so much time dealing with the bureaucratic red tape involved in her struggle to win American citizenship for herself and the baby. Because she had been married to an American citizen for more than five years, Tess hoped that she would qualify for citizenship. When Immigration and Naturalization Service bureaucrats rejected her application, she appealed to a Federal Court. The process was complicated and expensive. With her visitor's visa due to expire in mid-December, Tess was obliged to return to Geneva and from there pursue her citizenship application. As a result, the family had Christmas together, and for the first time since the March 1932 mishap in which he had lost the sight in his right eye William Shirer ventured onto the ski slopes at the Swiss alpine resort at Gstaad. Even in this storybook setting, Tess Shirer brooded about her stalled bid for American citizenship, while her husband remained downcast about the looming shadow of war: "The wealthy English and French [are] here in force and inanely oblivious of

Europe's state … Last night at the big Christmas ball I found the merry-makers so nauseating that we left early."[5]

In the opening weeks of 1939, it seemed to Shirer that all of his worst fears were coming true. With the pace of events quickening in Europe, political developments grew ever more ominous. Winston Churchill commented that it was as if everyone on the continent was aboard a runaway train speeding toward a precipice; such was the inevitability of war.

In New York, Ed Murrow was no less gloomy or fearful. When he met with his bosses at CBS, Murrow explained that his volume of work was fast becoming overwhelming. Ed Klauber's response was to suggest that Murrow employ an assistant, an idea he readily embraced. Murrow was eager to find someone with character, intelligence, and a flair for reporting events in the vivid language that would appeal to a diverse audience. With that in mind, he hired thirty-year-old Yale grad Thomas Grandin as the network's new man in Paris. Grandin had made a positive impression when he did some work for Murrow during the Sudeten crisis.

Like Shirer, Grandin was cerebral, soft-spoken, and prior to signing on with CBS had zero broadcasting or journalism training. Apart from their initial lack of on-air experience, Grandin and Shirer had something else in common: neither had a "natural" radio voice. Paul White complained that Grandin spoke too softly and that his voice was not "manly enough." However, White's opposition to Murrow's hiring of Grandin and the ensuing clash of egos only served to stiffen Murrow's resolve to add Grandin to his team. Murrow pressed ahead and prevailed because as CBS's brightest star he had both the ear and the confidence of William Paley. As another of Murrow's hires once noted, "[Ed] was always fighting New York on this business of voice and enunciation. He loved to throw it in their faces."[6]

"Murrow's boys," as Cloud and Olson dubbed them,[7] sat down together for the first time in early February 1939 in Paris. They were still in the midst of sorting out job responsibilities and logistical arrangements when word came from Rome that the health of Pope Pius XI had taken a marked turn for the worse, and his death now appeared imminent. This news put a hasty end to the Murrow boys' meeting. Although he was ill with flu, Shirer set off for Rome. The pontiff's death would be a major news story, and so CBS and NBC were scrambling to outdo one another in their coverage of the funeral and of the election of his successor.

Shirer, who was intent on atoning for his failures in Munich, was determined to get the story right in Rome. Because he was unfamiliar with the arcane world of Vatican politics and the rituals of papal succession, he recruited an American-born priest named Father John Delaney to help him explain and interpret the latest developments. Together, Shirer and Delaney did thirty-eight broadcasts, totaling more than twelve hours on air. However, the six-hour time difference between New York and Rome proved problematic.

When the pope's death was announced in Rome on 10 February, it was 4:30 a.m. local time. That was 10:30 p.m. New York time, too late in the day for CBS staff to set up a live shortwave broadcast. Owing to Max Jordan's foresight, rival NBC had made all of the necessary arrangements in advance. Thus, the network's Rome reporter was on the air with a news bulletin thirty-one minutes after the pope's death: "It seems hardboiled to talk of 'firsts' in connection with this solemn drama, but it is a matter of record that we got the news out first."[8] CBS was scooped yet again.

The American networks' self-imposed ban on the use of recordings in news broadcasting gave rise to another problem for Shirer, and for all reporters in the field since it increased the opportunities for embarrassing errors and unscripted moments. The latter happened during preparations for Pope Pius XI's funeral. When workmen ran out of solder to seal the Pontiff's casket, work was halted while they went off to find more. CBS commentator Delaney, who had the misfortune to be on air at the time, had no choice but to ad lib for two very long hours.

On other occasions, the fact that news reports were broadcast live and in "real time" proved serendipitous. That was the case on 2 March. Delaney had the good fortune again to be on air when word came that the College of Cardinals had elected Cardinal Eugenio Pacelli as the new pope, Pius XII. This was a watershed moment in Vatican history, the first time in the 1,900-year history of the papacy that such news was made known to the world as it happened. Gloating CBS publicity staff trumpeted that fact.

However, the ecclesiastical news out of Rome was but a prelude to the real developing story in Europe, which continued to be the rush to war. Thus, once his work in Rome was done, Shirer hastened to London for yet another meeting with Murrow. According to A.M. Sperber, Janet Murrow, who was becoming increasingly concerned about her husband's ill health, protested when Shirer and Murrow, both of them still suffering with flu, stayed up late drinking and talking. "Something ... disturbing was emerging in the patterns of [his] life-style: that of wearing himself out, then using doctors as palliatives,"[9] Sperber notes. In that regard, Murrow and Shirer were birds of a feather, workaholics driven by a relentless sense of duty to alert America to the dangerous situation that was developing in Europe. There was much to report.

Emboldened by his recent successes, Hitler remained intent on wiping Czechoslovakia from the map, and by mid-March he had succeeded. "Should go to Prague, but I haven't the heart," Shirer wrote in his diary. "Am I growing too soft-hearted, too sentimental to be a good reporter?"[10]

The run of depressing news continued two weeks later, when General Francisco Franco's fascist army claimed victory in the Spanish civil war. After five years of fighting that left more than 750,000 dead, the Republicans surrendered unconditionally. Franco, backed by military support from both Germany and Italy, now held the country in an iron grip. Having fond memories from nine months in 1933 that he and Tess had lived in Spain, Shirer felt a yet another profound sense of personal loss when he heard news of this development. The brevity of his diary entry for 29 March 1939 reflected his grim mood: "Madrid surrendered yesterday, the rest of republican Spain today ... There are no words to express what I feel tonight. Franco's butchery will be terrible."[11] Shirer was correct when he predicted there were still more ominous developments to come.

William Shirer stood among a cheering crowd two million strong who on 20 April jammed the streets of Berlin to view an awe-inspiring parade of Nazi military might. The day, Hitler's fiftieth birthday, was a national holiday. In that night's broadcast Shirer reported, "Today's parade of the cream of the new German army must certainly have been the greatest display of military power that modern Europe has ever seen."[12]

The looming shadow of the Third Reich was now dominating every aspect of Shirer's work. He had come to understand a fundamental truth that every journalist who works in a totalitarian state is obliged to accept: what is left unsaid in a news report is as important as what *is* said.

Tempting though it was to speculate on Hitler's military plans, Shirer ventured few opinions, even when he was outside of Germany: "I had to keep in mind that whatever I said abroad about the Third Reich and its imperious leader quickly got back to Berlin and that if Hitler and Goebbels disapproved too strongly, they might not let me return."[13]

Circumspect though Shirer and his colleagues were in their reporting, Nazi propaganda chief Josef Goebbels was irate over what he regarded as anti-German comments made by the announcers who read newscasts on the American radio networks. As Shirer had cautioned in a May 1938 letter to Paul White, Nazi agents in cities all across North America were tuning in to domestic radio broadcasts and sending reports back to Berlin.[14] Unless CBS and NBC tightened controls over what newscasters were saying, Goebbels was intent on curbing the activities of the Berlin correspondents of both networks; as a warning, he limited Shirer and Max Jordan's use of German state broadcasting facilities and denied CBS and NBC access to the live feed of an important speech by Adolf Hitler; only the Mutual Broadcasting network would be allowed to air the broadcast. However, when both of America's main networks refused to agree to Goebbels's demands, he relented. The propaganda benefits of having Hitler's message heard by a large American audience were too attractive to pass up.

Despite the warning signs, William Shirer still desperately *wanted* to cling to the hope that a way could be found to avoid war; "If I had known what Hitler would tell his generals in the greatest of secrecy [in spring 1939], and if I had learned of the direction a new wind was beginning to blow in Moscow, I would not have entertained such illusions."[15]

What the Nazi leader confided to his generals was that war was inevitable, and so he ordered them to begin planning in earnest. Poland, he insisted, would be attacked at the first good opportunity. In order to ensure this would not immediately draw Russia into the fray, Hitler instructed Foreign Minister von Ribbentrop to engage in secret negotiations with the Soviet Union for a non-aggression treaty. This would serve Hitler's ends until he had dealt with Poland and forced Britain and France to the sidelines.

With all this behind-the-scenes jockeying underway and the German habit of gearing-down during the summer months, Hitler retreated to his Bavarian Alpine chalet in late May for a holiday. A deceptive calm settled over Berlin and indeed all of Europe. Shirer took advantage of the lull to make a four-week trip home to the States. Tess and Eileen had returned to Virginia to press their case for American citizenship, and Shirer joined them there. He also planned to visit friends in New York and to meet with his bosses at CBS, for whom he had worked for almost two years but never met.

Shirer sailed from Liverpool on 7 June aboard the Cunard liner RMS *Mauretania*, which was on its maiden voyage. Shirer's spirits on the voyage home were lifted by good news he had received: a telegram from Tess informed him that her Federal Court appeal had been successful; she and Eileen – whom the family had taken to calling Inga – had won their American citizenships. Thus, it was an especially joyous celebration when the Shirer family gathered at John Shirer's home in McLean, Virginia. Older sister Josephine arrived from New York, where she was now teaching high school, and the family matriarch, Bessie Shirer, traveled by train from Cedar Rapids. Now sixty-eight, she continued to follow her elder son's broadcasting career, tuning into his news reports on the local CBS affiliate.

Bessie was delighted finally to meet Tess and to hold her first grand-child. However, she struggled to understand why Inga, who was now two, spoke no English. The reason was simple: in Geneva, Tess and Bill Shirer conversed in French, the first language of Inga's Swiss nanny. Happily, Bessie Shirer's puzzlement at this realization did not lessen the joy of the moment. This was the first and only time the whole family were together.

Reunited with his family, Shirer was understandably upbeat when he sat down with his CBS bosses in New York the last week of June. The Great Depression still had America in its grip, and at least 10 million people remained unemployed, yet Shirer saw signs of a return to better days. For one thing, the fortunes of CBS were on the rise. These were heady times for the network, which was making huge strides in catching rival NBC as America's most listened to – and profitable – broadcaster. NBC was still number 1 on the strength of its entertainment programming; however, the popularity of CBS's news broadcasts was eroding that primacy. In no small measure, this was due to the splendid work Shirer and Murrow were doing in Europe.

In the circumstances, William Paley and Ed Klauber rolled out the red carpet when Shirer came calling; news director Paul White was in London visiting Ed Murrow, and so it would be another week before Shirer and White met. Having been briefed by Ed Murrow on the corporate political situation in New York, Shirer understood the tangled relationships among the CBS senior management team. He quickly surmised that William Paley, whose word was final, grasped the importance of news and regarded this element of CBS's programming as being essential to the success of his network. Shirer found Paley approachable and friendly, something that changed for the worse as CBS grew and its management hierarchy became more rigid.

Ed Klauber was a different case entirely. Shirer found the CBS vice-president to be "dour, difficult and inclined to be autocratic, even tyranni-cal."[16] However, after spending some time with him and having a lengthy chat as they strolled the grounds at Klauber's country home, Shirer rec-ognized that Klauber was a seasoned journalist and a perfectionist with a solid understanding of radio and of its role as a news medium; in Shirer's mind this gave CBS an advantage over the competition. Years later, he explained to broadcast historian David Hosley, "There was no journalist over at NBC [in senior management] at that time. And Klauber made all the difference in the world because he had been an important journalist for *The New York Times*. It was a lucky break for Paley, and for CBS and for [Murrow and myself]."[17] Shirer realized that Klauber could be a powerful ally and a counterbalance to Paul White, who was inclined to a micro-manage and delve into areas in which he had no expertise.

Shirer left New York feeling good about the men heading CBS, but he was far less sanguine about the attitude of other Americans with whom he talked. Many of his journalist friends and colleagues felt certain there would be no war in Europe. A majority of the politicians in Washington held the same opinion; knowing this, Shirer decided the American government was "in a hopeless muddle, dominated by [politicians] who stood for no foreign policy at all."[18] Despite his concerns about Hitler's intentions, President Roosevelt was in no position to intervene, for he faced a hostile Congress that remained strongly isolationist. Shirer understood this, and so in conversations with Tess and with close friends, he poured out his frustrations about the situation. He could neither fathom nor accept the insularity of the American people at a time when so much of the world was looking to Washington for leadership and reassurance. Shirer's disillusionment in this regard was not new. He had felt the same way on his previous visit home, four years earlier. However, this time his feelings were even more pronounced: "I felt lost ... It is depressing and bewildering to feel yourself a stranger in your native land. It was now exactly fourteen years since I had gone abroad at twenty-one, and I had been back twice, both times briefly, in 1929 and 1935. Europe had become my home ... Where were we Americans going? No one knew. We were racing hell-bent to somewhere. That, to most people, seemed enough."[19]

The Shirers returned to Europe aboard the *Queen Mary*, sailing from New York on 5 July 1939. The voyage was smooth and uneventful, but memorable nonetheless. This was one of the few times since the birth of Inga that the family was united for an extended period. Tess and Bill Shirer spent time strolling the deck of the ship and socializing in the first-class lounge, where they played ping pong, a favorite pastime since their years in Vienna. In the evenings, they chatted with other passengers. Among them were the American singer Paul Robeson, whom Shirer had not seen since they had met in London in 1929, and the Soviet ambassador to Washington, a gruff diplomat named Constantine Oumansky. When the latter mentioned that he had been visiting some American students in the third-class passenger area to "enlighten them on the virtues of Soviet democracy," Robeson nodded in agreement.

Like many liberals and left-leaning Western intellectuals and artists in the 1930s, the singer was an unabashed admirer of Soviet Communism. Robeson joined Oumansky in trumpeting "Mother Russia's" opposition to fascism; Britain and France were the real villains in Europe, they insisted, for both countries were intent on isolating the Soviet Union and pushing Stalin into a war with Nazi Germany. (Of course, Ambassador Oumansky was careful to reveal nothing about secret negotiations for a non-aggression treaty between Russia and Germany.) Shirer did not believe such pronouncements any more than he accepted claims about the virtues of Stalinism, and he said so. Shirer had never visited the Soviet Union – he had been denied an entry visa each time he had applied – but he *had* talked with his friend Joe Barnes about life there. The *Herald Tribune*'s Berlin correspondent was fluent in Russian, having spent several years posted to Moscow. Barnes's view of life in the "great Socialist paradise" was far less rosy than that being described by Oumansky and Robeson. Not surprisingly, Shirer had had quite enough of the two by the time the Queen Mary reached England.

Once he was back in London, Shirer attended another meeting of the Murrow boys. Paul White was still in town, and the CBS news director took part in planning sessions and in discussions about the need for more staff. Competition in the radio news field was heating up. The upstart Mutual Broadcasting Company had joined the fray in earnest. Although resources at America's number 3 network were limited, it could now call upon a team of freelance correspondents in the capitals of Europe.

Rival NBC was taking a different approach to its news coverage from the continent. The network's senior management, still entertainment-oriented and acutely cost conscious, was not yet convinced of the value of news as a tool to build ratings or advertising revenues. NBC president Lenox Lohr was still struggling to decide the extent and nature of the network's informational programming. News director Abel Schechter, ever competitive, had added a third man to his overseas reporting staff, hiring Paul Archinard as the network's Paris correspondent. Fred Bate remained in London, while Max Jordan continued to roam Europe. However, that was the extent of NBC's operation, for now.

Seizing the moment, CBS opted to expand its news coverage and to hire new staff. The network's investment in news-gathering proved to be money well spent: it represented another step toward solidifying CBS's growing reputation as America's leader in radio news.

It was during the London deliberations that helped bring this about that Shirer finally had the opportunity to meet and assess Paul White. When he did, his preconceptions were confirmed. Shirer decided that White was not someone who could ever be his friend, nor was White the right man for the job. In part, this was because of his prickly personality;

however, even more limiting were what Shirer regarded as White's parochialism and his "old school" approach to journalism. Like those print journalists who are adrift in today's expanding online media universe, White was struggling to come to grips with changing technology and evolving consumer tastes. Shirer recognized that Ed Murrow was light years ahead in this regard, and so he accepted Murrow's advice, which was to get along with White and bide his time. For now.

Many later years, after his own falling out with Murrow, Shirer was forgiving in his assessment of White: "Like most American newspapermen who had never worked abroad, he was somewhat ignorant of Europe, and he could be occasionally a little insensitive to our problems of handling the news from there ... But on the whole I found him very supportive."[20] Indeed, White responded favorably when Murrow asked for the money to add news staff.

Acting on Shirer's suggestion, Murrow hired Arnold Eric Sevareid, yet another of the young men from the American Midwest who had traveled to Europe in the interwar years seeking adventure and work. Sevareid, twenty-six years old, had taken graduate courses at the London School of Economics and at the Alliance Française in Paris. Sevareid and Murrow, eight years his elder, had hit it off at first meeting. Thus, when the opportunity arose to add someone to his team, Murrow offered Sevareid a job.

The same eloquence and penchant for speaking the truth that might have held Sevareid back as a print journalist made him ideally suited to be a news broadcaster. He remained eternally grateful and loyal to Murrow for hiring him as one of what he always remembered as the "lucky young band of brothers" who worked for CBS in Europe in the golden years of radio news, during the Second World War.[21]

Although Sevareid would always consider himself to be a writer first and a broadcaster second, his hiring was yet another example of Murrow's knack for spotting talent. Like Shirer and Grandin, Sevareid was nervous to the point of being ill when he auditioned. Predictably, Paul White advised Murrow *not* to hire Sevareid. However, Murrow went ahead anyway, retaining Sevareid as Thomas Grandin's assistant (and eventual successor) in Paris. Sevareid, who became a Murrow friend and staunch loyalist, remained with CBS for thirty-eight years. After starting out in radio, he made a successful transition to television. Over the course of his long and distinguished career with the network, Sevareid earned a reputation as being one of the most gifted, literate, incisive, and well-respected American broadcast journalists of his era; in his silver-haired years, admirers referred to him as "the Gray Eminence."

Just as Shirer had been the ideal man for the job in 1937, Sevareid was an inspired choice to join the CBS team in Europe in summer 1939. Despite the thirteen-year age gap between them, Sevareid and Shirer became friends ever after.

Following his return to Geneva, Shirer welcomed the opportunity to spend downtime with Tess and Inga and to entertain visitors. Among them were Marcel Fodor and John Gunther, who dropped by. Gunther was riding high on the success of his new book, *Inside Asia*. While Shirer was happy for his friend's good fortune, he was also envious.

Over several bottles of wine, Shirer, Gunther, and Fodor debated the likelihood of war in Europe, a favorite topic. Gunther and Fodor remained optimistic about the prospects for peace; Shirer was pessimistic. The debate in Geneva settled nothing, and so Shirer and Gunther continued it a couple of weeks later, when they met on 11 August in the Polish port city of Danzig. Shirer was there to report on the growing tensions in the city that was at the heart of Hitler's demands in his territorial dispute with Poland. Gunther was in Danzig gathering material for a planned series of radio broadcasts. The two men idled away the afternoon on the pier at the Baltic seaside resort of Zoppot then passed the evening playing roulette at a local casino. Afterward, they adjourned to the bar where they drank and talked "a blue streak, settling the world's problems."[22]

Shirer and Gunther were now agreed that Europe's political crisis had passed the fail-safe point, and the last-ditch diplomacy that was taking place between Germany, France, and Great Britain was a delaying tactic rather than a serious bid to resolve the impasse. The grim reality was that there was no way out. Hitler was intent on having his way in Poland, and as he continued to escalate his demands it clearly was less a question now of *whether* he would strike than of *when*. Tensions in Europe rose another notch with each passing day.

We now know that Hitler spent the last two weeks of August agonizing over the timing of his order to attack Poland. However, as the world was about to learn, the German military was primed and ready to strike. Hitler's generals had drawn up plans for something they called "Blitzkrieg" – "lightning war," a high-speed, high-tech battle strategy the likes of which had never before been seen. The First World War was the first conflict in which armies employed twentieth-century technology to strip war of its last vestiges of romanticism and transform the battlefield into a human meat grinder. The war the German army was about to launch in late summer 1939 would be the first to marry this technology with the kind of assembly-line efficiency that made possible slaughter on an apocalyptic scale.

Shirer was in Berlin the last week of August to report on the mood there and to greet CBS news anchorman Hans Kaltenborn, who was touring Europe. In the wake of his on-air performance during the Munich crisis, Kaltenborn's popularity had grown to the point that he now had his own nightly commentary program on CBS. Unfortunately for Kaltenborn, Nazi officials were well aware of him. Shirer had received an initial affirmative reply when he asked his contacts at the Propaganda Ministry if the CBS commentator would be allowed into Germany. Regardless, Kaltenborn was denied entry when his plane landed at the Berlin airport. When Shirer raised an angry fuss, Nazi officials allowed Kaltenborn off the plane long, but only long enough to have for a drink with Shirer and Mrs Kaltenborn, who was German-born and had been in Berlin visiting family.

In the end, Hans Kaltenborn was turned away from Germany on the excuse that he had made unflattering comments about Hitler in a broadcast two months earlier. In retrospect, it is likely that Goebbels reversed the earlier decision to let the CBS news commentator into the country because of an announcement scheduled for later that same day: Germany and the Soviet Union had signed a non-aggression pact. News of that surprise agreement hit like a bombshell. The mood was somber at the Ristorante Italiano, where Shirer and his colleagues gathered each evening, but the German journalists there were "gloating, sputtering that Britain won't dare to fight now, denying everything they have been told to say those last six years by their Nazi lords."[23]

When he and Joe Barnes got into an argument with some Germans, the exchanges grew heated, so much so that the two Americans wisely decided to leave before the dispute turned violent. Shirer and Barnes, feeling agitated and deflated, walked and talked until almost dawn. When finally Shirer returned to his room at the Adlon Hotel, he looked out his window to see workmen erecting an anti-aircraft gun on the roof of the same building where other workmen had dismantled a similar weapon the previous autumn.

The shuttle diplomacy between London and Berlin continued all that week, with British Prime Minister Chamberlain traveling back and forth in a last-ditch effort to avoid the war that now seemed inevitable. The feeling was growing on all sides that there was no way out. By 25 August, the German government had severed radio, telephone, and cable communications with the outside world, and wartime rationing were already in effect. In his 26 August broadcast from Berlin, Shirer somberly declared,

"I don't know whether we're going to have war or not. But I can tell you that in Berlin tonight the feeling is that it will be war unless Germany's demands against Poland are fulfilled."[24]

The Poles held firm; on 30 August, the Warsaw government mobilized its army. Hitler responded by announcing he had formed a war cabinet to be chaired by Göring. Despite these ominous developments – underscoring Shirer's comment that Paul White still did not understand the gravity of the situation – the CBS news director sent word from New York that he wanted Murrow and Shirer to arrange a program of dance music from London, Paris, and Hamburg. Incensed by this, Murrow angrily told White it was insane to pretend all was well in Europe when the continent was on the brink of war.

From their posts in London and Berlin, Murrow and Shirer took to the airwaves three or four times each day to update CBS listeners on the latest news. At 2:40 a.m. on the morning of 31 August – 8:40 p.m. New York time – Shirer took to the airwaves to report that while the situation in Berlin remained tense and everyone knew "the showdown" was fast approaching, an ominous quiet had descended upon the city. "Tonight the great armies, navies, and air forces are all mobilized. Each country is shut off from the other," Shirer wrote in his diary.[25]

It was about 3:30 a.m. – 9:30 p.m. New York time – when Shirer returned to his hotel room once more and tumbled into bed. Within moments was fast asleep. It had been yet another exhausting eighteen-hour day.

Shirer was dead to the world when the telephone rang at about 6 a.m. It was still dark outside, and Shirer groggily fumbled for his bedside telephone. It was his friend and former *Chicago Tribune* colleague Sigrid Schultz calling. "It's happened," she announced. "The German army has invaded Poland." The memory of that moment remained with Shirer the rest of his life: "I was very sleepy – my body and mind numbed, paralyzed … I mumbled: 'Thanks, Sigrid,' and tumbled out of bed. The war was on!"[26]

19

A Pandora's Box of Horrors

The moral battle lines between good and evil were drawn from the opening salvos of the Second World War. However, William Shirer found himself awash in conflicting emotions, dreading the coming bloodshed and devastation while also recognizing that Hitler was a madman who had to be stopped. On the night of 1 September, unable to sleep, Shirer tossed and turned in his bed as he contemplated the day's events: "I felt a burning resentment against Hitler for so irresponsibly and deviously plunging [Germany] and Poland, and no doubt the rest of Europe, into a war which ... would be much more murderous than the last."[1]

Where Shirer and many of his colleagues erred was in continuing to assume that when faced with the combined might of the Allies, Hitler would back down. If not, most observers felt Germany would be defeated in a short, bloody war. However, German officials assured Shirer on 5 September, five days into the conflict, that not a single shot had been fired there. As proof, Shirer and NBC's Max Jordan were invited to visit the French-German border to see for themselves and to make sound recordings, for future use in their broadcasts. "American networks won't permit [this]," Shirer lamented in his diary, "a pity because it is the only way radio can really cover the war ... I think we're throwing away a tremendous opportunity, though God knows I have no desire to die a burning death at the front."[2]

Shirer also knew how pointless any rush to report on the war in Europe would be. Given the prevailing mood of isolationism in Washington, American involvement in Europe's latest conflict was a possibility that Hitler and his henchmen had either overlooked or scornfully dismissed as being so unlikely as to be irrelevant. That was confirmed for Shirer when one evening, two months after the German invasion of Poland, he and a group of American journalists encountered Hermann Göring at a social function at the Soviet embassy. The head of the German air force was in a genial mood as he drank beer and puffed on a cigar. Göring, ever pompous, could not resist boasting about the successes of his Luftwaffe in Poland. Göring chuckled when Shirer asked if he was concerned about a recent decision by the American Congress to repeal the neutrality law that forbade the selling of American airplanes to other countries – Great Britain and France in particular. "I got the impression he had given the matter little thought ... Unlike Hitler and Goebbels and Himmler, Göring obviously had no dislike of us American correspondents, no matter what our country did. He could not take America seriously as a military power."[3]

Nonetheless, being cognizant of the value of radio as a propaganda tool, the Nazis persisted in their efforts to sway American public opinion. When a German U-boat sank the British passenger ship *Athenia* off the coast of the Hebrides mere hours after the outbreak of war, 28 Americans were among the 112 casualties. It was obvious who was responsible for the atrocity, yet German propaganda ministry officials denied it. They asserted that a British sub had sunk the ship in hopes of stoking anti-German sentiments in the United States.

Shirer saw through the German deception, of course. He did not accept the Nazis' explanation for the *Athenia*'s sinking and confided to colleagues how "lousy" he felt even having to dignify the German claims by even reporting them. However, although he was now working under the cloud of wartime censorship and had been warned by his bosses in New York not to allow his personal opinions to influence his reports, Shirer found it increasingly difficult to comply. He had resolved never to compromise his journalistic integrity, and now felt that he was operating perilously close to the line: "I think my usefulness [in Berlin] is about over."[4] He remembered a rule that he had laid down for himself when he had arrived in Nazi Germany five years earlier: He would remain in Berlin only as long as he could "fairly report" what was going on. Increasingly, he felt that no longer was possible.

William Paley at CBS, like his counterparts at NBC and Mutual, was aware of German and British efforts to control the media. The head men at all three networks were also feeling pressure from Washington to ensure that their on-air staff refrained from comments that implied the American government favored one side over the other in the European conflict. So strong was this imperative that on 8 September NBC and Mutual announced they were suspending their war news reports. Thus, by default CBS became the only American network reporting on the fighting.

However, Ed Klauber did issue a four-page memo to CBS's on-air news staff in which he stressed that the network "as an organization, has no editorial opinions about the war." Correspondents in the field were cautioned to take "a balanced and fair approach"; at the same time, "What news analysts are entitled to do and should do is to elucidate and illuminate the news out of common knowledge or special knowledge possessed by them or made available to them by this organization through its news sources."[5] As broadcast historian Ed Bliss points out, Klauber's memo became a historic document in news broadcasting. For the first time, it attempted to articulate the specifics of that time-honored, but nebulous (and ultimately unattainable), journalistic ideal of objectivity, which is really a synonym for fairness.

In his book *Now the News*, Ed Bliss presents an excellent summary and an analysis of the situation at the outbreak of war in Europe: for several months, there were relatively few opportunities for serious controversy about issues of objectivity or fairness where American journalists in Germany were concerned. As Shirer later recalled, "All through that autumn and the rest of 1939 the *Sitzkrieg*, the sit-down, phony *drôle-de-guerre* continued. There was some action at sea, but almost no fighting on land or in the air. When British planes ventured over Berlin, it was to drop not bombs, but rather leaflets, which were 'in bad German!'"[6]

By 27 September, with Hitler's conquest of Poland complete, an uneasy calm settled over Europe. An anxious world waited to see what would happen next. Even with rumors of renewed peace initiatives continuing to swirl, the German people settled in for the duration of what most people hoped would be a brief conflict. Despite this, rationing, nightly blackouts, shortages of consumer goods, relentless government propaganda, and Gestapo terrorism quickly became the realities of daily life in Berlin and other German cities.

Shirer once described his own routine in one of the CBS news roundup broadcasts that had become a daily feature of the network's schedule. Outlining his "typical workday" in Berlin – to insofar as he had one – he noted that his days began about 9 a.m. After scanning the city's morning newspapers and telephoning his sources in the various government ministries, if there was breaking news, he sat down to type the rough notes for his first broadcast of the day. That was at 2 p.m. Berlin time (8 a.m. in New York). However, before traveling the five miles from his apartment to the studios of the German broadcast service, his habit was to attend the daily noon-hour press conference at the Propaganda Ministry. There was a Foreign Office press conference at 1 p.m.; however, because he had to get to the broadcast center and deal with the censors prior to his afternoon report, Shirer relied on a helper, a genial Alsatian German who was suspiciously well-connected. Fearful that his helper was a Gestapo informant, Shirer was careful to double-check any information the man provided.

One of Shirer's British journalist friends, who had made a hasty departure from Berlin on the eve of the war, had asked Shirer to keep his car "while he was away." Having the beat-up old Ford at his disposal was convenient, but Shirer found that obtaining the necessary permits to buy gasoline was a challenge, especially since he refused to cozy up to Nazi officials as so many of the other foreign journalists were doing, accepting as favors everything from preferred foreign exchange rates to special food allowances and help to find housing. For rationing purposes, foreign journalists were classified as "heavy laborers." This meant they could collect double rations and could also import Danish butter, eggs, and bacon for personal use.

When things were going well militarily, Nazi officials tended to be reasonable, even cordial, in their dealings with foreign journalists. That was especially true where Americans were concerned. The German government operated what Shirer's colleague Howard K. Smith described as "a posh restaurant for the foreign press," and like Berlin's most best private eateries – where only high-ranking Nazi Party officials and military officers dined – these government-run dining rooms were not subject to rationing, at least not in the early years of the war.[7]

Shirer's afternoon routine was a repeat of his mornings: to prepare for his nightly broadcast, he read more newspapers, made more telephone calls, and when possible he met with trusted informants. The latter was an activity fraught with danger. Shirer's travel was restricted, and Gestapo agents routinely monitored his activities or did all they could to make him believe they were doing so. To be seen talking with the CBS man in Berlin was a perilous proposition for German citizens, unless the interview was pre-approved, and such permissions were not easily obtained.

It was even more difficult for Shirer to gain access to high-Nazi leaders. Hitler, himself, gave no interviews and was seldom seen in public, apart from his occasional speeches in the Reichstag. Asked by his CBS bosses "to broadcast a [word] picture of Hitler at work," Shirer made numerous inquiries. His best efforts yielded but a few trivial details about the Nazi dictator's workaday routine; one of the most intriguing bits of information was the fact Hitler enjoyed American movies; the romantic comedy *It Happened One Night* – the winner of the Best Picture Oscar in 1934 – reportedly was one of his favorites.

Despite the tight grip of government control, Shirer was endlessly resourceful and always found news to report. At 5 p.m. each day he attended the Propaganda Ministry's second media conference of the day. Afterward, his habit was to make his way over to the German broadcast center to prepare for his second broadcast of the day. When he could not drive because of the blackout, he walked to the studio. Given his restricted vision, the blackout-darkened *Wilhelmstrasse* was not easy to navigate, especially in winter. With the wartime shortage of gasoline and public works trucks, snow was no longer being cleared from city streets, and footing was hazardous. "I'm not noted for my memory, and it took me three months to memorize the exact position of the [many obstacles] which lay along the sidewalk between my hotel and the subway station," Shirer reported in a September 1940 article for *Atlantic Monthly*. "It was a rare night when I did not collide with at least one obstacle or flop headlong into a snow pile ... If I had been walking fast and hit a lamp post, I would arrive at the studio with a lump on my forehead and a headache."[8]

When his day's work was finally done, Shirer invariably made his way to the Ristorante Italiano, where he savored the food and companionship. Most nights, he was back in his room at the Adlon Hotel and in bed by 3 a.m. after another eighteen-hour day.[9]

Maintaining such an onerous schedule was a drain, physically and emotionally. To sustain himself, Shirer took a break once every six to eight weeks, returning to Geneva for a few days of respite and recovery. When he departed Berlin in mid-October 1939 to fetch some winter clothing and "recover his senses,"[10] the relief he felt at being out of Germany was immense: "How dim in memory the time was when there was peace ... That world ended, and for me on the whole, despite its faults, its injustices, its inequalities, it was a good one. I came of age in that one, and the life it gave was free, civilized, deepening, full of minor tragedy and joy and work and leisure, new lands, new faces – and rarely commonplace and never without hope. And now darkness."[11]

The contrast between everyday life in wartime Berlin and neutral Geneva was stunning. After a week of spent with his wife and daughter, Shirer returned to Berlin. About the only thing he felt good about was the quality of his CBS reports. On air, his intonation remained "flat" and "timbre reedy," as his daughter Inga describes it,[12] but his self-confidence had grown immeasurably, and his technique was continuing to improve.

On numerous occasions, especially in the opening weeks of the war, Shirer reminded listeners of the parameters of his job. For instance, while reporting the sinking of the *Athenia* he explained, "I'd like to point out to you that I'm not here to try to report what is going on outside [of Germany]. My assignment is to tell you what news and impressions I can pick up here in Berlin."[13] A typical Shirer broadcast script was 700 words. His approach was informal, his tone conversational. Given the censorship and the technological restrictions under which he was operating – CBS still refused to let its correspondents use sound recordings – Shirer did not have access to voice clips from government or military officials, nor was he allowed to quote them directly or even to offer his own comments on the latest developments. At times, this created problems; the rule of thumb under which Shirer worked was that anything he mentioned in his broadcasts had to be news that had already been reported in the German media or that had been announced at a government press conference. As often as not, what Shirer left unsaid was as revealing as what he said. Like Ed Murrow, Shirer became adept at conveying information through the *tone* of his comments and the inflection of his voice. Regardless, his battles with the censors were now ongoing and at times heated. All scripts were vetted by two censors, who came from the Propaganda Ministry, Foreign Office, or military high command. However, as relations between the United States and Germany worsened, the level and intensity of scrutiny increased. A third censor joined the daily fray.

When Shirer's overseers objected to the content of his scripts, as they often did, it was usually because of his wording. On one occasion, the Nazi censors simply refused to allow one of Shirer's fill-ins (American newspaper reporters who skirted their employers' policies and picked up extra income by going on the air using pseudonyms) to do a scheduled afternoon broadcast; the only reason given was that the report might create a "bad impression" among CBS listeners. The fill-in meekly accepted this; Shirer did not. Upon hearing of the incident, he confronted Harald Diettrich, the director of German radio services. When Shirer threatened to stop broadcasting altogether if such interference continued, Diettrich relented. Uttering soothing words, he explained it had all been a "misunderstanding." Having made his point and won the day, Shirer returned to work.[14]

The logistics of CBS's broadcasts from Berlin are worth noting, at least in passing. Each week, Paul White in New York sent Shirer a list of his scheduled air times. There were two each day: a four-minute report that aired at the breakfast hour in North America's Eastern time zone. The other, longer and more in-depth, was heard around dinnertime. For each broadcast, Shirer carried into the studio with him two copies of his approved script; one was his to read on air, the other was for the broadcast technician, who sat with a finger on the mute button that would end the report instantly if Shirer deviated from the approved wording.

About five minutes before the scheduled airtime, the German technician would begin transmitting a shortwave signal across the Atlantic on the predetermined frequency. "This is DJL in Berlin calling CBS in New York," he would say. Once contact was made and the clocks at both ends were synchronized, everything was ready. At the exact moment in real time that the broadcast was to air, the technician would signal Shirer to start talking. "This is Berlin..." had become his signature introduction. When the allotted broadcast time was over, Shirer would end off with the words, "We now return you to the Columbia Broadcasting System in New York."

With no way of hearing the conversation between New York and Berlin, Shirer relied on the cue he received from the control room technician. By necessity, the process of broadcasting from Berlin required split-second timing and was dependent upon the weather and atmospheric conditions. As one of Shirer's associates pointed out, "We hoped we had caught the cues correctly. We never knew for certain unless there was a serious difficulty or error. We sat down before the microphone and spoke blindly."[15]

Things could and *did* go wrong. Sometimes cues were missed, and on at least one occasion, when a broadcast technician in Berlin hit a wrong button, part of a German opera was beamed to New York while Shirer's CBS report went out to listeners in Germany. Another time, because the CBS and NBC early broadcasts were aired at almost the same time each weekday, the reports were mixed up and were heard over the wrong networks.

By late 1940, a year into the war, broadcasting technology had improved. In Berlin, Shirer now wore headphones that enabled him to hear the CBS announcer in New York as well as the reports from other correspondents, including Ed Murrow in London.

"Though the Nazis don't like me, I suppose I shall never get kicked out of here ... The trouble is my radio scripts are censored in advance, so that whatever I say over the air cannot be held against me. The newspaper correspondents can telephone out what they please, subject to the risk [of being expelled]. This is almost a worse form of censorship than what we have since the New York offices of the press associations and New York newspapers do not like their correspondents to be kicked out."[16] Despite the restrictions under which he operated, during the first twenty-seven months of the war Shirer reported a surprising amount of real news. Propaganda Ministry officials often were secretive and selective about the information they released; at other times, they were shamelessly manipulative and boastful. So confident of victory were the Nazis in the early weeks of the war that they fell often victim to their own hubris and grew careless. On one occasion that autumn, he convinced a German U-boat captain to do a CBS broadcast in which he explained how he had sunk the British passenger ship *Royal Sceptre*. A few weeks later, when a German submarine crept into the waters of the British naval base at Scapa Flow and torpedoed the at-anchor British battleship HMS *Royal Oak*, the U-boat captain met with Shirer and other journalists to boast about how he had done it. On Christmas day 1939, Harald Diettrich arranged for Shirer to visit the Kiel naval dockyards. He was the first foreign journalist permitted to do so, touring the harbor and going aboard many of the warships to discuss with captains and other senior officers the progress of the war and their battle preparations.

Because Shirer's German was excellent, he enjoyed an easy rapport with many of the military people he met, especially those from the navy. When he inquired about one of the huge warships he saw Kiel shipyard workers were constructing, an obliging naval officer informed him that the vessel was the infamous *Bismarck*, a mammoth battleship the Germans were confident would enable them to break the Atlantic naval blockade that the British were working to put in place. "So this was the mighty *Bismarck*! ... The British would have liked to have my view, I mused. The *Bismarck* looked almost completed. A swarm of workers were hammering away on its decks."[17]

Shirer enjoyed a similar freedom of movement when he traveled to the front in the company of German army officers; he noted how they and the men in the ranks dined together in the communal mess hall. Shirer also saw that officers fraternized with their subordinates and were willing to listen to their ideas and complaints. The effect of this openness and camaraderie was that morale in the Wehrmacht was high, and the men appeared to have bought into and accepted the regime's rationale for the war. That, Shirer decided, helped to explain at least in part what he regarded as one of the great puzzles of the day: "These soldiers came from a country that had ruthlessly stamped out human freedom, savagely turned on its opponents, persecuted its Jews, whom it was planning to exterminate ... How could these soldiers fight so enthusiastically for such a barbarous regime? I could not understand it."[18]

In the spirit of the Yuletide season (and because other correspondents had done similar reports), Shirer ended his late broadcast on Christmas night

1939 by having the crew of a U-boat sing "Stille Nacht" – "Silent Night" – to the accompaniment of an accordion. "Well, let's look at the celebration on this ship," Shirer told CBS listeners. "I think the boys want to sing."[19] After the broadcast, some of the German sailors approached Shirer to ask, "The English, why do they want to fight us?" Shirer could offer no answer to that question: "Evenings like that depressed me, and there were more than one that dark, bitterly cold winter."[20]

Shirer's diary entries during this period reveal the extent of his despair and inner turmoil; there was scant joy in his life these days. A two-week Swiss ski holiday in February 1940 with Tess and Inga that provided temporary respite only served to remind him of how much he missed his wife and daughter; Inga was growing up without him. The familiar dark clouds over Shirer's psyche reappeared when he returned to Berlin two days before his birthday. More and more, Shirer was questioning the direction of his life. His diary entry for 23 February 1940 reads, "My birthday. Thought of being 36 now, and nothing accomplished, and how fast the middle years fleet by."[21]

Nonetheless, he understood that self-pity was a luxury he simply could ill afford. The awareness that so many other men of his age were in uniform and had been swept up in events beyond their control was a sobering thought. So, too, was the realization that with the coming of spring, the war on the Western Front would heat up and many people would die. Shirer later reflected, "What had I to be sorry about?"[22]

20

War on the Western Front

The war on the Western Front all but ground to a halt in winter 1939–40, one of the coldest on record in Europe. Strangely enough, the only venue where fighting raged was in the north, where Stalin's Red Army pushed through the snow in early December to attack Finland. Yet even with their huge superiority in numbers and firepower, the Russians took three months to overwhelm the plucky Finns.

When news of the Russian assault on Finland broke on 30 November, William Shirer arranged for American freelance journalist named Bill White to deliver on-the-spot reports on the fighting. If not for Tess Shirer's linguistic skills – Danish being one of the half-dozen languages she spoke – her husband never would have been able to pull things together. Burning up the telephone lines between Geneva, Helsinki, Stockholm, Berlin, Amsterdam, London, and New York added more than $1,000 to Shirer's telephone bill, while his cable and telegraph costs were half that much again.[1] Murrow had made it clear he wanted live reports from Finland, and so CBS was now spending about $10,000 per week to broadcast the news from Europe – NBC a similar amount.

While Paul White was pleased to have live reports from Finland, he worried they were too critical of Germany. Shirer feared his employer's angst might well be justified when, upon his return to Berlin on 7 December, the director of *Rundfunk*, the German broadcasting system, confronted him. The incident offers a vivid illustration of the uncertainties Shirer and his colleagues experienced when dealing with Nazi censors.

"Tall, thin, with wavy hair combed [into a] pompadour, heavy black eyebrows over large piercing eyes, [with] big ears and a protruding lower lip,"[2] Harald Diettrich generally was cordial in his dealings with Americans, so much so that Shirer regarded him as a "decent German." On this day, however, it was obvious that Diettrich was agitated, for he raced toward Shirer clutching in his fist a copy of the transcript of a recent CBS broadcast from Finland. Fixing a steely gaze on Shirer, the Nazi bureaucrat thrust the document forward. "Read this!" he demanded.

Having learned that the best way to respond to such belligerence was to push back with equal force, Shirer snapped, "Why? What's wrong with it?"

To Shirer's surprise, Diettrich smirked as he replied that there was *nothing* wrong with this particular report. It was "a wonderful broadcast, witty, but fair," he said. Diettrich then suggested that if Shirer should shelve his "personal antipathy to Nazism." "If I live in Germany for a hundred years I shall never understand these people," Shirer confessed in his diary.[3] At the same time, he confided that it was with a "heavy heart" that he continued to follow news of the fighting in Finland.

Each new day brought word of another German battlefield successes, each of which the Nazis were eager to trumpet. Luftwaffe chief Hermann Göring, in particular, boasted that for the first time Germany's land-based aircraft were triumphing over naval power; Great Britain's historic military trump card was in danger of being neutralized. Shirer reported this in his daily CBS reports, which were balanced, yet surprisingly frank. So confident of total victory were the Nazis that the censors permitted Shirer to point out the discrepancies between accounts of the fighting as reported in the British and German media, to take note of German setbacks – which admittedly were few and far between – and occasionally even to engage in a bit of editorial commentary. For example, in his evening broadcast on 8 December 1939, Shirer noted "The German radio reports tonight with some satisfaction that the latest Gallup Poll in America shows 96.5 percent of the American people against a war with Germany ... The radio commented that this showed what a failure the English propagandists are in our country. I was just wondering if there were any other questions in that poll."[4]

Despite the fact he sometimes succeeded in convincing his minders to allow him a modicum of editorial freedom, as the likelihood of German victory in the war grew, Shirer's morale plummeted. It did not help his mindset that Berlin's weather was unrelentingly cold or that he was feeling ever more sapped by the deprivations and isolation of his workaday life. The thoughts he was recording in his diary, written in an ersatz personal shorthand for security reasons, stand in marked contrast to his broadcast scripts from the period. The diary entries he wrote also offer insights into how he was able to continue doing his job in such a repressive police state. There was an emotional price to be paid, and Shirer was paying it.

Being perpetually on his guard, he was careful of whom he talked with and of where he went in Berlin; travel outside the city was forbidden without prior permission. With Germany's public telephone links to Western Europe and the United Kingdom severed, Shirer felt isolated. He was delighted to speak with Ed Murrow and other colleagues, however briefly, on CBS *World News Roundup* broadcasts. These programs, now being aired twice daily, were among the most popular on the CBS schedule, prompting a writer for *The New York Times* to comment that because of radio, "Now Europe sounds next door. To a listener the ocean seems to have dried up."[5] Unlike the situation in World War One, when the conflict in Europe was distant, the carnage was now terrifyingly real and immediate to North Americans.

The news reports by Shirer, Murrow, and the other radio foreign correspondents brought world events into North American homes in a way that many people found almost magical. "To hear a narrator describing scenes of devastation in Belgium then suddenly to hear his story interrupted by the roar of enemy planes, screams of people about him as a detonation blasts through the air when the bombs strike, makes the war resound as if just across the street," that aforementioned *New York Times* writer observed.[6]

As a nation of immigrants, America's appetite for news of the war in Europe was insatiable. Broadcast historian Ed Bliss notes: "For six years, from the German invasion of Poland to the final Japanese surrender ... air raid sirens, gunfire, and correspondents' voices were heard in the intimacy of American homes. Here the cliché about being 'glued' to the radio was born."[7]

With CBS expanding its coverage of war news, advertisers were now clamoring to sponsor the *World News Roundup* broadcasts. When Sinclair Oil became the first company to ante up, Murrow alerted Shirer and the other Murrow boys that henceforth whenever they took part in the program, they would receive a seventy-five dollar bonus. The irony in this arrangement was apparent, given that that CBS president William Paley had always been – and remained – adamant that all news reports on his network must be "objective," and so CBS correspondents were forbidden to editorialize. When Eric Sevareid in Paris questioned the propriety of the bonus arrangement, Ed Murrow advised him, "You'll get used to it."[8]

Where once, only a few years earlier, network executives had regarded news broadcasts as a "public service," that all changed quickly once the proverbial genie was out of the bottle. Sponsorship dollars were essential in American radio, and in a competitive marketplace the networks were loath to do anything that might drive those revenues elsewhere. The added financial resources they provided enabled CBS to extend the scope of its news operation and its corporate influence; the live hookups between Berlin and London were a prime example of that.

As was the case with daily news reports, censors vetted all scripts read by Shirer, Murrow, and their colleagues; however, outwitting their minders was a mental game at which CBS's star correspondents excelled. Rumor had it that the British had the speediest and most reasonable censors; the French were the hardest to deal with and were most picky. The Germans fell somewhere between those two extremes.

As noted, the American networks had set strict content guidelines for their reporters and announcers. Despite this and despite the censorship the faced, Shirer, Murrow, Sevareid, et al. managed to convey a wealth of information in their deftly chosen words. Understatement, humor, and clever inflection were the verbal tools used to make their points in subtle ways. Typical was Shirer's choice of words in a broadcast in which, tongue firmly in cheek, he described celebrations to mark one of Hitler's birthdays when a "crowd of about 65 persons ... *massed* outside the Chancellery."[9]

Listeners who tuned in to the on-air conversations between Shirer and Ed Murrow heard what sounded like a coffee-shop chat between two old friends. Their relaxed, offhand manner, which was informal, yet informative, was exactly what Murrow wanted. He and his team were striving to perfect what Eric Sevareid describes as "a new kind of pertinent, contemporary essay ... Familiar, very American voices now brought faraway scenes and issues into millions of living rooms ... giving not just the bones of the news, not an editorial ... nor a descriptive 'color' story by itself, but, in a very few minutes, putting it all in one package – the hard news of the day, the feel of the scene, the quality of the big or little men involved, and the meaning and implications of whatever had happened."[10]

As noted, one of the most trying aspects of Shirer's work in Berlin was his social isolation. He missed his family and the daily conversations with Ed Murrow that had been so much a part of his job in his early years with CBS; the two men had talked regularly via telephone, often several times each day. They did not have an opportunity for another such informal conversation until the third week of January 1940, when they again were able to meet face-to-face. Shirer and Murrow rendezvoused in neutral Amsterdam for a joyful reunion (at the same time that Murrow's wife, Janet, traveled to Geneva to visit Tess Shirer). What before the war would have been a two-hour junket for Shirer now took more than thirteen hours of travel and required a briefcase full of documents and permits. Murrow faced no less a challenge in journeying to Amsterdam from London.

The dangers and the logistical challenges of wartime red tape aside, the trip proved worthwhile, especially from a personal perspective. The official reason was to allow Murrow and Shirer to discuss and plan CBS's war coverage and to do a joint broadcast. At the same time – and even more importantly – it enabled the two men to get together for a midweek holiday in a neutral country where rationing and blackouts had not yet become the tiresome realities of everyday life, as they had in London and Berlin.

"Intoxicated by the lights at night and the fine food and the change in atmosphere, we have been cutting up like a couple of youngsters suddenly escaped from a stern old aunt or a reform school," Shirer recounted in his diary.[11] He and Murrow ate, drank, and went ice skating with Mary Marvin Breckenridge, a friend of Ed's from his New York days. Breckenridge had become one of the Murrow boys – the only woman ever to do so – and was the network's Amsterdam-based roving correspondent. Although she was well-versed in current affairs and was fluent in French, German, and Italian, Breckinridge was an unusual recruit for Murrow's team. She was thirty-four when she signed on with CBS in autumn 1939. New York City-born and a Vassar grad, she hailed from a wealthy family with extensive political and social connections. Despite her privileged background, "Marvin" – as family and friends called her – was no flighty debutante or social butterfly. In an era when most women of her age and social standing were content to marry and stay home to raise children, Breckenridge dared to be different. She had earned her pilot's license, worked as a political intern in Washington, helped found the National Student Federation of America, volunteered as a horseback courier in the Frontier Nursing Service, learned to make films, and was a top-notch photographer who worked for such magazines as *Life*, *Vogue*, and *National Geographic*.

It was Breckinridge who made the logistical arrangements for Shirer and Murrow to visit Amsterdam. Whatever she lacked in journalism experience prior to joining CBS, Breckenridge more than made up for in organizational skills, news instincts, and ability to paint an accurate and vivid picture with words; in Ed Murrow's mind, that latter talent was an essential skill for any broadcast journalist. "When selecting correspondents, [he] was not necessarily interested in them having experience in radio or even journalism ... He favored analytical skills, subject and foreign language knowledge, their connections, their writing skills, or their adventurous bent, all of which would serve them well in the dangerous years to come."[12]

Paul White, the archetypal "old-school" newsman, disagreed with this approach. However, Murrow was insistent; because he had William Paley's ear, he generally got his own way. But not always. After hiring the veteran journalist Shirer in August 1937, Murrow had further expanded his European news team by recruiting four more correspondents – Thomas Grandin in spring 1939 (to cover Paris), former United Press news service reporter Larry LeSueur (Rhiems, France), Eric Sevareid (to serve as Grandin's assistant in the French capital), and Breckinridge (northern Europe) in autumn 1939. Two of Murrow's first four hires had no journalism experience. That aside, it was Breckenridge's gender that some CBS officials found most nettlesome.

Ed Klauber was opposed to having female foreign correspondents work for CBS. As Cloud and Olson state, "In a letter to her parents dated June 11, 1940, [Janet Brewster Murrow] wrote, 'Marvin has been asked by the executive offices in New York to leave Columbia.' The letter went on to say the executives thought Breckenridge had been 'too sensational' in her reporting about the refugees pouring into France."[13]

Of course, that was merely the excuse Klauber used to justify his decision to get rid of Breckinridge and to order freelance journalist Betty Watson, who had succeeded Bill White as the CBS freelance contact in Scandinavia, to find a man to replace her. The same unabashed male chauvinism prompted Klauber to veto Murrow's plan in winter 1941 to hire veteran *Chicago Daily News* reporter Helen Kirkpatrick as the replacement in Paris for Eric Sevareid, who left the city when it fell to the Germans in June 1940. Interestingly, even today the Murrow boys' homepage on the CBS website makes no reference to Breckinridge, Watson, or Kirkpatrick.[14] Regardless, Breckinridge, in particular, deserves mention in any discussion of the early years of CBS radio news or of the Murrow legacy. In the fifty broadcasts she made for CBS, she proved herself to be one of the radio network's ablest and most intelligent voices. "I liked it more than any job I ever had," she said many years later.[15] There can – and should – be no ignoring Breckinridge's contributions to CBS or her role in arranging that January 1940 meeting in Amsterdam between Shirer and Murrow.

After a convivial dinner, the trio strolled back to their hotel, where Shirer and Murrow planned to write the script for an early-morning broadcast. It was snowing heavily, and Shirer, Murrow, and Breckinridge engaged in a spirited snowball fight in which Shirer lost his glasses and his hat. He and Murrow turned serious again a few hours later, when they went to the studios of the Dutch state broadcasting service for their broadcast to New York. Despite the restrictions imposed by Dutch censors, who insisted the American correspondents say nothing that might offend Germany, the report Shirer and Murrow delivered was memorable as much for its easy candor as for news content. Responding to a question from Murrow, Shirer reported that German attitudes toward the conflict had hardened; all talk of a peace treaty with England was now kaput. Shirer reiterated a point he had made often in earlier broadcasts from Berlin, noting that Nazi propaganda had convinced Germans there were only two possible outcomes to the war: complete victory or a defeat that "will make Versailles look like an ideal instrument of justice and fair dealing."[16]

Adolf Hitler was in a buoyant mood in the early months of 1940. With the German army having quickly occupied Poland, Denmark, and Norway, and with a non-aggression treaty with Russia in place, the Nazi dictator was confident that there would be no conflict on Germany's northern or eastern borders, at least not until it suited him. Thus, the German military was free to turn its attentions westward to France and England. The coming of spring marked the start of the long-anticipated German offensive on the Western Front.

A quarter century had passed since the opening salvos of the First World War, yet for military planners on both sides the goals remained essentially the same: the Germans were intent on finding a way to breach French defenses, drive deep into French territory, and seize Paris, while the French were determined to prevent any of that from happening.

After an initial flurry of attack and counter-attack, the so-called "war to end all wars" had become one of attrition. Both sides on the Western Front had gotten bogged down in a bloody stalemate. From early 1915 until autumn 1918, the fighting mostly involved static trench warfare. The armies laid siege to the other's vast network of trenches. Periodic attempts by both sides to break through the enemy lines failed, and the bloodletting was incredible. The First World War was a conflict fought by nineteenth-century military minds using twentieth-century weaponry. It has been estimated that 37 million people were killed in the carnage; millions of them were the soldiers who fought and died on the muddy battlefields of the Western Front.

German military planners in 1939 were determined to avoid the same mistakes their predecessors had made in 1914. However, it seems that the

French had learned nothing. French military leaders spent much of the 1930s building a line of supposedly impregnable concrete fortifications along France's borders with Germany and Italy. The Maginot Line – the 200-mile-long defensive barrier that separated France from Germany – was designed to repel attacks by cavalry and infantry. However, it was no match for tanks, motorized troop carriers, and modern military aircraft.

German military planners understood this well. Thus, they simply skirted the Maginot Line, attacking France by driving through Holland and Belgium. Seven elite panzer divisions made a dash through the narrow, hilly roads of the Ardennes Forest, which straddles the borders of France, stretching through southeastern Belgium and the Grand Duchy of Luxembourg to the German Rhineland. The speedy German move caught the French off guard. As a result, by 21 May the German military's "armored scythe" had cut a swatch all the way to the English Channel. There, in the French coastal town of Dunkirk, the battered remnants of the Belgian, French, and British armies found themselves trapped with their backs to the sea. They had no other choice than to make a desperate stand.

Tens of thousands of Allied soldiers died or were taken prisoner. The survivors in all likelihood would have been annihilated if it had not been for what became known as "the miracle at Dunkirk." For reasons that have never been entirely clear, on 24 May, with German panzer divisions closing in for the kill, Hitler ordered a pause in the advance. Perhaps it was because, as some historians insist, he still felt that he could make peace with England. Whatever the reason, as Shirer observes, "It was, as it turned out, the first major blunder made by the German High Command in World War Two – 'one of the great turning points' as General [Gerd] von Rundstedt, who was partly responsible for it, said he later realized."[17]

While military historians have endlessly debated the reasons for the German failure to smash the Allies at Dunkirk, there has never been any doubt about the results of not doing so. During the last week of May and the first few days of June a makeshift flotilla of Royal Navy ships and British civilian boats braved a muted but still deadly German attack to rescue more than 389,000 Allied soldiers, evacuating them to England, where they regrouped to fight again.

At this point in the war, the Nazi war machine seemed invincible. The Dutch and Belgians were beaten. With the French humbled and in full retreat, England stood alone against the German onslaught. But for how long? That was the crucial question. In his diary, Shirer lamented that among his colleagues in the foreign press contingent in Berlin, he alone clung to hope that Hitler could be stopped. Shirer's contacts in the German Foreign Office engaged him in a friendly wager that German troops would be in London within three weeks. Indeed, that prospect seemed frighteningly possible.

Nazi propaganda hailed "a new method of attack" being used by the German army. These references, deviously cryptic, were intended to confuse and intimidate the enemy. "I wish I could tell you what [this] new method is, but I can't. And the German army isn't telling," a frustrated Shirer reported.[18]

In Washington, the Roosevelt administration viewed developments in Europe with growing alarm. When the subject of American isolationism became an issue in the 1940 presidential election, GOP candidate Wendell Willkie declared, "The American people do not want war ... I stand with them. I am for keeping out of war."[19] Roosevelt, seeking an unprecedented third term in the White House, said nothing, even as he quietly continued to increase war aid to England. We now know that the president was convinced it was only a matter of time before America would be drawn into the conflict.

However, in spring 1940, any American involvement in Europe's war was still a long way off. For now, on balance, William Shirer accepted that. He feared that if the United States joined the Allied war effort, he and the other American journalists based in Berlin would be interned. Given his unabashed anti-Nazi sentiments, if that happened he knew he would not be well treated. He tried not to think about it, concentrating instead on his job. That involved reporting the news he gleaned at the twice-daily press briefings at the Propaganda Ministry and the Foreign Office, studying maps, reading German newspapers, listening to German radio news reports, and tapping his sources in hopes of learning what was really happening at the front. Shirer admitted in his broadcasts that he was "dazed" by the apparent pace and efficiency of the German advance. He reported in mid-May 1940 that the German press had confirmed "Hitler's army is using a modified form of the famous old Schlieffen Plan [from the First World War], which ... called for a 'swing door' movement across the lowlands ... And keep in mind when you visualize what's happening that it's not a vast frontal assault that's taking place ... but arrow-head thrusts at vital points led by tanks and airplanes."[20]

Whatever was happening, the reality was that the German military was enjoying unprecedented battlefield success. Italian dictator Benito Mussolini, ever the opportunist, entered the war on 10 June in support of Germany. This development prompted Shirer and other observers to speculate that the Wehrmacht would now sweep southward through Switzerland on its way to attack southern France, thus heading off any Italian advance in that area. When Tess Shirer telephoned her husband on 15 May with news that the Swiss army was mobilizing, Shirer set to work planning escape routes for her and Inga. However, barely a week after the opening shots of the ground war on the Western Front, there was no need for Germany to attack in southern France. With Allied Forces in Europe in total disarray, the rout was on.

To his wife's dismay, on 18 May Shirer went to observe "the Great Battle of Flanders" firsthand.[21] CBS, like NBC, allowed its staff to go on German-organized junkets, if they were allowed to pay their own way; the assumption was that this helped to preserve a degree of editorial independence, or at least the *appearance* of it. Regardless, on this occasion there was no doubt the German Sixth Army was on a relentless westward advance. Shirer and several colleagues traveled to Brussels, which the Germans had occupied a few days earlier. The Belgian capital having been spared the widespread devastation Shirer observed elsewhere, life here continued to be as normal as possible in the circumstances.

When the four-car press caravan and its military escorts stopped for lunch, it was at a tavern in Brussels that Shirer knew from pre-war visits. After savoring a meal of the quality and in the quantity that none of the journalists had enjoyed for months in Berlin, Shirer and his companions paid in German marks. They then bought out the restaurant's entire stock of American cigarettes. "I take three packages of Luckies ... I cannot resist, after a year of smoking 'rope' in Germany," Shirer recalled in an *Atlantic Monthly* article.[22]

He and the other foreign journalists were billeted in the German town of Aachen, just inside the Belgian-German border. Because there were no broadcast facilities there or in Brussels, Shirer hired a car to drive him to Cologne, and there he made his evening broadcast on 21 May. Earlier that same day, on the road from Brussels to Aachen, the journalists' caravan had come upon a column of British prisoners of war. They were a sad sight, given their situation and their recent ordeal. When the journalists stopped to speak with the Tommies, Shirer was shocked by their poor physical condition. "They were hollow-chested and skinny and round-shouldered. About a third of them had bad eyes and wore glasses," he later wrote, having made no mention of this in his broadcast for that day. These were realities that Shirer felt were reflective of their poor diet, sedentary lifestyle, and lack of adequate military training. "We didn't have a chance," one of them lamented in response to Shirer's questions. The CBS correspondent understood why when he considered their enemy. The comparison between vanquished and victor was striking: "Thirty yards away Germany infantry were marching up the road towards the front. I could not help comparing them with the British lads ... The Germans, bronzed, clean-cut, physically healthy-looking as lions, chests developed and all. It was part of the unequal fight."[23]

Shirer had an opportunity next day to see German soldiers in action on the battlefield. He and his companions made their way to the frontlines after General Walter von Reichenau, the commander of the German Sixth Army, received the journalists at his field headquarters. Reichenau, whom Shirer had seen occasionally in Berlin before the war, greeted his visitors on the porch of a chateau that he had commandeered. "He was tanned and springy as ever, his invariable monocle squeezed over one eye. With typical German thoroughness and with an apparent frankness that surprised me, he went over the operations thus far, stopping to answer questions now and then."[24]

A confident Reichenau was totally at ease. After patiently answering the journalists' questions, the general announced, "I've just given permission for you to go to the front ... You may be under fire. But you'll have to take your chances. We *all* do." For *Atlantic* magazine, Shirer reported, "[Reichenau then] turns us over to his adjutant, who wines us with an excellent red Bordeaux, no doubt from the cellar below. Then off to the front."[25]

The contrast between the serene, almost genteel scene at the general's headquarters and the one at the front, just a few miles distant was stunning. Mere minutes after meeting with Reichenau, Shirer and his companions were driving along a country road when they came upon "what was left of what must have been a retreating French column a day or two before."[26] The scene was one of utter devastation. Among the burned-out trucks, a couple of now-crippled light tanks, and some First World War-vintage artillery pieces were the abandoned personal effects of the French troops: articles of clothing, cooking utensils, helmets, tins of food, and letters. The bodies of fallen Frenchmen had been buried in shallow roadside graves. The bloody remains of a dozen horses that had been pulling supply wagons lay decomposing in the midday sun.

In Shirer's mind, the buzzing flies, the overpowering stench of death, and the visual shock of the battlefield carnage drove home with gut-churning clarity the cruel realities of war. Such firsthand observations enabled him to relate to CBS listeners the truths of the Blitzkrieg and of total war. The German army in 1940 was a fighting machine, well equipped, its soldiers in prime physical condition, and their leaders were competent and confident, almost to the point of being arrogant. The war was unfolding exactly as the German military had planned; for the first time ever, air power was being used to devastating effect in Europe. "I followed the German army into Belgium today as far as Brussels, and drove back here during most of the night to the first microphone I could find. There are two or three things I'd like to say," Shirer explained in an early-morning broadcast from the German city of Cologne.

"First, about how this Blitz Kreig [sic] is being fought. And let's face some hard truths. The tactics the Germans have used so far with such success are these: They attack Allied positions first with dive-bombers, then with tanks –and, if need be, artillery – and then the mechanized infantry delivers the final blow ... Another hard truth: So far as we would observe today, the Allied air force has done very little to hamper German communications in the rear. Though we drove for fourteen hours today along roads choked with columns of troops and supplies, we did not see a single Allied plane."[27]

The Luftwaffe controlled the skies over France. What precious few aircraft the French possessed were being marshaled in an effort to provide cover for the thousands of troops trapped on the beaches at Dunkirk, and most of the fighter planes of the Royal Air Force (RAF) were being held back for the last-ditch defense of England. This left the German army in France free to operate with impunity.

Shirer's words are revealing both for what they said about the military situation and about the scale of the German advance through Flanders. Back in Berlin for a broadcast on 24 May, he advised CBS listeners, "You have to see the colossal machine, which is the German army, in action – as I did earlier in the week – to believe it."[28]

After coming face-to-face with that army, Belgium's King Leopold was a believer. In fact, he concluded that further resistance would be futile and promptly agreed to an unconditional surrender. The guns of Belgium's army, 500,000 strong, fell silent on 28 May after only eighteen days of fighting. News of the capitulation was a grave blow to the Allied cause. Nonetheless, across the English Channel, Winston Churchill, who had succeeded Neville Chamberlain as England's prime minister merely two weeks earlier, remained resolute in his defiance. On 4 June 1940, he broadcast his most famous wartime speech, one of the great orations in history: "We shall fight on the beaches. We shall fight on the landing grounds. We shall fight in the fields and in the streets. We shall never surrender..."

Churchill's words went unreported in Germany, where the mood was one of quiet elation. Nothing could spoil the moment, not the escape of the rump of the Allied army from the beaches of Dunkirk, the inconveniences of wartime rationing, or even the occasional nighttime raids by RAF bombers. These were heady days indeed for Adolf Hitler and for the Third Reich.

Luftwaffe bombers and fighter planes attacked Paris for the first time on 3 June 1940. The next day, 40,000 Allied troops who remained trapped at Dunkirk surrendered en masse. Meanwhile in Germany Hitler ordered that Nazi flags be flown throughout the country and that church bells be rung in celebration. "But hardly were the Swastika banners hoisted," William Shirer reported, "when the German people were given word that a new offensive on the Western Front had started."[29]

This campaign, the "second phase" of Hitler's grand war strategy, began the morning of 6 June 1940. The immediate objective was the capture of Paris, a goal the Kaiser's army had failed to achieve in the four years of the First World War. This time, things were different. The German offensive rolled on relentlessly until 14 June. On that day, Paris fell into German hands, French government officials having fled, and all resistance melted away. Shirer was having lunch in the courtyard of the Adlon Hotel in Berlin when word of the German victory came over the radio. There were no great outbursts of emotion, no shouts of joy. The people of Berlin took the news of the fall of Paris as impassively as they had accepted everything else that had happened in the war to this point, although this victory, above all others, had special significance to Germans. It went a long way toward wiping out the bitter, humbling memories of the defeat of 1918.

News that Paris had fallen into German hands left Shirer feeling sick at heart. "Poor Paris! I weep for her. For so many years it was my home – and I loved it as you love a woman."[30] So distracted was he that during that night's blackout he slammed face-first into a door, gashing his nose. He was still dazed and at out-of-sorts the next day when he set off for the French capital in a car supplied by Harald Diettrich from the German radio service. "I did not want to see German jackboots tramping down the streets I loved … But then it hit me with a thud. I was slipping in my work. My burning hatred for these people, their Leader and what they were up to – and had been for so long – was getting the best of me."[31] He had vowed never to let that happen.

Tess Shirer took this picture of her husband playing with their daughter Inga in Geneva, 1939–40.

Shirer writing his broadcast report on the French surrender at the Compiègne, 22 June 1940.

Shirer discusses a script with censors at the Berlin broadcast centre, circa 1939.

Talking to a German policeman, Berlin, circa 1940.

Catching a few winks in the German government's studios prior to one of his early-morning (Berlin time) broadcasts, 1940.

Edward R. Murrow in uniform, circa 1944 (Edward R. Murrow papers, Digital Collections and Archives, Tufts University, MS025.002.045.00261b.00001).

Bill and Tess Shirer with their daughters Inga (left) and Linda, at their home in Bronxville, circa 1945.

Shirer visiting his mother for the last time in Cedar Rapids, Iowa, April 1944. She would die unexpectedly in 1945.

A CBS publicity photo showing (left to right) Robert Trout, John Daly, Paul White, William Shirer, and Larry LeSueur, probably late 1945 (from *News on the Air* by Paul White).

At work in the CBS studios, New York, circa 1946.

Ed Murrow and Shirer in the CBS studios, New York, circa 1946.

The Austrian-born actress-dancer and would-be painter Tilly Losch (The Tilly Losch Collection, Max Reinhardt Archives and Library, Special Collections, Binghamton University Libraries).

A portrait of Shirer as an astrologer by the Spanish painter
Luis Quintanilla, 1947 (courtesy of Paul Quintanilla).

The Shirer family farm at Torrington, CT.

NATIONAL BOOK AWARD WINNER

THE
RISE and FALL
OF THE
THIRD REICH

A HISTORY OF NAZI GERMANY

"One of the most important works of history of our time." — *The New York Times*

WILLIAM L. SHIRER

WITH A NEW INTRODUCTION BY RON ROSENBAUM

The 50th anniversary edition of *The Rise and Fall of the Third Reich*, issued in 2010.

An elderly Shirer reading Martine de Courcel's biography of Tolstoy (courtesy of Irina Lugovskaya).

Shirer with Mary Thomas, Lenox, MA, 1988 (courtesy of Mary [Thomas] Balle).

Shirer met Russian-born Irina Lugovskaya in 1982 when she was hired to tutor him in Russian. They married in 1988 – he was eighty-three, she was forty-nine (courtesy of Irina Lugovskaya).

Linda Shirer Rae and Inga Shirer Dean with Inga's dog Calypso, Lenox, MA, 2011 (photo by Ken Cuthbertson).

William L. Shirer's final resting place in Mountainview Cemetery, Lenox, MA (photo by Ken Cuthbertson).

21

Hitler Ascendant

William Shirer arrived in Paris at noon on 17 June 1940, on one of those sunlit summer days when the city is at its loveliest. However, as Shirer relates in his diary, "I had an ache in the pit of my stomach, and I wished I had not come."[1]

The normally bustling streets of the French capital were deserted and eerily quiet. The scene was in stark contrast to the chaos of a few days earlier, when the Champs-Élysées and other thoroughfares had been jammed with residents fleeing the city in advance of the impending arrival of the German army. The French military having placed its faith in the Maginot Line to repel a German attack, municipal officials had not bothered to prepare a contingency plan in the event of an enemy breakthrough.

"In the interests of morale, it was considered preferable to avoid evacuation and to endeavor to protect the large cities from attack," explains British historian Hannah Diamond.[2] What began as a trickle of refugees quickly became a great, seemingly endless torrent of humanity that in its collective panic clogged the roads leading south and west out of the French capital. "Most Parisians had no motor vehicles, nor hope of renting any," Demaree Bess of The Saturday Evening Post wrote. "They left their homes on foot, pushing baby carriages and laden bicycles, carrying packs on their backs, leading a child by one hand, and clutching a dog or gas mask with the other."[3]

In 1940, an exodus on such a mass scale was unprecedented. The scenes of human suffering left an indelible impression on those who were there – especially when German Stuka dive bombers roared down out of the sky to strafe the long columns of defenseless, desperate refugees. Sowing terror among civilian populations was an integral strategic element of the German Blitzkrieg.

Across America, millions of listeners tuned in to the radio news reports of the tragedy that was unfolding in France. CBS led the way in its news coverage. The network's reporting team was headed by Eric Sevareid – who joined the mass exodus from Paris – and Shirer, whom *Time* magazine was now hailing as "the ablest newscaster of them all."[4] It was with the deftness of chess masters that Paul White in New York and Ed Murrow in London moved their correspondents around Europe. Initially there were eight Murrow boys along with four part-time "stringers," on the job, but the turmoil in France led to a temporary reduction of the full-time staff by one.

Thomas Grandin had left Paris to escort his Romanian-born wife to Bordeaux, from where she planned to sail to safety in New York aboard an American ship. Upon learning that his wife would not be allowed into the States unless he accompanied her, Grandin rang Eric Sevareid in Paris to report that he, too, was leaving. Safe in far-off New York, Paul White accused Grandin of taking "the coward's way out." In Berlin, Shirer was no less judgmental, apparently having forgotten his own travails of a year earlier, when Tess Shirer had fought to gain American citizenship. He petulantly charged that Grandin "had turned chicken ... instead of sticking with Eric Sevareid."[5]

Ed Murrow alone chose to defend Grandin's decision, describing it as "entirely justifiable under the circumstances."[6] It may simply have been that he liked and respected Thomas Grandin – which, in fact, he did – or else he felt compelled to stick up for one of his staff, one whom Paul White had been opposed to hiring in the first place. Regardless, Murrow did "the right thing" then and again the following year when he recommended Grandin for a job with the foreign broadcast monitoring service of the FCC. Grandin would return to the airwaves in 1944, signing on with the newly formed American Broadcasting Corporation (ABC) and proving his mettle beyond any shadow of a doubt on D-Day, when he was among the first wave of American troops to storm ashore on Omaha Beach.

Grandin's sudden and unexpected departure left Sevareid on his own in Paris. Paul White and Murrow had planned for Grandin to follow the French government into exile and for Larry LeSueur, who had made his way back to Paris after Dunkirk, to join in the civilian exodus. The logical move, the CBS brass now decided, was for Shirer to report on the German occupation of the French capital, until someone else could be reassigned or a new correspondent recruited.

When the German army rolled into Paris on 14 June without firing a shot, they arrived "with their hands in their pockets," as Demaree Bess notes.[7] By the time Shirer got there three days later, the German army was firmly in control of the city, and so Shirer's escort, a group of Wehrmacht officers, were in high spirits. Their two-car caravan raced along the rue Lafayette without bothering to stop at intersections; the army drivers merely leaned on their car horns in celebratory fashion and carried on at full speed. Shirer pleaded with the soldier at the wheel of the vehicle in which he was a passenger to desist, and then he sat staring out the window. His mind drifted back to happier days in Paris, to times that were but wistful memories; blood-red Swastika flags and huge banners now festooned the city's public buildings.

Much to the displeasure of Shirer's hosts, no sooner had their cars arrived at German military headquarters than Shirer made a beeline for the American embassy, only a few doors away. Upon learning that Ambassador William C. Bullitt and the other diplomatic staff were out, Shirer left a note announcing his arrival in town. If he was underscoring the fact that as an American he was a neutral noncombatant and was concerned about his personal safety, he need not have worried. For now, Paris was quiet. The German army had imposed martial law, with a 9 p.m. curfew and full blackout in effect. Shirer noted that, once the shock of seeing German soldiers up close had worn off, most Parisians seemed resigned to the new realities of life in their occupied city. With the French resistance movement still in its nascent stages, some residents had even begun to fraternize with the enemy; most of the Wehrmacht soldiers out on Paris streets, Austrians who spoke French, were generally well mannered, polite even. In their off-hours, they behaved like typical tourists, snapping photos of historic and scenic landmarks.

Shirer did not, could not, share in their celebratory mood. The Paris he had known and loved had ceased to be, and so he sought solace in his work. He was relieved to discover that he was not the only American journalist in town. Checking in at the Scribe Hotel, where he had often stayed in happier times, Shirer met up with Demaree Bess of the *Saturday Evening Post* and Walter Kerr of the *New York Herald Tribune*. Like Shirer, they were scornful of the French government officials and military men who had fled, leaving the city and its residents to their fate. All three American journalists were taken aback by the news that Marshall Henri Philippe Pétain, one of France's national heroes in the First World War and now the prime minister, announced in a broadcast on 18 June that he had asked the German military for an armistice. Most French, who were shocked by how quickly their army had fallen apart, were angry and bitter over Pétain's unexpected decision. Subsequent events gave French patriots more reason to feel pain; Hitler, ever conscious of the power of symbolism, had a nasty surprise in store for France and for the rest of the world.

The treaty that ended the First World War had been signed in a railway dining car that was parked on a siding in the Compiègne forest, forty-five miles northeast of Paris. There at 5 a.m. on 11 November 1918, France's Marshal Foch had dictated the terms of surrender to a group of German generals. These were the same punitive terms Hitler railed about and had vowed to roll back. Now, after twenty-two years, the Nazi leader was intent on reversing that humiliation. One of Shirer's contacts, a friendly German colonel, advised him that the armistice would be signed in the same railway car in which the Allies had accepted Germany's 1918 surrender. With the tables now turned, Hitler was eager to trumpet news of his grand triumph and of France's ignominious defeat far and wide, especially to radio listeners in North America.

In his writings, Shirer provides a vivid eyewitness account of the French surrender, which took place on the afternoon of 21 June.[8] CBS and NBC cooperated on a rare joint broadcast, German army technicians having installed a dedicated phone line for them that was tied into a shortwave transmitter in the German city of Cologne. The microphones were set up only about ten paces from the railway car where history was being made. Shirer and NBC correspondent William C. Kerker had a clear view of proceedings and the story all to themselves.

Hitler intended to announce the armistice to the world the next day. With that in mind, he ordered all correspondents, German and foreign, to return to Berlin for a special news conference. However, Shirer's journalistic instincts told him there might be a better story to be found in the Compiègne forest. What if the French declined to sign the final text of the agreement or insisted on changes, he wondered? With such possibilities in mind, he made himself scarce when his colleagues were rounded up at their hotel for the flight back to Berlin. Shirer had arranged a ride out to the Compiègne in the car of the same German officer who had arranged his tour of the rail car in which the armistice was to be signed.

Shirer had been informed that any broadcasts from the site would be recorded in Berlin and then retransmitted to New York the next day, after Hitler had given his approval. Thus, Shirer's half-hour report that Saturday evening related the details of the scene as the French and German delegations signed their conditional agreement. Then, having finished his work, Shirer returned to his Paris hotel, intent on enjoying the first decent sleep he'd had in a week. He was awakened early next morning when Walter Kerr of the *Herald Tribune* came to his door with some unexpected but welcome news: Shirer's Saturday report had been broadcast live across the United States and parts of southern Canada. As a result, he had inadvertently scored a major journalistic success. Owing to "an error" by German radio technicians, a wrong switch had been thrown. Instead of sending Shirer's words to a recording machine at the broadcast center in Berlin, they had been relayed on to the CBS and NBC shortwave receivers in New York. Radio listeners in North America had learned of the French-German armistice even before people in Germany had and a full six hours before dispatches from reporters for the various American wire news services in Berlin arrived in New York.

Shirer never learned if his broadcast went out early due to a technician's error or because German generals who resented Hitler's attempts to claim credit for the recent battlefield victories had undercut his plans to do so: "There had been much more friction between the High Command and the Führer during the campaign than any of us knew."[9] Whatever had happened, Hitler was furious. Shirer was questioned by German officials and feared he would be expelled from Germany; however, to his relief and surprise the incident was quietly and quickly forgotten.

Like most observers, William Shirer had been stunned by the speed and the extent of the French collapse. In just six weeks of fighting one of the world's mightiest armies had been humbled and the country overrun by an enemy with whom the French already had fought two wars in less than a generation. The conflict that erupted in 1939 was the most destructive and traumatic of them all; it was also the first in which the French army had simply given up. That sad reality was a reflection of the extent of the divisions within French society in the 1930s, of the rot within the upper echelons of the military, and of the country's overall loss of direction. "What I saw at Paris was a complete breakdown of French society," Shirer confided in a letter he wrote to Paul White from Geneva.[10]

The more he thought about the situation, the more depressed Shirer became. His was a genuine and deep affection for the French people and for the city of Paris. Revealingly (and astonishingly), his diary entry for 23 June 1940 makes no mention of the appearance in the French capital of Adolf Hitler, who flew in from Berlin for a hasty early-morning tour. Hitler biographer Alan Bullock correctly makes the point that "No other tourist has ever paid his first visit to Paris as a conqueror. Hitler combined both roles."[11]

It may have been because there was no advance notice of the Nazi dictator's impending arrival in Paris. It may have been because William Shirer slept through the visit. Or it may have been because the circumstances of Hitler's visit were too painful for him to deal with, but Shirer ignored the event. Not that it really mattered; Hitler was on his way back to Berlin by nine 9 a.m. after spending merely four hours in Paris. He would never return, telling his aides that while he was impressed by the city's magnificent Opera House, he was mostly disappointed by the French capital.

Shirer did not do a broadcast on 23 June, the day of Hitler's historic visit to Paris. When he returned to the airwaves the following day, it was to bemoan the changes that had taken place in his beloved Paris (as much as the censor permitted), the plight of Parisians – many of whom were now displaced and starving – and the degree to which those who had stayed put were adapting to life under German rule: "Soldiers mingle in the streets with the Parisians, strike up all sorts of conversations with them on the sidewalk terraces of the cafés, and so far as I know there have been no incidents."[12]

Back in Berlin three days later, he found Germans were ebullient; it now seemed that Hitler that could do no wrong. German forces were mopping up in France and making plans for the final showdown with the English, who had retreated to their island fortress to hunker down and prepare for the invasion that now seemed inevitable, unless they accepted Hitler's terms.

If German forces attempted to invade England, Shirer knew he would be covering the battle. If that happened, it would be the biggest story of his career, yet he dreaded the prospect. Increasingly, he found his thoughts dominated by a growing sense of frustration and depression at how the war was unfolding and at the atrocities the Nazis were committing. He had been horrified by the extent of the carnage he witnessed in France and Belgium, particularly the senseless destruction of public buildings and facilities – libraries, town halls, hospitals, and homes[13] – and the abuse of Red Cross insignia, which were being painted on the cars of German army officers and delivery trucks hauling fuel and munitions supplies to troops at the front.

The fall of France having occasioned another brief lull in the war, Shirer seized the opportunity to travel to Geneva. So welcome was the respite that Shirer extended his planned two-day stay to a full week. He and Tess used the occasion to discuss the future and to celebrate Independence Day at a BBQ hosted by the American consul-general. The talk at this event was of life back home, the mood wistful and nostalgic. With the Stars and Stripes fluttering in the alpine breeze, Europe's war seemed far away, unreal even. However, as Shirer knew all too well, the nightmare was very real. It had become apparent that, as Hitler's territorial ambitions grew, those nations that submitted to Germany's will or pledged allegiance to the Third Reich were his friends; those that did not do so or even those that remained neutral – Switzerland being among the latter group – risked incurring Hitler's wrath.

With the German army otherwise engaged in France, Russian dictator Joseph Stalin's Red Army had invaded two oil-rich provinces of Romania and the Baltic nations of Estonia, Latvia, and Lithuania, on Germany's northeastern borders. Shirer's contacts within the German foreign office and military informed him that Hitler was enraged. Nonetheless, the censors were quick to stifle Shirer when he attempted to report the resulting chill in German-Soviet relations. The touchiness of this subject was made clear in mid-July when Ralph Barnes of the *Herald Tribune* wrote an article speculating about German plans for an attack on Russia. The Propaganda Ministry promptly ordered Barnes and his assistant Russell Hill (who also worked for Shirer) out of the country. The day before their departure, Barnes and Shirer met for a farewell drink. As they reminisced about their lives, their families, the war, and their careers, Shirer confided to Barnes his concern that he was losing his "edge" and his objectivity, both of which he regarded as essential journalistic requirement. As they parted, the two men vowed to meet again, in happier times. Sadly, that would never happen. Four months later, Barnes was killed when a British airplane in which he was a passenger was shot down over Yugoslavia.

What most observers assumed would be the final campaign of the war in Western Europe began in July 1940. The Battle of Britain, the greatest and most decisive air battle in military history, had begun in earnest. So confident of a successful outcome were the Nazis that construction crews in Berlin set to work building viewing stands for the victory parade that all of Germany was now anticipating. The British, bulldog stubborn, had other ideas. The fighting in the skies over England was fast and furious, with wave after wave of German aircraft winging westward from newly established bases along the French coast.

As the air war intensified, William Shirer joined in a German military press junket to the front. He hoped to observe the fighting and, if necessary, to ready himself to report on an invasion of the British Isles. That event, given the code name Operation Sea Lion by its German military planners, was without precedent for almost nine centuries, since 1066. Prior to leaving Berlin, Shirer visited the American embassy to meet with an American naval attaché who briefed him on what to look for when assessing German success in the battle. If they were winning and were ready to launch an invasion, the officer explained, the German military would be busy assembling an armada of transport ships, tugboats, and seagoing barges, and the harbors of French ports would be jammed with the vessels needed to transport troops, tanks, and supply vehicles. All of this would be a massive undertaking, the largest of its kind in military history. For that reason, the navy man advised Shirer that he was skeptical the Germans could muster the necessary resources, let alone succeed in crossing the English Channel. Not only were the logistical challenges of assembling the invasion armada problematic, the Luftwaffe was having difficulty delivering the knock-out blow to the RAF. The pesky British continued to disrupt invasion preparations by clawing back with nightly bombing raids on German shipping and supply concentrations in the French ports all along the English Channel.

Two days after the air war began in earnest, Shirer and a half-dozen colleagues traveled to the French port of Calais, arriving just as a battle was taking flight in the western sky. Heeding the advice he had received, as the journalists drove along the coast Shirer took careful note of German activities. What he saw confirmed his suspicions: there was little evidence of the kind of military buildup or naval preparations that suggested an invasion of the British Isles was imminent. In fact, Shirer noticed that German soldiers were busy shoring up defensive positions in the Channel ports. We now know that in the upper echelons of the German military a heated tactical debate was underway, for the window of opportunity for a 1940 invasion of the British Isles was fast closing. Autumn, with its problematic, uncertain weather, was mere weeks away.

When Hitler met with his generals, he was impatient to bring the war on the Western Front to a successful end. This was easier said than done for a variety of reasons, not the least of which were the rivalries between the high command of the German army and the navy, the egos of the personalities involved, political dictates, and the logistics of assembling and launching an invasion fleet. The distance between the French coast and the legendary White Cliffs of Dover was a mere twenty-one miles as the seagull flies; however, the English Channel seemed infinitely wider than that.

At the time, Shirer knew nothing of the squabbling that was occurring within the upper echelons of the Third Reich. His concerns were more immediate. He asked a host of questions about the epic air battle that was underway and about what was likely to happen next. The German military officials leading the media tour, acting on orders from Göring himself, were careful not to allow foreign reporters to interview German pilots. Even more restrictive from Shirer's perspective was the fact that he was unable to make any broadcasts until he returned to Berlin, where the censors could vet his scripts.

Despite these limitations, his observations of the bedraggled appearance of many of the Luftwaffe aircraft he saw returning to their bases made him skeptical of German claims the air war was going as well as claimed. A chagrined Hermann Göring was becoming ever more impatient for the victory that would not come. Thus, on 15 August – the very day Shirer and his party began watching the air war from the French side of the Channel – Göring adopted a crucial change of strategy that proved decisive. He ordered his aircrews to turn their attentions from attacking enemy naval installations and radar stations along the Channel to destroying the RAF. This was easier said than done. After three days of frantic aerial dogfights in which the losses on both sides continued to mount, Göring was forced to back off. A relieved British Prime Minister Winston Churchill told an aide, "They're making a big mistake in giving us a respite."[14]

What Churchill did not know was that the air battle was about to enter a new, even more deadly phase. Angered by the British refusal to surrender and frustrated at the Luftwaffe's inability to finish off the RAF, Hitler agreed with a new approach suggested by Göring: the saturation bombing of London and other industrial cities, a move that supposedly would cripple Britain's industrial output and traumatize and demoralize the civilian population. This strategy had considerable success in that first regard; in the second, not so much. In fact, despite the nightly pounding that London suffered and the death of more than 20,000 civilians, the ordeal only served to stiffen the resolve of the British people to stand firm against the Nazi onslaught.

The German change of tactics proved to be a turning point in the war. It also helped to galvanize American public opinion on the side of the underdog British. "It was the radio reporting from London ... which brought the Battle of Britain into the consciousness of America," writes broadcast historian Ed Bliss. "And it was Edward R. Murrow, more than any other radio reporter, who caught the listeners' attention."[15]

If this was Great Britain's proverbial finest hour, it was also Murrow's (and possibly CBS's). His dramatic eyewitness reporting of the Blitz enthralled listeners and proved conclusively that radio, with its immediacy and intimacy, had displaced print as the American public's news medium of choice. NBC's Fred Bate and his successor John MacVane reported the same news as Ed Murrow. So did James Reston of *The New York Times* and other newspaper reporters. However, it was the CBS broadcasts that America tuned into and that an entire generation would forever remember. With his unsurpassed oratorical skills, his energy, intelligence, and flair for the dramatic, this was a defining moment in Murrow's life and career. This was his opportunity to shine, and he seized it. He had learned well the journalistic lessons Shirer had taught him.

Night after night, Murrow risked his life to deliver eyewitness accounts of the death and destruction that rained down upon London. There was no defense against the bombs; who lived and who died was purely a matter of chance. Murrow knew this, and as Ed Bliss writes, Murrow advised Larry LaSueur, who was now helping out in London, that "the correct if undignified posture to assume when caught outdoors during a bombing was to lie flat in the gutter head down, mouth open, hands over the ears ... It was advice Murrow himself took five times in a single night. He had given up on going into bomb shelters except for stories, reasoning, 'Once you start going into shelters, you lose your nerve.'"[16]

Murrow's live broadcasts from London were as dramatic as they were unforgettable. Sometimes he ventured out into the streets – either on his own or in the company of colleagues – touring the city in an open car as bombs from the unseen German bombers 10,000 feet above pounded the British capital. Other times, from a vantage point atop the BBC building he described the surreal scene around him. Air-raid sirens wailed, anti-aircraft guns barked, searchlights swept the night skies, and thunderous explosions rocked the historic city. "Last night as I stood on London Bridge with Vincent ["Jimmy"] Sheean and watched that red glow in the sky, it's impossible to understand that that's fire, as a result of war. But the act itself, even the sound of the bomb that started the fire, was still unreal ... We could see the fire and hear the clanging of the fire-engine bells, but we hadn't seen the bomber, had barely heard him."[17]

Some of Murrow's friends and colleagues wondered if he had a death wish or if perhaps was out to test his mettle at a time when he and other journalists were watching from the sidelines as millions of other men were fighting a war in which the lines between good and evil were so clearly drawn. Regardless of his motives, Murrow's wartime broadcasts are classics that rank among the most memorable in broadcasting history.

This period of Murrow's career has been well documented, and his experiences reporting the Blitz have been recounted at length by his biographers. Murrow's extraordinary work during this period cemented his reputation as a fearless, incomparable, and utterly dedicated broadcast journalist. There also can be no doubt that his nightly reports from blitz-ravaged London made for powerful, compelling – even seductive – propaganda. The British, quick to realize this, had stopped censoring his scripts.

In Berlin, Shirer was unable to hear Murrow's CBS broadcasts, of course, although he secretly tuned into the BBC and knew what was happening in London. He was frustrated that Murrow was free to report facts as he saw them, while he was obliged to endure German harassment and intimidation. Shirer's scripts were subject to approval by three censors – one from the army, another from the Foreign Office, and a third from the Propaganda Ministry. He was no longer allowed to use the word "Nazi" in his broadcasts; the word supposedly sounded "negative" to American ears, and so the preferred term was now "National Socialist."

Shirer knew he risked being thrown out of the country or harassed by the secret police if he crossed that ill-defined, ever shifting line of what was acceptable to Nazi leaders and what was not. Despite this, he continued to react angrily to German attempts to control and direct his reports. William Shirer was nothing if not stubborn.

Following their whirlwind tour of the French coastal ports, on 16 August, Shirer and his colleagues traveled to Brussels. Here their military guides informed them that they could use telephone lines to file their reports. A German broadcasting service official and an army press officer advised Shirer that a telephone line to Berlin had been reserved for his use; he was now free to make an uncensored broadcast. To the surprise of his hosts, Shirer declined.

He had repeatedly been reminded in recent months that as an American he was to be scrupulously neutral in his news reports, as fair and objective as possible. When it was not to their advantage to allow him to describe all of what he was seeing and hearing, his scripts were rigorously censored. Now that the German military were eager to create the impression an invasion of the British Isles was imminent, those controls were dropped. Two of Shirer's print colleagues took the bait. Pierre Huss of INS – who was ever sympathetic to the Nazis – and Louis Lochner of the AP filed stories detailing German preparations for the invasion that was said to be imminent. Shirer declined to report this same news, which he regarded as nothing more than a "scare story."[18] When Paul White demanded to know why Shirer had missed the story, Shirer replied that the truth is more important than any scoop. In the highly competitive world of workaday journalism, such a stance is difficult to defend, let alone maintain. However, on this occasion Shirer was unwavering. It was just one more sign that his time in Nazi Germany was quickly running out.

Auf wiedersehen, Berlin

The tone and the temper of the war changed dramatically for Germans on the night of 25 August 1940. Shortly after midnight, for the first time, the wail of air-raid sirens and a barrage of anti-aircraft guns heralded the arrival of RAF bombers in the skies over Berlin.

Explosions began to rock the city an hour before Shirer's nightly broadcast. By chance, earlier that same evening he'd had a heated argument with a Propaganda Ministry censor, who had chided him for wanting to report that Berlin was awash with rumors the British were planning to bomb Berlin. The Nazi official had cut the offending words from Shirer's script, scoffing at any notion such a raid was probable or even possible. The wailing air-raid sirens, the barking of anti-aircraft guns, and the reverberations from explosions that rattled windows and shook the Berlin broadcast center now offered dramatic proof to the contrary.

Despite the tumult, the censors permitted Shirer to make only the briefest reference to what was happening all around him. "We're having an air-raid alarm here at the moment ... The sirens went off some time ago, about midnight, and afterward you could hear the big anti-aircraft guns going into action and see the searchlights trying to pick up the British planes. More details are not yet available."[1] Shirer was frustrated in his efforts to see for himself what was happening. "For his own safety,"[2] air-raid wardens prevented him from going outside, let alone up onto the roof of the broadcast center, from where he could have provided an eyewitness account of the action, as Ed Murrow was doing during German air raids on London.

When RAF bombers returned to the skies over Berlin on subsequent nights, the intensity and effectiveness of the bombardment grew. Shirer further angered his German hosts by declining to go on the guided tours

Propaganda Ministry officials organized to show how British bombers allegedly were targeting civilian neighborhoods. "Very annoyed that the German radio officials refuse to let me view the nightly air-raids," Shirer wrote in his diary on 5 September. "Nor can we mention them as they recur during our talk. Tonight when I arrived for my broadcast I found that the R[eichs] R[undfunk] G[esellschaft] had installed a lip micro-phone for us to speak in[to]. In order to make your voice heard you have to hold your lips to it. But the sounds of the anti-aircraft guns firing out-side do not register."[3]

Adding to Shirer's frustrations was the fact that reports being written by the Berlin-based correspondents of American newspapers and wire ser-vices included details of the RAF air raids. However, because the German Embassy in Washington monitored the American print media news reports coming out of Berlin, reporters exercised caution. "[I was] careful in what I wrote," Joseph Harsch notes, adding that "so long as one was rea-sonably discreet ... one could write freely – up to an invisible point."[4]

This double standard angered Shirer, who was vocal in his demands for more leeway in his broadcasts. When finally the censors had enough of his carping, they set out to teach him a lesson. By haggling longer than usual one evening, they caused him to miss his scheduled airtime. Shirer was livid, all the more so when he learned that Harald Diettrich had cabled Paul White in New York to complain that Shirer allegedly had arrived at the studio late. The German harassment of CBS's man in Berlin did not stop there.

When on 12 September Propaganda Ministry officials deported Shirer's assistant, Edwin Hartrich, Shirer protested even louder than usual. As usual, this was to no effect. However, his frustrations served to hasten a decision he had been agonizing over for months. Shirer concluded that the time had come for him to leave Nazi Germany. He had tired of his nightly verbal jousts with the censors, of the surveillance by the secret police, and of the simmering moral outrage he felt at being compelled to turn a blind eye to Nazi atrocities – in particular, their virulent anti-Semi-tism and persecution of "non-Aryan" minorities.

On a personal level, Shirer's life had never been bleaker. The monotony of his work, the uncertainties that were part of life in a police state, the tension of the now-routine British air raids, a chronic lack of sleep, and the loneliness were wearing him down; Shirer dared trust no one. He was living out of his suitcase at the Adlon Hotel, where many of the staff were Gestapo agents or police informers. Compounding his angst were the myriad minor irritations and deprivations in his workaday life, dietary limitations being primary among them. He and other foreign journalists received double rations and enjoyed other little perks; for example, a congenial waiter at the Adlon provided oranges and other fruit when they were otherwise unavailable. Despite such little kindnesses, the blandness of Shirer's daily diet was tiresome.

Other aggravations included the poor quality of German-made clothing, which cynics alleged was made of paper fibers rather than cloth, and the scarcity of tobacco. Being an inveterate pipe smoker, Shirer was perturbed that the only tobacco available was "like a poor grade of mattress filling."[5] When possible, he used his contacts in the American Embassy to obtain tins of Tuxedo, his favorite American pipe tobacco.

The cumulative effects of all these deprivations and stresses took their toll on Shirer. Minor irritations festered and grew into major concerns. As summer 1940 gave way to autumn and the hours of daylight waned, Shirer seriously questioned the value of the work he and the other American reporters were doing in Berlin. Shirer had always promised himself that when it was no longer possible to report events truthfully or completely he would leave Germany. In the circumstances, in September 1940 he concluded that time had come. He also suspected that if CBS threatened to withdraw its correspondent from Berlin, the Nazi censors would relax the rules. Paul White, much less certain of that, pleaded with Shirer to stay put for a while longer. White advised that for now Shirer should be content to report the latest Propaganda Ministry statements and to read the daily headlines from Berlin newspapers. As a serious journalist who took pride in the integrity of his work, Shirer bristled at both suggestions.

The day after Nazi officials expelled Edwin Hartrich from Germany, Shirer knew he could no longer stomach life in Berlin. Despite the fact there were rumors German forces intended to take advantage of the full moon and high tides on 15 September to attempt an invasion of England, Shirer traveled to Geneva for a frank telephone conversation with Paul White. Shirer was intent on taking an unpaid three-month leave of absence, during which he would return home to write a book based on a diary he had been keeping. New York publisher Blanche Knopf had suggested the project, and Shirer was eager to comply; he hoped to follow in the footsteps of his friend John Gunther, who had found fame and fortune with his trademark series of *Inside* books.

In addition to sorting out his future with CBS, Shirer had another compelling reason for traveling to Geneva: he wanted to spend time with his family. After months of discussion, soul-searching, and late-night phone calls, the Shirers had concluded it would be wise for Tess, Inga, and Inga's

Swiss nanny to take refuge in New York. There were widespread fears that the German army would occupy Switzerland before winter set in, and so Tess resolved to leave by no later than the end of October. It was a decision she agonized over for reasons both philosophical and personal.

In May 1940 Tess had written to her husband, "It's strange to remember happy, care[free] days now ... how sure and proud we all were ... my generation, at least how confident we felt in the world we had constructed for ourselves after the mess of the World War, how superior we felt to the generation that made the war, that fought the war. This was to have been a better world, a world in which war had no place. We were above that."[6] Sadly, she had learned otherwise. At the same time, Tess felt that if she left Europe she would in some measure be morally culpable for the evils that were happening there. "I feel as though I [am] running away from [the war], while this bitter struggle goes on – while my heart is in it," she lamented in a May 1940 letter. It troubled her "to be so far from it, safe, when one really hasn't got a right to be safe anymore than millions of other people."[7] Tess felt her place was in Europe, both because that was where she *belonged*, and because the strain of being separated from her husband was beginning to show. Doubts were creeping into her marriage. "How can you go on loving me if you never see me?" she asked him. "There is such danger in *friendships* developed at such times."[8]

Tess well understood how difficult it was for a relationship to survive the stresses and the workaday travails when one partner was on the road so much of the time. For that reason and because of the age-old gender-based double standard, a wife often turned a blind eye to her journalist husband's indiscretions, tolerating them as part of the normal course of affairs (pun intended) in the life of a foreign correspondent. At the same time, it was expected the women would be a dutiful spouse and mother who would keep the home fires burning while her husband was absent. The prevailing attitude of the day was that men would be men, while women were expected to remain stoic and chaste. The undeniable reality was that they did not and could not always do so.

That awareness had weighed heavy on Shirer's mind back in 1930–31 when he was in India and Tess remained in Vienna, where he knew would-be Lotharios such as his colleague Jay Allen and British journalist George Gedye had eyes for his wife. Shirer had been no less worried about the intentions of his friend John Gunther, and with good reason. He was a big, gregarious, amiable teddy bear of a man with a wandering eye and a fondness for the opposite sex.

Gunther was attracted to Tess Shirer, of that there can be no doubt. Nor can there be any doubt that Shirer's awareness of this played on his mind all the while he was in India and Tess remained in Vienna. Newly married, Shirer's uncertainties, conflicting emotions, and the passion in his heart are evident in his private correspondence from that period. He was by nature a private man, introspective, and at times was guarded. Yet he was human in his weaknesses, especially where his temper and his relation-ships with women were concerned. He'd had those youthful flings in Paris and Vienna; both women were older than him, and both were married. Following his marriage to Tess, Shirer did his utmost to remain true to his vows, which was not always easy; temptations were everywhere for him.

Tess Shirer knew the realities of being married to a foreign correspon-dent, who by necessity spent much of his time traveling. It is unclear whether in May 1940 she had anything specific in mind where her hus-band was concerned or if she was merely engaging in speculation. Veiled, cryptic references in her correspondence suggest that while she remained deeply in love with her husband, she feared his affections might wander – or already had. For example, in a 31 May 1940 letter she had cryptically mentioned how "this Whiteleather story has depressed me."[9]

Many years later, when her marriage was in its terminal stages, her love had died, and she was angry and bitter, Tess hurled at her husband the names of four women with whom she suspected he'd had extramarital relationships; one of them was a German woman in wartime Berlin. The truth of any of this is impossible to verify. What is undeniable is that the uncertainties of war intensified a live-for-the-moment mentality and that the life of an American journalist stationed in wartime Berlin was lonely, trying, and often traumat-ic, with the ever-present possibility of a sudden death. William Shirer was a good man, compassionate, principled, and moral. But he was no saint.

Although William Shirer was increasingly adamant in expressing his desire to leave Berlin, Paul White remained loath to grant his request. White's concerns are understandable. Shirer had become one of CBS's star foreign correspondents, second only to Murrow in luster and popularity. So it was only after much discussion, which at times grew heated, that White and Shirer reached a compromise: Shirer would stay in Berlin until a suitable replacement could be found. As a quid pro quo, White agreed to arrange passage for Tess, Inga, and Inga's nanny aboard a ship leaving from the Portuguese capital of Lisbon, the only European port from which merchant vessels were still sailing to New York.

Shirer accepted these arrangements, but his discontent remained. Thus prior to returning to Berlin he wrote once more to Paul White, reiterating the urgency of his desire to return home. He asked that White discuss his request with CBS vice-president Ed Klauber – and by implication with William Paley. "I realize that the next few weeks may decide the issue of the war, and that it is not the best time to threaten to pull out because of censorship ... If Germany should win, you will naturally want coverage of the events to follow that victory – a coverage that would largely come from the German side. For that reason I'm going back to have another crack at the job ... But if there is a stalemate this winter and the censorship is not relaxed, I personally cannot remain there, as I've already cabled you, and do the Nazi propaganda."[10] Shirer concluded by sarcastically suggesting that if CBS was content with having its Berlin correspondent report government press releases, the network could hire "a pro-Nazi American student for $50 a week and no expenses" to do his job.[11]

Predictably, Shirer's frustrations continued to build, as did his cynicism. Although it still seemed likely that Germany was destined to win the war, the British stubbornly refused to yield, and the RAF bombing raids on Berlin continued. In light of this and because he was aware of the profound impact of Ed Murrow's broadcasts from London, Nazi propaganda minister Goebbels took a new tack: he ordered his censors to allow Shirer and other American journalists to report details of the British attacks on "innocent civilians" in German cities.

Not only had the now nightly bombing raids become a huge embarrassment to the Third Reich, they were increasing in their intensity and effectiveness. Joseph Harsch, who replaced Edwin Hartrich as Shirer's emergency stand-in, notes, "When an air raid happened, the American group would tend to gather in Bill's room to watch the action. The same group would gather in my room at news time. I had a radio receiver that could pick up the BBC from London. Radio listening in my room became a feature of our lives, both morning and evening."[12]

Shirer's perspective was markedly different because he was obliged to leave the hotel each night to do his late broadcasts. "It was strictly *verboten* to circulate in the city during an alarm ... All transportation stopped and ... although my second broadcast was not until 1:45 a.m. – 6:45 a.m. [New York time] – I had to be at the station by eight in the evening and then just sit."[13] Although he never missed a broadcast because of an air raid, a feat he was justifiably proud of, if he was at the RRG broadcasting center when the air-raid sirens began to wail, he was now compelled to retreat to the building's underground shelter, where he came to realize that one of the other foreign nationals was a heavy-set Irishman who was making propaganda broadcasts for the Nazis. On air, William Joyce went by the name Fröhlich – which is the German word for "joyful." Seeing nothing to celebrate about Joyce, the British press had derisively dubbed him "Lord Haw Haw."[14] Shirer knew who Joyce was, and so in the long hours the two men sat together during various air raids they inevitably began to exchange small talk. Then on the evening of 26 September, in the midst of a punishing Allied air raid, Shirer found himself seated next to Joyce and his wife Margaret. When Mrs Joyce pulled a bottle of schnapps out of her purse, she offered Shirer a drink.

By the time the schnapps was gone, the sound of exploding bombs had started to die away. His courage fueled by alcohol, Shirer accompanied the Joyces when they made their way upstairs to Joyce's office. There they sat in the dark, watching out the window as explosions from the British bombs lit up the night sky over outlying areas of Berlin. The scene was surreal. During their conversation, Shirer questioned Joyce about his politics, his anti-Semitism, and his personal history, learning that Joyce was actually American by birth. He was Brooklyn-born; however, his family had moved to Ireland when he was three. As to why the British press had dubbed Joyce as "Lord Haw-Haw," Shirer was puzzled. On radio, the Irishman sounded like an English aristocrat, or a stage actor faking a blue-blood accent. In person, Joyce hardly looked the part. Shirer described him as being a "hard-fisted, scar-faced Fascist rabble-rouser."[15]

The incongruity of Joyce's appearance and his nickname were just part of Shirer's fascination with Joyce. Ever intrigued by the concepts of nationalism and patriotism, Shirer quizzed Joyce about what it was that had prompted him to "turn traitor." Joyce bristled at the question, insisting that he was no more of a turncoat than were those Germans who had emigrated to the United States or those American citizens who had renounced their citizenship and gone to experience life in the Soviet Union. Although he disagreed with almost everything Joyce said, Shirer had to acknowledge that Joyce, who was a University of London graduate, could be engaging company: "Haw-Haw can drink as straight as any man, and if you can get over your initial revulsion at his being a traitor, you find him an amusing and even an intelligent fellow."[16]

Regardless, Shirer could not stomach Joyce's politics and made no secret of it. While the two men agreed to disagree, they maintained a civil relationship. When Shirer presented Joyce with a copy of a novel entitled *The Death of Lord Haw-Haw* [17] (which Shirer had smuggled into Germany after a recent trip to Geneva), Joyce reciprocated by giving Shirer a copy of his German-language book *Dämmerung über England – Twilight over England*.[18]

In the end, Joyce's conviviality and sense of humor did not save him. When he fell into British hands in May 1945, he went on trial for treason in London. Found guilty, "Lord Haw Haw" went to the gallows on 3 January 1946.

William Joyce was certainly not the only traitor to make pro-Nazi broadcasts from Berlin. One of Shirer's colleagues from his Vienna days, United Press bureau chief Bob Best, also did so, albeit only occasionally in autumn 1940, and to much less dramatic effect. With the United States and Germany not yet at war, Best was guilty only of poor judgment. For now, most Americans who knew him regarded the big, genial South Carolinian as a crackpot, a fascist sympathizer who, like William Joyce, ranted about communists and Jews; Best also railed against Roosevelt, whom he decried as "a tool of the Jews." What Shirer found most unsettling about all of this was that Best was someone with whom he often had broken bread and raised many a glass. The two men had spent many hours socializing; try though he did, Shirer could not fathom what fueled Best's vitriol. Dorothy Thompson surmised that he had turned traitor because he was "intellectually lazy and ignorant."[19] Shirer was not so sure of that, and it was a subject that would continue to preoccupy him, most notably in his 1950 novel, *The Traitor*.

In the last week of October, William Shirer struggled with his emotions when he traveled to Geneva to bid farewell to Tess, Inga, and Inga's nanny.[20] He watched as his family boarded a bus for a six-hundred-mile ride to Barcelona, taking with them only what luggage and food they could carry.[21] The rest of their possessions, as well as Shirer's personal papers and files, some fifty boxes of them, were put into storage.

From Barcelona, Tess, Inga, and Inga's nanny traveled by train to Madrid, then Lisbon. There they waited until their ship sailed for New York the second week of November. Max Jordan of NBC had provided Tess with a letter of introduction to Manuel Barjano de Bivar, the director of the Portuguese national broadcasting service. Jordan's kindness was a measure of the mutual respect with which he and Shirer regarded each other. The two men were vocational rivals, but friends otherwise. In his letter, Jordan asked de Bivar to assist Tess Shirer in any way he could.[22] For her part, Tess was grateful, for as it turned out she sorely needed the respite she enjoyed in Lisbon; the two-day trip from Geneva to Barcelona had been an ordeal.

Both Tess and Inga had fallen ill with diarrhea and colds, and Spanish border guards refused to allow the Jewish passengers to enter the country; these unfortunate souls were turned back into France to face what was an uncertain fate at best. Spanish officials were only slightly less hostile to the refugees they did allow into the country. Writing to her in-laws in the United States upon her arrival in Lisbon, Tess Shirer noted that she had lost ten pounds on the journey from Geneva and had felt terrified the whole time she had been in Spain, where the pro-Nazi officials were surly and menacing: "I'd rather go through 50 air raids than ever set foot in Spain again. I was frightened every second of the time I was there."[23]

Tess's travails resumed when she, Inga, and the nanny finally boarded the American Export Line's ship *Excambion* for the nine-day voyage to New York. They traveled in the company of the American consul general in Geneva, John Carter Vincent, his wife Betty, and their two children, but Tess was ill much of time the ship was at sea. "I was on deck with my nanny, Mary Louise, who sat knitting happily while my mother was below and feeling seasick, as she did the whole trip," Inga recalls.[24]

The Shirers' Geneva farewell understandably had been tearful, for there was no way of knowing when they would be together again, or for that matter if they would *ever* be together again. "It was all I could do to get myself off to return to Germany the next day," wrote Shirer. "I remember on the train to Bern gazing with leaden heart through the window of my compartment ... I kept wishing I had taken that bus with Tess and Inga."[25]

Back in Berlin, Shirer fell into a funk. Emotionally adrift, he was more impatient than ever to be relieved of his CBS duties. Compounding his misery, the war had taken a personal turn for him. He received word that his dear friend Ralph Barnes had been killed when an RAF bomber in which he was a passenger crashed or was shot down over the mountains in Yugoslavia on 18 November.[26] Barnes thus became the first American journalist to die in the war and one of the sixty-nine journalists of all nationalities to do so.

Adding to Shirer's grief was the fact that on the heels of the news of his friend's death, Shirer learned that two of his sources in Berlin – a friendly clergyman and a German newspaper editor who helped Shirer decide what news the Propaganda Ministry decreed safe to report – were arrested by the Gestapo and condemned to death. Their sentences eventually were commuted to life in prison, but Shirer was shaken nonetheless by the awareness that at least in some measure it was their association with him that had gotten these individuals into trouble. This was not the only sign the Gestapo was keeping an eye on Shirer.

A German friend who worked in one of the ministries advised him to be "extra careful" in his activities. The secret police were said to be gathering information in advance of expelling him or possibly even arresting him as a spy. German embassy officials in Washington suspected Shirer was using code words in his CBS radio broadcasts to convey sensitive information to the American and British governments. In a bid to catch him out, Gestapo agents supposedly were recording Shirer's broadcasts and studying them for clues that could be used against him. Murrow biographers Cloud and Olson are skeptical of this; they quote Joseph Harsch: "I don't believe [Shirer] was ever really hassled. I think that was the result of his imagination. He wasn't all that much more critical of them overtly than any of the rest of us."[27] As further proof Shirer exaggerated the threat against him, Cloud and Olson offer this observation from Howard K. Smith, who was working as a UP reporter: "[Shirer] could feel the pressure. They were cutting his broadcasts. He wasn't going to be a star anymore because his scripts weren't going to be very good. He got out of Germany at the right time."[28]

It is impossible to know if Shirer really was a marked man; if so, he was by no means the first – nor would he be the last – American journalist whom the Nazis targeted for special treatment. It is worth noting that most of the correspondents who were thrown out of the country worked for newspapers. For a while, at least, their colleagues who were allowed to stay in Berlin were given leeway in their activities. "During [the] first phase of the war American correspondents had an easy time living, getting news, and transmitting it. We were allowed to travel more or less at will anywhere under German control," writes Joseph C. Harsch.[29] However, by late 1940 all that had changed. The war was no longer going all Hitler's way, and the Nazis were becoming increasingly unfriendly toward all foreign neutrals, Americans especially.

While Shirer may have been tabbed for special treatment, it could also have been that the Gestapo had something more ominous in store for him. Nazi officials knew that millions of people heard his daily reports on CBS, and so he had a wider and more immediate influence over American public opinion than did any print journalist. With German-American relations deteriorating and Germany's battlefield successes becoming fewer and further between, those Americans reporters who remained in Berlin found themselves in an increasingly uncomfortable position. Nazi thugs were harassing or even beating anyone heard speaking English in the street, and the Gestapo stepped up its intimidation of Americans. Their German sources and friends wisely began making themselves scarce. Telephones used by the American journalists were tapped. And censorship rules were tightened to the extent that it became impossible for any journalist to do their job.

Indicative of the rising level of tension was a March 1941 Gestapo raid on the UP bureau in Berlin. The office was ransacked, and shortly afterward Howard K. Smith's colleague Richard C. Hottelet was arrested and accused of being a spy. Hottelet, like Shirer, was staunchly anti-Nazi. Unlike Shirer, he was too indiscreet in making his opinions known and ignored warnings not to report the extent and nature of the damage inflicted by RAF bombing raids. If Nazi officials intended Hottelet's detention and the four months of imprisonment that followed as a warning to other American journalists, they succeeded; as Howard K. Smith reported, "One evening the same Wilhelmstrasse tipster who had once told Hottelet that he was growing dangerously unpopular with the Gestapo, came to me and suggested, 'My dear Smith, if I were you I would get out of Germany as fast as I could. If you do not leave soon, you will have reason to regret it.'"[30]

In the claustrophobic, emotionally charged atmosphere of wartime Berlin, William Shirer *believed* he was also in the Gestapo's crosshairs. This fueled a heightened sense of urgency on his part. He was tired. He was worn out emotionally and physically after having lived inside the Third Reich for six harrowing years. Wherever he looked, he saw telltale signs, real and imagined, that the Nazis were growing ever more suspicious and belligerent toward him and other American foreign correspondents in Germany, all of whom they regarded as being agents of the Roosevelt administration. "No other country receives regular broadcasts from both sides in this war," Shirer points out in an article for *The Atlantic*. "That we do is a tribute to the enterprise and sense of responsibility of American broadcasting and also a tribute to the American listener. If he did not *want* daily broadcasts from abroad, he probably would not get them, for they are costly affairs."[31] That said, there can be no doubt that the Nazis also benefited from the presence in Berlin of American radio correspondents; while they could be a nuisance to the regime, they provided a North American outlet for German propaganda.

In the United States, despite promises of continued neutrality from the two leading candidates in the 1940 presidential election campaign, the slow drift toward American involvement in Europe's war was taking on an air of inevitability. So, too, had Shirer's return home. His persistence in asking to be relieved in Berlin finally met with success when Paul White agreed to send a replacement to Berlin so Shirer could take his requested leave. To relieve Shirer in Berlin, White had recruited Harry W. Flannery, a staff announcer with the CBS affiliate in St Louis. Flannery, a bespectacled thirty-nine-year-old graduate of the University of Notre Dame, was three years Shirer's senior and an experienced newspaperman, but he had limited radio experience and none as a foreign correspondent. Even more problematic was the fact his knowledge of Germany was limited. Flannery's chief attribute, at least in Paul White's mind, was that in St Louis Flannery had been working in a city with a sizeable German-American community. According to *The Murrow Boys* authors Stanley Cloud and Lynn Olson, White soon "conceded his mistake – which looked all the worse when compared to the success of Murrow's hires,"[32] and so he set about finding someone better suited to the Berlin job. That person turned out to be the aforementioned Howard K. Smith. The former Rhodes Scholar, fluent in German, was already working in Berlin for the UP. Smith signed on with CBS in mid-1941; until then, Flannery was Shirer's replacement.

When Flannery arrived at Berlin's Tempelhof airport on 7 November, Shirer was there to meet him. Then, after settling Flannery into a room at the Adlon Hotel, Shirer escorted him on a tour of various government ministries and the broadcast center, where Flannery met Harald Diettrich and other officials. On this particular night, whether by chance or design, Shirer got into a loud argument with one of the censors who was vetting his scripts. Afterward, an awed Flannery tagged along when Shirer did his nightly broadcast. Flannery has left us with a detailed account of these events and of life inside the Third Reich in a 1942 book called *Assignment to Berlin*. Because he was viewing the situation through fresh eyes, his volume makes for interesting reading. Flannery's book provides an excellent complement to writings by Shirer and other American journalists who were in Berlin at the time.

The farewell was always bittersweet whenever another American journalist left Berlin, voluntarily or otherwise. William Shirer had taken part in the ritual more times than he cared to remember, yet doing so never got any easier. By late 1940, expulsions of foreign journalists had become rare. Nazi officials had adopted a new strategy: They were now neutralizing uncooperative reporters by limiting their access to sources, while other privileges were restricted or cut off. Being isolated made it difficult if not impossible for them to do their jobs, and so they left voluntarily. In the case of the Berlin-based radio correspondents of the three American networks, German censors and studio technicians were able to exert considerable control over the content, tone, and timing of broadcasts; for that reason Shirer pretty much had been left to carry on with his established routine. Nonetheless, he understood there were limits to what he could dare to say or not say on air. He also knew that he was being watched, yet it was easy – even for an old hand such as himself – to become complacent or sloppy; no longer was it easy to tell friends from enemies. Shirer was reminded of that at a farewell party that took place on 3 December after his final broadcast. An official from the Foreign Office, a German whom Shirer liked and trusted, after a few drinks had revealed that he was, in fact, an agent of the secret police. "I must say I hadn't suspected him, though I knew some of his colleagues were members."[33]

Feeling shaken and vulnerable, Shirer breathed a sigh of relief when his travel visas and passport arrived in his mailbox the next day. All that remained for him to do now was to pack the few belongings he could carry with him when he left. Although Shirer gave away most of his clothes and all of his books – another indication that he had no intention of returning to Berlin – he had one final and far more troubling concern to deal with.

Shirer feared his diaries and other personal papers contained enough incriminating material "to get me hanged."[34] With that in mind, he entrusted some pages, those with the most sensitive and incriminating entries, to American and Swedish officials who had agreed to smuggle the pages out of Germany for him in diplomatic pouches. Shirer was left to make his own arrangements for the balance of the material he wanted to take home. The plan he devised was as bold as it was risky: He gambled on his knowledge of the way Nazi officials went about their business.

Shirer packed his personal papers in two metal suitcases. On top of them, he piled copies of his broadcast scripts, all of which bore official-looking stamps indicating that government censors had vetted the documents. On top of his scripts, Shirer placed some old battlefield maps that he had obtained from contacts in the German high command. Once the cases were full, Shirer telephoned Gestapo headquarters. He asked the official he spoke with for permission to bring in for inspection two suitcases full of papers that he hoped to take with him when he left the country next day.

The two Gestapo men with whom Shirer met confiscated the military maps, just as he had anticipated. What Shirer had not expected was that the inspectors, neither of whom gave any hint of knowing who he was, would begin rummaging through the other papers in the suitcases. As they proceeded to do so, Shirer's anxiety increased. However, just as he had hoped, his salvation was those official-looking stamps the censors had put on his scripts. The Gestapo men were as lazy as Shirer had hoped they would be. Seeing the stamps was good enough for them, and so after asking a few more perfunctory questions they closed his suitcases, sealing them with metal tape. It was a lifesaver that they did.

Next morning at the Tempelhof airport check-in counter, Shirer's luggage drew inquiring looks from the Gestapo men who were screening travelers. One of them brusquely told Shirer to open *all* of his suitcases for inspection, including the two in which he had hidden his diaries. Having learned by experience that when being bullied by Nazi officials the best approach was to push back politely, but forcefully, Shirer protested. Outside the terminal, it was snowing and the flying conditions were deteriorating quickly as a storm approached. Making this point, Shirer complained that if he was held up he would miss his flight. Besides that, he insisted, there was no need to open two of the cases. He pointed to the metal tape and official seals that inspectors at Gestapo headquarters had affixed to them. Still not satisfied, a suspicious agent made a telephone call to confirm Shirer's story, after which he marked the two bags with chalk and then waved Shirer through: "The feared Gestapo, I knew, was really not very efficient."[35] Perhaps, but it is a safe bet that as Gestapo agents were inspecting his bags Shirer would not have been nearly as certain of that.

A few anxious minutes after this incident, the Junkers airliner with Shirer aboard rumbled down the runway and took off for Stuttgart, the first of three stops en route to Barcelona. Peering out the window of the aircraft, Shirer strained to catch a final glimpse of Berlin through a veil of falling snow. He could not decide whether to laugh or cry. Either way, he did not have much time to dwell on his emotions; his flight to safety was a white-knuckle experience. Ice on the plane's wings forced the pilot to drop down and fly at tree-top level. Hopelessly lost, the pilot then followed a major highway in hopes it would lead to an airport. It did, and the plane landed at Dresden, two hundred and fifty miles northeast of Stuttgart, well off course. As the shaken passengers and crew filed out of the plane and breathed a sigh of relief at having survived the ordeal, Shirer overheard the aircrew talking about how difficult it had been for the pilot even to keep the plane in the air.

Fortunately, the weather cleared enough for the plane to make it to Stuttgart and then Barcelona without further incidents. However, the next leg of Shirer's journey, Barcelona to Madrid, was another nightmare. The Spanish aircraft was buffeted by strong headwinds and almost ran out of fuel over the mountains. Two passengers who were not belted into their seats were seriously injured when they were thrown against the ceiling of the passenger compartment. Air travel in 1940 was still very much an adventure that was not for the meek.

Shirer finally reached Lisbon on 7 December, after two days of hard travel, only to find that all of the city's hotels were jammed with refugees. When finally he found a room, it was in the town of Estoril, a suburb of the Portuguese capital that enjoyed a reputation as being Portugal's royal Riviera. Here Shirer awaited the arrival of Ed Murrow, who flew in from London the following night. Janet Murrow noted in one of her letters home, "He's not very keen to go [to Lisbon] and wouldn't, but that he wants so much to see Bill."[36]

Ostensibly, Murrow had come to do one final broadcast with Shirer and to talk about CBS-related matters. In fact, he had made the risky journey from London to enjoy a few days relief from the grind of life in wartime London and to bid farewell to Shirer, with whom he felt a fraternal kinship. The two men spent the next five days together, talking and drinking late into the nights. They lounged at the beach during the days, played roulette in Estoril's casinos, and tried in vain to arrange for one last European broadcast together; in the end, Portuguese officials, fearful of offending Germany, refused to let them go on air. Regardless, Shirer and Murrow were thankful for the time together. They did not know when or even *if* they would ever see one another again; life in a time of all-out war was as uncertain as it was perilous. "[Ed] wasn't just a friend," Shirer told Murrow biographer A.M. Sperber many years later. "We had built up radio news from nothing ... [and] had been so close."[37]

With Shirer's ship, the SS *Excambion*, due to sail on the night of 13 December, Murrow accompanied Shirer to the dock. Daylight was fading as Shirer checked his luggage. The two old friends, in the time-honored tradition of veteran journalists, headed to the closest bar for a farewell drink. The place in which they found themselves was a rough-and-tumble open-air watering hole that catered to Portuguese dockworkers and sailors. "We crowded up to the bar and had some drinks," Shirer recalled – six shots of cheap brandy. By now, both men were growing nostalgic and tearful. "We fell silent. It got dark. I could no longer make out [Murrow's] face. It had been clouding up, taking on a familiar frown ... A loudspeaker blared a warning that all should be on ship. The crew started to pull up the gangplank. I shook hands with Ed. We found no words. I climbed aboard. I turned around. Ed had disappeared into the night."[38]

Shirer was relieved to discover that there were five other American foreign correspondents on board the New York-bound ship. The group of them adjourned to the ship's lounge for celebratory drinks. Shirer joined them briefly but was too restless to sit still. When his friends went to dinner, he excused himself. Instead, he went out on deck, where he could be alone with his hopes and fears. "A long, dark, savage night had settled over Europe," he reflected,[39] and yet he was escaping simply because of the fact he was lucky enough to have been born American.

There was a full moon, and as Shirer stood watching the lights of Lisbon receded into the night, his thoughts turned to home. His mind replayed the memories of those fifteen crazy, improbable, hectic, and historic years during which he had rambled around Europe, India, Afghanistan, and the Middle East.[40] The world, including America, had changed immeasurably, as had William Lawrence Shirer. His had been an incredible, astounding journey of self-discovery. From his front-row seat, he had witnessed history as it was being made.

23

Berlin Diary

William Shirer was among the throng of relieved, happy passengers standing on deck when the American Export Lines ship SS *Excambion* arrived in New York harbor the morning of 23 December 1940. As the ship steamed past the Statue of Liberty on this gray, sullen Monday, Shirer stood at the rail puffing his pipe, the collar of his overcoat turned up against a biting winter wind. Scanning the crowd of eager faces lining the pier, he broke into a smile when he caught sight of Tess and Inga waving in greeting. With Christmas just two days hence and the family reunited at last, there was much to celebrate.

On her previous visit to the United States, Tess Shirer had stayed with her brother-in-law and his wife in their home in Virginia. This time she did not; she was irked that it was only begrudgingly that John Shirer had loaned her money to help pay travel expenses.[1] So, upon their arrival in New York six weeks earlier, Tess, Inga, and the nanny had taken up residence in the St Moritz Hotel. "I think there were many Europeans there, and I remember that everyone on the staff seemed to speak French, which was my only language at the time," recalls Inga Shirer Dean.[2] The hotel, one of New York's poshest, was a luxurious way station for the family, especially Inga. "It will be good for her to get away from the hotel," Tess confided in a letter to her mother-in-law. "People [there] spoil her so, you know."[3]

The contrast between the circumstances of William Shirer's youthful departure for Europe and his triumphant homecoming was marked. In June 1925, he and his pal George Latta had sailed from Montreal, working their way over to Europe on a cattle boat. They had been two cash-strapped young men out for a summer of adventure. Now, fifteen years later, Shirer was returning home a celebrated foreign correspondent and a married family man.

Now in the eleventh year of the Great Depression, the United States was still struggling to right itself. The blind, unbounded optimism of the Jazz Age had been bludgeoned into submission by the familiar afflictions of our own era: a deep-seated cynicism that was reflected in cultural touchstones of the day. The acerbic tone of author John Steinbeck's proletarian novel *The Grapes of Wrath*, that year's winner of the Pulitzer Prize for fiction, struck a chord with many Americans.

Despite the fact isolationist sentiments still held sway in Washington, public interest in Europe's conflict was growing. This was largely due to the dramatic nature of wartime events and the sense of immediacy being fostered by the breathless live broadcasts that aired daily on the CBS, NBC, and Mutual radio networks. To millions of Americans and Canadians, star foreign correspondents and radio personalities – Edward R. Murrow and William Shirer in particular – had become household names and trusted figures. "To listeners, relaxed comfortably in their easy chairs at home, [Shirer's] voice from a nation at war has [become] but another taken-for-granted bit of radio magic," a *New York Times* reporter observed. "For them, the broadcasts from sources of world events involved only the snapping of a switch. For Mr Shirer the programs meant working at all hours of the day and night under the combined hardships of censorship, blackouts, air-raids, limited rations, and other wartime restrictions."[4]

New York Times reporter James "Scotty" Reston, Shirer's fellow passenger on the *Excambion* reported on the voyage in an article headlined "Shirer Back from Berlin."[5] Americans were eager to hear the uncensored details of the star CBS correspondent's experiences in Nazi Germany. So, after collecting his luggage and greeting his family, Shirer hopped into a cab and raced to the CBS studios at 485 Madison Avenue. In a dinner-hour broadcast – his first from American soil – Shirer recounted some of his experiences in wartime Berlin. He reported that any damage the city had suffered in RAF bombings was scattered, minor, and inconsequential, and he predicted it was unlikely Germans would go hungry that winter or that the Nazi war machine would run out of oil or other vital raw materials; the war would definitely continue.

As for any future expansion of America's involvement in the conflict, Shirer explained that, as the Nazis saw it, the Roosevelt administration was already "doing everything possible to help Great Britain – short of two things: a formal war declaration. And sending troops."[6] Thus, the key question many Europeans were asking was not whether America would enter the war, but rather if Germany would strike *first* if Hitler felt there was military advantage in doing so.

Audience reaction to Shirer's broadcast was such that when word got around in New York that he was planning to write a book about his experiences, publishers began courting him. Rumors were swirling that Fred Bate was writing a book, and publishers approached Ed Murrow to do likewise.

On John Gunther's recommendation, Shirer had signed on with Brandt & Brandt, one of New York's top literary agencies. Time being of the essence, in order to ensure that any Shirer book would be first on the market, Berenice Baumgarten, Shirer's agent at Brandt & Brandt, hastily negotiated a publishing deal on his behalf. Three weeks after his return home, Shirer signed a contract for a book to be published by Alfred A. Knopf in spring 1941.[7] In fact, the formal agreement was actually the culmination of a process that had begun almost four years earlier; Shirer and the Knopfs had been discussing the idea of him writing something for them since 1937.

Blanche Knopf had been appalled by the rising tide of anti-Semitism in Germany following Hitler's 1933 rise to power. By mid-1936, she was lamenting that there were no writers or publishers left in that country who were "worth thinking about." However, that did not stop her from seeking out writers whom she felt could make sense of what was happening in Germany. When she visited Paris in October 1937, one of the potential authors with whom she met was William Shirer, who chanced to be in town. Correspondence in the Knopf archives at the Harry Ransom Humanities Research Center at the University of Texas at Austin reveals that it was Shirer's friend Paul Gallico – a Knopf author – who alerted Mrs Knopf that Shirer was putting the finishing touches to a novel based on his experiences as a foreign correspondent in Germany. That Blanche Knopf was not all that familiar with Shirer or his work is evident; in the query letter she sent him, she misspelled his name: "Schirer."[8] If William Shirer even noticed, he failed to mention it when he sent Mrs Knopf a copy of his manuscript.

To Shirer's dismay, the publisher was unimpressed with his book, but she did offer suggestions on how he could improve it, the most significant being that he rewrite it as a first-person journalistic narrative. Shirer scoffed at that idea. "I'm not keen at all on making it straight personal reportage," he told Mrs Knopf. "I'll need some time to think over what, if anything, can be done to make the 'love story' fit better into the background."[9]

Shirer next sent a copy of his manuscript to his friend Paul Gallico, who expressed many of the same criticisms as Blanche Knopf had. Undeterred, Shirer asked Alfred A. Knopf for his opinion. Knopf obliged, but to Shirer's chagrin, he advised – as his wife had – that if Shirer was not prepared to make major changes to the book, he should "put it aside."[10]

Despite his disappointment, Shirer continued to hope he could publish with the Knopfs, and so he had met Blanche Knopf for lunch on 11 October 1937. By now, she was aware of Shirer's reputation as one of America's most high-profile foreign correspondents – and of the spelling of his surname. Mrs Knopf had also discovered that Shirer had grown up and gone to college in Cedar Rapids, the Iowa hometown of Knopf author Carl Van Vechten. Furthermore, Blanche Knopf knew Shirer was a friend of John Gunther, whose 1936 book *Inside Europe* had become an international bestseller for Knopf competitor Harper and Brothers. Like every other publisher in New York, the Knopfs were eager to find another big-name American journalist who might duplicate Gunther's commercial success. Mrs Knopf felt Shirer could be that person; if not, and if Shirer was amenable to editorial direction, she was hopeful that he could write the kind of book she was seeking. Shirer alluded to that notion when in a letter to Tess he noted that the publisher "was very different than I had expected, and she said the same frankly to me. She said she had expected I would look and act like Tom Wolfe."[11]

That was a strange statement; the two writers had little in common, other than their literary ambitions. Shirer was a veteran newspaper journalist from the Midwest who was now working in radio. Thomas Clayton Wolfe was a towering North Carolina-born playwright-turned-novelist, who had emerged as a major literary talent under the guiding hand of legendary Charles Scribner's Sons editor Maxwell Perkins; this was the editor who had shepherded Ernest Hemingway and F. Scott Fitzgerald to literary fame and fortune. Wolfe's novels *Look Homeward Angel* (1929), *Of Time and River* (1935), and the posthumously published *You Can't Go Home Again* (1940) had enjoyed huge critical acclaim and commercial success.

Wolfe, who was having a romantic fling with Martha Dodd, visited Berlin on several occasions in the mid-1930s and attended the 1936 summer Olympics. Shirer knew nothing of Wolfe's personal life or politics, and certainly not that Wolfe was one of those Americans who in their naiveté had admired Adolf Hitler early on. However, Shirer had read and admired Wolfe's writings, and when he expressed interest in meeting the author, Martha Dodd obligingly organized a get-acquainted lunch for the two men in the first week of September 1936. As Dodd anticipated, Shirer and Wolfe hit it off.

Shirer reported in his diary that Wolfe was "an immense fellow physically, boiling with energy; he developed a Gargantuan appetite, ordering a second main dish of meat and vegetables, and more bottles of wine than were good for us – or at least for me."[12] (In fact, Wolfe was an alcoholic.) The talk between Shirer and Wolfe flowed as easily as did the wine. The two chatted about the upcoming United States presidential election (in which they both favored Roosevelt), discussed writing, and mused about one of Shirer's favorite topics: why so many of America's best novelists stopped writing or were burned out at the point in their careers when their European counterparts were doing their best work.

Shirer summarized his impressions of Wolfe: "A very genuine person and more promising, if he can integrate himself, than any other young novelist we have."[13] The two men vowed to get together again next time they were both in New York. But that meeting was destined never to take place. Wolfe died in September 1938, falling victim to tuberculosis of the brain at the age of thirty-seven.

Blanche Knopf correctly sensed that Shirer was hungry to emulate Thomas Wolfe's success and to make a name for himself as a novelist. In autumn 1937, he still had misgivings about working in radio, something stopgap to pay the bills until he could achieve his real goal, which was to leave journalism and earn his living writing books. Blanche Knopf's rejection of his novel and his disappointment at the tone of their initial conversation colored his opinion of her. Aside from his assertion that Blanche Knopf was surprisingly tentative in her manner, "There was something in her I didn't like, but I don't know what it is," Shirer confided in a letter to Tess.[14]

Shirer's circumstances were markedly different in December 1940. That reality was reflected in the fact Blanche Knopf was ready to pay him a $10,000 advance for a book.[15] She understood how eager Americans were to read Shirer's inside account of life in Nazi Germany. Several of his friends had advised him to write "a research book that would be more solid, as scholars seek solidarity,"[16] but he rejected that idea. "Such a book would have meant a year of research and writing – at the least."[17]

Shirer had come to accept the wisdom of Knopf's suggestion that he write a first-person account of his experiences reporting from inside the Third Reich. That is what readers wanted, and he was now ready to provide it. When it was announced Shirer had signed a contract with Knopf, the media speculation was that his narrative would include some of the information that the Nazi censors had prevented him from conveying in his broadcasts from Berlin.

As a veteran newsman, Shirer accepted the need for haste, both because of the competition from forthcoming books by other writers and because he felt it was important to alert America to the growing threat posed by Hitler. The fact Shirer could now supplement his diary entries with information drawn from his own letters, from CBS broadcast scripts, and from newspaper clippings made his work easier. He had kept a diary in recent years and wrote in it every day. "A writer never stops," Shirer once told an interviewer. "He probably should, but he doesn't."[18]

Shirer had recorded details of the minutia of his daily life, his thoughts, and his experiences for his own "pleasure and peace of mind," as he explains in the foreword to his book, but also "to be perfectly frank ... with the idea that one day most of it might be published, if any publisher cared to commit it to print."[19] What had compelled him to keep a diary was that the "the kind of job I had ... appeared to be giving me a somewhat unusual opportunity to set down from day to day a firsthand account of a Europe that was already in agony and that, as the months and years unfolded, slipped inexorably towards the abyss of war and self-destruction."[20]

Tess Shirer found a rental house for the family near Chappaqua, a bedroom community about thirty-five miles north of Manhattan. It was here that William Shirer settled in and began work on his account of the six years he had spent in the capital of the Third Reich. He adopted a conversational tone straight off, plunging into his first-person narrative seven years earlier, on 11 January 1934: "Our money is gone. Day after tomorrow I must go back to work."[21]

At the time, he and Tess were broke and preparing to leave the Spanish seaside town of Lloret de Mer. Shirer euphemistically described his period of unemployment as a "sabbatical" that he and Tess had chosen to spend in Spain. He glossed over the fact that at the time he had been unemployed, like millions of other people.

Structuring his story as a diary allowed Shirer to be selective about the details of his experiences. He was intent on creating the impression that his Spanish adventures had been a continuation of the bohemian imperative that in the 1920s had prompted him and thousands of young Americans – Gertrude Stein's "Lost Generation" – to strike out for Europe in a search for adventure, romance, and meaning in life. As Shirer told it, in 1933 he and Tess had chosen to drop out once again. Such an explanation of why they were in Spain was more upbeat and compelling than admitting that he had been out of work and had no option other than to make the best of a bad situation. Having spent the time trying unsuccessfully to write a novel, he had been obliged to accept the first job offer that came along – one doing the same sort of ill-paying newspaper work he had left behind nine years earlier.

Shirer used literary license to full advantage while crafting an upbeat opening for his narrative. Writing in the first-person also allowed him to offer his perspective both on specific events and on the big picture. Shirer adhered to one of the golden rules of journalism: regardless of how grand or complex events are, focusing on the human elements of the story allows a writer to imbue it with a vital sense of drama, vitality, and timeliness.

In early May, Shirer delivered to Knopf a 220,000-word manuscript, which he dedicated "To Tess, who shared so much." There were the usual discussions between author and editor, and indecision about how much personal and family detail to include in the final text. The memos that passed back-and-forth between the book's editor and Mrs Knopf show that she agreed with the editor's assessment that Shirer displayed "an unfortunate habit of getting cute once in a while."[22] The editor added, "Nobody is interested in Mr Shirer's *weltschmerz* [world weariness], and nobody is interested in his attempts occasionally to make himself sound like a character in *The Sun Also Rises*."[23]

Shirer was privy to none of this, of course, and initially at least he had reluctantly acceded to the suggestions that he omit personal details and make his book a work of objective reporting. "Fortunately, William Allen White [the Pulitzer Prize-winning newspaper editor, politician and author] had read the manuscript uncut, and he was so strongly against having the personal parts removed that they later went back in."[24] At the same time, plans to title the book *This Is Berlin* – Shirer's signature radio sign-on from Berlin – were dropped; Ed Murrow had written a book called *This Is London* – his own trademark sign-on phrase. That title was appropriate since the book was a collection of recycled broadcast scripts, "a quickie" effort published by Simon & Schuster in hopes of capitalizing on Murrow's growing celebrity. However, sales were disappointing. For that reason, Knopf decided to market Shirer's book on its own merits and with a more distinctive and loftier title: *Berlin Diary: The Journal of a Foreign Correspondent, 1934–1941.*

The book, which went on sale across America in late June 1941, was the first attempt by a big-name American journalist to shed light on what was really happening inside Nazi Germany. *Berlin Diary* was also noteworthy because of Shirer's skillset. Here was a veteran journalist with a lively, compelling prose style and the ability to make a complex story understandable. It helped, too, that *Berlin Diary* received a welcome prepublication boost from the Book of the Month Club (BOMC). Berenice Baumgarten and Blanche Knopf scored a coup when they convinced BOMC founder Harry Scherman to offer the book as one of its featured selections for July. This was vitally important because, at 483 pages, *Berlin Diary* was a hefty volume. Without the BOMC's endorsement, it is likely that the book's size alone would have made it too daunting for popular success.

Berlin Diary benefited from its selection as a BOMC title, no question. However, the real secret to the book's popularity was in the writing; the public and critics alike were agreed on that. Word-of-mouth recommendations were strong, and the reviews were almost universally positive. It helped that Shirer had many contacts in the media. His old friend Joe Barnes, the former Berlin correspondent of the *New York Herald Tribune*, was among the first critics to review the book. He was enthusiastic in his praise, lauding *Berlin Diary* as being the "most important and the most exciting book written out of Germany since long before the war began. This is, first of all, an absorbing book."[25]

Many academics were no less effusive in their praise of *Berlin Diary*. This is worth noting since the tone of the response of professional historians to Shirer's later writings would be markedly different. In 1941, academics were still civil and positive in their assessment of Shirer's writing. For example, Hunter College president George N. Shuster, a prominent anti-fascist commentator of the day, wrote a laudatory review for *The New York Times Review of Books*: "Because Mr Shirer has been on the side of the angels, from the beginning of this struggle, the story he has to tell can be recommended with downright enthusiasm not because it is perfect or complete, but because it presents with honesty and firmness truth that must be known now if he and the rest of us are to survive."[26]

Buoyed by positive reviews, America's growing appetite for war news, and BOMC distribution, *Berlin Diary* climbed to the top of the bestseller lists in major cities from coast to coast in America and Canada (there was no such thing in either country as a "national bestseller list" at that time). The *Toronto Star* hailed *Berlin Diary* as one of the "grand books" of 1941 and reported that it was the bestselling nonfiction book in city bookshops.[27]

Congratulatory cards and letters also poured into Shirer's mailbox. From London came a letter from Ed Murrow that Shirer cherished above all others. Murrow praised *Berlin Diary* as a revealing account of life inside wartime Germany: "[It's] not easy to write about such things, but [the book] reveals in print the honesty, charity, tolerance, and humor that is you … You have no idea of the pleasure your friends here derive from your success and you'll not be surprised to know that those of here in the [CBS] office are in the forefront when there's applauding to be done."[28]

Given the favorable reception for *Berlin Diary*, Shirer finally felt he was in a position to break free of workaday journalism. He had no intention of returning to Berlin anyway. That was just as well for conditions for those few American correspondents still reporting from the city became increasingly tenuous and dangerous as the tensions between the United States and Germany grew. "If Bill Shirer thought Berlin was bad when he departed for the States a year earlier, he should have seen it in the fall of 1941," write Cloud and Olson. "Americans, whose government was still nominally neutral, were harassed on the street and in restaurants and sometimes beaten up. American journalists living in hotels were asked by nervous managers to leave."[29]

In the circumstances, as mentioned earlier, it is hardly surprising that Paul White and Ed Murrow had concluded Harry Flannery was not the right man to replace Shirer in Berlin. Thus, they reassigned him after only a few months on the job. In his place in early 1941 they installed former UP reporter Howard K. Smith. Unlike Flannery, he knew his way around the city and the Nazi bureaucracy. Smith was bright, talented, and resourceful. He was also a gifted writer with a keen eye for the human details that bring a story to life. In short, Smith was the kind of reporter Ed Murrow was keen to have on his staff, and he proved to be an inspired choice as CBS's man in Berlin.

As for Shirer, he had already moved on to the next phase of his career. His literary success further heightened his already lofty public profile; Knopf sold 600,000 copies of *Berlin Diary* in the first year after publication. A writer for *The New York Times* commented on the shift in public tastes that had made this possible: "The public began to desert the movies and theaters in favor of the radio's latest news flashes, and today the names of ... Shirer ... *et al.*, are as well-known as those of the reigning movie stars."[30] The *Times* writer went on to report that a year before the Munich crisis the four "major New York stations" broadcast only eight daily newscasts in the hours between 8 a.m. and 6 p.m. On the eve of Pearl Harbor, those same stations carried twenty-nine newscasts, plus talk shows and news commentaries.[31]

Shirer's take on the latest news from Europe aired three times each week on CBS in his fifteen-minute newscast at 5:15 p.m. on Sunday evenings, which was carried by sixty-seven network stations, and in five-minute commentaries heard in New York at 11:10 p.m. Monday and Wednesday. All of these broadcasts enjoyed solid ratings, with the Sunday network-wide program typically polling a 6.8 score on the ten-point Crossley scale.[32] In addition, now that he was no longer tied to the routine of daily deadlines, Shirer had time to cash in on his fame, delivering public lectures (for $1,500 plus expenses per engagement), writing a syndicated Sunday column for the *New York Herald Tribune*, and even making his screen debut. He appeared on camera with Dorothy Thompson and other well-known journalists in "What's the Shooting For?" – the first instalment in a series of one-reel films on current affairs. Such panel discussions are today standard fare on television; in 1941, they were novelty presentations – big-screen versions of the roundup broadcasts CBS radio had pioneered three years earlier – and were packaged with cartoons and Fox Movietone News film footage in the double-bill entertainment package shown in movie theaters across North America.[33]

Shirer basked in his growing celebrity. He was in demand, and honors flowed his way. In early June, he made a flying visit to Cedar Rapids – literally as well as figuratively. He returned to Coe College, his alma mater, for the first time since 1929 to accept an honorary Doctor of Letters degree and to pay his respects to his erstwhile mentor Harry M. Gage, who had announced his intention to retire as president of the college at the end of the school year.

Gage, Coe students and faculty, and many Cedar Rapids residents had tuned into Shirer's news reports on CBS, and this native son was regarded as a hero. A standing-room-only crowd of more than 1,000 people jammed the Sinclair Memorial Chapel for Shirer's public lecture, and his words were duly reported in the local media, the Coe alumni magazine,[34] and the student newspaper, the *Coe College Cosmos*; an account of the talk, which appeared on the front page of the next day's edition, provides a snapshot of Shirer's view on the war. Like most pundits, even those with some firsthand knowledge of events in Europe, his predictions proved yet again the folly of trying to guess Hitler's next moves.

Shirer was on safe ground when he "paint[ed] a vivid picture of the life of a radio correspondent in Germany," telling his audience that he felt the German people were intent on seeing the conflict through to what they were certain would be a victorious conclusion. That much was true. Where he missed the mark – and badly – was in his effort to foretell the course of the war. He was still convinced Hitler would launch an invasion of England, most likely before autumn and that the Nazi leader would "not provoke Russia until this war is over."[35] He was left to marvel at the folly of his words less than two weeks later when, on 22 June 1941, the German army turned eastward and attacked Russia: "These were dark days for those of us who hoped that Hitler would meet his match in Russia. Now it looked as though he had achieved his greatest conquest."[36]

Shirer's pessimism was on full display when on he met peers and colleagues at the annual dinner of the Headliners Club in Atlantic City on 28 June. Two years earlier, the journalists' association had honored both Shirer and Murrow for their 1938 coverage of the Austrian Anschluss, and now the assembled members bestowed a Silver Microphone Award on Shirer for his "general excellence in radio reporting."[37]

Despite this and all of the good things happening in his life, Shirer continued to feel downcast about the course of the war in Europe and the growing political tensions in the Far East. His uncertainties and worst fears were realized on the morning of 7 December 1941. The Japanese sneak attack on America's Pacific fleet in its base at Pearl Harbor in the Hawaiian Islands packed a devastating emotional punch, proving to be a watershed event in the history of the twentieth century and of the United States of America. As historian Arthur M. Schlesinger Jr observes, "The bitter wreckage of ships and planes at Pearl Harbor ended the illusion that the United States could be a world power and remain safe from a world conflict."[38]

The next morning, America declared war on Japan, and three days later Germany and Italy jumped into the fray on the side of their ally in the Far East. Shirer was dismayed by the scale of the danger America now faced: "The undefended west coast ... lay open to Japanese attack and invasion."[39] At the same time, he feared Hitler's Luftwaffe would strike the Eastern seaboard. Shirer predicted that as many as a 150 German bombers from a base in occupied France might attempt at least one "token raid" on New York City. Shirer should have known better. The notion that German air-

craft could fly such vast distances – as far as Charles Lindbergh had traveled on his historic 1927 transatlantic flight and then back again without
refueling was unrealistic to the point of being absurd. However, Shirer
feared it was possible, and it is a measure of the fears and uncertainty
of the times that others took him seriously; his words were duly reported
in *The New York Times* and elsewhere.[40] The flames of the conflict that
Hitler's invasion of Poland on 1 September 1939 had ignited were now
engulfing the entire planet.

24

The Price of Fame

On the eve of the war and awash in uncertainties, William Shirer pondered the direction of his career and his life: "When did family life start? ... A roving correspondent over these last years of crisis in Europe had little personal life."[1] Back home, as his frustrations abated and his priorities changed, Shirer's focus grew ever more introspective. He was living and working in New York, the world's most vibrant, prosperous, and exciting city. He had a plum job with CBS, and with the success of his first book he had at last realized his dream of establishing himself as an author. Shirer felt he had earned his successes. Yet he wondered if this life was what he *really* wanted. His confusion only intensified in the closing weeks of 1941.

Tess was in the final hours of her second pregnancy, and on 10 December, only three days after Pearl Harbor, she gave birth to the couple's second daughter. The arrival of a child on American soil was a watershed event for Tess and Bill Shirer. Neither of them would ever return to Europe to live; that phase of their life together was now behind them.

Congratulatory messages flowed in from family and friends far and wide. Janet Murrow agreed to stand as the godmother of the baby, whom her parents had decided to call Elizabeth Linda. She shared the given name of her paternal grandmother, while her middle name was chosen for its Hispanic ring, a reminder of the Shirers' Spanish sojourn.[2]

With two young daughters to care for, family concerns were now paramount, at least for Tess, who began searching for a new, larger home. She found what she was looking for in June 1942: a stately twelve-room brick house in the Sagamore Park section of Bronxville, an affluent suburban neighborhood about fifteen miles north of Manhattan. Domestic help was a luxury William Shirer could afford. As they had in Geneva, the family retained both a maid and a nanny, the latter being the young Swiss woman who had come over from Lisbon with Tess and Inga.

Despite his new affluence and the trappings of his success, Shirer was not content. For him, suburbia was the epitome of white, middle-class propriety and respectability; he felt out of place there. When Jack Goodman, Shirer's alter ego in his never-produced stage play about his Berlin years, bemoans "those stuffy New York suburbs ... where every other guy is a vice-president of something,"[3] he is voicing Shirer's sentiments.

For now, Shirer became a commuter, making the drive into Manhattan several times each week. Then, for convenience's sake, he leased a unit in a triplex located at 27 Beekman Place, the same upscale street on the Upper East Side where CBS president William Paley lived.

The Shirers settled into a moneyed lifestyle and all that it entailed, including holidays and summers in the country. At first, they vacationed at inns and guest cottages in the Lake Placid area of upstate New York or on Cape Cod. Years later, Shirer eventually purchased a 100-acre vacation property, which Paul Gallico recommended as an "absolute give-away" at $20,000.[4] Located three hours north of New York City, near the historic mill town of Torrington, Connecticut, "The Farm" included a quaint Revolutionary War-era "salt-box-style" house and was in the same area as rural properties owned by *New York Herald Tribune* books columnist Lewis Gannett, Columbia University scholar Mark Van Doren, and humorist James Thurber. Beginning in 1947, it was to The Farm that the Shirers retreated for long weekends and to escape the city's summer heat. Shirer's sister, Josephine – "Aunt Josie," as the Shirer girls affectionately called her – often joined them here for special occasions.

Despite his prosperity and fame, just as Shirer had feared, he found that reintegrating himself into workaday life in New York was not easy. He continued to wrestle with that most basic of questions: what did he want in life? After so many years abroad, he felt like a visitor in his own country, and that restlessness gave him a "sinking feeling in the stomach."[5] At the same time, he knew he was fortunate to be an American, especially because at age thirty-seven and with just one eye, he was deemed "unfit" for military service and was exempt from the draft lottery that came into effect in 1942. This was a mixed blessing. Just as was the case during the First World War, there was a stigma attached to *not* being in uniform, *not* being seen to do one's patriotic duty. Any man not in the military was expected to do his part to support the war effort. Ed Murrow felt strongly about this and made no secret of his scorn for what he felt was an unseemly eagerness on Shirer's part to take advantage of his privileged position. Murrow's resentment, heightened by Shirer's tardiness in honoring a personal commitment he had made to Murrow, opened a rift between them. For the first time, their relationship began to fray.

Prior to his 1940 return home and again in a 1941 letter, Shirer had agreed to stand in for Murrow in London as needed. However, once he was back home, Shirer was slow to make good on his promise. This nettled Murrow, who felt his old friend had grown lazy and was letting his ego get the better of him. Cashing in on one's celebrity and demanding VIP treatment did not sit well with Murrow, whose own self-image continued to be that of a blue-collar, no-nonsense guy. So strongly did he feel about this and about the morality of the war that prior to Pearl Harbor he contemplated quitting CBS to return home and take on an activist role in the fight to end America's isolationism; he even contemplated getting involved in politics. In the end, Murrow opted to continue working as a broadcaster, but he did donate to the Bundles for Britain charity all of the money he earned from an American lecture tour he did in late 1941 and early 1942. He was dismayed that some of his colleagues, Shirer among them, did not follow his example. In a letter to a friend, Murrow commented, "One of my age cannot go about ... making profits out of recounting the heroism of others, and then put the money in the bank."[6]

While such concerns were understandable, there may well have been an element of jealousy in Murrow's umbrage. During the years he and Shirer had worked together in Europe, they had fed off each other's energies and expertise. That changed following Shirer's 1940 repatriation. Now that he and Murrow were no longer a team and no longer communicating on a daily basis, an element of competition inevitably arose between them. These were men of strong character and sizable egos, and both were under considerable pressure in their lives. At the same time, there can be no denying that Shirer relished his celebrity and the influence he wielded as a CBS news commentator. Breathing the intoxicating air of the New York social scene served to distort his perspective and cloud his judgment.

Shirer sensed the chill in relations between himself and Ed Murrow; how could he not? On one occasion, as Cloud and Olson report, Shirer was back in London, attending a dinner Murrow hosted. When Shirer began expounding on conditions in Germany, Murrow interrupted him in mid-sentence to say that his dinner guests might prefer to hear from "someone who knows something about Germany." Eric Sevareid, who was present that night, recalls, "You could watch Shirer's face turning red."[7]

Shirer suspected Murrow was envious that *Berlin Diary* had become an international bestseller while his own book, *This Is London*, had not sold well. However, any such notion on Shirer's part was baseless; Murrow had praised *Berlin Diary* in his broadcasts and had bought dozens of copies to give to friends and colleagues. How much of this Shirer appreciated or conveniently forgot is unclear. Many years later, he acknowledged that his ego had gotten the better of him at the time: "It was easy with the notoriety and the constant publicity that radio brought, to get puffed up about yourself."[8]

Tess Shirer chided her husband when he confided his suspicion that Murrow was jealous of him. Shirer's daughter Inga remembered her mother relating how she had cautioned her husband not to let fame "go to his head." To his credit, Shirer heeded that warning, to a degree. "Dad once saw a photo of himself taken at the height of the popularity of *Berlin Diary* and when he was doing so well at CBS, and he asked my mother, 'Please don't ever let me look like *that* again.'"[9] This was easier said than done. Foreign correspondents were the glamor figures of journalism. In Berlin, Shirer had made his nightly broadcasts with his one good eye alternately on his script and on the Nazi officials who were ready to end the transmission if he deviated from the approved text. The whole process had had an air of unreality to it; at the time Shirer had no way of knowing what effect, if any, his words were having back home. Was anyone there listening? Shirer sometimes doubted it.

Once he was back on American soil, Shirer recognized that the impact of his words was immediate and palpable. CBS president William Paley certainly understood the enormous public influence wielded by the network's star correspondents and news commentators. A few days after Pearl Harbor, Paley had CBS news director Paul White circulate a memo to all CBS staff that echoed an Ed Klauber fiat from September 1939.[10] White reminded his on-air personnel of the importance of maintaining calm demeanor and of the network's ban on the use of recordings or evocative sound effects. The expression of personal opinions – "opinionating," as

White called it – likewise remained taboo. Yet, at the same time, "This is a war for the preservation of democracy. The American people must not only always be kept vividly aware of this ... but of the value of every man, woman, and child in the nation of preserving democracy."[11] Exactly *what* White was dictating is unclear. There also was more than a little subjectivity inherent in his approach to "objectivity," and so his demand for "non-opinionated commentary" did not sit well with some CBS staff. When White refused to back down, the rancor escalated. The essence of the debate remains a familiar one: is there such a thing as "objective" journalism? That concept was a utopian ideal that was difficult to achieve. And it was even more difficult to champion; the radio listener always had the option of turning off his or her radio, changing the station, or picking up a newspaper or magazine to find alternate viewpoints. White himself acknowledged as much in his 1947 book *News on the Air*: "Complete journalistic objectivity is only an ideal." However, he hastened to add: "The fact that it is difficult if not impossible to attain does not seem to me to impair the idea itself, or excuse the broadcaster for a constant and vigilant effort to try for it."[12]

William Shirer was one of the few big-name journalists to speak out in support of Paul White, defending CBS against charges the network was censoring its news commentators. In principle, Shirer and Ed Murrow were as one in the debate over objectivity and censorship; both knew there were no pat answers. As Murrow saw it, the real issue at the heart of the controversy was CBS's practice of allowing sponsors to choose the news commentators for the programs they supported. Murrow understood the economic necessity of having advertising support for any network programming, but he felt it would be better to say to potential corporate partners: "OK, you can have one of our men, but you can't choose some nitwit who will follow your party line."[13] The irony in those words would prove telling for both Murrow and for Shirer.

Despite their simmering personal antagonisms, where broadcasting was concerned there was never any real competition between the two men, certainly not in the public's mind. Ed Murrow's celebrity, popularity, and reputation eclipsed Shirer's and that of every other radio newsman of the day. The passage of time has done nothing to change that. However, Murrow insisted he was just an ordinary newsman. If there was one undeniable constant in his life, it was – as journalist Harrison Salisbury notes – that Murrow "didn't put on [airs]."[14] Of course, there was no need for him to do so; *others* exalted him. If there was royalty in broadcasting, it was Edward R. Murrow.

That was so whether Murrow was in London or New York. When he returned home in early December 1941 on a three-month furlough (with Robert Trout, *not* Shirer, standing in for him in London), William Paley feted Murrow at a gala dinner at New York's Waldorf Astoria Hotel. Also in attendance were other CBS luminaries including Klauber, Shirer, and Paul White, along with a who's who of New York journalism, business, labor, and academia. A writer for the show-business trade newspaper *Variety* described the event as "the most celebrity-studded [dinner] ever held for a radio employee."[15]

Despite his exalted status, Murrow continued to insist he did not expect any special treatment. He hoped – and expected – colleagues to take the same down-to-earth approach to their jobs. For that reason, he felt Shirer and some other newsmen were getting a little too full of themselves. Murrow could not, did not, hide how much this bothered him. Cloud and Olson report that one day as Shirer and Murrow were leaving a Manhattan restaurant where they had been drinking, Murrow – never one to shy away from physical confrontation – snatched Shirer's fedora off his head and threw it onto the street, where it was flattened by passing vehicles. "That old hat of Bill's got on my nerves," Murrow said later. "I told him that now, since he was in the money, he could afford a new one."[16] Cloud and Olson speculate that Murrow's sarcasm was his way of delivering a none-too-subtle message to Shirer: "Don't presume too much, old pal. I'm still the boss. As if to underscore the point, Murrow the next day presented Shirer with a brand-new hat."[17]

William Shirer could afford to buy new headwear or just about anything else he fancied. At a time when a typical industrial worker in America was earning forty dollars per week, Shirer was taking home $1,800 per week from his work as a radio broadcaster, his Sunday column in the *New York Herald Tribune*, freelance articles, and the fees from lectures for which he now earned $750 plus expenses. His pre-tax income for 1943 was $84,000[18] – roughly the equivalent of $1.4 million today.

Old friends sometimes tried to take advantage of Shirer's good fortune and largesse. For example, Jay Allen, who was down on his luck yet again, had gotten in touch to ask for a loan, even though he had failed to pay back $550 he had borrowed earlier. Shirer declined Allen's second request, making the excuse that he, too, was having financial troubles and had been obliged to cash in some investments and borrow from his brother in order to pay his bills and his taxes.[19] That was true.

It was Shirer's misfortune to begin earning big money just as the federal government initiated rigorous new fiscal measures that were intended to generate revenue for the country's war effort, which was costing Washington more than $6.6 billion per month.[20] To pay for it, the Roosevelt administration raised personal and corporate income taxes to unprecedented levels.

Shirer supported the war effort, but like many well-off Americans at the time he found himself in a tax dispute with the Internal Revenue Service (IRS). The nub of the disagreement was the agency's contention that he was a CBS employee. If so, he was subject to the "pay-as-you-go" provisions of the Income Tax Act. Shirer and his lawyers disagreed, arguing that as an "independent contractor" he was not covered by this provision of the tax laws. In the end, after two years of legal wrangling a judge ruled in Shirer's favor; however, his battle with the IRS caused him no end of aggravation and considerable expense.

In a bid to quell opposition to high taxes, in 1943 the government mounted an advertising campaign that was heavy on patriotism. Many celebrities were recruited to support the initiative. Songwriter Irving Berlin composed a tune entitled "I Paid My Taxes Today," while filmmaker Walt Disney created a cartoon in which Donald Duck paid his "taxes to beat the Axis." Although he was fighting the IRS, William Shirer also did his bit for Uncle Sam, contributing anti-Nazi articles pro bono to various publications and government propaganda booklets and lending his name to the victory bonds campaign. He also used both his weekly newspaper column and his Sunday evening newscast on CBS to advocate "a liberal or progressive American foreign policy."[21]

It is a measure of Shirer's celebrity during this period that the Spanish artist and revolutionary Luis Quintanilla asked to paint Shirer's portrait. Quintanilla, a friend of Jay Allen and Ernest Hemingway, had visited the Shirers during their 1933 sojourn in Spain. After fleeing his homeland in the wake of the fascist victory in the civil war, Quintanilla settled in New York City. He was painting a series of portraits of well-known American writers – people such as John Steinbeck, John Dos Passos, Dorothy Parker, and Arthur Miller – "as how they see themselves."[22] Shirer, perhaps because of his cynicism about organized religion or his Cassandra-like role as a news commentator, chose to be painted in the guise of an astrologer. Quintanilla's whimsical rendering depicts the mustachioed, bespectacled Shirer against a celestial backdrop. He is attired in an impressionistic robe of reds and violets that is decorated with astrological signs.

Perched atop his head as he puffs his pipe and studies a book with his one good eye is a star-bedecked pointy hat. The image is as arresting as it is cryptic.[23]

As was the case with Ed Murrow, albeit to a lesser extent, Shirer's reputation preceded him. This was true when finally he returned to London in June 1943 to spell Murrow, who was reporting from the frontlines. Hearing that Shirer was in town, playwright Noel Coward invited him to attend performances of his plays at the Hay Market Theatre. During this same London visit, Shirer had lunch with writer Rebecca West and her husband. Shirer had met West a decade earlier in Vienna, at one of the Gunthers' parties; now in the wake of the success of *Berlin Diary*, West invited him to renew acquaintances. At age fifty-one, West was a grande dame of the British literary scene. Shirer confided in his diary that he was "not quite myself" at the lunch, nervous of "being overwhelmed in my own mind by West's terrific literary reputation."[24]

Shirer, too, now had a literary reputation, something his British friends were quick to remind him about. When he visited with Nye Bevan and his wife Jennie Lee, the two British Labour Party MPs prevailed upon him for an introduction to John Steinbeck, who was the darling of left-leaning intellectuals and was in London for his work as a *New York Herald Tribune* war correspondent. Shirer had met Steinbeck as a result of their mutual support of anti-fascist causes.

Back in New York, Shirer was discovering that fame and money could be as addictive and debilitating as any drug. With many of his best friends also now living in Manhattan – including some CBS colleagues and old newspaper pals such as Dorothy Thompson, Joe Barnes, John Gunther, and Jimmy Sheean – Shirer's pattern of social activity changed. With too much time and too much money to spend, he fell in with a hard-drinking, fast-living social circle.

Shirer never was and never could be a bon vivant, not in the same way as friends such as John Gunther were. Yet Shirer began idling away his nights in Manhattan's fashionable restaurants and nightclubs. Like the coffee houses of pre-war Vienna, each of these establishments catered to distinct clienteles. Shirer became a frequent guest at John Gunther's table at the Stork Club, where champagne and witty conversation flowed freely. Shirer was also a regular at the lavish parties Gunther threw at his apartment, just a few blocks from Shirer's own place on the Upper East Side. In the circumstances and given his own high profile, it is not surprising that Shirer became acquainted with celebrities and with many of the beautiful women whom John Gunther was dating now that he was estranged from his wife.

Money, fame, and success are powerful aphrodisiacs, and Gunther had all three in excess, with a taste for the good life. His glitzy social life and many love affairs were grist for the gossip mills of Walter Winchell and *Evening Post* columnist Leonard Lyons. On the periphery of this whirlwind of social activity, Shirer felt himself being drawn into the vortex.

Change and Confusion

William Shirer's first meeting, in late August 1941, with Ottilie Ethel Leopoldine Losch – "Tilly" to her friends – marked the start of a long period of personal turmoil that was also the beginning of the end of his marriage to Tess. That summer, the Shirers had rented a beach house on Cape Cod. Tess, six months pregnant, remained at the seashore with daughter Inga to enjoy the waning days of summer when her husband returned to his job in New York. That is where he was one evening, preparing for his newscast, when John Gunther came calling. Out for another night on the town, he was accompanied by movie director Frank Capra, Russian-born filmmaker Anatole Litvak (with whom Capra was collaborating on the United States Army's *Why We Fight* film series), and Tilly Losch. The foursome had come to invite Shirer to join them for a nightcap at the 21 Club.

Losch caught Shirer's eye immediately; the Austrian-born actress, dancer, choreographer, and painter was an "extremely attractive-looking woman of about forty whose soft, slight Viennese accent I detected at the very instant she was being introduced."[1] Shirer was enthralled by Losch, whose reputation preceded her; she had been a star of Vienna stages in 1929 when Shirer was the *Chicago Tribune*'s man in the Austrian capital. Later, he had seen Losch acting in a Noel Coward play in London. Shirer found her beauty mesmerizing; however, although he had been single at the time, he had been too shy to act on his impulse to approach her. Instead, he had shelved his fanciful desires, which had resided in the recesses of his mind ever since. Or so he claimed.

A less romantic explanation for Shirer's reaction to meeting Losch is that in August 1941 he was at loose ends. Despite his recent literary success, he was unsettled and emotionally adrift, not entirely happy at being back home after almost sixteen years abroad. Nor was he was finding it

easy to settle down to a workaday routine that included family responsibilities, the trials and tribulations of an office environment, coping with
corporate politics at CBS, paying the bills, and dealing with income-tax
woes. It may also have been that monogamy did not come easily or naturally for a man who had grown used to a transient lifestyle. While there
was no smoking-gun evidence that he engaged in extramarital affairs in
the early years of his marriage, Shirer certainly had many opportunities to
stray; the peripatetic nature of a foreign correspondent's lifestyle was not
conducive of marital fidelity. While Tess had long had her suspicions in
this regard, she mostly had chosen to turn a blind eye.

In summer 1941, Shirer was thirty-seven, successful, and in good health
– but still struggling to resolve questions that were central to his life. He
suddenly found himself face-to-face with a glamorous woman about
whom he had fantasized for many years.

Losch was described as having "almond eyes and sensuous lips, [which]
with her disciplined talent and imagination, made her an exotic enchantress,
Oriental in appearance."[2] However, she was actually a native of Vienna. The
daughter of Russian émigré parents, as a child she had showed precocious
talent, making her dancing debut at age six in a children's ballet at Vienna's
Royal Opera House. In 1930, Losch was twenty-eight when she married
Edward James, an Anglo-American millionaire and arts patron who began
bankrolling dance productions that showcased his wife's talents. However,
these initiatives, like the marriage, ended abruptly; James was bisexual, or so
his wife alleged. According to legal documents filed in the subsequent
divorce proceedings, when James cavorted with male lovers, his wife did
likewise.

Losch came to New York in 1931 to dance with Adele and Fred Astaire
in a Broadway production of *The Band Wagon*. Auburn-haired, petite, and
graceful as a prima ballerina, she won effusive praise from critics. Brooks
Atkinson of *The New York Times* wrote that she "raise[d] musical show
dancing to the level of fine art."[3]

Following a messy, very public 1934 split from her husband, Losch
turned to acting, first in London, then in Hollywood. She enjoyed a successful, albeit brief, career on the big screen, appearing in a few films, most
notably *The Good Earth* (1937) – which starred Luise Rainer, another
actress whom Shirer had had a crush on during his Vienna days. According to a Losch biographical sketch written by Professor Herbert Poetzl
that can be found on the website of the State University of New York
(where Losch's papers are housed), "Tilly [like Rainer] was not particularly happy in the Hollywood dream factory. She recalled that it was a lone-

ly, isolated life with countless artists competing against each other for fame."[4]

In 1938, Losch was hospitalized in Davos, Switzerland, with depression. Once recovered, she remarried, becoming the wife of another wealthy Englishman. Henry Herbert, the sixth Earl of Carnarvon, was a major in the British army and the eldest son of the archeologist who along with Howard Carter in 1922 had co-discovered the tomb of the Egyptian pharaoh Tutankhamen. The Carnarvon's ancestral home is the backdrop for the popular British television series *Downton Abbey*. As Henry Herbert's spouse, Losch became a countess with the title Lady Carnarvon. Poetzl notes, "Due to her precarious health, her émigré status, and the dangers of war, Lord Carnarvon in 1940 shipped off his wife to the United States."[5] A 1945 *New York Times* news article tells a somewhat different story, reporting that "the Countess went to America and when she returned [to England] in 1940 she told the Earl she was not prepared to settle down [there]. The Earl said he did everything to dissuade her, but the Countess returned to America in June, 1940, and never returned."[6]

Either way, Poetzl is correct when he notes that "Tilly's newly acquired social status proved to be of great advantage in American society and in the furtherance of her career."[7] That career was no longer as a performer on stage or in films, but rather as a painter. Losch was intent on making it as a professional artist. New York was an ideal venue.

In the 1940s the city was a cultural Mecca. Most major American cities on either coast maintained a midnight curfew during the war years. Not the Big Apple; the doors of the city's nightspots officially remained open until 1 a.m., and unofficially until the last customer went home. Tilly Losch was very much at home in this milieu. At a cocktail party a stuffy New York socialite asked her, "I've heard of you, but why should I have?" Losch replied, "You've heard of me because I've never done anything *unimportant*."[8]

John Gunther, like Shirer, was much taken with Losch. That is why she came to be out on the town with Gunther, Capra, and Litvak the night they recruited Shirer to party with them. At Club 21, Shirer and Losch sat next to one another and sparks flew. "I was enthralled ... Tilly and I sat at one end of the table engrossed in talk, oblivious of the others. I became aware of my state when John Gunther, rather annoyed, suddenly yelled at us and asked if it wasn't time we joined them."[9]

Afterward, Shirer and Losch struck up a relationship that began with exchanges of cards and notes and quickly progressed to daily telephone calls. From there, things heated up quickly. When Losch invited the Shirers to tea, rather than bonding with her as another displaced Vienna native – as William Shirer had hoped – his wife took an instant dislike to Tilly Losch; Tess Shirer had sensed that here was a rival for her husband's heart.

Over his wife's protests, Shirer continued to see Losch. He and John Gunther worked in tandem to advance her career as an artist. When in April 1944 she staged the first American showing of her paintings, Gunther wrote a foreword for the catalogue while Shirer lobbied journalist friends to report on the exhibition. The opening night festivities drew a celebrity crowd and received wide media coverage, including an equivocal review in *Time* magazine, which opined that some of the twenty-eight paintings on display "looked as if they had been painted by the children in them; some were reminiscent of the French primitive Le Douanier Henri Emilien Rousseau, or of the French Modernist Marie Laurencin."[10]

As the affair between Shirer and Losch intensified, there was talk of marriage – mostly on Losch's part. By summer 1944, her union with Herbert was lurching inexorably toward divorce. Shirer, uncertain about the future of his own marriage, agonized over what to do. As yet, he could not, would not, seek a divorce; doing so would mean leaving behind his two young daughters. Wracked with guilt and unable or unwilling to resolve the emotional dilemma he had created, he sought escape in his work.

In the first week of October 1944, Shirer traveled to London on behalf of CBS and the *New York Herald Tribune*. His assignment as a uniformed correspondent was to spend a month reporting on the war, which in its final stages had become furious. As German defenses crumbled, the frequency and intensity of the Allied air raids grew. Like Shirer, Ed Murrow was wrestling with personal demons and had thrown himself into his work. Determined to tell "the full story" of what was happening at the front – to the dismay of family, friends, and CBS management – Murrow began flying on bombing missions with Allied air crews. His breathless eyewitness accounts of the war in the skies over Germany stand as classics of wartime reportage; as Howard K. Smith notes, Murrow's "forte was descriptive, rather than analytical, journalism."[11]

A.M. Sperber speculates on Murrow's rationale for placing himself in harm's way, concluding that he did so "for reasons he couldn't explain to himself, much less to others."[12] Murrow, like Shirer and so many of their friends, was struggling to make sense of what was happening to him and to the world. Janet Murrow shared none of her husband's uncertainties or his willingness to risk death. As Sperber points out, she had "made it clear she wanted to go home; she had had it with the expatriate life, belonging neither here nor there."[13] Whatever Murrow's reasons for tempting fate, it is clear they were part and parcel of the macho disdain he felt for those colleagues who were content to talk about the war or to profit from writing about it; that included his old friend Bill Shirer.

Murrow's behavior at this time in his career raises fundamental questions about the role of the media in news reporting and about the extent to which any journalist should become involved in the events they are reporting – i.e., how ethical is it for a journalist to be embedded in the military and to risk death in order to get closer to the "real" story?

Logistically, it was now much easier for Murrow to get away for prolonged periods, something he did with increasing frequency in the war's final months. The CBS presence in London had grown; the network's news staff there and in Europe was no longer a two-man operation. Murrow still served as bureau chief in London; however, veteran CBS newsmen such as Shirer, Eric Sevareid, Charles Collingwood, Larry LeSueur, and Bill Downs – "Murrow Boys," all – now rotated in and out, working alongside new hires who had increased the network's staff complement in the British capital to as many as ten full-time reporters. There was plenty of work for all of them; as Alexander Kendrick notes, "There were always enough CBS correspondents to be found in London ... for at least a small poker game."[14]

Back on familiar turf, Shirer resumed the routine of a workaday newsman. Even here, thousands of miles from home, the disquieting realities of the emotional discord he had stirred up continued to claw at his emotions; Tilly Losch was urging him to prod her English lawyers to speed up her divorce proceedings. If Shirer bothered to do so, it had little effect; the legal tangle was not finally sorted out until 1947. For now, Shirer remained ambivalent about what to do. With the war in Europe winding down and the inevitability of the Allied victory growing ever more likely, he devoted himself completely to his work. Sensing that he was in the midst of the biggest news story of his life, he was intent on making the most of the opportunity.

In the third week of October, Shirer returned to Paris, newly liberated from German occupation. Ed Murrow was there, too, but only briefly. Both men were relieved to see that the French capital had suffered little significant physical damage in the war. "How different this Paris [is] from the one I last saw in the tragic June days of 1940 ... when I came in with the German army," Shirer wrote in his diary. "Today the past is gone, the streets animated and full of bustling French, free again and drinking in lustily their freedom."¹⁵

From Paris, Shirer pressed on to northern France and Belgium before stopping in the German city of Aachen. Four years earlier, he had watched residents here cheer on local Nazis as they paraded through the streets. Now, on a somber day in early November, the survivors of the war – mostly the old and infirm, "pitiful specimens of humanity," as Shirer described them – cursed Hitler's very name.¹⁶

Back in Paris on 11 November, Shirer viewed the annual Armistice Day ceremonies, which commemorated the day in 1918 that the First World War had ended. On this, the twenty-sixth anniversary of that historic event, British Prime Minister Winston Churchill and General Charles De Gaulle, the leader of the Free French forces, headed the parade that was watched by Shirer and hundreds of thousands of jubilant spectators who lined the Champs-Élysées. Afterward, Shirer drove out to the Compiègne Forest for a ceremony in which American and French troops did their best to expunge some of the humiliations and hurt of the French surrender of June 1940.

Shirer stayed in France for another month. He visited the front and spent time at the headquarters of General Dwight D. "Ike" Eisenhower, the supreme commander of the Allied Forces in Europe. He also tended to personal matters in Paris, including the details of the belated publication in France of *Berlin Diary*, and a lunch with his "old sweetheart," Yvonne. The two had not seen each other since their tearful parting eighteen years earlier. It is either a testament to Shirer's investigative skills that he was able to reestablish contact with her, or else the erstwhile lovers furtively had kept in touch off and on over the years. "Time had changed her looks remarkably little," Shirer wrote in his diary, before adding cryptically, "but it had done a lot otherwise to us both, I felt."¹⁷

The military transport plane on which Shirer flew home landed in New York on the evening of 14 December. During the two eventful months he had been away, Shirer had the time to take stock of his life. He had come to the realization he was lucky to be an American and to be living in New York City: "This is almost too good to deserve ... Why, I keep asking, should I have it and not all those other men of my land, lonely in the strange towns and shivering in the foxholes of western Europe[?]"¹⁸

Reenergized, Shirer approached his work with a renewed zeal and focus; like Ed Murrow, who had started to earn extra income by writing freelance articles for various publications, Shirer was writing, broadcasting, and lecturing at every opportunity. Not only did he continue with his column in the *New York Herald Tribune*, he was plugging away at preliminary work on nascent book projects and turning out both pro bono articles for government agencies and paying ones for commercial publications. Typical of the latter was a piece he did for the November 1944 edition of *Harper's*: "What the Germans Told the Prisoners" delved into the way German propagandists were trying to influence American prisoners of war by publishing *The Overseas Kid – OK*, for short – a free weekly newspaper that was a conduit for misinformation and Nazi propaganda. Shirer's conclusion was that "The overall purpose of the paper seems to have been to amuse and interest the prisoners while deftly planting the seeds of doubt, mistrust, and fear for the future which might set them against their fellow Americans and their country's allies after the war – thus contributing in postwar America to the kind of dissension and internal weakness upon which the enemies of the United States have always – unavailingly – relied."[19]

Shirer did not and could not know or even dream that "the seeds of doubt, mistrust, and fear" he spoke of were planted (and nurtured) not by Nazi propagandists but rather by homegrown agitators. These people, mostly politicians and their mischievous henchmen, were intent on rooting out real or imagined Communist infiltrators and sympathizers in America. Being a man who subscribed to the democratic ideals that are enshrined in the United States Constitution – freedom of speech and thought, in particular – he naively believed that his individual rights always would be respected and protected. It never occurred to him that before long he would become a target and ultimately a victim of a poisonous paranoia.

Shirer was in Omaha, Nebraska, the second week of April 1944 to give a public lecture as a benefit for a local school. He took advantage of the opportunity to visit his mother in Cedar Rapids and to make a stop in Chicago. If Shirer hoped to get back in touch with his roots and to gain some fresh perspective on his life while he was in the Midwest, he came away disappointed. Instead, he found the trip disconcerting; he experienced an unexpected and sobering sense of disconnect as his train arrived at the Union Depot in Cedar Rapids. Ed Murrow had intimated to Shirer that he sometimes feared he had stayed in Europe too long and had lost touch with America. Shirer shared this same sense of displacement: "It was as though [I] came back in a trance and people said this is where you grew up, but you could not remember growing up there."[20] Here in the American heartland, Shirer now felt like a stranger and struggled to understand why. He had spent his formative years in Cedar Rapids, and many of the familiar landmarks, buildings, and faces of his youth were still here. Among them was his mother, Bessie Shirer, now age seventy-four and in failing health.

Shirer's sense of dislocation was further heightened on 12 April. That evening he was on his way to dinner with his mother and two old friends from his Coe College days when he heard that President Roosevelt had died in Warm Springs, Georgia, the victim of a massive cerebral hemorrhage. Shelving his dinner plans, Shirer hastened to the newsroom of the local CBS radio affiliate where he set to work writing a news commentary for his eleven o'clock network broadcast.

As America's longest-serving president, FDR's impact on the nation had been profound. Suddenly, at age sixty-three, he was gone. After the initial shock and sadness wore off, like most Americans, Shirer wondered about the future. Unlike most of Americans, his view of the president had been tempered by distance; he had not been in the United States to experience firsthand any of Roosevelt's four election wins, nor had he been exposed to the mudslinging and vitriol that had been part of those campaigns. In his thirteen years in the White House, Roosevelt had led America through three of the greatest crises in its history: the Great Depression, the Japanese attack on Pearl Harbor, and the war against the Axis powers. "These three things seem so logical, almost so simple to us now," Shirer later wrote. "But history will record – even if we forget – the great fight the President had to make to achieve them."[21]

The ultimate tragedy of Roosevelt's sudden passing, as Shirer saw it, was that FDR did not live to help make the peace that would define and shape the postwar era. Like Woodrow Wilson with the League of Nations in the closing scenes of the First World War, Roosevelt had pinned his hopes for a lasting peace on the new international body that would be the United Nations.

Shirer was still struggling to collect his thoughts and control his emotions when he returned to his mother's Cedar Rapids home. It was near midnight, and his mind was racing as fast as his body. He barely had time to pick up his bags and rush downtown to catch the night train for Chicago. Work was calling, yet again. As Shirer brushed his mother's cheek with a kiss and gave her a hasty goodbye hug, a bewildered Bessie Shirer uttered the question so many other Americans were asking at that moment:

"What will we do now?" Shirer shook his head. While he had no idea, he assured his mother that they would talk about it next time he came home. It was a conversation Bessie Shirer and her son would never have.

Shirer was back in New York only long enough to do his Sunday evening newscast before he flew west to San Francisco, where he reported on what was happening as delegates from fifty nations met beginning on 25 April for the United Nations Conference on International Organization. The importance and urgency of their task was underscored by events half a world away, where the Third Reich was in its death throes. When on 1 May Shirer heard the news of Hitler's suicide, the relief and joy he felt were bittersweet for they were tempered by the awareness the Nazi madman had escaped justice. "The world he poisoned [will not be] purified for a long time," Shirer wrote in his diary. "But at least he is dead. He can do no more evil on this earth."[22]

Shirer's emotions were equally mixed when the news came on 7 May that Germany had surrendered unconditionally. After six long, bloody years, the war in Europe was finally over. Fighting still raged in the Pacific, but most observers felt it was only a matter of time until Japan surrendered. Nonetheless, the question that remained to be answered was a gut-wrenching one: how many more people would die in any Allied invasion of the Japanese homeland? Estimates put that number to at least one million, and many of them would be Americans.

The end of fighting in Europe occasioned a major shift in news coverage by America's radio networks, of which there were now four – CBS, NBC, Mutual, and the new American Broadcasting Corporation (ABC). The latter had come into existence in 1943 when RCA, the parent corporation of NBC, was compelled to sell its Blue Network after a judge's decision went against RCA in an antitrust action.

Shifting its focus to the war in the Pacific, CBS reassigned Bill Downs from Europe, while over at NBC both H.V. Kaltenborn and Lowell Thomas began reporting on events there. Curiously, neither Ed Murrow nor Shirer followed suit. For now, Murrow remained in London; with the war in Europe finally over, he was still struggling to decide on the direction of his career. For his part, Shirer had minimal interest in the fight against Japan and admitted he had no special insights into that conflict. Thus, after having spent twenty-eight days on the West Coast, rather than traveling to the South Pacific, on 23 May he returned to New York, even though the delegates at the UN's founding conference still had not completed their work. It took them several more weeks to finalize details of the agreement that committed the world's nations to a set of basic rules that would, ostensibly at least, govern international relations from now on. In Washington, Congressional approval came on 28 July, when the Senate ratified the UN Charter. The UN officially came into existence three months later, on 24 October 1945.

Despite the new organization's many shortcomings, Shirer was an enthusiastic booster. He had little faith in President Harry Truman's ability to understand – much less deal with – the issues involved in ensuring a lasting and equitable peace. Some influential voices in America and elsewhere – mostly those who were uncomfortable with any alliance or even dealings with the Soviet Union – were urging that Germany be allowed to maintain enough military might to serve as a counterweight to Russian expansionism. Shirer disagreed adamantly, siding instead with those who were urging the president to insist that Germany be disarmed for good. The heated debate over this issue served as a reminder of the fragility of the Allied coalition that had won the war in Europe. If any further proof of that was needed, it came on 26 July when Britain's Labour Party confounded Shirer and most other supposed pundits by winning a landslide victory in the United Kingdom's first postwar election. Winston Churchill was out as prime minister, and so Labour leader Clement Attlee joined Truman and Stalin at a summit conference that was held in the town of Potsdam, near Berlin, from 17 July to 2 August 1945. The three men sat down to decide how to implement the decisions made at Yalta five months earlier and how postwar Germany should be governed. At the conclusion of the meeting, the United States and Great Britain issued an ultimatum to Japan: surrender unconditionally or face total annihilation. The latter, it would soon become apparent, was no mere threat.

While these events were unfolding, Shirer was gearing down for his annual summer vacation. Having settled into an uneasy truce in his marital difficulties with Tess, he joined his family for two weeks on Cape Cod. "On Monday, August 6, a pouring rain in New York had prevented my plane from taking off, and by the time I got to Hyannis by train and bus I was dead tired ... Tess had met me there that evening with the car. While waiting, she had picked up the tail end of a broadcast about something called an atom bomb having been dropped on Japan. Static from the storm had blotted out most of the broadcast and ... our car radio had gone dead."[23] Shirer noted the disquieting news in his diary: "I suppose it's important, but I'm too tired this night to care."[24]

It was only the next day, when he picked up the morning papers, that the mind-numbing reality of what had happened became apparent. "The bomb that would change history weighed five tons," writes Edward Bliss, Jr. "At its core was a package of Uranium 235 about the size of a football. Within nine seconds of the explosion, it had turned ground zero into a gridiron with temperatures rivaling those of the sun."[25] The blast that leveled the Japanese city of Hiroshima incinerated 100,000 people in a heartbeat and turned a four-square-mile patch of land into a radioactive inferno. The detonation of the first atomic bomb ushered in what the headline writers dubbed "the Atomic Age." What exactly this meant was as yet unclear, but, whatever it meant, it was underscored with stark and horrifying reality three days later. Another American aircraft dropped a second atomic bomb over the Japanese city of Nagasaki, instantly killing another 40,000 people. The shockwaves from these dramatic developments reverberated around the world, hastening the end of the war in the Pacific. Even Stalin, ever the opportunist, finally signed on to the Allied cause; on 8 August, he formally declared war on Japan and sent the Red Army into Manchuria.

It is difficult today for us to understand the horror and trepidation that gripped the world during these uncertain days in early August 1945. There was a widespread feeling of dread and uncertainty – well-founded as it turned out – that humanity had crossed some sort of terrible threshold from which there was no going back. Shirer said it simply and succinctly: "I think I was frightened."[26]

Despite all of the fear and uncertainties, the second-guessing began almost immediately. The seeds were planted for a vigorous and long-running historical debate about the morality of President Truman's decision to use "The Bomb" against Japan – the only times, thankfully, that atomic weapons have been used in a war. The further we are removed in time from the dark realities of the Second World War and the evils that confronted the world, the more emotional the debate over Truman's decision has become. Regardless of how one views the events of August 1945, this much is beyond debate: the use of nuclear weapons brought the war in the Pacific to a screeching halt.

Faced with the suddenly very real prospect of "total annihilation," Japanese Emperor Hirohito on 10 August waved a white flag. Japan surrendered unconditionally. That news – though neither unexpected nor unwelcome – left a great many people feeling unsettled. In London, Ed Murrow articulated a common sentiment: "Seldom, if ever, has a war ended leaving the victors with such a sense of uncertainty and fear, with such a realization that the future is obscure."[27] For his part, even as he watched the jubilant crowds that poured out into the streets of Manhattan amidst a cacophony of honking car horns and the peeling of church bells, Shirer's own sense of elation was tempered. He was saddened by the awareness of how much suffering and death six years of conflict had brought and by the stark realization of how close the Allies had come to losing the war.

Germany, too, had been racing to develop an atomic bomb; as Churchill noted, it was only "By God's mercy [that] British and American science outpaced all German efforts."[28] The reality was that Hitler's dreams of world conquest might well have succeeded and the world would be a very different and darker place had it not been for the American industrial might and knowhow that turned the tide in the Allies' favor, just as it had in the First World War. It was starkly evident that there could be no going back to the isolationism of the past. "Whether we like it or not, American power and American policy will be a major influence in the Europe that emerges [in the postwar era]," Ed Murrow observed.[29]

Shirer had similar thoughts on this night. His mind was busy with all that had happened and what possibly lay ahead. He stayed at work until the wee hours of the morning of 15 August 1945. Afterward, he joined his co-workers for celebratory food and drinks. Several hours later, as he stumbled home along Fifty-First Street, the sun was rising over the East River. His own troubles, his love affair with Tilly Losch, and all of the other cares in his life seemed a long way off and utterly insignificant.

26

The Banality of Evil

Amid the dizzying swirl of events that filled the first two weeks of August 1945, his family's annual Cape Cod vacation gave William Shirer an opportunity to collect his thoughts: "For those ... who had a fleeting moment to stop and think, it seemed ... as though we all had made a fateful plunge to a new planet where human life could not possibly ever be the same again, and would have to be, therefore, started anew with different precepts."[1]

He was still struggling to make sense of it all and to sort out the details of his personal life when on 1 October he sailed for Europe aboard the Cunard liner *Queen Mary*. Shirer's assignment for CBS was to report on the epilogue of the tragedy that was the Second World War: the German war crimes trials, which were about to begin in the historic Bavarian city of Nuremberg. Among Shirer's fellow passengers on the transatlantic voyage were several of the American judges who were to preside at the trials. Also aboard the ship were Canadian Prime Minister Mackenzie King (with whom Shirer had tea and a leisurely conversation about various issues, one of which was the daunting realities of what everyone was now calling "the Atomic Age"), and Ed Murrow. A photographer snapped a photo of the two men ascending the ship's gangway. Shirer, looking somewhat portly and every inch a civilian, is attired in a stylish three-piece wool suit. A fedora is perched atop his head, an overcoat draped over his left arm; he is peering back at Murrow quizzically. In contrast, Murrow, lean and dapper in an army war correspondent's uniform, appears self-confident and ready for action. He is gazing directly into the lens, his eyes filled with that trademark Murrow intensity. After a month in New York, he was returning to London, where his wife Janet was seven months pregnant with the couple's first child. Because both Murrow and Shirer were traveling without their spouses, for the first time in almost four years they had an opportunity to renew their friendship. Their reunion would be memorable, albeit for all the wrong reasons.

The *Queen Mary* reached Southampton on 7 October after an uneventful six-day crossing; however, soon after their arrival in England the simmering tensions between Shirer and Murrow – unarticulated, but undeniable – erupted in an ugly incident while they were en route to London. Shirer stopped off at hotel in Southampton to do a broadcast, but because the weather was poor, the shortwave signal failed to reach New York. That bit of bad luck was a harbinger of what was to come. After the failed broadcast, Shirer and Murrow partook of a liquid lunch. Among the many topics of their conversation on this day was the possibility of Murrow becoming a vice-president of cbs, a job offer William Paley had made. As their hired car sped across the fog-shrouded English countryside, Shirer and Murrow fell to quarreling about this and about other matters. Forty years later, Shirer recounted in an interview with Murrow biographer A.M. Sperber: "Ed was drunk, but we often got drunk together. We were young, drank hard, the pressures..."[2]

The reality was that Murrow had been smoking and drinking to excess in recent months. The stresses and uncertainties of six years of war had taken a heavy personal toll, and, while he refused to admit it, his health had suffered. All of Murrow's frustrations, doubts, and anger came pouring out in an unguarded moment. He lashed out at Shirer, punching and flailing away at his old friend. Bespectacled, blind in the right eye, and a head shorter than the six-foot-two-inch Murrow, Shirer did not, could not, fight back. In their cramped confines, neither of them was much hurt physically; the only real damage was to their friendship and to their bruised egos. And both of them knew it.

Following this outburst, the two men spent the rest of the drive to London in an uneasy, sullen silence. Early next morning, Murrow appeared at the door of the cbs flat where Shirer was staying. Now stone-cold sober and rueful, Murrow was there to apologize for his behavior. As they had so often in past, in better and more cordial times, the two old friends took a long walk together. On this day, they talked about their lives in the postwar world and about the growing gulf between them; Murrow was still Shirer's boss, true. However, they both knew that Shirer had ceased to be one of "the Murrow Boys" – if ever he truly had been one of them. Shirer was at heart a loner, cerebral and often aloof. Cloud and Olson report that on several occasions Shirer behaved petulantly in his dealings with co-workers at cbs in New York. There is no denying that in his impatience to get things done he often came across as being arrogant. There is also no denying that he sometimes snapped at underlings and demanded what others regarded as special treatment. For example, he had his own private secretary at the office and insisted she have a pristine copy of *The New York Times* ready for him when he arrived at the office each day. Ed Murrow resented such behavior and let Shirer know it. Nonetheless, an uneasy peace was restored between them following that October 1945 scuffle. The cracks in their relationship were papered over. At least for now.

Shirer was discreet about what had sparked the ugly incident with Murrow and made no mention of it in any of his public utterances. Murrow did likewise. Biographer Ann Sperber speculates on what prompted Murrow's angry outburst. Was it the alcohol talking? Jealousy at Shirer's literary success? Frustration at a drift of events over which Murrow felt he had no control? Anger at Shirer's apparent reluctance to spell him in London? Or was it "a reversion to childhood patterns, so long held in check – Egbert Roscoe Murrow lashing out against the brother figure in a burst of fury and depression that Lacey or Dewey Murrow would have recognized?"[3]

Regardless, although the two men spent parts of the next week together in London, each of them must have known that their relationship had undergone a seismic shift. As was the case with the world around them, they were forever changed.

From London, Shirer pressed on to Paris, where he reported on the first French elections in nine years, spent some time with novelist John Dos Passos, a fellow Chicagoan who chanced to be in town, and devoted some time to poking through the embers of his relationship with his erstwhile lover Yvonne, in whose company he again sought solace. Next, it was on for a week's visit to Berlin, where the Russian air traffic controllers now in control at the city's Templehof Airport denied landing permission for Shirer's plane. Instead, the flight was diverted to a landing strip 200 miles west. Shirer, with his intimate knowledge of Berlin, suggested to the pilot that they land at Gatow, a small airfield that had fallen under the control of British occupation forces. There Shirer's plane sat on the tarmac while officials worked all day to negotiate landing rights at Tempelhof. For Shirer, this incident served as a stark reminder of the new realities of life in postwar Berlin.

The city Shirer had known so intimately, the one ruled by the iron fist of the Nazis, had become an enclave in what in 1949 would formally become known as East Germany. The Soviet-dominated state included territory occupied (and pillaged) by the Red Army as it drove westward in

the closing days of the war. Berlin was shattered. Many of its great buildings lay in ruins, and the survivors among the city's four million pre-war
inhabitants were impoverished, hungry, and embittered. Adding insult to
injury for the German people was the fact the erstwhile capital of the
Third Reich had been partitioned. American, British, and French military
officials controlled the western half of the city, their Russian counterparts
the east. A Russian diplomat with whom Shirer spoke made it clear this
arrangement was by design, part of a grand strategy to ensure that Germany never again would be in a position to wage war on the Soviet
Union. At the same time, asserting Soviet control over those areas of Germany occupied by the Red Army – and indeed over the nations of Eastern Europe – salved the paranoia of Soviet dictator Joseph Stalin, who was
intent on expanding his own empire. As Winston Churchill so eloquently put it in an historic 5 March 1946 speech in Fulton, Missouri, "From
Stettin in the Baltic to Trieste in the Adriatic, an iron curtain has descended across [Europe]."[4]

When William Shirer finally arrived in Berlin on the evening of 3 November, he could scarcely believe the devastation he saw. The city was a waste-
land, "demolished almost beyond recognition."[5] His first broadcast from
postwar Berlin was as memorable as it was emotional. Working out of an
improvised studio, he could not help but be struck by the dramatic differences between his last news report from the heart of the Third Reich,
on 3 December 1940, and this one, delivered on the night of 4 November
1945. Shirer began as he had so many times in past, greeting CBS listeners
in America with his signature sign-on, "This is Berlin!" However, any similarities between the "then" and the "now" ended there. The old broadcast
center on Adolf Hitler Platz was now a bombed-out shell. At last, Shirer
could speak the truth. And there was much truth, past and present, to
report.

General Eisenhower, as the supreme Allied commander in Europe, had
decreed that all former Nazis should be removed from positions of
authority in areas of Germany that were under American control. However, that official order was not always obeyed to the letter. Many former
bureaucrats from the Nazi era – primarily mid- and low-level civil servants
and police officials – retained jobs in the postwar government, adminis-
tering what was left of the state machinery and serving as advisors to the
occupying forces. Although this troubled him, Shirer understood the
rationale. There was a need to restore order and get Germany back onto
its feet.

Shirer was fascinated by the events that had led to the downfall of Hitler and the Nazis, who once had seemed unstoppable in their dreams of world conquest. Intent on learning all he could about what had derailed their ambitions, Shirer set about interviewing scores of people and using his contacts to gather primary-source information. The latter included copies of Allied intelligence reports and captured German documents that laid bare the Nazi regime's innermost secrets, including the atrocities of Hitler's henchmen, details of Germany's wartime military strategy, the secret lives of Hitler and his inner circle, and even eyewitness accounts of the Nazi dictator's final days and his death. Some people, the Russians in particular, were skeptical that Hitler was really dead; Shirer was under no such illusions. He felt the information to which he had access was conclusive: Hitler had committed suicide. While Shirer was certain of that, he was less sure about other aspects of the situation in postwar Germany.

He had heard reports that Germans were remorseful for the war, and that they accepted blame for the evils and destruction the Nazis had wrought – in particular the death camps in which as many as six million Jews and other innocents had been systematically slaughtered. Thus, Shirer was by turns surprised, dismayed, and angered that so many Germans he met continued to deny any responsibility for what had happened. They instead viewed themselves as victims. Few were even willing to admit they had been aware of the atrocities being committed for "the greater good" of the Fatherland; "I was just following orders" was an oft-heard refrain. "The German people, I fear, have not – by a hell of a long way – learned the lessons of this terrible war," Shirer wrote. "They have no sense of guilt and are sorry only that they were beaten and must now suffer the consequences. They are sorry only for themselves."[6]

Another revelation for Shirer was the willingness of the soldiers of the Red Army to fraternize with Americans. When Shirer and two colleagues accepted an invitation to visit the Soviet sector of Berlin for a celebration marking the twenty-eighth anniversary of the Bolshevik revolution, Shirer was pleasantly surprised at the hospitality their Russian hosts displayed. Despite what he had heard about the surliness of Red Army soldiers and how they shunned contact with Americans, those he met were anything but hostile: "I have never drunk so many toasts in my life nor seldom seen such conviviality." Upon learning that Shirer was the author of *Berlin Diary*, one Russian major who was also a reporter for the Communist Party newspaper *Isvestia*, hugged Shirer like a long-lost brother. "It is you! You! You!" the Russian shouted. "Why, I used to read your diary day-after-day in the trenches at Stalingrad. It came out daily for weeks in one of our army papers there."[7]

William Shirer had never been fond of Berlin. Nor was he fond of Germans as a people, after his experiences in Nazi Germany. "I'm weary of the Berlin story I started to chronicle so long ago, which has been the core of my life for more than a decade."[8] For that reason, he was relieved to depart for Nuremberg, where he and CBS colleague Howard K. Smith were to report on what happened when "justice [tried] to catch up with some of the vile little men who have wrought this awful destruction to the human race."[9]

Whenever Shirer had visited Nuremberg in past, he had marveled at the town's rich history and its medieval architecture. Spiritually, he felt that Nuremberg had died when the Nazis began staging their annual party rallies here. Now, the streetscapes matched the residents' emotional despair. Many of the picturesque buildings that once made old Nuremberg one of Europe's scenic and historic jewels were in ruins, having been leveled by Allied bombing.

Berlin had been the initial preferred venue for any war crimes trials of Nazi leaders. However, Nuremberg was chosen instead mostly for logistical reasons. "The physical task alone of arranging a trial of this magnitude was enormous," Howard K. Smith observed. "It required a building to contain a courtroom with prison attached, plus offices for unusually large legal staffs from four nations and German defense attorneys."[10] In addition, space was required for a library of court documents (250 tons of them), a media center, cafeteria, and other facilities. All of these amenities were needed for the trials of the twenty-one high-ranking officials of the Third Reich who were charged with crimes against humanity.

Not everyone in the Allied camp agreed that such legal proceedings were advisable or even justified. Skeptics asked: were the war crimes trials at Nuremberg "victor's vengeance or the authentic pursuit of justice?"[11] A small but vocal lobby in the United States and Great Britain – academics, military men, and staunch anti-communists – concurred with German public opinion, which held that the Nuremberg war crimes trials were political theater, nothing more. There were also academics, legal scholars, and even some media people who argued that no Nazi official could ever receive a fair trial in a court set up by the victorious Allies. These same critics insisted there were no internationally recognized laws against the kind of war the German military had fought, nor against the atrocities that the Nazis had committed. Technically, while that may have been true, in 1945 animosities ran deep. So, too, did the feeling that justice demanded those who were responsible for so much death, destruction, and evil should be called to account and punished. Robert H. Jackson, the flamboyant, impassioned chief American prosecutor articulated those sentiments in his opening address to the eight judges – two each from the United States, Great Britain, France, and the Soviet Union – who presided at Nuremberg. Jackson made a compelling case for the argument that the crimes of the Nazi leaders and of the German military were so vile, so heinous, that they could not go unpunished.

Shirer had fallen ill with the flu and was not in the courtroom to hear Jackson's opening address, but after reviewing the transcript of the day's proceedings he concurred with Jackson's assessment. "I felt the thrill I had as a youth when I had taken to reading my father's law books, the texts of some of the great trial speeches of the past."[12]

Shirer was hawkish in his desire to see Nazi leaders punished for their crimes, and so he dismissed as "timid hairsplitters" the legal doves who opposed the show trials of the surviving Nazi leaders who had been responsible for so much misery and carnage. Nonetheless, to his surprise, he found he could muster little antipathy toward the men in the prisoners' docket. "Shorn of their power and the glory and the glittering trappings of Nazidom, how little and mean and mediocre they look."[13] Hannah Arendt's phrase "the banality of evil" has become something of a cliché in our own troubled times, but it was still new in 1945. In Shirer's eyes, the Nuremberg defendants, "nondescript-looking individuals, fidgeting nervously in their rather shabby clothes,"[14] appeared to be neither evil nor dangerous, but rather banal.

Shirer and Howard K. Smith covered the court proceedings for the next seventeen days, delivering their reports to an American public grown weary of war news, eager to get on with life, and to enjoy the fruits of victory. After a dramatic opening week in Nuremberg, things settled into a dull routine. As Smith observed, this was "a fact that may be unimportant to history, but was vital to a reporter trying to hold the interest of a milkman in Peoria."[15] Shirer, too, was finding it difficult to stay focused on the legal proceedings.

Cloud and Olson report that around this time Smith was writing to Ed Murrow to complain that Shirer had "raised hell because the army didn't provide him with special transportation, grumbled constantly at meals and accommodations [sic], and always managed to be ailing whenever I asked him to help me with the load of daily shows."[16] While there is an element of truth to the assertion that Shirer was "puffed up" and had objected to the treatment he and other journalists were receiving, there were reasons for his surliness. Reporters who were covering the trials were billeted in the former home of a local businessman, with as many as ten people to a bedroom bunking on army cots. Privacy was almost nonexistent, and the food that was provided was of dubious quality. Shirer commented on this in one of his weekly columns in the *New York Herald Tribune*, bemoaning "the most appalling conditions I have seen in 20 years of reporting from abroad." Shirer was ill with flu much of the time he was in Nuremberg, and his personal life remained in turmoil. He had gotten himself into a mess of marital woes because of his affair with Tilly Losch, and on the morning of 27 November his already fragile emotions suffered a body blow that sent him reeling.

Howard K. Smith awakened Shirer, still feverish and wan from the flu, to impart some sad news: Shirer's mother had died the previous day in Cedar Rapids. Bessie Shirer had been chatting with a neighbor when she collapsed. She was seventy-three. Shirer was heartbroken, and although the army doctor who was treating him advised him not to travel, Shirer refused to take no for an answer. Only when he was told there was no flight that would get him home in time for the funeral did he return to his sick bed.

Wracked with guilt, Shirer lamented his situation. Being the elder son in the family, it was his duty to deliver the eulogy. Instead, he could only send word that he had loved his mother and had respected her for having endured thirty-two years of widowhood, for selflessly raising three children on her own, and for making sure that all of them were able to attend university and to carve out successful careers for themselves.

The pastor of the First Presbyterian Church in Cedar Rapids, where Bessie Shirer and her parents before her had worshipped, read Shirer's telegram at the funeral. The knowledge that this was happening was cold comfort to Shirer, who spent the next two days grieving in his sickbed, "recalling a thousand family pictures of the past."[17]

Shirer was depressed, but physically he felt well enough to return to the courtroom on 30 November, when he resumed his CBS broadcasts and set to work on a lengthy article on the Nuremberg trial that he was writing for *Reader's Digest*. However, all of this activity, the pain of losing his mother, and his lingering health issues had taken a toll on him.

Physically and emotionally exhausted, Shirer departed for home in the wee hours of the morning of 10 December. He had a lot to think about on the long flight to New York. He wanted only to spend Christmas with his family and friends, and to take some time to pull himself together mentally. He continued the struggle to sort out his personal life and to make sense of the madness and evil in the world. "I cannot find much in my own rough notes in 1946 and the beginning of 1947 that provides encouraging answers to [these] questions ... The first two years of the peace were far from propitious."[18]

27

Changing Times

The end of the war in Europe altered the balance of power on the continent in unprecedented ways. Overnight, Russia went from being a reluctant partner in the Allied war effort to being a Red bogeyman, the new enemy of America and Western Europe. The world suddenly was cleaved into two blocs – one "Western," one "Eastern." The resulting mutual mistrust and hostility fueled a protracted struggle between capitalism and communism that ushered the world to the brink of nuclear Armageddon on several occasions. It also shaped many aspects of life on both sides of the Iron Curtain for forty-four years – from 1945 until 1989, when the Soviet Union collapsed under the weight of its own inefficiencies. The great irony in this, of course, was that the Soviet bogeyman to a large extent had been created and nurtured by the Western powers, the United States in particular. Although some observers, William Shirer among them, warned against the dangers of a resurgence of American isolationism, political hysteria and intellectual lethargy again were taking root in America as they had in 1919.

Post-1945 realities were stunningly different from those of the two decades between the two great wars of the twentieth century. The world had changed immeasurably and forever during the Second World War, and one area in which that change was reflected was in the broadcasting industry. CBS had the finest radio news service in America and perhaps in the world. Shirer's employer had built its reputation and its audience on the excellence of its overseas news gathering operation envisioned, nurtured, and developed by Ed Murrow with help from William Shirer and the rest of the Murrow Boys. Sustaining and building upon those strengths would not be easy in the postwar world. As the population boomed and new automobiles rolled off the assembly lines with radios as standard equipment, the airwaves grew ever more crowded with stations. The competition for listeners had reached a fever pitch.

It was in response to the needs of the returning veterans and their families (and *because* of them) that CBS and rivals NBC, Mutual, and ABC turned their attentions to domestic concerns. By 1946, the freewheeling pioneer days of radio news were history. So, too, were the days when Murrow and Shirer on CBS and their NBC competitors had engaged in a spirited, no-holds-barred contest to see who could be first to get the news. Both Max Jordan and Fred Bate were no longer on air as NBC transitioned to peacetime broadcasting. Jordan had left the network to become a priest. Bate, who had recovered after being badly injured in the London blitz, took a desk job at NBC headquarters in New York. "For Murrow," Sperber writes, "Bate's departure spelled the end to an era – that of the small radio community that had survived between Munich and the blitz, the all-for-one spirit of 1939–41, when overseas broadcasting had been almost a cottage industry, the end of the old days of Fred and Ed."[1]

William Shirer, struggling to deal with the transition from being a frontline foreign correspondent to a studio-bound news commentator, was also adrift emotionally and intellectually. He loathed the corporate bureaucracy at CBS with its stultifying hierarchy, yet he indulged himself in his own privileged situation because he believed he had earned his plum job and the money that came with it. Shirer was reluctant to accept Murrow's requests to stand in for him in London, and he flatly turned down Murrow's invitation to succeed him there.

Despite Shirer's advice to Murrow that he would be "wasting his talent" if he accepted William Paley's offer of a job as a CBS vice-president, Murrow returned home in March 1946 for two compelling reasons: one was his loyalty to CBS. The other was that he was fearful the news operation he had worked so hard to build would crumble in the postwar era or that it might even be intentionally dismantled in the rush to build ratings. Murrow's concerns in both regards were well founded. The radio industry was in flux; with the war over, CBS boss William Paley feared the American public would be less interested in news, especially world news. This was also an area of programming in which Paley had invested considerable time, effort, and money. Another of his fears, one that also preoccupied his counterparts at the other American networks, was that television, the new technology on the airwaves, would revolutionize the American broadcasting industry. "Paley had often talked with Ed and me about the prospects of television," Shirer recalled many years later. "He had urged us to start thinking of how news would be presented on the tube. It would be a new challenge – much greater and more exciting than radio had flung at us."[2]

Paley foresaw that, as television's popularity grew, fewer Americans would listen to radio. Inevitably, that would lead to a drop in advertising revenue, reduced operating budgets, lower profits, and the migration of top-flight news talent back to the print media, which still paid better and carried more prestige than did radio. Paley was unwilling to sit by and watch this happen or to do nothing while the competition revamped its executive lineup or its news operations in a bid to remain profitable. At the same time, he was more determined than ever to overtake NBC as America's number one radio network. Part of his plan involved shuffling his senior management team and bringing in new blood and fresh ideas to the CBS corporate offices on the nineteenth floor at 485 Madison Avenue in New York. One of the key changes he had in mind was elevating Ed Murrow to the job of vice-president and director of Public Affairs. Murrow, universally respected and revered, would bring a renewed gravitas and respect to the network's news operations. No less important was the notion that, as Ann Sperber points out, Paley felt that what CBS needed "was a centripetal force, commanding loyalty in a time of squeeze and leaner budgets."[3]

There was a big problem, however. Paley was offering a job that Ed Murrow had neither sought nor wanted, especially in the *new* CBS, which was larger, more bureaucratic, less averse to risk, and far richer than it was when he had signed on with the company in 1935. In the end, Murrow accepted the appointment begrudgingly – a mistake he forever regretted. His son Casey explains, "Dad was, at heart, a news guy completely and was much happier following a story than pushing papers and being in an office environment. He didn't like having to worry about budgets or the administrative side of the business."[4]

It was readily apparent to Murrow that his concerns were well founded: Sperber recounts how when Murrow attended his very first management meeting in spring 1946 he was informed that he had two pressing tasks: one was to fire the news director of CBS's Washington affiliate; the other was to get rid of Paul White, the former head of CBS news. Murrow reacted angrily, saying he would *not* serve as senior management's executioner. "You hired 'em, you worked with 'em, and you want to get rid of 'em, it's up to you," Murrow reportedly said. "But you're not going to tack it onto *me* – I won't do it!"[5]

Murrow was not the only one in the CBS executive offices who lamented the changing times and felt trapped. Paul White was having great difficulty coming to grips with, let alone accepting, his new role in the postwar world; that was especially true when it came to the new pecking order at CBS. A newsman of the old school, White was gruff, cynical, and at times uncouth, but he was also the consummate newsman. He was tough, savvy, competitive, and lived to beat the competition in getting the news on the air first and getting it right. He had no patience for corporate culture, management meetings, and reports. With Murrow's promotion in November 1945, White saw the proverbial writing on the wall as far as his own future at CBS was concerned. He felt slighted and resented the way he was being treated. After all, White reasoned, he had earned and was *owed* the job that Ed Murrow got. White had been with CBS since 1933, two years longer than Murrow. He had worked with Ed Klauber to build the network's news operation from scratch. White's myriad accomplishments were recognized by colleagues and competitors alike, who voted him the 1945 winner of the Peabody Award for Outstanding News Coverage. White turned to pills and the bottle for solace. The former was medication for his arthritis pain, the latter – a common succor for journalists of the day – helped him cope with the pressures and everyday frustrations of his work at CBS. "Paul started drinking more heavily after Ed [Murrow] became his boss," Shirer later told Murrow biographer Joseph Persico.[6]

White's addictions fueled the sort of behavior that gave rise to some embarrassing public incidents for him and for CBS; however, even more problematic was the fact that, as his mood darkened and his health declined, White grew increasingly disinterested in and scornful of workplace niceties and protocols. He made no secret of how he felt. An anecdote recounted in Robert Metz's 1975 book *CBS: Reflections in a Bloodshot Eye* illustrates that point in stark terms. Metz reports that one day when White decided he did not feel like attending another mind-numbing executive meeting he sent a note to his boss: "Dear Mr Paley, I am very sorry. But my little boy, Paul, cannot be at your meeting today as he is down very bad with his syphilis. Mrs White."[7]

The final straw for Paul White came in late April 1946 when he went on air to introduce CBS radio's new primetime fifteen-minute newscast *Robert Trout with the News till Now*. The Campbell Soup Company had signed on as show's sponsor, anteing up $1 million. This was Ed Murrow's first major initiative in his new job, and an envious Paul White was eager to grab a bit of the limelight. Unfortunately, when he went on-air to introduce that first broadcast, White was so inebriated and his speech was so slurred that listeners could barely understand him. According to Cloud and Olson, rumor has it that moments after the broadcast ended, an irate Ed Murrow stormed into White's office to fire him on the spot.[8] That story may be apocryphal, but what is certain is that Murrow sent White packing, just as he earlier had been told to do. A subsequent news release was diplomatic. It announced that White had resigned from CBS for "health reasons" and because he planned to write a book. There was some truth in both pronouncements.

Following his dismissal, White and his wife Margaret moved to San Diego, where White took a job as an editorial writer at the *San Diego Journal*, worked as the news director at the local CBS radio affiliate, and taught journalism at a local college. He also wrote the book he had long talked about: a journalism textbook called *News on the Air*. Out of the pressure-cooker environment at CBS headquarters in New York, White was more relaxed than he had been in years, so much so that he and Murrow became pen pals. White addressed his missives to "Muggsie Murrow" and affectionately signed them "Butch White."[9] The two men would continue their correspondence until 10 July 1955, when White died after a lengthy illness.[10]

Although he was now the CBS vice-president of News and Public Affairs, Ed Murrow longed for the good old days in London when he was in the broadcast studio every day. It was apparent to family, friends, and some of his colleagues that Murrow was unhappy in his new job. Sperber quotes Dorothy Paley, the then-wife of William Paley, as saying she sensed "a terrible weariness" in Ed Murrow, which resulted in him suffering from depression.[11] Just as many of the returning military veterans had trouble reintegrating themselves into peacetime life, Murrow was struggling to regain his sense of direction in the postwar world.

As far as the public knew, Murrow, Shirer, and the other "Murrow boys" continued to bask in the afterglow of all they had accomplished in Europe. The reality was much different. No longer did any of them have the intensity of focus or the sense of accomplishment they'd had when CBS news was still in a building phase and the news correspondents in the field were reporting on the latest wartime battle or political development. Life was simpler back then, and understandably so. The Second World War was a struggle between good and evil, dubbed "the last good war," which may well prove to be true in the moral sense at least.

Following his homecoming, Ed Murrow threw himself into his new job, maintaining a businesslike demeanor and generally remaining aloof. This could not have been easy because at heart Murrow was very much one of the guys. He drank, he smoked, and although he seemed distant and moody at times, he continued to enjoy the company of select colleagues and friends. This fostered a perception in the CBS radio newsroom that Murrow favored his old pals and was living on his reputation. Because of this, some of the younger members of the staff grew resentful, referring to themselves as being members of the "Murrow Isn't God Club." When he heard about it, Murrow applied for membership. He had not lost his sense of humor.

There was no denying that Ed Murrow gave preferential treatment to his "Murrow Boys." The longest serving among them was Shirer, of course. He and Murrow were no longer working together on a daily basis, nor were they as close as they had been in Europe. However, the two men and their families continued to socialize, and, like most of the other old hands, Shirer remained loyal to his boss and vice versa. Nonetheless, it was obvious that each man's priorities and expectations had changed. So had their friendship. Sperber writes, "For Murrow [his relationship with Shirer] was the only true peer relationship among his CBS colleagues in his broadcast career, marked, if anything, by a certain deference."[12]

Murrow was now locked into his corporate responsibilities. Shirer, ever a journalist (at least at heart), continued doing his news commentaries and writing his weekly Sunday column for the *New York Herald Tribune*. In his off-hours, he busied himself with various writing projects, in particular he was working on a novel and another stage play. The play, tentatively called *The Traitor*, was about treason, a subject Shirer found fascinating. Set in Berlin during the war, the play's dramatic focus was the relationship between an American newspaper reporter named Jack Goodman, the character who is Shirer's alter ego, and a disgruntled American radio correspondent named Oliver Knight, an amalgam of a thinly disguised Bob Best, the veteran United Press man in Vienna who had become a raging anti-Semite, and the infamous William Joyce, AKA Lord Haw Haw.

Shirer chose the surnames of his characters for obvious reasons, and he used the play as a vehicle to give voice to a lot of cynicism he was feeling at the time and to pose questions that he felt needed to be considered, even if he knew there were no answers. His own life remained in turmoil, and the stress was beginning to show.

Some people felt the quality of Shirer's work had slipped. Later, Murrow loyalists would opine that during this period Shirer had been living on his reputation and his insights were recycled from wire service copy rather than from news he reported personally. There is an undeniable element of truth to these accusations. However, the same charges could be leveled at many former war correspondents in the postwar era. With much less dramatic news to report or comment on, the wartime consensus that had provided a framework for news analysis and commentary had come apart at the seams.

Shirer's real sin was complacency. He naively took for granted that his close friendship with Ed Murrow and his track record gave him license to voice his opinions in his Sunday evening time slot on CBS. So smug was Shirer in this assumption that he regarded Murrow as his peer rather than as his boss; Murrow, he believed, would always side with him in any dispute with CBS management. Typically, when in January 1946 he fell ill and doctors advised that he was in need of elective surgery, Shirer opted to have the operation at a hospital in Lake Placid, the Adirondacks resort town. The Shirer family was vacationing there that summer, and Shirer continued to do his Sunday evening broadcasts from a studio at the local CBS affiliate station at – or so he later claimed – the insistence of his sponsor, the J.B. Williams Company.[13]

If Ed Murrow disapproved of this arrangement, he said nothing about it to Shirer. It was only nine months later, when the relationship between the two men had soured and Murrow was trying to rationalize what had gone wrong between them, that he articulated such concerns. In a letter to his friend Harold Laski, the British economist, Murrow commented, "For your own private information, Bill had become lazy. Nearly 20 per cent of his copy consisted of readings from newspapers and magazines. He had spent seven consecutive weekends at Lake Placid last summer, and whatever the benefits of Lake Placid might be, it is not considered the ideal place from which to report and interpret world affairs."[14] Murrow made no mention of Shirer's recent health issues, although he certainly knew about them.

Shirer did not help his own cause when he returned to New York in August 1946. Ed Murrow asked Shirer to take a trip overseas, do some broadcasts from London, gain some fresh perspective on postwar developments, and find out how European allies were viewing America's autumn's mid-term elections. To Murrow's dismay and anger, Shirer begged off on the trip, once again citing personal reasons. Around this same time, there was talk of an industry-wide strike by the Association of Federated Radio Artists (AFRA), which represented actors and other on-air performers. At CBS, Ed Murrow informed the network's team of news commentators that in the event of a labor stoppage they would be required to fill airtime. Around the clock, if necessary. Shirer was having none of it. "I told Ed flatly I would not strike-break against AFRA. I would respect its picket lines … Ed did not like that."[15]

None of these incidents was pivotal in souring relations between Shirer and Murrow; however, they are noteworthy because they were symptomatic of the growing gap between the two old friends. In Murrow's mind, Shirer's attitude had become a source of irritation. Then, too, there was an underlying clash of egos. Office gossip had it that in his work as a sponsored newscaster, syndicated newspaper columnist, and freelance writer, Shirer was making more than Murrow did in his $45,000-per-year job as a CBS vice-president. That surely must have rankled Murrow, even if he had always insisted that money was not important to him: "I am frankly not very much interested in making a lot of money," he wrote in a 1941 letter to Shirer from London, "although I would like to have a small nest egg so I won't be forced to look for a tin cup when I decide to come home for good."[16]

Had Ed Murrow's attitude to money changed since his return to New York? If so, there was no indication of it. What *had* changed was the Murrow-Shirer relationship. Now that the two men were no longer workmates, they had different priorities and drifted apart. Their egos and the cumulative weight of the differences between them then became problematic. William Shirer and Ed Murrow were on a collision course.

28

Tides of Intolerance

William Paley was in a restless mood when he returned home from the war in summer 1945. The CBS president had served in the psychological warfare branch of the Office of War Information in London, and he'd had lots of opportunity to plan for his return to postwar life. At the time, NBC still reigned as America's top radio network, both in terms of the size of audience and profits. Seeking to change all that, Paley had reorganized the senior management team at CBS, bringing in Murrow and other new executive blood, while taking on for himself the title of chairman of the network's board of directors. Paley also revamped CBS's primetime schedule, including new shows by popular entertainers such as singer Frank Sinatra and comedian Jack Benny, whom Paley had wooed away from NBC. In September 1947, Paley raided the NBC talent stable yet again, luring popular newscaster Lowell Thomas back to CBS, where he had begun his radio career in 1930. These moves and others were part of Paley's grand strategy to enable CBS to displace NBC as America's most popular and profitable radio network. As Joseph Persico notes, "In Paley's reckoning, [being number one] had a simple, unmistakable definition, the biggest audiences. And the route to mass audiences, to the highest ratings, was popular entertainment, pleasing the crowds, even if it meant displeasing the critics."[1]

By its nature, "popular" entertainment is safe. It is light-hearted, and as often as not it appeals to the lowest common denominator of taste and sophistication. William Paley knew and accepted this. It was one reason he had never been comfortable with news commentators on his network stating their opinions, especially if they stirred controversy or angered listeners. The second reason was the regulations governing radio broadcasting. The Federal Communications Commission (FCC) in 1941 had issued a ruling against the Mayflower Broadcasting Corporation after a listener complaint. "The Mayflower decision," as it became known, decreed that "The broadcaster cannot be an advocate."[2]

Cardinal Francis Spellman, the Roman Catholic archbishop of New York, was among the influential conservatives who took advantage of their social connections to complain personally to Paley whenever he felt CBS newscasters were violating FCC dictates. Spellman was particularly unhappy with some of the opinions William Shirer was expressing on air. (That Paley, who was Jewish, heeded Spellman's concerns is indicative of the power the archbishop wielded and of the acuity of Paley's business sensibilities.) Spellman was not the only one in Paley's social sphere who carped about Shirer's liberal politics. Another was a vice-president of J. Walter Thompson, one of Madison Avenue's most prominent advertising agencies and an important buyer of commercial time on CBS – including the 5:45 p.m. Sunday time slot in which Shirer's news commentary program aired. It also happened that the Thompson "Mad Man" was a rising star in the Connecticut Republican Party.

That reality underscored another of William Paley's concerns: the possibility that something said on a CBS news program might ruffle feathers in Washington. If that happened, it could attract the attention of meddlesome politicians or broadcast regulators, or even the scrutiny of agents from the FBI. This was a very real fear in the postwar era. With Cold War tensions rising, public tolerance was increasingly thin for opinions that were in any way critical of United States foreign policy or the "American way of life." As Alexander Kendrick notes, "The conversion from war to a suspicious peace had its inevitable effects on American radio."[3]

Senior management at NBC, no less aware and no less wary of the political chill that was sweeping the country, in December 1946 engaged in what trade unionists, some academics, and left-leaning media critics decried as a "cleaning out of liberal commentators." In a speech to members of the New York Newspaper Guild, FDR's former Vice-President Henry Wallace decried the "elimination of liberal newspapermen and commentators."[4] NBC executives countered by categorizing the moves as being the result of "commercial evaluation" – a euphemism for axing on-air staff whose shows had low ratings. None of these developments occurred in a vacuum, of course. When partisan observers saw what was happening, they sounded the alarm. In January 1947, the liberal-oriented journal *New Republic* reported that CBS, NBC, and some affiliated stations had dismissed two dozen reporters and newscasters who were perceived of as being too liberal: "The networks have been growing more and more worried about 'opinion' on their air ... Networks want to avoid 'trouble' – especially with their customers. Pressure to 'tone down' news which is sympathetic to organized labor and to Russia has increased rapidly in the last few months."[5] It did not help the cause of any of the suddenly unemployed broadcasters that the official Soviet news agency came to their defense. Tass reported that in the United States political pressure "was being applied to all broadcasting to 'get rid of liberals.'"[6]

It would be simplistic to conclude that political imperatives alone were behind the NBC housecleaning, the moves at Mutual, or William Paley's sensitivities. It is undeniable that market forces were also a factor. With radio ratings in steep decline, the networks were desperate to reverse that trend. The mood in the corporate offices of America's radio broadcasters reflected the prevailing mood of the nation, which had taken a turn to the right in the November 1946 mid-term elections. The popularity of the Truman administration had sunk so low that the expression "To err is Truman" had become a comedic catchphrase. As a result, the Republicans won a majority in both houses of Congress and for the first time since 1928 the GOP captured the governorship of twenty-five states. As Shirer later noted, "Among those elected that fall ... was a little-known local judge, Joseph R. McCarthy of Wisconsin, to the Senate, and an even lesser known local politician in California, Richard M. Nixon, to the House. Both had accused their opponents of sympathy with Communism and of having 'Communist' support."[7]

So disheartened were the Democrats by their electoral setbacks in 1946 that influential voices within the party began calling for the president to resign. However, Harry Truman was a scrapper and a savvy politician who was well aware of the rising tides of anti-communist hysteria and paranoia. In a bid to shore up his popularity, he took decisive steps to dispel any notions that he was soft on communism. For one, he appointed General George C. Marshall, a popular wartime military leader, to replace James F. Brynes as his Secretary of State. For another, Truman reached across the aisle for the bipartisan support of influential Republicans, one of whom was Michigan Senator Arthur H. Vandenberg, a leading conservative who had been an outspoken isolationist prior to Pearl Harbor.

The president garnered support from Vandenberg and other erstwhile critics when he appeared on Capitol Hill on 12 March 1947 to announce what the media dubbed "the Truman Doctrine": "I believe that it must be the policy of the United States to support free peoples who are resisting attempted subjugation by armed minorities or outside pressures."[8] The tough talk found a receptive audience in Congress. The Republican majority approved a bill granting $400 million in aid to Greece and Turkey, both of which were battling communist insurgencies. Hot on the heels of this initiative, urged on by hawkish advisors, Secretary of State Marshall proposed a bold new plan designed to restore economic prosperity to war-ravaged Europe and to thereby undercut the hunger, poverty, unemployment, and despair that were fueling communist sympathies in many countries.

In its day, the Marshall Plan was as controversial as the Obama administration's 2009 Wall Street bailout. It was also expensive and open-ended – characteristics that critics seized upon. Regardless, many Americans agreed that the administration had to do *something* to stem the perceived threat of world communism. This same ethos was about to give rise to the foreign policy doctrine known as "containment" – as American diplomat George F. Kennan (writing anonymously as "X") dubbed it in a July 1947 article in the influential journal *Foreign Affairs*; the purpose of containment was to block Soviet communism's attempts to occupy "every nook and cranny available to it in the basin of the world."[9]

William Shirer knew Kennan from their days together in Berlin, when Kennan had been on staff at the American embassy and he and Shirer had been regulars among the crowd of journalists and junior diplomats who gathered nightly to dine, talk shop, and socialize. Now, a decade later, when he learned the identity of "X," Shirer was dismayed by the strident tone of Kennan's foreign-policy pronouncements. Shirer continued to believe in the fundamental strengths and legitimacy of American democracy at a time when the nation was at the zenith of its power and international influence: "If the people of Europe want to swing 'left,' is there any good reason for us to fear it or try to prevent it? ... and since we have made a whacking success of democracy, why should an unholy fear of Communism grip us every time we look across the seas ... ?"[10]

What Shirer was arguing was that America was strong enough to withstand any challenge from the Soviet Union, and so there was nothing to fear in communism. Shirer felt that America was strong, and so engagement and dialogue were preferable to confrontation when it came to meeting the threat of Soviet expansionism.

Consistent with that belief, Shirer was outspoken in his opposition to the Truman administration's plan to give aid to Greece, a country headed by Georgios Papandreou, a leader who was widely regarded as being corrupt and authoritarian. At the same time, Shirer was critical of America's unwavering support of Chiang Kai-shek's Nationalist forces in China. It is worth noting that other liberal-oriented journalists and media commentators voiced similar misgivings; among them were the noted political commentator Walter Lippmann and Shirer's own CBS colleagues Howard K. Smith and Washington-based Joseph Harsch, who also had a columnist for the *Christian Science Monitor*. However, by dint of his decade of service at CBS, his association with Ed Murrow, and the fact he had his own weekly news program, Shirer enjoyed a loftier public profile than did many of his like-minded peers. He also reiterated his controversial opinions in his public lectures and in his personal correspondence with prominent political figures, including Henry Wallace (who in 1947 was editing the liberal journal *The New Republic*), and with 1944 GOP presidential candidate Wendell Willkie. In a letter to Republican senator Claude Pepper of Florida, a key member of the Foreign Relations Committee, Shirer asked if the politicians were "going to have a chance to question some of the so-called experts in the State Department on the President's proposals to pour money into Greece and Turkey? ... I think the President ought to be more frank with the people about the kind of 'democracy' we are supporting in Turkey and Greece."[11]

Such a query and citizen requests for transparency in government are to be expected and are even essential in a liberal democracy. However, given the tenor of the times in the Cold War era, many Americans had dwindling patience for those who insisted on voicing opinions that were out of step with the public mood. Shirer's opinions sometimes were *that* – particularly his pronouncements on American-Soviet relations. As Ann Sperber notes, "Shirer himself was a believer in 'the great diplomatic struggle against Russia and the spread of Communism,' as he called it – more flexible than some, however, more wide-ranging in his world view, less apt to close the door on discourse."[12]

In light of the growing Cold War tensions, Americans had little patience for dissent. As Cloud and Olson note, "Radio shows, movies, books, magazines, articles, and newspaper columns went beyond the reality of the Soviet Union's aggressive new international posture and suggested that Moscow had created a fifth column within the United States, abetted, consciously or unconsciously by American liberals."[13] The right to free speech notwithstanding, anyone who voiced a dissenting opinion was suspect on an ascending scale of culpability that included Communist "fellow travelers," "pinkos," and outright "Commies."

Elements of the media were eager to root out "subversives." And no one was keener in that regard than Shirer's erstwhile employer, Colonel Robert McCormick of the *Chicago Tribune*. In February 1947 the *Tribune* published a series of lengthy polemics by reporter Carl Wiegman about "foreign propaganda in the United States." One of the installments in the series took special aim at "one-worlders," the *Tribune*'s derisive term for "known pro-Communists" who supported the UN and opposed the spread of nuclear weapons. Louis Dolivet, the editor of a pro-UN journal called *Free World*, was singled out for criticism, as were high-profile supporters such as Shirer, Chinese-born writer Lin Yutang, and Orson Welles.[14]

Given *Tribune* publisher McCormick's ultra-conservative views, his paranoia about eastern liberals and other "pinko" troublemakers, and his partisan approach to the news, *Tribune* writers wrote with their boss's tacit approval, and even with his blessing. Their attacks helped to ratchet up the rhetoric and paranoia about communist infiltration of America. Sensing the public mood, those politicians in Washington who were eager to turn the situation to their own political gain were quick to condemn dissent of any kind as being anti-American, "pro-communist," or even treasonous. Thus, it is hardly surprising that Shirer and other prominent Americans who dared to speak their minds found themselves coming under scrutiny by the FBI.

It was J. Edgar Hoover who made anti-radical operations an FBI priority. To say that the FBI's first director was a controversial figure is an understatement. There can be no question that Hoover, who served under every president from Calvin Coolidge to Richard Nixon, made significant contributions to policing and to homeland security; however, we now know the extent to which he misused his position to build and shape the FBI as his own tool.

As the self-appointed guardian of the nation's security and morality, Hoover considered it part of his job and that of the FBI to keep an eye on opinion leaders – politicians, journalists, writers, scientists, entertainers, and sport figures, especially those whose opinions he did not approve of – to ensure they were not involved in "un-American activities." Thus, FBI agents collected dossiers on many public figures, disregarding or tiptoeing around the constitutional rights of these individuals. If it ever occurred to Hoover or any of his political masters that the kind of domestic surveillance FBI agents were involved was in itself anti-democratic, there was no hint of it.

Given his public profile, his liberal inclinations, and his feisty temperament, it was inevitable that William Shirer would attract FBI attention. The agency files on Shirer that have been declassified begin in 1941 and end in 1961. Curiously, there is scant evidence of FBI surveillance of Shirer from 1947 to 1956. While it may have been that he was no longer a "person of interest" during this period, it is no less likely that the files for these nine years remain classified. That supposition seems to be confirmed by the material about Shirer that has been released. For example, there is a three-page FBI internal memo about Shirer dated 10 June 1955 that has been redacted, but for a single paragraph that recommends information in the memo be referred to the FBI's Subversive Control Section. Another memo, dated 23 November 1956, and largely intact, includes among its seven pages information on Shirer's writings and incriminating details about his activities.

Those portions of the FBI's Shirer dossier that *are* available to the public under Freedom of Information laws have been censored. Large portions of many documents have been blacked out. Much of the information contained in the Shirer file is innocuous and so mundane that it would be amusing to behold, if the intentions of the individuals who gathered this material and meticulously chronicled it were not so sinister.

As far as can be determined, the FBI file on Shirer begins with a 17 July 1941 letter from T.J. Donegan, the acting assistant-director of the agency's New York office. Donegan wrote to J. Edgar Hoover to inform him that one of the agency's field agents in New York had "requested that this office obtain a copy of the book *Berlin Diary*," which the agent noted had been written by William L. Shirer, CBS's Berlin correspondent "during the years 1934 to 1941."[15] Given that he did not join CBS until 1937 – which is a fact that would have been clear to anyone who took the time to even scan a copy of *Berlin Diary* – one can only wonder at the veracity of the information in the Shirer file and of the acuity of the agents who gathered it. Regardless, Shirer was now on the radar as a "person of interest" for the FBI, though apparently not yet in a systematic or proactive way. In past, he had done his "patriotic duty" and spoken freely on various occasions with FBI agents who were gathering information on the treasonous activities of pro-Nazi journalists such as Bob Best, Douglas Chandler, Donald Day, and Mildred Gillars[16] and poet Ezra Pound. In 1943, Shirer turned the tables, approaching agents in the FBI's New York office for information he needed as background for a planned play about Bob Best. In the end, miffed at the lack of cooperation he received from the Bureau, Shirer dropped his request. Nonetheless, he was back in touch with the FBI later that same year after he received a profanity-laced letter from a deranged individual who said that he lived for the day when he would "be able to take care of [Shirer] in the manner in which you deserve."[17] While nothing more came of the threat, it did serve to remind Shirer of the depth of the passions his broadcasts and writings could spark.

Judging by the contents of those portions of the FBI file on Shirer that have been declassified, Hoover's men often clipped newspaper articles written by Shirer and those in which he was mentioned – "Shirer Blasts Enemy Agents" reads a typical headline.[18] The FBI also recorded and processed letters from various informants who raised specific concerns about Shirer's opinions. In March 1942, for example, an unidentified letter writer contacted J. Edgar Hoover to report that in a recent radio broadcast Shirer had referred to literature the letter writer deemed to be "against America's best interests." Among the pamphlets Shirer alluded to in passing was one that urged people to refuse to pay their income tax. The FBI informant did not report what Shirer said about this, nor did the person explain the context of Shirer's comments: "I was too indignant to be accurate enough to repeat to you their causes." He then suggested that the FBI contact Shirer for more details.[19]

Shirer again came under scrutiny nine months later because on his Sunday evening newscast on 3 January he read excerpts from a *Christian Science Monitor* newspaper article that speculated the German military might have advance knowledge of the sailing times of Allied merchant ships. Shirer recommended that FBI agents investigate the source of any such informational leaks. This piqued the interest of an FBI field agent in Chicago who had not heard the actual broadcast, but had been told about it after the fact and selectively at that. The agent wrote to Hoover to report that Shirer had not indicated the source of his information.[20]

J. Edgar Hoover received a subsequent complaint from an informant in Boston who objected that in his weekly syndicated newspaper column for 25 July 1943, Shirer had quoted from various German newspapers to explain how "Axis propagandists" had twisted facts about recent Allied bombing raids on Rome. The essence of Shirer's message was lost on both the informant and staff at FBI headquarters in Washington, who were also ignorant of the fact that in reporting information gleaned from foreign newspapers Shirer was doing something he had done in countless wartime broadcasts from Berlin – which were made under the watchful eyes of Nazi censors. It speaks volumes about the tenor of the times and the paranoia of J. Edgar Hoover's FBI that the type of information Nazis propagandist had no problems with was suspect in postwar America.

The Bureau's file on Shirer is filled with scores of similar documents. What is apparent is that while FBI agents were busy gathering information on him, no one at FBI headquarters in Washington really knew much about William L. Shirer. It was as if the FBI surveillance machine was operating on autopilot; only occasionally would anyone pay heed to the information being compiled. That happened in October 1946, when in a newspaper column Shirer commented on a speech Hoover had given to an American Legion conference in San Francisco. Shirer poked fun at the FBI director when he scoffed at the notion that Communism posed a threat to the United States "where the Bolsheviki can't collect enough votes to elect a single Congressman or lieutenant governor"[21] (or even a dog catcher, for that matter). Shirer speculated about Hoover's motives in sounding the alarm about the dangers of communism. "The tone and language of Mr Hoover somehow make one wonder whether he, able, energetic, and patriotic civil servant that he is, may not be stumbling into the role of [former Attorney General] A. Mitchell Palmer" whose "somewhat grotesque efforts to rescue the country from communism after the last war" in retrospect appeared to be "a painful, but clownish comedy."[22]

When one of his field agents drew Shirer's column to the attention of Hoover aide Clyde Tolson, he immediately alerted his boss. Hoover's reaction was predictable. On the bottom of Tolson's note, the FBI head scribbled: "Let me have memo on what we have on Shirer. He writes like a fool."[23]

Within a few days, FBI agents had compiled a detailed biographical sketch of Shirer. It was four pages of single-spaced type, complete with details about his personal life, work history, political involvements, and even his social activities. The report included a list of the clubs Shirer belonged to – everything from Tau Kappa Epsilon, his college social fraternity, to his membership in the Century Club of New York, which was made up of writers and other creative people. The sketch also listed some of the public dinners Shirer had attended recently, groups he had addressed, and even the names of some of the politically oriented publications he wrote for; among them was a left-leaning newspaper called *Free World*, which the sketch duly noted "has contained several articles written by individuals *reported* to hold Communist views."[24]

The word "reported" appears again and again in the biographical sketch, mostly in the expressions "*reportedly* Communist controlled" and "*reported* to have Communist sympathies." Of special interest to the G-men who were snooping into Shirer's life were his involvements in the India League of America (which supported Indian independence from Britain), the advisory council of the Association for the Prevention of World War Three (a coalition of groups opposed to a "soft peace" with Germany, headed by mystery writer Rex Stout), and in various anti-fascist organizations. Never mind that America had just fought a war against fascism, that none of the groups Shirer was involved with was illegal, or that all were very public in their activities; after all, that was how they publicized their causes. The names of such groups must have sounded exotic, and hence suspicious, to the straight-laced, uninformed agents of J. Edgar Hoover's FBI. Included on the list of questionable organizations were the "anti-Franco movement" Friends of the Spanish Republic,[25] the Joint Anti-Fascist Refugee Committee (an umbrella organization that in 1947 was included in a United States government list of subversive groups[26]), and the Action Committee to Free Spain Now.

There is no hard evidence the FBI did anything specific with the information it gathered on Shirer. However, it is clear that he was being watched by federal agents, and in all probability by investigators from the now-infamous House Un-American Affairs Committee (HUAC), the Senate's Internal Security Subcommittee, and by politicians eager to capitalize on the media attention the government hearings were attracting.

It was in 1947, under the chairmanship of New Jersey Democratic Congressman J. Parnell Thomas, that the HUAC launched hearings on Communist influence in the film industry. The committee's work resulted in the imprisonment of a group of writers, directors, and producers known as the Hollywood Ten. In 1948–49, future president Richard M. Nixon became known for his role in the HUAC's investigation of the alleged Soviet spy Alger Hiss. The committee became less active in the 1960s; its name was changed to the Committee on Internal Security in 1969, and it was disbanded in 1975.

The late 1940s and early 1950s – when Cold War anti-communist hysteria was at its peak – is now known as the McCarthy era; thanks to countless movies, books, and plays, McCarthyism and the HUAC have become synonymous in the public mind. However, the reality is that the HUAC was a Congressional committee, and Senator Joseph R. McCarthy had no formal ties to it, although he sympathized with the committee's work. McCarthy was an opportunist who, like Attorney General A. Mitchell Palmer in 1919, sought to tap into an existing groundswell of public uncertainties for his own political gain. Like most liberals, Shirer was disdainful, even scornful, of McCarthy and all that he stood for; however, as far as we know, Shirer never came directly into McCarthy's crosshairs. The reason is obvious: by the time McCarthy burst onto the scene, Shirer's CBS broadcasting career was in ruins, and he was no longer a high-value target for the senator. That said, in retrospect it is more surprising that Shirer was not investigated (as far as we know) by the HUAC. "I had never hidden what I thought … No congressional committee, not even the notorious HUAC nor its rival, the Senate Internal Security Subcommittee, nor any other government group obsessed with Communists and Communism ever expressed the slightest interest in calling me before them."²⁷

Ironically, while Shirer was not spattered by the mud thrown up by the HUAC or McCarthy, nor did he have any role to play in the 1954 showdown between McCarthy and Edward R. Murrow, there is a compelling argument to be made that Murrow finally decided to speak out against McCarthy at least in some measure because he was motivated by guilt at the fate of Shirer and others whose lives and careers were disrupted and in some cases ruined by the paranoia and fear that were undermining and poisoning democracy in America.

While much was made of it at the time and in the years since, it was not Shirer's liberal politics during the Cold War era that hastened the end of his time at CBS. True, his political views were the kindling wood for the blaze that consumed his radio career; however, the flashpoint for Shirer's troubles was as much personal as it was ideological. Shirer had made an enemy in the person of CBS boss William S. Paley, and the antagonisms between the two men had been building for years. However, because Ed Murrow was Paley's favorite and Murrow and Shirer were close, Paley tolerated Shirer as long as he made money for CBS and his views did not cause too many problems for the network. All of that began to change in autumn 1946, when Paley proposed to Shirer that he relocate to Chicago and do his Sunday evening program from there. Shirer's commentaries would be under the sponsorship of chewing gum magnate Phil Wrigley, Paley's friend and one of CBS's biggest advertisers. Paley's proposal bubbled with opportunity, but, after considering the offer, Shirer declined the boss's invitation to move to the Windy City. Shirer had settled into his life in New York; he had his weekly column in the *Herald Tribune*; his family was there, and so was Tilly Losch, with whom he was still infatuated. No less problematic from Shirer's perspective were his concerns that he would come to be regarded as a spokesman for the Wrigley Corporation.

William Paley begrudgingly accepted Shirer's rationale for rejecting a move west. For now. However, Paley was not a man to forgive or forget a slight, no matter how inadvertent or inconsequential. "After the Wrigley incident, things [were] never ... quite the same between Shirer and Paley," notes Joseph Persico. The Murrow biographer was correct about that, especially when Paley's animosities were combined with other concurrent developments. The cumulative effect proved disastrous for Shirer.

Paley was in a testy mood and was on edge because of criticism that advertisers were dictating the content, staffing, and scheduling of CBS news programs. Such accusations impugned the very credibility of the network's newscasts. This was an issue all broadcasters in America were sensitive to and which print journalists were ever-ready to write about, even if they had little reason to boast about their own objectivity or impartiality.

In 1947, like its competitors, CBS was wrestling yet again with the issue of objectivity and with what newscasters could or could not say on air. In the early years of CBS news, Ed Klauber had dictated a policy that said CBS would provide facts and let listeners make up their own minds about the meaning of events. The difficulty had always been to decide what is "fact" and what is "opinion." The dividing line between "objectivity" and "subjectivity" often is fuzzy. For that reason, when he became vice-president of CBS news, Ed Murrow made it one of his priorities to come up with a consistent editorial policy to end the ambiguity once and for all. With that in mind, he hired a former member of Wendell Willkie's campaign team, Russell Davenport, to draft a report and make recommendations. That document, which arrived on Murrow's desk in February 1947, suggested that CBS ensure that comments heard on its news programs be "fair" and that there be an "opportunity" for a wide range of alternate viewpoints, in effect like an "op-ed page of the airwaves."

Paley and Murrow were committed to that idea and set to work preparing the ground for a change of direction at CBS. However, before they could do so, the FCC announced it was planning to hold hearings where it would reconsider its 1941 Mayflower decision against on-air editorializing. Knowing this, CBS's lawyers advised that the Davenport proposal be shelved for fear that moving ahead on it would seem "impolite" – or even impolitic – and would create the impression the network was trying to outmaneuver or even defy the FCC. "To Murrow," notes Ann Sperber, "it became a memory that rankled, a nagging deep-lying disappointment and sense of lost opportunity."[28]

While all of this was happening, Paley and Murrow had another aggravation to deal with. New York Times radio critic Jack Gould had called into question the objectivity of CBS news and its editorial independence: "Only recently, one of the major conservative networks, at the behest of the sponsor, agreed to a complete change in format for a specific broadcast … The emphasis of the program was shifted from foreign to domestic issues and the old commentator replaced by a new one."[29] While Gould had not mentioned CBS by name, Paley was incensed. He suspected the reference was to his network, and Paley had little tolerance for criticism.

An editorial that appeared in *The New York Times* the following week rubbed salt into Paley's wound when it chided America's radio networks for linking corporations to particular newscasters or commentators: "Advertisers are being permitted to say what news is to be put on the air and who is to put it on the air ... No newspaper would tolerate for a moment such control of its news and opinions."[30] Despite the nonsensical nature of such a holier-than-thou pronouncement, the newspaper editorial further irked Paley, who urged Ed Murrow to write a reply to Gould's comments. "You say: 'Only recently one of the conservative networks at the behest of the sponsor agreed to complete change in format for a specific broadcast.' Which network, Mr. Gould? Wouldn't it be more responsible and effective criticism if you were to name names?"[31]

What Murrow was suggesting when he made use of the latter phrase is clear – that CBS was a victim, the target of a smear campaign of the sort being carried on by red-baiters. Gould ignored that and, of course, having the last word, he chided Murrow for failing to address one of the key points in *The Times'* criticism of CBS, namely "that news and opinion should be removed entirely from commercial sponsorship."[32]

Paley and Murrow emerged with figuratively bloodied noses from this very public verbal sparring match with Gould and *The New York Times*, and neither CBS man was happy about it. As Persico noted, the evidence is that Murrow had not been all that comfortable with the message he articulated in his letter to the editor or with being obliged to toe the corporate line. For his part, Paley was offended that his integrity had been questioned. He neither liked – nor did he accept – being challenged or told no. Gould had done both. William Shirer had also said no to Paley. Gould was out of reach; Shirer, a CBS employee, was not.

Shirer understood and later acknowledged that he should have been more aware of the dangers inherent in any clash of egos with the CBS president: "The controversy stirred up by *The Times* and Murrow's response did not, I admit, cause me any concern ... Perhaps it should have, but in those days, if not arrogant, I was rather self-confident. Perhaps I was guilty of what the ancient Greeks called hubris."[33] Others had reached the same conclusion.

Shirer's CBS colleague Charles Collingwood told Joseph Persico that in his opinion Shirer had become "a stuck whistle. He wasn't analyzing the news. He just kept preaching his own beliefs over and over."[34] Collingwood, like the other "Murrow boys," owed their primary allegiance to Ed Murrow, not to Shirer. What's more, when it became clear that Shirer was on the way out at CBS, given the temper of the times, it is perfectly understandable that the Murrow loyalists would side with their mentor and with CBS management; all of them knew who signed their paychecks.

Once the war ended, the American public's interest in foreign news waned. Even so, for the moment at least the ratings for Shirer's Sunday evening broadcasts on CBS remained strong; in fact, they were better than the ratings for many other network newscasters. At the same time, Shirer's status as one of America's most popular, influential, and widely respected radio news commentators was underscored in January 1947, when the French government awarded him a Medal of Chevalier in appreciation of the quality of his reports on France before, during, and after the war. In light of all this, it is impossible to know if Shirer's critics really felt that the quality of his work had slipped or if they formed this opinion in retrospect, when they tried to rationalize and explain the chain of events that hastened the end of Shirer's career at CBS and sealed the end of his friendship with Ed Murrow.

29

"Pride ruined the angels"

William Shirer's career at CBS ended almost as suddenly and unexpected-ly as it had begun a decade earlier. The chain of events that brought this about began on the evening of 10 March 1947. Shirer was at home when he received a telephone call from an executive of the J. Walter Thompson advertising agency, which represented the sponsor of Shirer's weekly newscast, the J.B. Williams Company. Shirer was on his guard when he received the phone call because, not long before this, a Thompson vice-president had complained to William Paley about Shirer's political views and had chided Shirer that he was "too liberal for his own good."

While Shirer had taken note of the ad man's criticism, he had not changed or tempered his opinions, despite the fact his fifteen-minute newscast on CBS provided him with a sizeable portion of his income – $1,300 per week – and a national forum for his views. Shirer had a more pressing problem than bowing down to the dictates of postwar conser-vatives: the alarming loss of listeners for all radio news programming. The number of news commentaries still being broadcast by America's four networks was dropping. Ratings were in freefall. "Long before the war ended I came to the conclusion the public would certainly become bored with us commentators if we continued to harangue four or five times a week," Shirer explained in a 1947 letter to a friend. "That is why as soon as the war ended I asked that my broadcast be cut down to one a week."[1]

Shirer's strategy seemed to pay off. After six years on the air, his news-cast remained one of the most popular shows in the CBS Sunday afternoon lineup, often attracting more than five million listeners. However, the pro-gram's ratings fluctuated from week to week, and the number of listeners was only about half of what it had been during the war. Despite this,

Shirer had heard no complaints from CBS, nor did he have any inkling that his sponsor was unhappy. Thus, the news the Thompson executive delivered to Shirer in that Monday evening phone call hit him like a bolt out of the blue.

The ad agency rep announced that the Williams Company was dropping its sponsorship of Shirer's newscast. The shaving cream maker supposedly was intent on appealing to a younger demographic, and so it wanted to sponsor a musical program in that Sunday time slot. The decision was presented to Shirer as being a fait accompli.

Back in December 1946, when lawyers for CBS and the Thompson agency had negotiated the contract for the show, they had included an out-clause for both parties. A thirteen-week option was standard industry practice at the time, and Williams was said to be acting on its out. It is worth noting that this was not the first time Shirer had lost his sponsor. In 1943, when General Foods had walked away, CBS had kept Shirer's show on the air on a "sustaining basis." The network had paid the costs until a new sponsor – the J.B. Williams Company – was recruited. In addition, the newscast had been moved around on the network's schedule before settling into its 5:45 p.m. Sunday time slot in June 1944. In the heat of the moment, Shirer apparently forgot all this.

His initial reaction to the loss of his sponsor, his time slot, and a sizeable portion of his income was, understandably, one of dismay and disbelief. "I was sceptical of [the Thompson executive's] explanation ... I was also taken aback and depressed at being thrown off the air suddenly and without warning. And I was surprised that there was no word from CBS about this."[2] What Shirer found especially galling was that the Thompson man who had called took it for granted that the fifteen minutes of airtime Shirer's newscast filled was owned by the Williams Company, and not by CBS or Shirer. He was no less dismayed that Ed Murrow had said nothing to him about CBS dropping the newscast. Shirer knew it was inconceivable that Murrow was not privy to Williams's plans. Thus, in Shirer's mind, all of this underscored a crucial issue in American broadcasting – that of editorial independence.

While he had not been involved in the recent controversy about sponsors and news programming sparked by *New York Times* radio columnist Jack Gould's sparring match with Paley and Murrow, Shirer had been an interested observer. Had he spoken out, he would have sided with Gould; like many journalists, Shirer was concerned about advertisers dictating the tone and content of news programming. The issue was a longstanding

one, and there were worrisome signs it would only become even more nettlesome as the new medium of television took over the airwaves. Thus,
Shirer recognized the direction of the political winds in the early months
of 1947. These were stormy times for American liberals, who were in disarray and were spending more time engaged in political infighting than
in battling political opponents.

With the return of peace and with the Great Depression now a fast-fading
memory, Americans' inherent mistrust of big government began to re-
assert itself. Conservatism was on the march all across the land with a newfound vigor. It is no coincidence that this Tea Party-like backlash came at
the same time that women, blacks, and organized labor, all of whom had
made huge strides during the war years, were pressing to solidify their
gains. A similar scenario had played itself out in the 1920s, in the wake of
the First World War.

Given his relationships with Ed Murrow and CBS president William
Paley and his decades of loyal service to the network, Shirer assumed –
naively, as he was about to discover – that he was insulated from any backlash against liberal media personalities. Less than two years after the death
of Franklin D. Roosevelt, the fractious coalition that had supported his
New Deal had disintegrated. The term "New Deal supporter" was now an
epithet that the resurgent opposition hurled at Shirer and other liberals.
This was the backdrop for the final act of Shirer's dramatic and bitter exit
from CBS.

His first move after receiving that distressing call from the Thompson
agency's spokesman was to telephone Ed Murrow to report the substance
of the conversation he had just had and to ask Murrow for reassurance
that his Sunday newscast would remain it its time slot on CBS. The real
question in Shirer's mind was this: was that particular fifteen minutes of
airtime *his*, and by extension CBS's, or did it belong to the sponsor? "To put
it bluntly – as [Murrow] and I always had put such matters between us in
the past, would he and Paley allow an advertiser to throw me off the air?"[3]

Shirer was taken aback by Murrow's response. His old friend did not
immediately rally to his side; instead, he hedged. Murrow promised to
look into the matter and get back to Shirer "in a day or two." This was not
satisfactory to Shirer whose next call was to CBS head William Paley himself. Paley, too, was noncommittal. He would say only that any decision
about the fate of the Sunday broadcast and of Shirer's future at CBS were
in Murrow's hands. This reply is at odds with what Paley said in an interview with Ann Sperber many years later. The CBS boss explained to her

that he and Murrow had "discussed [letting Shirer go] long before the thing blew. We were both conscious of the fact that Shirer just wasn't working at it."[4]

If that was indeed the case, it is odd – inconceivable, even – that neither Murrow nor Paley had ever broached this subject with Shirer. Similarly, if Paley had conveyed his concerns to Shirer when they spoke on the evening of 10 March, in all likelihood it would have short-circuited the ensuing bitter public controversy. However, Paley told Shirer none of this, and Shirer, a proud man, grew angrier by the minute as the conversation proceeded.

When Shirer called his agent, John Gude of the Stix & Gude agency, Gude was also taken aback to learn that Williams was dropping its sponsorship of Shirer's weekly newscast. However, Gude (who also represented Murrow) took a more dispassionate view of the situation. Murrow later insisted that Gude was aware that Murrow had concerns about the quality of Shirer's work, but there is no evidence this was true.[5] Regardless, Gude accepted that the Williams Company was within its rights to decline its option on continuing to sponsor Shirer's newscast. However, what *did* trouble Gude was CBS's handling of the situation; he felt that Ed Murrow, not someone from the Thompson agency, should have spoken with Shirer first to explain what was happening and why. Shirer agreed. In his mind, his friendship with Murrow trumped the employer-employee relationship. He felt he deserved better treatment.

Unfortunately, the reality was that Ed Murrow himself was conflicted and uncertain of what to do in this situation. When he had taken the corporate job at CBS and learned that one of his responsibilities was to fire people, Murrow balked. If there was "dirty work" to be done, he had said, it was not up to him to do it. He applied that same rationale now, when Shirer's hour of reckoning was at hand. Alexander Kendrick quotes Murrow as saying, "Who am I to be firing people, the Almighty Himself?"[6]

However, the situation with Shirer was different, and in his heart Murrow *must* have known it. He had hired Bill Shirer. They had worked together as colleagues, confidantes, and the best of friends. They had learned from and supported one another. They had eaten, drunk, and partied together countless times. During the four-year period from 1937 to December 1941 they had helped build CBS news into the industry leader. Yet it was also true that the dynamics of the Shirer-Murrow relationship had changed once Shirer had returned home from Berlin. Simmering petty differences and minor resentments, the egos of two hugely talented, strong-willed men, the corporate dynamics at CBS, and the political imperatives of the day all factored into the equation. Shirer and Murrow were locked into their respective roles by circumstances and their personalities. In hindsight, all of this is evident.

Exactly how the melodrama of Shirer's precipitous fall from grace unfolded long has been a subject of debate. The truism is that it is the victors who write the history of a conflict. However, if there was a victor in the struggle between Shirer and CBS it was the network, at least in the short term.

In the situation and with the personalities involved, it was unavoidable, inevitable even, that once battle lines were drawn, friends and colleagues of Shirer and Murrow would take sides. Given Murrow's journalistic reputation, his prominence as a media personality, and his corporate position, it is not surprising that most of "the Murrow boys" sided with him; among them were Eric Sevareid, Howard K. Smith, Charles Collingwood, and Larry LeSueur, all of whom Shirer regarded as close friends. "It was traumatic," LeSueur told Cloud and Olson. "I was a very good friend of Bill's, and I chose Murrow. I didn't see Bill after that."[7]

Then there was Frank Stanton. As Paley's right-hand man, when the boss moved up to become chairman of the board in 1945, Stanton became the president of CBS. Despite this, Stanton quietly egged Shirer on, assuring him that he was on the moral high ground in his disagreement with Murrow. It seems that Stanton either carried a grudge or else he continued to regard Murrow as a rival for Paley's ear. As a result, he was not at all unhappy to see Murrow in a tight spot. Stanton played no direct role in the Shirer controversy, but he was privy to what was happening in the CBS executive offices. Years later, he revealed that it was his understanding that the Williams Company *had* dropped Shirer mainly because their advertising agency, J. Walter Thompson, felt Shirer was "too liberal."[8] Furthermore, Stanton opined that Ed Murrow had "caved in quickly" when William Paley made it known that he wanted Shirer out of his Sunday evening time slot and gone from CBS.[9]

Shirer had ample time to contemplate what he regarded as Murrow's betrayal. The more Shirer brooded, the angrier and more bitter he became, especially after he received the letter from the Williams Company formally notifying him that his last newscast would be Sunday, 30 March 1947. By now, Shirer was convinced there was more going on here than he was being told. He suspected that he had been targeted for dismissal, just as other liberal news commentators had been.

Shirer was a fighter, stubborn and proud to a fault. He was not prepared to end his time at CBS meekly. On 19 March, he wrote to Murrow
seeking clarification on his status at the network: "When we last spoke –
a week ago today – you said you would let me know within a day or two
whether I was definitely off the 5:45 p.m. Sunday show, and therefore definitely off the air so far as an effective audience on CBS is concerned ...
Since the sponsor's agent had informed me that I am though a week
from Sunday [30 March], I would appreciate your confirming whether
this is Columbia's decision too, as Mr Paley informs me that the basic
final decision is yours, and not, as I had at first believed, that of the soap
company, I do not believe it is unreasonable to ask ten days' notice on an
affair such as this. Would you be kind enough, therefore, to send me definite word today?"[10]

Shirer got a response the following day. Murrow called him on the telephone. His old friend was "crisp and cool – most unlike the Ed I had
known for ten years."[11] Murrow told Shirer the decision was final: another announcer was being brought in to replace him on what once more
was a Sunday evening newscast. Shirer understandably did not take this
announcement well. At some point during the heated exchange that followed, Murrow floated the idea that Shirer might be given a new, late-
night time slot for another newscast; however, that suggestion only served
to fuel Shirer's rage. The conversation ended with the two men agreeing
on just one point: on 23 March, Shirer announced his impending departure from the Sunday newscast. "Next Sunday I will make my last broadcast on this program. I've been informed by the sponsor and by the
Columbia Broadcasting System of that decision."[12]

It was at this point that the situation spun out of the control of all concerned. What until that on-air announcement had been an internal matter at the network morphed into an issue of journalistic freedom and a
cause célèbre, at least in the New York media. Shirer was responsible for
this, at least initially, and in the end even he had to acknowledge that his
truculence did him more harm than good. Although he did not initially
recognize it, like Ed Murrow he had become swept up in a much larger
rush of events over which he had little control.

The moment Shirer ended his broadcast of 23 March, the CBS switchboard
was swamped with calls from hundreds of irate listeners who protested
the cancelation of Shirer's newscast. At the same time, a crowd of newspaper reporters was waiting outside the studio to interview him when he

emerged. "To suddenly change my [time] spot seems to me to be purely because of my editorial position," Shirer told them. "I certainly consider it a move to gag me."[13]

If he had been hoping to generate headlines, he succeeded. Shirer's words proved to be every bit as important as *how* he said them. His tone was accusatory. It was also inflammatory and embarrassing for CBS. William Paley and Ed Murrow were infuriated at finding themselves on the defensive and forced to deny that Shirer's newscast was being canceled for political reasons. Both Paley and Murrow were still smarting from the criticism that Jack Gould of *The New York Times* had hurled their way. They were no less upset that newspaper reporters had been waiting to interview Shirer when he emerged from the studio after his penultimate broadcast. Murrow and Paley suspected the newshounds had been tipped off about what was happening and that Shirer had set out to embarrass CBS. However, Shirer denied that he had been responsible or that he had appealed for the support of the critics who now began writing and calling Paley and Murrow, particularly the members of the Political Action Committee of the Congress of Industrial Organizations (CIO) who protested to the FCC about Shirer's dismissal and next day staged a noisy demonstration on the street outside CBS headquarters in New York.

Shirer may have been telling the truth about his role or lack thereof in these developments, although it certainly would not have been out of character for him to attempt to orchestrate either media interest in his situation or a public campaign to protest his dismissal. That said, it is just as likely that one of his friends or colleagues was responsible. Regardless, what had been intended as a controlled burn quickly grew into a raging out-of-control wildfire. And neither William Paley nor Ed Murrow could stand the heat given off by it.

If having union protesters outside the CBS offices had not been bad enough, the Voice of Freedom, a high-profile media monitoring group headed by writer Dorothy Parker came out in support of Shirer. The group, liberals all, condemned his removal from the 5:45 p.m. Sunday time slot on CBS as "a shocking blow to those who had faith in the freedom of the airwaves."[14] Among the celebrities who signed the protest telegram that Parker sent to William Paley were film star Gregory Peck, playwright Arthur Miller, and journalists John Gunther and Jimmy Sheean. In addition, playwright Robert Sherwood and poet Archibald MacLeish sent messages calling for Shirer's reinstatement. Paley, unaccustomed to and uncomfortable with being publicly pilloried, was outraged. So was Ed Murrow, who took the rebuke personally; some of the people who were now accusing him of censoring Shirer were friends. Murrow responded with a press release that denied Shirer was being gagged. But the statement did little to quell the controversy. As Sperber correctly notes, "[Murrow] was paying for his managerial blunder as he floundered in a middleman position for which his experience had given him no training."[15]

Murrow understood too late the mess into which he had gotten himself. He realized he had erred in abdicating his responsibilities initially – in not talking with Shirer before his friend and employee heard from the sponsor that he was being dropped from his newscast – and that he had underestimated the intensity of Shirer's reaction to losing what he had come to regard as "his time" in the CBS Sunday schedule. Murrow put on a brave face as he struggled to regain control of the situation and to do the right thing, whatever that was. He could not decide. The dispute had become personal, the raw, visceral emotions that had surfaced were clouding his judgment. Murrow agonized over what to do. Janet Murrow later told Joseph Persico, "I had never seen [my husband] so overwrought."[16] Sperber echoes that, quoting a Murrow associate as saying that Murrow was "absolutely destroyed" by the Shirer controversy. "[Ed] was in horrible shape, kept saying, 'I have no business in this job. I can't do this kinda thing to my friends.'"[17]

The essence of Murrow's dilemma was that he was a manager whose sensibilities were blue collar. While he accepted – admittedly, with initial reluctance – the perks, the power, and the prestige of his executive position at CBS and was loyal to his employer, Murrow was never entirely comfortable with the realization that he had become management. His sensibilities were those of the average Joe; that was at once his greatest strength and his greatest weakness as a broadcaster. As says Casey Murrow, "My dad was, at heart, a news guy completely, and he was much happier following a story than pushing papers and being in an office environment. He didn't like having to worry about the administrative details or the money side of the business."[18]

Beneath his anger, Ed Murrow was dismayed, rueful even, that he had become one of the corporate paper-pushers he and Shirer had once mocked. Coming from a devoutly religious family background, Murrow was imbued with a powerful sense of Christian morality that involved standing up for what was just. In his heart he must have been uncomfortable doing William Paley's bidding. Yet there can be no doubt that his differences with Shirer had become a contest of wills or that there was a lot of ego and testosterone involved here, especially with Paley pressuring Murrow to act. "Pride," Ralph Waldo Emerson once noted, "ruined the angels." It also ruined the Shirer-Murrow friendship.

The media loves nothing more than a scandal, especially one involving the high and mighty. Thus, the controversy at CBS attracted widespread attention. Various news commentators clucked their tongues and fanned the flames of controversy when they speculated that, despite Murrow's claims to the contrary, CBS had axed Shirer's newscast for political reasons. *Washington Post* syndicated columnist Drew Pearson observed, "So many denials and counter-denials have been issued by CBS officials that it is difficult to know whether CBS or the Williams Soap Co ousted Shirer."[18]

Murrow, frustrated and angry that the media were casting him in the unfamiliar role of villain, fought back. He personally called or visited friends and colleagues to tell his side of the story. In a bid to underscore the notion that Shirer's removal from the Sunday newscast was ratings-related and to assert that CBS, *not* the Williams Company, owned the air time, Murrow named Joe Harsch of CBS's Washington bureau as Shirer's replacement.

Harsch was a savvy choice. Known for his own liberal views, he had worked alongside Shirer in Nazi Germany and respected him as a colleague, a newsman, and a friend. Harsch's first move after hearing from Murrow was to telephone Shirer, who later stated that Harsch "said he would not accept replacing me unless I consented, which I did."[19] There was not much else Shirer could say. Nonetheless, it is revealing to note how very differently the two men recalled these events in later years. According to Shirer, he gave his consent at the time; Harsch was to claim this did not actually happen until after Shirer had left CBS. In 1990, in the third and final volume of his memoirs, Shirer was generous in his praise of Harsch, whom he described as a good journalist and as "a decent and honorable man."[20] Shirer was eighty-six at the time, and so this may have been an old man's way of making peace with Harsch, who in an interview with Ann Sperber four years earlier (and himself also an octogenarian) had lamented, "I've forgotten how it all worked out, but I suppose Bill [Shirer] never forgave me."[21]

However, Harsch *did* remember how upon his arrival in New York for a meeting with Murrow he had had to make his way through the crowd of protesters outside the CBS building. "Joseph Harsch is Murrow's choice. We want William Shirer's voice!"[22] they chanted. While Harsch went unrecognized, at least initially, he was rattled. Once inside the CBS building, he made a beeline for Shirer's office in hopes Shirer would reassure him that he would bear him no ill will if he took the job Murrow was offering him. In that Sperber interview, Harsch recalled that while he and Shirer were talking, a group of protesters led by Freda Kirchwey, the then-editor of the liberal journal *The Nation*, appeared at Shirer's office door. Recognizing Harsch, she shouted: "Joe Harsch, you're making it difficult for us to present this as a liberal issue."[23]

Spooked by this, Harsch beat a hasty retreat, making his way upstairs to Murrow's office. According to Harsch's account of the ensuing conversation, which he chronicled forty-five years later in his own memoir, Murrow claimed that he had suggested Shirer take a leave of absence to have an operation and time for convalescence. Harsch would be filling in for him on an *interim* basis. This, of course, was at odds with Shirer's account of events and with a letter from Murrow to his friend Harold Laski; Murrow complained to Laski about Shirer having done his weekly broadcast throughout summer 1946 from a studio at Lake Placid, where he was recuperating after having had some surgery. Harsch eventually realized the story Murrow told him was bogus, or else that his memory of the conversation was faulty. Regardless, at the time, Harsch agreed to take Shirer's spot on the Sunday newscast and to do the unsponsored newscast until it went off the air at the end of May for its annual summer hiatus. However, that proved to be the end of the newscast. When that autumn CBS replaced it with a quiz show, Shirer seized upon this as proof positive of Murrow and Paley's deceitfulness.[24]

Having convinced Harsch to fill in for Shirer, Murrow announced that the Sunday 5:45 p.m. newscast would be made better "having someone with Harsch's long experience in Washington ... will improve Columbia's news analysis in this period."[25] These words were akin to Murrow twisting the dagger that Shirer was convinced his old friend had plunged into his back. The words further poisoned relations between the two men and strengthened Shirer's belief that he was a wronged man, a martyr in the fight for freedom of the press and for the First Amendment right to free speech. That is how Shirer was portrayed by his friends in the media, by civil libertarians, and sympathetic political groups – including, much to Shirer's chagrin, American communists – who had jumped on his bandwagon in order to seize the moment and promote their own causes. To all of the Shirer supporters, the CBS controversy was just one more battle in what at the time was regarded as being a much wider war. Critics of commercial broadcasting charged that those who ran the radio networks were guilty of imposing on listeners their own standards, values, and political agenda and those of the networks' corporate sponsors.

30

Signing Off at CBS

In a 1975 interview with Ann Sperber, Shirer recalled how as the media attention and the political pressure on CBS increased, Murrow telephoned him to vent the anger and frustration he was feeling. According to Shirer, Murrow let fly with a "stream of language straight out of the logging camps of western Washington."[1] Shirer was himself no shrinking violet, and so it is not difficult to imagine the tone of the conversation.

Both men realized, albeit not until it was too late for either of them to exit gracefully, that their dispute had gone too far. There already had been too much hurt, but neither man was ready to swallow his pride and back down. Shirer apparently had the first chance to do so. He insisted that a J.B. Williams Company representative had contacted him to extend an olive branch and even to invite him to return to his spot on the Sunday newscast. John Gude remembered this incident differently, saying that Williams president Everett B. Hurlburt had telephoned Shirer to ask if he *might* be willing to return to doing the Sunday newscast.[2] Similarly, pollster Elmo Roper, a friend of both Shirer and William Paley, took Shirer aside one day and urged him to call the CBS chief, make peace, and seek a mutually acceptable compromise. Shirer stubbornly refused. He did not know it at the time, but such a call would have been for naught; in Paley's mind the situation had passed the point of no return.

Unaware of this, Murrow made one final effort to find an amicable solution to the situation. When he called Shirer, the two agreed to make a last-ditch effort to talk things out. These were two proud, macho, larger-than-life characters, each of whom believed that he was in the right. Yet, over conciliatory drinks, they cobbled together the text of a face-saving accommodation, to be jointly issued by Shirer and CBS: Shirer would stay with CBS, although he would have a new broadcast time at 6:30 p.m. on Saturdays.[3] Confident they had found a way out of what had become a thoroughly unpleasant situation for all concerned, Murrow and Shirer visited William Paley to get his approval on the deal; both men assumed this was just a formality.

However, Paley saw things differently and was not prepared to let bygones be bygones. He was angry with Shirer for having stirred up a hornet's nest of trouble, and he did not like that Murrow and Shirer felt *they* could patch things up and all would be well again. Paley was the boss, and he still felt slighted that Shirer had turned down that move to Chicago, where he would have done his newscast under the sponsorship of the Wrigley Corporation. Paley bore a grudge against Shirer for that perceived slight and for all the trouble and embarrassment he had caused of late. Now that Paley was in a position to have his pound of flesh, he was determined to get it. "We were villains and [Shirer] was the hero, caused very largely by his efforts to bring about this reaction," Paley said. "He was out to get even with us, I guess, and I was very upset by this because I didn't think this was fair ... It was too rough for him, I think, to admit to *himself* even that his job, and the quality of it, had been seriously questioned."[4]

Paley was being disingenuous. He had personal issues with Shirer; for him a business dispute had become personal. Thus Paley rejected the Murrow-Shirer agreement out of hand.

Shirer did *not* recount the scene in Paley's office that day. The only accounts we have come from Murrow biographers who interviewed Shirer and Paley many years afterward. Sperber reports that on 26 March Shirer wrote to Hans Kaltenborn, the president of the Association of Radio New Analysts (ARNA), wondering why the group had failed to speak out on his behalf: "ARNA's silence [is] growing eloquent."[5] Kaltenborn reportedly had shown the telegram to Paley, who was outraged and confronted Shirer about this when he and Murrow arrived at his office with their draft agreement.[6] However, there is no way to confirm if this really happened, or if, like so much about the timing of events, it was the product of a faulty or self-serving memory. In the end, all that really matters is what we know happened in Paley's office: the CBS chief fixed Shirer with an icy stare and announced, "As far as I'm concerned, your usefulness to CBS has ended. You're out!"

Shirer was stunned. For one of the few times in his life he was also speechless. When he looked to Murrow for support he saw that his old friend was no less taken aback. "We had an agreement," Murrow muttered as he sheepishly stared at Paley. "But if you don't like it, Bill, *you're* the boss."[7]

At that moment the Shirer-Murrow friendship was forever shattered. In Shirer's mind, the fact Murrow had meekly "caved in," as Frank Stanton later put it, confirmed that Murrow was firmly in the Paley camp. No longer was there any doubt about where he stood or where his loyalties lay. Shirer felt betrayed. Ever after, he derisively referred to Murrow as Paley's "toadie."

Murrow's reaction was markedly different. Sensing the significance of what had just happened and that the breach between himself and Shirer was now final and irreparable, he retreated in confusion, sorrow, and shame. Joseph Persico reports that the evening after Paley rejected the Murrow-Shirer compromise, Murrow dined with an old friend, an advertising executive named Joe Katz, and with Katz's son and daughter-in-law. In an interview in the late 1980s, the daughter-in-law told Persico that Murrow spent most of the dinner talking to the elder Katz, tearfully lamenting the end of his longstanding friendship with his Bill Shirer: "[That] episode had been the sorriest chapter in the unhappy history of Murrow the executive … He was willing to fly bombers into hell for what he believed. But the battles in the executive suite left him spiritually drained, limp with the fatigue that comes with fighting unfelt causes."[8]

That Murrow understood there were deeper issues at play in his dispute with Shirer is clear, also that he found them profoundly unsettling. In a letter to Edgar Ansel Mowrer, the veteran *Chicago Daily News* foreign correspondent – a friend of both Murrow and Shirer and one of journalists who had taken part in that historic CBS news roundup on the 1938 Anschluss – Murrow stated as much: "As we both know, there are very serious problems involved in sponsorship of news and opinions, and they go much deeper than anything involved in the case of Bill Shirer."[9]

There remained one last scene to play out in the sorry melodrama of Shirer's departure from CBS: his final newscast, which was scheduled for 30 March 1947. All week, the network's newsroom was alive with speculation that Shirer would seize the opportunity to blast CBS management for the way he was being treated. Despite the fact his at-times distant behavior had alienated some of his co-workers, there was still a lot of sympathy for him and for his position. A group of junior newsroom staff from CBS television's fledgling news operation sent Shirer a letter:

"We urge you most strongly to continue your fight to be restored to a satisfactory position here at Columbia."[10] They, too, felt pressured by senior management to tailor the content of newscasts to suit political orthodoxy, what we now call "political correctness," and the needs of advertisers.

Buoyed by such encouragement, by the thousands of letters from loyal listeners, and by the support of John Gunther and other friends, Shirer forged ahead with plans for his goodbye. He would not be deterred. With that in mind, he called Murrow the day before that final broadcast to discuss the wording of his script. Both men were now on the edge; Shirer was nearing a state of nervous exhaustion, and it showed. Murrow was no better off. Their conversation quickly grew heated. Murrow warned Shirer not to "try anything funny," reminding him that control room technicians could end his broadcast at any moment with the push of a button. Shirer responded by pointing out that Murrow had nothing to worry about. After all, Shirer said, he knew how to behave; he'd had lots of experience dealing with censors when he was broadcast from Nazi Germany.

An angry Murrow was taking no chances. When Shirer appeared in his CBS office on the afternoon of 30 March to prepare the text of his final script, two newsroom editors were there to review it. Murrow, who was in the building, chose to remain in his office on the nineteenth floor, from where he monitored Shirer's broadcast. The control room on this day was crowded with CBS executives who stood watching and listening intently to Shirer's every word. The technician on duty, on Murrow's orders, sat with a finger poised above the button that would have muted Shirer's microphone and aborted his final broadcast. "This was a much larger force that had ever been summoned to keep check on me in Berlin. It was all very familiar ... But I had not expected it here. I felt slightly repelled, but also slightly amused."[11]

Despite his inner turmoil, Shirer kept his emotions in check during that final newscast. When he came to the last page of his script, he paused, took a deep breath and continued: "This is my last broadcast on this program. The issues involved, which make it my last broadcast are – so far as I'm concerned – important, but I believe this is not the place nor the time to discuss them. I realize you listen to this program to hear the news. In conclusion, I would like only to say this: To you who have followed these Sunday afternoon broadcasts since 1941 – through the years of the war and the beginnings of peace – I thank you for having listened."[12]

With those words, Shirer's career at CBS came to an inglorious end. Exiting the broadcast studio for the last time, he was surrounded by a swarm of newspaper reporters. Shirer was ready with a prepared text in which he stressed that statements made by CBS management had made it clear to him that he had no future at the network. As a result, he had chosen to resign: "I had no intention of staying on with CBS so that Paley and Murrow could humiliate me further."[13] No sooner were those words out of his mouth than Shirer realized he had made a grave tactical blunder, one he would live to regret, no matter how much he insisted that Paley and Murrow had forced him out at CBS.

In later years, Shirer did his utmost to put a favorable gloss on his actions. He told Paley biographer David Halberstram in 1976 that "Both [Murrow] and Paley told me I was through and that if I tried to hold CBS to my contract, they would 'get me.'"[14] Perhaps. But semantics aside, the essential point was that Shirer *believed* that he had no choice but to fall on his sword, and he perpetuated that version of events even though he knew he had erred in doing so. It opened the door for Ed Murrow to seize the moment and to issue a statement of his own. Inelegant though it may have been, it was effective: "At no time has [Shirer] claimed to us that our decision was based upon any objection to the content of his broadcast or on what have been called his liberal views ... The Columbia Broadcasting System and no one else decided to place another news analyst in the period that has been occupied by Mr Shirer, and Mr Shirer doesn't like it, and that's all there is to it."[15]

CBS senior management, officials from J.B. Williams Company, those who had taken Murrow's side in the dispute, and even many people who were friends of both Murrow and Shirer now pointed to the fact that Shirer had not, in fact, been fired; he had *resigned*. That most people accepted this is made clear by the contents of a letter that Shirer received from Everett B. Hurlburt, the president of the Williams Company. It was a copy of a missive Hurlburt sent to an outraged listener who demanded to know why Williams had withdrawn its support for Shirer's newscast. In his reply, Hurlburt insisted the decision was made not for political reasons, but rather because of a change in direction for the company's advertising. Hurlburt ventured that he was confident "Mr Shirer would confirm this." Furthermore, Hurlburt added, the decision of whether or not Shirer remained with CBS was the network's decision.[16]

Ed Murrow, with help from the staff in the CBS publicity office, began spreading this same message, and together they did an effective job.

Understandably so; Murrow was America's most credible and respected newsman. He was not used to being criticized by the public, nor did he take it well; what had been especially stinging were the barbs that had been directed his way by people he had considered to be friends. Intent on getting his side of the story out, he made a concerted effort to speak with people whose opinions he knew Shirer respected and whose friendships he valued.

Shirer's CBS colleague Eric Sevareid was among those who accepted Murrow's version of events. Sevareid articulated as much in a letter he sent to Shirer the day after Shirer's final CBS broadcast: "I am intensely regretful that all this has happened and that you and Ed, both of whom have done so much to build radio the way we all want it, should fall on opposite sides of the fence, and, in effect injure the repute, one of the other ... It would be hypocritical of me, however, to say to you that I support your charges in this affair and that I feel you have been done an injustice. If I felt that way, I would have called you days ago. Trying to as objective about it as I possibly can, I still can't go along with your accusations against CBS. If time proves you right, I'll change my mind. Having said that, Bill, which I felt I must, I also want to say that my feelings about you as a person and a performer have not diminished at all, and that I earnestly hope that you will still consider me one of your loyal friends, as I consider you one of mine."[17]

Broadcaster Raymond Gram Swing – who in 1937 had advised Murrow to hire Shirer and who was now delivering his own liberal-leaning news commentaries on the Mutual radio network – was another one of the Murrow-Shirer circle who accepted Murrow's version of events. In a letter in which he tried to explain why he had not come out in support of Shirer, Swing struggled to steer clear of the politics of the situation: "If a man should tell me he was my friend and then *not* take up the cudgels for me in a crisis, I should wonder what kind of a friend he is. And you are entitled to wonder about me, I suppose ... The fact is that I never felt the sickness in the pit of my stomach over something affecting my friends that I now feel over this trouble between you and Ed. And since taking up the cudgels for you means [hurting] Ed, who is also my friend, I am paralyzed. If there was anything I could do for you [that] would not hurt a friend, I should do it, and I must hope that my failure to proceed for you will not hurt you. I still should crusade for you if I felt the issues were as clear as you state them. But the more I hear about the case, the more confused I get on the issues."[18]

Alexander Kendrick, a colleague of both Shirer and Murrow at CBS – another Murrow hire and his first biographer (while still on the network's payroll, as Shirer hastened to point out) – perpetuated the corporate line on Shirer's departure. Kendrick wrote that Shirer's ratings had been falling and his sponsor had become unhappy with his on-air performance, and so Shirer had resigned rather than be given a new time slot on CBS, one with a lower pay rate. Kendrick added insult to injury for Shirer when he repeated as fact the claim that, although Murrow had grown disenchanted with Shirer's on-air efforts and his "ivory towerish" approach to the news,[19] he had appealed to his old friend to stay with CBS. Kendrick never asked Shirer about this, nor did he make any reference to Shirer's version of events.

The reality was that Shirer had committed himself to a fight that he could never win. Even he must have understood that he was tilting at windmills. There was no way he could prevail in any contest of wills with CBS boss William Paley, who in 1947 was one of the most powerful men in the American media and in America. At the same time, Shirer's reputation as a broadcaster did not measure up to Ed Murrow's.

Regardless of any faults he may have had – no one would ever argue that Murrow was a saint – he was a fundamentally decent man, caring, and with a deep and abiding sense of right and wrong. By 1947 he was already a broadcasting legend, having redefined the very role and image of the foreign correspondent. Murrow's reputation for integrity and truthfulness grew even more after he made the transition from radio into the new medium of television. It was in this latter role that Murrow achieved his most lasting fame. The irony is that when finally Murrow decided to confront Senator Joseph R. McCarthy and reveal him as the phony he was – and it was not until after Murrow had meekly gone along with CBS's decision to investigate the patriotism of its employees and obliged each of them to sign a "loyalty oath" – he became a poster boy for freedom of speech and for American liberalism. There is a compelling case to be made that the events of March 1947 and lingering pangs of guilt about his own role in this affair and in the tragic end of his friendship with William Shirer played a pivotal role in prompting Murrow to finally take a stand against McCarthy.

While by 1947 Shirer was to a certain extent coasting and living on his reputation, he remained one of America's foremost journalists and news commentators. Politics and egos figured prominently in the end of his career at CBS. "On both sides there were undercurrents and hidden agendas, but the likelihood is that both Shirer's liberal views and his journalistic shortcomings were factors in his downfall," write Cloud and Olson.[20] That conclusion, which is supported by the facts and which was confirmed many years later by CBS executive Frank Stanton, is an element of the Edward R. Murrow story to which his biographers have given short shrift, if they have delved into it at all. Morality and guilt can be powerful motivators.

31

"May his voice be heard again"

Two weeks after his final cbs broadcast, Shirer was honored with a George Foster Peabody Award as the top news commentator of 1946. In many ways, winning this prestigious national honor was vindication for Shirer. In his mind, it served to confirm that cbs had treated him unfairly, that he *had* lost his job for political reasons and not because his work or his ratings had slipped. *New York Times* radio columnist Jack Gould opined that it was Shirer's "lively tiff" with cbs over his Sunday newscast that had won him a Peabody.

Those who agreed with Gould also shared Shirer's belief that his broadcasting career was not yet over; in fact, two radio stations in New York City had offered to pick up his weekly newscast. Shirer was grateful, but he knew he would never earn as much money at a local station as he had at cbs, nor could he reach as many listeners. Emotionally spent, he opted to take a summer hiatus, collect his thoughts, and weigh his options.

He did, however, attend the Peabody Award ceremony on the evening of 17 April 1947, in New York. A ripple of anticipation ran through the room as Shirer made his way to the dais to accept his award. Many people were anticipating a repeat of the Shirer-Murrow clash that had occurred a few days earlier at the weekly luncheon of the Overseas Press Club. Both men had been invited to speak, and Shirer seized the moment to reiterate the allegation that he had been forced out at cbs for political reasons. Murrow, bristling with anger, had responded by casting aside his prepared text – which, ironically, was about the dangers of allowing commercial sponsors to dictate news content. Instead, he verbally pummeled Shirer, reiterating his view that performance issues, *not* politics, had prompted the decision to drop Shirer's newscast. As for Shirer's Peabody Award,

Murrow pointed out that in 1944 he, too, had won this same honor. He had received it, he explained, in recognition of the quality of his wartime broadcasts from London. His implication was clear: Shirer was being feted for his reporting of events from inside Nazi Germany, *not* for his more recent work.

That was the backdrop to the Peabody ceremony, and so all signs pointed to more verbal fireworks. As he introduced Shirer, Peabody advisory board chairman Edward Weeks, the editor of *The Atlantic*, praised Shirer's integrity and stoked the fires of controversy by concluding his remarks with a nod in Shirer's direction: "May his voice be heard again." While Shirer doubtless savored that moment, he had no stomach just then for another confrontation with Murrow, who was in the audience along with a group of CBS executives. Instead, Shirer accepted his medal, said a quick thank you, and then sat down. He was content to let the audience's loud and sustained applause speak on his behalf.

Inevitably, as the controversy over Shirer's departure from CBS died down, he was left to contemplate his situation. Despite the assurances of his agent, who insisted Shirer would soon be back on the airwaves, the prospects for an unemployed forty-three-year-old were not all that promising. Shirer was still writing his weekly syndicated newspaper column and was in demand as a public lecturer, but he now found himself without a regular paycheck. He drew cold comfort from his belief that Ed Murrow would one day suffer a similar fate. Shirer had cautioned Murrow that, sooner or later, he, too, would be forced out at CBS for political reasons or because a commercial sponsor decreed it. In one of their angrier, profanity-filled exchanges, Shirer had reminded Murrow of his prediction. His words, which must have sounded like sour grapes in the heat of that moment, proved to be prophetic.

All Shirer knew or cared about in April 1947 was the harsh reality of his predicament: his career again was stalled. His income had dropped precipitously and, despite his bravado, his ego had suffered a crippling blow. As Tess Shirer was later to confide to Joseph Persico, "Times were very tough for us after Bill left CBS."[1]

The Shirer family had grown accustomed to an affluent lifestyle, and appearances were important. They had a posh apartment on Manhattan's fashionable Upper East Side and their weekend home in the country; paradoxically, one of the first things Shirer did after being fired by CBS was to spend $9,500 for The Farm, that aforementioned one hundred-acre hobby farm rural property in Connecticut.

Despite his growing financial woes, Shirer continued to travel and still frequented New York's best restaurants and trendiest nightspots. At home, he and Tess lived well, retaining a live-in housekeeper and other domestic help and entertaining often. "In those days, we, and many of our schoolmates, lived better than people do nowadays," Linda Shirer Rae observes.[2]

Linda and older sister Inga wanted for nothing materially and the girls attended Dalton School in New York, the same upscale private school attended by William Paley's son Jeff and the children of many other prominent New York families. Even when he was unemployed and money was tight, Shirer did his utmost to maintain the family's lifestyle. He and Tess did all they could to insulate their daughters from hardship. Linda avers, "We didn't become aware of any change in circumstances for a few years, not until the early 1950s."[3]

In the weeks after his departure from CBS, Shirer spent a lot of time musing about what had brought about his falling out with Ed Murrow, a man he once had felt as close to as a brother. Murrow went through a similar anguish, second-guessing himself, picking over the bones of his motivations, and contemplating his own future at CBS. The Shirer controversy continued to weigh heavy on Murrow's mind, as did his unhappiness with the drift of his own career. However, most unsettling of all for him was the nagging feeling that in becoming an executive he had sold his soul and compromised his commitment to quality, principled journalism. "Hard news reporting was simple enough," notes Murrow biographer Persico. "But what [Murrow] believed that he had failed to find was that elusive boundary separating legitimate news analysis from bias."[4]

Murrow could not hide his unhappiness. Seeing this, William Paley suggested Murrow return to full-time broadcasting. On 19 July – less than four months after Shirer's last CBS broadcast – Murrow ended his time as a member of the CBS senior management team. Not even his closest friends had seen this coming, and Murrow offered no explanation other than to say that he had not enjoyed his eighteen-month stint as an administrator. In a letter to Paul White, he confided, "I have been liberated."[5]

Shirer had no similar easy solution to his woes; with no acceptable job offer in hand, he left the city for the summer and shunned all contacts with those whom he felt had turned against him. When Eric Sevareid, now the reluctant CBS bureau chief in Washington, asked mutual friends about how Shirer was doing, he was told that no one had heard from him.

Sevareid sent Shirer a note: "I still think you were a crazy bastard to do what you did and say what you did … I still think you were wrong, but to hell with all that; I still prize your friendship … I may get to New York later, and don't get stiff and frosty if I call you on the phone."[6]

If Shirer replied, there is no record of it. That is hardly surprising; he was still hurting, still angry. He was also pouring all of his energies into writing a stage play and a nonfiction book called *End of a Berlin Diary*. The volume, which Shirer dedicated to the memory of his late mother, was a continuation of *Berlin Diary*: "[This] is the end of my own small contribution to the Berlin story."[7] It was also Shirer's attempt to make sense of and to come to grips with a world in which life had taken some unfortunate turns, both for himself and in terms of the peace that followed the destruction wrought by "Nazi and Jap barbarians."[8] Angry that the German people seemed to be unwilling to acknowledge their complicity in Nazi evils, Shirer cautioned against expecting that Germany could be a positive force in postwar Europe. Such a message did not resonate with the American public in 1947.

Cloud and Olson describe Shirer as "a lifelong collector of injustices."[9] He was a man of strong convictions, stubborn to a fault, and never one to temper his comments if he felt he had been wronged. In *End of a Berlin Diary,* he lamented what he regarded as the insularity and narrowness of mind in the American heartland, in Chicago especially. In his mind, the chief villains were Shirer's old nemesis Colonel McCormick – whom Shirer derisively referred to by his nickname, "Bertie" – and his *Chicago Tribune* minions. Shirer pointed out that one of the American "radio traitors" who had made broadcasts for the Nazis during the war (and escaped punishment afterward) was former *Tribune* correspondent Donald Day. Shirer also noted that when Roosevelt died in April 1945 every major newspaper in America, save one, had published a laudatory editorial about FDR and his legacy. That sole exception was McCormick's *Tribune*, "whose vicious attacks on the President," in Shirer's words, "were no credit to American journalism."[10] Tit for tat, the *Tribune*'s review of *End of a Berlin Diary* was downright hostile. "Shirer's views and opinions are no doubt colored largely by the atmosphere and environment in which he has spent most of his adult years … They reek of … eastern seaboard thinking."[11]

Other notices were more balanced and insightful, although the comments of some writers were as much influenced by their personal impressions of Shirer as by critical opinions of his work. Two reviews of *End of Berlin Diary* stand out for unexpected reasons. In *The New Yorker*, A.J.

Liebling observed that "a mighty smudge is going up from some prestigious smoke pots to obscure the memory of what the war was fought against, and Shirer's ability to interest a lot of people can be extremely valuable in laying the soot." Liebling then added – prophetically as it turned out: "If Shirer will devote some of the time his enforced departure from radio gives him to construct a careful book, planning each paragraph thoughtfully and going over it at least twice, we may live to thank whoever was responsible for firing him."[12]

The other review of *End of a Berlin Diary* that is worth special attention appeared in *The New York Times Book Review*. Allen Welsh Dulles stated that the book "is the writing of a man on the verge of disillusionment as he sees the beginnings of the failure of the peace."[13] Those words were ones that Shirer did not want to hear, yet in his heart he surely must have known they were true – for Shirer as much as for America. Dulles had touched upon one of the dominant themes of Shirer's life in 1947. He was not a man on "the verge of disillusionment"; he was a man *awash* in it, both in terms of his view of the world and his own future prospects. Still, it was not all bad news for Shirer.

In June 1947, *Billboard* magazine's annual ranking of America's best radio columnists and newspaper editors voted him "the most interesting news commentator on the air." Buoyed by this and by his determination to prove his critics wrong, Shirer was desperate for an opportunity to resume his radio career. However, he had only one firm job offer. It came from the United Electrical, Radio, and Machine Workers of America; the union was ready to sponsor a weekly Shirer newscast in a primetime slot on the ABC network. Shirer declined, mainly because of the union's reported ties to the American Communist Party.

When finally he returned to the airwaves at the end of November 1947, it was to do a weekly newscast for Mutual. Among the news stories that he reported and commented on during his time at Mutual was the 30 January 1948 assassination of Indian nationalist leader Mahatma Gandhi at the hands of a Hindu extremist. Shirer was shaken and profoundly saddened both by the mahatma's failures and his tragic death. In struggling to articulate his emotions, Shirer quoted the words that Plato had uttered upon hearing of the death of Socrates: "Such was the end of our friend; concerning whom I may truly say, that of all the men of his time whom I have known, he was the wisest and justest and best."

Gandhi's murder and the ensuing turmoil that rocked India were not the only big international news stories of the day. As the Cold War intensified, momentous events continued to shake and reshape the postwar world. Despite this, an America that was preoccupied with domestic concerns still had little interest in foreign news. For that reason and because Mutual – as America's fourth network – lagged well behind the competition in the number of affiliates, potential listeners, and prestige, Shirer faced an uphill, ultimately futile, battle to attract listeners. It is clear that he either failed to understand or refused to accept the reality that North America's listening habits were changing.

With television's popularity burgeoning (by 1948 there were already five million television sets in American homes), the radio industry was in steep decline. Despite the undeniable warning signs, Shirer clung to the belief that he could rebuild his audience and that once he did he could find work with NBC or ABC. One aspect of his contract with Mutual that fueled his hopes that he could regain market share was a clause that granted him free rein to comment on the news. Unlike CBS, which forbade its newscasters from editorializing, Mutual gave Shirer carte blanche to speak his mind. "I shall not try to make up your minds for you," he assured listeners. "But I shall not be dishonest with you by hiding my own opinions, which, I recognize, are, like everybody's, only human and therefore, often wrong."[14]

Shirer stayed with Mutual eighteen months. While ratings for his show were respectable, they were never what he had hoped for. When in April 1949 his sponsor finally dropped the show, even Shirer had to concede he was finished as a newscaster. The timing could not have been worse for him. With the Cold War intensifying and America continuing its shift to the political right – despite Truman's stunning, improbable win over GOP challenger Thomas Dewey in the 1948 presidential election – the media followed suit. With even the *New York Herald Tribune*, long known as a "liberal Republican" newspaper, now striking a more conservative tone, Shirer's opinions no longer fit in with the paper's editorial direction, and so the new publisher axed his syndicated column. Disheartened by this, in autumn 1949 Shirer set off on a two-month visit to continental Europe and the United Kingdom to gather information for the freelance articles and lectures that were now his only sources of income. He arrived on the continent at a time when the atmosphere in Germany was especially tense; with a Russian blockade of Berlin in effect, the only movement of people and supplies in and out of the city was by air. Shirer understood that many Americans were demanding to know why their nation, which in 1945 had been all-powerful and triumphant, four years later seemed ineffectual against, and even imperiled by, Soviet expansionism. "Some [people], resenting the complexity of history found a satisfactory answer by tracing all troubles to the workings of the communist conspiracy – unsleeping, omnipresent, and diabolically cunning," observes historian Arthur M. Schlesinger, Jr.[15]

In the wake of the loss of China to the Communists, as alarmists referred to it, military tensions were escalating on the Korean peninsula and throughout Southeast Asia. In Washington, Senator Joseph McCarthy, intent on exploiting the situation for political gain, set about whipping up fears of communist spies, infiltrators, and sympathizers, whom he alleged had corrupted the ranks of government, the media, and other influential sectors of American society. A series of sensational domestic spying cases (in particular the trials of Alger Hiss and of Ethel and Julius Rosenberg) underscored the seriousness of the situation. Stunning revelations of the extent of supposed communist infiltration fed a rising tide of opinion among the nation's military leaders and politicians that held that in order to avoid another Pearl Harbor, America might be forced to fight a "preventative war" – a strike-first, talk-later conflict. *Life* publisher Henry Luce now began pushing for a war with the Soviet Union and communism.

It was against this roiling backdrop that Shirer's situation and his employment prospects continued to worsen and his mood to darken. His broadcasting career was over. He had lost his weekly newspaper column. Once again, he was scrambling to earn a living. Compounding his woes was the disarray of his personal life. Shirer's relationship with Tess had settled into an uneasy peace; the damage he had inflicted and continued to inflict could neither be undone nor forgiven. Despite the unmistakable signs that his relationship with Tilly Losch was going nowhere, like a lovesick schoolboy, Shirer doggedly continued to pursue her.

Losch, beset by her own problems, could not decide if she was serious about Shirer. In any case, she enjoyed the attention he paid her, as long as it was on her terms. Ever eager for his help in advancing her career as an artist and would-be author, Losch was affectionate at times, distant at others; she often ignored his letters and phone calls. Shirer could not fathom her behavior. His uncertainties had heightened in January 1947, just prior to the end of his CBS career; he and Losch had had yet another big row. When her divorce finally came through, she spurned a proposal from Shirer, who announced that he was ready to end his own marriage. His letters to Losch reflect his disappointment; her replies, if there were any, have been lost.

Losch's rejection was a bitter pill for Shirer to swallow. "I am grateful, of course, that you finally spoke out honestly – after five years, though I realize you merely confirmed what I should have known for five years had I not been so blind," he lamented.[16] As for her suggestion that they remain "friends," he dismissed the idea, insisting that love is an "all or nothing" proposition: "Maybe in twenty years – when we are both in our sixties, and the passions are spent – we could have the sort of 'friendship' you seem to want."[17] Yet, in the next sentence, he promised to phone her "next week."

The Losch-Shirer correspondence also reveals that Shirer loaned or gave her money, even when he could ill afford it; he was living off his savings and a line of bank credit. Apart from the relatively modest salary that he earned from his Mutual newscasts, Shirer's only other regular source of income was from his public lectures. Thus when Losch asked him for money in spring 1948, Shirer begged off. In a letter written on the stationery of a hotel in Rochester, New York, where he was spending a night after a speaking engagement, he pleaded, "You know I would help out financially if I could. But at the moment I just haven't got anything."[18]

With his finances, employment prospects, and personal life in turmoil, Shirer suffered yet another blow when he found himself caught up in the anti-communist hysteria that was sweeping America. His troubles began in earnest in June 1950. He was traveling in Germany when he chanced to read a letter to the editor that appeared in the European edition of *The New York Times*; the American playwright-actor Howard Lindsay protested the inclusion of his name and those of a hundred and fifty other prominent Americans – actors, film-industry people, musicians, writers, journalists, and radio personalities – in an anti-communist pamphlet called *Red Channels: The Report of Communist Influence in Radio and Television*. The suggestion was that all of those individuals whose names were listed were communist sympathizers, or "fellow travelers" as they were termed.

Shirer's name was on the list. He was suspect for three reasons: he had once served as chairman of a group called the Friends of the Spanish Republic; he had attended a dinner of the left-leaning Voice of Freedom Committee, which had backed him in his dispute with CBS; and he was one of two hundred and four well-known artists, writers, and show business figures who had signed an amicus curiae brief that called upon the United States Supreme Court to undertake a judicial review of the case of the Hollywood Ten.[19] A Harvard Law School professor named Zechariah

Chafee had called him to enlist his support for the last initiative. Shirer did not know Chafee, was unfamiliar with the details of the case against the Hollywood Ten, and knew none of the accused personally. However, after conferring with publisher Cass Canfield, a longtime friend and a supporter of the brief, Shirer had agreed to add his name to the list of signatories.

What Shirer learned when he began looking into the details of the case of the Hollywood Ten was that they had been among the first and the most prominent victims of the chill that had arrived in October 1947. That was when the HUAC hearings into possible communist influences in the American film and entertainment industries got underway. Although the HUAC failed to uncover any hard evidence that communism had corrupted Hollywood or even that communist sympathizers were using movies as a propaganda tool, the anti-communist political chill of the late 1940s seeped into all aspects of American life. The hysteria was fueled by accusations and innuendos and by the fact that as members of the Hollywood Ten began serving their one-year prison sentences, one of them – Canadian-born director Edward Dmytryk – suddenly admitted that, yes, he had formerly been a communist. In a bid to show that he now recognized "the error of his ways," Dmytryk agreed to testify before the HUAC, revealing details of alleged communist subversion. When he named names, Dmytryk cited twenty-six individuals whom he alleged had been guilty of spreading communist propaganda in Hollywood. In return, Dmytryk was given early release from prison and was allowed to resume his own movie career.

In the wake of this and similar incidents, many more names were unofficially added to the blacklist, eighty-four in total. Those individuals who were implicated directly or because of their presumed guilt by association also found that for all intents and purposes they, too, were blacklisted. William Shirer was among this group.

Before his name appeared in *Red Channels*, Shirer had never even heard of the publication. He correctly assumed it was a byproduct of the growing movement to "out" people who were alleged to be communists or communist sympathizers. As Shirer noted in his diary, America was "in a state of the worst intolerance I have ever known."[20] Self-serving political opportunists and demagogues whom he scornfully denounced as "false and phony 'super-patriots'" were busy whipping up mass hysteria. Shirer felt that these people were intent on imposing on America the same kind of thought control and political orthodoxy in which Hitler

and Stalin engaged; Shirer, principled to a fault at times, was determined
to resist. Despite his cynicism, he continued to believe in the fundamental concepts that are the bedrocks of American democracy. He was
well aware of the bigotry and pettiness of McCarthy, of those who were
driving the HUAC, and of the camp followers who turned out publications such as *Red Channels*, yet he underestimated their power and their
influence. After all, Shirer wondered, how credible a publication was
Red Channels? In a different era that question would have been valid;
however, as Shirer was about to discover, neither credibility nor rationality had any role to play in this situation. Suddenly he was faced with
the task of defending himself against an indefensible accusation – the
kind of reverse onus proposition, so common in totalitarian states, that
puts the burden not on the accuser – the state – but rather squarely on
the accused.

In this case, the allegation against him had been made in a one-off publication put out by a shadowy company known as American Business
Consultants. Launched in 1947 by three ex-FBI agents: Kenneth Bierly,
John Keenan, and Theodore Kirkpatrick, the venture was bankrolled by a
wealthy businessman named Alfred Kohlberg. A self-proclaimed "patriot,"
Kohlberg had made his fortune by importing cheap Chinese textiles into
the United States. Now he was accusing the State Department of being
soft on communism and "losing China" to the Reds.

American Business Consultants Inc. had begun its anti-communist
crusade in 1947 by initiating a weekly newsletter called *Counterattack*,
the self-proclaimed "Newsletter of Facts to Combat Communism." That
for-profit publication directed its editorial scorn at a diverse range of targets that included public figures – politicians, journalists, entertainers,
and labor leaders; companies that sponsored radio and television programs on which alleged fellow travelers worked; some of America's most
renowned academic institutions; and a lengthy list of news agencies and
publications – everything from *The New York Times* to *The New Yorker*,
and even such quintessentially American magazines as *Time*, *Life*, and
Look.

Given the Cold War political hysteria that was sweeping America, *Counterattack* found an attentive audience on Madison Avenue. Anti-communist groups threatened to organize mass consumer boycotts of the prod-
ucts of any companies that sponsored radio or television programs in
which any performer appeared whose name was on the blacklist. Thus, so
brisk was the demand for the dollar-per-copy issues of *Counterattack* that
the editors of that publication issued a supplement in the form of the

aforementioned *Red Channels*. The cover illustration depicted a crudely rendered red hand – was it blood-stained or merely communist? – ready to seize a microphone. Inside the publication was a six-page introduction by anti-communist crusader Vincent Hartnett, an employee of the Phillips H. Lord radio-show production agency. It was Hartnett who first alleged that many popular radio and television shows were forums in which communists and their dupes, including "well-intentioned liberals," promoted such insidious causes as academic freedom, civil rights, the peace movement, and nuclear disarmament. What proof did Hartnett offer? None, because there was none. *Red Channels* should have been accorded as much credibility as a supermarket checkout tabloid. Yet many decision-makers took its allegations seriously.

The publication's editors were careful not to directly accuse anyone of anything. They had learned an expensive lesson when they were obliged to pay an out-of-court settlement to end a libel action brought against them by actors Frederic and Florence March, both of whom had been named as communists in the pages of *Counterattack*. Wiser and more cautious by 1950, Bierly, Keenan, and Kirkpatrick now shied away from making specific allegations. Nevertheless, the thrust of the suspicions they were sowing in *Red Channels* was undeniable.

In addition to William Shirer – and his friend and former CBS colleague Howard K. Smith – the list of names of those who were purported to be communist dupes was a who's who of American show business and letters. Among those who were included were Orson Welles, Edward G. Robinson, Burl Ives, Burgess Meredith, Zero Mostel, and Lee J. Cobb; musicians Leonard Bernstein, Aaron Copeland, Artie Shaw, Judy Holliday, and Lena Horne; and literary figures Arthur Miller, Dashiell Hammett, Lillian Hellman, and Irwin Shaw.

Historians have written at length about the HUAC hearings, McCarthyism, and other aspects of this dark period of American history. It was a prolonged time of fear, when civil liberties, the basic concepts of natural justice – and even common sense – were cast aside, supposedly in the name of national security and of saving democracy from communism. Lives were ruined. Careers were destroyed. The sad story of "the McCarthy era" stands as a stark reminder of the fragility of the principles upon which democracy in America is based.

The situation in which William Shirer found himself was by no means unique. True, he was not singled out in the same way that so many others were. Nor was he called to testify before the HUAC or any other government body. He was never publicly accused of any illegal activities, but after his name appeared in *Red Channels*, Shirer discovered that he was considered to be a "controversial" person. As such, he was persona non grata in the newsrooms of most publications and broadcast outlets. Editors who once had been delighted to have him write for them no longer called with work assignments and rejected his unsolicited articles. Even old friends in the editorial offices of magazines Shirer had written for were suddenly cool toward him.

Those who had been blacklisted or who, like Shirer, had been spattered with the muck of guilt by association could be "rehabilitated" if they were willing to confess – as Edward Dmytryk had done – that they were or had been communists or communist sympathizers. At the same time, they were expected to publicly "name names" and bear witness against others who allegedly were guilty of similar disloyalties. The irony in this, of course, is that these were the same tactics that Soviet dictator Joseph Stalin had employed against his enemies when he staged the political show trials that were integral to the mass political purges he had carried out.

Small wonder some of those who were blacklisted were willing to say or do whatever it took to clear themselves. However, seeking clearance or doing penance was out of the question for Shirer. Neither course was one he would ever have contemplated, let alone stomached. "It was as if I had committed some heinous crime against my country and had been convicted without trial. That puzzled me. I was not and had never been a Communist, nor had I ever been accused, even by the most hysterical witch-hunters, of being one ... I had never hidden what I thought. No congressional committee ... nor any other government group obsessed with Communists and Communism ever expressed the slightest interest in calling me before them. How then could one defend himself?"[21]

Shirer had nothing but scorn for the owners of America's mass media and advertising agencies. In his eyes, these people were cowards; none of them had had the courage to question the tactics, much less the truthfulness or motivations, of the politicians and their disciples who were bullying Congress, spreading fear, publishing lies, and defaming innocent people. In saner, more stable times the incendiary words printed in a journal such as *Red Channels* would have been read by few people, denounced by influential voices, and then quickly forgotten – unless they became the subject of a libel action.

When Shirer looked into suing the publisher of *Red Channels* for defamation, he was advised *not* to proceed, for any action would be long, expensive, and ultimately futile. While that was true, Shirer was puzzled why his lawyer, Morris Ernst, was so adamant about this. After all, Ernst had long been known as a passionate supporter of civil liberties, he was politically well connected, and he was known to be a staunch Democrat, pro-Roosevelt and pro-New Deal. Given Ernst's reputation, Shirer was perplexed when the lawyer suggested he have lunch with the publishers of *Red Channels* so they could talk about "his problem." Shirer was not inclined to break bread with his accusers. In his diary, Shirer lamented, "Morris does not seem to realize the enormity of the crime involved or the real danger to American liberties of such bigots and the facility with which they can stampede the bizmen who today run America."[22]

In fact, Ernst understood the situation all too well. His familiarity with the men who published *Red Channels* should have set alarm bells ringing for Shirer. Many years later, in the 1980s, the shocking truth about Shirer's lawyer and "friend" came out as a result of the investigative efforts of journalist Harrison E. Salisbury and others who made inquiries under the Freedom of Information Act. Their research revealed that in the late 1940s and throughout the 1950s, Morris Ernst had been an FBI informer. Not only had he cooperated with the HUAC and other government agencies, he had fed information to Senator Joseph McCarthy and FBI Director J. Edgar Hoover. Salisbury detailed Ernst's activities in a sensational article that appeared in the 1 December 1984 issue of *The Nation*.[23] Shirer found these revelations made for fascinating, albeit stunning, reading. He felt especially betrayed when he discovered that Ernst, whom he had regarded as a friend and trusted legal advisor, had provided the FBI with copies of letters Shirer had written to him about *Red Channels*.

However, there was no evidence that Ernst had discussed the specifics of Shirer's situation with Hoover or with anyone else from the FBI. "Perhaps my case was regarded ... as not important enough to take up their time," Shirer concluded. [24] Even so, the whole experience left a bitter taste in his mouth and a lingering anger. When he eventually came to see the bigger picture and to put things into perspective, Shirer did not blame the anti-communist hysteria of the McCarthy era on people such as Morris Ernst, or the opportunistic politicians who sought to exploit the situation for their own ends, or even J. Edgar Hoover and his FBI henchmen. Shirer concluded that the ones who really were responsible for the injustices that were committed had been the "shabby cowards" who had enforced the blacklist. They included the "big fish" Hollywood studio executives, the men who ran America's broadcasting networks, the moguls of Madison Avenue advertising, and the publishers and editors of the nation's newspapers and magazines. True, there had been a few brave men and women who had dared to speak out against the political chill that was sweeping America, but theirs had been lonely, ineffectual voices, and their resistance had been largely futile. It would be a long time before the thaw came and William Shirer again was able to earn a decent living.

32

Blacklisted

The thirteen years between 1947 and 1960 were the leanest and most trying period of William Shirer's life. Not only was he out of work, after 1950
he was blacklisted and found himself unemployable for no other reason
than his political views. Having reluctantly and begrudgingly conceded
that his journalism career was finished, he struggled to earn a living. He
did not and would not write under a pseudonym or work with someone
who would "front" for him in dealings with editors, as some blacklisted
writers did.

Being unemployed and without prospects, time was one of the few lux-
uries Shirer still enjoyed, and so he opted to try his hand at writing fiction. It was the writer John Hersey who helped inspire Shirer in this
regard. The two were among the speakers at a 1946 event in New York's
Carnegie Hall and afterward, they went for a drink. Like Shirer, Hersey
had been a war correspondent. Unlike Shirer, he had taken a significant
step toward becoming a novelist. After writing two nonfiction books
about the war in the Pacific, he had scored a literary breakthrough with
his debut novel, *A Bell for Adano*, which won the 1945 Pulitzer Prize for
fiction.

His conversation with Hersey provided Shirer with the inspiration he
needed to press ahead with work on a novel that he had been plugging
away at in a desultory way for more than a year. His original intention had
been to write a stage play on the theme of treason – a topic that he found
fascinating. At the heart of the drama he envisioned was the relationship
between two American journalists in wartime Berlin. One was an American newsman who served as Shirer's alter ego; Jack Goodman's name provides insight into Shirer's approach, which made up in earnestness what
it lacked in subtlety. The other main character was Oliver Knight, a Bob

Best-like cynic who had surrendered to his dark side and was earning his living by making propaganda broadcasts for the Nazis. When Best, the former UP correspondent in Vienna, went on trial in Boston for treason in March 1948, Shirer was one of the witnesses called to testify against him. The government's case shed scant light on what had prompted Best to turn traitor, but it did prove that he remained unrepentant. As a result, the court handed him a life sentence and he was behind bars in 1952 when he died after suffering a massive cerebral hemorrhage.

In his efforts to explore the motivations of Best and other traitors, Shirer had invested considerable time and effort in writing his stage play. However, after his conversation with Hersey, he concluded that the themes with which he was grappling might better be dealt with in a work of literary fiction. Once he accepted this idea, it took him almost two years to turn his play into a novel. Shirer dared to dream big, envisioning the book, which he called *The Traitor*, as the first in a planned series with the journalistic title of "Glimpses of the Times of the World War."

When Cass Canfield of Harper & Brothers, who was John Gunther's publisher and friend, asked to read Shirer's manuscript, it was with high hopes that Shirer sent him a copy. However, these hopes were dashed when Canfield pronounced the novel "Not saleable." Blanche Knopf was of the same opinion, despite the fact that she had published and sold almost a million copies of Shirer's two Berlin books. In a letter written forty years later, her son confided to Shirer: "You should know there was a faction in the shop who felt very strongly that whatever you wrote was deserving of publication, not only because you stick with an author, but also because it would take a number of unsuccessful books to make a dent in the profits Knopf made from both *Berlin Diary* books."[1] Alfred Knopf Jr's apologetic words are revealing. They underscore the fact that while Knopf editors had concluded *The Traitor* was unlikely to be a bestseller, they still felt that publishing it would have been the right thing to do. Knopf Jr's words are a reminder of the way publishers once did business.

Undeterred by these initial rejections, Shirer persisted in his efforts to find a publisher. He succeeded when Farrar, Strauss and Company agreed to publish the novel; however, no national magazine was willing to carry an excerpt of a book by a blacklisted writer, and so it was not surprising that, when copies of *The Traitor* appeared in bookstores in time for Christmas 1950, sales were discouraging. So were the reviews. Nevertheless, there was talk of a movie based on *The Traitor*, and so in November Shirer traveled to Hollywood to discuss the project, which tentatively was to star the well-known actor Richard Widmark. While plans for the film ultimately were scuttled in the face of blacklist paranoia, Shirer's western excursion was not a total loss. He was flattered to receive a lunch invitation from German novelist Thomas Mann, who had won the 1929 Nobel Prize in Literature. Mann had taken refuge in Los Angeles when the war began and in 1944 had become an American citizen. Having read *The Traitor*, Mann had some encouraging comments to offer. Praise from Mann was heady stuff indeed for Shirer, and it encouraged him to proceed with work on a second novel. First, however, because he was in dire need of money he heeded his agent's advice to return one more time to writing nonfiction.

Shirer was at times surprisingly philosophical about his situation, for he was well aware that he was not the only journalist of his generation who was struggling to earn a living. The postwar era was a period of transition and profound change in the American media, and Shirer knew that many of his peers – Dorothy Thompson, Vincent "Jimmy" Sheean, and Raymond Gram Swing, among many others – also were going through lean times. As he did each New Year's Day, Shirer took stock of his life on 1 January 1951: "It is puzzling how journalism, in which I made a certain mark, I think, has so little use for those who not so long ago were hailed as being near the top."[2]

Always in the back of Shirer's mind was that *other* reason for his woes: the de facto blacklisting that flowed from publication of his name in *Red Channels*. He remained embittered and angry.

On 5 March 1946, Winston Churchill had given his historic speech in Fulton, Missouri, in which he declared that "an iron curtain" had come down across Europe, with the imposition of "police governments" in the eastern part of the continent. Not only had his warning been timely, it seemed to have been prudent, for it appeared that communism was on the march across Europe and Asia. In London, the first sessions of the general assembly of the new United Nations had been meeting amid calls for nuclear arms control; only the United States had the atomic bomb at this time, and so many Americans saw such talks as an attack on the country's hegemony. In the circumstances, the news in September 1949 that the Soviet Union also had the atomic bomb and the outbreak of war in Korea just nine months later had a profound impact on the mood of the nation and on the financial markets. Americans were confused and fearful. They were also suspicious that communists were to blame for the world's troubles, especially those that were disrupting life domestically.

Senator Joseph McCarthy and his supporters were hurling wild, alarming allegations in all directions and warning that Soviet agents and com-

·munist sympathizers had infiltrated the upper echelons of the United States government. We now know that the Russian secret police, the KGB, were in fact actively recruiting spies and doing whatever they could to wreak havoc. However, it is no less clear that the impact of their efforts was more psychological than material.

Fears of communist infiltration of American government and society gave J. Edgar Hoover's FBI ample reason to step up its domestic surveillance operations. By the end of 1952, an astounding 6.6 million citizens had undergone security checks; more than 25,000 of these American citizens were being subjected to more extensive "field investigations." In the end, 490 federal employees were dismissed for "disloyalty," many of them having been adjudged on the flimsiest of evidence. Even more telling was that all of the FBI's spadework failed to uncover even one case of espionage. "It was not realized at first," then-Secretary of State Dean Acheson later wrote, "how dangerous was the practice of secret evidence and secret informers, how alien to all our conceptions of justice and the rights of the citizens."[3]

William Shirer understood all too well the insanity and injustice to which Acheson alludes. Crazy, maddening, and illogical though it was, the mere suggestion that Shirer at some time in his life *could* have been a communist sympathizer was enough to send his career into a tailspin. Had he continued to work at CBS and to enjoy the patronage of William Paley and Ed Murrow, it is likely that Shirer would have weathered the political storm – as did Howard K. Smith and Alexander Kendrick, whose names had also appeared in *Red Channels*.

An FBI internal briefing document dated 4 April 1950, made mention of Murrow and a "group [at CBS] believed to be communistically inclined or fellow travelers."[4] Such allegations, baseless though they were, aroused Hoover's suspicions. In June 1951, he ordered deputy director L.B. "Lou" Nichols to prepare a report on Murrow. In Hoover's eyes, CBS itself was suspect – indeed, in the corridors of FBI headquarters, the Paley network was referred to as the "Communist Broadcasting System"[5] – and Murrow, as its public face, was a marked man even if he seemed to be going out of his way to prove he was a loyal and true American.

Murrow biographer Joseph E. Persico notes that in the end, Nichols reported there was no evidence to suggest Murrow was unpatriotic. "Our files contain no information to the effect that [he] is a member of the group in CBS believed to be communistically inclined or fellow travelers," Nichols advised his boss. "Murrow was in fact instrumental in firing [name blanked out] because of the latter's failure to obtain good news coverage."[6] Persico surmises that the blanked-out name was that of William L. Shirer.[7] Despite this, Hoover remained wary and did not accept the idea that just because Murrow had fired Shirer, he was above suspicion.

For the FBI chief, the CBS decision to cut Shirer loose was prima facie evidence of Shirer's guilt. It also signaled to the Red-baiters that Shirer – one of "the Murrow boys" – was now on his own and could be cut down to size. Thus, when his name appeared in *Red Channels*, like sharks in a feeding frenzy, the zealots attacked. The timing could not have been worse for Shirer. The country was on edge. Americans were discontented and felt besieged. After all, the United States had led the Allies to victory in the Second World War. Something had gone terribly wrong, and the blame had to rest with someone. How else could the situation be explained? Conspiracy, like isolationism, is one of most pernicious and illogical recurring themes in American history.

In the circumstances, despite the supposed liberal bias of the mainstream media, right-of-center commentators ruled the radio airwaves in the late 1940s and early 1950s. Any discussion of the situation raises that vital, irresolvable question: does the media lead or follow public opinion? William Shirer certainly would have argued in favor of the former, since he – and others – continued to decry the rightward shift of America's mainstream media. Many of Shirer's colleagues likewise were feeling the heat to be "politically correct" in the Cold War sense of the term. The impetus for orthodoxy at CBS had intensified after December 1950, when in the face of demands from corporate sponsors the network had followed the lead of the federal government and instituted a compulsory loyalty oath for all employees. Civil libertarians, the Authors' League of America, and other like-minded groups protested. Some of Murrow's CBS colleagues – most notably Smith, Sevareid, and Kendrick – refused to sign the document, at least until Murrow pointed out that they had no choice if they wanted to continue working at CBS.

Ed Murrow met with his lawyer Morris Ernst and Ernst's son-in-law Mike Bessie, a prominent editor at Harper & Brothers publishing house, to discuss the situation. Ernst, whom we now know was an FBI informant, had urged Murrow to speak out against the loyalty oath, to condemn it as an infringement of First Amendment rights. Murrow biographer Joseph Persico quotes Ernst as asking Murrow "How could people in a weaker position stand up to this threat if a man of your stature did not?"[8] However, to the surprise of Ernst and a great many other people, Murrow refused to be drawn into the fray. For the time being.

Only later did the truth come out: not only had Murrow been aware of the specifics of the loyalty oath in its draft stages, he had read and approved the wording, implicitly if not explicitly. Murrow's family and friends had sensed he was not himself at the time and had lost his way. Although he was only forty-three, Murrow's health was already in decline; he was short of breath, chronically tired, prone to coughing spells, and suffering from insomnia and cold sweats. These symptoms were harbingers of the health issues that lay ahead for him.

At the time of their 1947 estrangement, Shirer had warned Murrow that it was only a matter of time until he, too, fell victim to a political witch hunt. Shirer's words continued to haunt Murrow, who explained his willingness to go along with that controversial CBS loyalty oath by stating that he preferred to pick and choose his battles. The truth was that in early 1951 Murrow had no stomach for a fight. He believed there were more pressing issues to deal with and that it would be pointless to risk his career and all that he had worked for in a futile bid to resist the tides of political orthodoxy. William Paley's former wife, Dorothy, told Ann Sperber how disappointed she had been that Murrow had not opposed the loyalty oath. "I don't know what it cost him ... I think a great deal. Of his own self-respect."[9]

Murrow's biographers have chronicled his predicament and his anguish. Joseph Persico makes the point that it is unfair to judge his actions from "a safe remove" – that is with the benefit of hindsight and through the eyes of a modern-day observer. "The hysteria of the '50s was real. Paranoia and suspicion were in the air," Persico points out.[10] Brooding and increasingly gripped by fears that he was betraying some of his own most cherished principles, Murrow knew he was in his enemies' crosshairs; it was exactly as Shirer had predicted. This is not to say that Murrow shied away from stating his beliefs or standing up for himself, only that he did so prudently and cautiously, now more than ever before. He continued to regard himself first and foremost as a newsman. For Murrow, it was a badge of honor that he drew fire on various occasions for stating his views and for challenging the prevailing political orthodoxy. Yet Murrow knew how tenuous his position was, and he surely knew or suspected that FBI agents were watching him. When in November 1953 he uttered a comment in a newscast that to suspicious ears sounded like a veiled criticism of the agency, Hoover ordered his agents to step up their surveillance of him.

Ed Murrow's popularity, prestige, and influence were still so robust that he was able to fend off the attacks of his conservative critics and enemies during the McCarthy era. That was the case even when he was assailed by the anti-red publication *Counterattack*, which accused him of being a communist dupe. It was no small feat that Murrow was able to tiptoe his way through the minefield of political orthodoxy. His reputation for being the consummate newsman, objective and dispassionate, afforded him a ready-made rationale for declining to take a stand on nettlesome issues and for refusing to get involved in the political fray – as he had when emotions were running high over the loyalty oath that in December 1950 CBS began requiring its employees to sign. The irony in this is that Murrow's reputation was, and in large measure remains, a function of his perceived integrity, courage, and devotion to principles. His dilemma was that in the postwar world it was not always easy to discern right from wrong, much less to take a stand. As Sperber notes, like William Shirer and a great many others, Murrow was "caught in the prototypical dilemma of the postwar liberal whose anti-communism was not of the traditional bred-in-the-bone variety but rather a gut repugnance for authoritarianism whether of the left or right."[11]

In the late 1930s, when Murrow and Shirer had been busy building CBS radio's news operations in Europe, and again during the war, the world had been much more black-and-white. The dichotomy between good and evil was clear: democracy versus totalitarianism. In that regard, those had been the best of times and the worst of times for Ed Murrow and for so many other Americans of his generation. Despite his own exalted status, he never forgot his hardscrabble early years or his youthful struggles to make something of himself. Nor was he willing to let others forget who he was or where he had come from. "In part, it was a social preemptive strike," Persico surmises. "There could be no surprised glances down long noses when [the subjects of] ancestors and schools came up in East Side salons."[12]

In many regards, Murrow was and remains an enigma; that is part of his appeal as an historical personality. He was a man's man who eschewed pretense and fuss. He enjoyed drinking, smoking, and playing poker with the boys; Murrow was in his element in the matey company of other males. In the postwar years, friends noticed that he seemed most at ease and was his old self when the Murrow Boys gathered in New York for their annual year-end roundtable broadcast on CBS. Murrow presided over the planning sessions, entertained the correspondents at poker nights, over meals, and on boozy nights out on the town.

Murrow had countless friends and associates. Yet few people, if any, knew the *real* Ed Murrow, for he was not a man inclined to confide his innermost thoughts and feelings. Despite this, there can be no doubt that the Murrow-Shirer friendship had been special or that it was as close as any either of them ever experienced. "We have worked together very close-ly ... and a bond grew that was very real, a kind you make only a few times in your life," Shirer wrote.[13] It was the closeness of this bond that had made the 1947 split between the two men so painful, profound, and traumatic.

That break was something from which Ed Murrow never truly recov-ered, a melancholy that, because of Shirer's obstinacy, Murrow carried with him to his grave. Murrow was not overtly religious; however, like Shirer, he had a deep and abiding sense of morality and social justice. Murrow's biographers recount numerous incidents in which he extended a helping hand to colleagues, former colleagues, and even to needy strangers. At the same time, Murrow could be brooding and intense, and like Shirer he had a long memory for slights and for wrongs done him. Clashing egos, confused loyalties, and a reluctance to jeopardize his own privileged position at CBS had led him to side with William Paley in the dispute with Shirer. The repercussions of that split-second decision were life-altering for both men.

For Shirer, it had been a dagger into the heart of his friendship with Ed Murrow, the ultimate betrayal. As such, it had signaled the end of his career at CBS. Although he never could have guessed or even dreamed it at the time, it also had marked the start of a crushing, humbling thirteen-year hiatus. This was a period in his life during which he would wander in the wilderness financially and vocationally.

The circumstances of his dismissal from CBS were to leave William Shir-er forever embittered, clouding his judgment. He retained a begrudging professional respect for Ed Murrow the newsman, but never again did Shirer think of Ed Murrow as a friend.

Shirer persisted in his belief that he had been fired for political reasons and that Ed Murrow could and should have stepped forward to side with him in his confrontation with William Paley. But what if Murrow had insisted on sticking with the compromise agreement that he and Shirer had worked out?

Would William Paley have fired Murrow as well as Shirer? Possibly. But given Ed Murrow's stature and the fact that at the time he was the public face of CBS news, that is unlikely. Paley was nothing if not an astute busi-nessman, and the loss of Murrow would have been a crippling blow for the network. Eric Sevareid, another of the Murrow boys who ran into political problems at CBS, said it well in a 1941 speech: "I have been impressed with how timid a million dollars' profit can make a publisher or a radio executive, instead of how bold it makes him."[14] The obverse of that was also true: any threat to the financial bottom line was enough to make William Paley or any other media mogul think twice about acting in a way that would jeopardize profits. Given the rivalry between CBS and NBC and given Paley's history of talent poaching, he surely would have known that an unemployed Ed Murrow would not have been out of work for long; in all probability, in a wink he would have found another job over at NBC or with the Mutual network, a move that would have given the latter instant credibility and raised its profile immeasurably. So it comes back to Murrow.

As for Shirer, what direction might his career at CBS have taken if Murrow had sided with him rather than Paley? While that is impossible to know, of course, the fate of Eric Sevareid offers an idea of how things might have unfolded. Unlike most of his colleagues, Sevareid had made no secret of his disdain for Senator Joseph McCarthy and other Red-baiters. On numerous occasions, Sevareid goaded the Wisconsin senator by making fun of him, comparing McCarthy to Winnie-the-Pooh. McCarthy and his supporters responded angrily, denouncing Sevareid as "Eric the Red." Sevareid believed his telephone was tapped by the FBI, as it doubtless was, and he and his family were routinely subjected to threats and abusive phone calls. In March 1950, Sevareid lost his sponsor and his six p.m. primetime slot on CBS radio; he was bumped to an unsponsored period at eleven p.m. Sevareid – ever the Murrow loyalist and having seen what happened to William Shirer – prudently said nothing. Soon enough he was rewarded with a new weekly fifteen-minute newscast that aired on Sunday afternoons. However, that program also was canceled in April 1951. While Sevareid managed to hang on at CBS, he eventually came to regret that he had not opted to quit broadcasting and spend his time writing as Shirer had done. The difference between the two, of course, was that Shirer had no choice.

Murrow's pangs of guilt about what had happened and his uncertainties about the man he had become and where his career was going prompted him to resign his job as vice-president and return to broadcasting. At various times over the years, Murrow made efforts to reach out to Shirer, indirectly. However, Shirer was too stubborn, too scarred, to forgive or forget. However, it is clear that Ed Murrow harbored a profound sense that in March 1947 he had erred when he had not stood with Shirer, right or wrong, and again in December 1950 when he had failed to speak out against the loyalty oath that William Paley compelled all CBS employees to sign. However, as Murrow's son Casey notes, "Time certainly mellowed my father's reaction to all that happened."[15]

The cumulative weight of events and Murrow's pangs of conscience provided impetus for his decision finally to confront the injustices he saw being perpetrated in the name of Cold War political correctness, which would put him on a collision course with the demagogues of the Red Scare, in particular that now-infamous junior senator from Wisconsin, Joseph McCarthy.

By autumn 1953, Senator McCarthy's influence and credibility were on the wane. The more people saw of him and heard him speak – and in good measure that was because of his exposure on the fledgling medium of television – the more apparent his true nature became. The impact was cumulative. The American people came to realize that McCarthy was a blowhard and a political opportunist who was far more of a threat to democracy than the Red bogeymen he was so intent on exposing. Despite the supposed threat the senator railed against, the reality was that support for communism in America was miniscule. The American Communist Party had been a legal entity for more than three decades, yet – as William Shirer repeatedly pointed out – no Communist had ever (or, for that matter, would ever) even come close to winning public office in the United States.

The long-anticipated confrontation between Murrow and McCarthy has been well documented by historians. The special report on Murrow's 9 March 1954 *See It Now* program that attacked McCarthy head on has become the stuff of broadcast history and an integral element in the Murrow legend. Ed Murrow lamented that the fear-mongering perpetuated by McCarthy and his supporters had done grave harm to America's international reputation and had given the country's enemies a boost: "[McCarthy] didn't create this situation of fear, he merely exploited it and rather successfully ... Cassius was right: 'The fault, dear Brutus, is not in our stars but in ourselves.'"[16]

This was potent stuff indeed. So, too, was the public response to Murrow's words, which was overwhelmingly favorable and enthusiastic. Immediately after the *See It Now* report aired, the CBS telephone switchboard was swamped with laudatory calls from viewers, and in the following days Murrow's mailbox overflowed with supportive cards, letters, and telegrams. Many historians and Murrow biographers have echoed the public's applause, and Ed Murrow has been widely hailed as a liberal poster boy for his role in taking down Senator McCarthy.[17] However, despite all of the plaudits, Murrow biographer Joseph Persico argues that, while Murrow's attack on McCarthy may have been the tipping point in the senator's decline, his star had already been fading when the *See It Now* broadside tore into him. This is not to suggest that Murrow did not take a huge chance in attacking McCarthy's credibility or that the newsman's actions were not pivotal, only that the events of March 1954 should be viewed in the broader historical context. "To credit Edward R. Murrow with the fall of Joe McCarthy would be an exaggeration," Persico writes. "[His] contribution to the defeat of the demagogue was that he had had the courage to use television against McCarthy. He had taken a young medium, skittish over controversy, and plunged it into the hottest controversy of the era."[18] Although Joe McCarthy's downfall did little to improve William Shirer's situation, he begrudgingly applauded Murrow's role in bringing it: "The hate and the fear and the intolerance [McCarthy] ignited and fostered lingered on in the country until the end of the decade when finally Americans, even the frightened rabbits in radio and TV and the films, not to mention those in the press and in Congress, came to their senses."[19]

33

End of an Affair

Following the expiration in 1948 of William Shirer's short-term contract with the Mutual radio network, three years passed before he was able to find another job, doing a tri-weekly newscast on the upstart Liberty network. However, with the popularity of radio in freefall, the ratings for his newscast were disappointing. Shirer's contract was not renewed when the show went on summer hiatus. Seeing the writing on the proverbial wall, he already had turned his efforts toward finding work in television, which fast was displacing radio as America's first choice for news and entertainment. Shirer had pitched an idea for a weekly newsmagazine show, which at the time was an innovative concept. However, decision-makers in the broadcast industry had rejected the initiative, in large measure because it was Shirer who had proposed it. Frustrated and angry at the runaround he was getting wherever he turned, Shirer approached Herb Rosenthal of MCA, his broadcast agent during his salad days, to ask if Rosenthal might be willing to represent him once again. The agent's reply was blunt: "MCA would not find it to their advantage to represent you today."[1]

This was the reality for Shirer. With no other option, he muddled through for much of the decade, barely eking out a living. Month after month, he was forced to dip into his savings to pay bills. His only steady source of income was lecturing, one of the few lines of work not closed off to him; but "I also began to realize that there was something insidious and terribly harmful in lecturing ... With all the adulation you got, you risked taking yourself seriously. There was no real debate to keep your wits sharpened, your ego dampened, and your mind clear of cobwebs. And practically repeating the same lecture night after night, week after week, was stultifying."[2]

Despite his reservations, Shirer drew solace from the knowledge that many celebrated authors before him had earned a substantial amount of money in this way; if lecturing had been good enough for Emerson, Dickens, and Twain, Shirer decided, it was also good enough for him. Then, too, there were some positives to the life of "an itinerant lecturer," as he now jokingly described himself. "Except that it took a good deal of time from writing, I rather liked the first couple of years of lecturing ... For one who had been away so long, it provided the opportunity of seeing large parts of the country for the first time."[3] The lecture circuit helped restore Shirer's faith in the fundamental decency and common sense of the American people, and he was pleased and flattered to see who came out to hear him speak.

On one occasion, retired General George C. Marshall was in the audience for a Shirer lecture in Pinehurst, North Carolina; when some retired army officers in attendance began to verbally attack Shirer for his liberal views, Marshall rose to his defense. Afterward, over drinks, the two men found they had much in common. Like Shirer, the general had been unjustly labeled as a "communist sympathizer." It mattered not that Marshall had been the army chief of staff during the war, that he had served in President Harry Truman's cabinet, or that he had won the 1953 Nobel Peace Prize for his work to rebuild Europe – and help check the spread of Communism – in the postwar world. None of this was enough to prove his patriotism in these crazy times. "[Marshall] complimented me for speaking out ... He seemed depressed about the state of the country, which McCarthy and his supporters were terrorizing."[4]

On another occasion, in April 1957, Shirer was speaking at a Rotary Club meeting in Independence, Missouri, when he spotted former President Harry Truman and his wife Bess in the hall. Afterward, the Trumans invited Shirer into their home for coffee, and next morning, the president gave his guest a personal guided tour of the new Truman Library, which at the time was still under construction prior to its dedication in July of that year.

Such encounters with eminent Americans were the exception rather than the rule, but they did add a welcome element of surprise and vitality to Shirer's life on the road. He traveled thousands of miles during the 1950s, visited scores of cities and university campuses – including his alma mater, Coe College – and he spoke before crowds large and small. While he savored the adulation he often received, Shirer ultimately found his life as a lecturer to be physically demanding and painfully lonely. Even more problematic was the fact that lecturing was seasonal work, and after deducting the booking fees he paid his agent and meeting his expenses – for travel, lodging, and income tax – Shirer was fortunate to net $7,500 per year. In better days, he made that much money in just a few weeks and with far less effort.

Print journalism had been Shirer's bread and butter early in his career, and even during his years with CBS he had supplemented his income by writing magazine articles and his syndicated weekly newspaper column. Once he was blacklisted, these markets were all but closed off to him. For almost a decade, his only sales were book reviews and occasional light-hearted, nonpolitical feature articles that he sold to sympathetic editors at *The New York Times* and the *Los Angeles Times*; more often than not, the articles for which he was paid were never published: "This being driven out of my profession by ... the hysteria of the times has puzzled me and troubled me ... And I have to fight hard – inside – to make sure it did not DEFEAT me."[5]

William Shirer felt embittered and very much alone as he struggled to maintain his lifestyle and dignity. Scratching out a living was anything but easy. Editors and broadcast executives no longer returned his phone calls or responded to his letters. Some former associates crossed the street when they saw him coming; others shunned him socially. However, what was most distressing of all, at least from an emotional standpoint, was the realization that his on-again, off-again affair with Tilly Losch was lurching toward its inevitable, unhappy end. Despite Shirer's best efforts to turn it into something more, the relationship had become platonic, and this was a source of endless frustration for him. That much is painfully clear from the letters he wrote to Losch, often to pass the long, lonely hours while he was traveling on lecture tours.

Shirer and Losch continued seeing one another, but always at times of her choosing and on her terms. Shirer bemoaned the fact she did not return his phone calls, nor was she ever home when he dropped by. The simple, unvarnished truth, so obvious to the dispassionate observer, is that Losch had no interest in a long-term relationship with Shirer. That he could not understand this is hardly surprising. Tilly Losch did not fit the prevailing female stereotype of the day – woman as homemaker, mother, and dutiful wife. She remained intent on building a career as an artist, author, and performer. Now that Shirer was no longer helpful in that regard, she had much less time for him. Despite this, it is clear Shirer filled an emotional void in Losch's life. She kept the scores of letters, telegrams, and cards that he sent her over the years, though no carbon copies of any of her own replies, if she ever sent any.[6]

Shirer and Losch had had their first major falling out in April 1946. The bloom having gone off the proverbial rose, she had announced it was all over between them. "So you have ended it all – for good," Shirer wrote in a letter. "Be assured that I accept your decision. I shall not ask to see you again, and this is the last you will ever hear from me."[7] Despite this, the pair soon reconciled. Within days, Shirer resumed his letter writing, even if he now professed a willingness to concede – or so he had claimed – that the relationship was purely "casual [and] platonic." It continued this way for five more years. Small wonder that Tess Shirer remained bitter and angry at her husband's behavior, which was outrageous and at times petulant. His infatuation with Tilly Losch persisted like a chronic illness.

On one occasion in April 1950, after spending an afternoon at her apartment watching her paint, Shirer wrote, "You were looking ravishingly beautiful ... I wanted to stay on there forever – until the end of time. You were nice to let me be there in the room while you puttered with the paint board. Perhaps if we made that arrangement more often – regularly – you would paint more, and even better! I would ask for nothing more. For that I was born. I can see it now; and I accept it, once and for all. That is the way it was meant to be between us."[8]

Despite this, it was not long before Shirer reverted to playing the role of the frustrated lover. In January 1951, he lamented in yet another plaintive letter that he had tried all that day without success to contact Losch. He was going through another especially difficult time and once more was thinking of ending his marriage. "I would give it all up – and everything. But I am not sure, and you probably are not sure yourself what you want ... And of course it hurts me to hurt others."[9]

As his angst deepened, Shirer had again broached with Losch the possibility of them being together. She had rejected the idea, saying she had no interest in hearing about his marital woes and dismissing any notion that she might become his wife. Shirer reacted angrily: "It has taken nearly ten years to get to this point – and now you say discussion of it BORES you ... You can't spare a minute even to talk it over at the most critical moment of all. If my giving up so much and hurting so terribly at least three human beings merely BORES you, as you said, you cannot blame me for wondering whether it is all a ghastly mistake. Don't you CARE about anything, or anyone?"[10]

There can be no rationalizing affairs of the heart, and Shirer's words speak volumes about his muddled perspective at the time. The situation came to a head the second week of July 1951. Tired of Shirer's theatrics, Losch announced she never wanted to see him again. "I am now quite willing to face the truth and admit the failure of our ten-year friendship to ripen into what we said we both wanted," he replied. "The casual, platonic relationship, which you have insisted on maintaining ... By all means, let us have it – for you it will be the same as before. For me, too, in practice, though not in feeling."[11]

Finally, mercifully, Shirer came to his senses. Ostensibly, at least. In 1990, forty years later, he would recall that his relationship with Losch had ended because *he* had made the painful decision and "finally broke for good with Tilly."[12] Shirer, the jilted lover, was putting his own spin on events – and evidently was unaware that Losch had saved many of his letters. Or perhaps time had dimmed his memory. Either way, his version of events does not ring true. What is true is that for two decades after their relationship ended, apart from a solitary greeting card that Shirer sent in 1953, there would be no further correspondence between the two of them (if there was, no copies exist). Their letter writing resumed in 1971, at a time when circumstances were markedly different for each of them. Losch by then was alone in the world and battling illness, and Shirer's personal life was once more in flux. But in the early months of 1951, sadder and at least somewhat wiser, Shirer resolved to do his best to get on with his life, writing, lecturing, and trying to either rationalize or resurrect his marriage.

Each summer throughout the 1950s, the Shirer family retreated to their rural property near Torrington, Connecticut. There, father, mother, and two daughters remained until Labor Day, away from the hassles and the pressures of Manhattan. Shirer refused to be humbled either by his enemies or by his situation. For the most part, he put on a brave face. That was the case in late 1951 when Ed Murrow extended an olive branch of a sort through mutual friend Raymond Gram Swing, who invited Shirer to contribute a statement of his beliefs to the popular "This I Believe ..." syndicated radio feature. Shirer accepted the invitation because it was Swing who approached him; however, there was also an undeniable element of vanity involved in his decision. Prominent Americans from diverse backgrounds were enlisted to write 500-word statements outlining their philosophy of life. These submissions, which Murrow introduced on air, were also published in newspapers across America. Shirer's statement provides insight into his mindset during this period: "Living in a totalitarian land taught me to value highly – and fiercely – the very things that dictators denied: tolerance, respect for others, and above all – the freedom of the human spirit." Shirer explained that reading history in "this Age of Anxiety" had given him a valuable sense of perspective. "I find that most true happiness comes from one's inner life, from the disposition of the mind and soul. Admittedly, a good inner life is difficult to achieve, especially in these trying times. It takes reflection and contemplation. And self-discipline. One must be honest with oneself, and that's not easy. You have to have patience and understanding. And when you can, seek God ... But the reward of having an inner life, which no outside storm or evil turn of fortune can touch, is, it seems to me, a very great one."[13]

Having that "inner life" had always been, and remained, a challenge for William Shirer. Being a skeptic by nature, he was constantly questioning and re-evaluating his own beliefs and those of people around him. Thus, one of the few unassailable constants in his life was the conviction that he had been wronged by CBS and that it was the cowardice and complicity of those who meekly went along with the blacklisting that prevented him from working as a journalist. Driven to prove to the world that he could not, would not, be cowed, Shirer did all he could to maintain a public profile. He served a two-year term (1956–57) as president of the Authors League of America, and he continued to speak out on foreign-policy issues whenever an opportunity presented itself. Despite these efforts, he was compelled to concede that apart from lecturing, for now at least, his only viable employment option was to continue writing books.

Force of habit, not to mention his need for income and self-respect, prompted Shirer to maintain a disciplined work regimen, even during the summer months at the family farm in Connecticut. He spent part of each day in the country tending to his vegetable garden, listening to his collection of classical music records, reading, and socializing with old friends who also summered in the area. However, he also took time to write, working in a makeshift study in a corner of the old barn that was on the property. The furnishings were Spartan: a long table that served as an ersatz desk and work surface, a couple of chairs, and a typewriter. He tapped away at his typewriter for seven or eight hours each weekday. His initiative was to pay off; he wrote five books during the six-year period from 1950 to 1956 – two works of nonfiction and three novels.

The first of those two nonfiction books was *Midcentury Journey*, published in autumn 1952. This was Shirer's attempt to resurrect the successful formula of the two Berlin diaries. Written in a quasi-diary format, but sans dates, *Midcentury Journey* was the author's assessment of the European political situation at the midway point of the century. In many ways, this "ruminative monologue," as a *New Yorker* reviewer described it,[14] proved yet again that Shirer was nothing if not a fighter. He had little to lose and refused to give his tormenters the satisfaction of seeing him humbled. Instead, he battled back, lashing out at the Red-baiters, isolationists, and those who had accused him of being a communist dupe or sympathizer. He had only scorn for those who ran the American media, who he charged were guilty of legitimizing the blacklist by not questioning its validity and by doing "a pretty poor job in furnishing readers with news from home and abroad."[15] Shirer disputed the allegations of alarmists who claimed the State Department had "sold out China to the Russians." He insisted that any such charge "was absurd and those who made it showed little knowledge of, or respect for, the facts of history, let alone the truth … With all our power we [in America] were not strong enough to dominate the course of events all over the world. China was a reminder of that – and of how helpful it would be to our understanding of a complex, erring world if we could develop a sense of history."[16]

Shirer mused that his recent travels had served as a reminder that the world into which he had been born in 1904 was gone forever. Uncertainty, fear, and intolerance had supplanted the certainties and relative peace of mind that were the intellectual and moral anchors of his parents' generation. While he argued that America should be willing to negotiate and to cooperate with allies, Shirer was no dove. As he saw it, this meant America should champion democratic ideals and be willing to fight to defend them if need be.

While the message Shirer offered in *Midcentury Journey* was a sobering one, it was tempered by an underlying note of optimism. He hoped the future would bring a return to peace and stability, and perhaps an even greater understanding in the world. However, he was enough of a realist to concede that it would not be painless: "No great age was easy or comfortable to live in."

Shirer felt somewhat vindicated when the Literary Guild chose *Midcentury Journey* as one of its featured monthly selections. He was no less pleased that reviewers, even some from conservative publications, which Shirer had expected would be hostile, had some kind things to say about the book. In particular, the words of conservative critic Henry Taylor set him smiling. Taylor was one of the regular reviewers on *Author Meets the Critics*, an unlikely primetime television program that aired on the now-forgotten Dumont Network.[17] Shirer's appearance on that show was arranged by his good friend, panel moderator Virgilia Peterson, whom

The New York Times described as "a rangy, erudite woman ... in the business of having a definite opinion on just about everything literary."[18]

Peterson knew that because Shirer was blacklisted, he was finding it difficult to earn a living, let alone promote his books. Despite this, she took a chance and did him a favor when she arranged his appearance on *Author Meets the Critics*. It was a program for which Shirer was a natural. The format was simple: an author sat down to chat with two critics, one of whom liked the author's book, the other who did not. When Henry Taylor, cast in the role of contrarian, showed up at the studio to talk about *Midcentury Journey*, he announced he could not in good conscience attack the book because he agreed with almost everything Shirer had written. The show's producers were understandably dismayed. "Typical of TV and radio," Shirer commented in his diary. "Neither of the two producers ... had bothered to read [my] book."[19] Shirer's appearance on *Author Meets the Critics* was less important than the fact it solidified his relationship with Gilly Peterson, which was destined to develop into something much more intense than a friendship.

Emboldened and feeling vindicated by the favorable reception for *Midcentury Journey*, Shirer decided the time was right for him to set the record straight about his departure from CBS. He was intent on telling the world his version of events and revealing how his erstwhile friend and colleague Ed Murrow had betrayed him by abandoning his own principles and throwing Shirer to the wolves in order to keep his own cushy job with William Paley's network. The key question in Shirer's mind was how to do this in a way that would enable him to tell his side of the story without being sued or ending up in another messy public debate that he knew he could not win; Ed Murrow had become an iconic figure, while Shirer was now all but forgotten.

The growing popularity of television was killing radio and eroding the public's interest in print as a medium of information and entertainment. Sales of Shirer's recent nonfiction books had been disappointing. For that reason, he opted to tell the story of his departure from CBS in a work of fiction. He hastened to do so, for in the months leading up to his fiftieth birthday in February 1954, he faced a new worry: the feared loss of his creativity. As a young man, Shirer had mused in an academic way about why it was that "American writers stop writing (or they stop writing anything good or important) at middle-age, in marked contrast to Europeans, who usually just get into their stride at forty-five or fifty."[20] The specter of dissipated creativity now loomed in Shirer's mind as a very real and pressing concern. All of this had come sharply into focus and taken on fresh relevance for him on 11 January 1951, when he heard the news that novelist Sinclair Lewis had died in Rome. Shirer never forgot the winter day in 1933 that he and Lewis had spent drinking and discussing the essence of literary creativity. This was a topic on which Lewis could expound eloquently and with authority. The author of five of the most widely read and influential novels of the Jazz Age, he won the Nobel Prize for Literature in 1930 at age forty-five. Lewis's last important book had appeared in 1935, when the author was fifty; *It Can't Happen Here* was a cautionary tale about the dangers of fascism in America. While Lewis had continued to write, Shirer noted that never again did the author enjoy critical or popular success; his troubled personal life had exacted a high toll – Lewis and Dorothy Thompson had divorced in 1942, the toxic combination of alcohol abuse and cynicism having sapped Lewis of his happiness, his health, and his creativity. He was only sixty-six when he died.

Like some other literary luminaries of the era – Thomas Wolfe and F. Scott Fitzgerald being two of the more prominent ones – Sinclair Lewis had flamed-out by middle age. Ernest Hemingway, whose literary style and larger-than-life persona cast a giant shadow across an entire generation of writers, likewise spiraled downward professionally and personally after having won the Nobel Prize for Literature in 1954 at age fifty-five.

While the rationality of the notion that the half-century mark represents a creative dividing line in a writer's career is dubious, such were Shirer's fears during this uncertain, lean time in his life. Determined not to suffer his own ignominious and disastrous descent into irrelevance, he set about telling his side of the story of his departure from CBS in a work of fiction, a roman à clef entitled *Stranger Come Home*. The publisher advertised the book as being "the story of a veteran foreign correspondent turned radio commentator who returns to his native land and meets head-on the political pressures of the day ... [and] whose democratic heritage and principles make him unalterably opposed to Communism yet [he] is accused of being a Communist when he stands by these principles." Shirer felt the need to include an author's note – in effect, a disclaimer – on the front flyleaf of the dust-jacket: "This is the imaginary journal of an imaginary person, and all the other characters in its pages are likewise imaginary. If there is any resemblance whatsoever to persons living or dead, it is purely coincidental."[21]

Like Shirer's Berlin diaries, *Stranger Come Home* is written as a journal, complete with dates. Narrator Raymond Whitehead, a former American diplomat-turned-foreign-correspondent, returns home from Europe in 1949 to a job as a radio news commentator with the Federal Broadcasting Company (FBC). However, to his dismay he discovers he feels alienated and profoundly out of touch; he is a stranger in his own land – hence the book's title. At one point Whitehead comments, "People here haven't the faintest idea how well off they are – at least compared to those in Europe, not to mention Asia, where the squalor would be beyond the comprehension of our well-fed, neatly dressed, cleanly housed, gaudily entertained, automobile owning citizens, unless they saw it, which they have not."[22]

When Whitehead's news commentaries attract the attention of conservative critics who chide him for having "lived abroad too long," he is labeled a "communist sympathizer." Given the prevailing climate of fear and paranoia in America at the time, what follows for Whitehead is a nightmare. He loses the sponsor for his newscast and sees his name appear in an accusatory way in an anti-communist newsletter called *Red Airwaves*. Whitehead, like Shirer, declines to be cowed and even has the audacity to support a colleague who has been similarly accused. This draws the attention of an opportunistic Red-baiting United States senator named O'Brien, who is the chairman of the Orwellian-sounding Committee on Security and Americanism.

Amid all of the controversy and adding insult to injury, Whitehead's erstwhile friend and colleague Bob Fletcher, who has risen to become an executive with the FBC, declines to support him. Then, as public pressure mounts, Fletcher throws Whitehead to the wolves when he fires him from his job. Whitehead is hurt and feels betrayed; in his mind, Fletcher has sold out his principles and his friend in order to protect his privileged position. "I do my job, Raymond, as I see it," Fletcher rationalizes.[23] Despite Shirer's insistence to the contrary, it does not take much of a leap of imagination – if any – on the reader's part to see the parallels between the novel's plot and Shirer's own situation in real life.

Stranger Come Home was published in spring 1954, around the time Ed Murrow was confronting Joseph McCarthy and emerging as the hero of all those who had been waiting for someone to reveal the junior Senator from Wisconsin for the demagogue he was. As a result, public opinion was squarely in Murrow's corner.

Those who were unfamiliar with the details of Shirer's departure from CBS or of his falling out with Ed Murrow read *Stranger Come Home* as a cautionary tale about the dangers of the political paranoia that was sweeping America. Reviewers who *were* familiar with Shirer's story correctly saw the novel for what it was: a thinly disguised attempt to even the score with those people whom Shirer felt had wronged him.

As had been the case four years earlier with *The Traitor*, there was some initial interest in a movie version of the novel; again, it all came to naught. Despite the fact that Senator McCarthy's influence was on the wane, the political situation in the country remained in flux.

Sales of *Stranger Come Home*, while respectable, were not what Shirer had hoped for. His need for income prompted him to return once more to his bread-and-butter for so many years: reportage.

Having already analyzed the political situations in France, Germany, and the United Kingdom, Shirer turned his attention northward to Scandinavia for a second work of nonfiction written during the blacklist years. *The Challenge of Scandinavia* encompassed in its coverage Norway, Sweden, Finland, and Denmark – the last of which, as Shirer explained, was included in the narrative although at the time it was not generally regarded as being part of Scandinavia.

At first blush, this was an odd choice of subject matter for a journalist who had never lived in or even spent much time in the region. However, the reality was that Shirer had long been intrigued by life in Scandinavia. He regarded the countries of the region, with their social-welfare systems and planned economies, as pathfinders in efforts to track a middle course between "unbridled private enterprise and the strait jacket of Communist tyranny."[24] Shirer's curiosity had been piqued when Winston Churchill in his acceptance speech for the 1953 Nobel Prize for Literature lauded Scandinavia for its "healthy way of life."

Since Shirer had no other projects in the works, both his lecture and literary agents urged him to tour the region, which he did in summer 1953. The resulting book was Shirer's attempt to emulate the formula John Gunther had perfected in his popular *Inside* series, which examined life in various parts of the world. Unfortunately for Shirer, who was more serious and analytical than Gunther, he had none of his friend's bonhomie and not enough of his ear for the kind of gossipy human details that made the *Inside* books so appealing to a general audience. The type of informal writing that was Gunther's forte did not come easily to Shirer. Nonetheless, some critics lauded *The Challenge of Scandinavia* when it was published in May 1955; one reviewer even hailed it as "a Guntherian 'inside' job."[25] Despite this, sales of the Shirer book paled when compared to the numbers for John Gunther's *Inside* books. This only added more fuel to Shirer's uncertainties and angst about the future.

Still hopeful of somehow finding a way to return to broadcasting, he wrote to Pat Weaver, then-president of NBC, sounding him out on some fresh ideas he had for a weekly television news show that would be "entirely different from Murrow's."[26] Weaver was not interested; even with Senator McCarthy's influence on the wane, Shirer remained a pariah to the American broadcasting industry. He was reminded of that and of the harsh realities of the business when he heard that Paul White, the former vice-president and news director at CBS, had died on 9 July 1955, after a lengthy illness. He was fifty-three, just two years older than Shirer and had been living in self-imposed exile in San Diego since his 1947 departure from the network.[27]

News of White's death and the disappointing sales for his Scandinavia book left Shirer downcast and wallowing in self-doubt. Unsure of how best to proceed and hoping to reinvent himself, once more he turned to writing drama and fiction – the former because the theater was less affected by the blacklist than either movies or broadcasting; the latter because he still harbored dreams of achieving success as a novelist. All his life, Shirer loved to read and to draw inspiration from the classics, in particular the novels of Dickens, Austen, Hardy, Conrad, Balzac, and Tolstoy. Like most literary-minded people of his generation, Shirer subscribed to the myth that "real writers" wrote novels, and he stubbornly clung to the belief he had it in him to write creatively. He plunged into work on another book of fiction, this one rooted in his experiences as a young reporter in India. Initially, he had intended to write a stage play about Gandhi and the struggle for Indian independence. When that idea for a play did not work out, he instead focused on other aspects of the drama that had been unfolding in the British colony. Thus, from time to time in the early 1950s, bits of news appeared in the New York newspapers, usually in the gossip columns, reporting that Shirer was at work on a stage play that was destined for Broadway. Those reports inevitably proved to be premature, or perhaps they were nothing more than wishful thinking on Shirer's part. He had written and rewritten drafts of a drama that was set against the backdrop of colonial India; however, in the end he'd had no luck in finding a producer for the play.

Shirer's efforts as a dramatist suffered from the same shortcomings as his novels. As is the case with so many journalists who delve into fiction or drama, too often his characters emerged as two-dimensional caricatures who mouthed the author's views on politics, society, life, or love. In the case of Shirer's Indian story, most of the action took place in the

American consulate, where diplomat Harold Leighton was in the twilight of a thirty-year career in the service of the State Department and had some weighty issues to deal with. The plot that unfolded provided Shirer with opportunities to expound on the decline of colonialism in Asia and more generally on the upsurge of nationalism in the developing world. In the mid-1950s these were timely themes for a playwright to tackle and for theatergoers to contemplate.

However, Shirer needed money and could ill afford to spend time writing anything he might not sell. Thus, he did with his India play what he had done with his drama about journalists in wartime Berlin: he rewrote the story, turning it into a novel with the working title *Pawancore*, that being the name of his fictitious British colony where the Hindu and Sikh inhabitants were struggling to achieve independence. He was confident the novel to which he put the finishing touches in the early weeks of September 1955 was the best fiction he had ever written. After perusing the manuscript, John Gunther concurred. Despite this, Gunther advised that, in his opinion, the book would be more commercial with a snappier title; *Perhaps the Monsoon* was his suggestion.

Taking Gunther's advice to heart, Shirer adopted the title *Spent Monsoons*. He could have saved himself the creative effort, because the editors at Little, Brown and Company, the novel's publisher, convinced him to rename it yet again. When it went appeared in bookshops in February 1956, it was with the title *The Consul's Wife*.[28]

Shirer's high hopes for this, his third novel, were quickly dashed. Even those critics who applauded the book's brisk pace offered what can only be described as qualified praise; most reviewers panned it. To Shirer, it seemed that his luck was going from bad to worse. Nothing he wrote brought him the kind of success he so desperately wanted or needed. In his diary on 2 January 1958, he reviewed the year just ended, his fifty-fourth. He continued to be unemployed and had few prospects; his savings were all but gone, and his chequing account was empty. Not surprisingly, his assessment of his situation was bleak: "Another year gone by ... I continue to lose ground ... My capital is almost exhausted ... For the last 10 years ... I have simply not earned enough to meet our modest expenses."[29]

Shirer's income for the year 1957 had been only $6,600; a decade earlier, before losing his job at CBS, he had been making close to $100,000 per year. Adding insult to injury was the fact that two-thirds of what he had earned in 1957 had come in the form of advances from his publisher. The nub of Shirer's problems was that his expenses continued to exceed his income; he could no longer pay his bills. Shirer received a cold and very vivid reminder of that fact when the furnace at the farmhouse in Connecticut died. He had no money to repair or replace it; when the Shirers retreated to the country to celebrate New Year's Eve with the Thurbers and a few other close friends, the only heat in the house came from the living room fireplace and a kitchen woodstove.

To say that these were lean days for William Shirer is an understatement. He had all but reached the end of his rope financially and emotionally. However, he still refused to give in. Shirer doggedly continued to believe that somehow he would find a way out of his troubles. It was with that goal in mind that he began work on another nonfiction book, a big, ambitious effort that he had been musing about for several years. He believed this book would be his salvation. Others did not share his enthusiasm, nor were they confident there was a market for it. Shirer was determined to prove them wrong. After all, he reasoned, what other choice did he have?

34

A Book for the Ages

William Shirer knew that his publisher was fast losing faith in him after the disappointing sales of his recent books. Stanley Salmon, the vice-president and chief editor of Little, Brown and Company, had delivered that message personally one day in spring 1955. As he and Shirer were reviewing the final proofs for Shirer's book about Scandinavia, Salmon casually asked the author what he planned to write after he finished the novel he was working on, which was *The Consul's Wife*.

Seizing the moment, Shirer pitched his idea for a book on the history of Nazi Germany. This was a project he had first envisioned back in autumn 1945, while reporting on the Nuremberg trials. Shirer had returned home from Germany with suitcases bulging with copies of documents used by the prosecution in building cases against the Nazi leaders. In the decade since then, a vast amount of fresh information on Hitler's regime had become available.

Shirer long had puzzled over many of the events he had reported on in the run-up to the outbreak of the war and in the first two years of conflict. Like many observers, he had wondered about Hitler's true intentions – had the Nazi dictator blundered into a war or planned it? – and about some of the peculiar strategic decisions taken by the German military. Fast forward sixteen years, and with so many once-secret documents now accessible, Shirer was eager to find answers to questions that lingered in his mind, to understand *how* and *why* the German people had succumbed to the collective madness and barbarism of Nazism.

Shirer's interest in knowing more had only grown the more he delved into the evidence. He had gathered additional primary-source documents during his 1950 trip to Europe, and following his return home had continued to amass information. While he still had no firm plans for a book, the research process was taking on a momentum of its own. That became clear the day in January 1954 when Shirer wrote a to-do memo to himself that included a book on the history of Nazi Germany; he even had a title in mind: *The Rise and Fall of the Third Reich*. However, Shirer understood that recounting the full story of the Hitler regime would be a Herculean task that would involve sifting through thousands of pages of disparate primary-source material in hopes of making sense of the seemingly incomprehensible. No less problematic was the awareness that his bills were piling up and he would not be earning any money while researching and writing a history of Nazi Germany. Nevertheless, Shirer's every journalistic instinct told him that here was the story of a lifetime, a story so compelling, so terrifying, so bizarre, and so historically important that he had to tell it.

After listening to his sales pitch, Stanley Salmon stated that he had no interest in a history of Nazi Germany. In an October 1960 interview with *The New York Times*, Shirer related a different version of this story. He claimed to have outlined his proposal for the German book in a letter to an unidentified publisher: "By return mail there came a note remarking in effect, Lordy, don't ask us to publish anything like that."[1]

Given the tenor of the times, Little, Brown and Company's lack of interest in the proposed book is understandable. Cold War tensions were at their height. The Soviet Union had emerged as America's number one enemy, and fear of nuclear annihilation had become a national preoccupation. The presumption also was that people were "war weary," and as such were tired of hearing about Nazis, Japanese imperialism, and horrors of the Holocaust. While that certainly was true in 1945, American book publishers a full decade after the war were wrong to assume that readers were still uninterested in knowing what had happened or, more importantly, *why* it had happened. Through all of the pain, sorrow, death, and destruction, the conflict had exerted a powerful, life-altering impact on all those who had lived through it. A decade later, Americans were finally ready to know more about a war in which good and bad had been so clearly defined.

It is unlikely that Shirer analyzed the situation in any systematic way. His perspective was far more pragmatic: here was a compelling news story that he felt cried out to be told, and he was in a unique position to tell it. At the same time, the journalist in him sensed that the inside story on Nazi Germany was one readers would be interested in.

Oxford University historian H.R. Trevor-Roper had written a 1947 book on the final days of Hitler,[2] and in 1952 his academic colleague Alan

Bullock had crafted a massive biography of the Nazi dictator.[3] Both books had won favorable reviews and relatively wide readership – for works of history. Both had also generated so much discussion in academic circles that other scholars had set to work recounting various aspects of the Nazis rise to power, the Holocaust, and the war's various military campaigns. Still others were intent on deconstructing Nazism and understanding how it fit into a broader academic paradigm that explained the rise of totalitarianism in the middle decades of the twentieth century. However, no one had attempted to write the book Shirer envisioned: a complete history of Nazi Germany.

Shirer's agent, Paul Reynolds, set about pitching the project to publishers in hopes of securing the $10,000 advance Shirer felt he would need to pay his bills while he worked on the manuscript. Shirer was frustrated to find that, at first, there was zero interest in his proposal. However, Shirer's persistence finally paid off. Simon & Schuster agreed to ante up the requested advance, in large measure because of Shirer's friendship with Joe Barnes, who was now one of the company's senior editors. Harvard educated, left-leaning politically – and therefore, like Shirer, politically suspect in the postwar era – Barnes had been the *New York Herald Tribune*'s Moscow (and later Berlin) correspondent in the 1930s. After serving as a speechwriter for 1940 Republican presidential candidate Wendell Willkie, Barnes worked as a newspaper editor before "the rising tide of McCarthyism washed him up [in the late 1940s] in a small office at Simon & Schuster, with a part-time secretary he shared with another editor," as his then-colleague Michael Korda later recalled, explaining that book publishing did not seem important enough to draw the attention of anti-communist zealots.[4]

Under the terms of the contract Shirer signed with Simon & Schuster in mid-April 1956, he was to collect $1,000 per month for each of the next ten months – although after his agent took a 10 percent fee, Shirer netted only $900 each month. Still, he hoped that would be enough to meet basic living expenses and buy him enough time to write his book on the Third Reich. However, when he plunged into the preliminary research that summer he was dismayed to realize that the project was far bigger and more involved than anything he had ever done, let alone envisioned.

The volume of available material, already problematic, was growing at a dizzying pace. After the Nuremberg Trials, the Allies had published a forty-two-volume set of books called *Trial of the Major War Criminals*. These weighty tomes contained the verbatim testimony from the courtroom and supporting documents that prosecutors had entered into the official record. In addition, the Allies made available another ten volumes titled *Nazi Conspiracy and Aggression*,[5] which included additional documents, affidavits, and the transcripts of pre-trial interrogations of many Nazis leaders. This material – like almost all of what was found in the court records – was in German and was unindexed. This was also the case with most of the other documentation collected by the Library of Congress in Washington.

Shirer might never have succeeded in sifting through this mountain of information had he not met Dr Fritz T. Epstein, a fifty-seven-year-old German-born, German-educated scholar who worked in the Library of Congress's Slavic and Central European Division. Epstein, an expert on the Soviet Union, had fled Nazi persecution, immigrating to the United States in 1936. Following a teaching stint at Harvard, he joined the State Department during the war, and afterward spent three years at Stanford University before joining the staff at the Library of Congress in 1951. Like Shirer, Epstein was intent on unlocking the dark secrets of Hitler's Germany. For that reason, he had made it his business to familiarize himself with the contents of the Library's holdings of Nazi documents and papers. Epstein was delighted to be Shirer's guide as he sifted through all the historical records. This was only the jumping-off point in terms of the necessary research.

In addition to the records of the Nuremberg trial, the United States Army had collected a huge number of uncatalogued documents, all which were warehoused in Alexandria, Virginia. Two army photographers charged with the task of copying this huge mass of information had poked through the storage crates, as had a few curious academics; however, no one had done this in any systematic way. Being the first to do so, Shirer was surprised and sometimes astounded at what he found: "One day a group of the ranking librarians at the Library of Congress, obviously pleased that someone was interested in their unique holdings, trundled out a whole [library cart] full of Hitler's personal papers. I was astonished that they had not been opened since being catalogued. We took to untying the ribbons that bound them. Out fell what to me were priceless objects: among others, scores of drawings and paintings that Hitler had done in his vagabond youth in Vienna."[6]

In addition to the treasure trove of captured German war documents available in the Washington area, Shirer found repositories of information at venues around the country. For example, the Hoover Library and Archives at Stanford University had a cache of papers from the files of Gestapo head Heinrich Himmler. In New York, the Public Library and the

Council on Foreign Relations had amassed extensive collections of captured Nazi documents. So, too, had individuals such as Brigadier General Telford Taylor, one of the Allied prosecutors at Nuremberg. Shirer gained access to much of this material and more. He also sought out individuals who could answer his specific questions and help him understand the archival material he was reviewing. Having lived in Nazi Germany for seven years – two of them when the country was at war – Shirer still had many contacts in Berlin. He knew whom to approach for bits of information he needed to help him piece together the at-times puzzling events and the strategic decisions that had dictated the course of the conflict. One such person was General Franz Halder, the chief of the General Staff of the Supreme High Command of the German Army from August 1939 to September 1942.

Halder, a Roman Catholic and an aristocrat, had never been a Hitler supporter. In fact, had the Nazi dictator known the general was involved in a plot to topple him on the eve of the war, Halder surely would have been killed, as were so many other dissenters. Shirer wrote to Halder asking for his help in solving one of the war's greatest military mysteries: why had Hitler ordered the German Army on 24 May 1940 to halt its westward advance on Dunkirk when the Allied armies were surrounded with their backs to the sea? In all probability, the German military could have delivered a knockout blow, yet they had looked on as British and French troops were evacuated from the Dunkirk to live and fight another day.

According to Halder, there were two reasons the German advance had been halted. One was the political infighting in the upper echelons of the Nazi regime. The other was Hitler's own bizarre priorities; he still believed that he could come to an accommodation with the British. Halder had recorded in his diary his impressions and the details of his daily activities in this period. He gave Shirer access to this material, and the general later defended him against German critics who accused Shirer of distorting the truth and of being "anti-German."[7]

Gaining access to Halder's journals was not Shirer's only coup. He managed to locate journals kept by some other key figures in the Third Reich, including Propaganda Minister Joseph Goebbels, Finance Minister Count Schwerin von Krosigk, and General Alfred Jodl, Chief of the Operations Staff of the High Command of the Armed Forces (OKW). Because the Nazis were such meticulous record keepers, a wealth of sundry documentary evidence fell into Allied hands at war's end – the German Naval Archives, for example, as well as records kept by the OKW and the Naval High Command, and even Hitler's calendar book, which a sharp-eyed American soldier plucked from the ruins of the Nazi dictator's Berlin bunker. Shirer reviewed all these sources and thousands more pages of diverse records, everything from the transcripts of telephone conversations between Hitler and his underlings to documents that laid out plans for the death camps and the Nazis' "Final Solution to the Jewish problem."

William Shirer's biggest problem in chronicling the true history of the Third Reich was not a shortage of information, but rather the sheer volume of material available to him. Compounding his difficulties was the fact he had to struggle not to get sidetracked in the arcane details of his research: "Reading the captured documents showed how little we – the correspondents and diplomats – really knew about what went on [in Hitler's Germany] ... I lived with [the Nazis] for seven ... years, but when you read over the papers, you change your ideas. They were both more evil and more intelligent than we [ever] realized."[8]

The sheer volume of information that Shirer was trying to understand and process was daunting, almost to the point of being overwhelming, as was the nature of what he was learning. Having lived and worked in Nazi Germany, Shirer found it utterly fascinating to read primary documents that cast new light on events that had long puzzled him or that he had not known about at all. At times, what Shirer discovered was eye-opening. Other times, it was utterly depressing. That was especially so with the nightmarish details of Hitler's planned "New Order for Europe" and his "Final Solution" for dealing with Jewish people.

In summer 1956, Shirer settled down to begin writing in the studio he had set up in the old barn at his farm. His typical workday commenced at 9 a.m. and ran until 3 p.m. He would then stop for a late lunch and clear his mind by working in his garden or listening to classical music. Each evening after dinner, he returned to his typewriter for several more hours of work.

When the weather turned cool in the autumn, Shirer retreated to the family's apartment in New York. There he continued working apace, maintaining the same exhausting schedule he followed in summer. Regardless of where he worked, Shirer tried to stick to his goal of writing at least a thousand words each day. That was easier said than done. Notwithstanding the fact that the flow of historical events dictated the chronology of his narrative, Shirer constantly found himself considering new revelations, each of which necessitated that he spend precious hours revising or rewriting chapters he thought he had completed. Despite this, by September 1957 Shirer had about 150,000 words on paper – more than 600 pages of manuscript. The book was taking on a life of its own, and this had given rise to some pressing concerns.

Shirer found himself plagued by self-doubts. He wondered if any of what he had written was any good or interesting. Would readers find it relevant? In hopes of getting answers to those questions, Shirer sent what he had written so far to Joe Barnes, the book's editor. Shirer knew that Barnes, who was both knowledgeable and blunt-talking, would not soften his criticisms just because he and Shirer were old friends. Barnes, "tall, well-dressed, debonair, and deeply dignified,"[9] sat in his office each day chain-smoking as he pored over the incomplete draft manuscript. Quietly excited by what he read, he said as much in his memos to publisher Max Schuster: "I'm more enthusiastic about this book than anything I've read in a long time."[10]

Buoyed by Barnes's encouraging words, Shirer pressed ahead with renewed vigor. Six months later, he had 800 pages of manuscript but estimated that the book was still only half done. By now, some of the editors at Simon & Schuster doubted that Shirer would ever finish, and so they urged Max Schuster to cancel the contract. That he did not do so was only because Barnes continued to insist that Shirer's book was going to be "an extraordinary and unorthodox combination of personal reportage and scholarship."[11]

Shirer was heartened by Barnes's faith in him, but he was plagued by a new concern: although he was putting in fourteen-hour work days, his researching and writing were taking far longer than he had ever expected or could afford. By mid-1957, the advance money from Simon & Schuster was gone. With his popularity as a lecturer fading – how many times could he deliver the same talk? – Shirer again was struggling to make ends meet. Tess, still smarting from her husband's infidelity, refused to look for a job, and the Shirers' household bills continued to pile up, especially with two daughters still in school. By now, Inga was a junior at Radcliffe College, after having graduated from the Dalton School in New York, the private school at which Linda was now in her senior year.

Fortunately for Shirer, the paranoia of the McCarthy era was finally beginning to fade, and the Shirer name was no longer anathema to *all* magazine editors. Paul Reynolds, Shirer's agent, managed to sell a couple of his articles for $3,000. While that money provided Shirer with temporary respite, his desperation grew as his bank balance continued to shrink. With Simon & Schuster refusing to provide any more advance money, Shirer began casting around for another $10,000. He got nowhere with the applications he submitted to large foundations or the various organizations that provided grants to needy writers – save for one unexpected, bizarre offer that came from the Ford Foundation. Shirer's contact, a former *New York Times* editor named Shepard Stone, who was now the foundation's director of International Affairs, suggested they might be willing to provide $1 million to bankroll an ambitious academic research project; Shirer would lead it, heading a team of academics. But Shirer, who never fancied himself to be a professional historian, much less as a scholar, rejected the idea. Instead, he turned his attentions once more to the national magazines in hopes of selling more articles. Again, his efforts mostly came to naught; the conservative-minded editors of mass-circulation publications such as *The Saturday Evening Post*, *Life*, and *Reader's Digest* remained unwilling to do business with him.

Shirer's mood spiraled ever downward; he realized that soon he would have to stop work on the Nazi book and go back to paid work full-time, *if* he could find a job. Shirer floated the suggestion that he could serve as foreign editor for the liberal journal *The Nation*; he also proposed to Joe Barnes that the two of them start a publishing house that would specialize in bringing the works of British and European writers to American readers – as Blanche Knopf had done in the late 1930s.

Neither idea came to anything, nor did the prospects of jobs for Shirer with the Mutual radio network or with *Foreign Affairs* magazine. However, when word got around that Shirer was in dire straits financially and might be forced to abandon work on his book, Hamilton Fish Armstrong, the editor of *Foreign Affairs*, advised Shirer to approach a man named Frank Altschul for grant support. Altschul, a wealthy Wall Street investment broker and philanthropist, was a key member of the Council on Foreign Relations, the organization that published the journal *Foreign Affairs*. He also operated a family trust called the Overbrook Foundation. On Armstrong's recommendation, and after listening to Shirer's pitch for funding, Altschul agreed to grant him $5,000 immediately; he would receive a like sum six months later, in early 1959, if he could show that he had made progress on his manuscript. "This saved my life and my book," a grateful Shirer later wrote.[12]

Freed now from his most pressing money worries, Shirer plunged into the writing of his manuscript with a renewed sense of urgency. He worked every day for as many hours as he could endure. So preoccupied with the effort was he that for one of the few times in his life he abandoned his routine of making daily entries in his journal; only later did he realize this. If not for a 31 August letter to his old friend Kay Boyle, the author-poet he had known since Paris in the 1920s, Shirer would have had no written record of finishing *The Rise and Fall of the Third Reich*. He reported to Boyle that this had happened on the evening of 24 August 1959. After five years of work, he finally typed the words "The End" on the last page of his manuscript, page 1,795. That done, he sent daughters Inga and Linda to a nearby liquor store for a bottle of celebratory champagne.

Shirer was exhausted, but exhilarated. He felt as if a monumental weight had been lifted off his shoulders. He also felt an incredible sense of accomplishment. *The Rise and Fall of the Third Reich* would stand the test of time to become one of the definitive books of its era and something of a trailblazer. It was one of the first books of popular history to reach a mass audience and helped pave the way for such authors as Barbara Tuchman, John Toland, Stephen Ambrose, Erik Larson, Simon Winchester, and David McCullough in the United States, Andrew Marr in the United Kingdom, and Pierre Berton in Canada, all of whom popularized the genre and made it not only respectable but also lucrative.

At the time, no one – not Joe Barnes, Max Schuster, or even William Shirer – had any inkling of how successful *The Rise and Fall of the Third Reich* could be. The original plan called for a press run of 5,000 copies for *Hitler's Nightmare Empire: The Rise and Fall of the Third Reich*, as the book was originally titled. The dustjacket artwork featuring that title spelled out in "spiky letters of barbed wire"[13] was originally to be included in Simon & Schuster's spring 1960 catalogue. However, those plans changed abruptly when Joe Barnes convinced Schuster that Shirer's book was something special. An astute Simon & Schuster staffer named Nina Bourne (who went on to become a legendary figure in the American publishing industry) suggested the book's title be shorted to *The Rise and Fall of the Third Reich*, which was the very title that Shirer himself had come up with in 1954. Despite a "volcanic eruption" by Frank Metz, Simon & Schuster's art director,[14] the original cover artwork was scrapped. Metz then begrudgingly devised a new dustjacket, solid black with a Nazi swastika in a white circle and the title and author's name in muted gold. That design, stark, provocative, and eye-catching, became iconic in the history of book publishing.

Initially, not everyone appreciated the genius of Metz's work, and many booksellers balked at displaying the book. The swastika was imbued, as it still is, with a powerful symbolism. Publication and sales of *The Rise and Fall of the Third Reich* went ahead only because Max Schuster insisted and refused to accept the dictates of retailers. This proved to be an astute business decision.

In good part, the success of *The Rise and Fall of the Third Reich* is attributable to the fact its author was *not* a professional historian. William Shirer was a journalist who chanced to be in a unique position to write a history of the Nazi regime, with personal knowledge of many of the relevant events and personalities. Likewise, no other non-German had the depth of understanding, the necessary journalistic and linguistic skills, or the dogged determination to craft a work that was as readable or as authoritative. Sensing as much, Shirer opined in conversations with family and friends that the book was the best thing he had ever written: "I thought it might interest a lot of people not only because of its revelations based on the secret documents, but also because of the way I tried to write it: history as literature, not cut-and-dried history as so many academics wrote."[15]

Despite this, Shirer harbored doubts his book would sell. He feared it was too weighty, too serious for the average reader; at the time, only academics read books with footnotes. London-based publisher Secker and Warburg knew this; however, the company's marketing people thought Shirer's book *might* appeal to some readers in the United Kingdom, and so they purchased the British rights for a mere $5,000.

Gardiner ("Mike") Cowles, Jr, the owner-publisher of *Look* magazine, also surmised that Shirer's book might be of interest to his readers. *Look*, a bi-weekly, large-format magazine, competed with industry leader *Life* by appealing to the same broad demographic – everyone from business executives to factory workers, males and females, young and old alike. When the first issue of *Look* hit newsstands in 1937, its per-issue circulation was about 700,000. By 1960, *Look* was still number two to *Life*, but the circulation of Cowles's magazine had grown to four million copies per issue; Americans were still buying and enjoying picture magazines. Cowles knew his market, and his suspicions about potential reader interest in *The Rise and Fall of the Third Reich* were borne out when *Look* offered an excerpt from the book as the cover story for its 1 September 1959 issue. To the surprise of many people – and to Shirer's delight – *Look* outsold that week's competing issue of *Life*, which featured a cover photo of a pretty girl in a bathing suit. Cowles, urged on by Max Schuster, invited Shirer to write a 25,000-word article on the life of Adolf Hitler based on material from his new book. Cowles also agreed to publish a series of three more 5,000-word excerpts, with an option for a fourth installment. The fee for each of these articles was a dollar per word – $5,000. Shirer was ecstatic; he needed the ego boost almost as much as he needed the money.

Given that his new book was more than 1,200 pages and included end-notes – thirty-five pages of them, plus another ten pages of bibliographi-cal citations – Shirer worried its ten-dollar cover price would limit sales. (This was before the age of mass-market paperbacks. When the first such "pocketbooks" – most of which were reprints – appeared in the 1940s, they proved popular with millions of American GIs serving overseas. However, because these inexpensive editions typically sold for a dollar each, publishers regarded them as a threat to sales of pricier hardcover edi-tions, which retailed for as much as five dollars each.)

Shirer was no less apprehensive about possible negative critical reaction to his book; his experiences in recent years suggested his fears were well-founded. Indeed, when Simon & Schuster sent Oxford University histori-an A.J.P. Taylor the proofs for *The Rise and Fall of the Third Reich* in the hope he would offer an endorsement to appear on the cover, Taylor replied with a testy note. He praised Shirer's industry and initiative but chided the author for his wordiness, faulting Simon & Schuster for opt-ing to publish such a hefty tome. America, Taylor observed, was an "out-sized nation," and so the book's size was "all right for you." Reflecting on this snub many years later, Shirer could not resist pointing out that Tay-lor's own book, *English History, 1914–1945*, published merely five years after *The Rise and Fall of the Third Reich*, weighed in at 708 pages.[16] Taylor had a reputation among American historians for being demanding and at times cantankerous. That, and Shirer's nationality, perhaps explains his antipathy to the Shirer book. The fact he was a journalist and not a pro-fessional historian, only compounded Shirer's perceived sins. These extra-neous factors aside, Taylor was not the only reviewer who would take issue with aspects of Shirer's book.

For all concerned – and no one more than the author – there was a lot riding on the commercial success of *The Rise and Fall of the Third Reich*. Shirer's efforts to stir advance interest in the book had caused tempers to grow short and misunderstandings to flare at Simon & Schuster. Joe Barnes and Shirer got into a shouting match one day while socializing at the Shirers' farm. The disagreement grew so loud that the men almost came to blows. Barnes accused Shirer of disloyalty for having sold those book excerpts to *Look* magazine, a move the editor saw as being a short-sighted cash grab that would hurt book sales; Barnes was unaware the idea for the excerpts was Max Schuster's. The incident provides telling insight into the depths of the confusion and uncertainties surrounding publica-tion of *The Rise and Fall of the Third Reich*. Even Schuster was quietly hedg-ing his bets.

The publisher had revised his plans and opted for an initial press run of 20,000. Nonetheless Shirer was disappointed; he had hoped for a much larger number. Adding insult to injury for him was the revelation that the publisher had sent 7,500 books to Secker and Warburg for sale in the United Kingdom. This left only 12,500 copies for distribution in the United States.

Shirer dreaded the prospect of yet another failure, especially a book in which he had invested so much time, effort, and emotional capital. Once more, he faced an uncertain future. Once more, he was grappling with the humbling realization that he might have to seek full-time work. Shirer was contemplating a possible return to broadcasting if anyone would hire him. Radio was dying, and Shirer had to concede that he was ill-suited for a switch to television. For all his expertise, public profile, and on-air experience, the truth was that he was not the kind of pretty face that is tailor-made for television. At age fifty-six, Shirer was bespectacled and soft-spoken; his waistline was growing as his hairline receded. Then, as now, television was more about style and appearance than about substance.

If not a return to broadcasting, then what? Many years before, Shirer had been scornful of the idea of returning to school to earn a graduate degree and then working in academia. Now he hoped that his varied experience and his celebrity might be enough to help him land a job teaching journalism. That held little appeal for him, but he knew his options were limited, and he was in dire need of a job. The prospect of starting over again was as worrisome as it was problematic and embarrassing, even if he was broke and struggling to make ends meet. In addition to their household bills, the Shirers faced several unexpected expenses. For one, Inga had become engaged to a Harvard law graduate named Timothy Dyk. With the wedding set for the third week of June 1960, the Shirers needed money to pay for it. At the same time, after two years of trying, Shirer still could not afford to repair or replace the furnace at the farmhouse in Connecticut; any winter visit there was an arctic adventure.

Seeking time alone to consider his options and clear his head, Shirer packed his warm clothing and retreated to the farm the last week of March. There he spent seven days in chilly solitude, puttering around the property, readying the garden for planting and contemplating his options. Given his uncertain future, he was feeling his age. His sister Josephine, four years his senior, had announced her retirement that spring after a twenty-eight-year career teaching high school English in New Jersey. Unlike her brother Bill, after graduating from Coe College and teaching in Cedar Rapids for a few years, "Josie" had gone on to further her education, earning a Master of Arts degree at Columbia University in New York in 1932. "Surely there can have been no more important job in our time and in our society than teaching in a public school," Shirer praised in a letter to his sister.[17]

Shirer was still in a reflective mood on Friday morning as he packed for his return to the city. However, his preparations were interrupted by a telephone call from Joe Barnes, who had good news to share: The Book of the Month Club (BOMC) had just announced that *The Rise and Fall of the Third Reich* would be a "featured selection" for November 1960. The logistics of this meant that the book's release date would be pushed back to autumn and the BOMC edition would retail for just $5.99, but the delay would be more than worthwhile. Shirer was guaranteed a $20,000-dollar advance and sales of his book would benefit from the publicity and the marketing push the BOMC was planning. All of this seemed almost too good to be true, and because it was April Fool's Day, he suspected Barnes was being mischievous.

Shirer insisted on confirming the BOMC details, telephoning his agent as well as his good friend Irita Van Doren, the editor of the *New York Herald Tribune*'s Sunday book section, who both reassured him. In a heartbeat, Shirer's financial woes were behind him. For now, at least, he felt as if sunshine had at long last broken through the clouds of despair that had hung over him for most of the previous fourteen years. His three-hour drive home on this day seemed incomparably shorter than usual. Back in the city, he made his way to meet with a group of friends who had gathered for celebratory drinks.[18]

Despite the sudden reversal of his fortunes and the fact that in his heart he felt *The Rise and Fall of the Third Reich* was the best work he had ever done, Shirer remained guarded in his hopes for the book's success. These concerns were well-founded since his recent books had not sold well despite receiving some favorable reviews. The nub of it was that because he was no longer on network radio or writing for national magazines, Shirer was in danger of being forgotten. A mention of Shirer in the "Where Are They Now?" column in the back pages of a November 1957 edition of *Newsweek* magazine had underscored his fears in that regard. The article reported that, "William L. Shirer, made famous by his nightly radio reports from Berlin during the early years of the war and by his book *Berlin Diary*, has been off the air nearly ten years and is now a writer and part-time lecturer." The *Newsweek* writer had gone on to add that Shirer was "working on a book."[19] Those latter words had stung. "Wasn't that what the press usually said about someone consigned to oblivion? ... That he 'was working on a book'? A sort of face-saving expression for those [who were] considered 'finished'?"[20]

If any further evidence of Shirer's slide into obscurity was needed, it could be found in the fact *The New York Times Book Review*, one of the most influential publications in the world of American letters, had not even bothered to review his last two books. To Shirer, this was problematic. There was an undeniable element of vanity involved here, but his concerns were also pragmatic. He understood the effect that reviews could have on book sales. Thus, he hoped *The Rise and Fall of the Third Reich* would be well received, even if the odds were against it. Shirer could only wait and hope that readers would judge his latest book on its merits and not by its bulk or price.

The editor of *The Times* books pages asked the eminent Oxford University historian H.R. Trevor-Roper to review *The Rise and Fall of the Third Reich*.[21] The fact that Trevor-Roper's colleague A.J.P. Taylor had reacted negatively when Max Schuster had sent him a proof of the book raised a red flag in Shirer's mind. So, too, did the commonly held perception in the United States at the time that British academics were biased against the work of American authors. Shirer feared that he was in for a rough ride. However, he was pleasantly surprised by Trevor-Roper's assessment of *The Rise and Fall of the Third Reich*. While he criticized aspects of the book, Trevor-Roper wrote that here was "a splendid work of scholarship, objective in method, sound in judgment, [and] inescapable in its conclusions ... Not that Mr Shirer states his conclusions; he leaves them to be deduced."[22]

Trevor-Roper's critical assessment of *The Rise and Fall of the Third Reich* was one of the first and one of the most high-profile. To Shirer's delight, it proved to be a harbinger of many of the reviews to come. Alan Bullock, another prominent and highly respected British academic and Hitler biographer, followed Trevor-Roper's lead a few weeks later when he weighed in with a similarly favorable opinion in *The Guardian*. Bullock noted that "Mr Shirer has hardly drawn on a single source or employed a quotation which is not already familiar to him ... Nor is there anything original in the story he has to tell." Given the depth of Shirer's research and his reliance on primary documents, that was a stunning allegation. However, any slight that Shirer felt was soothed when Bullock continued, "Neither Mr Shirer nor the reader has any reason to regret ... the hard work he put into writing [this book]. There are a dozen books on Nazi Germany which I should rate higher as historical studies of particular aspects, but I can think of none which I would rather put in the hands of anyone who wanted to find out what happened in Germany between 1930 and 1945, and why the history of those years should not be forgotten."[23]

Many of the reviews of *The Rise and Fall of the Third Reich* that appeared in newspapers and mainstream magazines in America were equally laudatory. For example, Nuremberg prosecutor Telford Taylor wrote in the *Saturday Review*: "The level of factual accuracy is high ... Mr Shirer is a journalist, and his book carries the marks of his profession at its best ... The style throughout is simple and direct and despite the necessary bulk, the book is immensely readable from cover to cover."[24] Such an assessment, coming from such an important source, was heady praise for Shirer. So, too, was the surprising review that appeared in the 16 October edition of the *Chicago Tribune*, his former employer.

Colonel Robert McCormick, the newspaper's irascible owner and Shirer's longtime nemesis, had died five years earlier, on 1 April 1955, and the old antagonisms evidently had been laid to rest with him. The *Tribune* devoted page 1 of its Sunday book section to a review of *The Rise and Fall of the Third Reich*. Professor S. William Halperin, the editor of the *Journal of Modern History*, praised Shirer's erudition as being "impressive without being obtrusive." Halperin went on to laud Shirer's psychological insights as being "superb" and his "descriptions of situations and events [as being] among the finest in contemporary reportorial writing." Halperin concluded, "For those reasons *The Rise and Fall of the Third Reich* may be regarded as the crowning achievement of Shirer's distinguished career."[25]

While Shirer balked at any notion that his career was over, he was otherwise pleased with Halperin's review. For him, it provided a measure of closure on an angry, unhappy chapter in his life. He derived no small measure of satisfaction at having outlasted his nemesis, Colonel McCormick. Shirer was no less proud of having been strong enough to refuse to accept defeat when so many others who had been blacklisted in the 1950s had given in or given up. Even so, there was no danger of Shirer becoming smug or taking himself too seriously. *The Rise and Fall of the Third Reich* also drew negative reviews.

A prime example was Princeton University historian Gordon A. Craig's assessment, which appeared in the *Herald Tribune*. Craig, who had written extensively on Germany history, praised Shirer for returning "at last to a subject that made him famous" (namely, Nazi Germany) and for crafting an immensely readable book.[26] However, the historian went on to question Shirer's decision to focus on the Second World War rather than on the Nazi Party's formative years, prior to Hitler's 1933 rise to power. Craig also charged that Shirer had "concentrated on those aspects of Nazi history that have been most written about and skipped over the periods about which it is time history had something new and fresh to say."[27]

Craig's review stung Shirer less because of what the professor had to say than because he voiced his opinions in a publication that was edited by Irita Van Doren, who sent Shirer an apologetic note. Meanwhile, novelist Kay Boyle sprang to Shirer's defense in a contrary review for the *New York Post*. Boyle offered a laudatory assessment of the book and took Craig to task for what she termed his "patronizing attitude."[28]

The review of *The Rise and Fall of the Third Reich* that was published in *Time* served to remind Shirer that to some media people he was still a pariah. The anonymous writer dismissed Shirer as a writer of "only modest writing gifts" whereas the person needed to write the history of Nazi Germany was "another Dante or a new Wagner." The *Time* reviewer went on to describe Shirer's book as a "breezy journalistic surrogate for many better books on specialized aspects of Nazism."[29] This was essentially the same comment Trevor-Roper had made, only the professor had made it in a more eloquent and reasoned manner and had extolled Shirer's book for being, essentially, more than the sum of its parts, and therefore unique. As Shirer himself later pointed out, the writer of the *Time* review failed to elaborate on his criticism or to offer the titles of any of the "better books" to which he alluded.

Craig's comments and those advanced in *Time* were typical of the bad notices for *The Rise and Fall of the Third Reich*. Just as Shirer had feared, some professional historians found much in the book to criticize. So, too, did readers in West Germany. As historian-author Ron Rosenbaum notes, at that time "[r]eminders of Germany's recent past were not welcome, especially if they emphasized some kind of malevolent Germanness."[30]

Sales of *The Rise and Fall of the Third Reich* in North America exceeded all expectations. In the first year after publication, Simon & Schuster sold the initial allotment of 12,500 copies and then went through thirteen more printings.[31] Boosted by some highly positive reviews, word-of-mouth advertising, and an unprecedented demand from BOMC members, *The Rise and Fall of the Third Reich* jumped onto the national bestseller lists, where it remained into early winter 1961. During this period, about a million copies of the book were sold in the United States alone – two-thirds of them to BOMC subscribers.[32] An illustrated coffee-table edition based on the text of a three-part *Reader's Digest* abridgment (published in March, April, and May 1961) added thousands of books to the total sales. The book remains in print and in the public consciousness; American readers have bought an estimated ten million copies of *The Rise and Fall of the Third Reich*. In a 2010 episode of the Fox television series *The Simpsons*, Lisa has a nightmare about Nazis after reading a copy. When Simon & Schuster published a special fiftieth-anniversary edition in 2011, the book attracted a whole new generation of readers. Its influence has extended far beyond the English-speaking world, with translations into German, French, Chinese, and Russian.

In February 1961, *The Rise and Fall of the Third Reich* book won the Carey-Thomas Award, a prestigious publishing industry honor,[33] and the following month Shirer garnered a National Book Award.[34] It is worth noting that one of the members of the judging panel for this latter honor was Virgilia Peterson. This is not to suggest that Peterson had a hand in Shirer winning the award, only to note that she knew how much effort Shirer had put into writing *The Rise and Fall of the Third Reich*.

The book's unprecedented success as a work of popular history inevitably attracted the attention of academic historians; as Fairfield University professor Gavriel Rosenfeld notes, "*The Rise and Fall of the Third Reich* has become more than just another work of history. A singular literary institution, it has acquired a reputation as 'the best-selling historical work ever written in modern times.'"[35]

Some professional historians praised Shirer's book for its scholarship and for the author's narrative skills, but others questioned his methodology and conclusions: "Strongly influenced by the so-called 'Luther to Hitler' view of German history," Rosenfeld writes in an insightful 1994 article published in the *Journal of Contemporary History*, "Shirer's book was based on the simple, yet controversial postulate that 'nazism and the Third Reich ... were but a logical continuation of German history.'"[36]

This notion of a "special path" – a *Sonderweg* – was a commonly held view in American academic circles at the time. In noting this, Rosenfeld points out that many of the reviewers who were critical of Shirer's book had come to it with "expectations shaped by a different historiographical paradigm – one which explained nazism under the broader phenomenon of totalitarianism."[37] At the same time, Rosenfeld explains, that paradigm was influenced and shaped by Cold War geopolitical realities. The rivalry between the United States and the Soviet Union was intense – the Cuban missile crisis in summer 1962 brought the world to the brink of nuclear war – and relations between the Kennedy administration in Washington and the West German government were frosty. The upshot of all this was that some of America's most influential academic journals had not even bothered to review *The Rise and Fall of the Third Reich*. Those that had tended to be biased to the point of being hostile. Brown University historian Klaus Epstein's review, which appeared in the April 1961 edition of *The Review of Politics*, was typical.

Epstein downplays the value of Shirer's primary research and insights, dismissing *The Rise and Fall of the Third Reich* as being fatally flawed owing to the author's failure "to describe, or adequately comprehend, the nature of a modern totalitarian state."[38] That was really the essence of it: Shirer had failed to make mention of – much less discuss – political scientist Hannah Arendt's seminal book *The Origins of Totalitarianism*, a work that has exerted a profound and lasting influence over academic thought, particularly during this period. The key question was this: was Nazism a uniquely German movement, or can it best be understood in a broader context, as part of Zeitgeist of the 1930s?

University of Oregon historian William O. Shanahan picks up on that theme in a review for the October 1962 edition of *The American Historical Review*, a full year after Shirer's book was published.[39] Shanahan hails *The Rise and Fall of the Third Reich* as a "literary *tour de force*," but he then proceeds to dismiss the book as trivial and "woefully inadequate" as a work of history. By failing to answer the basic question "What is Nazism," Shanahan argues, Shirer had written a work that failed to rise "above the most commonplace level of understanding."[40]

Other American academics piled on, offering similar criticisms of *The Rise and Fall of the Third Reich*. From the perspective of the professional historian, it is true that in terms of historical analysis Shirer's writing came up short. However, the reality is that he did not set out to write an analytical study of Hitler and the Nazis. Rather, he approached his task as a journalist, focusing on personalities – in this case Hitler and his henchmen – and on the dramatic events of the Nazi era, of which there was no shortage. Readability was crucial to Shirer and to his book's commercial viability: "I had wanted, within my limitations, to write narrative history as literature … and I hoped I had succeeded to some extent."[41]

Shirer intended his book as a cautionary tale on the dangers of underestimating the threat of German militarism and evil; he was convinced it still had not been extinguished, even after two devastating world wars. He insisted – and not without reason – that Germans continued to delude themselves by denying the self-incriminating truths of the Nazi years. Now that Germany was being rebuilt and was on the road to economic recovery, at least in those areas under Allied occupation, Shirer feared "the Germans would do it again" if only they were not terrified of a war in which they did not possess nuclear weapons. This was a warning Shirer reiterated in lectures, media interviews, and his writings.[42] He also inflamed passions with a 1961 article for *Look*. "If Hitler Had Won the War"[43] was part of a speculative series the magazine featured.

Shirer drew upon his personal experiences as well as primary documents he had read during the course of his book research. While the scenario he painted was mere opinion, many readers found his words unsettling and even objectionable. Shirer maintained that because Hitler had had only contempt for President Roosevelt, the Nazi dictator would not have hesitated to attack America if there had been an opportunity to do so. If it had, and if German troops and the SS had reached American soil, Shirer opined they would have set to work enslaving and slaughtering Americans just as they had Poles and Slavs.[44]

This was strong stuff, meant to be provocative, and it succeeded. The *Look* article, like *The Rise and Fall of the Third Reich*, stirred up raucous debate. Despite the evils of the Third Reich and all of the blood that had been shed during the war, there were still people in the Pentagon and the American intelligence community who felt the Allies should have cooperated with the German military in spring 1945 to hold back the Red Army's westward advance. There were influential voices in Washington at the time who favored the idea of offering safe haven to German intelligence officers and scientists, who were to become instrumental in helping to develop America's missile and space programs. Wernher von Braun, the head of Germany's missile program, was the most high-profile figure among this group.

The full story of American involvement in shielding select ex-Nazis and Nazi sympathizers from prosecution remains to be told. A November 2010 report in *The New York Times* revealed the existence of a draft 600-page secret United States government document, written in 2006, that chronicles how successive administrations provided refuge to suspected Nazi war criminals for strategic reasons.[45] This is worth mentioning in any discussion of William Shirer's postwar writings since it provides insight into some of the imperatives that were at play in the early 1960s and that colored public reaction to some of the themes in his work. In keeping with the tenor of the times, conservatives and pro-German elements in America regarded any criticism of Germany as being pro-Soviet. Shirer – still suspect in some people's eyes as a communist dupe or sympathizer – became a target of their vitriol. For example, in reviewing *The Rise and Fall of the Third Reich*, a writer for the journal *The American-German Review* denounced Shirer for his "one-sided style of history" and charged that many of his journalistic sources in Germany had been left-leaning or communists.[46] Similarly, a book reviewer for the conservative journal *Modern Age* elaborated that the logical conclusion of Shirer's line of reasoning was that all Germans were inherently bad, and so the West should refrain from allowing Germany to rearm.[47]

Predictably, nowhere was the negative reception for *The Rise and Fall of the Third Reich* louder or more strident than in West Germany. Both the media and the government expressed outrage and attacked Shirer for being "anti-German," which Professor Rosenfeld documents in the afore-mentioned *Journal of Contemporary History* article.

Interestingly, a German-language edition of *The Rise and Fall of the Third Reich*[48] was published in October 1961. Despite the many negative reviews that appeared in big-city newspapers, the book sold briskly, climbing as high as number 5 on the top ten bestseller list. (Lawsuits filed against Shirer by neo-Nazi groups doubtless helped to heighten the book's profile and piqued people's curiosity.) Much of the media criticism of Shirer was based on an insistence that he was neither qualified to write about German history, nor was he an objective observer: "I was struck by the fact that the outbursts against the book and me seemed to be of one piece, as if orchestrated and directed from some center. All the criticisms resembled each other."[49]

There was a reason for this. The West German government was acutely aware of and sensitive to American public opinion. Thus, the government of Chancellor Konrad Adenauer did all it could to stir up resentment against *The Rise and Fall of the Third Reich* and its author as being "anti-German." Media reports in West German newspapers fanned the flames of outrage. In reviewing *The Rise and Fall of the Third Reich*, a writer for *Die Zeit* of Hamburg accused Shirer of "oversimplifying history" and of being guilty of telling "half-truths,"[50] while the New York correspondent of the *Frankfurter Allgemeine Zeitung* wrote a lengthy article chronicling what she reported was a growing "anti-German feeling" in the United States; Shirer was singled out as being one of the main culprits in this regard.[51] Sciz-ing on this, the Adenauer government's media relations people circulated quotations from negative German reviews of the book, and the Chancellor himself denounced it in media interviews and in his conversations with influential Americans. *Look* publisher Mike Cowles told Shirer that, on a visit to New York City, the West German Chancellor invited Cowles to his hotel for a chat. Adenauer then chided his guest for publishing excerpts from *The Rise and Fall of the Third Reich* and the "If Hitler Had Won the War" article. When Cowles volunteered to print a retraction if

Adenauer could prove that any of Shirer's writing was untrue, the Chancellor reportedly explained, "The point is not whether it's truthful or not. The point is that it is turning out to be extremely harmful to German-American relations. It is stirring up in America hatred of the Germans."[52]

When reporters asked Shirer to respond to the German criticisms, Shirer said he preferred to let his work "speak for itself."[53] He also surmised that any controversy about his book would only help sales, and the royalty income that came rolling in helped to erase the pain and the humiliation of the long years during which he had been unemployed and unemployable.

In the circumstances, the Shirer family's celebrations during the 1960 Christmas season were especially joyous and carefree. With his money woes behind him – for good, he hoped – Shirer could pay off his debts, ante up for Inga and Linda's college tuition, and he could even afford to have that much-needed new furnace installed in the farmhouse in Connecticut. His biggest concern suddenly was how to follow up on the success of *The Rise and Fall of the Third Reich*. All things considered, especially with what he had been through in recent years, that must have been a relatively pleasant problem to have.

35

"The transientness of our existence"

With the success of *The Rise and Fall of the Third Reich*, editors and publishers who for years had been slow to respond to William Shirer's queries – if they bothered to do so at all – again were approaching him with suggestions for magazine articles and even for possible books he might write. Suddenly, the media were interested in soliciting his views on everything from European affairs to the need to build fallout shelters. All of this was gratifying to Shirer, who again was able to pay his bills and had his choice of writing projects.

However, with his days devoted to lectures and public appearances, he had scant time to write. Instead, he savored his success and coasted for almost two years. It was an incongruous course of action for a man who obsessed about losing his creativity. The only writing Shirer did during this period was a handful of articles on sundry topics in which he had special interest including a piece on the "folly" of Americans racing to build fallout shelters: "Our mind and our imagination and our energies, it seems to me, must be turned not to groveling under the ground like moles, on a gamble that a few may survive a nuclear holocaust to eke out a miserable, degrading, inhuman existence on the burnt-out crust of the earth, but to keep the peace ... Admittedly [keeping the peace] is a difficult, complicated, often discouraging task, whose achievement does not depend on us alone. But it is the only alternative we have."[1]

This was vintage Shirer. It was also Shirer the commentator making the kind of pronouncements that only a few years earlier would have led to renewed allegations that he was a communist dupe or sympathizer. However, in the harsh light of Cold War realities and faced with the threat of a nuclear war in which survival, not victory, was the only realistic outcome, many readers now saw the logic in Shirer's argument and in the wisdom of the new, more cautious worldview he was articulating. In many ways, this was part-and-parcel of the changing times, which were reflected in John F. Kennedy's victory in the 1960 presidential election.

America's new political leader was bright, witty, literate, and a decorated war hero. At age forty-three, he was also the youngest man and the first Roman Catholic ever elected to the White House. The Kennedy presidency initially held forth the promise of a fresh beginning for America and the world, a Camelot-inspired period of renewed optimism, idealism, and hope.

Kennedy recognized the implausibility of the United States, with its 180 million residents – merely 6 percent of the world's three billion inhabitants – militarily imposing its will on the rest of humanity. Instead, the president proposed to lead by example; he regarded nuclear war as a no-win option that in all probability would bring about the end of civilization. For that reason, he preferred negotiation and dialogue whenever possible, and he stressed that "civility is not a sign of weakness." At the same time, Kennedy advised, "Let us never negotiate out of fear. But let us never fear to negotiate."

Shirer applauded the general thrust of Kennedy's foreign policy, which echoed themes Shirer had articulated in his 1952 book *Midcentury Journey*. At that time, such notions had been considered to be politically naïve, heretical even, and so they had attracted renewed FBI scrutiny. Now, eight years later, here was the president of the United States voicing many of the same ideas. Small wonder Shirer was filled with fresh hope: "Although I had some reservations about him as a president ... [Kennedy] was the first occupant of the White House since FDR who inspired me with much confidence and hope, and even affection."[2]

Despite his ebullience, when Shirer got down to work he continued to focus his energies on writing about what he knew best: the past. This prompted him to sign a contract with Doubleday for a book on his encounters with Gandhi in India in the early 1930s. The mahatma had influenced Shirer profoundly, and in ways that three decades later he was still struggling to understand. As a result, when he began to reflect on his Indian experiences in a serious way, Shirer realized he still was not ready to write about Gandhi. Once more, Shirer was in another period of intense intellectual and emotional turmoil. He turned fifty-seven a few weeks after Kennedy's inauguration; just as the nation was taking stock and reassessing its options, Shirer was again questioning his own values and the meaning and direction of his life. Writing about Gandhi would have to wait.

Shirer's next book after *The Rise and Fall of the Third Reich* was another Nazi-themed effort, a short biography of Adolf Hitler for the young adult (YA) market. Shirer wrote *The Rise and Fall of Adolf Hitler* at the request of Bennett Cerf. The Random House publisher had invited him to do a couple of books for a popular illustrated series called "World Landmark Books," which were aimed at readers ages ten to fourteen. Other prominent authors, John Gunther and Pearl S. Buck among them, had written books in the series, and Cerf felt Shirer was also a natural fit. For his part, Shirer signed on because he wanted to make use of some of the surplus information he had collected while researching his book on Nazi Germany. He assumed that presenting this material in a way that would appeal to a young audience would be easy and fun, a kind of paid vacation for him. However, much to his chagrin, Shirer learned the hard way that writing for young readers is more difficult than it seems. He toiled for several months over his 47,000-word manuscript. It was a struggle not to talk down to his audience and to strike the right tone; he did not want paint Hitler as a sympathetic character.

It took considerable effort for Shirer to hit his stride and get comfortable writing in the YA genre. In addition to the Hitler book, he also wrote a second book commissioned by Cerf: an account of the May 1941 British pursuit of the German super-battleship the *Bismarck*. That book, *The Sinking of the Bismarck*, like the Hitler biography, proved popular with reviewers and readers alike. In fact, *The New York Times* hailed the *Bismarck* book as one of the Best YA Books of 1962.

Shirer was perplexed by the reaction of some YA readers to his writing; as he would later explain to a *Boston Globe* reporter, after his Hitler biography appeared, "I [got] two or three letters a week from teenage boys saying, 'Gee, that was a great book. You actually knew [the Nazi dictator]? Could you send me a lock of his hair or something?'"[3] Shirer was doubtless engaging in a bit of hyperbole for dramatic effect, but there can be no doubt he preferred writing for adults. Those two Random House books would be his only forays into YA literature. They were more work than he had anticipated, and soon he was too busy with other projects.

Taking advantage of the resurgent interest in his opinions, in March 1961 Shirer hit the road on yet another lecture tour, which took him as far west as Los Angeles. There "the relaxed, scholarly, wispy-haired journalist" sat down for some discussions with producer John Houseman and Metro-Goldwyn-Mayer (MGM) studios head Louis B. Mayer. MGM had snapped up the film rights to the Third Reich book the previous December for an undisclosed sum, although Shirer told an inquisitive reporter that he received "considerably less than $100,000."[4] Exactly how much he pocketed was never made public. Regardless of the sum, there was talk Shirer would relocate to California long enough to write the screenplay for what was being touted as the most elaborate documentary film ever made in Hollywood.

While it was true that MGM was ready to invest big money in the project, it is unclear exactly how serious the studio really was about making a film. The day Shirer and Houseman went to meet Louis Mayer in his office – which a bemused Shirer described "as big as a barn" and painted garish pink – the MGM boss kept his visitors waiting. When finally they sat down to talk, Mayer proceeded to gush about how much he had enjoyed reading *The Rise and Fall of the Third Reich*. However, at one point he paused in mid-sentence to take a phone call. As Shirer and Houseman sat cooling their heels, Houseman leaned over and whispered in Shirer's ear, "Don't believe a word of [what he says]. The s.o.b. can't read."[5]

Regardless, MGM accorded Shirer VIP treatment. The studio paid for his stay in a swank Beverly Hills hotel and for numerous meetings with Houseman and with director George Roy Hill, who had been brought in from Broadway to work on the planned film. In the end, Shirer accomplished nothing of lasting significance in Tinseltown.

When he was not in meetings, Shirer was squired around the MGM backlots to visit the sets of several movies. On the set of *Judgment at Nuremberg*, a fictional account of the 1948 trial of Nazi war criminals, he chatted with some of the actors, Judy Garland and Spencer Tracy in particular. Garland, who was playing a prostitute in the film, approached Shirer to ask his advice on how such women dressed and behaved in Germany. Tracy, cast in the role of a judge, questioned Shirer on the look and deportment of the Nuremberg judges.

All of this was great fun for Shirer, even if he was not much of a movie fan. He was even less so when he learned that all the talk of an MGM documentary based on *The Rise and Fall of the Third Reich* had come to nothing. Shirer was back home in June when he heard the first rumblings that, although the studio had spent more than $1 million on pre-production work, Louis B. Mayer had concluded that with several other Hollywood films about the Nazi era already in theaters, the market was saturated. Rumors became reality in early July 1962, when MGM abandoned the *Third Reich* film project, selling the rights to the renowned documentary film producer David L. Wolper, who unlike Mayer, was serious about filming a movie based on Shirer's book. Wolper spent the next five years crafting a television mini-series that won critical acclaim when it was broadcast on ABC in 1967–68. Shirer, who had no involvement in the making of the Wolper documentary, admitted that he was disappointed that MGM had abandoned plans for a feature film. But, he allowed, he was also relieved: "I would rather have no movie than a bad one."[6]

William Shirer's need for money was constant, but he had yet another reason for forging ahead with new book projects: writing was integral to his life. The clickety-clack of his battered old Royal manual was as much a part of his daily routine as breathing or talking. Shirer wrote every day of his adult life, even if it was only to dash off letters to friends or make notes in his journal. He long had been aware of what he called "the transientness of our existence." However, with each passing year his sense of urgency grew. He was acutely aware that many of the iconic figures of his time, including some of the greatest American writers of the 1920s had already made their exits. The roll call of the departed was growing ever longer, including men he had encountered and admired. Thomas Wolfe had died in 1938, F. Scott Fitzgerald in 1940, Sinclair Lewis in 1951, and Ernest Hemingway by his own hand in July 1961. Then in November of that same year humorist James Thurber – that "lanky, owl-eyed man with thick glasses,"[7] as Shirer described him – had died at the age of sixty-seven. Shirer was particularly saddened by Thurber's passing. The two men had been friends since their Paris days. Thurber and his wife Helen owned a vacation home not far from the Shirers' farm, and whenever the two couples were in the area at the same time they got together on Saturday evenings for drinks and dinner.

This had happened less often in the late 1950s because Thurber's final years were not easy. Blind and in failing health, he had been unable to draw, write, or work. He found his physical limitations frustrating, and it showed. While he was still widely respected and even revered, he could be demanding company. This man who was known for his whimsy and gentle good humor often seemed sullen, consumed by inner rage. Sadly, the Shirers' daughters, Inga and Linda, remember Thurber this way. "He always seemed so ... angry. I think that he was a very frustrated and angry man toward the end of his life," Inga recalled.[8]

William Shirer, like Thurber, brooded, although not in the same way or to the same extent. The realization that time was running out for him and his physical stamina was declining was underscored by a series of pivotal events that served to remind him of how cruel life could be. Ultimately these travails prompted him to reassess his own values and priorities in ways that were life-altering.

The first of these events was the 22 November 1963 assassination of President John F. Kennedy. Shirer was at his farm in Connecticut when he heard the news bulletins out of Dallas, Texas. Like millions of Americans and people around the world, Shirer spent the weekend in front of his television set feeling numbed and in a state of near shock. His sense of loss, disillusionment, and anger was deep and profound: "As I sat watching the little screen, I kept thinking that this was the clinching proof that not only is there no sense in human life, but that all the talk of religious men about there being a righteous God that rules the universe is humbug."[9]

No less disconcerting to Shirer, albeit in a very different way, was the departure from his life once and for all of Ed Murrow. The two men had never reconciled after their acrimonious split in March 1947, and Shirer's bitterness had only deepened during these long years. Although he begrudgingly admitted his admiration for some of the pioneer work that Murrow had done after making the transition from radio to television, Shirer was adamant that his old friend had "sold his soul" to the corporate interests at CBS and had been slow to speak out against McCarthyism. Better late than never, Shirer allowed; even so, he nodded approvingly when he read David Halberstam's 1979 book *The Powers That Be*, which delved into the office politics that had shaped the CBS empire during its formative years. Unlike so many other writers who had seen only the good in Murrow's decision finally to confront McCarthy, Halberstam took a more critical view; he chided Murrow for his reticence to take a stand sooner, just as Shirer once had.

In a fit of pique and anger, one day in March 1947, Shirer had warned Murrow that what was happening to him sooner or later also would happen to Murrow: CBS president William Paley would terminate him the moment his usefulness to the corporation ended. Murrow did his utmost to push Shirer's words to the back of his mind. However, the evidence is that he never forgot that admonition, which was as caustic as it was cautionary.

Shirer continued to follow Murrow's career from afar throughout the 1950s, always with a mixture of envy, admiration, and regret; he imagined what might have been if only he and Murrow had continued their partnership in television. But it is unlikely a Murrow-Shirer team ever would have accomplished anything greater than what Murrow did working in concert with producer Fred Friendly, his partner on the *See It Now* broadcasts. The Murrow-Shirer collaboration was one of the great teams – arguably *the greatest* – in the early history of news broadcasting. But by autumn 1941 it had run its course. We can only speculate about what could or might have been had it continued in the postwar world. What we *do* know is that Ed Murrow's crowning achievement in television, his decision to confront Senator McCarthy, was also the beginning of the end for him at CBS.

He had long been skeptical of the direction the network was taking and of the general direction of news and public affairs broadcasting in America. The seeds of Murrow's discontent, planted and nurtured during his radio days, continued to sprout following his migration to television. They burst into full bloom in 1955, the year after the landmark McCarthy broadcasts, when Alcoa, the sponsor of *See It Now*, withdrew its advertising support; Americans were more interested in tuning in to quiz programs and variety shows than they were in watching news or current affairs programming, and the ratings reflected that reality. At the same time, Murrow's edgy, no-nonsense approach to the news increasingly brought him into conflict with his old foe Frank Stanton – who by now was CBS president – and eventually with chairman of the board William Paley, who in past had been inclined to give Murrow whatever latitude he needed to do his work. No more. The two men got into a shouting match one day in summer 1958. Murrow demanded to know if he would have a free hand to continue doing *See It Now* his way or if CBS was intent on second-guessing his every move by providing equal airtime to those corporate interests and influential voices who felt Murrow had wronged them. When Paley declined to promise Murrow the level of support he demanded and felt he needed, Murrow opted to end his involvement in *See It Now*. The final edition of the show aired on 7 July 1958, at a time of year when few viewers were tuning in.

The antagonisms between Murrow and CBS continued to simmer until summer 1959, when Murrow took a leave of absence from CBS with no firm plans to return. Murrow returned to the airwaves briefly, helping out with CBS's coverage of the 1960 presidential election, but it was obvious that his time at CBS was done. That angry admonition that Shirer had hurled Murrow's way in March 1947 surely must have been ringing in Murrow's ears for he confided to his old friend and CBS colleague Charles Collingwood, "You're only important around here as long as you're useful to them ... When they're finished with you they'll throw you out without a further thought."[10]

Shirer and Murrow chanced to meet on Madison Avenue in New York one cold day in December 1960. At the time, *The Rise and Fall of the Third Reich* was topping the bestseller lists, and Shirer's career finally had been resurrected. Meanwhile, Murrow's fortunes, his mood, and his health were at a low ebb, and it showed. At various times over the years Murrow had reached out to Shirer, always through mutual friends, in hopes of a possible reconciliation. Shirer, stubborn to a fault, had never reciprocated, other than to write that 1951 segment of the syndicated feature "This I Believe." Now, meeting his old friend face-to-face for the first time in a decade Shirer was taken aback by Murrow's appearance: "His deeply lined face was emaciated; his trim body seemed shrunken. A cigarette dangled from his lips. He coughed."[11]

Murrow congratulated Shirer on the success of *The Rise and Fall of the Third Reich* and then after a bit of small talk the conversation turned, inevitably, to Murrow's situation at CBS. Shirer reported that Murrow told him he was "washed out" at the network. "In the end, I got what you got," he said. "I remember you told me I would. I should have known it."[12] There is no way of knowing if Murrow actually said this to Shirer, at least in so many words, but Shirer's account squares with Charles Collingwood's recollections of Murrow's sentiments and with Murrow's decision to leave CBS for good not long afterward, wishing his viewers "Good night, and good luck" – his signature sign-off – for the final time in January 1961.

Murrow ended his twenty-seven-year CBS career to accept a job offer from newly elected President John F. Kennedy. Murrow moved to Washington to head the United States Information Agency. Unbeknownst to Murrow, Frank Stanton had been offered the same job, but when he turned it down he suggested Murrow as a candidate.

Murrow, who complained of a lack of energy and of feeling ill, struggled in his new role. In September 1963 he went into hospital complaining of what he assumed was a bad case of laryngitis. Tests revealed that Murrow was suffering from lung cancer; his many years of heavy smoking – three packs of Camels per day – had caught up with him. On 6 October, doctors removed Murrow's left lung – the same surgery his brother Lacey, another heavy smoker, had undergone a few years earlier. Murrow then endured radiation therapy in a desperate attempt to kill the cancer. He also was forced to give up smoking, finally. "Since I have been in [the broadcasting] business I have smoked 60 to 70 cigarettes a day. I doubt very much that I could spend a half-hour without a cigarette, with any comfort or ease," he lamented.[13]

Murrow was still at home recovering on the day that President Kennedy was assassinated in Dallas. Murrow was devastated by the news; although he wanted to return to the office immediately, he was too weak. Uncharacteristically, he broke down in tears. Those who knew him were shaken;

Murrow's behavior was a measure of how frail he had become, physically and mentally.

Shirer had heard from mutual friends that Murrow's health was failing, yet after that chance 1960 meeting in New York, the two men did not see one another again for almost four years. Then one day in August 1964, Janet Murrow called the Shirer farm in Connecticut. Janet and Tess Shirer had much to talk about. Like their husbands, they had been close – Janet Murrow was godmother to Linda Shirer – but Tess and Janet had not seen much of one another in recent years. Now Janet was calling to invite the Shirers for lunch at the Murrow's vacation home at Pawling, New York. Shirer knew Murrow was dying, and he surmised that Murrow was eager to reconcile with him and, if possible, to make amends for the bitterness and hurt that had ruined their friendship. However, Shirer remained unwilling to talk about the past with Murrow. He still could not bring himself to forgive or forget.

As had been the case when the two men met on the street in New York in 1960, Shirer was stunned by the changes in Ed Murrow's appearance. He was just a shell of his former self, frail, skeletal, pale, and coughing incessantly. However, both Bill and Tess Shirer saw the old spark in Murrow's eyes when they sat down over lunch.

Casey Murrow, nineteen at the time and a junior at Yale University, was home for the summer, and so he joined his parents and their guests for the meal. This was the first time he had met the Shirers, though he had grown up hearing his parents talk about them. The younger Murrow's recollection is that the conversation on this sunlit summer day was lively and lighthearted. The adults reminisced about the many good times they had spent together in Europe: "The plan was for my dad and Shirer to go for a walk after lunch, but it ended up being a drive … That's when the conversation that my dad had in mind [to have with Shirer] took place."[14]

Ed Murrow was too weak to walk very far, and so he and Shirer rode in an old army Jeep that Murrow used to get around on the farm. Shirer later recalled that on at least two occasions Murrow stopped the vehicle, took a deep breath and started to talk about "the old days together." He was sweating profusely and spoke with difficulty. Sadly, there would be no Hollywood happy ending on this day. There were no hugs, no tearful mea culpas uttered by either man. "I changed the subject as quickly and gracefully as I could," Shirer later wrote. "We fell silent and drove back to the house."[15]

After rejoining their wives for tea, Shirer and Murrow said their goodbyes, and the reunion ended. The Murrows stood waving in the driveway until the Shirers' car disappeared down the road in a cloud of dust. That was the last time Shirer and Murrow were together or spoke. Murrow died the following spring, in 27 April 1965, two days after his fifty-seventh birthday. The cancer that had ravaged his lung had metastasized and spread to his brain.

If Shirer was among the 1,200 mourners who packed St James Episcopal Church in New York on 30 April for Murrow's funeral, he failed to say so in his writings. Nor did his name appear among the list of prominent media personalities, politicians, and other public figures who were mentioned in news reports. However, Inga Shirer Dean has a "vague recollection" that her father *did* attend, probably all but unnoticed in an inconspicuous back corner of the church: "He was very good about [attending] funerals of old friends, and I think he would have gone for Janet's sake, if for no other reason."[16]

Shirer was never eager, or even willing, to talk about that final meeting with Ed Murrow or their relationship. Even years later, when Inga Shirer Dean attempted to broach with him the subject of the events of that final, painful meeting with Murrow, he remained unwilling – or unable – to discuss it. In the third and final volume of his memoirs he offered a brief, almost clinical, account what had transpired. As Inga recalls, "the first thing he wrote when he began work on his memoirs was the Murrow chapter because he was afraid he might not live long enough to finish. He wanted that one thing to be done."[17]

Shirer's refusal to make peace with the terminally ill Ed Murrow is difficult to understand. We will never know what was going through Shirer's mind, what emotions he was feeling as he bid farewell to Ed Murrow. The nearest he ever came to articulating them was in a 1991 interview with Cloud and Olson. He was eighty-nine and in failing health: "[Shirer] admitted that few days in his life went by when he didn't think fondly of Murrow and their pioneering days together."[18]

William Shirer was somewhat more forthcoming about another death that touched him in a very different kind of way. This was the sudden, shocking disappearance from his life of Virgilia ("Gilly") Peterson.

Shirer and Peterson had known each other for two decades, having met at a 1932 party thrown by their mutual friend John Gunther in Vienna. "A very attractive American woman – tall, statuesque, with bright hazel eyes and brown hair and radiant personality,"[19] as Shirer recalled her, Peterson was the daughter of a prominent New York psychiatrist. Named after the wife of Coriolanus in Shakespeare's play of the same name, she majored in foreign languages during two years of study at Vassar before attending the University of Grenoble in France. Thrice married – the first time to writer Malcolm Ross in 1926, the second to a Polish prince Paul Sapieha in 1933, and the third to magazine editor Gouverneur ("Govey") Paulding around 1950 – Peterson was also a talented writer; her credits include a candid bestselling memoir in 1940 about her life in Poland as well as a 1943 novel, which she later dismissed with a succinct two-word self-review: "It stinks."[20]

In 1947, Peterson was working for a New York public-relations firm, and it was in that capacity that she contacted Shirer on a work-related matter; the two, who had not spoken for fifteen years, fell to talking about the old days in Vienna. There had been something there between them from the beginning, the sparks of mutual attraction. It was still there in 1947, and so Shirer and Peterson began meeting socially as well as professionally. Initially, it seems their relationship was mostly platonic – a friendship fed by occasional lunches, meeting for drinks, and lively conversations about people, books, literary matters, and classical music. Shirer enjoyed Peterson's company and found her attractive. Bright, passionate, and sophisticated, she was a talented writer with an intriguing air of nobility about her. Others evidently also found her engaging, for she began appearing on television, first a guest on various programs and then in 1952 as moderator of *Author Meets the Critics*, the program on which she arranged Shirer's appearance to promote his book *Midcentury Journey*.

It is unclear if Tess Shirer knew about her husband's long-simmering relationship with Virgilia Peterson. Tess did her best to forgive and forget the hurt and humiliation caused by her husband's infidelities and love affairs, but not surprisingly the emotional wounds remained unhealed. Both of the Shirers' daughters had left home by now, having finished college and married. Inga, the older of the two, had given birth in August 1966 to her first child, a daughter she named Deirdre, and Shirer was now a grandparent and well aware of his own mortality.

With Tess and Bill Shirer left to spend more time alone together, all of the old antagonisms, frustrations, and hurt that had been building for so many years began spilling out with alarming frequency. The arguments and recriminations grew ever louder and more bitter. Sometimes when the Shirers were both at the farm in Connecticut and there was no escape for either of them, the confrontations that flared up would go on for hours, all night even. Shirer had started preliminary work on a new book, an account of the 1940 collapse of the French republic, and he was fearful that Tess in a fit of anger might destroy the manuscript. To guard against this, he would snatch up the pages and his research notes before fleeing, taking refuge in a nearby motel. His actions speak volumes both about his priorities and about the dysfunctional state of the marriage at the time.

Shirer later wrote, "I no longer remember, if I ever knew just when or how Gilly and I ... fell in love. All I know is that it happened suddenly, sometime in the early part of 1966."[21] He spelled out the details of the affair in his own writings, recalling that he and Gilly Peterson began seeing one another at every opportunity. They would steal away to Connecticut for trysts at the little-used vacation home of mutual friends. There, Shirer and Peterson spent nights and weekends together. Despite the intensity of the relationship, Shirer was wracked by guilt. Even so, he could not bring himself to break off with Peterson or to ask Tess for a divorce.

William Shirer himself eventually acknowledge how insensitive and selfish his behavior had become. Unfortunately, as he later admitted, he did not or could not grasp this at the time, when it counted most. The situation came to a head in December 1966 when a mutual friend invited Shirer and Peterson to spend Christmas at her vacation home in the West Indies. Shirer declined. Still unable or unwilling to make the final break with Tess, he begged off, saying he was too busy with work and that he was expected to attend his family's annual gathering at the Connecticut farm. Peterson accepted the news begrudgingly and informed Shirer that she was going to spend Christmas at the home of her daughter and son-in-law in Sharon, Connecticut, a half-hour drive northwest of Torrington.

Shirer spent the day at the farm with his own family, just as they had every year for the past two decades. Outside, a snowstorm was turning the countryside into a winter wonderland. Inside the old farmhouse, there were gifts, a big dinner, a beautifully decorated tree, and a fire blazing in the hearth; family members took turns readings from Dickens's classic *A Christmas Carol*. This was the last Christmas Eve the Shirer family spent together. It also marked the end of married life as Tess and Bill Shirer had known it for the past thirty-five years. Late on the afternoon of Christmas Day, Shirer received a telephone call from Gilly Peterson's daughter with some terrible news: her mother had committed suicide on Christmas Eve, having swallowed an overdose of sleeping pills. Shirer was devastated. He was also overcome by feelings of guilt at his own perceived role in his lover's decision to end her life.

Initial media reports of Gilly Peterson's death were vague. They simply stated she had died while "visiting her daughter."[22] It later was reported that she had been felled by a heart attack. Shirer knew better, as the circumstances of her death were spelled out in a suicide note. It was painful reading for him; Peterson lamented that she had concluded she was an expendable element in Shirer's life – after all, she said, he had his writing and his marriage – and knowing this she was too tired to go on living. She assured him that her decision to end her life was not his "fault," but she also made it clear that if only he had been prepared to commit to her or even to "come flying" sometimes when she most needed him, she would not have killed herself.

Peterson's death and the issues it raised in Shirer's mind shook him to his core. He was a cerebral and deeply spiritual man who spent much of his life seeking answers to the ultimate questions. For better and for worse, he endlessly analyzed ideas and every aspect of his life. In the wake of Peterson's death he began yet another reexamination of his core values and priorities. The conclusions he reached after ten long, agonizing months of introspection were anything but pleasant. He had been selfish and deceitful, and he needed in some way to atone. Shirer's life was forever changed by the tragedy of his ill-fated love affair with Gilly Peterson. Now in what amounted to an act of contrition – or was it self-flagellation? – he resolved to sort out the tangled ends of his own life. He set out to do what he now admitted that he should have had the integrity and strength to do years earlier: end his troubled marriage. It was now beyond salvation, and Shirer could no longer deny it. He had known for many years that his infidelities, his insecurities, and his ceaseless quest for answers to questions for which there ultimately were no answers would inevitably destroy his marriage. Tess had been the love of his life and his partner in so much that he had accomplished professionally. Now he acknowledged that neither of them could or wanted to go on as they had. Not after all that had happened.

36

An Ending and a New Beginning

William Shirer spent most of the year 1967 agonizing over the final break with his wife. There was no denying that his infidelities had poisoned their love, irreparably shattering the bonds that had united them in their marriage. After much soul-searching and self-recrimination, one day in early November he finally moved his belongings out of the couple's Manhattan home. Not long after that he also vacated the farm in Connecticut, a place that he dearly loved. It was at this point, with battlelines drawn, that the situation turned nasty. "The trauma of getting a divorce was not spared us," Shirer wrote. "Not the usual sordid haggling over money. Not the wrangling of the lawyers, whose fees year after year soaked up much of our modest lifetime savings. Not the bitter recriminations."[1]

Compounding the Shirers' angst was the sense that even as their own world was coming apart at the seams, chaos was all swirling around them. America itself seemed to be on the verge of being torn asunder. In his inaugural address in 1960 President John F. Kennedy had predicted, "Before my term is ended we shall have to test anew whether a nation organized and governed such as ours can endure. The outcome is by no means certain." Kennedy could not possibly have imagined how prophetic those words would be. Within two years, circumstances compelled Americans to re-examine some of their core values and their nation's place in the world.

By the mid-1960s, the United States of America was a house divided. It was an unnerved, uncertain nation that struggled to find its way forward, lurching through of one of the most tumultuous decades in the history of the Republic. Social and political unrest the likes of which had not been experienced since the Civil War years were threatening to shred the fabric of civil society. The hope and optimism that had brightened the dawn of the new decade had faded to black by the end of 1963 as a storm of national despair broke in the wake of the JFK assassination. The anger, hatreds, old animosities, and political differences that had been dividing Americans deepened and spread.

Democratic President Lyndon Johnson's ambitious vision for his "Great Society" fell by the wayside in the autumn elections of 1966. The Republicans regained control of Congress and the mounting cost of the Vietnam War, both in terms of the national psyche and financially – the latter tally now being more than $20 billion annually – became ever more problematic. By 1967, there were more than 485,000 American troops in Vietnam, and planeloads more arriving daily. As the fighting intensified, annual casualty figures rose at a horrifying rate, up from 4,179 in 1966 to 12,588 in 1968. More than a thousand young Americans were dying in combat each month. Opposition to the Vietnam War grew exponentially as the sons of more and more middle-class families were drafted or returned home in body bags. Angry protests flared on college campuses and in towns and cities across the country. The turmoil did not stop there.

On 4 April 1968, civil rights leader Martin Luther King Jr was assassinated in Memphis, Tennessee and rioting flared in black, inner city neighborhoods across America. Just two months later in Los Angeles, on 6 June, presidential hopeful Robert F. Kennedy was murdered on the day he won the California Democratic primary. The long, hot, tumultuous summer of 1968 continued with yet another explosion of hatred and violence as crowds of young protesters clashed with police on the streets of Chicago, where Democrats had gathered to choose their candidate for that autumn's presidential elections. An embattled Lyndon Johnson had quit the race, having been vilified for his role in getting the United States ever more embroiled in the war in Vietnam – a course of action that we too often forget had been supported at the time by a sizeable majority of Americans. No less bizarre was the fact that Republican candidate Richard M. Nixon, who had been more hawkish than Johnson, succeeded in completing an astonishing political comeback. Nixon won that autumn's election after convincing voters that he was the man to bring the Vietnam War to a successful and honorable conclusion. His margin of victory in the popular vote was razor thin; furthermore, he was the first president since Zachary Taylor in 1848 to be elected to the White House when his party controlled neither the House nor the Senate.

In many ways, William Shirer's personal situation paralleled that of the nation. His decade, which had begun on such a high note with the success of *The Rise and Fall of the Third Reich*, by 1967 was dissolving in a welter of upheaval, unhappiness, and personal loss. Yet despite all of the turmoil in his own life, Shirer remained a keen observer of the events that were reshaping America and the world. Just as so many young people were doing, and just as he had done all his adult life, he questioned the nation's political agenda. Some of its priorities, he argued, were expensive and wasteful beyond reason; others were destructive. A prime example of the former was the 20 July 1969 moon landing. Shirer shared in the national sense of pride in the fact Americans had gotten there first. Nonetheless, he lamented the $35 billion dollar cost of sending men to "so dismal a place,"[2] and he wondered if the money might not have been better spent on social and healthcare programs that might have improved the lot of the poor, the homeless, and the elderly. As Shirer saw it, there was no more troubling example of waste than the Nixon administration's ongoing military involvement in Southeast Asia. Shirer was especially vocal in his condemnation of the May 1970 bombing of Cambodia. "I do not for one moment compare President Nixon with Hitler," he wrote in an impassioned letter to the editor that appeared in *The Washington Post*. "But the shabby propaganda out of Washington since our going into Cambodia is bound to remind one of the Nazi propaganda used to justify the Germans going into Poland, Denmark, and Norway."[3]

Shirer was at a loss to understand the appeal of rock music, "recreational" drugs, and most other aspects of the counterculture, yet he empathized with many of the political demands of the nation's youth. There can be no doubt that had he been forty years younger, he would have been in the streets, taking part in protest marches. "I like today's kids. I'm unable to find a generation gap," he told a *New York Times* reporter in December 1969.[4] The rebel in Shirer applauded the protest movement that was being led by students and black militants on the campuses of America's colleges and universities. In some cases – especially when violence flared – he conceded that the protesters were going too far: "But on the whole, shaking up the staid and insensitive administration ... was probably overdue ... I liked young people who stood for something beyond achieving safe careers and were willing to risk life and limb against the billy clubs and bayoneted rifles of the police and the National Guard to express it. I joined them in their opposition to the Vietnam War."[5]

As his dismay grew, Shirer began writing plaintive articles and letters and speaking out against what he warned were the dangers of unbridled militarism, a subject with which he felt all too familiar, having witnessed firsthand the march to war in the late 1930s. "The military have played an increasingly dominant role in getting [America] bogged down in a disastrous and meaningless war in Vietnam," he raged in a *New York Times* op-ed article, "and in putting over the staggering increase in defense expenditures from twelve billion dollars in 1948 to $80 billion" in 1969, "while our cities have rotted and the needs of the poor and the young and old and the black have been neglected for lack of funds."[6] Shirer feared that America was drifting toward fascism. "I'm not saying all flag-wavers are fascists, but are the flag-wavers thinking about patriotism or are they really expressing opinions against war dissenters, blacks, [and] the long-haired young?" he wondered in a December 1969 interview. "Many of the flag wavers have been so brainwashed by the Government they think anyone who holds a differing view is un-American."[7] Communism, Shirer never tired of pointing out, had failed in Russia and the countries of Eastern Europe: Communism's "greatest triumph was in the way it befuddled the American people and their government."[8]

It was with an anti-Vietnam War message on his lips that in May 1968 Shirer traveled to Berkshire Community College in Pittsfield, Massachusetts, to speak in support of Democratic presidential hopeful Eugene McCarthy. The Minnesota senator, an outspoken critic of the war, was in the midst of an ill-fated run for his party's nomination, which he ultimately lost to Hubert Humphrey. What happened during Shirer's appearance in Pittsfield is less important than what grew out of the evening.

One of the event organizers was a fifty-three-year-old divorcee named Martha Pelton (née Quisenberry). Kentucky-born, she had grown up in the Chicago suburb of Evanston and attended Mount Holyoke, the elite women's college in South Hadley, Massachusetts. Pelton, well-to-do, ambitious, and vitally interested in politics and the arts, belonged to the local historical society and various civic-minded groups and causes. On the evening of Shirer's lecture, Pelton sat front and center in the audience. Intrigued by what Shirer had to say, she invited him for a drink afterward. Sparks flew. "Who can say why?" says her daughter Suzanne Pelton-Stroud. "All we can say for certain is that they fell in love."[9]

The fact that Shirer's mind was in turmoil doubtless was a factor. His relationship with Martha Pelton blossomed quickly. "I think Bill was attracted all his life to high-strung women," observes Elaine Steinert, who was Shirer's secretary for almost a decade beginning in 1977. "He was always drawn to what I'd describe as *unusual* women."[10]

Pelton lived in nearby Lenox, an historic town sandwiched between Pittsfield, five miles to the north along scenic Route Seven, and Stockbridge, the same distance to the south. Located in the Housatonic Valley, in the heart of what has been described as "America's Lake District," Lenox is one of those historic, postcard-perfect New England towns of the Berkshire Hills. Shirer found the area and the town very much to his liking. He felt at home in the Berkshires, forty miles south of the farm at Torrington. Politically, it is conservative, but it is also laid back, and its ambience genteel. From the start, Shirer was accepted in the community, where his celebrity status made him a welcome, even coveted, guest in the homes of the Berkshire county elite. Martha Pelton, who in the early 1940s had raised money for the first birth-control clinic in Connecticut, was active in the Lenox Town Democratic Committee in the 1950s and had marched with Jesse Jackson for fair housing practices in Chicago's southside in 1966, enjoyed a renewed degree of celebrity when she began appearing around town with Shirer as her escort. It was not long before he was renting the guest apartment in Pelton's home; Breezy Corners is a rambling white 1872 frame house on Cliffwood Street in the heart of Lenox. Although Pelton and Shirer insisted that he was a lodger, it soon became apparent their relationship was more than that of landlady and tenant; Pelton hired a carpenter to build bookshelves for Shirer and created a writing space for him.

Shirer was a man who needed a woman in his life. He was most content and productive when he had a partner who was willing to provide him with an emotional anchor and a measure of stability. It almost goes without saying that he was not an easy person to live with; Tess, who had been his rock for so many years, could attest to that. Nor was Shirer able to curb his libidinous impulses or his insecurities. Monogamy had not been part of the lifestyle of a roving foreign correspondent, a job at which he had worked for so many years. Shirer was not the only one of his circle of journalistic friends and colleagues – and that includes the other Murrow Boys – who experienced marital woes or had relationship problems.

Once his marriage crumbled, Shirer was at loose ends and adrift emotionally. At sixty-four, he was acutely aware of his age. Paunchy, bespectacled and with a balding pate, he sported a Van Dyke-type beard. An unruly spray of gray hair spilled down over his ears and collar, reflecting both his liberal political and rebellious social leanings. Ever in hand was his briar pipe, on which he puffed whenever he sat down to converse or write. Many people who met Shirer for the first time assumed he was an academic, an artist, or a literary man; he looked like central casting's idea of a bohemian.

As the confusion and uncertainty in his personal life intensified, Shirer sought solace in the one element over which he maintained control: his writing. In 1961, he had begun preliminary work on an ambitious book about the collapse of France's Third Republic. His research had shifted into high gear by 1965. Although it was now two decades since the end of the war, the French people were still puzzling over how and why their country, so proud, cultured, and resolute, had collapsed like a house of cards in the face of the German army's May 1940 onslaught. In less than six weeks, France – which at the time was regarded as being one of the world's great powers – had been reduced to an occupied land. The dramatic, unforgettable spectacle of millions of French refugees fleeing Paris before the advancing German army had been as unprecedented as it was humbling.

Having chronicled the rise and fall of the Third Reich, Shirer felt the logical next step for him was to explain what had brought about the French defeat and to chronicle that nation's tortured history under the wartime Vichy regime. After all, he'd had the singular good fortune to be an eyewitness to many of the key moments of both the rise of Nazi Germany and the demise of the Third Republic. Although he had watched events unfold and had reported on what he saw, Shirer admitted that, as a journalist who was working under the pressure of daily deadlines and not privy to the secrets of state, there was much he did not know or understand at the time. However, as he explained, he believed "[t]he lack of perspective of time for all who labor in the field of contemporary history is more than compensated ... by the experience of having lived through the events themselves."[11]

Regardless, finding answers to the pivotal questions about the 1940 fall of France was not easy. Researching a book on the Third Reich had been a momentous task, but it was one that was relatively straightforward. The Nazis were meticulous record-keepers, and, because they had lost the war, nothing was secret; no subject was too sensitive or off-limits to Shirer as he did his research. Not so in France; the French are a proud people. By the terms of "*la loi de cinquante ans*" – "the fifty-year law" – which kept secret all sensitive information for a half-century, the postwar French government had forbidden access to many wartime documents and records.

At first, Shirer found this secrecy problematic. But then as he got into his research, being both a skilled journalist and fluent in French, he realized there were ways around the official secrecy. For one thing, much of the information he sought was available in a roundabout way. French legislators had held their own inquiry into the collapse of the Third Republic. The hearings, which had dragged on for five years, were exhaustive in their scope: "Dozens of generals and admirals took the [witness] stand clutching bulging briefcases full of classified documents they hoped would back up, in retrospect, the actions they had taken during the crisis … The documents became part of the unclassified hearing record, while at the same time they remained classified secret under the 50-year rule. It's a comic opera situation that only the French could dream up."[12]

Shirer was further aided in his research by the fact that many of the same retired politicians, diplomats, military men, academics, and other public figures who appeared before the parliamentary hearings kept file copies of the materials to which they had referred in their testimony. Because *The Rise and Fall of the Third Reich* had garnered wide readership in France, Shirer's name was well known. It was in hopes of further pleading their own cases that many of the same witnesses who had given evidence to the French legislators were willing to assist him in his research and to help him interpret the information he was uncovering: "This was all the more remarkable because I was prying into an unpleasant subject for the French: their failures, mistakes, shortcomings, that had brought their country down."[13]

Because most of the primary source material and the individuals to whom he needed access were in France, Shirer made numerous visits, spending considerable time in Paris. There he made extensive use of resources found in the Bibliothèque de Documentation Internationale Contemporaine, visiting the collection so often that the staff came to know him by name, and vice versa. They even provided him with a desk in the librarian's office.

While William Shirer did research in France, back in New York his estranged wife continued to live in the family's comfortable Upper East Side home at 27 Beekman Place. Tess Shirer filled her days by painting, reading, and spending time with her two daughters and their families. She also resumed her study of foreign languages, enrolling in courses in Greek at New York University. Unlike her husband, Tess Shirer never wrote an account of this new phase in her life, much less one that chronicled the end of her marriage; she had always been and to the end remained a private person. Curiously, while her husband previously had never been one to make public the details of his personal life, for a variety of reasons, he now had a change of heart. Wracked by guilt at the failure of his marriage, sorry for all the pain he had caused with his serial infidelities, and haunted by the circumstances of Gilly Peterson's suicide, Shirer grew ever more introspective.

As is the case in most marital breakdowns, family and friends took sides. Initially, at least, the Shirers' daughters, Inga and Linda, sided with their mother. In their eyes, Tess Shirer was the wronged party. Their father did not disagree; so remorseful had he grown that he no longer tried to make excuses or argue. There was no fight left in him, only sorrow. As the lawyers wrangled over the final details of the end of the Shirers' marriage, William Shirer continued to seek escape by channeling his energies and time into his work.

The book on France had grown to epic proportions. At 1,620 pages, the manuscript was almost as voluminous as that for *The Rise and Fall of the Third Reich*. By the time he finished writing late on the night of 3 February 1969, Shirer was emotionally and physically exhausted. The exertion of completing the book and the stresses in his personal life left him feeling so drained that he landed in hospital in early March. He had been polishing the final chapter of the manuscript when he received devastating news from California: his younger brother had died after suffering a heart attack while playing golf. John Shirer was only sixty-two.

Although John and Bill Shirer had not seen much of each other in John's latter years, they had remained close. They had always kept in touch, although as typical men of their era and culture neither of them had ever been inclined – much less able – to articulate their affection for one another. Inga Shirer Dean recalls, "There was a kind of Yankee stiff-upper-lip spirit in the [Shirer] family. They were emotionally cool and didn't express their feelings."[14] Nonetheless, William Shirer was profoundly saddened by his brother's death. He was well aware that John had never really been content or found inner peace; in that regard, the brothers were alike. "You were by temperament easily the most bookish of us children and the most intellectual," William Shirer once opined in a letter to John.[15] For that reason, Shirer had always felt that his brother had underestimated his own creative abilities. John had enjoyed a successful career as a senior economist in various federal agencies and had taught economics at the University of Arizona. However, like his famous brother, he had aspired to a literary career. In 1966 he had ended his teaching career at age fifty-nine and moved to the West Coast to write plays and novels. Sadly, he ran out of time before he could fulfill his dreams.

Given his own health problems, William Shirer was in no condition to attend his brother's funeral. Shirer and his sister Josephine, now sixty-nine and retired, could only commiserate from afar when a sorrowful Erna Shirer buried her husband on the other side of the continent.

The sudden loss of his only brother tore yet another gaping hole in Shirer's life. He responded predictably, seeking diversion in his work. He got busy with the details of *The Collapse of the Third Republic*, which was scheduled for late autumn publication, until the Book of the Month Club chose it as a featured selection for January 1970. That decision all but guaranteed the success of the book, which Shirer dedicated to his brother's memory.

To Shirer's delight, *The Collapse of the Third Republic* appeared on the national bestseller list the same week it went on sale, and some of the initial notices were laudatory, for example, *Atlantic* reviewer Anthony Sampson's: "Shirer succeeds magnificently in the main [task] he sets himself ... He is fair, scholarly, and superbly dramatic."[16] Unfortunately for Shirer, that was as good as it got; the book lacked the drama and the grand sweep of *The Rise and Fall of the Third Reich*. Even Shirer was willing to concede that his latest effort had shortcomings, but overall he felt it was still a work of considerable merit. Thus, he was disappointed and even angered when reviewers for some publications – ones that he considered pivotal – panned the book employing terms that Shirer felt were unfair and even mean-spirited.

Two of the most troubling notices appeared in *The New York Times*. Shirer felt the criticisms offered there were especially damaging. Following the 1966 demise of the *Herald Tribune*, *The Times* enjoyed what Shirer decried as a "near-monopoly in the greater New York area insofar as reviewing books was concerned."[17] While the newspaper's writers could not entirely kill a book with a negative review, they certainly could cripple sales. In Shirer's mind, *The Times'* reviewers clobbered *The Collapse of the Third Republic* with a devastating one-two critical punch.

In the newspaper's Sunday book review section in early November, Columbia University historian Owen Paxton lambasted Shirer's work on three grounds: for failing to provide a straight-forward explanation of the reasons for the Third Republic's sudden, shocking collapse in spring 1940; for failing to differentiate between the important and the "merely colorful" in his narrative; and for the book's ungainly size: "Size is not authority, and *The Collapse of the Third Republic* can please only those for whom scholarship, like medicine, is supposed to go down hard."[18]

Christopher Lehmann-Haupt, *The Times'* senior daily book reviewer, picked up on that same theme in a second review, which appeared a little over a week later. Not only was he critical, he was downright sarcastic. "To begin with, the fall of France seems of dubious significance for a work of this size. I don't mean to be callow: I understand that it was one of the traumas of the twentieth century ... But I submit that it was of greater psychological meaning than historical."[19] He went on to chide Shirer for his repetitiveness, suggesting that readers only needed to peruse about a third of *The Collapse of the Third Republic* to grasp its essence: "Tear out the rest of the pages and use them to line the gerbil's cage, or something."[20]

Livid, Shirer dismissed Lehmann-Haupt as being ignorant of history and, therefore, not qualified to pass judgment on a book as complex and detailed as *The Collapse of the Third Republic*. At the same time, Shirer decried Paxton as "an academic lightweight" who only compounded his shortcomings by being condescending and envious of Shirer's success as a writer of popular history. Shirer felt many other American academics were guilty of the same intellectual sin. There was an undeniable element of truth to that notion; however, there is also a case to be made that Shirer was inclined to find malice where none existed. British academics were no less critical of *The Collapse of the Third Republic*. Their French counterparts similarly found much to quibble with in the book, although they judged it "on its contents," Shirer pointed out, rather than because he was not a professional historian.[21]

Adding insult to injury for Shirer was an unflattering article about him that appeared in *The New York Times* the last week of December 1969. Shirer felt the offending article, which bore the headline "After 2 Tomes, Shirer Leans Back Thinking of No. 3," left readers with the impression he was a pompous old curmudgeon who was bereft of ideas ("My well is dry," he was quoted as saying) and energy ("I don't really know when I'll feel like writing again"). The article depicted Shirer as bemoaning the fact he had to do his own research "because I simply can't trust someone else to do it."[22] Taken out of context, such an outburst seemed ill-tempered at best, arrogant at worst. Despite the fact he had at long last finished the massive French book, this was not a happy time for Shirer.

After his six week "barnstorming" promotional tour of France, Shirer returned home in mid-February 1970. He was intent on slowing down and immersing himself in what he envisioned as a Thoreau-like life of writing, reading, and quiet contemplation. He had always wanted to learn Russian and read in their original versions the novels of Tolstoy and the other greats of Russian literature. He also hoped now to have time to mend fences with his daughters and their families, whom he had not seen since his split with Tess. Shirer planned to garden, sail, ski, and enjoy performances at the annual Tanglewood music festival in Lenox: "I drifted slowly, and, for the most part happily, actively, and in relative good health, into old age."[23]

That was only partly true. With his marriage to Tess still in its death throes, he suffered the loss of two more of his dearest friends, who died in quick succession. The first to go was Joe Barnes, who had edited both *The Rise and Fall of the Third Reich* and *The Collapse of the Third Republic*. Barnes was only sixty-two when he fell victim to cancer on 28 February 1970. Shirer spoke at the memorial service in New York, a private affair attended only by the immediate family and a few of Barnes's closest friends, Shirer and John Gunther being among them. Afterward, the two men adjourned to a bar on Lexington Avenue for drinks. They had not seen each other for a couple of years "for certain personal reasons."[24] They had previously quarreled over misunderstandings from years earlier, and with Shirer no longer spending much time in New York, their paths did not cross as often as they once had. As was the case when he chanced to meet Ed Murrow on the street in New York in December 1960 after having not seen him for several years, Shirer was stunned by Gunther's gaunt appearance.

They had been friends for more than forty years. They had always had a lot in common and enjoyed each other's company. Both were natives of the Windy City, had similar worldviews, were keen students of history, and both dreamed of writing The Great American Novel. Along with the footloose Vincent ("Jimmy") Sheean, who was cut from a similar bolt of Midwestern cloth, the trio referred to themselves as "the Chicago kids."

John Gunther, six-foot-two, with twinkling blue eyes and an athlete's build, had cut an impressive figure in his youth. Women had adored him, so much so that at times Shirer was envious, jealous even. Gunther's love of life had always been as unabashed as it was infectious. However, on that cold day in February 1970 when Shirer and Gunther sat down for a drink, it was apparent to Shirer that his old friend was ailing.

Gunther had just returned from a research trip to Australia, where he had gone to gather material for yet another of his *Inside* books. After having written about all of the other continents, he conceded this would be his last book. In fact, he did not live to complete it. "I saw that he was a sick man," Shirer writes. "His face had no color and he was breathing heavily as he talked, and [he was] coughing. He said that he had given up smoking, but it was obvious he [still suffered with his] emphysema."[25] Gunther complained about feeling tired and about his failing eyesight. Despite his distress, the two old friends had a long chat and shook hands as they parted. "That was the last time I ever saw him," Shirer recalled. "He was dead a few weeks later."[26]

Gunther died in a New York hospital on 29 May 1970, three months short of his sixty-ninth birthday. It was not emphysema, but rather cancer that killed him. It had started in his esophagus and soon spread to his liver.

The passing of two of his dearest friends fed Shirer's own sense of mortality and a fresh desire to resolve the lingering problems in his personal life. By summer 1970, he and Martha Pelton were contemplating marriage, and so Shirer asked his lawyer to proceed with the paperwork for his divorce. When everything was ready, he and Tess and their respective lawyers met in New Haven, Connecticut, to sign the final agreement. All that remained to be done was for Tess, as the aggrieved spouse, to fly to Mexico for a quick divorce. She did so on 31 July 1970, thus formally putting an end to their thirty-nine years of marriage. Shirer's diary entry for that day reflected his inner torment: "I feel an awful void, a deep ache in the heart."[27]

A week after their divorce was finalized, the former spouses met at the family farm at Torrington one final time. After a lunch and a nostalgic last glass of wine together, Shirer departed, carting a load of his books and papers in a U-Haul van. He occasionally returned to the farm in coming years, but only as a visitor. It was never easy when he did; his presence there was a reminder of all that once had been and no longer was. Tess Shirer never remarried, never reverted to using her maiden name. It was evident to family and friends that however much pain her former husband had caused her, she loved him to her dying day. The feelings were mutual. Yet both of them knew they could no longer live together as husband and wife.

"Even after the bitterness of the divorce had died down, [my parents] continued to be close, and they kept in touch. Dad always sent mom flowers on her birthday. I saw some of the letters he'd sent her, and they talked regularly on the telephone. They always had a lot to say to each other," says Inga Shirer Dean. "All marriages have problems, but the good stuff between our parents was so good it's really sad that in the end the bad stuff outweighed it. We always thought [our parents] should have stayed married because they really were good together. Whenever they were, they'd talk and talk."[28] Inga's sister, Linda Shirer Rae, echoes those comments: "Whenever [our parents] were at the farm they'd often be talking away, and we'd call, 'Mummy! Daddy! Yoohoo! Hello!' They always had so much to say to each other. At the end of each day, they'd have cocktails, Mummy would always make a lovely warm hors d'oeuvre, and they'd sit and talk endlessly. Even if neither of them had been out that day, they always had a lot to talk about."[29]

As was the case more often than not, Shirer recorded in his journal his activities and his feelings during this emotional period; confessional writing was self-therapy for him. Years later he included in the third and final volume of his memoirs excerpts from his diary and snippets from his personal letters to Tess. Reading what he chose to include is the literary equivalent of passing the scene of a bad car accident; the reader almost feels guilty looking but is hard pressed to resist. Shirer's own account of his divorce and what he was thinking, which he edited for publication, is at times rambling, disjointed, and reflective of the tangled state of his emotions. Why did he choose to sift through the still-smoldering ruins of his marriage in such a public way? Being an inveterate journalist, did he do so reflexively, in the interests of telling the whole story? Was it penance, to show that he was sorry for his actions and all of the hurt he had caused? Or did he have other, more personal reasons? The answer most likely is some combination of all those factors. Whatever his motivation, Shirer was selective in what he reported. There is not a word in his memoirs or any of his writings about his love affair with Tilly Losch or about his relationship with or his marriage to Martha Pelton. Similarly, he did not bother to announce to his daughters that he planned to remarry. Inga Shirer Dean received a letter from her father in which he announced his relationship with Pelton and volunteered information about her: "But as I remember, [he] didn't mention that he was actually going to get married, and so I didn't even know the date."[30]

Shirer and Pelton formalized their relationship, marrying in a quiet ceremony on 24 February 1972, a day after Shirer's sixty-eighth birthday. For the next three years, the couple lived together as husband and wife. However, it was not long into the relationship before there were signs of unrest. It was evident the marriage had been a huge mistake for both of them. "I'm not sure Martha Pelton knew what she was getting into when she married Shirer," says author Rinker Buck, a then-young *Berkshire Eagle* newspaper reporter whom Shirer befriended in summer 1974. As Buck recalled in his irreverent 2002 memoir about this period in his life,[31] the two men were introduced by one of Buck's girlfriends – an *Eagle* graphic designer – who enjoyed Shirer's company and sometimes ran errands for him. "Everybody in town knew or knew of Bill Shirer. There were a lot of older, well-to-do people among the Berkshire County elite, and they readily invited him to all the 'right' parties. Martha was already part of that social scene, and when she and Shirer attended together, he became a center of attention. The women would sometimes fuss over him. I don't know this for sure, but I wouldn't be surprised if Martha was upset by this ... The thing is, too, that Shirer was of an earlier generation of journalists, mostly men, who in their work as foreign correspondents had traveled widely and lived life to 'the fullest,' as they say."[32]

Shirer was not much different from his peers, at least in that regard, and his old habits were not easily broken or changed. However, there was an added element to Shirer's life in Lenox that complicated things in his mind: his struggle to rationalize his past and to adjust to his new realities. His divorce from Tess and the circumstances surrounding the death of Gilly Peterson had affected him deeply and in ways he was still struggling to understand. Shirer's situation was complex, his behavior at times puzzling, bizarre even. On the one hand, he continued his quest for answers to some of the big questions and spiritual concerns that had troubled him for so many years; these were issues that remained largely unresolved to the very end of his life. On the other hand, his lifestyle and habits remained unchanged, even if he was no longer living the life of the peripatetic foreign correspondent. Buck recalls several incidents that were indicative of Shirer's mindset at the time.

For example, Shirer had been a hobby sailor ever since his Berlin days, and when he settled in Lenox he had the time and the money to buy an old "faded blue Day Sailor with a wobbly mast and tattered sails," as Rinker Buck describes it.[33] Shirer moored the boat at Stockbridge Bowl, the lake where the town's yacht club was located. Given his poor eyesight and arthritis, Shirer needed company when he sailed, and so he took to inviting along Buck and whatever young woman Buck was dating at the time. On these outings, Shirer would bring a bottle of red wine, and he and his companions sipped as they sailed and talked. One day, as Buck's date was sunbathing in the bow of the boat, he and Shirer began chatting about life. Buck lamented that he sometimes got depressed; after all, here he was, age twenty-three and "had not yet done anything with his life." Shirer chuckled as he advised his young friend to stop worrying: "Oh, my Lord, son. I'm 71 years old, and I'm still trying to figure out my life."[34]

On another occasion, Buck was in bed with one of his girlfriends one night – the same *Eagle* workmate who had introduced him to Shirer – when the bedside telephone rang. It was Shirer, calling for a goodnight chat with the young lady. Buck says he "twiddl[ed] his thumbs under the sheets for 15 or 20 minutes" before he finally grabbed the phone in exasperation to complain that Shirer was being intrusive. If Shirer was offend-

ed, he did not let on. Instead, he mockingly chided Buck for being "puri-
tanical" about his girlfriend. "We can share her," he insisted. He then
quizzed Buck about a recent article Buck had written.[35]

This kind of overly friendly behavior irked Buck at first, but he soon
came to accept it for what it was. He realized Shirer was often lonely;
while he was married, he remained an incurable flirt who was not at all
upset if people in town buzzed about his behavior. By this stage in his life,
that was who William Lawrence Shirer was. There was no changing him.
Buck and his young friends doubtless found that easier to accept than did
Shirer's wife Martha, especially when she discovered he had developed a
fondness for a young, married friend of one of Martha's daughters. Shirer
had met the woman on a winter vacation trip he and Martha took in Florida. Despite the distance between them in both years and geography, the
relationship between Shirer and the young woman soon moved beyond
mere friendship or flirtation.

If Shirer had been taken aback by Richard Nixon's win in the 1968 presidential election, it is no exaggeration to say that he was shocked when
Nixon was re-elected in 1972, defeating Democratic challenger George
McGovern. The American public seemed disinterested in the scandal the
media had dubbed "the Watergate affair." For Shirer, the matter summoned to mind disquieting echoes of Nazi "dirty tricks." He regarded
Nixon as being a devious, dishonest, and dangerous man. On 8 November
1972, the day after the election, Shirer wrote in his diary: "As [historian]
Henry Commager said in a recent piece, no Administration in history has
been so crooked, so lying, *etc.*, but the citizens didn't care."[36]

Shirer was correct. At the time, most Americans were oblivious or apa-
thetic to the burgeoning scandal that less than two years later led to
Nixon's forced resignation. The voter turnout in the 1972 election – 55
percent of the electorate – was the lowest since 1948. While the Democrats managed to retain control of both the Senate and the House of Representatives, Nixon won re-election in a landslide. His margin of victory
in the Electoral College was a staggering 504 votes.

The political situation in Washington was not the only source of angst
in Shirer's life. On 28 October 1973, he received more bad news of a personal nature. His sister Josephine, at seventy-three years of age, had died in
hospital in Westwood, New Jersey. While Josephine had always been the
most gregarious of the Shirer siblings and had "a lively personality and
enjoyed life," as Inga Shirer Dean recalls,[37] she had never married. Thus, it
fell to her brother to look after the funeral. He arranged the burial and a

graveside service in which one of his sister's teaching colleagues and one of her former students spoke. So, too, did Shirer and his daughters. Inga and Linda read some of Josephine's favorite poems.

With his sister gone, William Shirer was the last surviving member of his immediate family. He had always been introspective and prone to periodic bouts of melancholy. Now, with his seventieth birthday looming, he was increasingly preoccupied with thoughts of his own mortality and with his efforts to rationalize and make sense of his life and the world – if there was any sense to be made of either. The inner turmoil he was experiencing was reflected in his behavior, which was ever more problematic and puzzling, even to those who knew him best.

Memoirs

It is not clear exactly when William Shirer's marriage to Martha Pelton began to unravel. Martha, who led a busy life and often traveled solo, was dismayed to hear rumors that in her absence her husband was being seen around town in the company of various women. At times he was indiscreet about it, recklessly – or perhaps even willfully – so. As a result, by spring 1975 tongues were wagging in Lenox, a town of fewer than 4,000 residents.

Despite the resulting strains on his marriage and his own emotional turmoil, Shirer continued to feel at home in Lenox. As John Hess, a writer for *The New York Times Book Review*, notes, "The setting is America as she would like to see herself. The Berkshires, Hawthorne Country."[1] William Shirer relished the laid-back pace of life here and the genteel ambience. The area's political sensibilities were also to his liking; while not exactly liberal, they were moderate Republican. Two of the best friends Shirer made in Lenox were *Berkshire Eagle* publisher Lawrence K. ("Pete") Miller and editorial page writer Roger Linscott. Miller was renowned for publishing what *Time* magazine once hailed as being one of the best small dailies in the nation and for opposing McCarthyism in the 1950s. Linscott won a Pulitzer Prize in 1973 for his passionate editorials, which included a ringing endorsement of Democratic presidential hopeful Senator George McGovern, one of Shirer's favorite politicians.

Following his move to Lenox, Shirer – like America itself – was going through a period of bewildering uncertainty. As had been the case when he returned from Germany in December 1941, Shirer struggled with issues of self-identity and purpose. This gave him all the more reason to savor his status as one of the celebrity residents in his adopted hometown. He was highly visible and recognizable as he ambled around town puffing on his briar pipe, a blue beret perched atop his head. He walked back and forth to the post office and local shops each day, and he was a familiar figure in the reading room of the Lenox public library.

Shirer had a mystique. Locals regarded him as "a somebody," as did many of seasonal residents and tourists who flocked to the Lenox area each summer. In a small community where everyone knew everyone, Shirer's profile was both a blessing and a curse. Whenever he attended public events and social functions his presence was noted. People listened when he spoke. Those who were old enough to remember his days as a CBS war correspondent or who had read his books were eager to meet and talk with him. There can be no doubt that he basked in the attention, especially when his audience was female. On such occasions, he usually could be found telling stories about the old days, when he had rambled around Europe and India. Rinker Buck recalls Shirer relating his encounters with Churchill, Hitler, and Gandhi; while Shirer was not one to swear or tell off-color jokes, when he was regaling a younger crowd with tales he sometimes talked in a matter-of-fact way about the famous women he had known and "if you were willing to believe him," about how "he'd bedded many of them."[2]

Some locals who knew Buck or knew of him when he lived in Lenox maintain that he is guilty of exaggeration, if not outright sensationalism – especially in what he writes about life in the town in the mid-1970s. Buck denies such charges, countering that he researched and verified everything in his book. Perhaps he did, but Shirer's friends and associates from this period insist that to the best of their knowledge, in public and in his dealings with townspeople he was always well mannered, the very model of decorum. Elaine Steinert, Shirer's former secretary, remembers him that way: "Bill was very personable ... He was always nice, whether you were a visitor or a tradesperson who came to the door to do work for him, he'd sit down and start talking with you."[3]

Martha Nordstrom and her husband Stephen Fay have similar memories. Fay worked as a bureau reporter at *The Berkshire Eagle* in the mid-1970s; because Shirer became friendly with some of the staff at the paper, Fay heard through the grapevine in early 1976 that Shirer was looking for a secretary (this was before he hired Elaine Steinert). When Fay told his wife about the job, she applied for and got it. For the next year, Martha Nordstrom spent about four hours each weekday at Shirer's house. She did some typing for him, handled routine correspondence, filed papers, ran errands, did his shopping, made some meals, and ate lunch with him on weekdays: "I had heard that Shirer liked to flirt, and when I started to work for him people said to me, 'Be careful, he likes blondes!' I was a cute little blond myself back then, but I never, ever had a problem with him. He was a perfect gentleman."[4] What Stephen Fay remembers best about Shirer is that he was an enthralling storyteller: "He wasn't one of those stodgy old guys who sat around telling 'war stories.' He didn't lecture or hold forth … He was extremely well read, had a bright, active mind, and he usually had something interesting to say. People listened when he spoke."[5]

The Nordstrom and Fay recollections of Shirer square with Rinker Buck's in at least one important regard: Shirer exuded what Buck describes as "perennial youth and spontaneity."[6] Buck writes that Shirer enjoyed youthful company: "He seemed revived by the attention this brought him. The year I met him [in summer 1975], Shirer was 71, and it was enjoyable spending time with someone that age; he still enjoyed pretty girls and night-time drinking. We offered him the companionship of the young that he craved, and he offered us great stories and the thrill of knowing an older, famous man."[7]

Shirer had a solid income from his writing and he had money to spend, and consequently he enjoyed the good life. He would sometimes treat his young friends to dinner at the historic Red Lion Inn in Stockbridge or at the Curtis Hotel in Lenox. At other times, Buck remembers Shirer sitting around with young people at a table in Alice's Restaurant in Stockbridge; that was the iconic eatery made famous by Arlo Guthrie's anti-Vietnam War folk song of the same name.

Shirer, being an incurable flirt, enjoyed spending time with Buck and his circle of friends, which always included young women. Buck admits to sometimes being uncomfortable with and even jealous of the attention Shirer paid to Buck's girlfriends, in particular Rachel, a dark-haired young woman from New Jersey who was working as a design artist at *The Berkshire Eagle*. Shirer took a shine to Rachel, and she apparently relished the attention. Buck was jealous until finally he came to realize that Shirer was simply an old man who loved female company. There was an undeniable undercurrent of sexual energy between Shirer and Rachel; however, beyond an occasional peck on the cheek, their relationship probably was not physical.

Buck also came to understand that while Shirer's libidinous urges had gotten the better of him in the past – too often – he was now a septuagenarian who was hobbled by arthritis and talked a far more energetic game than he played, even if he himself was loath to accept that reality. Shirer still had a wandering eye.

Over the years, his infidelities had one common denominator: they all had ended badly. Shirer bore the emotional scars of his dalliances. He put on a brave face, as most men of the time would have, but the undeniable truth was that he had not learned his lesson, not even after he was hurt in his ill-fated pursuit of Tilly Losch.

Until 1973 there was no further contact between the pair. However, the reality was that through it all and for all that time Shirer had continued to carry a torch for Losch. It was work on a new book that sparked his desire to reconnect with her.

Despite a lack of interest from his publisher,[8] in his "semi-retirement" Shirer set to work on writing an autobiography following his move to Lenox. "My family and friends kidded me for never throwing anything away. But as I plunged into 'Memoirs,' as I called [the book], I was glad I never had. My diaries, my correspondence, my clippings, were not only invaluable – without them I never could have written the books."[9] Throughout his working life, Shirer maintained a disciplined daily writing schedule, and that had continued in Lenox. By autumn 1973, he already had 400 pages of manuscript, and he was still only writing about his youthful years in Paris in the 1920s.

Delving into his memories gave Shirer an excuse to explore his family history in a way he never had before. It also gave him occasion to be nostalgic. As he got into the spirit of things, Shirer did something that many people do as the awareness of their own mortality begins to grow more acute: he reached out to rekindle relations with an old flame. After an eighteen-year hiatus in their relationship, in 1971 Shirer sent Tilly Losch a Christmas card. If she responded, there is no record of it. What we do know is that, as was her habit, Losch filed Shirer's card. She had kept every piece of correspondence he had sent her over the years; in the end, memories were all she had in life. Losch had never remarried after her second divorce, had never found peace, and had never achieved the level of fame or success she had so craved. In many ways, Shirer was a kindred spirit.

He, too, was a restless soul who had spent much of his life seeking happiness and answers to fundamental questions about spirituality and the human condition. His journalistic career had been mercurial, marked by soaring highs and crushing lows. On the personal level, his marriage to Tess had disintegrated, largely due to his own follies and weaknesses of character. He had gone through the worst agonies of a lengthy divorce battle before settling into what at first blush had promised to be a long-term happy-ever-after relationship with Martha Pelton. For better and worse, that fairytale ending was not to be.

Shirer persisted in sending special-occasion greeting cards to Losch; she eventually responded. The two met and renewed their acquaintance at a 1973 social event in the home of mutual friends in New York. That Christmas, Tilly Losch sent Shirer a card inscribed with a cordial message. He responded with an invitation to have lunch when next he was in New York, "just the two of us, this time."[10]

Over lunch one afternoon in early February 1974, the conversation between the two of them flowed as freely as it ever had. However, there was a disquieting note to the occasion; Losch revealed she was having serious health problems of an as-yet-undetermined nature. Shirer sent her a note following his return to Lenox: "It was awfully nice to see you again. You were as beautiful as of old and full of the same charm ... I was depressed at what you said of your health, though of course I could not notice anything myself and you spoke only generally."[11]

Shirer's version of events, which he offered for public consumption, is that he'd had no contact with Losch until early 1975 when one day, out of the blue, he received a cryptic telegram from her. "Please call me. Situation serious," it supposedly read. Like the cavalry riding to the rescue, Shirer claimed to have hastened to New York where he found Tilly Losch very much alone and feeling downcast after her doctor diagnosed her as being terminally ill with cancer. In desperation, after all those years apart, as Shirer told the story, she had turned to him in hopes he could find another doctor, who would offer a second opinion, hopefully one with a more optimistic prognosis. Shirer did succeed in finding another doctor for Losch. However, it was to no avail; the second opinion only confirmed the original diagnosis. No one could offer Tilly Losch anything more than palliative care.

Shirer agonized over the realities of her illness. At the same time, once again he was struggling to rationalize the course of his own life and to deal with the realities of his marriage to Martha Pelton. The details of what happened between Shirer and Pelton are unclear, but Shirer's attentions and his affections wandered, and he made no effort to hide it. Rinker Buck recalls visiting Shirer at his Breezy Corners home one day around this time. Buck was interviewing Shirer for an *Eagle* news story when Pelton stormed into the room. "Don't forget to tell him that we're getting a divorce!" she snapped at her husband.[12]

Shirer spent a few weeks in summer 1975 traveling across Europe in the company of Mary Thomas, a young woman from Florida with whom he had begun a relationship. Shirer surely knew that traveling to Europe with a female companion who was thirty years his junior and not his wife would be the end of his marriage. He seems not to have cared. At various times in his life, Shirer behaved so outrageously that he must have known it would provoke a reaction from others with whom he had differences.

Shirer was drawn to strong-willed, opinionated women who were willing to help organize his life and support him in his work; Mary Thomas fit that description and was happy to take on the role. Shirer and Thomas were drawn to one another and were determined to be together. Shirer informed his daughters and friends that Thomas's husband in Florida tolerated her relationship with him. "By this point, I don't think my husband *cared* what I did," Thomas confirms.[13] It was apparent to both partners that their marriage was over. Martha Pelton had come to the same conclusion about her own union with Shirer, but, unlike Mary Thomas's spouse, Pelton was anything but indifferent or willing to accept the situation.

Pelton confronted Shirer when word got back to her that he and Thomas had traveled together in Europe. Angered by whatever excuse Shirer offered, Pelton reacted decisively. On 15 July 1975, Shirer returned home from one of his daily outings to discover his belongings had been heaped on the lawn of Breezy Corners. Pelton had locked him out of the house. News of the Shirers' marital woes quickly became the talk of the town. With the conflict escalating, Shirer's attorney swore out a criminal complaint against Pelton, charging her with conversion – the legal term for taking illegal possession of another person's property. This development attracted media attention far and wide, and a 15 August article in *The New York Times* reported Shirer had "told the court he hasn't been able to get his clothes, check books, or manuscripts since his wife changed the door locks."[14]

After deliberating for five days, a judge of the Berkshire Probate Court ruled in Shirer's favor. He was allowed to retrieve the rest of his belongings from Breezy Corners. Apart from personal effects, what he most cared about were the manuscript and notes for his memoir. Shirer resumed writing when he found a house of his own on Sunset Avenue, a tree-lined street a short drive from where he and Pelton had been living. This new residence, a spacious two-story frame home with oversized windows and a two-acre lot, was built on a rise and had scenic views of the surrounding countryside. From the picture window of his second-floor study Shirer had a panoramic view of the wooded Berkshire Hills "that soak up the summer music of Tanglewood."[15] He would call this place his home for the rest of his life.

Shirer and Pelton divorced only a month after their split, the minimum statutory waiting period. There could be and were no attempts at reconciliation. Their estrangement was final, the hurt enduring. Given Shirer's behavior, it is surprising that he was the one who petitioned for divorce, alleging that he had suffered "cruel and abusive treatment"[16] at the hands of his wife. The name Mary Thomas is conspicuously absent from the court documents. When a few years later an inquiring reporter asked Shirer about his marriage to Pelton, he remarked that it was an aberration: "A man of my years should have known better."[17]

The lesson was a hard-learned one for both parties. For Shirer, the trauma of his second divorce in five years was as costly emotionally as it was financially. He was already paying Tess 40 percent of his annual income under the terms of their divorce agreement, and now Pelton was claiming a percentage of what was left. Shirer's income during this period was still substantial. In the fiscal year March 1975 to March 1976, he received more than $497,000 in royalties from the sales of *The Rise and Fall of the Third Reich* alone,[18] and he earned varying lesser amounts from his other books that remained in print, mostly in paperback.

Despite his travails, Shirer carried on with his life in Lenox. He continued to be vitally interested in domestic politics and in matters of American foreign policy. Included among his papers are copies of many of the letters he wrote to other well-known writers and to various politicians on a variety of concerns; United States-Spanish relations was one matter in which he had taken special interest since 1933, when he and Tess had sojourned in Spain. Thus, in November 1975, upon the death of General Francisco Franco, the fascist dictator who had ruled the country with an iron fist for four decades, Shirer joined with other American liberals in urging President Gerald Ford to press the Spanish regime for democratic reforms. However, this was but a momentary diversion for Shirer.

Work on his memoirs had become the focal point of his life. Shirer had always had an astounding sense of self-discipline where his writing was concerned, and he was now spending a minimum of six hours each weekday at his typewriter. So preoccupied was he with his efforts in this regard and with his evolving long-distance relationship with Mary Thomas that he did not see Tilly Losch again that autumn, nor were they in touch during this period, which turned out to be her last weeks of life. A Christmas card and the flowers Shirer sent her drew no response, and phone calls to her apartment went unanswered. Losch had no immediate family, and so there was no one to relate the news to Shirer that her health was failing quickly, and that she had gone into a New York hospital for the last time. Tilly Losch died there, very much alone, on Christmas Eve 1975.

Although he had known the end for Losch was near, Shirer was stunned by news of her death. Having finally sold the farm at Torrington, the Shirers gathered at the home of one of the Shirer daughters for a family Christmas. It was Tess who handed her former husband the obituary page from the Christmas Day edition of *The New York Times*. There, across three columns was a report headed "Tilly Losch, Exotic Dancer, Is Dead."[19] Given the circumstances of Gilly Peterson's tragic death on Christmas Eve nine years earlier, the timing of Losch's passing was not lost on William Shirer. He did not spell out in detail his reaction to these events other than to write in the final volume of his memoirs, "I felt a tremendous loss. And I felt remorse."[20]

Shirer made no mention of Tilly Losch in the first volume of his memoirs, which was finished in early 1975 but not published until September 1976. Despite the best efforts of Shirer's agent, Paul Reynolds, the head of Simon & Schuster remained lukewarm to the book, although he did eventually agree to publish it. As the title suggests, *Twentieth Century Journey: A Memoir of a Life and Times – The Start (1904–1930)* is an account of Shirer's early life in the Midwest and of his experiences as a young journalist in the Paris of the 1920s. However, Shirer intended this first volume of his life story to be "a memoir not only of a life, but of the times."[21] The book is an informative and engaging read that offers a wealth of background on the history of the period. Many reviewers commented favorably on this.

In *the Saturday Review*, Pulitzer Prize-winning journalist Ted Morgan lauded *Twentieth Century Journey* as a "meditation on America," noting that "the 'small-town-boy-makes-good" story is only one of the things that makes the book "so affecting and so eminently worth reading." Morgan especially liked the "sweet-and-sour reconstruction of the climate of life in the Midwest at the turn of the century" and Shirer's personal view of "the [foreign] correspondent's Europe it unfolds" in the 1920s.[22]

Even the review of *Twentieth Century Journey* that appeared in *The New York Times* – a newspaper whose writers had in the past been harsh in their critical assessments of Shirer's writings – had kind things to say. The editor of the Sunday book pages enlisted Malcolm Cowley, the eminent literary critic and chronicler of the "lost generation," to render an opinion, and his review was generally positive, especially where Shirer's account of Paris in the 1920s is concerned. If Cowley was less enthusiastic about the overall tone of the narrative, it was only because he felt the narrative voice was too distant and impersonal. "The book keeps looking outward at public events and famous people: it is another contemporary history rather than a true memoir ... While meeting as many characters as at a crowded cocktail party, a reader is likely to feel that someone is absent. The missing person is William L. Shirer."[23]

Other reviewers echoed Cowley's comment, but Shirer was not bothered by this criticism. He could afford to be sanguine; not only was *Twentieth Century Journey* attracting media attention, sales of the book were unexpectedly strong. Regardless, the decision-makers at Simon & Schuster remained skeptical about the market for future books by Shirer, especially two or three more planned volumes of autobiography. Book one of his personal saga ended in Vienna in 1931 with *Chicago Tribune* publisher Colonel McCormick sending Shirer a cable that reads "SHIRER FLY INDIA." Shirer planned for book 2 to pick up his story with his coverage of the Indian revolution and the life and work of Mahatma Gandhi, whom Shirer venerated as "the greatest man of our time."[24]

Frustrated by what he felt was a lack of respect from both his agent and his publisher, Shirer began casting around for new representation. In summer 1978, he left Paul Reynolds and signed on with Don Congdon, a veteran agent with the Harold Matson literary agency in New York. Among Congdon's high-profile clients were science-fiction writer Ray Bradbury, whose career Congdon had helped build, bestselling novelist William Styron, and historian William Manchester; in fact, it was Manchester who recommended Congdon to Shirer, and with good reason. Pennsylvania-born Congdon, a former editor at Simon & Schuster, was a veteran of more than thirty years in the agency business, and he had won a well-deserved reputation as a shrewd, tough negotiator. Congdon had made a name for himself in 1966 when he sold to *Look* magazine the serial rights to William Manchester's book *Death of a President*, a study of the JFK assassination, for the then-unprecedented sum of $600,000.

When Congdon went to work on Shirer's behalf, after much negotiation, he secured a deal by which Simon & Schuster agreed to pay Shirer a $75,000 advance on the second and presumably final volume of his memoirs. The deal was that in this book, to be completed within two years, Shirer would chronicle the events that led to the outbreak of the war, recount his wartime experiences in Berlin, and conclude with his views on and analysis of postwar Europe. Any account of events in India and Shirer's experiences with Gandhi could wait; Peter Schwed suggested this material might be recast as a standalone memoir or perhaps as a biography of the mahatma. Shirer was pleased with the monetary aspects of the deal that Congdon had worked out on his behalf, but he stubbornly clung to his original plan: he wanted to include the Gandhi material in the second volume of his memoirs. He doubted he had the energy to complete a separate Gandhi biography or that he would live long enough to do so.

When Shirer delivered his revised manuscript to Simon & Schuster in spring 1979, it was a year early. It was also 600 pages of text. The early chapters dealt with Gandhi, while the rest of the narrative related Shirer's story up to the end of 1932. This was not the book Shirer had promised to write. For that reason, the Simon & Schuster editor who was assigned to work on the book rejected the manuscript. However, Congdon was able to calm the waters, this time convincing Simon & Schuster to publish Shirer's account of his relationship with Mahatma Gandhi as a standalone volume. Quid pro quo, Shirer supposedly would agree to press ahead with the writing of the second volume of his memoirs, which would follow the outline that the publisher had stipulated. The plan was a reasonable one; however, there was now a new problem.

All the wrangling between Shirer and his publisher had eaten up the better part of three years. Shirer, who turned seventy-five on 23 February 1979, was beginning to feel his age and to look it. His health was fast becoming a major concern for him. That autumn, during a routine checkup, his doctor in Lenox discovered Shirer was suffering from angina. A stress test gave no indication of an immediate problem, but he was still feeling lethargic when he traveled to Florida to spend Christmas with Mary Thomas.

Shirer's wan appearance bespoke the trouble that lay ahead. Thomas, who took a keen interest in his health, urged him to visit a cardiologist before returning to Lenox. He agreed to do so, albeit reluctantly, on 5 January 1980. In all probability that decision saved his life. Tests at this time revealed major problems. "Bill had occlusions in two spots on the main descending artery to his heart; it was 98 percent blocked," recalls Mary Thomas. "The cardiologist who saw him advised us that if he didn't have immediate surgery, he could die at any time."[25]

Faced with such a dire prognosis, Shirer opted to undergo open-heart surgery. The Florida specialist provided Shirer with a referral to Dr Dudley Johnson, one of America's top cardiologists. Johnson was based at Mount Sinai Medical Center in Milwaukee, and so it was to that facility that Shirer now traveled. The operation he underwent, a triple bypass, proved to be far more complicated than expected and took more than eight hours to complete.

Shirer's recovery, even with Mary Thomas nursing him, put him on the shelf for almost six months. With work on volume two of his autobiography at a halt, he had time to brood about the treatment Simon & Schuster had been according his Gandhi book. Originally, *Gandhi: A Memoir* was to have been published in June 1979. When the date was pushed back to autumn, Shirer was dismayed, but he accepted the change of schedule because the book – which he dedicated to Mary Thomas – would be available in time for Christmas. For that reason, Shirer was irate when Simon & Schuster announced a second delay in publication, this one to mid-January 1980. Adding insult to injury, the book's cover price was increased by $3 – from $9.95 to a more problematic $12.95. The upshot was predictable: despite the fact the Gandhi memoir was an "alternate selection" by the Book of the Month Club, sales of the book lagged.

This was a bitter blow for Shirer; *Gandhi: A Memoir* was a book that had special meaning for him. It was one of the most intensely personal writing tasks he had ever set for himself. "It is difficult, if not impossible, at least for me, to sum [Gandhi] up, his mind and personality and soul, from which he drew such inner strength and purity, difficult to understand or reconcile the strange contradictions of his life and teachings, to grasp the nature and source of his genius."[26]

The time he had spent in Gandhi's company was relatively brief, yet those days were among the most affecting and meaningful of Shirer's life; his experiences in India had proved to be pivotal, and he had come away forever changed. "I think my father was a receptive student, and Gandhi was an eager teacher," explains Inga Shirer Dean. "I doubt that Bill Shirer, the individual, was important to Gandhi in any way, but because he was an American journalist who wrote for a major daily newspaper and for a news service, Gandhi knew that he could help him spread his message to a wide audience."[27]

Shirer was also a skeptic by nature, and at the time that "fate took me to" Gandhi, he was struggling to understand some of the big-picture concerns in his life.[28] To Shirer's receptive eyes, Gandhi was Christ-like, a man of puzzling contradictions – much like life itself. The mahatma was frail, yet his strengths were as oversized as his shortcomings. While he could offer Shirer no definitive answers in life, Gandhi did impart the notion that, as often as not, questions are as important as answers. He insisted there are no absolutes, and so no religion, no philosophy, has a lock on truth. The best that anyone can do is to compare, weigh, and sift ideas in the hope of gaining understanding. This message resonated with Shirer, who at times was cerebral to a fault. He was also enough of a realist to acknowledge and accept his personal shortcomings as a thinker: "That my own effort was not very successful was not [Gandhi's] fault ... Perhaps my reaction to a rather narrow Presbyterian upbringing dulled my capacity to be very religious ... I count the days with Gandhi [as being] the most fruitful of my life. No other experience was as inspiring and as meaningful and as lasting. No other so shook me out of the rut of banal existence and opened my ordinary mind and spirit, rooted in the materialist, capitalist, West as they were, to some conception of the meaning of life ... No other so sustained me through the upheavals and vicissitudes that I lived through in the years after I left India."[29]

Shirer accepted that not everyone regarded Gandhi with the same reverence he did. Thus, while sales of *Gandhi: A Memoir* were weak, Shirer was pleased to see that many of the reviews for the book were positive. However, it was one that appeared in *Newsweek* that came closest to understanding the true essence of the book. Reviewer Jean Strouse applauded Shirer's efforts to offer readers a personal perspective of Gandhi but noted that the author ultimately "cannot say what he learned" from the Indian holy man.[30] There was more truth to that observation than Strouse ever could have realized. Despite his best efforts and the fact he had spent more than forty years reflecting on that very question, Shirer continued to search for the words to express what he was feeling and thinking. In the end, he had to be content with what he had written about Gandhi, for he had come to accept that perfection and truth are ideals to be sought, not realities that can ever be attained.

Shirer was angered by what he perceived of as a lack of respect accorded him by the new management at Simon & Schuster. He wanted nothing more to do with them; Don Congdon understood that "for some reason [Shirer] had taken a dislike to Richard Snyder, the new head of the company."[31] The antipathy was mutual. Sensing this, Shirer balked at living up to the terms of the deal that his agent had worked out with the publishing house. The manuscript he delivered in mid-1979 was essentially the same one that the editors already had rejected. "While he never said so," Congdon writes, "I thought Bill was behaving this way to get out of his contract with Simon & Schuster."[32] If that was the case, he was successful.

An angry Simon & Schuster editor called Congdon to inform him that the manuscript Shirer had submitted was unacceptable and to demand that the author repay half of the $75,000 advance he had received, plus interest on the money. The latter request further angered Shirer, who was adamant in his refusal to comply. He pointed out there was no penalty clause for "non-performance" in his contract with Simon & Schuster. He also noted that the publisher retained in a "pool account" $700,000 in royalties from sales of *The Rise and Fall of the Third Reich*, which the company was doling out to Shirer in annual installments of $40,000, and he received no interest on the money being held back. The ensuing dispute between Shirer and Simon & Schuster dragged on for several months, growing ever more acrimonious. In the end, Shirer repaid $37,500 in advance money – but no interest – and he and the publisher parted ways.

Fortunately for Shirer, Little, Brown and Company, the same publisher that almost two decades earlier had rejected *The Rise and Fall of the Third Reich*, stepped forward to publish the second volume of his memoirs, providing the book covered at least the years up to the start of the war. If Shirer made those changes, Little, Brown agreed to publish a third volume of Shirer autobiography, which would chronicle the war years and beyond. In return, Shirer received an advance of $100,000 on the two books. In an era of inflated, at times incomprehensible, publishing deals, by no means was this big money. However, at age seventy-six, Shirer was gratified that Little, Brown and Company believed in him. He was still not ready to retire, although he now had the undeniable feeling that he was living on borrowed time. "I won't say I'm ready to go. I'm not," he wrote in his diary in January 1981, as he was doing his annual New Year's review of his life. "I'd like to finish the Memoirs ... And maybe [spend] a few more years in such a pleasant place as Lenox, with the music at Tanglewood, the gardening and sailing, and M[ary]'s love."[33]

38

A Twenty-Year-Old Mind
in an Eighty-Year-Old Body

His heart surgery had given him a new lease on life, and so William Shirer was determined to use his remaining years to full advantage. He dreaded dying with unfulfilled dreams and ambitions, as his brother had. However, the two men were different in one vital regard: William Shirer's self-discipline had always been monk-like, and that continued to be so – at least as far as his writing was concerned. Shirer was at his desk five days per week, often more. He was intent on completing two more volumes of memoirs as well as the stage play that he had been begun thirty years earlier.[1]

A typical day for Shirer now began at about 7 a.m. with a session of physical activity. After a light breakfast and a quick read of the morning papers, by 9:30 a.m. he was at work in his cluttered second-floor study. For the next four hours, he would tap away at the keys of his battered old Royal manual typewriter. A one-hour lunch and a thimbleful of wine (usually savored in the company of his secretary), followed by a brief walk, and an afternoon nap gave him the energy for a couple more hours of work. His workdays invariable ended with a drink as he watched the evening news on television. He was in bed with the lights out by 11 p.m.

In winter, Shirer seldom strayed from his routine; on summer weekends he took it easy, preferring to spend his days sailing, pottering in his well-tended flower and vegetable gardens, enjoying musical concerts at Tanglewood, or spending time with family and friends. Despite the infirmities of old age, which for him included an arthritic knee, hearing loss (for which he wore a hearing aid in one ear), and failing vision in his one good eye, Shirer's zest for life remained undiminished, as did his intellectual acumen.

Throughout this period, he continued his relationship with Mary Thomas, who cohabited with him in Lenox for several months each summer and visited for long weekends at other times. However, the reality for both of then was that the relationship had begun to wear thin. According to Don Congdon, Mary "tried to run his life, interfering with a couple of overseas deals that we made while Bill was [recovering from his bypass surgery]."[2]

Elaine Steinert, Shirer's secretary at the time, has similar memories, but "I'll say one thing in [Mary's] favor: she took very good care of Bill and saw to it that he went to doctors ... She was very good about anything medical."[3] Steinert and Thomas had their minor differences, but what ultimately led to their falling out was the degree of control over Shirer's business affairs that Thomas seemed intent on exercising. If Shirer was concerned about Thomas's assertiveness, he said nothing about it to Thomas herself. What ultimately scuttled their relationship was her refusal to get married; Thomas was having second thoughts about formalizing her ties to a man three decades her senior. Thomas – who became Mary Balle when she subsequently remarried – insists that she and Shirer parted as friends: "I still had a great fondness for Bill. I learned a lot from him ... I feel truly blessed to have known him. I am what I am today because of him. He used to say to me, 'Lady, you're beautiful, and you're talented.' Bill taught me to write (she has become a published author) and to believe in myself. My time with him was for me the Camelot period in my life. I'll never forget that."[4]

Following his break with Mary Thomas, much to the bewilderment of his family and friends, despite his advanced age and various infirmities, Shirer had a brief romance with a New York food writer, and he continued to seek out female companionship. One of Shirer's new lady friends was Marge (née Belcher) Champion Sagal, the Hollywood-born dancer-actress who had been the model for the fluid movements of the title character in Walt Disney's iconic animated films *Snow White*, of the Blue Fairy in *Pinocchio*, and of the dancing hippo in *Fantasia*. Marge had married dancer Gower Champion in 1947 and had enjoyed a stellar career as his wife and dance partner in several big-budget 1950s movie musicals in which the two performed and choreographed, most notably the 1951 version of *Show Boat*. By the early 1980s, the Champions were long divorced. Marge had remarried and, after being widowed, settled in the Berkshires. She and Shirer met at a social event in Stockbridge, "probably in 1981, I think it was," Champion recalls. "Bill always had a thing for and liked dancers. He'd met Isadora Duncan in Paris back in the 1920s, and she had fascinated him. He thought she was one of the most beautiful women he'd ever seen."[5]

Shirer and Champion had many mutual interests. In her early sixties, Champion was still a dynamic, energetic woman with boundless passion for life; in fact, she continued to dance into her nineties. Champion became one of Shirer's regular companions for afternoon outings in his sailboat; his physical condition was such that he could no longer sail on his own. Sometimes Shirer and Champion also traveled together. Thus, when she was planning an October 1982 trip to the Soviet Union with the Society of Stage Directors and Choreographers, Champion suggested Shirer come along. Learning Russian so he could read the novels of Tolstoy in the original versions and visiting the great writer's estate were two of the items on Shirer's bucket list; however, whenever he had applied for a visitor's visa in the past, Soviet authorities had turned him down. He had never been told why, although he suspected it had to do with his criticisms of the Nazi-Soviet pact of August 1939; the KGB had a long memory. The irony of being persona non grata in the Soviet Union could not have been lost on Shirer in light of his blacklisting as a supposed Communist sympathizer.

In late 1982, the Soviet army was bogged down in its ill-fated invasion of Afghanistan; there also were fears of a new arms race with the United States, and President Ronald Reagan soon began referring to the Soviet Union as "the evil empire." With tensions between Washington and Moscow simmering, veteran *New York Times* foreign correspondent Harrison Salisbury, Shirer's friend and neighbor and formerly *The Times*' man in Moscow, advised Shirer not to travel to Russia. Salisbury was well aware of the potential perils; while his advice was not to be taken lightly, Shirer had made up his mind to go ahead with the trip.

Tour groups visiting the Soviet Union were escorted by "tour guides" who generally were considered to be KGB officers. Not surprisingly, two days into the Society of Stage Directors and Choreographers' tour, the Russian woman charged with escorting the group called Shirer aside and began questioning him on the "real purpose" of his visit to the Soviet Union. It was obvious that he was not a dancer, and by now the authorities had realized who he was. Shirer feared he would be expelled. He was not, but his trip did take an unfortunate turn when he fell ill with flu and had to cancel the one activity on his itinerary that he most wanted to do: visit the country home of writer Leo Tolstoy.

Given Shirer's abiding interest in politics and his populist ideals, he had been dismayed by the presidency of Richard Nixon. Gerald Ford's term in the White House, he had tolerated. Jimmy Carter's, he had puzzled over. Where Ronald Reagan was concerned, Shirer gritted his teeth and did his utmost to endure. Reagan was "one of the great phenomena of modern politics,"[6] as Shirer noted, although he readily admitted to being at a loss to fathom why.

Shirer was especially critical of President Reagan's foreign policy. In 1983, Shirer railed against the American invasion of the Caribbean island of Grenada. However, he accepted that his was a voice crying in the wilderness; the more Reagan's shortcomings became apparent, the more popular "the Great Communicator" was with the American people. Shirer found this maddening; when he could no longer restrain himself, he vented his frustration in letters to the editor, usually sent to *The New York Times*.

In April 1985, Shirer traveled to Europe one final time, visiting London, Paris, and Berlin for celebrations to commemorate the fortieth anniversary of the war's end. In London, he took part in a CBS television broadcast of a round-table discussion that reunited five of the Murrow Boys – sans Murrow, of course.[7] The nostalgia and joys of the occasion were dampened when Charles Collingwood, another of "the boys" and one of Shirer's oldest friends, revealed he was terminally ill with cancer.

The specter of death continued to follow Shirer as he revisited many of his old haunts in Paris. He pined for friends now gone and lamented that his infirmities prevented him from savoring the delights of his favorite city. "I was simply getting too old and too decrepit to partake any longer of the moveable feast here that Hemingway had written about and from which I had taken large portions in the heady 1920s in Paris."[8]

That sojourn in the City of Light, which he knew would be his last, left him feeling glum, although not as much as did his return to Germany, where he attended a reunion of war correspondents. Ronald Reagan, who was also in the country on an official visit, took part in a ceremony honoring the memory of the 2,800 German soldiers who were buried at Bitburg Military Cemetery; among them were members of the Waffen SS, who had been some of Hitler's most rabid devotees. When journalists queried Reagan about the ethics of him taking part in the memorial service, he opined that the German soldiers buried at Bitburg were as much victims of the Nazis as were those millions of people who had been murdered in the concentration camps. Those ill-informed remarks sparked a heated controversy. Shirer weighed in on the side of the American Legion and spokespeople for various Jewish groups, voicing his revulsion over Reagan's "retouching" of history. "As one of the few Americans still living who went into Poland in 1939 and into the Netherlands, Belgium, and France in 1940 with the German Army as a neutral war correspondent," he wrote in an angry letter to *The New York Times*, "I can testify that not one of the hundreds of German soldiers I talked to during those campaigns considered himself a 'victim of Nazism.' On the contrary, the German soldiers fought for the Führer [and] the Fatherland ... with immense enthusiasm and dedication, and very bravely. They appeared to me to believe fanatically in Hitler's cause and the leader himself. [Even] during my sojourn on [the Western Front] in the fall and early winter of 1944, I helped a number of German prisoners, some of them teenagers, a few hours after their capture, when they were still under the shock of being taken. I cannot remember one who did not express his utter loyalty to Hitler and the Third Reich."[9]

Shirer had accurate memories about this. Although he had turned eighty on 23 February 1984, he remained razor-sharp mentally and still had vivid recollection of the run-up to the war, the evils of the Nazi regime, and the fighting on the Western Front. As Inga Shirer Dean told a *Boston Globe* reporter, her father had "a 20-year-old mind locked up in an 80-year-old body" and remained vitally interested in current events.[10] While researching his memoirs, he had spent more than three years reviewing primary source material, perusing books, and combing through his notes and other personal papers from the late 1930s and the war years. Shirer had always prided himself on getting the story right, and he remained meticulous about details. He knew that his reputation and his ability to earn a living depended on it. He was intent on telling as fully and accurately as possible the personal side of the history he had recounted in *The Rise and Fall of the Third Reich* and thus to uphold his end of the agreement with Little, Brown and Company. His falling out with Simon & Schuster had served as a stark reminder that the relationship between a writer and a publisher is ultimately a business one; sentiment counts for nothing. In the end, he succeeded on both counts, producing a great book and fulfilling his contractual obligations.

The Nightmare Years: 1930–1940 ranks with Shirer's finest work. Arguably, in some regards it is his best book. At times, the narrative is chilling; at times, it is heart-warming. It is one of Shirer's most readable books.

In the past, ever the consummate old-school journalist, Shirer had resisted all suggestions that he include more personal stuff in his writing. Now, for the first time, he injected himself into the story he was telling; this adds dramatic tension to the narrative and raises to another level what easily could have been just more "war stories" from another old journalist. *The Nightmare Years* is a compelling and provocative read, for Shirer observed disquieting parallels between Nazi propaganda and the growing tendency on the part of postwar governments and politicians of all stripes to twist the truth and spin information for their own purposes. Beyond the book's cautionary tone, it is a reminder of what a skilled reporter William Shirer was. In the middle decades of the last century – truly a golden age of journalism – he was one of the stars in the small but glittery galaxy of American foreign correspondents.

William Shirer was never a great literary stylist, but, whatever his shortcomings were in that regard, he more than made up for them in the acuity of his insights, his gift for storytelling, his shrewd judgment of human nature, and his sense of the grand sweep of history. In all those regards, *The Nightmare Years* is the work of a consummate elder craftsman, one still at the top of his game. The book recounts Shirer's experiences as a frontline reporter in India, Afghanistan, and Europe – Nazi Germany in particular – in the 1930s. He does a superb job of giving readers a sense of what it was like to have lived through this period, which he brings to life with his words. That was and remains the appeal of *The Nightmare Years*. People evidently recognized this, and the book became a national bestseller.

One sharp-eyed reader, a *Chicago Tribune* reporter, noted that Shirer had never received his severance pay from the newspaper after his October 1932 firing. Now, each autumn *Tribune* reporters who had done exemplary work were honored with cash prizes drawn from a memorial trust fund set up in memory of former managing editor Edward Beck. It took five years to happen, but to Shirer's delight, his name was included among the 1989 list of honorees. Because Shirer's poor health prevented him from traveling to Chicago, *Tribune* managing editor Richard Ciccone and assistant managing editor Howard Tyner journeyed to Lenox to present Shirer with a check for \$1,250.[11] Seldom in his life had he been more pleased to receive money owed to him; although it was fifty-seven years late, the irony of the moment was sweet: the funds Shirer received came from the memorial trust fund honoring the same man who had fired him.

Shirer's run of good luck did not end with the popularity of *The Nightmare Years*. He was delighted by the tone of reviews of the book, which were positive and "many of them were discerning, showing a deep understanding of what I had tried to do."[12] One such reviewer was Naomi

Bliven of *The New Yorker*. Bliven heaped praise on *The Nightmare Years*: "Some Americans – unfortunately some in government – forget that freedom of the press and freedom of information and expression are not frills or electives or accessories; they are not privileges bestowed but rights essential to the working and preservation of modern political democracy. Mr Shirer has produced an exceptionally powerful argument for these freedoms: in his prose we live through what happens without them."[13] Cultural writer-critic Herbert Mitgang expressed a similar sentiment in a piece for *The New York Times*: "Mr Shirer stirs the ashes of memory in a personal way that results in both a strong view of world events and of the need for outspoken journalism."[14]

One review in which Shirer took special delight appeared in the journal *The American Scholar*. Although the writer was not fond of Shirer's informal prose style, he conceded, "I can think of no other narrative that gives you the disturbing sensation of having lived in suspense throughout the period, not knowing how it was to end."[15] In Shirer's mind, that was high praise indeed. Despite the mass popularity of some of his books, academics often had scoffed at and dismissed his writing; for the most part that was still the case. Reviewing *The Nightmare Years* in *The Boston Globe*, Professor William Sheridan Allen from the State University of New York at Buffalo repeated a stock criticism of Shirer's books, opining that they were journalistic, and as such were "simplistic in interpretation," "unbalanced in coverage," and "superficial."[16]

Such assertions nettled Shirer for obvious reasons, but also because at heart he was, despite his denials, an intellectual. It rankled him to be chided and dismissed out of hand by America's academic historians. Over the years, Shirer had often stated that it was his observation that British and European scholars did not differentiate between journalists and historians, at least not to the same extent their American counterparts did, and they were less snooty. "The greatest history is great literature, and most [American] academics insult the language every time they write," he once told a *Washington Post* reporter. "I don't have anything but a BA degree, and British and French historians consider me a colleague."[17]

In retrospect, it is evident that Shirer's umbrage said as much about his own insecurities and prejudices as it did about the ever-uneasy relationship between history and journalism. Historian Barbara Tuchman observes, "Bill Shirer represents in his person the evolution of journalist into historian."[18] The sort of criticisms American academics leveled at Shirer are essentially the same as those that have been directed at other "popular historians" – writers such as Barbara Tuchman herself. However, the debate about the relative merits of "popular history" is today so shop-worn as to be almost a non-issue; most professional historians – "acade-mics" – today regard as de rigueur the need for writing in an engaging style to enlighten an audience that extends beyond the halls of academia.

William Shirer, ever the diligent researcher, got serious about finally learn-ing Russian, both as a matter of personal interest and because he had another book project in mind. Thus, in autumn 1982 he had asked his sec-retary to find him a tutor. The person Elaine Steinert recruited was a Russ-ian émigré named Irina Lugovskaya, a teacher at a community college in nearby Great Barrington. The match was ideal in more ways than one.

Lugovskaya, a native of the Russian city of Nizhniy Novgorod (known as Gorky during the Soviet period) – like Shirer – had grown up in a single-parent home. Lugovskaya's father had been murdered in one of Sovi-et dictator Joseph Stalin's purges, a few months before Irina's 1939 birth. Her mother, Zinaida Lugovskaya, gave her baby daughter her own sur-name and moved to Moscow to be near the Lugovskaya family. Their already bleak life in the Russian capital took a turn for the worse with the outbreak of war and the German invasion of the Soviet Union. When mothers with young children were evacuated from Moscow, Zinaida Lugovskaya and her daughter were "relocated" to a remote village in the southern Urals. They knew no one there, and life was hard and lonely. Even finding enough to eat was a daily struggle. Mother and daughter sur-vived and after the war returned to Moscow, where Irina completed her early schooling.

Being a bright and diligent student, she was admitted to the Lenin Ped-agogical Institute in 1957. For the next five years, Irina majored in mathe-matics. Despite this, it was not her abilities in this discipline that would shape her life, but rather her linguistic talents. Lugovskaya had started learning English in the fourth grade. Fascinated by the language, she also studied it on her own, committing to memory favorite pieces of poetry and prose. Her efforts paid off. Lugovskaya's fluency in English won her a spot in the Russian equivalent of the United States Peace Corps; only six of her eighty classmates achieved this coveted honor. "In the middle 1960s, the Soviet Union started courting Third World countries," she recalls. "Doctors, teachers, engineers, [and] agricultural specialists were sent out to work in these countries."[19]

Ostensibly these young people were dispatched to help with foreign aid projects; their real job was to foster the global spread of communism. At that time, Soviet citizens had few opportunities for foreign travel, and so

Irina – being more intent on traveling than proselytizing – was happy to do a tour of duty teaching in the West African nation of Ghana.

She returned to Moscow afterward, spending three years there before leaving on another deployment, this time to rural Zambia. As it happened, an hour's drive down the road from where she was working was another school in which some of the teachers were Americans. It was at a gathering of staff from the two schools that Lugovskaya met Chicago-born Philip Freund. The two fell in love, got married in 1970, and, when Lugovskaya obtained a Soviet exit visa, she joined her husband in the United States. The couple lived in the Berkshires, where Freund taught at a private school and in 1971 the couple's first child, a son, was born. However, Philip Freund's wanderlust had not yet subsided, and when his job contract expired in 1972 the Freunds moved to El Salvador. A year later, it was on to Jamaica, where Irina gave birth to second child, a daughter. By 1980, the Freunds were back in the Berkshires. "Staying in one place was boring for [my husband]," recalls Lugovskaya, who had grown tired of the nomadic lifestyle. "In 1981, Philip left for Saudi Arabia ... Our marriage was already falling apart, and so I refused to go."[20]

That is how Irina Lugovskaya came to be living in the Lenox area. Needing to support her family, she responded to Elaine Steinert's appeals for a Russian tutor for William Shirer: "I'd never heard of him, but I thought he must be important if he couldn't call me himself."[21]

The day she was scheduled to give Shirer his first ninety-minute lesson, Lugovskaya fell ill after eating some berries from her backyard. When Shirer heard about this he quipped, "I feel as if I've just met a heroine from a Dostoyevsky novel."[22]

The following week, when Shirer and Lugovskaya finally met, they hit it off for a very practical reason. By this point in Shirer's life, his eyesight was so poor that he was having difficulty seeing, let alone deciphering the research materials for his Tolstoy book. So Lugovskaya began reading to him, for hour after hour. Predictably it was not long before he began flirting with his Russian teacher. She was charmed. Their relationship intensified as they discovered their mutual passion for classical music, books, and gardening. Shirer was drawn to his blue-eyed, diminutive tutor. Soft-spoken and dignified, she emanated a quiet intensity that fascinated him. Just as he aspired to become proficient in Russian, Lugovskaya had taken it upon herself to become competent in English. She had also taught herself to play the piano; after saving the money to buy her own instrument, she had mastered it by practicing endlessly, spending as long as five hours at the keyboard every day while still in Moscow.

By summer 1986, when Lugovskaya accompanied Shirer on a research trip to the Soviet Union, romance had blossomed between them. The couple formalized their relationship two years later, on 7 February 1988, when they married in a quiet civil ceremony held at Shirer's home in Lenox. He was eighty-three; she was forty-nine.

The 1980s in North America were a period of heightened public interest in and appreciation of history. In some measure this is attributable to the popularity of the television mini-series, which in the late 1970s was all the rage as an entertainment form. The format, which had its origins in the serials that long have been a staple of television in the United Kingdom, spread to North America in 1974. However, it was really the phenomenal success of the 1977 adaptation of Alex Haley's black history novel *Roots* – the highest-rated program in television history to that time – that opened people's eyes to the potential of the mini-series as a genre and sparked the mass interest in genealogy that persists to this day. The public appetite for well-told history continues with the success of made-for-television adaptations of Stephen Ambrose's Second World War-era chronicles and the sundry documentary series created by Ken Burns and other like-minded filmmakers.

The success of *The Nightmare Years* led readers and publishers alike to rediscover some of Shirer's earlier writings – especially *Berlin Diary* and *Twentieth Century Journey*, which were reissued in paperback. All of this activity inevitably brought Shirer's books to the attention of television executives and producers. One who was especially intrigued was Jerry Rafshoon, the former media strategist for President Jimmy Carter. Rafshoon saw potential in *The Nightmare Years* as "an ideas-driven mini-series." He felt there was a message in the book that was as relevant in the late 1980s as it had been in the late 1930s: "We've come to a time in our public and political life where the message is probably the most important factor in electing people and keeping [them] in office … And the use of tools to expand the message and to emotionally and dramatically get it into people's minds has become paramount."[23] For that reason, he felt it was imperative that good reporters maintain a sense of objectivity, as much as is possible, by not becoming too cozy with politicians and their spin doctors; Shirer had striven to do that in Nazi Germany, but many of his colleagues had not. Rafshoon was dismayed that far too many modern journalists were allowing themselves to be swayed and used to deliver a political message rather than report the facts.

This was the message Rafshoon took to cable television pioneer Ted Turner in summer 1988 when he presented Turner with a proposal to adapt *The Nightmare Years* as an eight-hour mini-series for the Turner-owned TNT cable service. Turner liked the idea for several reasons, not the least of which was that this would be a new venture for him and for cable television. Until that point, high-profile mini-series such as *Roots*, *War and Remembrance*, and *The Thorn Birds* had been produced by and aired on the mainstream television networks.

When Turner bought Rafshoon's proposal, negotiations between the producer and Shirer's agent, Don Congdon, netted Shirer a $25,000 consultant's fee and an additional payment of $30,000 for each hour of the mini-series, a substantial sum in 1988 dollars. Rafshoon hired *Washington Post* reporter Bob Woodward – of Watergate scandal fame – and Christian Williams, a former reporter and editor at the newspaper, to write the screenplay for the mini-series. The two were intrigued by Shirer and by his experiences in Nazi Germany, especially after they read *The Nightmare Years* and *Berlin Diary*. For Woodward, learning about what Shirer had endured gave him a fresh perspective on his own experiences: "It was like a glass of cold water to realize what a reporter does in America versus the obstacles that Shirer had to deal with … In America we have obstacles. But the obstacles [Shirer] had to deal with and the stakes are sobering. We worry about whether we will be called in by some court to disclose a source. When you lay it up against the history of [the Nazi era] and [Shirer's] books, you realize that he was working in the real evil empire."[24]

The challenge for Williams and Woodward as they crafted their screenplay for the mini-series and for experienced British television series writer Ian Curteis, who turned their words into a shooting script, was to make the life of a reporter interesting. "The American storytelling tradition involves action. A journalist lives in the world of ideas," Williams explains. "We had to constrain ourselves from inventing moments in Shirer's life that were only dramatic. We resisted the temptation to have him pick up a machine gun and start shooting."[25]

As they worked, Williams, Woodward, and Rafshoon visited Lenox several times to talk with Shirer. The experience proved to be not what any of them had expected. As Williams told a newspaper interviewer, "There's a dispassionate quality about Bill. He's a newspaper reporter who grew up in the Midwest, that classic American autodidact, the man of few words."[26]

Shirer might have been somewhat more forthcoming – although that is no certainty – had he not been so immersed just then in work on the third and final volume of his memoirs. The world of this man who had roamed so far and wide in his career as a foreign correspondent was gradually, inexorably shrinking. The cluttered second-floor study of his Lenox home, where he now spent most days, had become the focal point of his life. Although it seemed that every square inch of space was filled with books, papers, and files – none of which appeared to a visitor to be in any kind of systematic order – Shirer knew where to find everything he needed. Elaine Steinert recalls: "Intellectually and even academically, Bill had the room organized in his mind. But physically it was kind of helter-skelter. I tried to keep things sorted out for him. That's really what my job was."[27]

Health concerns had also become pivotal for Shirer; as is the case with most octogenarians, his body was beginning to betray him. His last years were punctuated by repeated visits to doctors and hospitals for a variety of ailments, both minor and major. Despite having undergone successful bypass surgery, he was slowed up by the effects of congestive heart failure. He had problems with his gall bladder. Even more concerning was that during a checkup in late autumn 1986 his doctor discovered that a growth that had appeared on his leg was a rare form of cancer. The surgery to remove the tumor and the follow-up treatments left him too weak to work for several months. He spent his eighty-third birthday convalescing.

Shirer still had much that he wanted to say and knew that time had become his enemy. In addition to a final volume of memoirs, he had one more book in mind that he desperately wanted to write: the strange story of the marriage of the iconic Russian writer Leo Tolstoy and his wife Sophia, which Shirer had come to believe had many parallels to his own marriage to Tess. Small wonder that he was impatient in dealing with any distractions that kept him from his work, including the visits from Bob Woodward and Christian Williams.

When he tired of their questions Shirer suggested that the writers look for answers to their queries in the cartons of personal papers that he had kept from the period, which they did while Shirer napped each afternoon. Williams later expressed surprise and some disappointment that nowhere did he and Woodward find among Shirers' effects an actual diary in which he had recorded his daily movements and innermost thoughts; rather there were bits of information Shirer had scribbled on sundry file cards and scraps of paper. There were also old press cards, invitations to Nazi cocktail parties, and other ephemera. Nevertheless, Woodward and Williams managed to satisfy their curiosity and find most of the background information needed to flesh out their screenplay; whatever they failed to find, they invented.

Once the screenwriters had done their work, the two actors hired to play the lead roles for the mini-series followed the now well-trodden path to the door of Shirer's Lenox home. New England-born Sam Waterston had been cast as Shirer, while the Swiss film star-opera director Marthe Keller was to portray Tess Shirer. The pair proved to be inspired choices for their roles, even if Shirer initially knew nothing about either of them; he was not much of a moviegoer. No matter, having read Shirer's books, both Waterston and Keller were well aware of his story and his reputation. Waterston recalls, "We certainly knew who Shirer was. In person, he was white-haired, frail, and seemed somewhat reserved. I found him to be extraordinarily gentlemanly."[28]

Waterston, a lanky, classically trained actor with an impressive body of stage and screen work to his credit, is today widely known for his recurring role over the course of sixteen seasons in the popular television series *Law & Order*. However, he was already a star in 1989, having appeared in more than thirty movies. Among his most notable performances was a lead role in the 1984 Academy Award winner *The Killing Fields* – for which Waterston received an Oscar nomination for his portrayal of *New York Times* foreign correspondent Sydney Schanberg. No less important was the fact Waterston was regarded as a "serious actor" who enjoyed a well-earned reputation as a humanitarian and a man of conscience; he had also been cast as Abraham Lincoln in an eponymously named 1988 made-for-television movie on the life of the sixteenth president of the United States.

Keller brought a much different background to *The Nightmare Years* mini-series She had studied ballet as a girl growing up in her native Switzerland, but had stopped after a teenage skiing accident (something to which Shirer could relate, having lost his right eye on the slopes in that 1932 mishap). Afterward, Keller became a stage actress in Berlin and in 1966 started making movies. Although she appeared in several high-profile Hollywood films starring opposite the likes of such A-list leading men as Al Pacino and Dustin Hoffman, she had done most of her work in European films and appropriately brought an Old World sensibility and charm to the her *Nightmare Years* role as Tess Shirer.

Both Waterston and Keller found it helpful to meet Shirer in order to get a feel for his character. They did so initially in late summer 1988, when they performed at Tanglewood, where they narrated a concert by the Boston Symphony Orchestra. Shirer, who still had "a thing" for dancers, even former ones, was thrilled that Keller had been cast in the role of his wife; he felt she was perfect for the part. In conversation with family and friends he mistakenly referred to her as "a beautiful Austrian woman, like Tess."[29]

The insights into Shirer's character and motivations that both actors garnered when they met him proved useful when it came time to film the mini-series. The six-hour production was shot in Hungary, with Budapest and its old buildings standing in for Berlin in the late 1930s. Waterston says the experience of filming behind the Iron Curtain, which was in the process of crumbling, was memorable for a variety of reasons. He recalls shooting one scene in the Budapest train station, which had been festooned with huge Nazi banners for the occasion: "I wondered how people passing through the station would react to that, but they seemed to take it all in stride ... Later I was talking with one of the film crew who told me that he'd overheard a conversation in which an elderly traveler whispered to his companion, 'You see, I told you they'd be back!'"[30]

While the Nazis were not on the march in Europe again, for four nights in September 1989 they were back in the consciousness of the American public as *The Nightmare Years* mini-series was presented in two-hour segments on the TNT cable network. The mini-series drew respectable ratings and won several favorable reviews; however, for a variety of reasons, it failed to capture the public's imagination. Geraldine Fabrikant of *The New York Times* pinpointed a likely reason why: "[*The Nightmare Years*] does not have the grit of battle scenes or the tragedy of the Holocaust. It deals with a subtler, but equally insidious struggle: the fight by the Nazi Ministry of Propaganda and Public Enlightenment to control the dissemination of news both within Germany and beyond its borders, and how the media at the time, and one reporter in particular (William Shirer), responded to the barrage of Nazi propaganda."[31] These were the very reasons that producer Jerry Rafshoon had been drawn to *The Nightmare Years* as the basis for a mini-series. Subtlety and nuance evidently do not play well in prime-time television programming in America.

For his part, Shirer approved of that aspect of *The Nightmare Years*, and he told inquiring reporters that he liked the small screen adaptation of his book; however, the truth was that he had serious reservations about aspects of the screenplay, especially Woodward and Williams's use of dramatic license. That was the case with one scene in particular: the Shirers' traumatic June 1938 departure from Berlin. Inga Shirer Dean recalls, "My mother had terrible problems when I was born. She'd had surgery and was heavily bandaged. At the Berlin airport, I was left with my nurse when the Gestapo officers took her away to strip-search her. She got very upset and called out to my father, 'Bill, they're taking me away!' My father must have felt terribly impotent because he couldn't do anything and they undid mom's bandages, and it really was a nightmare. It would have been a pretty exciting scene without any embellishment. I mean, the aircrew were holding the plane for us out on the runway and all of that. Anyway, the script had the guards taking my father into a side room, where he reacted by brandishing chairs and leaping across tables in an effort to rescue my mother. When my dad read this part of the script, he laughed. I started laughing too, but he laughed much harder than I did. He laughed so hard that he had tears rolling down his cheeks."[32]

39

Tenacious to the End

William Shirer was a proud man who was not inclined to forgive and forget. Despite all his successes in life, to his dying day he smarted from the pain of his dismissal from CBS and from what he believed was his betrayal by Ed Murrow; Shirer felt Murrow's actions had put him in the vulnerable position that had indirectly led to him being blacklisted and to his long years of unemployment and financial hardship. People who met Shirer late in his life puzzled over his tenaciousness, which bordered on an obsession to have the last word on this issue. "He was a fascinating man and at heart was a good person, but I was astounded that he could be so bitter about some things that had happened long ago," says Martha Nordstrom, who preceded Elaine Steinert as Shirer's secretary.[1]

Nordstrom also recalls Shirer's ultra-competitiveness, a trait she attributes to in his background as a journalist who came of age in an era when "beating the competition" was paramount. Shirer's drive to excel extended to all aspects of his life, even to a leisure activity such as gardening. "I remember that he had a next-door neighbor who kept a nice garden and grew tomatoes; Shirer loved tomatoes, and he was envious of the ones his neighbor grew. I found that level of competitiveness in him curious, puzzling even."[2]

Shirer may have been roleplaying and having a bit of fun with his gardening. However, in Nordstrom's mind it seemed consistent with his character because he applied the same no-nonsense, win-at-all-costs attitude to his work, especially the writing of volume 3 of his memoirs. In the late 1980s, that book became the focus of his life, his raison d'être. Above all, he was determined to provide his account of his 1947 departure from CBS and his falling out with Ed Murrow. It was a task he was obsessed with completing, especially after his battle with cancer in early 1987, his ongoing concerns about the health of his heart, and the 1988 surgery to repair a tear in the retina of his left eye, his one good eye. The latter affliction further limited his ability to read and write. All of this doubtless factored into his decision to abandon a book project for which his agent had negotiated a $500,000 contract with Bantam Books. The proposed volume was a series of interviews with Americans who had been born around the start of the twentieth century; this was a genre of historical narrative that oral historian Studs Terkel – another celebrated Chicagoan – had elevated into an art form and a commercial success; the editors at Bantam felt Shirer could emulate Terkel's success. Despite this and despite the easy money he would have made, Shirer's heart was not in the project, and he abandoned it.

Preoccupied now with his health, Shirer made no secret of his desire to spend whatever time he had left writing the final volume of his memoirs. Inga Shirer Dean recalls her father's steely determination to finally tell his side of how he had been fired by CBS for what he insisted were political reasons and to reveal the role that Ed Murrow had played in this drama: "One day my dad said to me, 'I want you to type something for me because before I die I want to set down on paper my side of what really happened.' And so I did. I typed what he told me."[3]

Shirer's account of the end of his CBS career was just one element of a much broader story. *A Native's Return: 1945–88* covers the events of the forty-three years that spanned more than half of Shirer's life to that point. The book's title, a variation of that of English author Thomas Hardy's 1878 novel *The Return of the Native*, is revealing for what it says about Shirer's mindset. Among the classic works by such authors as Dickens, Austen, Chekhov, Zola, and Proust, he had read in his youth, he had also read Hardy's writings, which he explained had helped to illuminate the nineteenth century for him "leaving indelible impressions of what life was like in that time and what the human experience, with its comedies and tragedies, its ups and downs and uncertainties, and its baffling mysteries, was."[4] Shirer, like Hardy, was a man of unfathomable sensitivity and complexity, as well as of puzzling contradictions.

Both authors were voracious readers whose intellectual inquiries led them to question their faith and ultimately to doubt the existence of God. Both were excoriated by critics; both lived a tangled personal life, and both spent their final years struggling to make sense of – or perhaps it was to *justify* – some of the things they had done and the mistakes they had made. One well-known literary critic observes of Hardy, "He wrote forceful studies of life in which his characters are continually defeated in their struggle against their physical and social environment, against their impulses, and against the malevolent caprices of chance."⁵ While it would be putting too fine a point on it to make too much of any comparison of the lives and careers of Thomas Hardy and William Lawrence Shirer, there are some undeniable similarities.

Like Diggory Venn, the protagonist of Hardy's novel *The Return of the Native*, Shirer was a man who was ever groping for answers and struggling to understand his place in a world from which he had become alienated. Since his 1941 return to New York from Berlin, Shirer had never truly felt at home in America, the land of his birth. "For much of my adulthood," he explains in *A Native's Return*, "Europe had been the center of my life and work."⁶ The reality was that he had spent only fifteen years – 1926 to 1941 – living abroad, yet those years defined the man and shaped the rest of his life.

Surprisingly, *A Native's Return* offers only a passing mention of Shirer's wartime life in New York. Having touched upon aspects of these experiences in his earlier writings, he must have felt that he had nothing more of any importance to say on the subject. Despite this, the third and final volume of his memoirs includes some of Shirer's most intensely personal writing. In fulfilling his desire to have the last word on the subject, he devotes almost a third of the book to an impassioned account of the background to and circumstances of his departure from CBS, his alienation from Ed Murrow, and the lean years that he spent struggling to scratch out a living and maintain his self-respect after being blacklisted. The balance of the book recounts the story behind the writing of *The Rise and Fall of the Third Reich*, delves into the reasons for the failure of Shirer's marriage to Tess, and chronicles his struggles to resolve the philosophical and theological questions he had puzzled over for much of his life. None of this was easy for him to write about, especially the details of his private life.

The breakup of his marriage to Tess was something he had come to accept, but regretted with all his heart and soul. While both husband and wife bore some responsibility for the collapse of their relationship, Shirer conceded that, if there was blame to be apportioned, the lion's share was his. Reflecting that, his account of the breakup, the divorce, and its grim aftermath – selective though it may be – is candid and visceral to the point of being painful to read. His hurt is palpable; it is as if Shirer, older, sadder, and wiser after all that had happened, was doing literary penance.

Shirer bared his soul in the last chapter of *A Native's Return*, musing about the meaning of life, his own mortality, and the spiritual void into which he had slipped because he could not bring himself to believe in heaven or hell: "I could not prove that they did not exist nor could I prove the opposite … At the moment, I am content to wait and see."[7] Shirer had begun to lose his faith early in life, following his father's premature death. Subsequently, his extensive readings on questions of religion and faith and his conversations with Gandhi and other spiritual people had only served to accentuate his skepticism about the credibility of religion. However, it was really his wartime experiences – having seen firsthand and up close the unspeakable horrors of the Nazi-orchestrated Holocaust – that solidified his doubts and convinced him there is no such entity as a "just and powerful God." Ever the rationalist, he searched elsewhere for answers to the big questions in life: "But if … I faced soon departing this life without the consolation of religion and a belief in a life hereafter … I felt enriched by the poetry and the philosophy which I had found in the religions I knew."[8]

Many readers were not sure what to make of *A Native's Return*. The book had little of the chronological flow or dramatic arc of *The Nightmare Years*. Apart from the story of Shirer's dramatic departure from CBS and his falling out with Ed Murrow, which was emotional ground he had already covered in his 1954 novel *Stranger Come Home*, the narrative is at times shapeless and discursive to the point of being problematic. The ultimate reaction of readers and reviewers alike reflected those shortcomings.

A Native's Return was not nearly as commercially successful as *The Nightmare Years*. In large measure, this was due to the book's subject matter and its desultory structure. At the same time, publisher Little, Brown and Company was less than optimistic about the prospects for commercial success; others evidently were of the same opinion. Bantam Books purchased the paperback rights for merely $10,000, a pittance when compared to the $400,000 that Bantam had paid for the same rights to *The Nightmare Years* or the $500,000 it had promised for the book of oral history that Shirer had opted not to finish.

The media reception for *A Native's Return* echoed and affirmed the publishers' indifference to the book. On balance, the reviews were unfavorable; several chided Shirer for being wordy and repetitious. Some reviewers focused on that portion of *A Native's Return* in which Shirer offered his version of the events that ended his CBS career. Prior to this, a history of the incident had been recited by Murrow himself, repeated by his "Boys," by various Murrow biographers, and by CBS boss William Paley. The essence of this version of events was that by March 1947 Shirer had lost his way, grown lazy, and was losing his audience. In 1988, Murrow biographer Joseph Persico – whose biography is arguably the definitive book on the life and career of Ed Murrow – had been the first to raise serious doubts about aspects of Murrow's assessment of Shirer's situation.

Nonetheless, most people – at least those who still cared about what had happened – continued to accept the party line.[9] As history professor Alan Brinkley of the Graduate School of New York University speculates in an article for *The New York Times Book Review*, "Shirer's recounting of Edward R. Murrow's role in his demise at CBS may come as a shock to those who revere Murrow as the saintly patriarch of broadcast journalism."[10] Other reviewers picked up on that significant theme. Writing for *The New York Times'* daily edition two weeks later, Herbert Mitgang observes, "*A Native's Return* is full of hurt feelings and misunderstandings; the executives who denied [Shirer] his livelihood and, by his lights, lacked courage. In places the memoir reads like a combination of Paddy Chayefsky's *Network* and [Martin Ritt's] *The Front* – except that this is not a film, but real-life recollection."[11]

Journalist Harrison Salisbury takes a broader view of *A Native's Return*, musing in a *Washington Post* review about what he calls "the taming of the airwaves": "Shirer's third volume [of memoirs] tells how the superb generation of WWII reporters was destroyed and, with occasional exceptions such as Walter Cronkite and Howard K. Smith, replaced by second raters, thought to be more acceptable to advertisers and audiences."[12] Salisbury includes a judicious criticism of Shirer that was also a backhanded compliment, noting that "if this prickly, sometimes ill-tempered, [and] ego-conscious man had been more malleable, he could have continued his career in electronic journalism." But then, Salisbury adds, in all likelihood, he would never have written *The Rise and Fall of the Third Reich* or *The Nightmare Years*, two of the definitive books on Hitler and the Nazi era.[13]

Shirer did not dispute Salisbury's analysis, most of which he begrudgingly accepted. And doing so in no way diminished the sense of satisfaction he derived from knowing that he would have the last word on the story of his 1947 departure from CBS. Ed Murrow was long gone, and CBS boss William Paley was now eighty-nine and in failing health; he died after a fatal heart attack suffered on the night of 26 October 1990, nine months after the publication of *A Native's Return*.[14]

Despite his satisfaction at having finally finished his memoirs, Shirer was disappointed by the overall tone of the critical reception for the final book. Over nearly a half century as an author, he had learned to accept the good with the bad; he was savvy enough to understand that as often as not reviews of his books and any articles that were written about him were colored by the writers' opinions of him or his politics, which he had never been shy about voicing. What Shirer had never accepted – and never would accept – was the indifference with which publishers had treated his work, especially in his later years.

Shirer's umbrage only deepened when his agent, Don Congdon, pitched Little, Brown and Company a proposal for the book Shirer dearly wanted to write next – an account of the ill-fated marriage of Sonya and Leo Tolstoy. The company "shocked us by turning it down cold, with no explanation."[15] That disappointment fed Shirer's growing impatience with the publisher and fueled his decision to buy his own newspaper ads to tout *A Native's Return*, which he felt Little, Brown and Company had failed to promote properly. After an initial series of newspaper advertisements that coincided with the book's January arrival in bookstores, the publisher had done nothing to keep the book in the public's eye. Although he complained that he "could not afford it,"[16] Shirer purchased his own ad space in the 16 September 1990 editions of both *The New York Times Book Review* and the *Los Angeles Times*. "Notice," the plaintive display announcements read, "Perhaps because there was no follow-up advertising, some readers may have missed the January publication of the third and last volume of my memoirs."

Corporate executives at Little, Brown and Company were embarrassed and angered by Shirer's self-promotion. "It obviously doesn't make us look very good," Arlynn Greenbaum, the company's director of trade book marketing, told a reporter from *Publishers Weekly*.[17] Not surprisingly, the incident hastened the end of Shirer's relationship with Little, Brown and Company. It also left Don Congdon no choice but to seek another publisher for Shirer's Tolstoy book, which Congdon and Shirer knew would be his last.

40

The Final Act

By 1990, the ravages of time had taken a heavy toll on William Shirer. He was virtually blind. He was hard of hearing, hobbled by arthritic knees, plagued with congestive heart failure, had undergone gall bladder surgery, and had endured two bouts with cancer. Through it all, as was his habit, he continued to tap away at his typewriter each and every day.

For a time, Shirer had considered writing a stage play about Tolstoy. However, he had abandoned that idea when his agent succeeded in pitching the Tolstoy book to Bantam Books for $50,000 in advance money. Congdon felt he still could do better and was proved right when two other publishers made superior offers. While Shirer was gratified, money was no longer the deciding factor in his career decisions, if it truly had ever been. As a young man, he had chafed at prohibition, prudery, Midwestern parochialism, and what he described as "the cant of the bourgeois who dominated our land and made it, [I] thought, such a mindless, shoddy place to live in."[1] In a 1990 interview with New England-based *Yankee Magazine*, Shirer echoed that comment when he lamented, "These days it seems that making money is all that's really important to people." Then after a dramatic pause, he added, "To Americans."[2] He had become a stranger in his own land. Mentally, he remained an expatriate.

True to the spirit of his ideals, Shirer felt he owed a measure of loyalty to Steve Rubin, the president of Bantam Books. Rubin forgivingly had opted not to penalize Shirer for abandoning the book of oral history he had been working on for Bantam. At Shirer's urging, Don Congdon reached an agreement with Rubin on the planned Tolstoy book, although not until he had convinced the publisher to increase the advance payment to $100,000; it was not without good reason that Congdon was renowned as being one of New York's shrewdest literary agents.

Shirer was already hard at work on Tolstoy research by the time he signed the contract. He had long dreamed of writing a book about the iconic Russian writer. His fascination with Russian literature had begun in his youth, when he had devoured classics by Gogol, Dostoyevsky, Turgenev, Chekhov, and Tolstoy. Especially Tolstoy. Shirer's passion for the count's writings and his life story had received fresh impetus in India in 1931 when Shirer fell under the spell of Gandhi, who explained to Shirer how he – like so many others in the opening decade of the twentieth century – had been swayed by Tolstoy's utopian vision and his ideas on the power of passive resistance. Tolstoy and Gandhi biographers have delved into the complex relationship between the two men. In 1909, Gandhi had written to the Count asking for advice and for permission to reprint some of Tolstoy's nonfiction writing. When Tolstoy gave his approval, the two men began a correspondence in which they discussed practical and theological aspects of nonviolent protest. Gandhi had adopted elements of Tolstoy's philosophy as tools in the struggle for Indian independence. A half-century later, Martin Luther King, Jr was inspired by Gandhi's ideas, employing them in the 1960s struggle for black civil rights in America.

Shirer found all of this intriguing; however, for him what most resonated about Tolstoy's life and ideas was the story of the great writer's stormy marriage, in particular its tragic final chapter. In his dotage, Tolstoy had attempted to simplify things, living by the fruits of his own physical labors and renouncing materialism. This proved problematic since his wife Sonya, sixteen years younger and fearful of falling into poverty once when her husband was gone, shared none of his enthusiasm for an ascetic lifestyle. The couple's quarrels became so heated, so embittered, that Tolstoy fled the family estate intending never to return. He was eighty-two at the time, and we can only speculate about his mental competency. That aside, what history tells us is that mere days after running away, accompanied by his doctor and soon by his youngest daughter, Tolstoy fell ill with pneumonia. He died early on the morning of 7 November 1910, in the stationmaster's house in the isolated village of Astapovo, 240 miles southeast of Moscow. It was a bizarre, forlorn ending for Russia's greatest writer.

The story of how Tolstoy's marriage had unraveled and of his final days appealed to the romantic in Shirer. Acknowledging the errors he had made in his own life, he identified with Tolstoy and with his marital woes. Inga Shirer Dean, who by now was herself divorced and had remarried, moved to Lenox with her second husband, John W. Dean (*not* the one who served as President Richard Nixon's counsel during the Watergate scandal). She intended to pursue her own writing career[3] and be near her father, who, as Inga recalled, had come to feel that – like Tolstoy – he had been "a misunderstood husband with [a] difficult wife."[4] Inga says her parents "had once had great passion for each other, as the Tolstoys had; however, things were not at all happy between them in the end."[5]

Shirer's fascination with Tolstoy had also been fired by his friendship with Joe Barnes, who had edited *The Rise and Fall of the Third Reich* and had played a pivotal role in that book's success. Inspired and encouraged by Barnes's knowledge of Russian, Shirer was keen to learn the language. However, finding the time had always been a problem for him; in his younger years, Shirer had studied Russian in a desultory way. Now he decided that having access to the diaries of Tolstoy's wife and other primary source material in the original editions would be the key to any Tolstoy book that he might write: "For years Tolstoy's biographers saw the Countess ... through [her husband's] eyes ... But all this changed when her diary appeared in a definitive Russian edition in 1978."[6]

Irina Lugovskaya helped her husband hone his Russian skills and do the research for the Tolstoy book, while daughter Inga now served as her father's secretary. Given his frailties, work on the Tolstoy book was slow at times. The realities of Shirer's advanced age and fading health were underscored in early December 1990 when his heart failed. After a week in a local hospital, he returned home, although he was still not fully recovered. A few nights later, Irina called an ambulance to rush her husband to Massachusetts General Hospital in Boston, two hours to the east. There he remained in critical condition for three days. With Irina and his daughters Inga and Linda at his bedside, Shirer clung to life by the slimmest of threads. Irina whispered encouragement in his ear, reminding him that he still had work to do, a book to finish. As a vivid, tangible reminder, she put on his feet his favorite socks, which were a gloriously cheerful red.

Fortunately for Shirer, he came under the care of Dr John R. Levinson, the top cardiac specialist at Massachusetts General Hospital and one of America's best. In large measure, it was because of Levinson's medical expertise that Shirer made a remarkable, improbable recovery. Nonetheless, he faced a long period of convalescence when he returned home after a month's hospital stay. He had lost thirty pounds as well as his mobility.

With his wife's love, help, and encouragement, Shirer began a program of rehabilitation, hobbling around the house each day to rebuild his stamina and his motor skills. He was more determined than ever to somehow find the strength to finish this one last book, which took him almost two more years of laborious effort. While the manuscript was hardly vintage Shirer, it did recount the story that its author wanted to tell. Shirer was a frail eighty-nine years of age when he finished writing in the summer of 1993. Well aware that he was living on borrowed time, Shirer dedicated his Tolstoy book to the two people whom he knew had helped him live long enough to finish it: his wife Irina and Dr John Levinson. "I asked him if he had solved the riddle that he had set out to solve," recalls Irina. "His reply was 'No,' but he was happy ... We celebrated by donning *lapti* [Russian peasant footwear made out of tree bark fibre] and raising glasses of champagne."[7]

Having made such a monumental effort to finish his Tolstoy book, Shirer suffered a rude shock when Bantam rejected the manuscript. Steve Rubin had left the company, and his successor had no interest in the project. Happily for Shirer, ever the master agent, Don Congdon sold the book to Simon & Schuster, albeit for a smaller advance than the $100,000 Bantam had offered. Very significant and positive from Shirer's perspective was the fact that Simon & Schuster editor-in-chief Michael Korda personally took on the job of editing the manuscript.

London-born and the fifty-nine-year-old scion of an artistic family, Korda had studied history at Magdalen College, Oxford University, and had served in the Royal Air Force. By 1992, he had been with Simon & Schuster for almost thirty-five years and was a legend in the American publishing world for his work in editing the memoirs of high-profile public figures such as former presidents Richard Nixon and Ronald Reagan (and he had offered some input when Joe Barnes was editing *The Rise and Fall of the Third Reich*). Ever flamboyant and opinionated, Korda also had a rare talent for shaping and refining a manuscript to best advantage. He was the ideal man to hammer into shape Shirer's Tolstoy tale, which was wordy, repetitive, and cried out for the guiding hand of a strong editor. The book was meant to be, as Shirer himself explained, "an inquiry into why Leo Tolstoy's long and productive life ended as it did: strangely, irrationally, and in tragedy."[8] Korda understood that; however, he also recognized the broader theme that coursed through the narrative. On one level, he saw Shirer's book as the story of a grand romance that had spanned almost a half-century. On another level, Korda recognized that Shirer had crafted a study of a creative genius who had grappled in his personal life and in his writings with the universal themes of love, sex, marriage, and aging.

Inga Shirer Dean credits Korda with a brilliant editing job; he cut superfluous material, cleaned up the verbal infelicities, and sharpened the book's focus. What Korda did not and could not do was inject the necessary literary perspective, which could have raised the book to a higher level of excellence and relevance. While Shirer understood and accepted this, he appreciated the changes that Korda did make. In his acknowledgments, written in June 1993, Shirer thanked his editor "for his many helpful suggestions and for his encouragement when I most needed it."[9] Shirer knew that *Love and Hatred* was his swan song. After fifty-two years as an author, he was no longer up to the sustained intellectual and physical effort of writing a book: "I've been lucky. But I shall be ninety early in 1994. Time to quit."[10] Those were the final words William L. Shirer wrote for publication.

In the following weeks, he did everything he could to generate interest in his Tolstoy book, which he correctly surmised Simon & Schuster suddenly had minimal interest in promoting, despite Korda's involvement in it. After all of the effort Shirer had put into the manuscript, this was a cruel, embarrassing blow. The angst he was feeling inevitably took a toll on his health, which took a sharp turn for the worse one day in early December 1993. When he began having difficulty breathing, Irina called for an ambulance again to rush him to Massachusetts General Hospital in Boston, where he again came under the care of Dr John Levinson. For more than three weeks, Shirer stubbornly battled for his life. However, even the good doctor could not work another miracle: "[Shirer] knew he would not live to see his ninetieth birthday or the publication of his last book."[11]

Shirer's final days were traumatic and difficult. Sedated, he slipped in and out of consciousness, and the true extent of his wartime emotional traumas became painfully clear: "He cried out, shouting about German planes coming, German bombs falling," recalls Irina.[12] William L. Shirer's suffering came to an end on 28 December 1993. Thirteen years after his bypass surgery, his ailing heart failed him for the final time.

Following his death, Shirer's body was returned to Lenox for a family funeral and burial in Mountain View Cemetery. His hilltop gravesite is next to that of his first wife, Tess (who died in 2008).[13] From up there, a visitor's eyes take in a panoramic Berkshires view that is as tranquil and unspoiled as it is timeless. It is a scene that Shirer would have loved for it harkens back to earlier times, when life was simpler and less frenetic. During "the American Century," as *Time-Life* Books publisher Henry Luce described it, the land of Shirer's birth had been a place of boundless optimism and brash self-confidence. By the time of Shirer's death in 1993, America and the world were forever changed, and not always for the better.

Two hundred family and friends gathered on the afternoon of 15 January 1994 for a memorial service that celebrated William Shirer's life and myriad accomplishments. The music for the event, held in the nondenominational Church on the Hill, a white-frame, postcard-perfect structure on the town's Main Street, was performed by Shirer's seventeen-year-old grandson Alex Rae. The son of Shirer's daughter Linda played piano pieces by Tchaikovsky and Beethoven and a well-known work for classical guitar entitled "Spanish Romance," which was a composition that guitar virtuoso Andrés Segovia likely played for Tess and Bill Shirer when he was their neighbor during the couple's idyllic 1933 sojourn in Spain.

David Murray, a journalist friend; Shirer's cardiologist, Dr John Levinson; and Shirer's longtime neighbor and friend James MacGregor Burns, the noted historian and biographer of President Kennedy, delivered eulogies. Burns said it eloquently and well when he remembered Shirer as an acute observer who had "chronicled some of the most splendid and the most terrifying events of the [twentieth] century," noting that Shirer "had shaped Americans' views of Hitler, Gandhi, and other important historical figures who had shaped and changed our world."[14]

Had William Shirer lived to see publication of *Love and Hatred: The Troubled Marriage of Leo and Sonya Tolstoy*, he would not have been surprised by the reviews. As was the case with each of his books, the critical reception was mixed. A reviewer for *Publishers Weekly* lauded *Love and Hatred* as a "darkly magnificent dual portrait" of the Tolstoys,[15] while Michiko Kakutani at *The New York Times Book Review* praised the work for being "highly readable," but she hastened to add that it was too narrow in its focus, was poorly organized, and ultimately failed to "add appreciably to our knowledge of the [Tolstoys]."[16]

Shirer doubtless would have been happier with the critical reception for a collection of scripts from his wartime radio broadcasts, which his daughters put together five years after his death. Published in autumn 1999 under the title *"This Is Berlin": Radio Broadcasts 1938–40*, the volume featured an introduction by British historian John Keegan and a preface by Inga Shirer Dean, who edited the text and reinserted words that German censors had excised.

Reviewers praised the deftness and eloquence of Shirer's radio scripts. *Publishers Weekly* hailed them as being "one of the great pillars of broadcast journalism."[17] For *The National Review*, Mike Potemra observed that reading *"This Is Berlin"* will "give you a sense of how much scarier WWII was before the outcome was known. It makes the heroism of our American soldiers even more striking and proves there is no such thing as being 'on the right side of history.'"[18] Richard Mullen of *Contemporary Review* lamented, "It is sad to reflect when reading these scripts that such broadcasts are not possible today as journalists lack Shirer's knowledge and most of the audience would not understand such allusions."[19]

The Spanish-American philosopher George Santayana cautioned that those who forget their history are condemned to relive it. That William Shirer understood and agreed with this sentiment is clear, for he included Santayana's oft-quoted epigram as a caveat in *The Rise and Fall of the Third Reich*. Others have paid heed.

For example, writing in a 2009 article that appeared in *The Providence Journal*, John R. MacArthur, the president of the charitable foundation that publishes *Harper's Magazine*, wonders if President Barrack Obama has ever heard of William L. Shirer. If so, MacArthur speculates, it is unlikely Obama knows anything more than the fact that Shirer chronicled the history of Nazi Germany and the folly of the Allies' failure to confront Hitler sooner rather than later: "You can't read Shirer or any other standard account of Germany between the wars without concluding that given stronger French and British political will, Hitler could have been stopped (and maybe even overthrown by an internal coup), either in March 1936 ... or at some other point before the Munich agreement in September 1938."[20]

MacArthur is forgetful – or else he is charitable – when he excuses the United States from culpability. However, there was a rationale for America's failure to get involved in Europe: for two decades after the First World War, isolationists held sway in Washington and in the court of American public opinion. History tells us there was a lamentable degree of sympathy – and, yes, even admiration – for what Hitler and the Nazis were up to in post-Weimar Germany. At the same time, there was an undeniable undercurrent of anti-Semitism in the ranks of the United States diplomatic corps and of the State Department.

Pulitzer Prize-winning author and historian David McCullough, among others, has decried Americans' ignorance of history. In a 1983 appearance before a Senate committee that was studying the need for programs to educate history and civics teachers, McCullough warned that such ignorance is no triviality; it can and does pose a threat to national security. "[He] pointed out that only three United States colleges require a course on the Constitution and they are all military institutions: the United States Military Academy at West Point, the Naval Academy at Annapolis, and the Air Force Academy."[21]

Countless studies over the years have validated and underscored McCullough's concerns, The situation is only marginally better in Canada, where the Dominion Institute, which regularly commissions surveys to measure Canadians' knowledge of their country's history, has found that 40 per cent of adults cannot name the country's first prime minister let alone pinpoint the year Confederation occurred.[22]

In the 1930s, radio displaced newspapers as our preferred source of news; William L. Shirer's career reflected and was shaped by that change, just as he himself played an important part in shaping radio news. Television then eclipsed radio in the 1950s, and social media today is reshaping the media landscape once again. The new reality is that anyone with a smart phone and the urge to do so – a "citizen journalist" – can use the internet to create and disseminate news and information. In theory, whenever such material is posted online, it comes under scrutiny in the worldwide forum that is cyberspace. Underlying the faith many people have in this process is the assumption that the truth will come out when any statement is challenged, in what effectively is a kind of online intellectual free-for-all. However, any such approach is at best imprecise and is rife with uncertainties and peril. The validation process is ill-defined. And even more problematic is the degree to which it is subject to abuse in an age of digital manipulation.

For better and worse, the emergence of social media has changed our world irrevocably. The internet and social media have become ubiquitous, even in countries where the ruling elites reject the tenets of traditional Western democracy – think Russia and China – and in areas such as the Middle East. In the Western world, especially in North America and Europe, the rise of the internet and social media have brought about – and continue to bring about – profound cultural change that is as significant and wide-reaching as Johannes Gutenberg's invention of moveable type in the fifteenth century. Indeed, the e-revolution that is swirling around us is redefining virtually every aspect of our daily lives: how we communicate, acquire and consume knowledge, shop, seek entertainment, and even how we control the utilities and services that make our homes and cities run smoothly.

Just as broadcasting – first radio and then television – displaced print as society's medium of choice, the internet is today displacing traditional forms of broadcasting and is fundamentally altering long-established business models for both radio and television. Likewise, the growth of digital media threatens to drive print culture to extinction. Professor Douglas Mann, who teaches media studies and pop culture at Western University in London, Ontario, aptly speaks of how it is "almost midnight" for print culture.[23]

The familiar model of news gathering and dissemination that thrived in the twentieth century is being swept aside by the digital tsunami. And the explosive growth of the internet as information highway is giving rise to new sources of news and to some excellent journalism as presented by *Slate*, *Huffington Post*, *Salon*, and *The Tyee*. What will ultimately replace the old, familiar journalistic model remains to be seen. However, this much does seem certain: the influence and importance of what has been dubbed "citizen journalism" will only continue to grow.

Morley Safer, the Toronto-born television journalist (and author of the foreword for this book) a fifty-year veteran at CBS television who has become famous as a correspondent for the network's popular newsmagazine program *60 Minutes*, cautions, "I'd trust citizen journalists as much as I'd [trust] a citizen surgeon." Safer is no impartial observer and, as an octogenarian, he is definitely of the old school. However, he does raise a fundamental and vitally important concern when he questions the reliability and the critical standards of those who "report" and post information and opinions online. Whom can we trust? What should we believe? The potential for manipulation and disinformation is infinite – now and as history is being written.

Will there ever again be a place in our world for professional journalists and interpreters – people such as William L. Shirer, Edward R. Murrow, Dorothy Thompson, Harrison Salisbury, or Teddy White? Their time is past.

In our headlong rush to the future, there are dangers in forgetting where we have been and how we got where we are. The life and career of William Shirer – and the complex fate of the United States of America in the "American century" – provide us with an unsettling reminder of that inconvenient, uncomfortable reality.

Acknowledgments

This book is the fruit of more than eight years of research and writing; however, it would not have been possible for me to complete it without the help, kindness, and encouragement of the many people who generously shared with me their time, ideas, primary source materials, and photographs. Heading the list of people to whom I owe an incalculable debt of thanks are the daughters of William and Tess Shirer: the late Eileen Inga (Shirer) Dean, Lenox, MA, and Linda (Shirer) Rae, Cross River, NY, the torchbearers for the memory of their father's many accomplishments and his legacy.

When I began my research, I had no idea of how much work I had ahead of me. It was Inga who steered me in the right direction and encouraged me whenever I began to have doubts. An accomplished writer in her own right – she was the author of a critically acclaimed novel and various other writings – Inga provided me with sage advice, introduced me to many of the people with whom I needed to consult, gave me unfettered access to her father's personal papers, and generously, patiently, and with unfailing good humor answered my myriad questions. To her, I am eternally grateful. What began as working collaboration, developed into a friendship. If I have any regrets about this book, they are that I was unable to finish it in time for Inga to see it published. Sadly, she was only seventy-three when she lost her courageous battle with cancer in July 2011.

Following Inga's passing, her younger sister, Linda, stepped into the breach, patiently responding to my queries and reading and critiquing draft chapters. I owe a sincere and huge thank-you to Linda and her husband Noel Rae, who is himself an author.

I would also like to offer special thanks to two individuals who were near and dear to William Shirer and who provided me with invaluable information and assistance: William Shirer's widow, Irina Alexandrovna Lugovskaya, and his longtime assistant-secretary, Elaine Steinert, both assisted me in chronicling and understanding Shirer's final years of life in Lenox, Massachusetts.

Of enormous help to me in a very different way was Shirer's personal archive. Like many journalists, he was a packrat, an inveterate collector of letters, documents, newspaper and magazine clippings, photos, and ephemera. A significant volume of this unsorted and uncatalogued material, which was stored at Inga Dean's home in Lenox, MA, is now held by the Literary Trust of William L. Shirer, PO box 145, Cross River, NY, 10518.

William Shirer donated the bulk of his personal papers (including correspondence, photographs, diaries, book manuscripts, and photos) to Coe College in Cedar Rapids, IA, his alma mater. All of these materials – the starting point for any in-depth research into Shirer's life and work – can be found in the William L. Shirer Papers, George T. Henry Archives, Stewart Memorial Library, Coe College, Cedar Rapids. Faculty and staff at Coe have been endlessly helpful to me, particularly the now-retired Director of Library Services Professor Emeritus Richard Doyle and his colleagues Jill Jack, Harlene Hansen, and Hongbo Xie, *Coe College Courier* alumni magazine editor Lonnie Zingula; Assistant Director of Alumni Programs Kate Rose and staff at Clark Alumni House; and, 2008 Coe College alumnus Charles Showalter, who did yeoman service in helping me with some follow-up research at the Stewart Memorial Library.

Closer to home, I am indebted to my eagle-eyed colleague Marjorie Bousfield for her help with proofreading and fact-checking, to writer-editor Lindy Mechefske for her suggestions and help, to my friend Britton C. Smith, who answered any and all questions regarding ships and nautical matters, and to my friend and mentor Queen's University Professor Emeritus (History) Geoffrey S. Smith. In my student days, Geoff provided me with a solid grounding in the principles of historiography, and more recently he took time to critique some draft chapters of this book and helped me to see events and people in the broader context that proved essential in the writing of this book.

I also wish to thank author-poet Mark Abley, the McGill-Queen's University Press acquisitions editor who acted as my guide when I set about preparing my manuscript for consideration and then for publication. Mark has been helpful and patient beyond measure in offering his counsel, and I am grateful to him and to Claude Lalumière, who served as my copyeditor, reined in my excess enthusiasm, and helped me to view my material through fresh eyes.

The list of other individuals who have assisted me with my research and to whom I also owe thanks is a long one. It includes: Mary Balle (William Shirer's erstwhile companion and friend), Stockbridge, MA; William Bell (retired *Berkshire Eagle* reporter), Lenox, MA; the late Don Boyd (Shirer family historian), Centerville, OH; Rinker Buck (former *Berkshire Eagle* reporter and now bestselling author), Hartford, CT; Professor Emeritus James MacGregor Burns (Shirer's friend and a Pulitzer Prize-winning historian), Williamstown, MA; Marge Champion (legendary dancer and Shirer's friend and traveling companion), Lenox, MA and New York, NY; Professor Emeritus (Art) Paul Clervi (colleague of Shirer's friend George Latta), William Woods University, Fulton, MO; Michael Congdon (literary agent and the son of Donald Congdon, Shirer's former agent), New York, NY; Stephen Fay (former *Berkshire Eagle* writer); Milanne Hahn (freelance researcher), Austin, TX; Lesley Martin, Reference Librarian, Chicago History Museum Research Center, Chicago, IL; the late Herbert Mitgang (eminent journalist and author), New York, NY; Charles ("Casey") Murrow (educator-author and the son of Edward R. Murrow), North Brattleboro, VT; Martha Nordstrom (Shirer's former assistant); Suzanne Pelton (the daughter of Shirer's second wife, Martha Pelton), Lenox, MA; Edward R. Murrow biographer Joseph E. Persico, New York, NY; Tilly Losch authority Professor Herbert Poetzl, Translation, Research, and Instructional Program, Binghamton University, Binghamton, NY; Cynthia Romanin (daughter of George Latta, William Shirer's friend and traveling companion on his 1926 trip to Paris), St. Louis, MO; Professor Gavriel D. Rosenfeld, Fairfield University, Fairfield, CT; archivist Elizabeth Schau, formerly of the Russell D. Cole Library, Cornell College, Mount Vernon IA; Coe College Professor Emeritus (History) Arthur Schmidt, Washington, DC; Academy Award-nominated actor Sam Waterston (who portrayed Shirer in the 1989 television miniseries *The Nightmare Years*), West Cornwall, CT; and Pilar Wolfsteller (freelance writer-translator), formerly of Zurich, Switzerland.

In the course of my research I also received kind help from the staffs of the following agencies and organizations: the reference desk of the Cedar Rapids Public Library, Cedar Rapids, IA; ETH *Zürich/Archive fur Zeitgesschichte*, Zurich, Switzerland; Archives and Special Collections, Mount Holyoke College, South Hadley, MA; Freedom of Information Record Information/ Dissemination Section of the Federal Bureau of Investigation, Washington, DC; the Harry Ransom Center, The University of Texas at Austin, Austin, TX; the Interlibrary Loans Office, Stauffer Library, Queen's University, Kingston, ON, Canada; Linn County Historical Society, Cedar Rapids, IA; Special Collections, Regenstein Library, University of Chicago, Chicago, IL; and, Digital Collections and Archives, Tufts University, Medford, MA.

A special thank you to New York–based Furthermore: a program of the J.M. Kaplan Fund, for its kind and generous financial support for the publication of this book.

And finally, I would like to offer thanks to my wife Marianne Hunter for her unwavering support, love, and understanding during this book's long gestation period.

Notes

FOREWORD

1 www.winstonchurchill.org/learn/speeches/speeches-of-winston-churchill/104-neville-chamberlain

INTRODUCTION

1 Address at Sioux Falls, SD, 8 September 1919.
2 markedtreeschools.com/?page_id=1490.
3 Cited in *Inside: the Biography of John Gunther* by Ken Cuthbertson (Bonus Books, 1992), xviii. Eric Sevareid was speaking on CBS radio on 2 June 1970, memorializing his friend John Gunther, who had died four days earlier. However, Sevareid was referring not only to Gunther but also to the inordinate number of influential American journalists – Shirer and Sevareid being prominent among them – who hailed from the American Midwest.
4 *Life*, 17 February 1941, 61.
5 Barbara Tuchman, "William L. Shirer," *Book of the Month Club: Sixty Years of Books in American Life*, edited by Al Silverman (Little, Brown and Company, 1986), 152.
6 Shirer, *A Native's Return*, 467.
7 M.R. Montgomery, "William L. Shirer's Century," *Boston Globe*, 30 December 1993, 45.
8 Virginia Woolf, "The Art of Biography," *The Death of the Moth, and Other Essays* (Harcourt, Brace and Company, New York, 1942).

CHAPTER ONE

1 From Carl Sandburg's 1916 poem "Chicago."

2 Shirer, *Twentieth Century Journey*, 63. The street address is now 6500 South Greenwood Avenue. The building has been demolished, and the site is now a vacant lot.

3 William L. Shirer's great-nephew, the late Don Boyd from Centerville, Ohio – a grandson of Shirer's aunt Mabel and her husband James Craig Boyd – compiled an extensive and richly detailed history of the family.

4 William G. Shirer letter to William L. Shirer, 6 January 1931 (William L. Shirer Papers, George T. Henry Archives).

5 According to William L. Shirer's uncle, William G., Johann's brother immigrated to the New Orleans area, and for many years thereafter that branch of the family lost contact with the Scheurers who had settled in New York. William G. reported in his 1931 letter to his nephew that "About 1915 in my regular work as a school-book peddler, I was asked by the Superintendent of Schools in Nashville, Illinois, to OK a recommendation for the adoption of a book. I found this gentleman to be a hardware merchant by the name of Scheurer and discovered that he was evidently the son of my great-uncle ... who came to New Orleans in 1845."

6 Shirer, *Twentieth Century Journey*, 78.

7 Carrie Triem's mother, Elizabeth Huppert, was born in the Palinate on 25 July 1829. She was one of the three children of Henry Huppert and his wife Margaret. The Hupperts and the first two of their three children immigrated to the United States in 1842. Their descendants, who now number more than four hundred, today are scattered across North America. Henry and Margaret Huppert were William L. Shirer' maternal great-grandparents.

8 Shirer, *Twentieth Century Journey*, 79n.

9 William G. Shirer evidently was "a character." A whimsical entry in the 1903 Cornell College yearbook, *The Royal Purple*, says this about him: "WILLIAM G. SHIRER – The small but mighty subject of this sketch first made 'goo-goo' eyes at the lasses of La Porte City in 1880. For two years his parents resided with Willie in Des Moines and later in Mt. Vernon. Shirer can hustle some, and while still a youth edited (or sold) Chicago papers. For two years he was employed in the Mt. Vernon bank and besides that has taught school. He will certainly make his mark – if somcone else writes his name." The cryptic reference to the Shirers living in Des Moines for two years doesn't fit with information gathered by family historian Don Boyd or with other sources.

10 *Cedar Rapids Republican*, 21 January 1899.

11 Lexington Avenue, renamed in 1914, is now called University Avenue.

12 Author interview with Inga Shirer Dean, William Shirer's elder daughter, 8 April 2006.

13 Shirer, *Twentieth Century Journey*, 113.

14 Ibid., 92.

15 Ibid., 76.

16 Ibid., 120.

17 *Chicago Tribune*, "Seward S. Shirer Dies at Hospital," 18 February 1913, 9.

18 Shirer, *Twentieth Century Journey*, 125–6.

CHAPTER TWO

1 Shirer, *Twentieth Century Journey*, 129.

2 Ibid., 134–7.

3 Frank Tanner, whose mother was Sophorana (née Ames), was born 24 March 1844.

4 Shirer, *Twentieth Century Journey*, 138.

5 According to Cedar Rapids city directories, the Tanners lived initially in a house at the northeast corner of South Harrison and Park Avenue in 1880. In 1883, they were living at 221 Second Avenue. However, by 1913, when daughter Bessie arrived home with her three children, the Tanners had moved to 881 Second Avenue.

6 Shirer, *Twentieth Century Journey*, 186.

7 Ibid., 138.

8 Author interview with Inga Shirer Dean, 8 April 2006.

9 Shirer, *Twentieth Century Journey*, 155.

10 William Shirer's Camp Funston diary, 1 July 1919 (William L. Shirer Papers, George T. Henry Archives).

11 Ibid., 10 July 1919.

12 Shirer, *Twentieth Century Journey*, 151.

13 Chautauqua contract (William L. Shirer Papers, George T. Henry Archives).

14 Shirer, *Twentieth Century Journey*, 155.

15 Ibid., 159.

16 Ibid., 161.

CHAPTER THREE

1 Shirer, *Twentieth Century Journey*, 165.

2 Ibid., 166.

3 Albert Saye et al., *Principles of American Government*, 49.

4 Ibid., 167.

5 William Shirer to Ethel Outland, 30 July 1924 (The Literary Trust of William L. Shirer).

6 Shirer, *Twentieth Century Journey*, 178.

7 *Coe College Cosmos*, "It's Fun to Be an Editor." 21 May 1925.

8 Shirer, *Twentieth Century Journey*, 207.

9 Ibid., 213.

10 The 1926 *Acorn* yearbook (226) includes a satirical write-up headed "Escaped from Marshall Hall: The Sing-Sing of Coe College." Four well-known students were mentioned, one them being "Willie Shirer." The tongue-in-cheek biographical blurb about him that appears beside a police mug-shot of a shifty-looking felon, reads as follows: "Age, Awkward; Complexion, yes; Nationality, Bolshevik ... Precautions should be taken to apprehend this man, as he would not hesitate to shoot off his mouth ... is convicted of smoking on the Coe campus."

11 Shirer essay, "Confessions of a College Boy," *Coe College Cosmos*, 10 June 1925.

12 This article and others by Shirer can be found in the archives of the *Coe College Cosmos*, which are posted online at coecollege.newspaperarchive.com.

13 Shirer had been dating a young woman whose surname was Potts. In later years, he referred to her as "Love Potts." Whether "Love" was her given name or a nickname is unclear. There is a reference to a young woman who is identified as "Love Potts" in a wedding report (Crocker-Kremer) that appeared in the *Coe College Cosmos* on 3 February 1922. However, she evidently was not a Coe student because her name does not appear in the student directories from this period or in the College's alumni records.

14 Shirer's traveling companion was five months his junior. George Haworth Latta was a part-time linotype operator at the Cedar Rapids *Daily Republican*, where Shirer worked as a sports reporter. The two had also attended Coe together and became good friends, although Latta was a year behind. Instead, after returning home to Cedar Rapids in autumn 1925, Latta dropped out of Coe and moved to Chicago where he found work as a linotype operator, married Marie Cecilia Ryson in September 1932, and began taking art courses. Eventually Latta earned a Bachelor of Fine Arts degree from the School of Art Institute of Chicago in 1937 and then in 1945 a Master's degree in Fine Arts from the University of Chicago. He subsequently went on to head the Art Department at William Woods University in Fulton, Missouri. After retiring in 1990, Latta moved to Los Angeles, where he lived the last six years of his life with his daughter Cynthia Romanin and her family.

CHAPTER FOUR

1 Cowley, *And I Worked at the Writer's Trade*, 26.
2 Shirer, *Twentieth Century Journey*, 229.
3 Ibid., 219.
4 Hemingway, *A Moveable Feast*, as quoted on the book's title page.
5 Shirer, *Twentieth Century Journey*, 216
6 Malcolm Cowley, "A Place in Paris between James Thurber and Elliot Paul," *The New York Times Book Review*, 10 October 1976, 244.
7 Shirer, *Twentieth Century Journey*, 215.
8 Ibid., 62.
9 Stearns, *The Street I Know*, 286.
10 Shirer, *Twentieth Century Journey*, 350.
11 *Chicago Tribune*, "Army Edition of *The Tribune*." 4 July 1917, 1.
12 Root, *The Paris Edition*, 15.
13 Shirer, *Twentieth Century Journey*, 230.
14 Ibid., 232.
15 Ibid., 233.
16 Ibid., 236.
17 Ibid.
18 Ibid., 238.
19 Author interview with William L. Shirer, Lennox, MA, 10 November 1986.

CHAPTER FIVE

1 Root, *The Paris Edition*, 55.
2 Shirer, *Twentieth Century Journey*, 268.
3 Allen, *Only Yesterday*, 220.
4 Shirer, *Twentieth Century Journey*, 337.
5 Henry Wales, "'Am I Here', He Asks...." *Chicago Tribune*, 22 May 1927, 1.
6 Shirer, *Twentieth Century Journey*, 339.

CHAPTER SIX

1 Shirer, *Twentieth Century Journey*, 347.
2 Katherine van Etta "Kate" McCormick (née Medill), 1853–1932.
3 Shirer, *Twentieth Century Journey*, 352.
4 Ibid., 360.
5 Ibid., 422.
6 Gunther, *Fragment of Autobiography*, 5.

7 Root, *The Paris Edition*, 85

8 Seldes, *Witness*, 232–3.

9 Shirer, *Twentieth Century Journey*, 393.

10 Shirer, *A Native's Return, 1945–1988*, 464.

11 Ibid., 398–9.

12 Ibid.

13 *Dictionary of Literary Biography, Volume 4*, 353–6.

CHAPTER SEVEN

1 Shirer, *Twentieth Century Journey*, 427.

2 Ibid., 430.

3 Ibid., 468.

4 Ibid., 465.

5 Shirer and his Hungarian lover remained friends and kept in touch until the outbreak of World War Two. Sadly, Zora died in the turmoil of the Red Army's occupation of Budapest in the closing weeks of the war.

6 Shirer, *Twentieth Century Journey*, 472.

7 Ibid., 482

8 Ibid., 483.

9 Ibid., 489.

10 John Gunther, "Dateline Vienna," *Harper's*, April 1930, 198–208.

11 Ibid., 201.

12 Shirer, *Midcentury Journey*, 53.

13 *Time*, "Back to the Balkans," 14 August 1944, 90.

14 Sheean, *Dorothy and Red*, 263.

15 Shirer, *Twentieth Century Journey*, 459.

16 Hank Wales letter to William Shirer, 13 March 1930 (William L. Shirer Papers, George T. Henry Archives).

17 According to the information on the passport she carried at the time (The Literary Trust of William L. Shirer).

18 Inga Shirer Dean email to author, 15 August 2007.

19 Tess Shirer in conversation with her granddaughter Deirdre Van Dyk, 15 November 2007.

20 Linda Shirer Rae email to the author, 19 February 2010.

21 Ibid.

22 Author interview with Inga Shirer Dean, 20 May 2008.

23 Linda Shirer Rae email to the author, 19 February 2010.

24 William Shirer letter to Colonel McCormick, 22 May 1930 (William L. Shirer Papers, George T. Henry Archives).

CHAPTER EIGHT

1 Upton Close, "Gandhi: The Prophet Who Sways India." *The New York Times*, 19 January 1930, 77.
2 William Shirer letter to Tess Stiberitz, August (undated) 1930. (The Literary Trust of William L. Shirer).
3 Ibid.
4 Shirer, *Twentieth Century Journey*, 492.
5 Morris, *Farewell the Trumpets: An Imperial Retreat*, 280.
6 Gilbert, *Churchill: A Life*, 499–500.
7 Shirer, *A Native's Return, 1945–88*, 464.
8 Shirer, *Gandhi: A Memoir*, 15–16.
9 The Short S.8 Calcutta was the first stressed-skin metal-hulled flying boat. It was flown by two pilots, who sat in an open cockpit, while the radio operator and as many as fifteen passengers rode in the cargo hold. The plane had a maximum range of 650 miles.
10 The first airliner with a pressurized fuselage, the Boeing 307, was built in 1938. But only ten were produced. It was not until after World War Two – when the technology was perfected for use in military planes and the jet engine was fully developed – that pressurized cabins became common in commercial passenger air service.
11 Miller, *I Found No Peace: The Journal of us Foreign Correspondent*, 227.
12 William L. Shirer, "Flies to India from London in 6 ½ days," *Chicago Tribune*, 17 August 1930, 1.
13 In his initial account of the meeting, which was published in the *Chicago Tribune* on 20 October 1930, 1, Shirer incorrectly described the prince as being nineteen years old. In fact, he had been born 15 October 1914, in Kabul, Afghanistan, meaning that he was nine days short of his seventeenth birthday when Shirer met him.
14 Amanullah Khan (1892–1960) ruled Afghanistan from 1919 to 1929, first as Emir and after 1926 as king. He led the country to independence over its foreign affairs from Great Britain, and his rule was a period of dramatic political and social change inspired by Western ideals. However, Amanullah Khan was deposed and in January 1929 he abdicated, fleeing to India as civil war raged in Afghanistan. He eventually went to Europe where he died in Zürich, Switzerland, in 1960.
15 Shirer, *The Nightmare Years*, 15.
16 The Anglo-Afghan Treaty of 1919, which is also known as the Treaty of Rawalpindi, was an armistice made between the Great Britain and Afghanistan that ended the Third Anglo-Afghan War (May to August 1919).

Signed on 8 August 1919, it was an ambiguous document that acknowledged British recognition of Afghanistan's independence, stated that British-
India would never extend past the Khyber Pass, and ended all British financial support of Afghanistan.

17 *The Nightmare Years*, 8.

18 Ibid., 17.

19 *Chicago Tribune*, 29 December 1930.

20 William Shirer, "Marco Polo's Old Time Route Is Speeded Up," *Chicago Tribune*, 1 February 1931, G-9.

21 Shirer, *The Nightmare Years*, 38.

22 Ibid., 40.

CHAPTER NINE

1 In his 1984 memoir *The Nightmare Years*, Shirer misspelled the surname of
Hungarian-born Emil Vadnay. In the early 1930s Vadnay was the number 2
man in the Vienna bureau of *The New York Times*. In an obituary for the
newspaper's edition of 2 April 1939, 62, G.E. Gedye described Vadnay as
being personable, genteel, and "an inimitable raconteur."

2 Shirer, *The Nightmare Years*, 41.

3 It was and still is possible in Austria for the two witnesses to a marriage to
be male.

4 Inga Dean email to the author, 15 August 2007.

5 William Shirer to Bessie Shirer, 5 January 1931 (William L. Shirer Papers,
George T. Henry Archives).

6 William Shirer to John Shirer, 9 February 1931 (William L. Shirer Papers,
George T. Henry Archives).

7 William Shirer to Bessie Shirer, 5 January 1931 (William L. Shirer Papers,
George T. Henry Archives).

8 Shirer, *The Nightmare Years*, 42.

9 William Shirer to Tess Shirer, undated February 1931 letter (William L. Shirer Papers, George T. Henry Archives).

10 William Shirer to John Shirer, 9 February 1931 (William L. Shirer Papers,
George T. Henry Archives).

11 William Shirer to Tess Shirer, 15 February 1931 (William L. Shirer Papers,
George T. Henry Archives).

12 Shirer, *Gandhi: A Memoir*, 27.

13 Ibid., 28.

14 Ibid., 29.

15 Ibid., 31.

16 Ibid., 46.

17 William Shirer to Tess Shirer, 25 February 1931 (The Literary Trust of William L. Shirer).

18 Shirer, *Gandhi: A Memoir*, 46.

19 William Shirer, "Mystery Hides Britain's Peace Offer to Gandhi." *Chicago Tribune*, 1 March 1931, 7.

20 Shirer, *Gandhi: A Memoir*, 54.

21 William Shirer, "British Empty Cells in India as 'War' Ends," 6 March 1931, 1, 10.

22 Ibid.

23 Shirer, *Gandhi: A Memoir*, 56.

24 Ibid., 55.

25 William Shirer to Tess Shirer, 6 March 1931 (The Literary Trust of William L. Shirer).

26 William Shirer to Tess Shirer, 26 February 1931 (The Literary Trust of William L. Shirer).

27 Ibid., 65.

28 W. Elsfelder to Shirer, 27 February 1931 (William L. Shirer Papers, George T. Henry Archives).

29 William Shirer to Tess Shirer, 27 February 1931 (William L. Shirer Papers, George T. Henry Archives).

30 William Shirer to Tess Shirer, 26 March 1931 (The Literary Trust of William L. Shirer).

31 William Shirer to Tess Shirer, 6 March 1931 (The Literary Trust of William L. Shirer).

32 Shirer, *Gandhi: A Memoir*, 73–4.

33 William Shirer, "Lord Willington, New India Viceroy, Arrives in Bombay," *Chicago Tribune*, 17 April 1931, 21.

34 Shirer, *Gandhi: A Memoir*, 145.

35 John Kenneth Galbraith, *The New York Times Book Review*, 14 July 1974, 2.

36 William Shirer, "Gandhi Balks at Dominion Status in India," *Chicago Tribune*, 12 September 1931, 1, 4.

37 Shirer, *Gandhi: A Memoir*, 158.

38 William Shirer, "English Cotton Workers Talk about Gandhi," *Chicago Tribune*, 1 November 1931, G-8.

39 William Shirer, "India's Chances for Liberty Go Up in Smoke," *Chicago Tribune*, 9 October 1931, 3.

CHAPTER TEN

1 William Shirer, "Socialist Vienna to Vote: Predict Victory for Reds," *Chicago Tribune*, 23 April 1932, 13.

2 Robert R. McCormick to William Shirer, 27 April 1932 (William L. Shirer Papers, George T. Henry Archives).

3 Shirer, *The Nightmare Years*, 46.

4 William Shirer, "Actress and Song Writer Held by Austrian Police: Car Strikes Child," *Chicago Tribune*, 12 September 1932, 3.

5 Ibid.

6 E.S. Beck memo to Colonel McCormick, 30 September 1932 (William L. Shirer Papers, George T. Henry Archives).

7 William Shirer to John Steele, 17 October 1932 (William L. Shirer Papers, George T. Henry Archives).

8 While being interviewed about his 1984 book *The Nightmare Years* by Don Swaim of CBS radio, Shirer said that in upcoming visit to Chicago he planned to drop by the *Tribune* newsroom. He quipped that while he was there he might ask the editors for the month's severance pay he never got when he was fired in 1932. Shirer could only laugh when Swaim asked if he planned to ask for interest or to hire a lawyer.

9 Shirer, *The Nightmare Years*, 58.

10 Colonel McCormick to William Shirer, 30 December 1932. As quoted in *The Nightmare Years*, 56. Shirer initially claimed that the letter was dated 20 December, but in subsequent references he refers to it as being dated ten days later.

11 William Shirer to John Steele, 17 January 1933 (William L. Shirer Papers, George T. Henry Archives).

12 Shirer diary, 19 February 1933 (The Literary Trust of William L. Shirer).

13 Miller, *F.D.R.: An Intimate History*, 306.

14 Shirer diary, 22 March 1933 (The Literary Trust of William L. Shirer).

15 Shirer, *The Nightmare Years*, 70.

16 Ibid., 67.

17 William Shirer to Ethel Outland, 19 January 1934 (William L. Shirer Papers, George T. Henry Archives).

18 William Shirer, "A Record," 1 February 1934. Shirer incorporated this narrative into his 1941 bestseller *Berlin Diary: The Journal of a Foreign Correspondent, 1934–40*. The original record, which is among the Shirer papers at the Stewart Library at Coe College in Cedar Rapids Iowa, provides revealing insights into the writing of that book.

19 Ibid., 3 February 1934.

20 Shirer, *The Nightmare Years*, 82.

21 For a brief time after McCormick sold the *Tribune*, some disgruntled employees continued to publish a weekly paper of the same name. Some of

those people eventually were hired by the *Herald*. Some joined the *Tribune* FNS, while others found new jobs or returned to the States.

22 According Eugene Weber' book *The Hollow Years*, 102, in 1939 there were only 300,000 Jews in France, representing 0.7 percent of the country's 41 million citizens.

23 Shirer, *Berlin Diary*, 7.

CHAPTER ELEVEN

1 Shirer, *Berlin Diary*, 12.
2 Shirer, *The Nightmare Years*, 138–9.
3 Larson, *In the Garden of Beasts*, 136.
4 Smith, *Last Train from Berlin*, 49.
5 Shirer, *The Nightmare Years*, 116.
6 Ibid., 119.
7 Ibid.
8 Ibid., 124.
9 The foreign media derisively gave Hanfstaengl the nickname "Putzi." Shirer described him as being Hitler's "court [piano player] and jester" (Shirer, *Nightmare Years*, 138). After falling from grace, Hanfstaengl fled to Washington, where he was detained as an enemy alien while serving as an "advisor" to the American government during the war.
10 Shirer, *The Nightmare Years*, 126.
11 Ibid., 126–7.
12 Ibid., 127.
13 Dodd, *Through Embassy Eyes*, 107.
14 Ibid., 108.
15 Ibid.
16 Ibid.
17 Shirer adopted the phrase as the title of his 1984 memoir *The Nightmare Years*.
18 Shirer, *Berlin Diary*, 13.

CHAPTER TWELVE

1 Shirer, *Berlin Diary*, 33.
2 Isherwood, *Berlin Stories*, 204.
3 Shirer, *Berlin Diary*, 34
4 Ibid., 54.

5 Wolfe completed his quartet of semi-autobiographical novels with *The Web and the Rock* (1939) and *You Can't Go Home Again* (1940). His bibliography includes five other books: a short story collection, a book about writing, and three books that were published posthumously.

6 Shirer, *The Nightmare Years*, 256.

7 George Kennan (1904–2005) also achieved eminence as an educator, teaching at the Institute of Advanced Studies at Princeton, and enjoying considerable literary success. He won the Pulitzer Prize in history and the National Book Award for his book *Russia Leaves the War* (1956), part of a two-volume study of Soviet-American relations, 1917–20. Kennan also won the Pulitzer Prize in biography and the National Book Award for *Memoirs: 1925–1950* (1967).

8 Barnes was three years younger than Shirer, having been born 21 July 1907 in Montclair, NJ. He was only sixty-two when he died in March 1970.

9 Like Shirer, Howard K(ingsbury) Smith wrote about his Berlin years. His 1942 bestseller, *Last Train from Berlin: An Eye-Witness Account of Germany at War*, recounts his life in Berlin in the months leading up Pearl Harbor. Following the liberation of France in 1944, he signed on with CBS as one of the "Murrow boys." In the late 1940s, Smith was one of the American journalists whom conservative groups in the United States accused of having pro-Communist sympathies. However, because he was working overseas as the chief of CBS news in Europe, the allegations did Smith minimal harm. When he finally returned home in 1957 he enjoyed a second career on television, first with CBS and then from 1961 onward with the American Broadcasting Corporation (ABC). Smith left CBS when his bosses edited out a line of his narration of the Civil Rights documentary *Who Speaks for Birmingham?* Smith's commentary included a pointed quotation from Edmund Burke: "All that is necessary for the triumph of evil is for good men to do nothing." When CBS chairman William S. Paley supported the deletion, which he termed "editorializing," Smith quit in disgust and moved over to rival ABC.

10 The CIA was active internationally during Helms's tenure as chief, carrying out a vigorous campaign of covert operations against left-leaning regimes.

11 Shirer, *The Nightmare Years*, 193.

12 Persico, *Edward R. Murrow: An American Original*, 110–11.

13 Jordan, *Beyond All Fronts*, 69.

14 Arendt, *Origins of Totalitarianism*.

15 Shirer, *The Nightmare Years*, 147.

16 Ibid., 117.

17 Douglas Chandler, "Changing Berlin," *National Geographic*, February 1937, 131–77.

18 Author Steve Wick offers a more detailed account of the Shirers' efforts on behalf of Helene Katz in his 2011 book *The Long Night: William L. Shirer and the Rise and Fall of the Third Reich*, 128–36.

19 Shirer, *The Nightmare Years*, 160.

20 Ibid., 162.

21 Ibid., 161.

22 Ibid., 225.

23 Smith, *To Save a Nation*, 89.

24 Shirer, *The Nightmare Years*, 233–4n.

25 Ibid., 232.

CHAPTER THIRTEEN

1 Shirer, *Nightmare Years*, 261.

2 A total of thirty-six people were killed – thirty-five on board the aircraft and one member of the ground crew. Amazingly, sixty-two passengers and crew survived the crash.

3 William Hallman to William Shirer, 16 March 1937 (William L. Shirer Papers, George T. Henry Archives).

4 Shirer, *Berlin Diary*, 45.

5 Ibid., 45.

6 Toland, *Adolf Hitler*, 430.

7 Shirer, *Nightmare Years*, 268

8 William Shirer to Tess Shirer, 14 August 1937 (The Literary Trust of William L. Shirer).

9 Shirer, *Nightmare Years*, 272.

10 INS telegram to William L. Shirer, 24 August 1937 (William L. Shirer Papers, George T. Henry Archives).

11 Harsch, *The Hinge of History*, 41.

12 William Shirer interview with Don Swaim on CBS radio, 1984, www.wiredforbooks.org/williamlshirer/.

CHAPTER FOURTEEN

1 Allen, *Since Yesterday*, 77

2 Shirer, *The Nightmare Years*, 273.

3 Sperber, *His Life and Times*, 104.

4 Ibid., 11.

5 Kendrick, *Prime Time*, 75–7.

6 Edwards, *Murrow and the Birth of Broadcast Journalism*, 26.

7 Ibid., 24.

8 Kendrick, *Prime Time*, 131.

9 On 29 April 1929, Toronto radio station CFRB began carrying programming from CBS, having made an exclusive arrangement with the American network for a coverage area that took in Toronto, Hamilton, and surrounding areas. The Gooderham and Worts distillery-owned station in Toronto, CKGW, made a similar arrangement with NBC. In total, five Canadian stations were broadcasting programs from CBS and NBC. Thus, prior to the May 1932 passage of the Canadian Radio Broadcasting Act, many Canadian nationalists feared the growing popularity of American radio in Canada. In a debate that has echoes to this day, critics of this situation urged the Conservative government of Prime Minister R.B. Bennett to put an end to these arrangements. For more information on this aspect of Canadian broadcasting history, please visit www.broadcasting-history.ca/index3.html.

10 Persico, *An American Original,* 130.

11 Shirer, *Berlin Diary*, 64.

12 Shirer, *The Nightmare Years*, 274.

13 William Shirer to John Shirer, undated 1933 letter (William L. Shirer Papers, George T. Henry Archives).

14 Kendrick, *Prime Time*, 144.

15 Sperber, *His Life and Times*, 102

16 Kendrick, *Prime Time*, 145.

17 Elizabeth McLeod, "Max Jordan – NBC's Forgotten Pioneer," www.midcoast.com/~lizmcl/jordan.html.

18 Shirer's recollection of the date of his initial meeting with Murrow was faulty. In his 1942 book *Berlin Diary*, he described his firing from INS and the arrival of Murrow's telegram in an entry headed "Berlin, August (undated)" and then, in a subsequent entry dated 20 August, he recounted the circumstances of his first meeting with Murrow. Shirer corrected himself in his subsequent writings and interviews. The sequence of events and their timeline has been confirmed by Murrow biographers.

19 Edwards, *Murrow and the Birth of Broadcast Journalism*, 33.

20 Shirer, *Berlin Diary*, op. cit., 65.

21 Shirer, *The Nightmare Years*, 275.

22 Shirer, *Berlin Diary*, 64.

23 William Shirer to Tess Shirer, 29 August 1937. (The Literary Trust of William L. Shirer).

24 Ibid.

25 Shirer interview with Don Swaim, CBS radio, 1984.

26 Shirer, *The Nightmare Years*, 278.

27 Ibid., 279.

28 Sperber, *His Life and Times,* 103.

29 Shirer, *The Nightmare Years,* 280.

30 Ed Murrow to William Shirer, 13 September 1937 (The Literary Trust of William L. Shirer).

31 William Shirer undated 1937 letter to Tess Shirer (The Literary Trust of William L. Shirer).

32 Ibid.

33 Sperber, *His Life and Times,* 103.

34 Shirer, *The Nightmare Years,* 281.

35 Persico, *An American Original,* 247.

CHAPTER FIFTEEN

1 Shirer to Ed Murrow, undated, although it is apparent the missive was written shortly after 10 September 1937, when Murrow extended a job offer. (William L. Shirer Papers, George T. Henry Archives.)

2 Shirer, *Berlin Diary,* 68.

3 Culbert, *News for Everyman,* 15.

4 Hosley, *Foreign Correspondence on American Radio, 1930–1940,* 9.

5 Shirer, *Nightmare Years,* 284.

6 Ibid., 285.

7 Cloud and Olson, *The Murrow Boys,* 40.

8 Author telephone interview with George Seldes, 20 January 1989.

9 Dodd, *Through Embassy Eyes,* 107.

10 Cancer claimed both of Shirer's old friends: Gunther in 1969 at age sixty-eight and Sheean six years later at age seventy-five.

11 Sperber, *His Life and Times,* 281.

12 Shirer, *Nightmare Years,* 285.

13 Shirer, *"This Is Berlin,"* 5.

14 Shirer, *Nightmare Years,* 286.

15 Bryan III and Murphy, *The Windsor Story,* 392.

16 *The New York Times,* "US Will Not Act in Austria Crisis." 12 March 1938: 2.

17 Shirer, *Nightmare Years,* 292.

18 It is a measure of how close the Shirers were to Agnes and H.R. Knickerbocker that Agnes stood as the baby Eileen's godmother.

19 Shirer, *Berlin Diary,* 77.

20 Following the war, in a handwritten pencilled letter dated 10 June 1947, Maass bemoaned his situation and pleaded with Gunther for help. When

Shirer read the letter he advised Gunther, "[Maass is] the bastard who whipped out a swastika button in the Café Louvre after it seemed certain that night that the Nazis were in." Shirer had a long memory and did not easily forgive. Shirer to John Gunther, 24 June 1947. (Both letters: Special Collections Research Center, University of Chicago Library.)

21 Shirer, *Berlin Diary*, 77.
22 William Shirer, "Berlin Speaking," *Atlantic Monthly*, September 1940, 309.
23 Shirer, *Berlin Diary*, 82.
24 Shirer, "Berlin Speaking," 309.
25 Hosley, *As Good As Any*, 44.
26 Shirer, *Berlin Diary*, 83.
27 Jordan describes the broadcast in detail his 1944 book *Beyond All Fronts*.

CHAPTER SIXTEEN

1 Paper, *Empire*, 74.
2 Paley, *As It Happened*, 130.
3 Ibid., 130–1.
4 Elizabeth McLeod, "CBS World News Roundup – Facts and Fiction," email posting to old.time.radio@oldradio.net.
5 Ibid., 75.
6 Shirer, *The Nightmare Years*, 304.
7 Ibid., 306.
8 Ibid., 307.
9 The first broadcast of CBS's World News Roundup, 13 March 1938, is available online at https://www.youtube.com/watch?v=WoGYXiyNWRM.
10 Paley, *As It Happened*, 133.
11 Sperber, *His Life and Times*, 119.
12 Shirer, *The Nightmare Years*, 308.
13 Sperber, *His Life and Times*, 120.
14 White, *News on the Air*, 45–6.
15 Paley, *As It Happened*, 134. Paley also noted that "the European Roundup" soon became *World News Roundup*, a daily feature on CBS radio for many years.
16 The Radio Hall of Fame honored CBS's *World News Roundup* when the program was "inducted" in October 1995. Selected editions of the program, including segments of the very first broadcast, can be heard at www.archives.museum.tv/archives.
17 Hosley, *As Good As Any*, 47.
18 Cloud and Olson, *The Murrow Boys*, 36.

19 Shirer, *Berlin Diary*, 91.

20 Kendrick, *Prime Time*, 158.

21 Manchester, *The Last Lion*, 265.

22 Shirer, *The Nightmare Years*, 311.

23 The Rothschilds were allowed to flee Austria on condition they leave behind their art collection. The Nazis then plundered the family's home, stealing priceless paintings and antique musical instruments, carpets, and other objets d'art. Fittingly, the Austrian and Swiss governments, which eventually came into possession of the treasures, returned them to the Rothschilds in February 1999.

24 Shirer, *The Nightmare Years*, 313.

25 Ibid., 314.

26 Shirer, *Berlin Diary*, 90.

27 Shirer, *The Nightmare Years*, 320.

28 Sperber, *His Life and Times*, 124.

29 Ibid., 321.

30 Shirer, *Berlin Diary*, 95.

CHAPTER SEVENTEEN

1 Shirer, *Berlin Diary*, 91.

2 Shirer, *The Nightmare Years*, 332.

3 Ibid., 337.

4 Shirer, *Berlin Diary*, 102.

5 Schechter and Anthony, *I Live on Air*, 206.

6 Shirer, *Berlin Diary*, 101.

7 Cloud and Olson, *The Murrow Boys*, 38.

8 Sperber, *His Life and Times*, 126.

9 Shirer, *Berlin Diary*, 108.

10 Ibid., 110.

11 Ibid., 114.

12 Ibid., 119.

13 Ibid., 117.

14 Jordan offers a detailed explanation of how he did this in his book *Beyond All Fronts*.

15 Ed Murrow to William Shirer, 26 October 1938 (The Literary Trust of William L. Shirer).

16 William Shirer, "Berlin Speaking," *Atlantic Monthly*, September 1940, 309.

17 Sperber, *His Life and Times*, 129.

18 Shirer, *Berlin Diary*, 120.

19 Elizabeth McLeod, "Max Jordan – NBC's Forgotten Pioneer," www.midcoast.com.

20 Ibid.

21 Cloud and Olson, *The Murrow Boys*, 39.

22 Kendrick, *Prime Time*, 167.

23 According to information posted on the Tufts University archival webpage "Murrow at CBS, Europe, 1935/37–1946", a *Scribner's Magazine* article reported that CBS and NBC spent a combined total of about $195,000 to cover the crisis in Czechoslovakia. "To put this into perspective: a well-paid factory worker in the Midwest earned about a hundred and twenty-five dollars a week" at that time, dca.lib.tufts.edu/features/murrow/exhibit/CBSeurope.html.

24 McLeod, *Max Jordon.*

25 Robert Landry, "Edward R. Murrow," *Scribner's Magazine*, December 1938.

26 Sperber, *His Life and Times*, 131

27 Paper, *Empire*, 75.

CHAPTER EIGHTEEN

1 Shirer, *The Nightmare Years*, 393.

2 Ibid., 370.

3 Shirer, *Berlin Diary*, 120.

4 Ibid., 121.

5 Shirer, *Berlin Diary*, 125.

6 Cloud and Olson, *The Murrow Boys*, 42.

7 The origin of the term "Murrow boys" is unclear. However, it has become familiar, and Stanley Cloud and Lynne Olson borrowed the term as the title of their 1996 book on Murrow and his World War Two broadcast team.

8 Cloud and Olson, *The Murrow Boys*, 42.

9 Sperber, *His Life and Times*, 134.

10 Shirer, *Berlin Diary*, 128.

11 Ibid., 130.

12 "*This Is Berlin,*" 39.

13 Shirer, *Nightmare Years*, 395.

14 "I thought maybe you in New York would like to know that you were being spied upon, but naturally please treat this as confidential," Shirer told Paul White in a letter dated 8 May 1939, as quoted in "*This Is Berlin,*" 46.

15 Shirer, *The Nightmare Years*, 403.

16 Ibid., 414.

17 Hosley, *As Good As Any*, 68.

18 Shirer, *The Nightmare Years*, 410.

19 Ibid., 410–11.

20 Shirer, *The Nightmare Years*, 414. If Shirer recorded his impressions of his bosses, he deleted them from his diary before the text was published in book form as his 1942 bestseller *Berlin Diary*.

21 Sevareid used this expression in his final broadcast for CBS television news, which took place on 30 November 1977. The video clip can be viewed on YouTube, www.youtube.com/watch?v=lHGHm8iPeUY.

22 Shirer, *Berlin Diary*, 41.

23 Ibid., 145.

24 Ibid., 149.

25 Ibid., 155.

26 Ibid., 155.

CHAPTER NINETEEN

1 Shirer, *The Nightmare Years*, 450.

2 Shirer, *Berlin Diary*, 164–5.

3 Shirer, *The Nightmare Years*, 464.

4 Shirer, *Berlin Diary*, 435

5 Bliss, *Now the News*, 107.

6 Shirer, *The Nightmare Years*, 463.

7 Smith, *Last Train from Berlin*, 86.

8 William Shirer, "Berlin Speaking," *Atlantic Monthly*, September 1940, 315.

9 Shirer, Ed Murrow, and Thomas Grandin described their daily routines in an article titled, "The Censors in Three Capitals," *The Living Age*, November 1939, 220–3.

10 Shirer, *Berlin Diary*, 188.

11 Ibid., 188.

12 Shirer, *"This Is Berlin,"* 3.

13 Ibid., 77.

14 Shirer, Berlin Diary, 191.

15 Flannery, *Assignment to Berlin*, 27.

16 Shirer, *Berlin Diary*, 201.

17 Shirer, *The Nightmare Years*, 417.

18 Ibid., 548.

19 Shirer, *"This Is Berlin,"* 171.

20 Ibid., 475.

21 Shirer, *Berlin Diary*, 233.

22 Shirer, *The Nightmare Years*, 475.

CHAPTER TWENTY

1 Shirer, *Berlin Diary*, 205.
2 Flannery, *Assignment to Berlin*, 16.
3 Ibid., 206.
4 Shirer, *"This Is Berlin,"* 157.
5 Orrin E. Dunlap Jr, "Distance Shrinks." *The New York Times*, 26 May 1940: X-10.
6 Ibid.
7 Bliss, *Now the News*, 106.
8 Cloud and Olson, *The Murrow Boys*, 61.
9 "Censorship and Danger," an article posted on the Murrow exhibit homepage, Tufts University, dca.lib.tufts.edu/features/exhibit/boys.htm, accessed July 2013.
10 Sevareid, *Not So Wild a Dream*, 178.
11 Shirer, *Berlin Diary*, 223.
12 "An adventurous bent," an article posted on the Murrow exhibit homepage, dca.lib.tufts.edu/features/exhibit/boys.htm.
13 Cloud and Olson, *The Murrow Boys*, 78.
14 www.cbsnews.com/2100-500164_162-1343638.html.
15 Cloud and Olson, *The Murrow Boys*, 79.
16 Shirer, *"This Is Berlin,"* 188.
17 Shirer, *Nightmare Years*, 520.
18 Shirer, *"This Is Berlin,"* 271.
19 Beard, *The Beards' New Basic History of the United States*, 432.
20 Shirer, *"This Is Berlin,"* 280.
21 Tess's diary entry for 21 May 1940 reflects her fears. "It seems such a silly thing to risk your life in [this] way, just to give the American public another sensation … If [Bill] was in the government service, or if he was fighting for his country, it would be another thing. I would accept that; it would be his duty. But what will [CBS] care if he is killed or maimed?" In a letter to her husband penned on 26 May 1940, Tess confided how fearful she had been that something bad would happen to him when he was at the front: "I can't tell you how relieved I was to hear that you'd got back … I was so scared for you. I was sick to my stomach all the time. Darling, don't do that again. I'd go mad with worry. I used to look at Eileen and see her as an orphan already." (The Literary Trust of William L. Shirer.)
22 William Shirer, "With the German Armies: A War Diary," *The Atlantic*, March 1941, 266.
23 Ibid., 271.
24 Ibid., 272.

25 Ibid.
26 Shirer, *The Nightmare Years,* 512.
27 Shirer, *"This Is Berlin,"* 288
28 Ibid., 293.
29 Ibid., 313.
30 Ibid.
31 Shirer, *The Nightmare Years,* 525.

CHAPTER TWENTY-ONE

 1 Shirer, *Berlin Diary,* 328.
 2 Diamond, *Fleeing Hitler: France 1940,* 18.
 3 Ibid., 67.
 4 *Time,* "Radio: War Babies," 17 June 1940, 85.
 5 Cloud and Olson, *The Murrow Boys,* 80.
 6 Ibid.
 7 Demaree Bess, "With Their Hands in Their Pockets," *Saturday Evening Post,*
    31 August 1940, 29.
 8 A full description of the day's events appears in Shirer's 1984 book *The
    Nightmare Years,* which draws on *Berlin Diary.* An even more vivid account
    can be found in the script of Shirer's 21 June 1940 joint CBS-NBC broadcast.
    The full text is reproduced in the 1999 book *"This Is Berlin,"* 328–33.
 9 Shirer, *The Nightmare Years,* 543.
10 William Shirer to Paul White, 5 July 1940, *"This Is Berlin,"* 339.
11 Bullock, *A Study in Tyranny,* 591.
12 Shirer, *"This Is Berlin,"* 335.
13 A BBC news report estimated that the ratio of soldiers to civilians killed was
    10:1 in World War One. In World War Two, that figure was 1:1. In today's
    wars, the ratio is ten civilians killed for every combatant. *The Globe and Mail,*
    13 August 2009: L-6.
14 Gilbert, *Second World War,* 119.
15 Bliss, *Now the News,* 129.
16 Ibid., 130.
17 Kendrick, *Prime Time,* 201.
18 Shirer, *Berlin Diary,* 383.

CHAPTER TWENTY-TWO

 1 Shirer, *"This Is Berlin,"* 385.
 2 Shirer, *Berlin Diary,* 390.

3 Shirer, *Berlin Diary*, 398. The Reichs-Rundfunk-Gesellschaft (RRG) – the Reich Broadcasting Corporation – was a national network of German regional public broadcasting companies that was active from 1925 to 1945.

4 Harsch, *At the Hinge of History*, 42.

5 Flannery, *Assignment to Berlin*, 23.

6 Tess Shirer to William Shirer, 12 May 1940 (The Literary Trust of William L. Shirer).

7 Tess Shirer to William Shirer, 31 May1940 (The Literary Trust of William L. Shirer).

8 Ibid.

9 Ibid.

10 Shirer, *"This Is Berlin,"* 405.

11 Ibid.

12 Harsch, *At the Hinge of History*, 41.

13 George Mooney, "Behind the Scenes...," *The New York Times*, 12 January 1941, X-10.

14 British historian Ian Crofton explains in his book *Traitors & Turncoats*, 126, that it was a columnist for the London newspaper the *Daily Express* who dubbed Joyce "Lord Haw Haw." Because "he speaks English of the haw, haw, damn-it-get-out-of-my way variety."

15 Cole, *Lord Haw-Haw*, 175.

16 Shirer, *Berlin Diary*, 419.

17 Brett Rutledge, *The Death of Lord Haw-Haw*. In fact, the book was written by Shirer's old friend Eliot Paul (1891–1958), with whom Shirer had worked in Paris.

18 Cole, *Lord Haw-Haw*, 175. Joyce's book was published in 1940 by the Nazi publishing house Internationaler Verlag.

19 *Time*, "The Press: Worst Best," 15 February 1943, 42.

20 The Shirers' apartment, at 29 Avenue de Miremont, was in a fashionable area of Geneva, a city Shirer regarded as being too fusty and staid for his liking.

21 The twice-weekly buses that carried passengers from Geneva to Barcelona were packed for each westward leg of the trip. The lineup to get on board was long, with thousands of refugees – many of them displaced Jews – desperate to flee.

22 Max Jordan to Manuel Barjano de Bivar, Director Tecnico de Emissora Nacional de Radiodifuasao, Lisbon, 11 June 1940 (The Literary Trust of William L. Shirer).

23 Tess Shirer to her in-laws, 3 November 1940 (The Literary Trust of William L. Shirer).

24 Eileen Shirer Dean email to the author, 7 July 2009.

25 Shirer, *The Nightmare Years*, 603.

26 "US Reporter Dies in Bomber Crash," *The New York Times*, 20 November 1940: 7.

27 Cloud and Olson, *The Murrow Boys*, 100.

28 Ibid.

29 Harsch, *At the Hinge of History*, 41.

30 Smith, *Last Train from Berlin*, 352.

31 William L. Shirer, "Berlin Speaking," *Atlantic Monthly*, September 1940, 308.

32 Cloud and Olson, *The Murrow Boys*, 136.

33 Shirer, *Berlin Diary*, 475.

34 Ibid., 608.

35 Ibid., 609.

36 Sperber, *His Life and Times*, 185.

37 Ibid., 185.

38 Shirer, *The Nightmare Years*, 614.

39 Shirer, *The Nightmare Years*, 615.

40 Ibid.

CHAPTER TWENTY-THREE

1 Tess Shirer to William Shirer, 21 June 1940 (The Literary Trust of William L. Shirer).

2 Inga Shirer Dean email to the author, 24 September 2009.

3 Tess Shirer letter to Bessie Shirer, 5 November 1941. (The Literary Trust of William L. Shirer).

4 George A. Mooney, "Behind the Scenes… " *The New York Times*, 12 January 1941, X10.

5 James Reston, "25 Child Refugees…" *The New York Times*, 25 December 1940, 7.

6 Ibid.

7 "Books and Authors." *The New York Times*, 16 January 1941, 19.

8 Blanche Knopf to William Shirer, 22 July 1936. Letter in the Blanche Knopf papers at the Harry Ransom Humanities Research Center, The University of Texas at Austin.

9 William Shirer to Blanche Knopf, 12 November 1936. (Knopf papers.)

10 Anonymous writer – but almost certainly Alfred A. Knopf – to William Shirer, 10 December 1936. (Knopf papers.)

11 William Shirer letter to Tess Shirer, 12 October 1937 (William L. Shirer Papers, George T. Henry Archives).

12 Shirer, *Berlin Diary*, 54.

13 Ibid.

14　William Shirer letter to Tess Shirer, 12 October 1937 (William L. Shirer Papers, George T. Henry Archives).

15　Alfred Knopf J. letter to William Shirer, 2 February 1990. The younger Knopf recalled that when his mother agreed to pay Shirer a ten-thousand dollar advance "She had to call my father in to get an OK." (Knopf papers.)

16　Robert Van Gelder, "An Interview with William L. Shirer." *The New York Times Book Review*, 18 January 1942, 2.

17　Ibid.

18　William L. Shirer in a 1984 interview with Don Swaim, CBS radio, www.wiredforbooks.org/williamlshirer.

19　Shirer, *Berlin Diary*, v.

20　Ibid.

21　Ibid., 3.

22　B. Smith memo to Blanche Knopf, 18 March 1941 (Knopf papers).

23　Ibid.

24　Van Gelder, "An Interview," 2.

25　Joseph Barnes, *Books*, 22 June 1941.

26　George N. Shuster, "Six Fateful Years in Germany." *The New York Times Book Review*, 22 June 1941, 1.

27　"Plethora of Grand Books Make 1941 Notable Year," *Toronto Star*, 6 December 1941, 10

28　Edward R. Murrow letter to William Shirer, 27 July 1941 (William L. Shirer Papers, George T. Henry Archives).

29　Cloud and Olson, *The Murrow Boys*, 135.

30　"About the Newscasters," *The New York Times*, 16 November 1941, X-10.

31　Ibid.

32　Tess Shirer letter to John Shirer, 5 November 1941 (The Literary Trust of William L. Shirer). The Crossley Ratings were used to determine the size of a radio audience from 1930 and 1935. A polling firm telephoned a random sample of homes in a market area to "count the house" by asking what programs the residents of that house had listened to the previous evening. The Crossley system was not all that reliable since only those with telephone service were contacted – the well-to-do during the Great Depression – and the accuracy of the measurements depended on the memory and whims of the person being surveyed. The Crossley system was replaced in 1935 by the Hooper ratings, which involved calling listeners while they were actually tuned into a program.

33　*The New York Times*, "Journalists Are Signed," 28 January 1941, 23.

34　An account of Shirer's remarks, written by Roy McHugh, a member of Coe

College's Class of 1941, appeared on pp. 3–4 of the July 1941 edition of *The Coe College Courier* alumni publication. "Shirer's … listeners heard him outline a Nazi plan for world conquest that will culminate in the economic, social, and political downfall of the United States as we know it today, unless Great Britain successfully holds out," McHugh reported. Shirer went on to say he felt it was essential that the Roosevelt administration intervene decisively to ensure an Allied victory.

35 *Coe College Cosmos*, 9 June 1941, 1.
36 Shirer, *The Nightmare Years*, 618.
37 "15 Awards Bestowed by Headliners Club." *The New York Times*, 29 June 1941, 32.
38 Blum et al., *The National Experience*, 679.
39 Shirer, *The Nightmare Years*, 619.
40 "Shirer Predicts Token Raid Here." *The New York Times*, 29 January 1942, 14.

CHAPTER TWENTY-FOUR

1 Shirer, *The Nightmare Years*, 393.
2 Author interview with Inga Dean and Linda Rae, Lenox, MA, 20 May 2008.
3 Shirer used this line in a play he was writing *The Traitor*.
4 Paul Gallico to William Shirer, 18 March 1942 (William L. Shirer Papers, George T. Henry Archives).
5 Shirer, *End of A Berlin Diary*, 26.
6 Cloud and Olson, *The Murrow Boys*, 143–4.
7 Ibid., 269.
8 Ibid.
9 Author interview with Inga (Shirer) Dean and Linda (Shirer) Rae, Lenox, MA, 20 May 2008.
10 Klauber abruptly resigned from CBS on 6 August 1943, at age fifty-six, for health reasons. The reality seems to be that personality issues were the real reason; Klauber was a good newsman, but he was abrasive to a fault and a poor manager of people. Sperber points out that when Klauber took a job in Washington as associate director and administrator of the Office of War Information, his ill health did not slow him down.
11 Bliss, *Now the News*, 139.
12 White, *News on the Air*, 204.
13 Ibid., 226. Murrow wrote these words to Shirer on 15 October 1943.
14 Sperber, *His Life and Times*, 228.
15 Kendrick, *Prime Time*, 238.
16 Cloud and Olson, *The Murrow Boys*, 144.

17 Ibid.

18 This figure is mentioned in correspondence Shirer received from the New York legal firm Greenbaum, Wolff, and Ernst, which was representing him in a tax dispute he was having with the Internal Revenue Service.

19 William Shirer to Jay Allen, 11 May 1944 (William L. Shirer Papers, George T. Henry Archives).

20 This dollar figure comes from a 2008 Congressional Research Service Report on the United States' spending in the various wars in the country's history. http://www.history.navy.mil/library/online/costs_of_major_us_wars.htm. The total estimated cost of the Second World War is $296 billion. Based on forty-five months of conflict (December 1941 to August 1945), that is $6.6 billion per month. Taking inflation into account, in today's dollars that is about $4.9 trillion.

21 This is the phrase B. Smith of Alfred A. Knopf used in a November 1943 memo to Blanche Knopf, and it is a fair and valid assessment (Knopf papers).

22 To view Quintanilla's portraits of writers visit www.lqart.org/portsfold/writports.html.

23 Quintanilla painted Steinbeck as a sea serpent, Dos Passos as a hobby painter, Parker as a modern-day Betsy Ross, and Miller as Abraham Lincoln. Quintanilla's original intention was to exhibit the paintings and publish them in a book. Unfortunately, neither project came off. In the end, Quintanilla either sold the portraits or gave them to the writers who had posed. For more information on the artist's portraits of writers "as they see themselves," please visit the webpage www.lqart.org/portsfold/writports.html.

24 Shirer's diary, 23 June 1943.

CHAPTER TWENTY-FIVE

1 Shirer, *A Native's Return: 1945–48*, 271.

2 Peter Flint, "Tilly Losch, Exotic Dancer, Is Dead," *The New York Times*, 25 December 1975. 48.

3 Ibid.

4 Herbert Poetzl, "Biographical Note: Biography and Career of Tilly Losch" (May 2000), website of the Max Reinhardt Archives, State University of New York (Binghamton), library.binghampton.edu/special collections/findingaids.

5 Ibid.

6 "Carnarvon Trial Halts." *The New York Times*, 6 October 1945, 6.

7 Herbert Poetzl. "Biographical Note."

8 Flint, "Tilly Losch, Exotic Dancer."

9 Shirer, *A Native's Return*, 273.
10 "Art: Losch Launched." *Time*, 15 May 1944, 39.
11 Smith, *Events Leading Up to My Death*, 146.
12 Sperber, *His Life and Times*, 234.
13 Ibid., 256.
14 Kendrick, *Prime Time*, 271.
15 Shirer, *End of A Berlin Diary*, 6.
16 Ibid., 8.
17 Ibid., 17.
18 Ibid., 22.
19 William Shirer, "What the Germans Told the Prisoners." *Harper's*, November 1944, 542.
20 Shirer, *End of A Berlin Diary*, 28.
21 Ibid., 36.
22 Shirer, *End of A Berlin Diary*, 48.
23 Shirer, *An August to Remember*, 14.
24 Ibid., 15.
25 Bliss, *Now the News*, 173.
26 Shirer, *End of A Berlin Diary*, 100.
27 Sperber, *His Life and Times*, 256.
28 "Thanks to Hitler." *The New York Times*, 8 August 1945, 22.
29 Kendrick, *Prime Time*, 284.

CHAPTER TWENTY-SIX

1 Shirer, *End of a Berlin Diary*, 112.
2 Sperber, *His Life and Times*, 257.
3 Ibid.
4 Shirer, *A Native's Return*, 296.
5 Shirer, *End of a Berlin Diary*, 132.
6 Ibid., 146.
7 Ibid., 186.
8 Ibid., 287.
9 Ibid., 287.
10 Smith, *Events Leading Up to My Death*, 183.
11 Persico, *Nuremberg: Infamy on Trial*, xi.
12 Shirer, *End of a Berlin Diary*, 301.
13 Ibid., 293.
14 Ibid., 301.
15 Smith, *Events Leading Up To My Death*, 196.

16 Cloud and Olson, *The Murrow Boys*, 269.
17 Shirer, *End of a Berlin Diary*, 314.
18 Ibid., 359.

CHAPTER TWENTY-SEVEN

1 Sperber, *His Life and Times*, 212.
2 Shirer, *A Native's Return*, 99.
3 Sperber, *His Life and Times*, 259.
4 Author interview with Casey Murrow, 16 October 2009.
5 Sperber, *His Life and Times*, 262.
6 Persico, *Edward R. Murrow*, 250.
7 Metz, *CBS: Reflections in a Bloodshot Eye*, 110.
8 Cloud and Olson, *The Murrow Boys*, 245.
9 Persico, *Edward R. Murrow*, 251.
10 "Paul White Dies." *The New York Times*, 10 July 1955, 72.
11 Sperber, *His Life and Times*, 267.
12 Ibid., 281.
13 Ibid.
14 Perscio, *Edward R. Murrow*, 253.
15 Shirer, *A Native's Return*, 114.
16 Ibid., 100.

CHAPTER TWENTY-EIGHT

1 Persico, *Edward R. Murrow*, 244.
2 Bliss, *Now the News*, 140.
3 Kendrick, *His Life and Times*, 285.
4 "Wallace Bewails Perils to Freedom." *The New York Times*, 7 January 1947, 25.
5 Cloud and Olsen, *The Murrow Boys*, 271–2.
6 Ibid.
7 Shirer, *A Native's Return*, 115.
8 Blum et al., *The National Experience*, 715.
9 George Kennan (writing under the pseudonym "X"), "The Sources of Soviet Conduct," *Foreign Affairs*, July 1947, 566–82.
10 Undated *New York Herald Tribune* column by Shirer in FBI files.
11 William Shirer to Claude Pepper, 17 March 1947 (William L. Shirer Papers, George T. Henry Archives).
12 Sperber, *Murrow: His Life and Times*, 282.

13 Cloud and Olson, *The Murrow Boys*, 271.

14 Carl Wiegman, "One-Worlders Prattle..." *Chicago Tribune*, 22 February 1947, 6.

15 T.J. Donegan, acting assistant-director in New York, letter to FBI Director J. Edgar Hoover, 17 July 1941 (FBI files).

16 Chandler, a former *Baltimore Sun* journalist, made pro-Nazi wartime propaganda broadcasts under the pseudonym Paul Revere. Donald Day, the *Chicago Tribune's* one-time correspondent in Riga, delivered anti-Russian diatribes over German radio. Mildred Gallars broadcast pro-German propaganda as "Axis Sally." Shirer knew all of these individuals and provided information on them to the FBI. Chandler and Gillars were tried and convicted of treason after the war – Chandler received a life sentence, Gillars ten to thirty years. Day escaped prosecution.

17 The undated letter, written on letterhead from a hotel in Columbus, Ohio, was probably the work of a deranged individual who posed no real danger to Shirer. However, the tone of the missive was so unnerving that he went to the FBI with it.

18 *New York Herald Tribune*, 16 March 1942.

19 Anonymous letter writer to J. Edgar Hoover, 17 March 1942 (FBI files).

20 S.J. Drayton letter to J. Edgar Hoover, 6 January 1943 (FBI files).

21 *New York Herald Tribune*, 20 October 1946, Section II, 1.

22 Ibid.

23 Clyde Tolson memo to J. Edgar Hoover, 22 October 1946 (FBI files).

24 FBI "Memorandum Re: William Lawrence Shirer, 25 October 1946" (FBI files).

25 The FBI biographical sketch on Shirer noted that the Friends of the Spanish Republic were "reported to be closely connected with *The Nation* magazine ... sent a telegram on one occasion ... to President Truman urging him to break diplomatic relations with the Spanish government and to intervene on behalf of Republican Spain." Shirer had signed the telegram, and this apparently made suspect his loyalties to the United States.

26 "Accused Groups Deny Disloyalty," *The New York Times*, 5 December 1947, 18.

27 Shirer, *A Native's Return*, 164.

28 Sperber, *His Life and Times*, 278.

29 Jack Gould, "Commercial Comment," *The New York Times*, 5 January 1947, X9.

30 "Sponsored News." *The New York Times*, 12 January 1947, E8.

31 "Sponsored News: CBS States Position." *The New York Times*, 26 January 1947, XII.

32 Ibid.

33 Shirer, *A Native's Return*, 97.

34 Persico, *Edward R. Murrow*, 253.

CHAPTER TWENTY-NINE

1 William Shirer to Dorothy Thompson, 9 April 1947. (The Literary Trust of William L. Shirer.)

2 Shirer, *A Native's Return*, 93.

3 Ibid., 95.

4 Sperber, *His Life and Times*, 288.

5 If Gude had raised such concerns with Shirer, it is likely that Shirer would have mentioned it in his own writings. He did not. Likewise, Gude said nothing in his conversations with Murrow biographer Ann Sperber.

6 Kendrick, *Prime Time*, 294.

7 Cloud and Olson, *The Murrow Boys*, 281.

8 Harsch, *At the Hinge of History*, 221.

9 Cloud and Olson, *The Murrow Boys*, 273.

10 William Shirer to Ed Murrow, 19 March 1947 (William L. Shirer Papers, George T. Henry Archives).

11 Shirer, *A Native's Return*, 95.

12 Ibid., 95.

13 Cloud and Olson, *The Murrow Boys*, 274.

14 Sperber, *His Life and Times*, 283.

15 Ibid.

16 Persico, *Edward R. Murrow*, 253.

17 Sperber, *His Life and Times*, 292.

18 Drew Pearson, "Merry Go-Round," *Washington Post*, 4 April 1947, 11.

19 Shirer, *A Native's Return*, 105.

20 Ibid.

21 Sperber, *His Life and Times*, 285.

22 Ibid., 284.

23 Harsch, *At the Hinge of History*, 222.

24 Shirer implied that this was also a convenient way to get rid of Harsch. Whether or not this is true is impossible to say. However, it is a fact that when Harsch's contract with CBS expired on 1 March 1949, he was "declared redundant." That was Harsch's version of events. In *A Native's Return*, the final volume of his memoirs, Shirer quotes from a letter from Harsch in which he said he had quit CBS before he was "booted out." According to

Shirer, Harsch told him, "The one thing that I resent above all is that they took the Sunday show away from me on the ground that I had not been able to attract a sponsor when they themselves had deliberately withheld the time from sale ... They then announce that I am unsalable" (196n). When Harsch left CBS he found work with the Liberty radio network, remaining there until that network folded in 1953. He then he moved over to NBC for a fourteen-year stay.

25 "Harsch Will Succeed Shirer on CBS Time." *The New York Times*, 25 March 1947, 50.

CHAPTER THIRTY

1 Sperber, *His Life and Times*, 287.
2 Shirer wrote nothing about this. Ann Sperber reports that Gude told her that he had been at Shirer's apartment when the president of the Williams Company called. He claimed to have just returned from vacation and wanted to get Shirer's side of the story. Shirer was polite, apologizing for having caused trouble, but he insisted he had no control over the situation. That is a claim that Gude felt was untrue. For his part, Shirer remembered the incident differently. As he told it, a representative of the Williams Company came to his door one evening to personally appeal to him to return to the Sunday newscast and also suggested to Shirer that he call CBS boss William Paley in hopes of finding a mutually acceptable compromise. Shirer said he declined to do so. It is not clear which version of events is to be believed, or perhaps both incidents happened. The important point is that regardless of whether or not the management of the Williams Company *wanted* to rescind their decision not to continue sponsorship of Shirer's newscast, it was too late. Nothing came of these efforts.
3 It was later pointed out that time slot in the CBS schedule was filled by a newscast hosted by Larry LaSueur, another of the "Murrow boys." However, so keen was Murrow to bring Shirer back into the fold and to defuse the controversy that he was prepared to make this move unilaterally. He hoped to patch things up later with LaSueur.
4 Sperber, *His Life and Times*, 289.
5 Ibid., 290.
6 Ibid., 289.
7 Perscio, *Edward R. Murrow*, 254.
8 Ibid., 256.
9 Cloud and Olson, *The Murrow Boys*, 280–1.

10 Henry Cassirer, Roy Smith, Henry Rose, Fred Rickey, Chester Berger, and Mary T. Stack to William L. Shirer, 28 March 1947. (The Literary Trust of William L. Shirer.)

11 Shirer, *A Native's Return*, 107.

12 Ibid., 108.

13 Ibid., 109.

14 William Shirer to David Halberstram, 6 April 1975. (William L. Shirer Papers, George T. Henry Archives.)

15 "Shirer Quits CBS at Last Broadcast," *The New York Times*, 31 March 1947, 38.

16 Everett Hurlburt to William L. Shirer, 2 April 1947 (The Literary Trust of William L. Shirer).

17 Eric Sevareid to William Shirer, 31 March 1947 (The Literary Trust of William L. Shirer).

18 Raymond Gram Swing to William Shirer, 14 April 1947 (The Literary Trust of William L. Shirer).

19 Kendrick, *Prime Time*, 295.

20 Cloud and Olson, *The Murrow Boys*, 280.

CHAPTER THIRTY-ONE

1 Persico, *Edward R. Murrow*, 256.

2 Author interview with Linda Shirer Rae and Inga Shirer Dean, 20 May 2008.

3 Ibid.

4 Ibid.

5 Sperber, *His Life and Times*, 294.

6 Eric Sevareid to William Shirer, 1 July 1947. (William L. Shirer Papers, George T. Henry Archives.)

7 Shirer, *End of Berlin Diary*, vii.

8 Ibid., viii.

9 Cloud and Olson, *The Murrow Boys*, 282.

10 Shirer, *End of Berlin Diary*, 33.

11 George Scharschug, "Mr Shirer's..." *Chicago Tribune*, 21 September 1947, C11.

12 *The New Yorker*, 27 September 1947, 109.

13 Alan Welsh Dulles, "Postscript to a Berlin Diary," *The New York Times Book Review*, 21 September 1947, BR1.

14 Shirer, *A Native's Return*, 129.

15 Blum et al., *The National Experience*, 727.

16 William Shirer to Tilly Losch, 8 January 1947. (Binghamton University Special Collections.)

17 Ibid.

18 William Shirer to Tilly Losch, 8 March 1948. (Binghamton University Special Collections.)

19 The Hollywood Ten: screenwriters Alvah Bessie, Lester Cole, Ring Lardner Jr, John Lawson, Albert Laltz, Samuel Ornitz, and Dalton Trumbo, director Edward Dmytryk, screenwriter-director Herbert Biberman, and screenwriter-producer Adrian Scott.

20 Shirer, *A Native's Return,* 159.

21 Ibid., 163.

22 Ibid., 164fn.

23 Harrison E. Salisbury, "The Strange Correspondence of Morris Ernst and J. Edgar Hoover," *The Nation,* 1 December 1984, 575ff.

24 Shirer, *A Native's Return,* 170.

CHAPTER THIRTY-TWO

1 Alfred Knopf, Jr, to William Shirer, 8 February 1990. (The Literary Trust of William L. Shirer.)

2 Shirer, *A Native's Return,* 179.

3 Ibid., 163–4.

4 Blum et al., *The National Experience,* 727.

5 Cloud and Olson, *The Murrow Boys,* 301.

6 Persico, *Edward R. Murrow,* 333.

7 Ibid., 333.

8 Persico, *Edward R. Murrow,* 342.

9 Sperber, *His Life and Times,* 364.

10 Persico, *Edward R. Murrow,* 342.

11 Sperber, *His Life and Times,* 305.

12 Persico, *Edward R. Murrow,* 364.

13 Shirer, *Berlin Diary,* 482.

14 Cloud and Olson, *The Murrow Boys,* 304.

15 Author interview with Casey Murrow, Brattleboro, VT, 16 October 2009.

16 As quoted in *Now the News.* 241.

17 Historians have endlessly chronicled and analyzed the details of the Murrow-McCarthy confrontation. Joseph Persico's superb 1988 Murrow biography, cited above, is arguably the definitive text. Persico's treatment of Murrow, while sympathetic, is also balanced and less hagiographic than some of the other narratives. The George Clooney-directed 2005 feature film *Good*

Night and Good Luck is an entertaining must-see for those who are interested in the period. However, as history, the film has its limitations.

18 Persico, *Edward R. Murrow*, 393.

19 Shirer, *A Native's Return*, 192.

CHAPTER THIRTY-THREE

1   Shirer, *A Native's Return*, 182.

2   Ibid., 191

3   Ibid., 185.

4   Ibid., 190.

5   Ibid., 192

6   Included in the Shirer correspondence file that is included in the Losch papers, which are housed in Special Collections the State University of New York at Binghamton, are eighty-four letters, eleven telegrams, and nine Christmas cards.

7   Shirer to Tilly Losch, 10 June 1946 (Binghamton University Special Collections).

8   Shirer to Tilly Losch, 26 April 1950 (Binghamton University Special Collections).

9   Shirer to Tilly Losch, 27 January 1951 (Binghamton University Special Collections).

10 Shirer to Tilly Losch, May 1951 (exact date unspecified). (Binghamton University Special Collections.)

11 Shirer to Tilly Losch, 12 July 1951 (Binghamton University Special Collections).

12 Shirer, *A Native's Return*, 272.

13 William Shirer, "This I Believe." *The Washington Post*, 30 December 1951, B5.

14 *The New Yorker*, 13 September 1952, 146.

15 Shirer, *Midcentury Journey*, 288.

16 Ibid., 291.

17 *Author Meets the Critic* debuted on NBC in 1948, moved to ABC in 1949, returned to NBC in 1951, and from January 1952 to early 1954 aired on the Dumont Network.

18 "Distaff Moderator," *The New York Times*, 12 April 1953.

19 Shirer, *A Native's Return*, 194.

20 Ibid., 197.

21 Shirer, *Stranger Come Home*.

22 Ibid., 25.

23 Ibid., 162.

24 Shirer, *The Challenge of Scandinavia*, 3.

25 *San Francisco Chronicle*, 23 May 1955, 25.

26 William Shirer to Pat Weaver, 19 May 1955 (William L. Shirer Papers, George T. Henry Archives.)

27 "Paul White Dies; Radio Newsman," *The New York Times*, 10 July 1955: 72.

28 Shirer, *The Consul's Wife*.

29 *A Native's Return*, 202.

CHAPTER THIRTY-FOUR

1 Nichols, "Talk with William L. Shirer," *New York Times Book Review*, 16 October 1960, 18.

2 Trevor-Roper, *The Last Days of Hitler*.

3 Bullock, *Hitler: A Study in Tyranny*.

4 Korda, *Another Life: A Memoir of Other People*, 97.

5 *Nazi Conspiracy and Aggression*.

6 Shirer, *A Native's Return*, 216n.

7 *Chicago Tribune*, 24 December 1961, C6. Halder issued a statement praising William Shirer for writing *The Rise and Fall of the Third Reich*, and Simon & Schuster for having the courage to publish the book, which was one he felt Germans needed to read and understand.

8 Nichols, "Talk with William L. Shirer."

9 Korda, *Another Life*, 96.

10 Shirer, *A Native's Return*, 228.

11 Ibid.

12 Ibid., 234.

13 Korda, *Another Life*, 97.

14 Ibid., 98.

15 Shirer, *A Native's Return*, 235.

16 Ibid., 239n.

17 William Shirer to Josephine Shirer, 25 March 1960. (The Literary Trust of William L. Shirer.)

18 Ibid., 242.

19 *Newsweek*, 25 November 1957.

20 Shirer, *A Native's Return*, 183n.

21 It is interesting to note how many of the reviews of *The Rise and Fall of the Third Reich* that appeared in mainstream newspapers and magazines were written by academics. Shirer was writing for a lay audience, yet editors reflexively sought out professional historians and political scientists to assess the book.

22 Trevor-Roper, "Light on Our Century's Darkest Night," 1.

23 *The Guardian*, 11 November 1960.

24 *Saturday Review*, 15 October 1960, 23.

25 S. Halperin, "Shirer Crowns His Career with Superb History," *The Chicago Tribune*, 16 October 1960, BR-1.

26 Gordon Craig, *New York Herald Tribune Book Review*, 16 October 1960, 1.

27 Ibid.

28 Shirer, *A Native's Return*, 245.

29 *Time*, 17 October 1960, 108.

30 Rosenbaum, xvii.

31 Gavriel D. Rosenfeld, "The Reception of William L. Shirer's *The Rise and Fall of the Third Reich* in the United States and West Germany, 1960-62," *Journal of Contemporary History*, Volume 29, 1994, 95–128.

32 According to a 1989 article in the *Washington Post* ("William Shirer at Journey's End," 10 August 1989, C-1), to that time, *The Rise and Fall of the Third Reich* was the Book of the Month Club's all-time bestseller – fiction or non-fiction.

33 *Publishers Weekly*, 13 February 1961, 123–5. The book's dustjacket, stark black with bronze type, featured a large black swastika in a white circle. The same motif was repeated on the book's spine. This cover, a masterwork of simplicity, was profoundly, stunningly evocative – so much so that it continues to influence the work of graphic designers a half-century later.

34 Kennett Love, "3 Receive National Book Awards for 1960," *The New York Times*, 15 March 1961, 34.

35 Rosenfeld, "*The Reception*", 98.

36 Ibid., 101.

37 Ibid., 103.

38 Klaus Epstein, "Shirer's History..." *The Review of Politics*, April 1961, 230–45.

39 Shanahan, William. O. "*The Rise and Fall of the Third Reich*: A History of Nazi Germany," *American Historical Review*, October 1962, 126–8.

40 Ibid., 126.

41 Shirer, *A Native's Return*, 250.

42 Kennett Love, "3 Receive National Book Awards for 1960," *The New York Times*, 15 March 1961, 34.

43 *Look*, 19 December 1961, 36ff.

44 In 1940, Shirer speculated that New York City might be attacked by the Luftwaffe. Military historians – and common sense – suggest this was impossible. However, such was the mood of the times that Shirer had given it some serious thought and had even voiced his concerns in public.

45 *The New York Times*, 13 November 2010. This news article ("Nazis Were Given 'safe haven' in United States, Report Says"), written by reporter Eric Lichtblau, prompted the Simon Wiesenthal Center to call upon the Obama administration to release the full report.

46 Marcia L. Kahn, "William Shirer's *The Rise and Fall of the Third Reich* Three Years Later: A Critical Appraisal of Non-Objective History," *The American-German Review*, October-November 1962, 39.

47 Felix Morley, "Those Incorrigible Germans," *Modern Age*, spring 1961, 193.

48 The German edition of *The Rise and Fall of the Third Reich* was titled *Aufstieg und Fall des Dritten Reiches*.

49 Shirer, *A Native's Return*, 258.

50 "German Edition of Shirer Book..." *The New York Times*, 13 October 1961, 8.

51 Gerd Wilke, "Anti-Bonn Feeling..." *The New York Times*, 24 December 1961, 5.

52 Shirer, *A Native's Return*, 260.

53 "German Edition of Shirer Book..." *The New York Times*, 13 October 1961, 8.

CHAPTER THIRTY-FIVE

1 William Shirer, "Let's Stop the Fall-Out Shelter Folly!" *Good Housekeeping*, February 1962. 56ff.

2 Shirer, *A Native's Return*, 190.

3 R.S. Kindelberger, "At 80, Author William Shirer Continues to Craft with Words," *Boston Globe*, 15 May 1984, 2.

4 Murray Schumach, "MGM Shifts Plans for Shirer's Book," *The New York Times*, 10 July 1962, 29.

5 Shirer, *A Native's Return*, 267.

6 Schumach, "MGM Shifts Plans for Shirer's Book," *The New York Times*, 10 July 1962, 29.

7 Shirer, *A Native's Return*, 314.

8 Author interview with Inga Dean and Linda Rae, Lenox, MA, 20 May 2008.

9 Shirer, *A Native's Return*, 290.

10 Halberstam, *The Powers That Be*, 150.

11 Shirer, *A Native's Return*, 118.

12 Ibid.

13 Kendrick, *Prime Time*, 497.

14 Author interview with Casey Murrow, 16 October 2009.

15 Shirer, *A Native's Return*, 119.

16 Author interview with Inga Dean, 9 April 2006.

17 Ibid.

18 Cloud and Olson, *The Murrow Boys*, 391.

19 Shirer, *A Native's Return*, 333.

20 "Virgilia Peterson Is Dead at 62," *The New York Times*, 27 December 1966.

21 Shirer, *A Native's Return*, 336.

22 "Virgilia Peterson Is Dead at 62; Was Author and Literary Critic," *The New York Times*, 27 December 1966, 52.

CHAPTER THIRTY-SIX

1 Shirer, *A Native's Return*, 341.

2 Ibid., 376.

3 William L. Shirer, "William L. Shirer on Cambodia," *The Washington Post*, 14 May 1970, A-18.

4 Albin Krebs, "After 2 Tomes," *The New York Times*, 29 December 1969, 36.

5 Shirer, *A Native's Return*, 375.

6 William Shirer, "When Militarists Dominate Democracies," *The New York Times*, 8 November 1969, 32.

7 Albin Krebs, "After 2 Tomes," *The New York Times*, 29 December 1969, 36.

8 Shirer, *A Native's Return*, 395.

9 Author telephone interview with Suzanne Pelton-Stroud, 15 February 2011.

10 Author interview with Elaine Steinert, 19 May 2008.

11 Shirer, *The Collapse of the Third Republic*, 11.

12 Albin Krebs, "After 2 Tomes," 36.

13 Shirer, *A Native's Return*, 348.

14 Author interview with Inga Shirer Dean, 8 April 2006.

15 William Shirer to John Shirer, 16 August 1944. (William L. Shirer Papers, George T. Henry Archives.)

16 *The Atlantic*, 29 December 1969, 143ff.

17 Shirer, *A Native's Return*, 360.

18 Owen Paxton, "The Collapse of the Third Republic," *The New York Times Book Review*, 9 November 1969, 66. Paxton's own 1972 book on the same subject was half the size of Shirer's.

19 Christopher Lehmann-Haupt, "Half Military History, Half Wastepaper," *The New York Times*, 17 November 1969, 45.

20 Ibid.

21 Shirer, *A Native's Return*, 364.

22 Albin Krebs, "After 2 Tomes," 36.

23 Shirer, *A Native's Return*, 373.

24 Ibid., 323.

25 Ibid.

26 Author interview with William L. Shirer, Lenox, MA, 10 November 1986.

27 Shirer, *A Native's Return*, 342.

28 Author interview with Inga Shirer Dean and Linda Shirer Rae, Lenox, MA, 20 May 2008.

29 Ibid.

30 Inga Shirer Dean email to the author, 4 February 2011.

31 Buck, *First Job*, 309.

32 Author telephone interview with Rinker Buck, 8 March 2011.

33 Buck, *First Job*, 315.

34 Ibid., 316.

35 Author telephone interview with Rinker Buck, 8 March 2011.

36 Shirer, *A Native's Return*, 378.

37 Author interview with Inga Shirer Dean, 9 April 2006.

CHAPTER THIRTY-SEVEN

1 John Hess, "William Shirer: 'A Matter of Character,'" *The New York Times Book Review*, 24 July 1977, 1.

2 Buck, *First Job*, 309.

3 Author interview with Elaine Steinert, Lenox, MA, 8 May 2009.

4 Author telephone interview with Martha Nordstrom, 30 March 2011.

5 Author telephone interview with Stephen Fay, 10 March 2011.

6 Buck, *First Job*, 309.

7 Ibid.

8 Simon & Schuster was bought out in January 1975 by the Gulf and Western media conglomerate. The move was part of a wave of changes that swept the publishing industry as one after another, the aging owners of many of America's best-known publishing houses sold out and moved on to other ventures or retired.

9 Shirer, *A Native's Return*, 384.

10 William Shirer to Tilly Losch, 21 January 1974 (Binghamton University Special Collections).

11 William Shirer to Tilly Losch, 6 February 1974 (Binghamton University Special Collections).

12 Author telephone interview with Rinker Buck, 8 March 2011.

13 Author telephone interview with Mary Balle (formerly Thomas), 25 May 2011.

14 "Notes on People," *The New York Times*, 14 August 1975, 23.

15 Fisher, Mark, "William Shirer at 'Journey's End,'" *Washington Post*, 10 August 1989, C1.

16 Commonwealth of Massachusetts Probate Court Order (#15083), 15 August 1975.

17 R.S. Kindelberger, "At 80, author William Shirer..." *The Boston Globe*, 15 May 1984, 2.

18 William Shirer to Tess Shirer, 27 January 1977 (The Literary Trust of William L. Shirer).

19 Peter Flint, "Tilly Losch, Exotic Dancer, Is Dead," *The New York Times*, 25 December 1975, 48.

20 Shirer, *A Native's Return*, 274.

21 Shirer, *Twentieth Century Journey*, 9.

22 *Saturday Review*, 21 August 1976, 38.

23 Malcolm Cowley, "Twentieth Century Journey," *The New York Times Book Review*, 10 October 1976, 244.

24 Shirer, *A Native's Return*, 389.

25 Author telephone interview with Mary Balle (formerly Thomas), 25 May 2011.

26 Shirer, *Gandhi: A Memoir*, 228–9.

27 Author interview with Inga Shirer Dean, 9 April 2006.

28 Shirer, *Gandhi: A Memoir*, 245.

29 Ibid., 239–40, 244.

30 Jean Strouse, *Newsweek*, 28 January 1980, 71.

31 Congdon manuscript.

32 Ibid.

33 Shirer, *A Native's Return*, 395.

CHAPTER THIRTY-EIGHT

1 That play *The Consul's Wife* was based on Shirer's 1956 novel of the same name. The play, which premiered at a theater in Great Barrington, MA, in autumn 1985, has rarely (if ever) been staged in the years since.

2 Congdon manuscript.

3 Elaine Steinert email to author, 20 May 2011.

4 Author telephone interview with Mary Balle, 25 May 2011.

5 Author telephone interview with Marge Champion, Lenox, MA, 27 December 2011.

6 Shirer, *A Native's Return*, 394.

7 Shirer, Eric Sevareid, Charles Collingwood, Richard C. Hottelet, and Winston Burdett were in attendance. Among the missing were Thomas Grandon, who had died in 1977, Bill Downs – who had died in 1978, and Howard K. Smith, who was now with ABC. Also absent were Mary Breckinridge and Cecil Brown, whom Murrow biographers Cloud and Olson note "CBS had long since forgotten," Cloud and Olson, *The Murrow Boys*, 375.

8 Shirer, *A Native's Return*, 459–60.

9 William Shirer, "Loyal to Hitler," *The New York Times*, 25 April 1985, A-26.

10 *The Boston Globe*, 5 May 1984, 1.

11 Steve Moore, "Better Late Than Never," A-1.

12 Shirer, *A Native's Return*, 399.

13 *The New Yorker*, 2 July 1984, 99ff.

14 Herbert Mitgang, "Books of *The Times*," *The New York Times*, 3 February 1990, C-24.

15 Vernon Young, "The Nightmare Years," 414.

16 Shirer, *A Native's Return*, 400.

17 Marc Fisher, "William Shirer at 'Journey's' End," *Washington Post*, 10 August 1989, C-2.

18 Barbara Tuchman, "William L. Shirer," 150.

19 Irina Lugovksaya fax to the author, 14 June 2011.

20 Ibid.

21 Author interview with Irina Lugovksaya, Lenox, MA, 20 May 2008

22 Ibid.

23 Geraldine Fabrikant, "Hitler's Berlin..." *The New York Times*, 17 September 1989, H-33.

24 Ibid.

25 Ibid.

26 Marc Fisher, "William Shirer at..." *The Washington Post*, 10 August 1989, C-2.

27 Author interview with Elaine Steinert, Lenox, MA, 19 May 2008.

28 Author telephone interview with Sam Waterston, 23 February 2011.

29 Marc Fisher, "William Shirer at..." C-2.

30 Waterston interview, op. cit.

31 Geraldine Fabrikant, "Hitler's Berlin..." H-33.

32 Author interview with Inga Shirer Dean and Linda Shirer Rae, Lenox, MA, 20 May 2008.

CHAPTER THIRTY-NINE

1 Author telephone interview with Martha Nordstrom, 31 March 2011.

2 Ibid.

3 Author interview with Inga Shirer Dean and Linda Shirer Rae, Lenox, MA, 20 May 2008.

4 Shirer, *A Native's Return*, 133.

5 *Benét's Reader's Encyclopedia*, 425.

6 Shirer, *A Native's Return*, 416.

7 Ibid., 465.

8 Ibid., 466.

9 As Fred Friendly told columnist Susan Anderson of *The New York Times*, 9 January 1990, B-4, "I was told by Ed that the reason Shirer was fired was because he had gotten lazy." William Paley, who was himself eighty-nine and in his last months of life, offered no public comment.

10 Alan Brinkley, "In the Grip..." *The New York Times Book Review*, 21 January 1990, 15.

11 Herbert Mitgang, "After War..." *The New York Times*, 3 February 1990, 19.

12 Harrison E. Salisbury, "Memoirs of an Iconoclast," *The Washington Post Book World*, 9 February 1990, D-3.

13 Ibid.

14 "William S. Paley Dies at 89..." *The Washington Post*, 27 October 1990, A2.

15 Congdon manuscript.

16 *Publishers Weekly*, 26 October 1990, 10.

17 Ibid.

CHAPTER FORTY

1 Shirer, *Twentieth Century Journey*, 17.

2 James Dodson, "The Lessons of History," *Yankee Magazine*, January 1990, 120.

3 Inga Shirer Dean's first book, a novel entitled *Memory and Desire* (Viking, 1985), was widely reviewed and won critical praise. For example, *Publishers Weekly* hailed the author as "a talented new novelist," 10 May 1985, 233.

4 Inga Shirer Dean email to the author, 27 April 2011.

5 Ibid.

6 Shirer, *Love and Hatred*, 11–12.

7 Author interview with Irina Lugovskaya, Lenox, MA, 20 May 2008.

8 Shirer, *Love and Hatred*, 11.

9 Ibid., 372.

10 Ibid., 373.

11 "At Memorial Friends Remember..." *The New York Times*, 17 January 1994, A-15.

12 Author interview with Irina Lugovskaya, Lenox, MA, 20 May 2008.

13 Tess outlived her former husband by fifteen years, dying at her New York home on 25 January 2008 at the age of ninety-seven.

14 "At Memorial Friends..." *The New York Times*, 17 January 1994, A-15.

15 *Publishers Weekly*, 30 May 1994, 40.

16 Michiko Kakutani, "Scenes from a marriage..." *The New York Times*, 8 July 1994, C-28.

17 "*This Is Berlin*..." *Publishers Weekly*, 29 November 1999, 62.

18 Michael Potemra, "Shelf Life." *National Review*, 5 June 2000, 50.

19 *Contemporary Review,* February 2000, 100.

20 John R. MacArthur, "History Promises," Providence Journal, 18 November 2009

21 Education Reporter, www.eagleform.org/educate/2003/june03/history.shtml.

22 M. Chalifoux and J.D.M. Stewart, "Canada is Failing History," The Globe and Mail, 16 June 2009, A17.

23 Douglas Mann, "It's Almost Midnight For Print Culture," *Toronto Star*, 7 July 2013.

Bibliography

ARCHIVAL SOURCES

Federal Bureau of Investigation archives, United States Department of Justice, Washington, DC – William L. Shirer holdings.

Harry Ransom Center, University of Texas at Austin – Blanche W. Knopf papers.

The Literary Trust of William L. Shirer.

Special Collections Research Center, Regenstein Library, University of Chicago – John Gunther papers.

The Tilly Losch Collection, Max Reinhardt Archives and Library, Special Collections, Binghamton University.

William L. Shirer Papers, George T. Henry Archives, Stewart Memorial Library, Coe College, Cedar Rapids.

BOOKS

Allen, Frederick Lewis. *Only Yesterday: An Informal History of the 1920s.* New York and London: Harper and Brothers Publishers, 1931.

– *Since Yesterday: The 1930s in America.* New York; Harper & Brothers, 1939.

Arendt, Hannah. *Origins of Totalitarianism.* New York: Harcourt, Brace and Company, 1951.

Barnouw, Erik. *The Golden Web.* New York: Oxford University Press, 1968.

Beard, Charles A., and Mary Beard (updated by William Beard). New York: *The Beards' New Basic History of the United States.* Doubleday and Company, 1960.

Benét's Reader's Encyclopedia (3rd Edition). New York: Harper & Row, 1987.

Bliss, Edward, *Now the News: The Story of Broadcast Journalism*. New York: Columbia University Press, 1991.

Blum, John, Edmund Morgan, et al. (editors). *The National Experience: A History of the United States Since 1865*. (Part II, Third Edition). New York: Harcourt Brace Janovich, Inc., 1973.

Brown, Cecil. *Suez to Singapore*. New York: Random House, 1942.

Buck, Rinker. *First Job*. New York: Public Affairs, 2002.

Bullock, Alan. *Hitler: A Study in Tyranny*. New York: Harper and Brothers, 1952.

Casey, Steven. *Cautious Crusade: Franklin D. Roosevelt, American Public Opinion, and the War against Nazi Germany*. New York: Oxford University Press, 2001.

Cerf, Bennett. *Try and Stop Me*. New York: Simon and Schuster, 1944.

Chaplin, Charles. *My Autobiography*. London: The Bodley Head, 1964.

Cloud, Stanley, and Lynne Olson. *The Murrow Boys: Pioneers on the Front Lines of Broadcast Journalism*. Boston: Houghton Mifflin Company, 1996.

Cole, J.A. *Lord Haw-Haw*. London: Faber and Faber, 1964.

Coolidge, Olivia. *Gandhi*. Boston: Houghton Mifflin Company, 1971.

Cowley, Malcolm. *And I Worked at the Writer's Trade: Chapters of Literary History, 1918-78*. New York: Viking, 1978.

Crofton, Ian. *Traitors & Turncoats: 20 Tales of Treason from Benedict Arnold to Ezra Pound*. London: Quercus, 2009.

Cronkite, Walter. *A Reporter's Life*. New York: Knopf, 1997.

Culbert, David H. *News for Everyman: Radio and Foreign Affairs in '30s America*. Westport, CT: Greenwood Press, 1976.

Cuthbertson, Ken. *Inside: the Biography of John Gunther*. Chicago: Bonus Books, 1992.

DeSpain, Robert G. *The Impact of Blacklisting on American Radio History: The Experiences of William L. Shirer*. (Unpublished MA thesis.) Iowa City, IA: University of Iowa, July 2007.

Diamond, Hanna. *Fleeing Hitler: France 1940*. New York: Oxford University Press, 2007.

Dictionary of Literary Biography (*Volume IV: American Writers in Paris, 1920-1939*). Farmington Hills, MI: Gale, 1980.

Dodd, Martha. *Through Embassy Eyes*. New York: Harcourt, Brace and Company, 1939.

Edwards, Bob. *Edward R. Murrow and the Birth of Broadcast Journalism*. Hoboken, NJ: John Wiley & Sons, 2004.

Flannery, Harry W. *Assignment to Berlin*. New York: Alfred A. Knopf, 1942.

Ford, Hugh (editor), *The Left Bank Revisited: Selections from the Paris Tribune 1917-1934*. University Park, PA: Pennsylvania State University Press, 1972.

Gallico, Paul. *Confessions of a Story Writer*. New York: Alfred A. Knopf, 1946.

Gandhi, M.K. *Collected Works of Mahatma Gandhi*. (*Volume 45*). Ahmedabad, India: Navajivan Trust, 1967-84.

- *An Autobiography: The Story of My Experiments with Truth*. Boston: Beacon Press, 1957.

Gentry, Curt, J. *Edgar Hoover: The Man and His Secrets*. New York: Norton and Company, 1991.

Gilbert, Sir Martin. *Churchill: A Life*. London: Heinemann, 1991.

- *Second World War*. London: Stoddart, 1989.

Gunther, John. *Fragment of Autobiography*. New York: Harper & Row, 1962.

- *Inside Asia*. New York: Harper & Brothers, 1939.

- *Inside Europe*. New York: Harper and Brothers, 1936.

- *Inside USA*. New York: Harper and Brothers, 1947.

Halberstam, David. *The Powers That Be*. New York: Alfred A. Knopf, 1979.

Harsch, Joseph C. *At the Hinge of History: A Reporter's Story*. Athens, GA: University of Georgia Press, 1993.

Hemingway, Ernest. *A Moveable Feast: Sketches of the Author's Life in Paris in the '20s*. New York: Charles Scribner's Sons, 1964.

Hess, Stephen. *International News and Foreign Correspondents*. Washington, DC: Brookings Institution, 1996.

Hoffman, Frederick J. *The '20s: American Writing in the Postwar Decade*. New York: Viking Press, 1955.

Hosley, David H. *As Good As Any: Foreign Correspondence on American Radio*. Westport, CT: Greenwood Press, 1984.

Isherwood, Christopher. *Berlin Stories*. New York: New Directions Publishing, 1946.

Jordan, Max. *Beyond All Fronts: A Bystander's Notes on This 30 Years War*. Milwaukee, WI: Bruce Publishing, 1944.

Kaul, Channdrika. *Communications, Media and the Imperial Experience: Britain and India in the Twentieth Century*. London: Palgrave Macmillan, 2014.

Kelly, Fred C. *The Wright Brothers*. New York: Farrar, Straus and Young, 1950.

Kendrick, Alexander. *Prime Time: The Life of Edward R. Murrow*. Boston: Little, Brown and Company, 1969.

Kluger, Richard. *The Paper: The Life and Death of the New York Herald Tribune*. Knopf. 1986.

Korda, Michael. *Another Life: A Memoir of Other People*. New York: Random House, 1999.

Laney, Al. *The Paris Herald: The Incredible Newspaper*. New York: D. Appleton-Century Co., 1947.

Larson, Erik. *In the Garden of Beasts: Love, Terror, and an American Family in Hitler's Berlin*. New York: Crown Publishers, 2011.

Leitz, Christian. *Nazi Foreign Policy, 1933-41*. New York: Routledge, 2004.

Manchester, William. *American Cesar: Douglas MacArthur, 1880-1964*. Boston: Little, Brown and Company, 1978.

Metz, Robert. cbs: *Reflections in a Bloodshot Eye*. Chicago: Playboy Press, 1975.

Miller, Nathan. *F.D.R.: An Intimate History*. New York: Doubleday & Company, 1983.

Miller, Webb. *I Found No Peace: The Journal of as Foreign Correspondent*. New York: The Literary Guild, Inc., 1936.

Mitgang, Herbert. *Dangerous Dossiers*. New York: Primus, 1996.

Morris, Jan. *Among the Cities*. New York: Oxford University Press, 1985.

– *Farewell the Trumpets: An Imperial Retreat*. London: Faber and Faber, 1979.

– *Manhattan '45*. New York: Oxford University Press, 1987.

Mowrer, Edgar A. *Germany Puts the Clock Back*. New York: John Lane Company, 1933.

Murrow, Edward. *This Is London*. New York: Simon and Schuster, 1941.

Nazi Conspiracy and Aggression. Washington, DC: Office of the Chief Counsel for the Prosecution of Axis Criminality, United States Publishing Office, 1947.

Paley, William. *As It Happened*. New York: Doubleday and Company, 1979.

Paper, Lewis J. *Empire: William S. Paley and the Making of cbs*. New York: St Martin's Press, 1987.

Payne, Robert. *The Life and Death of Adolf Hitler*. New York: Praeger Publishers, 1973.

Persico, Joseph E. *Edward R. Murrow: An American Original*. New York: McGraw-Hill Publishing, 1988.

– *Nuremberg: Infamy on Trial*. New York: Penguin Books, 1994.

Root, Waverley. *The Paris Edition: The Autobiography of Waverley Root, 1927-34*. (Edited and with an introduction by Samuel Abt.) San Francisco: North Point Press, 1987.

Ross, Walter. *The Last Hero: Charles A. Lindbergh*. New York: Harper & Row, 1976.

Rutledge, Brett. *The Death of Lord Haw-Haw*. New York: Random House, 1940.

Saerchinger, César. *Hello, America: Radio Adventures in Europe*. Boston: Houghton Mifflin, 1938.

Sanders, Marion K. *Dorothy Thompson: A Legend in Her Time*. Boston: Houghton Mifflin Company, 1973.

Schechter, A.A., with Edward Anthony. *I Live on Air*. New York: Stokes, 1941.

Schorer, Mark. *Sinclair Lewis: An American Life*. New York: McGraw-Hill, 1961.

Seldes, George. *Eyewitness to a Century: Encounters with the Noted, the Notorious, and Three sobs*. New York: Ballantine Books, 1987.

Sevareid, Eric. *Not so Wild a Dream*. New York: Alfred A. Knopf, 1946.

Sheean, Vincent. *Dorothy and Red*. Boston: Houghton Mifflin Company, 1963.

Shirer, William. *Berlin Diary: The Journal of a Foreign Correspondent, 1934-40*. New York: Alfred A. Knopf, 1942.

– *The Challenge of Scandinavia: Norway, Sweden, Denmark, and Finland in Our Time*. Boston: Little Brown and Company, 1955.

– *The Collapse of the Third Republic*. New York: Simon & Schuster, 1969.

– *The Consul's Wife*. Boston: Little, Brown & Company, 1956.

– *End of a Berlin Diary*. New York: Alfred A. Knopf, 1947.

– *Gandhi: A Memoir*. New York: Simon & Schuster, 1979.

– *Love and Hatred: The Stormy Marriage of Leon and Sonya Tolstoy*. New York: Simon & Schuster, 1994.

– *Midcentury Journey*. New York: Farrar, Strauss and Young, 1952.

– *A Native's Return*. Boston: Little, Brown and Company, 1990.

– *The Nightmare Years: 1930-1940*. Boston: Little, Brown and Company, 1984.

– *The Rise and Fall of Adolf Hitler*. New York: Random House, 1961.

– *The Rise and Fall of the Third Reich*. New York: Simon & Schuster, 1960.

– *The Rise and Fall of the Third Reich: 50th Anniversary Edition*. New York: Simon and Schuster, 2011.

– *Stranger Come Home*. Boston: Little, Brown and Company, 1954.

– *The Sinking of the Bismarck*. New York: Random House, 1962.

– *"This Is Berlin."* New York: Overlook Press, 1999.

– *The Traitor*. New York: Farrar, Straus and Company, 1950.

– *Twentieth Century Journey: The Start, 1904-1930*. New York: Simon and Schuster, 1976.

Siemon-Netto, Uwe. *The Fabricated Luther: The Rise and Fall of the Shirer Myth*. St. Louis, MO: CPH, 1993.

Silverman, Al (editor). *Sixty Years of Books in American Life*. Little, Brown and Company, 1986.

Smith, Geoffrey. *To Save A Nation: American Countersubversives, the New Deal, and the Coming of World War II*. New York: Basic Books, 1973.

Smith, Howard K. *Events Leading Up to My Death*. New York: St. Martin's Press, 1996.

– *Last Train from Berlin*. New York: Alfred A. Knopf, 1942.

Smith, R. Franklin. *Edward R. Murrow: The War Years*. Kalamazoo, MI: Western Michigan University Press, 1978.

Speer, Albert. *Inside the Third Reich*. New York: Avon Books, 1971.

Sperber, A.M. *Murrow: His Life and Times*. New York: Freundlich Books, 1986.

Stearns, Harold E. *The Street I Know*. New York: Lee Furman, 1935.

– (editor). *Civilization in the United States: An Inquiry by 30 Americans* New York: Harcourt, 1922.

Sterling, Christopher H., and Kittross, John M. *Stay Tuned: A History of American Broadcasting* Mahwah, NJ: Lawrence Erlbaum Associates, 2002.

Swanberg, W.A. *Luce and His Empire*. New York: Charles Scribner's Sons, 1972.

Taylor, Telford. *The Anatomy of the Nuremberg Trials: A Personal Memoir*. Boston: Little, Brown and Company, 1992.

Thomas, Hugh. *The Spanish Civil War*. New York: Harper and Row, 1977.

Thompson, Dorothy. *I Saw Hitler*. New York: Farrar & Rinehart, 1932.

Thurber, James. *The Thurber Carnival*. Harper and Brothers, 1945.

Toland, John. *Adolf Hitler*. New York: Doubleday and Company, 1976.

Trent, Herbert. *France since 1918*. London: B.T. Batsford, 1970.

The Trial of the Major War Criminals. London: Published under the authority of H.M. Attorney General by His Majesty's Stationary Office, 1946.

Truman, Harry S. *Years of Trial and Hope* (Vol. II). New York: Doubleday and Company, 1956.

Waldrop, Frank C. *McCormick of Chicago*. Englewood Cliff, NJ: Prentice-Hall, 1966.

Weber, Eugene. *The Hollow Years*. New York: W.W. Norton & Company, 1994.

White, Paul. *News on the Air*. New York: Harcourt, Brace, 1947.

Wick, Steve. *The Long Night: William L. Shirer and the Rise and Fall of the Third Reich*. New York: Palgrave Macmillan, 2011.

Williams, W.A. *Americans in a Changing World*. New York: Harper and Row, 1978.

ONLINE SOURCES

Huttner, Markus, "Norman Ebbutt," *Oxford Dictionary of National Biography*, www/oxforddnb.com.

MacLeod, Elizabeth, "Max-Jordan – NBC's Forgotten Pioneer," www.midcoast.com/~lizmcl/Jordan.html.

Murrow exhibit homepage, the Tufts University website, dca.lib.tufts.edu/features/exhibit/ boys.html.

Luis Quintanilla home page, "Portraits of Writers as They See Themselves," www.lqart.org/portsfold/writports.html.

Schwartz, Professor Richard A., "How the Film and Television Blacklists Worked," comptalk.fiu.edu/blacklist.html.

William Shirer interview with Don Swaim on CBS radio, 1984, www.wiredforbooks.org/williamlshirer/.

Index